PREFACE

Today, when law courses are more popular than ever before, students can have real difficulty in getting at the materials they need. Libraries are often not large enough, or not sufficiently well stocked, to cater for all those who want to use them. Part-time students can be at a special disadvantage. In the end, the struggle to find materials as well as the time to read them can prove too much, and lower results are obtained in the examination than a student deserves.

I cannot hope to cure this completely in one volume. But I have placed substantial emphasis on reports of cases and have aimed to present as much of a chosen case as space allows. Wherever possible I have tried to let the facts emerge from the report. Short summaries may make for easy reading, but they are also apt to mislead. This is particularly true of evidence, where, perhaps more than in other topics, the old model of law as a system of rules is being replaced by a discretionary approach which involves the application of principles to complex factual situations. The student of this subject who has ignored the complexities of arguments about facts is likely to do poorly not only in the examination but also later when conducting cases in court. At the same time, I have kept to a minimum my own introductory material and I have avoided the sort of minute commentary on cases that, for the undergraduate at least, tends to generate more heat than light. I hope that an inevitably brief selection from the excellent articles that have been written will be of special use in preparing for essay questions.

The topics covered are those encountered in the syllabus for most evidence examinations; they follow the order adopted in the recent edition of my book on evidence in the Cavendish Q & A Series. Experience of lecturing and examining in evidence has persuaded me that most students would greatly improve their performances if they concentrated on the main areas favoured by examiners and read carefully some of the cases in those areas. It is for these students, especially, that I have prepared this selection. But I hope that others may find it a convenient collection which will save them time for wider reading.

I should like to thank Jon Claydon for his excellent work in word processing and checking my manuscript.

Finally, I should like to express my appreciation to Cavendish Publishing Limited for all their help in the production of this book.

CJWA
Gray's Inn
March 1996

ACKNOWLEDGMENTS

Grateful acknowledgment is made for permission to reproduce from the following sources:

Carter, PB, 'Forbidden Reasoning Permissible: Similar Fact Evidence a Decade after Boardman', (1985) 48 *Modern Law Review* 29. (Reproduced by kind permission of Blackwell Publishers.)

Dworkin, RM, 'Is Law a System of Rules?' in *The Philosophy of Law*, RM Dworkin (ed), (Oxford University Press, 1977). (Reproduced by kind permission of the Author.)

Guest, Stephen, 'The Scope of the Hearsay Rule', (1985) 101 *Law Quarterly Review* 385. (Reproduced by kind permission of Sweet & Maxwell.)

Munday, Roderick, 'The Paradox of Cross-Examination to Credit', (1994) 53 *Cambridge Law Journal* 303. (Reproduced by kind permission of the Author and Editorial Committee.)

Smith, JC, 'The Presumption of Innocence', (1987) 38 *Northern Ireland Legal Quarterly* 223. (Reproduced by kind permission of the Author.)

Spencer, JR, 'Hearsay, Relevance and Implied Assertion', (1993) 52 *Cambridge Law Journal* 40. (Reproduced by kind permission of the Author and Editorial Committee.)

Twining, William, *Theories of Evidence: Bentham and Wigmore*, (Wiedenfeld and Nicolson, 1985). (Reproduced by kind permission of the Author.)

Williams, CR, 'The Problem of Similar Fact Evidence', (1979) 5 *Dalhousie Law Journal* 281. (Reproduced by kind permission of the Author and Editorial Board.)

Williams, Glanville, 'The Logic of "Exceptions"', (1988) 47 *Cambridge Law Journal* 263. (Reproduced by kind permission of the Author and Editorial Committee.)

Grateful acknowledgment is also made to the Controller of Her Majesty's Stationary Office for permission to reproduce Crown Copyright materials; to the Incorporated Council of Law Reporting for England and Wales for permission to reproduce extracts from the *Law Reports* and the *Weekly Law Reports*; to Butterworths for permission to reproduce extracts from the *All England Law Reports*; and to Sweet & Maxwell for permission to reproduce extracts from the *Criminal Appeal Reports*.

CONTENTS

TABLE OF CASES

TABLE OF STATUTES

CHAPTER 1

BASIC CONCEPTS

In this chapter I shall deal with two matters that seem to me to be fundamental in any study of the law of evidence. First, I shall try to say something about the nature of the subject matter. This is not as obvious as is sometimes assumed. The concept of evidence is an ambiguous one, and this has to be appreciated in order to avoid misunderstanding when reading evidence texts.[1] In the second section I shall consider relevancy. The understanding of this concept is vital. It is needed for the preparation and presentation of cases generally. In addition, the law which governs the admissibility of testimony often depends on an exact assessment of the probative job in the case as a whole – ie the relevancy – of any contested item.[2]

THE NATURE OF THE SUBJECT MATTER

The word 'evidence' is used in different ways, and what 'evidence' refers to will depend on how it is used in any particular context. Consider these examples:

(1) 'In August of last year Bywaters, according to the evidence, made a statement to his mother about the unhappy life of Mrs Thompson, and the evidence showed, if the jury accepted it, as they apparently did, that on more than one occasion Bywaters had called at the warehouse where Thompson was employed ...'

(2) [Of a brother and sister charged with incest] 'Their passion for each other was as much evidence as was their presence together in bed of the fact that when there they had guilty relations with each other.'

(3) '"You must not tell us what the soldier, or any other man, said, sir," interposed the judge; "it's not evidence".'

In the first of these examples 'evidence' was used to refer to *testimony that had been given by a witness in court.* In the second, the same word was used to refer to a *relationship of relevancy* between the facts of mutual passion and the occupation of the same bed, and the fact that had ultimately to be proved: the commission of incest. In the third example 'evidence' was used to refer to *legally admissible testimony.*

This dependence on context for reference is true of other expressions associated with evidence which are sometimes used in attempts at classification; examples are 'primary evidence' and 'direct evidence'. The difficulties to which

---

1. By 'evidence texts' I intend to refer to writings, such as law reports, which are regarded as sources of evidence law, and also to writings, such as textbooks, articles and reports of commissions, which may be broadly described as being about evidence law.

2. See, eg the law relating to similar fact evidence and to hearsay.

1

use in a variety of contexts can give rise were noted by James Fitzjames Stephen.[3]

JF Stephen, *The Indian Evidence Act* (1872)

The ambiguity of the word 'evidence' is the cause of a great deal of obscurity ... In scientific inquiries, and for popular and general purposes, it is no doubt convenient to have one word which includes:

(1) the testimony on which a given fact is believed

(2) the facts so believed, and

(3) the arguments founded upon them.

For instance, in the title of *Paley's Evidences of Christianity*, the word is used in this sense. The nature of the work was not such as to give much importance to the distinction which the word overlooks. So, in scientific inquiries, it is seldom necessary ... to lay stress upon the difference between the testimony on which a fact is believed, and the fact itself. In judicial inquiries, however, the distinction is most important, and the neglect to observe it has thrown the whole subject into confusion by causing English lawyers to overlook the leading distinction which ought to form the principle on which the whole law should be classified. I mean the distinction between the relevancy of facts and the mode of proving relevant facts.

The use of the one name 'evidence' for the fact to be proved, and the means by which it is to be proved, has given a double meaning to every phrase in which the word occurs. Thus, for instance, the phrase 'primary evidence' sometimes means a relevant fact, and sometimes the original of the document as opposed to a copy. 'Circumstantial evidence' is opposed to 'direct evidence'. But 'circumstantial evidence' usually means a fact, from which some other fact is inferred, whereas 'direct evidence' means testimony given by a man as to what he has himself perceived by his own senses. It would thus be correct to say that circumstantial evidence must be proved by direct evidence – a clumsy mode of expression, which is in itself a mark of confusion of thought.[4]

The student of evidence needs, therefore, to read critically any attempt by textbook writers to define and classify 'evidence', and to observe carefully how any term which seems to belong to such a classification is used when it appears in a reported case or other evidence text. Particular care should be taken to avoid what may be called *the fallacy of justification by labelling*. I use this expression to refer to the kind of argument which attempts to justify, without more, the legal admissibility of an item of evidence by labelling that item with the name of some category such as 'original evidence' or 'real evidence'. A satisfactory argument for admissibility which relies on classification requires that the student make clear what he refers to by his use of a particular classification, why he says that the disputed item of testimony falls within it,

---

3. Sir James Fitzjames Stephen (1829-94) Criminal law reformer, writer and judge. Appointed 1869 as legal member of the Governor General's Council in India where he became a leading codifier of criminal law. Drafted the Indian Evidence Act. Returned to England 1872 and began work on the codification of English evidence law at the request of the Attorney General, Coleridge. A code proved to be impracticable, but his work was reflected in his *Digest of the Law of Evidence* (1876) and *Digest of the Criminal Law* (1877). Appointed judge of QBD 1879. Uncle of Virginia Woolf.

4. Stephen, *Indian Evidence Act*, pp 6-7.

and why it follows that the disputed item should be admitted. For example, to say merely that an item of evidence is admissible because it is not 'hearsay' but 'real evidence' tells the examiner almost nothing – except that she is dealing with a weak candidate. In practice it will be found that perfectly good arguments for admissibility can be constructed by relying on the function of an item of contested evidence.

Students should not, therefore, begin their studies of evidence by trying to memorise a list of classifications. Rather, they should try to see their subject as part of a wider whole. Stephen realised this and attempted to put the law of evidence in context in the following way.[5]

JF Stephen, *The Indian Evidence Act* (1872)

All rights and liabilities are dependent upon and arise out of facts.

Every judicial proceeding whatever has for its purpose the ascertaining of some right or liability. If the proceeding is criminal, the object is to ascertain the liability to punishment of the person accused. If the proceeding is civil, the object is to ascertain some right of property or of status, or the right of one party, and the liability of the other, to some form of relief.

In order to effect this result, provision must be made by law for the following objects. *First,* the legal effect of particular classes of facts in establishing rights and liabilities must be determined. This is the province of what has been called substantive law. *Secondly,* a course of procedure must be laid down by which persons interested may apply the substantive law to particular cases.

The law of procedure includes, amongst others, two main branches. (1) the law of pleading, which determines what in particular cases are the questions in dispute between the parties, and (2) the law of evidence, which determines how the parties are to convince the court of the existence of that state of facts which, according to provisions of substantive law, would establish the existence of the right or liability which they allege to exist.[6]

There is a problem, which Stephen in part recognised, with the description of the law of evidence as something 'which determines how the parties are to convince the court of the existence of ... facts which ... would establish the existence of the right or liability which they allege to exist'. This is a function of the law of evidence, but it is not a function of the law of evidence alone. On most occasions when we need to decide if A tends to prove B, we rely not on law, but on ordinary principles of reasoning. One way of acknowledging this is to make a distinction between 'natural evidence' and 'judicial evidence'. The former term has gone out of fashion, but the latter is still to be found and may serve to remind us of the minimal function served by law in matters of proof. Best, for example, in his *Treatise* noted how the word 'evidence' had been defined as 'any matter of fact, the effect, tendency or design of which is to produce in the mind a persuasion, affirmative or disaffirmative, of the existence

---

5. In reading this account it should be remembered that the usual effect of a 'not guilty' plea in criminal proceedings is that 'everything is in issue and the prosecution have to prove the whole of their case, including the identity of the accused, the nature of the act and the existence of any necessary knowledge or intent': *Sims* [1946] KB 531, 539, *per* Lord Goddard CJ.

6. Stephen, *Indian Evidence Act*, pp 7-8.

of some other matter of fact'. Evidence outside a judicial or jurisprudential context he referred to as 'natural' or 'moral' evidence. 'Judicial evidence' he defined as 'the evidence received by courts of justice in proof or disproof of facts, the existence of which comes in question before them'. Such evidence was 'a species of the genus "evidence"' and was 'for the most part nothing more than natural evidence restrained or modified by rules of positive law'.[7]

This point was emphasised by two American scholars, Thayer and Wigmore.

JB Thayer, *A Preliminary Treatise on Evidence at the Common Law* (1898)

In seeking to ascertain the unknown from the known, a judicial tribunal is called on to use, apply, reflect upon, and compare a great body of facts and ideas of which it is already in possession, and of which no particle of 'evidence', strictly so called, is ever formally presented in court. And then, in addition, it has to be put in possession of new material. It is this necessity, that of furnishing new matter, which gives occasion for rules of evidence. On the other hand, the function of scrutinizing the material which it has once got, of observing its implications, and the effect of one part on another, of comparing and inferring, does not belong to the region of the law of evidence. To the hungry furnace of the reasoning faculty the law of evidence is but a stoker.

Let it be distinctly set down, then, that the whole process of legal argumentation, and the rules for it, essential as these are, and forever pressing upon the attention, are mainly an affair of logic and general experience, not of legal precept. I say mainly, because the reasoning process, in its application to particular subjects, gets always a tincture from the subject matter. Undoubtedly there are rules of legal practice and procedure, qualifying and restraining the free processes of reason; so that it is a proper qualification, when we use the phrase *legal* reasoning; not because, as compared with reasoning in general, it calls into play any different faculties or involves any new principles or methods, or is the creature of technical precepts; but because in law, as elsewhere, in adjusting old and universal methods to the immediate purposes in hand, special limitations, exclusions, and qualifications have to be taken into account. In particular and emphatically, in legal reasoning, such peculiarities spring from the practical aims of a court of justice and the practical conditions of its work; eg from the nature of such a tribunal as a jury, and the exigencies of time, place, and subject matter which control its operations. In dealing with litigation, courts are not engaged in an academic exercise. With them the search for truth is not the main matter; their desire to know this, and their ability to use it, are limited by the requirements of their main business, namely, that of awarding justice, ie awarding it so far as they may, under rules of law, and according to established usages and forms ... And again, whether it be out of regard to the general want of time and convenient opportunity; or to the nature of the questions discussed, and the ordinary methods of mankind in judging of the practical problems of life and business, and the practical impossibility of running an inquiry out into fine details; or to the nature of the popular tribunal, the jury; or for whatever reason; we have principles of exclusion which limit the inquiry, and so the evidence, to matters that have a clear and obvious bearing and a plainly appreciable weight, as contrasted with what is slight, conjectural, and remote; and to matters which

---

7. WM Best, *A Treatise on the Principles of the Law of Evidence* (1866, 4th edn), pp 31–32.

do not unnecessarily tend to complicate and confuse the determination of the issue. These I call principles, rather than rules, because of their necessarily indeterminate form, and their appeal to the general sense and judgment of the tribunal; as contrasted with definite legal rules, in the application of which it is reasonable to expect a near approach to unanimity among competent minds.

We have no treatise and no chapters of treatises that deal separately and specifically with the topic of legal reasoning in the ascertainment of facts. Copious books on evidence, on procedure, and on the many branches of substantive law, we have, but none upon the nature and methods of that art by which all the rules of all these various subjects are applied and developed. It is not my purpose now to furnish one, but only to bring this subject out into the light, to mark its characteristics, and to emphasize its separate place and distinctive character.

Why is any such exposition needed? Certainly not, as I have said, because legal reasoning differs in any fundamental respect from any other reasoning, or because lawyers have any peculiar organs or methods for tracking and apprehending the truth. What is called the 'legal mind' is still the human mind, and it must reason according to the laws of its constitution ...

But while legal reasoning, at bottom, is like all other reasoning, yet a thousand practical considerations come in to shape it. There is one grave reason for discriminating this topic and remarking its characteristic methods and its separate place which has been too little observed; namely, that it has a tendency to run over and mingle with other subjects, and to distress all attempts to clarify them. In particular this has happened with the subject of evidence. Rules, principles, and methods of legal reasoning have taken on the color and used the phraseology of this subject, and thus disguised, have figured as rules of evidence, to the perplexity and confusion of those who sought for a strong grasp of the subject. A bastard sort of technicality has thus sprung up, and a crop of fanciful reasons for anomalies destitute of reason, which baffle and disgust a healthy mind ...

... [T]he great characteristics of the art of reasoning and the law of thought still remain constant. As regards the main methods in hand, they are those untechnical ways of all sound reasoning, of the logical process in its normal and ordinary manifestations; and the rules that govern it here are the general rules that govern it elsewhere, the ordinary rules of human thought and human experience, to be sought in the ordinary sources, and not in law books. And so a knowledge of these processes and methods is presupposed in all judges and lawyers. When Abraham Fraunce, therefore, the friend of Sir Philip Sidney, published, in 1588, *The Lawyer's Logic*, it turned out to be only a rather novel sort of treatise on the general subject, illustrated by examples from Plowden's recent volume of 1571, and other law books. He had first written his book under the name of *The Shepherd's Logic*, taking his example from Spenser's poem, 'The Shepherd's Calendar', published in 1579. The illustrations differed; the thing illustrated was the same.

We may dismiss, then, any notion that legal reasoning is some non-natural process by which the human mind is required to infer what does not logically follow. Expressions that import this are to be regarded as mere phrases for what may be and should be accurately stated. The technicalities of legal reasoning merely grow out of the material, the subject matter, in which it works.[8]

---

8. Thayer, *Preliminary Treatise*, pp 270-73, 275-76.

JH Wigmore, *The Principles of Judicial Proof* (1931, 2nd edn)

The study of the principles of evidence, for a lawyer, falls into two distinct parts. One is proof in the general sense – the part concerned with the ratiocinative process of contentious persuasion – mind to mind, counsel to judge or juror, each partisan seeking to move the mind of the tribunal. The other part is admissibility – the procedural rules devised by the law, and based on litigious experience and tradition, to guard the tribunal (particularly the jury) against erroneous persuasion. Hitherto, the latter has loomed largest in our formal studies – has, in fact, monopolized them; while the former, virtually ignored, has been left to the chances of later acquisition, casual and empiric, in the course of practice.

Here we have been wrong; and in two ways:

For one thing, there is, and there *must* be, a probative science – the principles of proof – independent of the artificial rules of procedure; hence, it can be and should be studied. This science, to be sure, may as yet be imperfectly formulated. But all the more need is there to begin in earnest to investigate and develop it. Furthermore, this process of proof represents the objective in every judicial investigation. The procedural rules for admissibility are merely a preliminary aid to the main activity, *viz* the persuasion of the tribunal's mind to a correct conclusion by safe materials. This main process is that for which the jury are there, and on which the counsel's duty is focused.

And, for another thing, the judicial rules of admissibility are destined to lessen in relative importance during the next period of development. Proof will assume the important place; and we must therefore prepare ourselves for this shifting of emphasis.[9]

The last paragraph quoted from Wigmore was, at least in relation to English law, prophetic. In later chapters we shall see several examples of a shift away from interpreting evidence law as a system of rules to its interpretation as a body of principles, whose application depends on the probative job that the questioned item of testimony is put forward to do. The law relating to similar fact evidence is an obvious example. The distinction between a rule-based and a principle-based approach to law is important because it governs the form which arguments about admissibility should take. If a part of evidence law is seen as being rule-based there will be less room for manoeuvre because argument will tend to be founded on the wording of statutes or on decisions in previous cases which may be seen as binding. By contrast, where part of evidence law is seen as not being rule-based, but based on principle, there will more room for manoeuvre in its application. The reason for this has been explained by Ronald Dworkin. In practice, of course, it may not be clear which of these approaches should apply. But a good advocate will be able to see which approach is more likely to be useful and to develop an argument accordingly.

RM Dworkin, 'Is Law a System of Rules?' in *The Philosophy of Law*, RM Dworkin (ed) (1977)

The difference between legal principles and legal rules is a logical distinction. Both sets of standards point to particular decisions about legal obligations in particular circumstances, but they differ in the character of the direction they give. Rules are applicable in an all or nothing fashion. If the facts a rule stipulates

---

9.   Wigmore, *Principles*, pp 3-4.

are given, then either the rule is valid, in which case the answer it supplies must be accepted, or it is not, in which case it contributes nothing to the decision.

This all or nothing is seen most plainly if we look at the way rules operate, not in law, but in some enterprise they dominate – a game, for example. In baseball a rule provides that if the batter has had three strikes, he is out. An official cannot consistently acknowledge that this is an accurate statement of a baseball rule, and decide that a batter who has had three strikes is not out. Of course, a rule may have exceptions (the batter who has taken three strikes is not out if the catcher drops the third strike). However, an accurate statement of the rule would take this exception into account, and any that did not would be incomplete. If the list of exceptions is very large, it would be too clumsy to repeat them each time the rule is cited; there is, however, no reason in theory why they could not all be added on, and the more that are, the more accurate is the statement of the rule.

If we take baseball rules as a model, we find that rules of law, like the rule that a will is invalid unless signed by three witnesses, fit the model well. If the requirement of three witnesses is a valid legal rule, then it cannot be that a will has been signed by only two witnesses and is valid. The rule might have exceptions, but if it does it is inaccurate and incomplete to state the rule so simply, without enumerating the exceptions. In theory, at least, the exceptions could all be listed, and the more of them that are, the more complete is the statement of the rule.

But this is not the way ... principles ... operate. Even those which look most like rules do not set out legal consequences that follow automatically when the conditions provided are met. We say that our law respects the principle that no man may profit from his own wrong, but we do not mean that the law never permits a man to profit from wrongs he commits. In fact, people often profit, perfectly legally, from their legal wrongs. The most notorious case is adverse possession: if I trespass on your land long enough, some day I will gain a right to cross your land whenever I please. There are many less dramatic examples. If a man leaves one job, breaking a contact, to take a much higher paying job, he may have to pay damages to his first employer, but he is usually entitled to keep his new salary. If a man jumps bail and crosses state lines to make a brilliant investment in another state, he may be sent back to jail, but he will keep his profits.

We do not treat these – and countless other counter-instances that can easily be imagined – as showing that the principle about profiting from one's wrongs is not a principle of our legal system, or that it is incomplete and needs qualifying exceptions. We do not treat counter-instances as exceptions (at least not exceptions in the way in which a catcher's dropping the third strike is an exception) because we could not hope to capture these counter-instances simply by a more extended statement of the principle. They are not, even in theory, subject to enumeration, because we would have to include not only these cases (like adverse possession) in which some institution has already provided that profit can be gained through a wrong, but also those numberless imaginary cases in which we know in advance that the principle would not hold. Listing some of these might sharpen our sense of the principle's weight (I shall mention that dimension in a moment), but it would not make for a more accurate or complete statement of the principle.

A principle like, 'No man may profit from his own wrong', does not even purport to set out conditions that make its application necessary. Rather, it states a reason that argues in one direction, but does not necessitate a particular decision. If a man has or is about to receive something, as a direct result of something illegal he did to get it, then that is a reason which the law will take into account in deciding whether he should keep it. There may be other principles or policies arguing in the other direction – a policy of securing title, for example, or a principle limiting punishment to what the legislature has stipulated. If so, our principle may not prevail, but that does not mean that it is not a principle of our legal system, because in the next case, when these contravening considerations are absent or less weighty, the principle may be decisive. All that is meant, when we say that a particular principle is a principle of our law, is that the principle is one which officials must take into account, if it is relevant, as a consideration inclining in one direction or another ...

Principles have a dimension that rules do not – the dimension of weight or importance. When principles intersect ... one who must resolve the conflict has to take into account the relative weight of each. This cannot be, of course, an exact measurement, and the judgment that a particular principle or policy is more important than another will often be a controversial one. Nevertheless, it is an integral part of the concept of a principle that it has this dimension, that it makes sense to ask how important or how weighty it is.

Rules do not have this dimension. We can speak of rules as being *functionally* important or unimportant (the baseball rule that three strikes are out is more important than the rule that runners may advance on a balk, because the game would be much more changed with the first rule altered than the second). In this sense, one legal rule may be more important than another because it has a greater or more important role in regulating behaviour. But we cannot say that one rule is more important than another within the system of rules, so that when two rules conflict one supersedes the other by virtue of its greater weight. If two rules conflict, one of them cannot be a valid rule. The decision as to which is valid, and which must be abandoned or recast, must be made by appealing to considerations beyond the rules themselves. A legal system might regulate such conflicts by other rules, which prefer the rule enacted by the higher authority, or the rule enacted later, or the more specific rule, or something of that sort. A legal system may also prefer the rule supported by the more important principles. (Our own legal system uses both of these techniques).

It is not always clear from the form of a standard whether it is a rule or a principle. 'A will is invalid unless signed by three witnesses' is not very different in form from 'A man may not profit from his own wrong', but one who knows something of American law knows that he must take the first as stating a rule and the second as stating a principle. In many cases the distinction is difficult to make – it may not have been settled how the standard should operate, and this issue may itself be a focus of controversy. The First Amendment of the United States Constitution contains the provision that Congress shall not abridge freedom of speech. Is this a rule, so that if a particular law does abridge freedom of speech, it follows that it is unconstitutional? Those who claim that the first amendment is 'an absolute' say that it must be taken in this way; that is, as a rule. Or does it merely state a principle, so that when an abridgement of speech is discovered, it is unconstitutional unless the context presents some other policy or principle which in the circumstances is weighty enough to permit the abridgement? That is the position of those who argue for what is called the 'clear and present danger' test or some other form of 'balancing'.

Sometimes a rule and a principle can play the same role, and the difference between them is almost a matter of form alone. The first section of the Sherman Act states that every contract in restraint of trade shall be void. The Supreme Court had to make the decision whether this provision should be treated as a rule in its own terms (striking down every contract 'which restrains trade', which almost any contract does) or as a principle, providing a reason for striking down a contract in the absence of effective contrary policies. The Court construed the provision as a rule, but treated that rule as containing the word 'unreasonable' and as prohibiting only 'unreasonable' restraints of trade. This allowed the provision to function logically as a rule (whenever a court finds that the restraint is 'unreasonable' it is bound to hold the contract invalid) and substantially as a principle (a court must take into account a variety of other principles and policies in determining whether a particular restraint in particular economic circumstances is 'unreasonable').[10]

RELEVANCY

What is relevant in any process of proof or disproof is generally, as Thayer put it, a question of 'logic and general experience', not one of law. Our first task, therefore, is to try to clarify the ways of 'logic and general experience'.

JH Wigmore, *The Principles of Judicial Proof* (1931, 2nd edn)

9. Form of Inference is Inductive. The process of passing upon judicial evidence is and must be based ultimately on the canons of ordinary reasoning, whether explicitly or implicitly employed. It is therefore necessary to review the distinction which logic makes between the two great types of argument or inference – the deductive and the inductive forms.

The deductive form is this (known as a 'syllogism'): 'Persons related by blood to a party are biased in their testimony' (major premise). 'This witness is related by blood to a party' (minor premise). 'Therefore, this witness is biased in his testimony' (conclusion). The inductive form is this: 'This witness is related by blood to a party' (thesis). 'Therefore, he is biased in his testimony' (conclusion). Modern logic looks at this distinction without prejudice. Its tendency is to accept both types as capable of reduction to a single one. Nevertheless the distinction is a practical and substantial one, particularly in litigious proof. It is set forth with clearness and brevity by an eminent authority.

Professor Alfred Sidgwick, *Fallacies: A View of Logic from the Practical Side* (1884) pp 212ff:

> 'The real foundation of proof is always the recognition of resemblance and difference between things or events known and observed, and those which are on their trial – whether such recognition is based (1) on knowledge already reached and formulated in names or propositions or (2) on direct observation and experiment. (1) In proportion as we openly and distinctly refer to known principles (already generalized knowledge) is proof *deductive* ; (2) in proportion as we rapidly and somewhat dimly frame new principles for ourselves from the cases observed is proof *inductive, empirical,* or (in its loosest form) analogical ... The whole history of the rise and growth of knowledge (it has been also already remarked) is a record of fruitful rivalry and interaction between two opposite processes ... '

A brief examination will show that in the offering of evidence in court the form of inference is usually inductive.

---

10. Dworkin, *Philosophy of Law*, pp 45-49.

Suppose, to prove a charge of murder, evidence is offered of the defendant's fixed design to kill the deceased. The form of the inference is: 'A planned to kill B; therefore, A probably did kill B.' It is clear that we have here no semblance of a syllogism. The form of inference is exactly the same when we argue: 'Yesterday, Dec 31, A slipped on the sidewalk and fell; therefore, the sidewalk was probably coated with ice'; or, 'Today A, who was bitten by a dog yesterday, died in convulsions; therefore, the dog probably had hydrophobia'. So with all other legal evidentiary facts, whether circumstantial or testimonial, we may argue: 'Last week the witness A had a quarrel with the defendant B; therefore, A is probably biased against B'; 'A was found with a bloody knife in B's house; therefore, A is probably the murderer of B'; 'After B's injury at A's machinery, A repaired the machinery; therefore, A probably acknowledged that the machinery was negligently defective'; 'A, an adult of sound mind and senses, and apparently impartial, was present at an affray between B and C, and testifies that B struck first; therefore, it is probably true that B did strike first'. In all these cases, we take a single or isolated fact, and upon it base immediately an inference as to the proposition in question. This is the inductive, or empiric, process.

It may be objected, however, that in all the above instances, the proposed inference is implicitly based upon an understood law or generalization, and is thus capable of being expressed in the deductive or syllogistic form. Thus, in the first instance above, is this not the true form: 'Men's fixed designs are probably carried out; A had a fixed design to kill B; therefore, A probably carried out his design and did kill B'?

There are two answers to this objection:

(1) It has just been seen that every inductive inference is at least capable of being transmuted into and stated in the deductive form, by forcing into prominence the implied law or generalization on which it rests more or less obscurely. Thus it is nothing peculiar to litigious inference that this possibility of turning it into deductive form exists here also. But it is not a question of what the form *might* be – for all inductive may be turned into deductive forms – but of what it *is*, as actually employed; and it *is* actually put forward in inductive form.

(2) Even supposing this transmutation to be a possibility, it would still be actually undesirable to make this transmutation for the purpose of testing probative value; because it would be useless. We should ultimately come to the same situation as before. Thus, in one of the instances above: 'A repaired machinery after the accident; therefore, A was conscious of a negligent defect in it'; suppose we turn this into deductive form: 'People who make such repairs show a consciousness of negligence; A made such repairs; therefore, A was conscious of negligence.' We now have an inference which sounds (in form, at least) deductive, ie if the premises be conceded. But it remains for the court to declare whether it accepts the major premise, and so the court must take it up for examination, and the proponent of the evidence appears as its champion and his new inference becomes: 'The fact that people make such repairs indicates (shows, proves, probably shows, etc) that they are conscious of negligence.' But here we come again, after all, to an inductive form of inference. The consciousness of negligence is to be inferred from the fact of repairs – just as the presence of electricity in the clouds was inferred by Franklin from the shock through the kite string, ie by a purely inductive form of reasoning. So with all other evidence when resolved into the deductive form; the transmutation is useless, because the court's attention is merely transferred from the syllogism as a whole to the validity of the inference contained in the major premise; which presents itself again in inductive form.

For practical purposes, then, it is sufficient to treat the use of litigious evidentiary facts as generally inductive in form.

10. Same: Occasional Deductive Form. Nevertheless, the deductive form occasionally may be used – even must be used, in seeking to discover the real points of weakness of inference. The two commoner cases of this use are, (1) in circumstantial evidence, inferences involving a supposed general truth of natural science; and (2) in testimonial evidence, inferences involving a supposed general truth of testimonial psychology.

(1) Suppose a case of tracking an offender by a bloodhound; the hound has been put on a scent and has trailed the accused. The evidence is then offered in the form: 'This hound, put on the scent at the place of the offence, has gone to the accused; therefore the accused was at the place.' But here the evidential fact is seen to rest implicitly on some generalization about hounds; and that generalization needs to be made explicit. Doing this, we obtain the following: (a) bloodhounds when put on a scent at the place of an offence can find a person who was there; (b) this bloodhound, being so put, found this accused; (c) therefore this accused was there. But now, with our attention on premise (a), and studying it as a *probandum*, it may turn out to be loose and unacceptable. Perhaps it can be acceptable only in this form: bloodhounds of *recorded pedigree* and *oft-tested qualities*, when put on a scent, etc. In this (supposedly) correct form, as an accepted truth of canine zoology, we now perceive that the minor premise (b) does not fit ; for the offer does not state that this hound has pedigree and experience. Thus the weakness of the inference is exposed.

   In this way, the deductive form may prove serviceable, and may more readily enable the inference to be valued.

(2) Suppose a witness testifying to the brown color of the suit of clothes of a person to be identified; the sun was low in the west, and the witness was looking westward. The offer is: 'This witness, in the above circumstances, saw a man wearing a brown suit; therefore the man was wearing a brown suit.' Now, put deductively, the offer becomes: (a) A person looking west under the above circumstances and seeing a brown suit sees accurately; (b) This witness did so look; (c) therefore he saw accurately. Thus phrased, it may now develop from expert testimony that the major premise is unacceptable, because a person looking westward into bright sun cannot distinguish between black and brown, and thus black will seem brown under those circumstances. Here, by forcing the underlying generalization into the open, we are able to discover its lack of foundation, and the inference is found to be valueless.[11]

It is worth breaking into Wigmore's exposition at this point to emphasise how important it is to force underlying generalisations into the open when considering questions of relevancy.

William Twining, *Theories of Evidence: Bentham and Wigmore* (1985)

V is found dead from a stab wound in the back. W, a forensic scientist, testifies that a particular knife was the murder weapon. He also testifies that there was one clear set of fingerprints on the weapon with characteristics x, y, z etc and that M's finger patterns conform precisely to the prints. In this simple example, particular scientific findings establish the cause of death, the identity of the

---

11. Wigmore, *Principles*, pp 17-22.

murder weapon and the identity of a person who had handled the weapon. They all form part of a chain of reasoning which has strong, but not necessarily conclusive, probative force despite the length of the chain. It is possible that W is lying or mistaken, or that the prints were planted, or that M's fingerprints were there innocently or that V was killed by accident or in self-defence. In short, the argument is open to attack at a number of points. Nevertheless, most people would agree there is a strong *prima facie* case against M.

How do we arrive at this judgment? The standard answer lies in the fact that several, but not all, of the links in the chain are backed up by a body of well-founded *general* scientific knowledge. In ordinary discourse we tend to gloss over the background generalisations that support such inferences. For example, we tend to move directly from the fact that M's finger patterns coincide with the prints on the knife to the conclusion that it was almost certainly or very probably M who killed V. If called on to justify such inferences and our assessments of their strength we invoke generalisations of the kind 'a finger pattern x, y, z etc can be borne by one person only' or, more cautiously, 'Where a person's finger patterns coincide with a set of clear fingerprints it is very probable indeed that the prints were that person's'. The generalisation thus forms the major premiss of a syllogism:

A finger pattern x, y, z can be borne by one person only.

M bears that finger pattern.

M is that person.

In this instance the major premiss is based on a well-developed body of scientific knowledge; yet it is striking that even in this context forensic scientists are very reluctant to give precise numerical estimates of the chances of more than one person in a given population having the same fingerprints. It is only exceptionally that we are in a position to appeal to such scientific generalisations as a basis for making inferences from evidence. Typically we have to appeal to our own personal or vicarious experience, often referred to as 'common sense', 'general knowledge' or 'experience of the common course of events'. Some of the problems surrounding such generalisations can be illustrated by another example.

Edith Thompson was accused of inciting her lover, Frederick Bywaters, to murder her husband, Percy. Edith was twenty-eight years old at the time, Freddy was only twenty. Is his discrepancy in age relevant to the *probandum* of incitement? Many people would intuitively feel that it is; counsel for the prosecution in the case, the trial judge and many commentators have all assumed it to be relevant. Yet an argument which goes: 'X was older than Y, therefore she incited Y' seems highly dubious. Can the inference be justified analytically and, if so, how?

The standard answer to this kind of question is that the *factum probans* is linked to the *factum probandum* by an implicit generalisation. Common sense does suggest that there is some connection between age and influence in human relationships but this is too vague. What precisely is the generalisation? Let us consider just two possible candidates:

(i)   All older women always dominate younger men in all circumstances.

(ii)   There is a tendency for the older person in an intimate relationship to be the dominant partner.

The first proposition provides the major premiss for a syllogism proving that Edith dominated Freddy. The argument is valid, but the premiss is easily falsified. There is no scientific evidence to support such a broad generalisation and most people can produce counter-examples from their own experience to show that (i) is at the very least grossly over-generalised. Furthermore, it appears to be both prejudiced and prejudicial.

At first sight, (ii) seems to meet these objections. It is not framed in sexist terms and it is more likely to be true than (i). However, it is open to some further objections. First, it is very vague: it does not even differentiate between often, sometimes and occasionally, let alone quantify the estimate of frequency; secondly, how are we to know whether it is true or not? and thirdly, it is not universal. It therefore does not establish a necessary connection between the fact that Edith was older than Freddy and the allegation that she incited him to murder.

Thus (i), if it were true, would establish a very strong probative relation between the *factum probans* and the *factum probandum*; but it is not true. On the other hand, (ii) might be true, but its strength as a bridge between the *factum probans* and the *factum probandum* is both weak and indeterminate. To complicate matters (i) and (ii) are by no means the only possible generalisations that might provide a link between the relative ages of Edith and Freddy and the allegation of incitement. Indeed, taken in isolation from a whole mass of other general and particular background information it is not possible to make any confident judgment about the probative value, if any, of this particular fact ...

Binder and Bergman state a commonly held view: 'A generalisation is, then, a premiss which rests on the general behaviour of people or objects. How does one formulate generalisations? Usually, one adopts conventional wisdom about how people and objects function in everyday life. All of us, through our own personal experiences, through hearing about the personal experiences of others, and through knowledge gained from books, movies, newspapers and television, have accumulated vast storehouses of commonly held notions about how people and objects generally behave in our society. From this storehouse one formulates a generalisation about typical behaviour. The generalisation, in turn, becomes the premiss which enables one to link specific evidence with an element one hopes to prove.'

Sociologists of knowledge, sceptics and relativists of various kinds have done much to heighten our awareness of the difficulties and dangers of accepting 'common sense' generalisations and the like as constituting 'objective knowledge'. In respect of any such generalisation one should not assume too readily that there is in fact a 'cognitive consensus' on the matter. The stock of knowledge in any society varies from group to group, from individual to individual and from time to time. Even when there is widespread consensus, what passes as 'conventional knowledge' may be untrue, speculative or otherwise defective; moreover 'common sense generalisations' tend not to be purely factual – they often contain a strong mixture of valuation and prejudice, as is illustrated by various kinds of social, national and racial stereotypes.[12]

Because relevancy depends on some underlying generalisation, which itself may be wrong or at least questionable, the detection of generalisations is a useful weapon in the hands of an advocate who wishes to exclude potentially damaging evidence. The reason for this is that while there is a general principle that evidence is admissible if it is logically relevant to an issue in question[13] that

---

12. Twining, *Theories of Evidence*, pp 142–46.
13. *Sims* [1946] KB 531, 537, *per* Lord Goddard CJ.

is not the end of the story. Relevancy 'does not result in evidence being admissible: it is a condition precedent to admissibility'.[14] It follows that if evidence is not relevant, it is inadmissible. Thus if you can show that the relevancy of a piece of evidence that your opponent wishes to tender depends on the truth of a generalisation that is wrong, or at least questionable because that generalisation is itself unsupported by evidence, you will have good grounds for arguing that the evidence in question should be excluded.

Suppose you are satisfied that an item of evidence is relevant to an issue in question, and that it cannot be excluded by some principle or rule of law. There may still be considerable room for argument about the inferences that should be drawn from it.

JH Wigmore, *The Principles of Judicial Proof* (1931, 2nd edn)

11. Practical Requirements of the Inference-Process, to Avoid Fallacious Inference. The next inquiry is, What are the peculiar dangers of the inference, the loopholes for error, the opportunities for false inference? By ascertaining these we shall learn what safeguards or tests ought to be applied by the jurors in weighing the evidence, and what opportunities of counter-inference are offered to the opponent.

These peculiar dangers and necessities are thus set forth by the same eminent authority: Professor Alfred Sidgwick, *Fallacies* (1884) p 270.

> 'There is at bottom one primary source of fallacy in the inductive argument, call it by whatever name may be most convenient. We may name it, for instance, the danger of overlooking plurality of causes, or of neglecting possible chance or counteraction, or the possibility of unknown antecedents, or of arguing either *"post hoc ergo propter hoc"* or *"per enumerationem simplicem"*,[15] or of neglecting to exclude alternative possibilities, or of forgetting that facts may bear more than one interpretation ... or of failing to see below the surface, or – perhaps on the whole the best of all – of unduly neglecting points of difference ...
>
> [The form of proposed inference is] a case or cases brought forward, of which a certain conclusion is asserted to be the best explanation. If, then, some better explanation is possible, the theory as stated is impeachable ... By the "best" explanation is meant ... that solitary one out of all possible hypotheses which, while explaining all the facts already in view, is narrowed, limited, hedged, or qualified, sufficiently to guard in the best possible way against

---

14. *Turner* [1975] QB 834, 841, *per* Lawton LJ.

15. *Post hoc ergo propter hoc*. Literally, 'After this, therefore because of this'. The name given to the fallacy of supposing that event B is due to event A, merely because event B occurred after event A. For example, Alice feels depressed and anxious after the death of her husband. She has weekly sessions of psychotherapy at considerable expense for five years. At the end of that period she no longer feels anxious or depressed. She attributes this to the powers of her psychotherapist, arguing that before she went to him she was suffering from depression and anxiety and after five years of sessions she was not. But her anxiety and depression might well have disappeared naturally by the time five years had elapsed. An argument *per enumerationem simplicem* is an inductive argument by simple, ie mere, enumeration, and consists in arguing that what is true of several instances of a kind is true universally in that kind. For example, every swan I have ever seen is white. From this I conclude that all swans are white. But I am wrong. Black swans exist, though I have never seen them. For a short, readable introduction to these and other problems of logic, see Wesley C Salmon, *Logic* (Englewood Cliffs, New Jersey: Prentice-Hall Inc, 1984, 3rd edn).

undiscovered exceptions ... All positive proof depends ... on the care, the precautions with which observation has been interpreted and experiment conducted. So far only as these exclude alternative possibilities are they of real value ...

The real important point is, always, to show that all other possible theories are weighed in the balance and found wanting – that is to say, that all precautions have been taken against that crudest kind of unchecked generalization which the least-trained mind possesses in the greatest abundance ... And the right of the theory chosen, over all its possible rivals, depends entirely upon the depth of our insight into the conditions under which the experiment or observation was really made. This is the main lesson of logic as regards induction ... The immediate question in each case is, What certainty can we obtain that the alternative chosen is the right one put out of all those conceivable? The method of inductive proof may be viewed as attempts to answer this question.'

The peculiar danger, then, of inductive inference is that there may be *other explanations*, ie possible inferences, than the alleged *probandum* one, from the fact taken as the basis of proof.

Let us now examine this principle from the point of view of the opposing parties in a legal trial. Since our system of procedure is based on the method of leaving the production of evidence to the parties themselves, the proceeding is an antiphonal one: proponent and opponent in turn offer evidence. Both counsel and jury therefore need to examine each piece of evidence, first, from the proponent's point of view, next, from the opponent's point of view, and, finally, from the jury's point of view.

12. Same: from the Viewpoint of the Proponent of Evidence. If the potential defect of inductive evidence is that the fact offered as the basis of the conclusion may be open to one or more other explanations or inferences, the failure to exclude a single other rational inference would be, from the standpoint of *proof*, a fatal defect; and yet, if only that single other inference were open, there might still be an extremely high degree of probability for the *inference* desired. When Robinson Crusoe saw the human footprint on the sand, he could not argue inductively that the presence of another human being was absolutely proved; there was at least (for example) the possible inference of his own somnambulism. Nevertheless, the fact of the footprint was, as a basis of inference, evidence of an extraordinary degree of probability. The provisional test, then, from the point of view of valuing the inference, would be something like this: *Does the evidentiary fact point to the desired conclusion* (not as the only rational inference, but) *as the inference* (or explanation) *most plausible or most natural out of the various ones that are conceivable*? Or (to state the requirements more weakly), is the desired conclusion (not the most natural, but) *a* natural or plausible one among the various conceivable ones? After all the other evidential facts have been introduced and considered, the net conclusion can be attempted. But in dealing with each separate fact, the only inquiry is a provisional one: How probable is the *probandum* as the explanation of this *probans*?

This test for the probative value of a proposed inference may be illustrated from various sorts of evidentiary facts:

(1) The fact that A left the city soon after a crime was committed will raise a slight probability that he left because of his consciousness of guilt, but a greater one if his knowledge that he was suspected be first shown. Here the evident notion is that the mere fact of departure by one unaware of the charge is open to too many innocent explanations; but the addition of the fact

that A knew of the charge tends to put these other inferences into the background, and makes the desired explanation or conclusions – ie a guilty consciousness – stand out prominently as a more probable and plausible one. Even then there are other possible inferences – such as summons from a dying relative or the fear of a yellow-fever epidemic in the city; but these are not the immediately natural ones, and the greater naturalness of the desired explanation makes it highly probable.

(2) The fact that A before a robbery had no money, but after it had a large sum, is offered to indicate that he by robbery became possessed of the large sum of money. There are several other possible explanations – the receipt of a legacy, the receipt of a debt, the winning of a gambling game, and the like. Nevertheless, the desired explanation rises, among other explanations, to a fair degree of plausibility.

(3) The fact that A, charged with stealing a suit of clothes, was a poor man is offered to show him to be a thief. Now the conclusion of theft from the mere fact of poverty is, among the various possible conclusions, one of the least probable; for the conclusions that he would preferably work or beg or borrow are all equally or more probable, and the inference of stealing, being also a dangerous one to adopt as the habitual construction to be put on poor men's conduct, has the double defect of being less probable and more hard upon the innocent. Such evidence, then, is of slight value to show that conclusion.

(4) A person of unbalanced delusions asserts on the stand that he saw A strike B. Nowadays it is recognized that a delusion may affect the powers of observation and memory to a limited extent only, and may not concern the subject of the testimony. If it does concern that subject, the inference that the act occurred as he stated it is too feeble and improbable, alongside of the inference that his delusion is the only source of his statement. But if the delusion does not concern that subject, then his statement may prove something, even though it is still possible that his statement has been affected by the delusion. Thus the notion is, as before, that the evidentiary fact – ie the assertion on the stand – is of probative value as far as the correctness of the assertion is at least one among probable inferences.

(5) The fact that A makes his statement on the witness stand in response to a leading question of his counsel is not of great value to show the fact asserted by him, because in experience the chances are so great that his answer is based on the counsel's suggestion and not on his own knowledge. On the other hand, where the leading question deals merely with the preliminary matters of his name, age and residence, the answer is fairly probative, because, there being so little motive for falsification on those subjects, the conclusion that he answered truly is far the most probable one.

(6) The fact that A, the witness, has had a lawsuit with B, the defendant, is offered to show that A has feelings of animosity towards B which make it probable that he cannot testify correctly against him. Yet the inference of such animosity is a forced and unnatural one; the mere fact of a lawsuit is consistent with so many other more probable inferences that the evidence does not reach a great degree of probative value.

Thus, throughout the whole realm of evidence, circumstantial and testimonial, the theory of the inductive inference, as practically applied, is that the evidentiary fact has probative value only so far as the desired conclusion based upon it is a more probable or natural inference, and as the other inferences or explanations of the fact, if any, are less probable or natural. The degree of strength required will vary with different sorts of evidentiary facts, depending somewhat upon differing views of human experience with those facts, somewhat upon the practical availability of stronger facts. But the general spirit and mode of reasoning of the courts substantially illustrates the dictates of scientific logic.

13. Same: from the Viewpoint of the Opponent of Evidence. The pure scientist works alone in his laboratory; there is no one at hand to dispute his every step of inference. But in judicial trials, there are always two parties; the partisan proponent offers his evidence, without pointing out its weaknesses; the partisan opponent points out the weaknesses, ie, the possible explanations. Therefore it is important to notice the double treatment of which every offer of evidence may admit.

Where the scientist is dealing with the subject of proof in logic, the single stage of the inquiry is whether the argument offered as involving proof does really fulfil the logical requirements. But wherever, in the application of logical principles to specific practical purposes, two parties are found contending, the proponent and the opponent – as in a formal debate, and, pre-eminently, a trial at law – the treatment of the inference falls into two stages. Whenever, on the evidential fact offered by the proponent, a single other inference remains open, complete proof fails; the desired conclusion is merely the more probable, or a probable inference; the other possible inferences, less probable or equally probable, remain open. It is thus apparent that, by the very nature of this process, a specific course is suggested for the opponent. *He may now properly show, by adducing other facts*, that one or another of these inferences, thus left open, is not merely possible and speculative, but is more probable and natural as the true explanation of the originally offered evidentiary fact. That fact has been admitted in evidence, but its force may now be diminished or annulled by showing that some explanation of it other than the proponent's is the true one.

Thus every sort of evidentiary fact may call for treatment in a second aspect, by the opponent, *viz: What are the other possible inferences which are available for the opponent as explaining away* the force of the fact already admitted? To illustrate:

(1) In showing the defendant's connection with a murder, the fact is admitted of the finding of a knife, bearing his name, near the body of the deceased; the defendant, to refute the claimed conclusion that he was present with the knife at the murder, may show that he lost the knife a month before; thus giving greater color of probability to the inference that someone else was present with the knife.

(2) To show the defendant's animosity against the deceased, the fact of a serious quarrel ten years before is offered; the claimed conclusion, namely, that the animosity existed at the time of the killing, is an inference of low relative probability; for the opponent may show, by the fact of a reconciliation in the interim, that the fact of the quarrel does not lead to the conclusion claimed.

(3) To show the injurious vibrative qualities of a bridge in causing cracks in adjacent buildings, the fact of the existence of cracks in other adjacent buildings is received; this may be explained away by the fact that the operation of a railway, and not the bridge vibrations, had been their cause.

(4) A witness may appear to have had adequate opportunity to observe accurately the facts related; but he may be mendacious by disposition, and if the opponent can show his bad character, it will tend to explain away all his assertions as those of a confirmed liar.

(5) The rest of a conversation or writing, of which a part has been received, may be presented by the opponent to explain away the apparent effect of the fragment; thus, to adopt Algernon Sidney's famous illustration (frequently

used by Erskine in his arguments for the accused in the sedition trials of the 1790s), the prosecution, on a charge of blasphemy, might offer a statement of the defendant: 'There is no God'; but this might be instantly explained away as being merely part of a quotation from the Bible of the passage: 'The fool hath said in his heart, "There is no God".'

Such is the complementary process of explanation, by the opponent.

How does the opponent use this process, in practice? *By offering evidentiary data tending to prove one more of the explanations.* The explanation, which is at first only a possibility, may thus become a fact. The greater the value of the opponent's inference to the explanation, the less the value of the proponent's inference to the *probandum* ...

14. Other Processes For the Opponent. Thus far, in considering the process of inference from a particular evidentiary fact, we have noticed that its weaknesses give rise to the opponent's process of explanation.

But are there no other processes used by the opponent, in opposing this proposed inference?

There are, indeed, two other processes, and only two. He has three processes in all. He may (1), as already seen, seek to *explain* away the proposed inference. Or, (2) he may deny the existence of the evidentiary fact itself. Or, (3) he may offer some *new and rival* evidentiary fact, tending independently to disprove the *probandum*.

But in neither of the latter two cases is he using any new logical principle. In (2) he is not contesting the logical value of the proponent's inference, but is denying that its basis, the evidentiary fact, is a fact; and thus for that purpose he becomes a proponent of new data, and offers inferences from new evidentiary facts tending to disprove the proponent's original evidentiary fact. In (3) he neither explains away the force of the proponent's inference nor disputes the fact on which it rests; he offers a new fact, with an inference pointing directly at the *probandum*, but negatively; he thus becomes a proponent, in turn, as to that new rival evidentiary fact; and the same logical principle applies, in valuing his new proposed inference, that applied to the proponent's original inference.

To illustrate:

To charge A with murder, the prosecution shows a specific threat, an old quarrel, and traces of blood on his clothes. The defendant may answer:

(1) *Explaining* away the old quarrel by showing an intervening reconciliation; explaining away the blood traces by showing the recent killing of a chicken; this is the complementary process of explanation suggested by the evidentiary facts of quarrel and blood, and is directed to diminishing their force; this complementary process depends for its conditions and possibilities upon those original facts;

(2) *Denying* the specific threat; this in itself does not affect the logical probative value of the threat as circumstantial evidence; it introduces a new issue of evidence, raising a doubt as to the very existence of the circumstantial fact;

(3) *Advancing the rival facts* of an alibi and of good character for peaceableness; here the defendant is simply a proponent of new evidentiary facts, just as the prosecution was for its own evidence; this new question of relevancy depends on precisely the same tests as the prosecution's original evidence.

All an opponent's modes are reducible to these three. In the first, he is an opponent by logical nature of his argument. In the second, he is an opponent from the contradictory point of view, but this may require him to become a proponent of

either a new circumstance or a new witness. In the third, he becomes himself the proponent of a new argument, which the original proponent may now attack as an opponent. The first is inherent in the probative use of the proponent's original fact; the other two are not inherent, and may or may not be resorted to.

We have thus cleared the ground by discovering that *all of an opponent's processes fall into one of these three modes*. No matter how voluminous or complex the mass of evidence, the opponent's processes must take one or another of these three forms. It thus begins to be possible to analyze disentangle, chart, and think out a mass of evidence with greater clarity.

15. Summary View of the Four Probative Processes. It has been seen thus far, that every evidentiary fact or class of facts may call for four processes and raise four sets of questions, which may be grouped as follows. (P) represents the proponent, and (O) the opponent.

(P) The first process, assertion, consists in offering a fact tending *to prove* a specific conclusion or *probandum*. This is subject to the test whether the claimed conclusion is a probable or a more probable one, having regard to conceivable other interpretations of the fact. The process we may label PA.

(O) The second process, explanation, consists in *explaining away the original fact's force* by showing the existence and probability of other hypotheses; for this purpose other facts affording such explanations are receivable from the opponent. This process we label OE.

(O) The third process, denial, consists in *negating the original proponent's evidentiary fact* as such, either testimonially or circumstantially; and thus (O) as proponent offers a new witness or circumstance. This process we may label OD.

(O) The fourth process, rivalry, consists in adducing a new fact, circumstantial or testimonial, which by a *rival inference* tends to *disprove* the proponent's *probandum*. This process we may label OR. Here the opponent becomes in turn a proponent, and the fact offered by him is now open to the same processes as above from the original proponent, *viz*: OE, OD and OR.

Such are the forms of probative processes available for each single fact as offered. For each new fact the processes may be repeated, though they may not be actually used in each instance. Just as modern chemistry has analyzed the nutritive processes, and has discovered that the multifarious aspects of the daily menu are reducible to the three fundamental elements of proteins, fats and carbohydrates (to which the more recent science has added the vitamins), so we find that, amidst the multifarious varieties of evidence, our mental processes thereupon are reducible to four fundamental types, constantly repeated.[16]

Logic and general experience alone are not always enough to determine questions of relevancy that arise in legal proceedings. Some items of evidence which would be regarded as logically relevant may be excluded for reasons of policy or principle.[17] This may happen where the evidence falls within a more or less obvious area of public interest immunity, such as evidence on matters of state security, but it can also happen on other occasions.

---

16. Wigmore, *Principles*, pp 22-31.

17. In using these terms I follow Dworkin's usage in 'Is Law a System of Rules?' ie, a policy is 'that kind of standard that sets out a goal to be reached, generally an improvement in some economic, political, or social feature of the community'. A principle is 'a standard that is to be observed ... because it is a requirement of justice or fairness or some other dimension of morality'. (*Ibid*, pp 43-44.)

Hollingham v Head (1858, Court of Common Pleas)

This was an action for goods sold and delivered, tried, before Williams J at the last assizes for the county of Sussex, when it appeared that the plaintiff was the agent for the Sussex Farming Society, and attended markets for the purpose of selling a new kind of guano, called 'Rival Guano', and that the defendant, a farmer residing at Lindfield, in that county, had purchased a quantity of it, for the price of which this action was brought. The defence was, that this guano was a new kind, which the plaintiff, being anxious to introduce into the market, and in order to induce the defendant to become a purchaser, sold to him at £7 a ton, on condition that if it was not equal to Peruvian guano, the price of which was £14 a ton, the defendant was not to pay for it. With a view to establish this defence, the plaintiff was asked, on cross-examination by the defendant's counsel, whether he had not sold parcels of this same guano to other persons upon the same condition. The question was objected to by the plaintiff's counsel, but the learned judge allowed it to be put for the purpose only of pressing the witness's memory. The plaintiff having denied that he had ever sold any of this guano upon that condition, evidence was tendered as part of the defendant's case to prove that the plaintiff had done so. This evidence was also objected to by the plaintiff's counsel, and rejected by the learned judge. The jury returned a verdict for the plaintiff.

Montagu Chambers now moved for a new trial on the grounds that the evidence was improperly rejected.

Willes J: ... The question is, whether in an action for goods sold and delivered, it is competent for the defendant to shew, by way of defence, that the plaintiff had entered into contracts with other persons in a particular form, for the purpose of inducing the jury to come to the conclusion that the contract sued upon was in that particular form, and so to defeat the action; and I am of the opinion that it is not competent for the defendant to do so. The plaintiff's case in the present instance was, that he had sold to the defendant a quantity of guano at a certain price and without any condition. The defendant's case was, that it was sold on condition that he was not to pay for it unless it was equal to Peruvian guano. The plaintiff having been called as a witness in support of his own case, was asked on cross-examination, whether he had not sold the same quantity of guano to other persons on the same condition? As I understand it, this question was disallowed, if put for the purpose of shewing it was more probable that the defendant's account of the transaction was correct. And I also understand that my Brother Williams rejected similar evidence-in-chief, offered on the part of the defendant, on the ground that such evidence was not pertinent to the issue between the parties; and I think he was right in rejecting it on that ground. It may be often difficult to decide upon the admissibility of evidence, where it is offered for the purpose of establishing probability, but to be admissible it must at least afford a reasonable inference as to the principal matter in dispute. No doubt the rule, confining evidence to that which is relevant, is one of great importance; not only with regard to the particular case in which it has to be applied, but with reference to saving the time of the court, and preventing the minds of the jury being prejudiced, and distracted from the point in issue ... It appears to me that the evidence, which was proposed to be given in this case, would not have shewn that it was probable that the plaintiff had made the contract, which the defendant contended he had made; I do not see how the fact that a man has once or more in his life acted in a particular way makes it probable that he so acted on a given occasion. The admission of such evidence would be fraught with the greatest inconvenience. Where, indeed, the question is one of guilty knowledge or intent, as in the cases of uttering forged documents, or base coin, such evidence is admissible as tending to establish a necessary ingredient of the crime. But if the evidence were admissible in this case, it would be difficult to say that in any case, where the question was whether or not goods had been sold upon credit, the defendant might not call evidence to prove that the other persons had received credit from the plaintiff; or in an action for an assault, that the plaintiff might not prove that the defendant had assaulted other persons generally, or persons of a particular class. To obviate the prejudice, the injustice, and the waste of time to which the admission of such evidence would lead, and bearing in mind the extent to which it might be carried, and that litigants are mortal, it is necessary not only to adhere to the rule, but to lay it down strictly. I think, therefore, the fact that the plaintiff had entered into contracts of a particular kind with other persons on other occasions could not properly be admitted in evidence, where no custom of trade to make such contracts, and no connection between such and the one in question, was shewn to exist ...

Byle J: I am of the same opinion. This appears to me to be a perfectly clear case ... Such evidence, when offered as part of the defendant's case, was totally inadmissible. To have admitted it would have been contrary to all principle, and to what has been the universal practice so long as I have known the profession.

Williams J: ... As to the evidence offered by the defendant, there can be no doubt whatever that that was inadmissible. It would lead to the greatest inconvenience if we were once to relax the rule, which requires the evidence to be confined to the points in issue, by allowing other transactions to be inquired into.[18]

Willes J said: 'I do not see how the fact that a man has once or more in his life acted in a particular way makes it probable that he so acted on a given occasion.' One can only conclude that if he meant what he said, he was a very short-sighted man. There clearly may be circumstances where the fact that someone has done X in the past makes it more likely that, where X has been committed, he, *rather than someone who has not done X before*, has committed X on this occasion. If my cat Rimsky has in the past caught birds in the garden and brought them into the house, but my other cat Romanov has not, Rimsky's past behaviour is relevant if I want to know who has brought in the sparrow which I have just found in the kitchen. That, of course, was not the type of question asked in *Hollingham v Head*. What the defendant wanted to do apparently – it is not wholly clear from the report – was to establish that the contract which he had made with the plaintiff was part of a campaign of promotion for 'Rival Guano' which the plaintiff was engaged in at the time. In those circumstances it would surely have been relevant to establish the existence of such a campaign by showing that contracts had been made by the plaintiff with other persons on identical terms.[19]

The real reason for exclusion appears to have been pragmatic: inconvenience would be caused if such evidence were to be admitted. The length of trials would have tended to increase, and this would have been an important

---

18. (1858) 27 LJCP 241.
19. It is not clear whether the other transactions fitted a product promotion pattern; the report does not give details of alleged times and places.

consideration in the mid-19th century when the assize system was threatening to break down under an increasing case load.

A recent decision of the House of Lords shows pragmatic considerations affecting relevancy in a more subtle way. The leading speech, with which all the other Law Lords concurred, was delivered by Lord Bridge.

R v Blastland (1985, House of Lords)

Lord Bridge of Harwich: My Lords, at about 6 pm on Thursday, 9 December 1982 a 12 year old boy named Karl Fletcher left his home in Gainsborough after an argument with his mother. Later in the evening his mother became alarmed when he did not return and set about to look for him without success. Shortly after midnight she reported to the police that her son was missing. Karl's body was found the following morning on some open ground about half a mile from his home lying face down in a drainage ditch. He had been forcibly buggered and strangled with a scarf. His death by strangulation occurred on the Thursday evening, but the precise time of it was not established by the evidence.

On 4 October 1983 the appellant was arraigned before Bush J and a jury in the Crown Court at Lincoln on an indictment charging him with both buggery and murder. After a trial which lasted seven days he was convicted on both counts.

The prosecution case against the appellant was an extremely cogent one, but since its details are not germane to any issue arising in the present appeal it would serve no useful purpose to summarise it here. The appellant's own evidence, shortly stated, was that he admitted meeting the deceased boy at some time between 6 and 7 pm on the Thursday not far from where the body was later found. He engaged in homosexual activity with him, to which, according to the appellant, the boy consented in return for a money payment. He first attempted to bugger the boy but, when the boy complained of pain, desisted before achieving penetration. He then had oral intercourse with the boy. Very shortly after this the appellant said he saw another man nearby who, inferentially, could have seen what had happened between the boy and the appellant. Fearing that he had been observed committing a serious offence, the appellant panicked, ran away, and returned to his home. He gave a description of the other man which corresponded closely to a man who is, in a sense, the central character in this appeal and whom it will be appropriate in the circumstances to identify simply by his Christian name as Mark.

If the appellant's account was true, then Karl Fletcher, at some time in the evening after his encounter with the appellant, must have been buggered and murdered by another man. A central feature of the presentation of the appellant's defence at the trial was to invite the jury to draw the inference that that other man was Mark. It was certainly known to the jury that Mark had come under suspicion after Karl's murder, since there was a formal admission by the prosecution in the following terms: 'Mark was fully investigated by the police after the death of Karl Fletcher, including medical examination and submission of his clothing for forensic examination.'

The medical examination revealed an injury to Mark's penis, the significance of which was canvassed with the medical experts who gave evidence. The forensic examination disclosed nothing to connect Mark with Karl. In addition there were formal admissions by the prosecution showing Mark to have been known to engage in the past in homosexual activities with adults but not with children. There were also both formal admissions and evidence relating to Mark's movements on the evening of Karl's murder. All this was, I have no doubt, properly put before the jury as relevant and admissible material which they could be invited to weigh in the scales against the powerful case adduced for the Crown in deciding whether it might have been Mark, not the appellant, who murdered Karl Fletcher.

What the jury did not know was that, in a series of interviews with police officers, Mark had successively made and withdrawn admissions of his own guilt of the offences with which the appellant stood charged. Your Lordships are not in any way concerned with the reasons which prompted those responsible for investigating these horrifying crimes to conclude that Mark's admissions were untrue. Indeed, for a reason which will shortly become apparent, the detailed evidence of what was said at these interviews has not been included in the material put before your Lordships. At the trial counsel for the appellant sought to put the material in these interviews before the jury, first by an application to call a police officer and elicit from him directly what was said; second, by an application to call Mark, treat him as a hostile witness, and cross-examine him about what he had said at the interviews. Both applications were refused by Bush J.

The prosecution had very properly made available to the defence the statements of a number of witnesses to the effect that Mark had said to them that a little boy had been murdered. A woman named June, with whom Mark was living, was alleged by another woman to have told her that Mark came home about 8 pm on the Thursday evening of the murder, that at the time Mark was shaking like a leaf, covered in mud, and wet from his knees downwards, and that he then told her that a young boy had been murdered. Other witnesses said that they had been told by Mark on the Friday morning before the finding of Karl Fletcher's body that a boy had been murdered, and according to one witness that the murdered boy lived at an address which, though not in fact the address of the Fletcher family, was only a short distance from it in an adjoining street. The defence wished to call the woman, June, and the other witnesses mentioned in order to elicit from them what Mark had said about the boy's murder. The judge ruled that this evidence, like the evidence of what Mark had said to the police, would be hearsay and therefore admissible.

The appellant appealed against his conviction on the ground that the judge had been wrong to exclude the evidence both of what Mark said in the police interviews and of what he said on Thursday evening and Friday morning, 9 and 10 December 1982, about the murder of a boy. No complaint was made of the judge's refusal to allow the defence to call Mark and treat him as hostile. The appeal was dismissed by the Court of Appeal, Criminal Division ...

The argument most attractively presented to us by counsel for the appellant may, I hope without doing him injustice, be summarised as follows. The authorities relating to the application of the hearsay rule contrast two distinct situations. In the first situation evidence is sought to be adduced of a statement made to a witness in order to prove the truth of the facts stated. This is hearsay evidence and must be excluded, unless it can be brought within one of the recognised exceptions to the hearsay rule. In the second situation evidence is sought to be adduced of a statement made to a witness in order to prove, not the truth of any facts stated, but the state of mind either of the person who made the statement or of the person to whom it was made. This evidence is not within the hearsay rule at all; it is direct and primary evidence of the state of mind of the maker or recipient of the statement. Applying this distinction to the statements here in question leads to the following conclusions. Knowledge is a state of mind. What Mark said to the witnesses on the Thursday evening when Karl was murdered and on the following morning was direct and primary evidence of his knowledge of the murder before the body had been found. Accordingly, the evidence was direct and primary evidence of that which it was called to prove. It was not excluded by the hearsay rule and should have been left to the jury, together with all the other evidence, for them to draw such inferences from it as they saw fit.

This argument seems to proceed from its premises to its conclusion by a formidable chain of reasoning. Yet, if it is right, the argument does appear to lead to the very odd result that the inference that Mark may have himself committed the murder may be supported indirectly by what Mark said, though if he had directly acknowledged guilt this would have been excluded. In giving his ruling that the disputed evidence be not admitted, Bush J succinctly and graphically expressed this view of the matter in the following words: 'The real purpose and relevance of calling the evidence as to the state of mind is to say that in effect that was an implied admission of the knowledge of the crime, which is an implied admission of the crime itself and that too I regard as hearsay evidence and inadmissible.'

I shall in due course need to examine the authorities on which counsel for the appellant relies to see how far they support him. But I prefer to approach the matter initially as one of principle. Hearsay evidence is not excluded because it has no logically probative value. Given that the subject matter of the hearsay is relevant to some issue in the trial, it may be potentially probative. The rationale of excluding it as inadmissible, rooted as it is in the system of trial by jury, is a recognition of the great difficulty, even more acute for a juror than for a trained judicial mind, of assessing what, if any, weight can properly be given to a statement by a person whom the jury have not seen or heard and which has not been subject to any test of reliability by cross-examination ...

It is, of course, elementary that statements made to a witness by a third party are not excluded by the hearsay rule when they are put in evidence solely to prove the state of mind either of the maker of the statement or the person to whom it was made. What a person said or heard said may well be the best and most direct evidence of that person's state of mind. This principle can only apply, however, when the state of mind evidenced by the statement is either itself directly in issue at the trial or is of direct and immediate relevance to an issue which arises at the trial. It is at this point, as it seems to me, that the argument for the appellant breaks down. The issue at the trial of the appellant was whether it was proved that the appellant had buggered and murdered Karl Fletcher. Mark's knowledge that Karl had been murdered was neither itself an issue, nor was it, *per se*, of any relevance to the issue. What was relevant was not the fact of Mark's knowledge but how he had come by that knowledge. He might have done so in a number of ways, but the two most obvious possibilities were either that he had witnessed the commission of the murder by the appellant or that he had committed it himself. The statements which it was sought to prove that Mark made, indicating his knowledge of the murder, provided no rational basis whatever on which the jury could be invited to draw an inference as to the source of that knowledge. To do so would have been mere speculation ...[20]

This was a case which raised two problems: one of hearsay, the other of relevancy. We do not need to consider the hearsay point now, but we do need to think about what Lord Bridge said concerning relevancy. As he saw it, the

---

20. [1985] 2 All ER 1095.

question was whether Mark's state of mind was 'of direct and immediate relevance' to an issue which arose at the trial. If the evidence didn't satisfy that test, it was inadmissible because of the general principle that relevancy is a precondition of admissibility.

A problem that at once arises is what we are to understand by the qualifying words 'direct and immediate'. What the prosecution had to prove in this case was that the defendant had murdered Karl. You might have thought that anything that tended to prove or disprove that proposition was relevant. What does the requirement that the relevancy be 'direct and immediate' add? Some things, of course, point more clearly to a particular conclusion than others. In Twining's example of murder by stabbing, the presence of the defendant's fingerprints on the murder weapon points quite strongly to his guilt. If, instead, the only evidence against the defendant was that he disliked the deceased and had been seen in the neighbourhood at about the time of death, that information would point a good deal less clearly to his guilt. But it would still be relevant to the question, 'Did the defendant murder the deceased?' because it provides some evidence of motive and opportunity. What we are left with is a difference in weight, not relevancy. Ought we to take Lord Bridge, then, as stipulating that for evidence to be relevant it must reach some minimum weight? But while 'weight' in relation to evidence can usually be understood, it is doubtful if the metaphor can be pressed so far. A requirement of a minimum weight demands the ability to measure exactly, and it is at this point that the metaphor ceases to be usable. While physical objects can be measured, evidence cannot.

Another way of reading what Lord Bridge said is to stress the inconclusiveness of the information. Mark's knowledge was relevant because it opened up a possibility that he had come by it in a way that was inconsistent with the guilt of the accused. But because the jury had no means of telling whether that possibility was likely to be right or not, it was 'irrelevant'. Evidence does not, of course, have to be conclusive to be admissible. But where there are no means of resolving an ambiguity, such evidence will be 'irrelevant' because, like the evidence in *Hollingham v Head* (1858), its admissibility would be 'fraught with the greatest inconvenience'. It would waste time, because it could never lead to anything more than speculation on the part of the jury. But then, as we shall see in the next chapter, the relevancy of Mark's knowledge will depend on how you express the question for the jury's consideration. Most people would say, in light of the standard of proof borne by the prosecution in a criminal trial, that the proper question for the jury was not, 'Did Blastland murder Karl?', but rather, 'Has the prosecution proved beyond reasonable doubt that Blastland murdered Karl?' Can we be as certain as Lord Bridge seems to have been that an unresolved ambiguity is incapable of providing a reasonable doubt?

CHAPTER 2

BURDEN AND STANDARD OF PROOF

THE BURDEN OF PROOF IN CIVIL CASES

Questions about the legal burden of proof, and about the standard of proof that has to be reached by the person on whom the legal burden lies, do not arise in relation to cases as a whole, although in criminal cases this fact can be obscured by the absence of pleadings. Instead, these questions arise in relation to discrete issues in each particular case. In many civil cases, and in some criminal cases also, one party will bear the legal burden of proof on some issues and the other party will bear it on others. What the issues are in any particular situation will be determined by the substantive law in a criminal case, and by a combination of substantive law and pleadings in a civil action. You will recall from Chapter 1 that in a criminal action the effect of pleading 'not guilty' is simply to put in issue every element of the offence alleged against the defendant.[1] There are in general no documents corresponding to civil pleadings. But in civil actions each party sets out in the pleadings the basic facts relied upon to establish a claim, defence or counterclaim, though not the details of the evidence relied upon in support.

Take, for example, the following pleadings in a simple case of negligence based on a road traffic accident.

IN THE BARCHESTER COUNTY COURT   Case No S 123
BETWEEN

OBADIAH SLOPE   *Plaintiff*

and

FRANCIS ARABIN   *Defendant*

PARTICULARS OF CLAIM

1. On 1 April 1994 the plaintiff was driving his Ford motor car, index number GFK 970, along Newbridge Road Barchester at the junction with Apsley Road when there was a collision between his car and a motor car, index number OLL 234, driven by the defendant.
2. The said collision was caused by the negligence of the defendant.

---

1. *Sims* [1946] KB 531, 537. But now there are informal procedures for clarifying issues in any complex criminal case at a pre-trial hearing, and there are statutory procedures for the same purpose at preparatory hearings in cases of serious or complex fraud. See Practice Rules 25 October 1994 and the Criminal Justice Act 1987, ss 7-11.

Particulars of Negligence

(a) Driving too fast.

(b) Emerging from Apsley Road into Newbridge Road without keeping any or any sufficient lookout for other vehicles.

(c) Failing to maintain a safe distance between his motor car and the car driven by the plaintiff.

(d) Failing to give way to the plaintiff.

(e) Failing to stop, slow down or take any or any sufficient action to avoid the said collision.

3. By reason of the matters aforesaid the plaintiff has suffered pain and injury, loss and damage.

Particulars of Personal Injury

The plaintiff suffered bruising to the chest and upper arms, lacerations to the forehead and shock, by reason whereof he was unable to work for 2 weeks.

Particulars of Loss and Damage

Cost of repair to motor car	£2,500
Loss of earnings net of tax	£1,500
Medical expenses	£800

AND the plaintiff claims:

(1) Damages

(2) Interest pursuant to section 69 of the County Courts Act 1984.

HAPHAZARD & CO

(Solicitors for the plaintiff)

DATED 28 September 1994
To the Barchester County Court
and to the defendant

IN THE BARCHESTER COUNTY COURT   **Case No S 123**
BETWEEN

OBADIAH SLOPE   *Plaintiff*

and

FRANCIS ARABIN   *Defendant*

DEFENCE AND COUNTERCLAIM

1. Paragraph 1 of the Particulars of Claim is admitted.

2. Paragraph 2 of the Particulars of Claim is denied. The said collision was caused, alternatively contributed to, by the negligence of the plaintiff.

Particulars

(a) Driving too fast.

(b) Failing to maintain any or any sufficient lookout for other vehicles.

(c) Failing to stop, swerve, slow down or take any or any sufficient action to avoid the said collision.

3. No admissions are made as to paragraph 3 of the Particulars of Claim. If, which is not admitted, the plaintiff suffered the alleged or any pain or injury, loss or damage, the same was contributed to by the plaintiff's failure to wear a seat belt.

COUNTERCLAIM

4. The defendant repeats paragraph 2 hereinabove.

5. By reason of the matters aforesaid, the defendant has suffered pain and injury, loss and damage.

Particulars of Personal Injury

The defendant suffered whiplash injury, shock and 2 broken teeth.

Cost of repair to motor car	£2,000
Loss of earnings net of tax	£500
Medical and dental expenses	£4,500

AND the defendant counterclaims:

(1) Damages

(2) Interest pursuant to s 69 of the County Courts Act 1984

HARDING & QUIVERFUL

(Solicitors for the defendant)

DATED 5 November 1994

To the Barchester County Court

and to the plaintiff.

On these pleadings the following issues arise:

(1) Whether the collision was caused solely by the defendant's or solely by the plaintiff's negligence. (Particulars of Claim para 2, Defence and Counterclaim para 2.)

(2) Whether the plaintiff suffered the alleged or any pain or injury, loss or damage as a result of the collision. (Particulars of Claim para 3, Defence and Counterclaim para 3.)

(3) Whether, even if the defendant is guilty of some negligence, the plaintiff is guilty of some contributory negligence also. (Defence and Counterclaim para 2.)

(4) Whether the plaintiff contributed to his own injuries by his failure to wear a seat belt. (Defence and Counterclaim para 3.)

(5) Whether the defendant suffered the alleged or any pain or injury, loss or damage as a result of the collision. (Defence and Counterclaim para 5.)

Note that it is *not* in issue that there was a collision between the two cars on the date and at the place alleged in the Particulars of Claim. (Particulars of Claim para 1, Defence and Counterclaim para 1.) Note, also, that none of the above issues would arise unless there were certain provisions of substantive law about duties of care and the effect of breaches of those duties on liability to pay damages for negligence.

It is a general principle that 'the burden of proof lies on the person who affirms a particular thing' rather than on the person who denies it. In *Joseph Constantine SS Line Ltd v Imperial Smelting Corpn Ltd* (1942) Viscount Maugham said that this was 'an ancient rule founded on considerations of good sense', which 'should not be departed from without strong reasons'. But he emphasised that this was only the general rule, saying that 'the burden of proof in any particular case depends on the circumstances under which the claim arises'.[2] The pleadings in *Slope v Arabin* show, as is usual in such cases, that the defendant not only denies any responsibility for the plaintiff's injuries and loss but puts in a claim of his own (the 'counterclaim') against the plaintiff, saying that the latter should compensate him for the injuries and loss which he himself has suffered as a result of the accident. In this situation the general rule about burdens of proof applies and the burden on the various issues will be distributed as follows:

(1) The plaintiff has the burden of proving that the collision was caused wholly, or at least partly, by the defendant's negligence.

(2) The plaintiff has the burden of proving that he suffered pain and injury, loss and damage as a result of the collision.

(3) The defendant has the burden of proving the allegation in his counterclaim that the collision was caused wholly or partly by the plaintiff's negligence.

(4) The defendant has the burden of proving that the plaintiff failed to wear a seat belt. (Once such a failure is shown, it will generally be presumed that the failure contributed to the injuries suffered.)

(5) The defendant has the burden of proving for the purposes of his counterclaim that he suffered the alleged pain and injury, loss and damage as a result of the collision.

A burden of proof can rest on only one party *in relation to any one issue*. Thus, in relation to a single issue, you cannot have a burden on one party to prove the existence of a state of affairs and a burden on another to disprove its existence. Do not be misled by the presence of a counterclaim; it raises quite separate issues. If the plaintiff fails to satisfy the judge that the accident was caused by the negligence of the defendant, the plaintiff fails to recover from the defendant, but the defendant does not automatically recover from the plaintiff. To do so,

---

2. *Constantine (Joseph) SS Line Ltd v Imperial Smelting Corpn Ltd* [1942] AC 154, 174.

the defendant must satisfy the judge that the accident was the plaintiff's fault. He may fail to achieve this. It might be a perfectly rational result for both claim and counterclaim to fail because on neither side was the evidence strong enough to persuade a judge that one party was at fault rather than the other. Courts have acknowledged that there may be cases where the evidence on each side appears to be evenly balanced, and that in those circumstances the distribution of the burden of proof may determine the issue.

Morris v London Iron and Steel Co Ltd (1987, Court of Appeal)

May LJ: ... A judge or a tribunal of fact should make findings of fact in relation to a matter before it if they can. In most cases, although in some it may be difficult, they can do just that. Having made them, the tribunal is entitled to draw inferences from the findings of primary fact where appropriate. In the exceptional case, however, a judge conscientiously seeking to decide the matter before him may be forced to say, 'I just do not know': indeed to say anything else might be in breach of his judicial duty. In this connection, however, I would say this. Speaking from my own experience, some people find it easier to make up their minds than others and it should not be thought that a swift reliance on where the burden of proof lies and a failure to decide issues of fact in the case ought in any way to be considered an easy or convenient refuge for anybody who does find it difficult to make up his mind in a particular case. Judges should, so far as is practicable and so far as it is in accordance with their conscientious duty, make findings of fact. But it is in the exceptional case that they may be forced to reach the conclusion that they do not know which side of the line the decision ought to be. In any event, where the ultimate decision can only be between two alternatives, for instance negligence or not, or, as in the instant appeal, dismissal or resignation, then when all the evidence in the case has been called the judge or the tribunal should ask himself or itself whether, on that totality of evidence, on the balance of probabilities, drawing whatever inferences may be thought to be appropriate, the alternative which is necessary for the plaintiff to succeed is made out. If it is not, then the operation of the principle of the burden of proof comes into play and the plaintiff fails.[3]

Unless you are dealing with the interpretation of a clause in a standard form of contract that has already been considered by the courts, it is well to be aware that the question where the burden of proof lies in any particular case is a matter of interpretation which may be more or less directed by principle or policy. For example, it was early decided that the burden of proof (and hence the right to begin at trial) would not be determined on the basis of mere formalism.

Soward v Leggatt (1836, Court of Exchequer)

Covenant – The declaration stated that the plaintiff, and Jane Soward, deceased, demised to the defendant a certain messuage, &c, and that the defendant covenanted to repair the messuage, &c, and to paint the outside wood-work once in every three years, and the inside wood-work within the last six years of the termination of the lease. Breach – That the defendant did not repair the said messuage, &c, and did not paint the outside wood-work once in every three years, and did not paint the inside wood-work within the last six years of the said term, 'but on the contrary thereof, &c, suffered and permitted the messuage,

---

3. [1987] 2 All ER 496.

&c, to become, &c, and the same during all that time were ruinous, prostrate, dilapidated, fallen down, and in decay, and in very bad state, order, and condition, for want of needful and necessary reparations and amendments thereof, and the same, at the end or expiration of the said term, were left by the defendant so ruinous, prostrate, dilapidated, fallen down, and in decay, and in such bad state, order, and condition, as last aforesaid,' contrary to the covenant, &c.

Plea – That the defendant did from time to time, at his own proper costs, &c, well and sufficiently repair the said messuage, &c; and that he did paint the outside wood-work once in every three years during the said term, that is to say (specifying the times); and that he did paint the whole of the inside parts that were usually painted within the last six years of the termination of the said term, to wit, on the 1st day of June, 1831, 'according to the tenor and effect of the said indenture, and of his covenant therein in that behalf contained; and that the defendant did not suffer and permit the said messuage, &c, to become and be, nor were the same ruinous, prostrate, dilapidated, fallen down, and in decay, and in a bad state of order and condition for want of needful and necessary reparations and amendments thereof, nor were the same at the end and expiration of the said term left by the said defendant so ruinous, prostrate, dilapidated, fallen down, and in decay, and in such bad state, order, and condition, as is in the said declaration alleged; and of this the said defendant puts himself on the country', &c.

Carrington, for the plaintiff, having opened the pleadings,

Bompas, Serjt, [for the defendant] claimed the right to begin ...

Lord Abinger CB: Looking at these things according to common sense, we should consider what is the substantive fact to be made out, and on whom it lies to make it out. It is not so much the form of the issue which ought to be considered, as the substance and effect of it. In many cases, a party, by a little difference in the drawing of his pleadings, might make it either affirmative or negative, as he pleased. The plaintiff here says, 'You did not repair'; he might have said, 'You let the house become dilapidated'. I shall endeavour by my own view to arrive at the substance of the issue, and I think in the present case that the plaintiff's counsel should begin.[4]

It may be particularly difficult to predict how a judge will distribute the burden of proof in a case where contractual provisions purporting to exclude or limit liability have to be interpreted.

The Glendarroch (1894, Court of Appeal)

[When reading this case, the following points should be noted:

- The court dealt with the action on the basis that the contract was on the terms of an ordinary bill of lading.

- The court implied a term so as to provide an exception to an exception already expressed.

- The court placed considerable reliance on earlier decisions about the burden of proof in cases where this standard contract had been litigated.]

APPEAL by the defendants, Wainwright Brothers & Co, against a decision of the President (Sir FH Jeune) in favour of the plaintiffs, JC Johnson & Co and HF

---

4.   7 Car & P 613; 173 ER 269.

Currie & Co, shippers and consignees respectively of certain sacks of cement damaged by water whilst being conveyed by the defendants in the steamship *Glendarroch*.

At the trial before Sir F Jeune, President, assisted by two of the Elder Brethren of the Trinity House, it appeared that the action was for breach of duty and breach of contract in and about the carriage of the cement which had been shipped in the defendants' vessel. The vessel stranded on St Patrick's Causeway in Cardigan Bay, and the cement sustained such damage as to be valueless.

No bill of lading had in fact been signed; but the learned judge found that the plaintiff's goods were carried on the terms of an ordinary bill of lading excepting perils of the sea, but not excepting negligence.

The defendants relied upon the exception in the bill of lading exempting them from liability in respect of perils of the sea; but after argument ... the learned judge ruled that, in order to excuse themselves for the damage to the goods, it lay on the defendants to shew, not only a peril of the sea, but a peril of the sea not occasioned by their negligence. Thereupon counsel for the defendants declined to call any evidence, and counsel for the plaintiffs asked for and obtained judgment for the agreed value of the goods, *viz* £335 16s 1d.

Lord Esher MR: We have to treat this case as if the contract were in the ordinary terms of a bill of lading. The contract being one on the ordinary terms of a bill of lading, the goods are shipped on the terms that the defendant undertakes to deliver them at the end of the voyage unless the loss of the goods during the voyage comes within one of the exceptions in the bill of lading.

The exception relied upon by the defendants is that the goods were lost or damaged by a peril of the sea; and upon that, it is alleged that, even though that be true, yet that peril of the sea was the result of negligent navigation on the part of the defendants' servants.

The law is that if that be made out the defendants have no defence, and the plaintiffs are entitled to succeed, and the real question is, how is that to be made out? By which of the parties is it to be made out?

It is to be decided according to the practice of the law courts; and the question is, how is that result to be arrived at? The terms of the bill of lading as they stand on paper are, except the loss be from perils of the sea. But then it is said that, nevertheless, if the perils of the sea are produced by the negligence of the defendants' servants, then that loss cannot be relied on by the defendants. How can that be unless there be an irresistible inference that such exception does exist in the contract, though it is not written in it, so that the exception must be read into it as if it were in it? Therefore, we must try and see whether this stipulation as to negligence must be written in, or be considered as written in.

The liabilities of shipowners under a bill of lading are in that part which precedes the exceptions. Is this stipulation about the loss being the result of the negligence of the shipowners' servants – although within the terms of the exception – is that to be written in before the exceptions or not? The first thing that strikes one is that in that part of the contract it is not wanted. It is immaterial. Before you come to the exceptions the liability of the shipowner is absolute. He has contracted that he will deliver the goods at the end of the voyage. If there were no exceptions, it would be utterly immaterial whether the loss was caused by his servants or not. Even if there were no negligence whatever he would be liable. It cannot be, therefore, that this irresistible inference ought to be written into that part of the contract. It is not wanted there; therefore you must write it into that part which contains the exceptions.

When you come to the exceptions, among others, there is that one, perils of the sea. There are no words which say 'perils of the sea not caused by the negligence of the captain or crew'. You have got to read those words in by a necessary inference. How can you read them in? They can only be read in, in my opinion, as an exception upon the exceptions. You must read in, 'Except the loss is by perils of the sea, unless or except that loss is the result of the negligence of the servants of the owner'.

That being so, I think that according to the ordinary course of practice each party would have to prove the part of the matter which lies upon him. The plaintiffs would have to prove the contract and the non-delivery. If they leave that in doubt, of course they fail. The defendants' answer is, 'Yes; but the case was brought within the exception – within its ordinary meaning'. That lies upon them. Then the plaintiffs have a right to say there are exceptional circumstances, *viz*, that the damage was brought about by the negligence of the defendants' servants, and it seems to me that it is for the plaintiffs to make out that second exception.

In my opinion, you find in all the books, down to the most modern times, that the pleading followed that view of the burden of proof. The declaration stated the bill of lading, and, relying on the first and substantive part of the bill of lading, alleged non-delivery. Strictly speaking, the declaration could not properly have stated anything about negligence, because negligence was immaterial. The plea followed the terms of the exception construed in their ordinary sense – that is, that the loss was a loss by perils of the sea. No plea that can be found in the books ever went on to say that the loss by perils of the sea was not caused by negligence. Yet, if the contention be true that the burden of proof to that extent lies on the defendant, every one of those pleas without that allegation was no answer to the declaration, and was open to demurrer. There is no such case in which a demurrer was brought forward and supported. As that was so, it shews that it was no part of the proof which the defendant was bound to give.

Then you have a long succession of cases, all setting out a replication, and that replication in the given case is: 'Yes, it is true there was a loss by perils of the sea within the *prima facie* exception; but that was brought about by the negligence of your servants – ie, by your captain and crew.' The plaintiff could not depart from his declaration; but he could support it by shewing that the exception was not satisfied, because there had been negligence.

That being the state of things, is there any case to the contrary of that constant course of pleading, and of that result of the principle of construction of a bill of lading? I know of none; but I think there are cases which distinctly shew that the course of pleading did give the right view of the different shiftings of the burden of proof ... [5]

Lopes and Davey LJJ delivered concurring judgments.

Hurst v Evans (1917, King's Bench Division)

By a policy of insurance dated 4 May 1915 the defendant and others insured the plaintiff, a jeweller, from 1 May 1915 to 30 April 1916, to an amount of £21,301. against loss of or damage to jewellery and other property 'arising from any cause whatsoever whether arising on land or water save and except breakage of furniture, china, earthenware, glass, and brittle articles, and save and except

---

5.   [1894] P 226.

loss by theft or dishonesty committed by any servant or traveller or messenger in the exclusive employment of the assured'.

On 3 May 1915 a robbery was committed at the plaintiff's premises and jewellery to the value of £725 18s 1d was stolen and damaged. The defendant's proportion of this loss amounted to £51 2s 5d for which sum this action was brought.

The defendant pleaded that the loss was caused by the theft or dishonesty of one Mason, a servant in the exclusive employment of the plaintiff.

The following facts were proved: The plaintiff employed two servants, namely, Brown, the manager, and Mason, who acted under him. In the plaintiff's shop was a safe containing four trays for holding jewellery. There were duplicate keys to the door of the shop and also to the safe. The plaintiff and Brown kept each one key of the shop and one key of the safe. Evidence was tendered and admitted to show that on Sunday, 1 May, two days before the robbery, Mason was seen in a public house in close conversation with three highly skilled safe-breakers who were well known to the police. On the same night Mason told Brown that he knew of a possible purchaser of some jewellery and arranged that they should go to the plaintiff's shop on Sunday, 2 May, at 11 am and remove the jewellery in order that Mason might show it to this person. Mason called for Brown on Sunday at 9 am. Brown was in bed. Mason asked for and obtained the keys of the shop and safe. These he took away and, returning later, restored to Brown.

On Monday, May 3, Brown and Mason remained longer than usual at the plaintiff's premises in order to repair some defect in connection with the electrical light. Brown was anxious to remain until the work was finished, but at about 8.30 pm Mason became very insistent that they should leave and finish the work next morning. They left shortly afterwards. At about 8.45 a violent explosion occurred at the premises. Firemen arrived and found the shop locked up. They kicked open the door and went in. They found that the safe had been blown open. One of the neighbours gave evidence that no one came out of or went into the premises before the arrival of the firemen. The police arrived soon afterwards and found that of the four trays which had previously been in the safe one was still in it; two were on the floor, and one was on a table in a recess. Soap had been applied to the keyhole of the safe and was found scattered about the room and upon the trays on the floor, but not on the tray in the safe. The jewellery which had been in the safe was all gone. The learned judge drew the inference that the trays had been withdrawn from the safe before the explosion. The examination by the police showed that there had been no breaking into or out of the premises. Neither Mason nor the proposed purchaser of the jewellery was called as a witness for the plaintiff.

Lush J: In this case I have to see what light is thrown upon the occurrence by what is known of Brown and Mason. There is no suggestion that Brown took any part in the theft. As to Mason, the defendant tendered evidence of his character which I rejected as inadmissible. The defendant also tendered evidence to prove that at or near the date of the theft Mason was associating with notorious and highly-skilled safe-breakers. Mr Hart [for the plaintiff] objected to the admission of this evidence. I doubt whether the evidence would have been admissible in a criminal prosecution, not because it was irrelevant, but because in a criminal case evidence is frequently rejected which tends to prejudice the defendant and prevent a fair trial. I admitted the evidence because, although taken by itself its weight is slight, I cannot say that it is irrelevant in this case, where the whole question is whether Mason was acting dishonestly and in complicity with the actual thieves. The evidence was that two days before the occurrence a detective saw Mason in a public house in an earnest conversation with three noted safe-breakers.

Mr Hart has contended that the onus is on the defendant to prove that Mason was dishonest and that he was either the actual perpetrator of the theft or an accomplice of the thieves; and he asks me to hold upon the evidence that, although the circumstances may be very suspicious, there is not sufficient evidence to warrant a conclusion of fact that the loss was due to Mason's dishonesty.

Mr Hastings [for the defendant] says that the onus is on the plaintiff to negative the dishonesty of his servant. If so, I have no hesitation in saying that the plaintiff has not discharged the onus.

The question therefore which I have to decide is this: Is the onus on the plaintiff or the defendant? Mr Hart cited two authorities which he said supported his contention that the onus was on the defendant. The first case was *Thurtell v Beaumont* (1823). That was an action against an insurance company where the burden of proof undoubtedly lay on the defendants. But I would point out that the terms of the policy in that case were not similar to those of this policy. It was an ordinary fire policy, and the defence pleaded was that the plaintiff had himself set fire to his premises and was fraudulently claiming against the insurance company to recover a loss which had been caused by his felonious act. I can quite understand that in a case of that sort the onus would be on the defendant; but the decision is no guide in the present case.

The other case relied on by Mr Hart was *Gorman v Hand in Hand Insurance Co* (1877). That was also an action on a fire policy ... and it was held that the burden of proof lay on the defendants. Palles CB said: 'When, therefore, it is once shown that the loss resulted from fire, the plaintiff has established a *prima facie* case, and the onus is thrown upon the defendants to prove that the act which caused the fire was within the proviso. The defence is not in any sense a traverse of an allegation comprised within the general averments of the plaint; it is a plea in confession and avoidance, and the proof of it is upon the defendants.' Again in my opinion that case is not really in point. The policy was not like this one. It was an ordinary insurance against fire, subject, no doubt, to the conditions in the policy. The defendants did not traverse the allegations of the plaintiff, but pleaded in confession and avoidance, and had therefore undertaken the burden of proving the facts necessary to support their plea. I think that the general law applicable to the present case can be best ascertained by considering what the plaintiff has to prove, and in *Bullen and Leake on Pleading* (3rd edn) p 182, the requisites of a declaration on a marine policy are stated thus: 'Care must be taken to state the contract accurately, with all the exceptions and qualifications of the defendant's liability, *Dawson v Wrench* (1849), and the declaration must negative that the defendant comes within the exceptions.' The learned authors then say 'but see' and cite two cases, which were not actions on policies of insurance but on charterparties, and I cannot treat those cases as authorities binding on me in this case, even if they do negative the effect of the passage immediately preceding.

The Glendarroch (1894) has also been cited, but I cannot find anything in Lord Esher's judgment which militates against the accuracy of the statement in *Bullen and Leake.* No case has been produced which precludes me from expressing my own view on this question, having regard to the terms of this policy. Looking at the policy, it is impossible to hold that the onus is on the defendant. To do so would produce absurd results. This is not a case of an insurance against loss caused by some specified reason, such as fire or theft. It is an insurance against loss due to any cause except the two specified, namely, breakage and dishonesty of servants. If the contention of the plaintiff is right, he need only aver a loss of jewellery, and it would be for the defendant to prove that, amongst the multitude of causes which might have occasioned the loss, the actual cause was either breakage or dishonesty of servants. In my opinion the plaintiff must allege facts to show that the lost goods were covered by the policy, that the loss was one against which the defendant had agreed to indemnify the plaintiff.

I therefore hold that on this policy it was for the plaintiff to prove that the loss was one against which the defendant had agreed to indemnify him. The plaintiff has not proved that. He has proved a loss, but has left, to say the least, the gravest suspicion whether his own servant was not the cause of the loss ... '[6]

Joseph Constantine SS Line Ltd v Imperial Smelting Corpn Ltd (1942, House of Lords)

Viscount Simon LC: My Lords, by a charterparty, dated August 5 1936 the appellants, who were the owners of a steamship called the *Kingswood*, chartered the ship to agents for the respondents for a voyage with a cargo of ores and concentrates from Port Pirie in South Australia to Europe. The vessel duly sailed for Port Pirie to load her cargo. On January 3 1937 while she was anchored in the roads at Port Pirie, but before she became an 'arrived ship', there was an explosion of extreme violence in the neighbourhood of her auxiliary boiler, which caused such damage to the steamer that she could not perform the charterparty, and the appellants gave notice to the respondents to that effect. The respondents claim damages from the appellants, alleging that the latter have broken the charterparty by failing to load a cargo. The appellants set up the defence that the contract was 'frustrated' by the destructive consequences to the *Kingswood* of the explosion.

The dispute was referred to the arbitration of Mr HU Willink KC, and the learned arbitrator has made an interim award in the form of a special case. He finds that the explosion was one 'of an unprecedented character' and that no probable sequence of events had been suggested as capable of having given rise to it ... It is not disputed that the time needed to repair the damage and to make the *Kingswood* fit for her voyage was so great as to frustrate the commercial object of the adventure. The respondents, however, contend that this frustration does not suffice to excuse the appellants from having to pay damages for non-performance unless the appellants establish affirmatively that the explosion occurred without any fault on their part. The appellants, on the other hand, contend that, once the frustrating event is proved, the onus is on the respondents to establish such default on the part of the appellants as would deprive the latter of their right to rely upon it.

After examining three principal theories which were suggested in evidence as possibly accounting for the disaster, the arbitrator declares himself unable to decide whether any one of them provided the true explanation, and he goes on to say that he is not satisfied that the direct cause of the disaster has as yet been suggested at all. His conclusion is that he was not satisfied that any of the

---

6. [1917] 1 KB 352.

servants of the appellants were guilty of negligence. On the other hand, neither was he satisfied that negligence on the part of the servants of the appellants did not cause or contribute to the disaster. It is this nicely balanced conclusion on the facts which provides the question of law which this House has now to decide. That question is whether, when parties have contracted in such circumstances as require a term to be implied in the contract that it shall be determined, and the mutual obligations of the parties discharged, by supervening destruction of essential subject matter of the contract, the party alleging frustration must prove affirmatively that the destruction has not been brought about by his own neglect or default ...

The question here is where the onus of proof lies; ie, whether, when a supervening event has been proved which would, apart from the defendant's 'default' put an end to the contract, and when at the end of the case no inference of 'default' exists and the evidence is equally consistent with either view, the defence fails because the defendant has not established affirmatively that the supervening event was not due to his default.

I may observe, in the first place, that, if this were correct, there must be many cases in which, although in truth frustration is complete and unavoidable, the defendant will be held liable because of his inability to prove a negative – in some cases, indeed, a whole series of negatives. Suppose that a vessel while on the high seas disappears completely during a storm. Can it be that the defence of frustration of the adventure depends on the owner's ability to prove that all his servants on board were navigating the ship with adequate skill and that there was no 'default' which brought about the catastrophe? Suppose that a vessel in convoy is torpedoed by the enemy and sinks immediately with all hands. Does the application of the doctrine require that the owners should affirmatively prove that those on board were keeping a good lookout, were obscuring lights, were steering as directed, and so forth? There is no reported case which requires us so to hold. The doctrine on which the defence of frustration depends is nowhere so stated as to place this onus of proof on the party relying on it ...

In this connection it is well to emphasize that when 'frustration' in the legal sense occurs, it does not merely provide one party with a defence in an action brought by the other. It kills the contract itself and discharges both parties automatically. The plaintiff sues for breach at a past date and the defendant pleads that at that date no contract existed. In this situation the plaintiff could only succeed if it were shown that the determination of the contract were due to the defendant's 'default', and it would be a strange result if the party alleging this were not the party required to prove it.

The doctrine of discharge from liability by frustration has been explained in various ways – sometimes by speaking of the disappearance of a foundation which the parties assumed to be at the basis of their contract, sometimes as deduced from a rule arising from the impossibility of performance, and sometimes as flowing from the inference of an implied term. Whichever way it is put, the legal consequence is the same. The most satisfactory basis, I think, on which the doctrine can be put is that it depends on an implied term in the contract of the parties ... Every case in this branch of the law can be stated as turning on the question whether from the express terms of the particular contract a further term should be implied which, when its conditions are fulfilled, puts an end to the contract ...

If the matter is regarded in this way, the question is as to the construction of a contract taking into consideration its express and implied terms. The implied term in the present case may well be: 'This contract is to cease to be binding if the vessel is disabled by an overpowering disaster, provided that disaster is not brought about by the default of either party.' This is very similar to an express exception of 'perils of the seas', as to which it is ancient law that by an implied term of the contract the shipowner cannot rely on the exception if its operation was brought about either (a) by negligence of his servants, or (b) by his breach of the implied warranty of seaworthiness. If a ship sails and is never heard of again the shipowner can claim protection for loss of the cargo under the express exception of perils of the seas. To establish that, must he go on to prove (a) that the perils were not caused by negligence of his servants, and (b) were not caused by any unseaworthiness? I think clearly not. He proves a *prima facie* case of loss by sea perils, and that he is within the exception. If the cargo owner wants to defeat that plea it is for him by rejoinder to allege and prove either negligence or unseaworthiness. The judgment of the Court of Appeal in *The Glendarroch* is plain authority for this ...

[Viscount Simon LC moved that the appeal be allowed and the original order of Atkinson J restored. That judge had held that the onus was on the charterers to prove that there had not been frustration. By contrast, the Court of Appeal had held that a party relying on frustration to avoid liability for failure to perform his contract had the burden of proving that the frustration had occurred without his default.]

Lord Russell of Killowen: ... The question raised on this appeal is whether, on the facts as found by the arbitrator, the doctrine of frustration applies, with the result that the appellants are released from liability under the charterparty. The answer seems to me to depend on what is the correct statement of the doctrine, ie, on the correct statement of what the law requires to be established in order that the promisor should be relieved from liability. The respondents contend that it must be affirmatively established, as a condition precedent to the application of the doctrine in the promisor's favour, that, in respect of the destruction of the corpus, he is free from fault or default. In other words, he must prove that he is not responsible for that destruction. The appellants contend that on the destruction of the corpus, the doctrine applies in the promisor's favour unless it is established that he is responsible for the destruction. The rival contentions may be stated thus: (1) The appellants say: 'Frustration will excuse unless it is proved to be self-induced'. (2) The respondents say: 'Frustration will not excuse unless it is proved not to be self-induced'.

My Lords, in my opinion the appellant's contention is correct. In coming to this conclusion I am influenced by three considerations. First, the proving of a negative, a task always difficult and often impossible, would be a most exceptional burden to impose on a litigant. Secondly, I know of no case of frustration in the books, in which an attempt has been made, or called for, to prove the suggested negative. Thirdly, the statement of the doctrine in the authorities does not in any way compel us to adopt the contention of the respondents ...

Lord Wright: ... In more recent days the phrase more commonly used is 'frustration of the contract' or more shortly 'frustration'. But 'frustration of the contract' is an elliptical expression. The fuller and more accurate phrase is 'frustration of the adventure or of the commercial or practical purpose of the contract'. This change in language corresponds to a wider conception of impossibility, which has extended the rule beyond contracts which depend on the existence, at the relevant time, of a specific object, as in the instances given by Blackburn J, to cases where the essential object does indeed exist, but its condition has by some casualty been so changed as to be not available for the purposes of the contract either at the contract date, or, if no date is fixed, within any time consistent with the commercial or practical adventure. For the purposes of the contract the object is as good as lost. Another case, often described as frustration, is where by State interference or similar overriding intervention the performance of the contract has been interrupted for so long a time as to make it unreasonable for the parties to be required to go on with it. Yet another illustration is where the actual object still exists and is available, but the object of the contract as contemplated by both parties was its employment for a particular purpose, which has become impossible, as in the coronation cases. In these and similar cases, where there is not in the strict sense impossibility by some casual happening, there has been so vital a change in the circumstances as to defeat the contract. What Willes J described as substantial performance is no longer possible. The common object of the parties is frustrated. The contract has perished, *quoad* any rights or liabilities subsequent to the change. The same is true where there has been a vital change of the law, either statutory or common law, operating on the circumstances, as, for instance, where the outbreak of war destroys a contract legally made before war, but which, when war breaks out, could not be performed without trading with the enemy. I have given this bare catalogue to illustrate the application in practice of the doctrine of frustration in order to show how wide and various is the range of circumstances to which it may extend and how manifold are the complications involved in the rule laid down by the Court of Appeal that there is an affirmative onus of disproving fault on the party claiming to rely on frustration ...

... [T]he court is exercising its powers, when it decides that a contract is frustrated, in order to achieve a result which is just and reasonable. It would indeed be strange if it clogged its decision with the qualification which the Court of Appeal would impose, but which seems to me ... inconvenient and unreasonable ... [7]

[Lord Maugham and Lord Porter also delivered speeches in favour of allowing the appeal.]

Levison v Patent Steam Carpet Cleaning Co Ltd (1977, Court of Appeal)

Lord Denning MR: It was a fine Chinese carpet worth £900, but it needed cleaning. Mr and Mrs Levison, the plaintiffs, had it in their home. On July 5 1972 Mrs Levison telephoned the cleaners and told the young lady that she had a carpet and curtains for cleaning and asked them to come and collect them. The young lady said, 'Yes. The van will call on July 17'. She made a note of the particulars on a printed form, giving the date, name, address and, in addition: 'Date for collection, 17/7/72; Date for return, 31/7/72; Instructions: Collect heavy Chinese carpet for cleaning, and velvet curtains for cleaning.'

Then, on July 17, the young lady in the office gave this printed form to the van-driver, but she wrote on it these further words for him: 'Get order.' This meant that he was to get the householder to sign the back of the form.

When the van-driver arrived at the house, Mrs Levison was out, but her husband was in. He stayed in so as to see the carpet off. By that time they wanted a rug washed as well. So Mr Levison gave the van-driver both the carpet and the rug. He added these words on the front just beneath the carpet: 'One white rug to be washed.'

---

7.   [1942] AC 154.

Mr Levison also signed that form on the back in the space provided for signature. He did not read the print but it contained many lines of small print containing 'Terms and Conditions of Processing', by the defendants, of which I will quote a few: Clause 1 gave the cleaners power to sub-contract any of the work or storage. Clause 2 (a) said: 'The maximum value of any carpet, rug or tapestry delivered to the company for any purpose whatsoever shall if the area thereof exceed four square yards be deemed to be £2 per square yard, and if the area does not exceed four square yards shall be deemed to be £10.'

This carpet was five yards by four yards, that is 20 square yards. So, under this condition, the maximum value was deemed to be £40. Clause 5: 'All merchandise is expressly accepted at the owner's risk and the owners are recommended either to insure such merchandise in such manner as to cover them whilst in the company's hands or to instruct the company to insure it as their agents in such sum and in such manner at their cost as they shall specify.'

Clause 8: 'The company shall only be liable to execute services or to account in any way to the owner if the order for such services is on the company's official order form and the owner signs the same in accordance with these conditions ... '

Clause 9 deals with delay and adds: '... If the company is liable for any delay its liability shall not exceed the limits imposed by clause 2 (a) hereof.' Finally the form said: 'I/We the undersigned agree to the terms and conditions set out above and on the face of this document. I H Levison (Signature of Owner).'

So Mr Levison signed the form. The driver took the form, the carpet and the rug. A week or so later the rug was returned washed. But the carpet was not. Mrs Levison telephoned several times. The first time she was told: 'It is not ready yet.' The next time she was told: 'It is in the corner of the warehouse and we cannot get it out.' Then: 'We cannot find it and we are looking for it.' Finally: 'We are sorry but it has been stolen.' The one letter was on September 12, 1972, from the cleaners: 'I understand that we are having difficulty in returning your Chinese carpet after cleaning and, despite a number of detailed searches, this item cannot be traced at present.'

Mr Levison approached his insurers. They took up the matter with the cleaners, who replied on October 5 1972: '... Under the terms and conditions of contract, upon which these goods were accepted, our total liability in this event is £2 per sq yd, which limits our liability to £44. We are enclosing a copy of the terms and conditions ... for your perusal.'

Mr and Mrs Levison sued the cleaners for loss of the carpet, claiming the full sum of £900. The county court judge gave judgment against the cleaners. They appeal to this court ...

If a party uses his superior power to impose an exemption or limitation clause on the weaker party, he will not be allowed to rely on it if he has himself been guilty of a breach going to the root of the contract. In other cases, the court will, whenever it can, construe the contract so that an exemption or limitation clause only avails the party when he is carrying out the contract in substance: and not when he is breaking it in a manner which goes to the very root of the contract ...

This brings me to the crux of the case. On whom is the burden of proof? Take the present case. Assuming that clause 2 (a) or clause 5, or either of them, limits or exempts the cleaners from liability for negligence: but not for a fundamental breach. On whom is the burden to prove that there was a fundamental breach?

Upon principle, I should have thought that the burden was on the cleaners to prove that they were not guilty of a fundamental breach. After all, Mrs Levison does not know what happened to it. The cleaners are the ones who know, or should know, what happened to the carpet, and the burden should be on them to say what it was. It was so held by McNair J in *Woolmer v Delmer Price Ltd* (1955); and by me in *J Spurling Ltd v Bradshaw* (1956) ... A contrary view was expressed by this court in *Hunt & Winterbotham (West of England) Ltd v B R S (Parcels) Ltd* (1962). And there is a long line of shipping cases in which it has been held that, if a shipowner makes a *prima facie* case that the cause of the loss was one of the excepted perils, the burden is on the shipper to prove that it was not covered by the exceptions: see *The Glendarroch* (1894) and *Munro, Brice & Co v War Risks Association Ltd* (1918). To which there may be added *Joseph Constantine Steamship Line Ltd v Imperial Smelting Corporation Ltd* (1942) on frustration.

It is, therefore, a moot point for decision. On it I am clearly of the opinion that, in a contract of bailment, when a bailee seeks to escape liability on the ground that he was not negligent or that he was excused by an exception or limitation clause, then he must show what happened to the goods. He must prove all the circumstances known to him in which the loss or damage occurred. If it appears that the goods were lost or damaged without any negligence on his part, then, of course, he is not liable. If it appears that they were lost or damaged by a slight breach – not going to the root of the contract – he may be protected by the exemption or limitation clause. But, if he leaves the cause of the loss or damage undiscovered and unexplained – then I think he is liable: because it is then quite likely that the goods were stolen by one of his servants; or delivered by a servant to the wrong address; or damaged by reckless or wilful misconduct; all of which the offending servant will conceal and not make known to his employer. Such conduct would be a fundamental breach against which the exemption or limitation clause will not protect him.

The cleaning company in this case did not show what happened to the carpet. They did not prove how it was lost. They gave all sorts of excuses for non-delivery and eventually said it had been stolen. Then I would ask: By whom was it stolen? Was it by one of their own servants? Or with his connivance? Alternatively, was it delivered by one of their servants to the wrong address? In the absence of any explanation, I would infer that it was one of these causes. In none of them would the cleaning company be protected by the exemption or limitation clause ...

I think the judge was quite right in holding that the burden of proof was on the cleaning company to exclude fundamental breach. As they did not exclude it, they cannot rely on the exemption or limitation clauses. I would, therefore, dismiss this appeal.

Orr LJ (read by Sir David Cairns): ... On the final and crucial issue as to the burden of proof I agree that as a matter of both justice and of common sense the burden ought to rest on the bailee who, if the goods have been lost while in his possession, is both more likely to know the facts and in a better position to ascertain them than the bailor, and I would on this issue follow the decision of McNair J in *Woolmer v Delmer Price Ltd* (1955), and the view expressed by Denning LJ in *J Spurling Ltd v Bradshaw* (1956). In my view nothing in the judgments of this court in the later case of *Hunt & Winterbotham (West of England) Ltd v B R S (Parcels) Ltd* (1962), or in the shipping cases to which we were referred in argument, precludes us from so doing.

Sir David Cairns: ... This is one of those rare cases where the result must depend on which side had the onus of proof.

If the decision of McNair J in *Woolmer v Delmer Price Ltd* (1955) was right it must in my opinion follow that the onus in the present case was on the defendants.

While some doubt was cast on the correctness of that decision in *Hunt &*
Winterbotham (West of England) Ltd v B R S (Parcels) Ltd (1962), it appears to have
been distinguished ... on the ground that it was a case of deposit and not of
carriage of goods. But even in relation to carriage of goods the judgment of the
court, while dismissing the plaintiff's appeal in that case, contained ... the words:
'The position might no doubt be different where a fundamental breach is
specifically pleaded by the consignor ...'. This at least leaves it open to this court
to hold that when a fundamental breach is pleaded by the owner of the goods, as
it was in the reply in this case, the onus is on the bailee to disprove fundamental
breach.

In *J Spurling Ltd v Bradshaw* (1956) Denning LJ said: 'A bailor, by pleading and
presenting his case properly, can always put on the bailee the burden of proof. In
the case of non-delivery, for instance, all he need plead is the contract and a
failure to deliver on demand. That puts on the bailee the burden of proving
either loss without his fault (which, of course, would be a complete answer at
common law) or, if it was due to his fault, it was a fault from which he is excused
by the exempting clause: see *Cunard Steamship Co Ltd v Buerger* (1927) and
Woolmer v Delmer Price Ltd (1955). I do not think the Court of Appeal in *Alderslade
v Hendon Laundry Ltd* (1945) had the burden of proof in mind at all.'

I respectfully agree with that passage. Parker LJ ... expressly refrained from
considering whether *Woolmer v Delmer Price Ltd* was wrongly decided. It is in my
judgment open to this court either to approve or to overrule McNair J's decision
and for my part I would approve it because, however difficult it may sometimes
be for a bailee to prove a negative, he is at least in a better position than the bailor
to know what happened to the goods while in his possession.

The considerations applicable to bills of lading and to policies of marine
insurance (see *The Glendarroch* (1894) and *Munro, Brice & Co v War Risks
Association Ltd* (1918)) are not in my judgment applicable to cases such as the
present.

Accordingly I would hold that the onus was on the defendants, that they did not
discharge it and that the appeal should be dismissed.[8]

THE BURDEN OF PROOF IN CRIMINAL CASES

The basic principle was laid down by Viscount Sankey LC in *Woolmington v
DPP* (1935):

Throughout the web of the English Criminal Law one golden thread is always to
be seen, that it is the duty of the prosecution to prove the prisoner's guilt subject
to what I have already said as to the defence of insanity and subject also to any
statutory exception. If, at the end of and on the whole of the case, there is a
reasonable doubt, created by the evidence given either by the prosecution or the
prisoner, as to whether the prisoner killed the deceased with a malicious
intention, the prosecution has not made out the case and the prisoner is entitled
to an acquittal. No matter what the charge or where the trial, the principle that
the prosecutor must prove the guilt of the prisoner is part of the common law of
England and no attempt to whittle it down can be entertained.[9]

---

8.   [1978] 1 QB 69.
9.   [1935] AC 462, 481.

The generality of this principle was emphasised again by the House of Lords in *Mancini v DPP* (1942), when Viscount Simon LC said:

> *Woolmington's* case is concerned with explaining and reinforcing the rule that the prosecution must prove the charge it makes beyond reasonable doubt, and, consequently, that if, on the material before the jury, there is a reasonable doubt, the prisoner should have the benefit of it. The rule is of general application in all charges under the criminal law. The only exceptions arise, as explained in *Woolmington's* case, in the defence of insanity and in offences where onus of proof is specially dealt with by statute.[10]

As Lord Sankey noted, Parliament can expressly override the general principle. But there have been challenges to the idea that it accords with justice to place the burden of proof on defendants.

Glanville Williams, 'The Logic of "Exceptions"', *Cambridge Law Journal* 47 (1988)

> I could understand (though I would not agree with) an argument that in some respects the burden of proof resting on the prosecution should be lightened to a burden on the balance of probability. What I am unable to comprehend is how a believer in the rule of law in a free society can countenance convictions that are not supported by evidence even on the balance of probability. This is what reverse onuses allow. Yet it seems that no one who speaks in their favour (whether judicially or otherwise) has yet frankly acknowledged it.
>
> At one time, reverse onuses were part of the common law. In the pre-*Woolmington* era, not only the civil but the criminal courts frequently (though not invariably) regarded the burden of proof of defences as resting on the defendant. It was *Woolmington* that effected a revolution in the criminal law on their subject – for all that Viscount Sankey pretended that he was only stating the existing position. Consequently, it is only since that celebrated decision that the anomaly of the reverse onus provisions has become pronounced.
>
> Typically, reverse onus provisions state that the defendant can be convicted unless he 'proves' some fact or other. The question is what is meant by the word 'proves'. If one looks at a selection of the statutes in which the provision appears, it becomes obvious that what was primarily in the draftsman's mind was a desire to make the defendant produce evidence to neutralise a *prima facie* presumption against him: in other words to impose on him a burden of producing evidence (or, as we now express it, an evidential burden). Why did not the draftsman do just this?
>
> One can rarely find out who is responsible for the precise wording of Government legislation. Do parliamentary counsel write in reverse onuses whenever they think this may be convenient? Or perhaps whenever they think it will not occasion parliamentary criticism? Are they specially instructed, and if so by whom? By the department's legal adviser? The permanent secretary? Other senior administrative adviser? The minister, prodded perhaps by the police? If the person who takes the decision is not a lawyer, does he know what he is doing? Is the difference between an evidential and persuasive burden explained to him? Suppose that whoever was responsible for a reverse burden had been asked the question: 'If the defendant produces enough evidence to put the fact into genuine doubt, do you want him to be convicted?' I think it quite possible

---

10. [1942] AC 1, 11.

(to put it no higher) that the reply would be: 'In that case he would have sufficiently satisfied the burden of proof I am imposing on him.'

The word 'proof' is open to different shades of meaning. It can mean 'proof up to the hilt':

> So prove it.
>
> That the probation bear no hinge nor loop
>
> To hang a doubt on.

But it can mean something less than this. Indeed, the courts hold that when a burden of proof is placed on the defendant, it is merely a burden of proof on the balance of probability. So proof can be of various degrees; and the so-called reverse onus provisions do not simply put on the defendant, in negative terms, the burden that would otherwise lie on the prosecution.

The reduced burden on the defendant still leaves him open to conviction although the charge as a whole has not been proved against him. Should not the courts say that the burdens of proof placed on the defendant mean burdens of proof of his defence sufficient to take it to the jury? They would then be what are called evidential burdens.

Take as an example the Prevention of Corruption Act 1916, section 2. Essentially it provides that 'where it is proved that any consideration has been given to a person in the employment of His Majesty, the consideration shall be deemed to have been given or received corruptly unless the contrary is proved'. The word 'proved' where it first here appears means 'proved beyond reasonable doubt'. Where it secondly appears it is interpreted as 'proved on the balance of probability' – which appears to signify that the odds in the defendant's favour on this issue must be better than evens. The courts see no objection to giving the word these two different meanings in the same section, because this is necessary to fit the different positions of the prosecution and the defendant. Having swallowed this camel, why strain at the remaining gnat? Why should not the concluding words 'unless the contrary is proved' be taken to mean 'unless sufficient evidence is given to the contrary'? 'Sufficient evidence' would bear the meaning that it usually bears in relation to defences, *viz* evidence that, if believed, and on the most favourable view, could be taken by a reasonable jury to support the defence. It is, of course, the judge who decides this issue; the jury are not instructed on the evidential burden. They are told to consider whether the case as a whole has been proved beyond reasonable doubt. If the proposed change were made, the law would retain efficiency; the jury's task would be simplified, and our sensibilities on the score of justice would be spared.

A reform along these lines was proposed by the Criminal Law Revision Committee, in its neglected Evidence Report (now repeated, in regrettably diluted form, by the Law Commission's codification team) [Cmnd. 4991 of 1982, paras 140-141; Law Com. No 143 cl 17.] No one would say that the CLRC was soft on crime; on the contrary, the Evidence Report caused the committee to be regarded in certain circles (with little justice) as hard-nosed; but it was unanimously in favour of this liberal change, and gave a number of reasons in favour of it. One that appealed particularly to the experienced judicial members of the committee was that the minds of the jury become numbed when they are directed in terms of two different burdens of proof, one involving a double negative and both rather hard to grasp and apply: 'You will return a verdict of guilty if you are satisfied beyond reasonable doubt that the defendant made a gift to the tax officer, unless you are satisfied on the balance of probability that he did not make it corruptly.'

The committee looked to legislation rather than judicial action to effect the reform it wanted, but its expectation of a statute has been disappointed (for reasons apparently unconnected with this particular proposal). At one time it was a possible view that the Law Lords might execute the reform in default of legislation, but any hope that might have been pinned upon them has died since [R v] Hunt. [See below.] Lord Griffiths referred to the CLRC's proposal and dismissed it from consideration, saying, 'such a fundamental change is a matter for Parliament'. Lord Ackner agreed 'without hesitation'.

This is the answer regularly given by the Lords to pleas for the judicial extension of defences. But Parliament, as we know, is uninterested in the criminal law, apart from occasionally wanting to sharpen it; and much the same thing is true of the Home Office. It may be asked: is the proposed change any more fundamental than the step already taken of reducing the quantum of proof required from a defendant in a criminal case? (Normally, the rules of evidence for the two sides to a prosecution are the same, yet here an exception has been made). Are not the arguments for this proposed change much the same as those for the lesser change already accomplished? The idea that the defendant must prove a defence on the balance of probability introduced an unfamiliar concept into the criminal law; in contrast, a rule that the defendant must prove his defence to the extent necessary to create a reasonable doubt as to his guilt would utilise the traditional concept of criminal evidence. And as to the notion that the change is beyond the competence of the Law Lords, we see on sundry occasions that the courts, including the Appeal Committee, extend the scope of the criminal law and increase its efficacy in producing convictions. When the courts improve the law at the defendant's expense they have to disregard the *nulla poena* maxim,[11] which is generally taken as a fundamental principle of justice. Why is it so out of the question that they should sometimes alleviate the defendant's position in the interests of justice?[12]

Just or unjust, there is at least no problem in interpreting a statute providing, for example, that an accused person shall be guilty of an offence 'unless the contrary is proved', or 'unless the accused proves ...', or where a defence is provided, 'the proof whereof shall lie on the accused'. The question whether Parliament in any given case has *impliedly* overridden the *Woolmington* principle is likely to be more difficult to resolve. The starting point is the Magistrates' Courts Act 1980, s 101 (formerly the Magistrates' Courts Act 1952, s 81). In *R v Edwards* (1975) counsel for the prosecution successfully submitted that the Magistrates' Courts Act 1952, s 81 (now s 101 of the 1980 Act) was a statutory statement of a common law rule applicable in all criminal courts. In this case Lawton LJ referred to the need to 'construe the enactment under which the charge is laid' in determining where the burden of proof lay. The task of interpretation was subsequently emphasised by the House of Lords in *R v Hunt* (1987).

Magistrates' Courts Act 1980

101 Where the defendant to an information or complaint relies for his defence on any exception, exemption, proviso, excuse or qualification, whether or not it

---

11. *Nulla poena sine lege.* The maxim conveys the idea that there should be no punishment in the absence of a law declaring the action under consideration to be criminal.
12. Williams, 'Logic of "Exceptions"' (1988) *Cambridge Law Journal* 47 pp 261, 263-67.

accompanies the description of the offence or matter of complaint in the enactment creating the offence or on which the complaint is founded, the burden of proving the exception, exemption, proviso, excuse or qualification shall be on him; and this notwithstanding that the information or complaint contains an allegation negativing the exception, exemption, proviso, excuse or qualification.

R v Edwards (1975, Court of Appeal)

Lawton LJ: ... Over the centuries the common law, as a result of experience and the need to ensure that justice is done both to the community and to defendants, has evolved an exception to the fundamental rule of our criminal law that the prosecution must prove every element of the offence charged. This exception, like so much else in the common law, was hammered out on the anvil of pleading. It is limited to offences arising under enactments which prohibit the doing of an act save in specified circumstances or by persons of specified classes or with specified qualifications or with the licence or permission of specified authorities. Whenever the prosecution seeks to rely on this exception, the court must construe the enactment under which the charge is laid. If the true construction is that the enactment prohibits the doing of acts, subject to provisoes, exemptions and the like, then the prosecution can rely upon the exception.

In our judgment its application does not depend upon either the fact, or the presumption, that the defendant has peculiar knowledge enabling him to prove the position of any negative averment. As Wigmore pointed out in his great *Treatise on Evidence* (1905), vol 4, p 3525, this concept of peculiar knowledge furnishes no working rule. If it did, defendants would have to prove lack of intent. What does provide a working rule is what the common law evolved from a rule of pleading ... Like nearly all rules it could be applied oppressively; but the courts have ample powers to curb and discourage oppressive prosecutors and do not hesitate to use them.

Two consequences follow from the view we have taken as to the evolution and nature of this exception. First, as it comes into operation upon an enactment being construed in a particular way, there is no need for the prosecution to prove a *prima facie* case of lack of excuse, qualification or the like; and secondly, what shifts is the onus: it is for the defendant to prove that he was entitled to do the prohibited act. What rests on him is the legal or, as it is sometimes called, the persuasive burden of proof. It is not the evidential burden.[13]

R v Hunt (1987, House of Lords)

Lord Griffiths: My Lords, on 26 February 1985 in the Crown Court at Lewes the appellant pleaded not guilty to an indictment charging him with possessing a controlled drug contrary to s 5(2) of the Misuse of Drugs Act 1971, the particulars of the offence being that he on 13 July 1984, at Eastbourne in the county of East Sussex, unlawfully had in his possession a controlled drug, namely 154 mg of a powder containing morphine, a Class A drug.

The prosecution called two police officers who gave evidence that on 13 July 1984 they executed a search warrant at the appellant's home and there found, under an ashtray in the bedroom, a paper fold containing a white powder. The appellant told the police that he had bought the powder in Shaftesbury Avenue and that it was amphetamine sulphate. The only other evidence for the

---

13. [1975] QB 27.

prosecution was contained in the report of an analyst which was by agreement read to the jury. The report showed that the powder was not amphetamine sulphate and that it contained morphine. The report read: 'On 19 July 1984 the following sealed item was received at the laboratory from Sussex Police, Eastbourne: RSE.1 Paper fold with powder. The paper fold, item RSE.1, contained 154 milligrams of off-white powder. This powder was found to contain morphine mixed with caffeine and atropine. Morphine is a controlled drug within the Misuse of Drugs Act 1971, Part I of Schedule 2 (Class A drugs). Caffeine and atropine are not controlled under the Misuse of Drugs Act 1971.'

At the close of the prosecution case counsel for the appellant submitted that there was no case to answer. In order to understand the basis of that submission it is necessary to set out the relevant statutory provisions which I take from the judgment of the Court of Appeal:

> The defendant was charged with an offence under s 5(2) of the Misuse of Drugs Act 1971. Section 5(1) and (2) provides as follows: '(1) Subject to any regulations under section 7 of this Act for the time being in force, it shall not be lawful for a person to have a controlled drug in his possession. (2) Subject to section 28 of this Act and to subsection (4) below, it is an offence for a person to have a controlled drug in his possession in contravention of subsection (1) above.' The expression 'controlled drug' is defined in s 2(1)(a) of the Act, which provides that in the Act – 'the expression "controlled drug" means any substance or product for the time being specified in Part I, II or III of Schedule 2 to this Act ... ' Part I of Sch 2 is concerned with Class A drugs. Paragraph 1 of Part I contains a list of 'substances and products', including morphine. Paragraph 5 specifies: 'Any preparation or other product containing a substance or product for the time being specified in any of the paragraphs 1 to 4 above.' It follows that the powder of which the defendant was found to be in possession was a controlled drug by virtue of being a preparation or other product containing morphine. It is to be observed that s 5(1) of the Act is expressed to be 'subject to any regulations under section 7 of this Act'. Section 7(1) of the Act provides as follows: 'The Secretary of State may by regulations – (a) except from section 3(1)(a) or (b), 4(1)(a) or (b) or 5(1) of this Act such controlled drugs as may be specified in the regulations; and (b) make such other provisions as he thinks fit for the purpose of making it lawful for persons to do things which under any of the following provisions of this Act, that is to say sections 4(1), 5(1) and 6(1), it would otherwise be unlawful for them to do.' In 1973 there came into force the Misuse of Drugs Regulations 1973, SI 1973/797, made in pursuance of various sections of the 1971 Act, including s 7. Part II of the regulations is headed 'Exemptions from Certain Provisions of the Misuse of Drugs Act 1971', and contains regs 4 to 13 inclusive. For present purposes, the regulation which is of immediate importance is reg 4(1) which provides as follows: 'Sections 3(1) and 5(1) of the Act (which prohibit the importation, exportation and possession of controlled drugs) shall not have effect in relation to the controlled drugs specified in Schedule 1.' The amended Sch 1 to the regulations, which was in force at the relevant time, is headed as follows: 'Controlled Drugs Excepted from the Prohibition on Importation, Exportation and Possession and Subject to the Requirements of Regulation 23'. The schedule consists of nine paragraphs. Each paragraph specifies a particular controlled drug in the nature of a preparation or powder or mixture. The relevant paragraph for present purposes is para 3, which reads as follows: 'Any preparation of medicinal opium or of morphine containing (in either case) not more than 0.2 per cent of morphine calculated as

anhydrous morphine base, being a preparation compounded with one or more other active or inert ingredients in such a way that the opium or, as the case may be, the morphine, cannot be recovered by readily applicable means or in a yield which would constitute a risk to health.' It follows, therefore, that a controlled drug, being a preparation as described in para 3, is a controlled drug excepted from the prohibition on possession contained in s 5 of the Act. It was the submission of counsel for the defendant at the trial that there was no case to answer because the prosecution had called no evidence as to the proportion of morphine contained in the powder found in the defendant's possession, or to the effect that the powder was not compound as specified in para 3 of Sch 1 to the regulations, and that it was not therefore open to the jury to hold, on the evidence, that the defendant was unlawfully in possession of a controlled drug contrary to s 5(2) of the Act.

The judge ruled against the submission. The appellant changed his plea to guilty and after being formally convicted by the jury he was sentenced to three months' imprisonment suspended for two years.

The judge did not give reasons for rejecting the submission of no case to answer but it is apparent from the discussion between the judge and counsel during the course of the submission that the judge rejected the submission because he was of the opinion that Sch 1 only applied to possession by such persons as doctors, dentists, veterinary surgeons and pharmacists. For the reasons given by the Court of Appeal this was an erroneous view of the scope of the regulations and the prosecution do not seek to uphold the construction of the regulations adopted by the trial judge.

The Court of Appeal, however, concluded that the ruling that there was a case to answer was correct, albeit it had been made for the wrong reason. The unchallenged evidence of the prosecution established that the appellant had had morphine in his possession, and in these circumstances the Court of Appeal held that if the appellant wished to escape conviction the burden lay on him to prove on the balance of probability that the preparation of morphine fell within the relevant exception contained in the Misuse of Drugs Regulations 1973. As it was obvious that the appellant neither intended to nor could discharge this burden of proof, the Court of Appeal upheld the conviction.

The Court of Appeal gave leave to appeal to your Lordships' House and certified the following point of law of general public importance: 'Whether in a prosecution for possession of a preparation or product containing morphine under section 5 of the Misuse of Drugs Act 1971, where the morphine is of an unspecified amount and compounded with other ingredients, and where the defence seeks to rely upon the exceptions to the said section 5 set out in regulation 4(1) of and paragraph 3 of Schedule 1 to the Misuse of Drugs Regulations 1973 (as amended) the burden falls upon the defence to show that the said preparation or product comes within the said exception ...'

I would summarise the position thus far by saying that *Woolmington v DPP* did not lay down a rule that the burden of proving a statutory defence only lay on the defendant if the statute specifically so provided; that a statute can, on its true construction, place a burden of proof on the defendant although it does not do so expressly, and that if a burden of proof is placed on the defendant it is the same burden whether the case be tried summarily or on indictment, namely a burden that has to be discharged on the balance of probabilities.

The real difficulty in these cases lies in determining on whom Parliament intended to place the burden of proof when the statute has not expressly so provided. It presents particularly difficult problems of construction when what might be regarded as a matter of defence appears in a clause creating the offence rather than in some subsequent proviso from which it may more readily be inferred that it was intended to provide for a separate defence which a defendant must set up and prove if he wishes to avail himself of it. This difficulty was acutely demonstrated in *Nimmo v Alexander Cowan & Sons Ltd* (1968). Section 29(1) of the Factories Act 1961 provides: 'There shall, so far as is reasonably practicable, be provided and maintained safe means of access to every place at which any person has at any time to work and every such place shall, so far as is reasonably practicable, be made and kept safe for any person working there.'

The question before the House was whether the burden of proving that it was not reasonably practicable to make the working place safe lay on the defendant or the plaintiff in a civil action. However, as the section also created a summary offence, the same question would have arisen in a prosecution. In the event, the House divided 3 to 2 on the construction of the section, Lord Reid and Lord Wilberforce holding that the section required the plaintiff or prosecution to prove that it was reasonably practicable to make the working place safe, the majority, Lord Guest, Lord Upjohn and Lord Pearson, holding that if the plaintiff or prosecution proved that the working place was not safe it was for the defendant to excuse himself by proving that it was not reasonably practicable to make it safe. However, their Lordships were in agreement that if the linguistic construction of the statute did not clearly indicate on whom the burden should lie the court should look to other considerations to determine the intention of Parliament, such as the mischief at which the Act was aimed and practical considerations affecting the burden of proof and, in particular, the ease or difficulty that the respective parties would encounter in discharging the burden. I regard this last consideration as one of great importance, for surely Parliament can never lightly be taken to have intended to impose an onerous duty on a defendant to prove his innocence in a criminal case, and a court should be very slow to draw any such inference from the language of a statute. When all the cases are analysed, those in which the courts have held that the burden lies on the defendant are cases in which the burden can be easily discharged. This point can be demonstrated by what, at first blush, appear to be almost indistinguishable cases that arose under wartime regulations. In *R v Oliver* (1943) the defendant was prosecuted for selling sugar without a licence. The material part of the Sugar (Control) Order 1940, SR & O 1940/1069, by art 2 provided: 'Subject to any directions given or except under and in accordance with the terms of a licence permit or other authority granted by or on behalf of the Minister no ... wholesaler shall by way of trade ... supply ... any sugar.'

The Court of Criminal Appeal held that this placed the burden on the defendant to prove that he had the necessary licence to sell sugar. In *R v Putland and Sorrell* (1946), the defendant was charged with acquiring silk stockings without surrendering clothing coupons. The material part of the Consumer Rationing (Consolidation) Order 194, SR & O 1944/800, art 4 provided: 'A person shall not acquire rationed goods ... without surrendering ... coupons.' The Court of Criminal Appeal there held that the burden was on the prosecution to prove that the clothing had been bought without the surrender of coupons. The real distinction between these two cases lies in the comparative difficulty which would face a defendant in discharging the burden of proof.

In *R v Oliver* it would have been a simple matter for the defendant to prove that he had a licence if such was the case but in the case of purchase of casual articles of clothing it might, as the court pointed out in *R v Putland and Sorrell*, be a matter of the utmost difficulty for a defendant to establish that he had given the appropriate number of coupons for them. It appears to me that it was this consideration that led the court to construe that particular regulation as imposing the burden of proving that coupons had not been surrendered on the prosecution.

In *R v Edwards* (1974) the Court of Appeal expressed its conclusion in the form of an exception to what it said was the fundamental rule of our criminal law that the prosecution must prove every element of the [offence] charged. It said that the exception: 'is limited to offences arising under enactments which prohibit the doing of an act save in specified circumstances or by persons of specified classes or with specified qualifications or with the licence or permission of specified authorities.'

I have little doubt that the occasions on which a statute will be construed as imposing a burden of proof on a defendant which do not fall within this formulation are likely to be exceedingly rare. But I find it difficult to fit *Nimmo v Alexander Cowan & Sons Ltd* into this formula, and I would prefer to adopt the formula as an excellent guide to construction rather than as an exception to a rule. In the final analysis each case must turn on the construction of the particular legislation to determine whether the defence is an exception within the meaning of s 101 of the 1980 Act, which the Court of Appeal rightly decided reflects the rule for trials on indictment. With this one qualification I regard *R v Edwards* as rightly decided ...

With these considerations in mind I turn now to the question of construction. The essence of the offence is having in one's possession a prohibited substance. In order to establish guilt the prosecution must therefore prove that the prohibited substance is in the possession of the defendant. As it is an offence to have morphine in one form but not an offence to have morphine in another form the prosecution must prove that the morphine is in the prohibited form for otherwise no offence is established. The Court of Appeal recognised the strength of this argument for it said: 'The offence, it will be remembered, is created by s 5(2) of the 1971 Act, under which it is an offence for a person to have a controlled drug in his possession in contravention of s 5(1). Section 5(1) provides that, subject to any regulations under s 7 of the Act for the time being in force, it shall not be lawful for a person to have a controlled drug in his possession. By virtue of para 4(1) of the regulations, s 5(1) of the Act shall not have effect in relation to the controlled drugs specified in Sch 1. If we restrict ourselves to the form and wording of these provisions, a strong argument can be advanced in favour of the proposition that this is simply a case where the possession of certain controlled drugs is prohibited, and the possession of others is not; that it must therefore be for the prosecution to prove that the controlled drug in the possession of the defendant is one the possession of which is prohibited; and that the prosecution must therefore negative the possibility that the drug in question is a controlled drug excluded from the prohibition in s 5(1) because it falls within Sch 1.'

The Court of Appeal rejected this construction primarily because it considered that all the regulations made pursuant to s 7 of the 1971 Act should be similarly construed as placing a burden on the defendant. But this approach does not, in my view, give sufficient weight to the difference between the two regulatory powers given to the Secretary of State by s 7(1). Under s 7(1)(a) a power is given to provide that it shall not be an offence to possess certain drugs; this is achieved by exempting them in reg 4. Under s 7(1)(b) a power is given to clothe certain persons with immunity for what would otherwise be unlawful acts and this is achieved by the remainder of the regulations in Pt II of the 1973 regulations. These latter regulations provide special defences to what would otherwise be unlawful acts and would, I accept, place a burden on defendants to bring themselves within the exceptions if it were necessary to do so. I say 'if it were necessary to do so' because of the extreme improbability that an exempted person would be charged with an offence.

However, I regard reg 4 as in a quite different category from the other regulations in Pt II. It deals not with exceptions to what would otherwise be unlawful but with the definition of the essential ingredients of an offence. This can be strikingly demonstrated by reference to reg 4(2), which provides: 'Section 4(1) (which prohibits the production of and supply of controlled drugs) and 5(1) of the Act shall not have effect in relation to poppy-straw.'

Poppy-straw is shown in Pt I of Sch 2 to the 1971 act as a Class A drug. But, Parliament having removed poppy-straw from the schedule by the regulation, where is there room for any burden to lie on a defendant if he is charged with possessing poppy-straw? The defendant's answer is simply that it is not an offence to possess poppy-straw. Clearly, one cannot approach the problem of poppy-straw by saying that the prosecution establishes a *prima facie* case by proving the possession of poppy-straw because it is a controlled drug within Pt I of Sch 2 to the 1971 Act when poppy-straw has been withdrawn from the schedule for the purposes of an offence under s 5(1). Both parts of reg 4 must be similarly construed and by parity of reasoning the prosecution cannot establish a *prima facie* case of possessing morphine by pointing to morphine in the schedule when the regulation has provided that it is not an offence to possess morphine in a particular form. The prosecution must prove as an essential element of the offence the possession of a prohibited substance and the burden therefore lies on the prosecution to prove not only that the powder contained morphine but also that it was not morphine in the form permitted by reg 4(1) and Sch 1 made thereunder.

I do not share the anxieties of the Court of Appeal that this may place an undue burden on the prosecution. It must be extremely rare for a prosecution to be brought under the 1971 Act without the substance in question having been analysed. If it has been analysed there will be no difficulty in producing evidence to show that it does not fall within Sch 1 to the 1973 regulations. I pause here to observe that the analyst was in court during this trial and could, no doubt, have given this evidence if called on to do so. In future the evidence can, of course, be included in the analyst's report. On the other hand if the burden of proof is placed on the defendant he may be faced with very real practical difficulties in discharging it. The suspected substance is usually seized by the police for the purpose of analysis and there is no statutory provision entitling the defendant to a proportion of it. Often there is very little of the substance and if it has already been analysed by the prosecution it may have been destroyed in the process. In those cases, which I would surmise are very rare, in which it is intended to prosecute without an analyst's report there will have to be evidence from which the inference can be drawn that the substance was a prohibited drug and such evidence may well permit of the inference that it was not one of the relatively harmless types of compounds containing little more than traces of the drugs which are contained in Sch 1 to the 1973 regulations.

Finally, my Lords, as this question of construction is obviously one of real difficulty I have regard to the fact that offences involving the misuse of hard drugs are among the most serious in the criminal calendar and, subject to certain special defences the burden whereof is specifically placed on the defendant, they are absolute. In these circumstances, it seems to me right to resolve any ambiguity in favour of the defendant and to place the burden of proving the nature of the substance involved in so serious an offence on the prosecution.

For these reasons, my Lords, I would answer the certified question in the negative. I would allow this appeal and quash the conviction ...

Lord Ackner: ... My Lords, in giving my reasons for allowing this appeal, answering the certified question in the negative and quashing the conviction which are substantially the same as those of my noble and learned friend Lord Griffiths, I have made no mention of *R v Edwards* (1974). I have not done so firstly because I agree with the Court of Appeal that this case does not fall within the principle stated in that case and secondly because it is clear that the statement of principle is not intended to be exclusive in its effect. Lawton LJ in giving the judgment of the Court of Appeal stated in terms: 'Whenever the prosecution seeks to rely on this exception, the court must construe the enactment under which the charge is laid.'

R v Edwards provides, to my mind, a most helpful approach; but it still leaves to be answered in every case where Parliament has made no express provision as to the incidence of the burden of proof, the question: what is the proper construction of the enactment?[14]

But the task of interpretation is a difficult one, making prediction in a novel situation almost impossible. There are at least four reasons for this:

- The question whether a given statutory provision falls within the class of 'any exception, exemption, proviso, excuse or qualification' is inherently problematic: see for example, *Nimmo v Alexander Cowan & Sons Ltd* (1968).
- Section 101 has been only haphazardly applied.
- It may be that the whole project of distinguishing for s 101 purposes between rules and exceptions is logically flawed.
- The reliance on policy authorised by *Hunt* makes prediction particularly uncertain.

Nimmo v Alexander Cowan & Sons Ltd (1968, House of Lords)

Lord Reid: ... The pursuer, the present appellant, avers that on May 18 1964 he had, within a factory, to unload railway wagons filled with bales of pulp. In doing this he had to stand on some of the bales, and while he was standing on one of the bales it tipped up and caused him to fall and fracture his skull and three ribs. He founds on s 29(1) of the Factories Act, 1961, which is in these terms: 'There shall, so far as is reasonably practicable, be provided and maintained safe means of access to every place at which any person has any time to work and every such place shall, so far as is reasonably practicable, be made and kept safe for any person working there.'

He avers that the bales were insecurely placed in the wagons, so that the place at which he had to work was not made and kept safe for his working there. He

---

14. [1987] 1 All ER 1. Lord Keith agreed with Lord Griffiths. Lord Templeman and Lord Mackay also delivered speeches in favour of allowing the appeal.

deliberately avoids averring that it was reasonably practicable for the respondents, his employers, to make that place safe. He says that he has averred a relevant case because under this section it is for the defender to aver and prove, if he can, that it was not reasonably practicable to make the place safe. The respondents, of course, had no control over the loading of the bales in the wagon: that no doubt was done by the seller who was sold the pulp to them. They make averments to show that it was not reasonably practicable for them to make the place safe, and they also plead that, the pursuer's averments being irrelevant, the action should be dismissed. This plea to the relevancy was sustained by the Lord Ordinary (Lord Hunter) and the second Division adhered to his interlocutor.

This matter is not a mere technicality. It has important practical consequences. If the respondents are right the pursuer must not only aver in general terms that it was reasonably practicable to make the place safe – such an averment without more would be lacking in specification – he must also make sufficient positive averments to give notice to the defender of the method of making the place safe which he proposes to support by evidence. If the appellant is right, however, he can simply wait for the evidence which the respondent would have to lead to discharge the onus on him to show that it was not reasonably practicable to make the place safe, and then cross-examine the respondent's witnesses in any relevant way he chooses. He would have to make positive averments only if he intended to lead evidence that some particular method of making the place safe could have been adopted by the defender. In my opinion this question should be approached by considering first what a prosecutor would have to allege and prove in order to obtain a conviction. For civil liability only arises if there has been a breach of the statutory duty, and I cannot see how a pursuer could succeed in a civil action without averring and proving all the facts essential to establish the commission of an offence. It is true that the standard of proof is lower in a civil case, so that the pursuer has to show only that it is probable that an offence was committed; that cannot mean that the onus of proof is different with regard to any of the essential elements of the offence.

The appellant's argument is that, although the statute says that every working place 'shall, so far as is reasonably practicable, be made and kept safe', a prosecutor need only allege and prove that the place was not made and kept safe, leaving it to the accused to show that this was not reasonably practicable ...

It would be very convenient if one could avoid examination of the method of drafting and have a general rule either that in all these cases the onus is on the pursuer or that it is on the defender; but I do not think that that is possible. On the one hand, where the provision is that it 'shall be a defence to prove' something it would not be reasonable to require the pursuer to disprove that defence. On the other hand, take for example s 31 of the Factories Act, 1961, which requires that 'all practicable steps shall be taken' to prevent an explosion, to restrict its spread, and to remove fumes, etc. I cannot see how a prosecutor or pursuer could frame a relevant complaint or condescendence by merely alleging that an explosion occurred, or that it spread, or that fumes were not removed, leaving it to the accused or the defender to show that no practicable steps could have been taken to avoid that. The offence here must be a failure to take practicable steps and the prosecutor or pursuer must allege and prove such failure. I get no assistance in this case from any general presumption that a person is not required to prove a negative or that a person is required to prove facts peculiarly within his own knowledge. I do not lay any stress on the fact that if the appellant is right the defender would have to prove a negative – that it was not reasonably practicable to make the place safe; and I do not think that the question whether this was reasonably practicable is a matter peculiarly within the knowledge of the defender – an expert witness for the pursuer should be just as well able to deal with this as the defender. I would dismiss this appeal.

Lord Upjohn: My Lords, the appellant, pursuer in the action, claims against his employers, the respondent company, damages for injuries received in the course of his employment while working in the respondents' factory. He pleads as the respondents' ground of fault a breach of s 29(1) of the Factories Act, 1961 ... The pursuer avers that the place at which he had to work was not made and kept safe for him to work there. He has deliberately refrained from averring that it was reasonably practicable for the respondents to make and keep the place of work safe for any person working there. The question at this stage is one of relevancy. Is it essential for the pursuer to make that averment and, if he fails to do so, does his action fail for irrelevancy? The question of onus of proof will of course also arise at the trial. The question is one of some general importance, for if the pursuer has to aver that the respondents must make and keep the working place safe so far as is reasonably practicable, the pursuer must specify with the necessary particularity the manner in which the respondents could and should have discharged that obligation. Much the same situation would arise in England, for if the obligation is on the plaintiff to allege that the place could be made and kept safe so far as is reasonably practicable, he would no doubt be asked for some particulars of that allegation, although in practice it is likely that the burden on him would not be so heavy as under the much stricter rules of pleading in Scotland.

My Lords, the Lord Ordinary (Lord Hunter) examined the English and Scottish cases in some detail and came to the conclusion, not without some hesitation, that it was necessary for the pursuer to aver that it was reasonably practicable to make the working place safe; so the action failed on the ground of irrelevancy. In the First Division the matter was dealt with entirely as a question of the construction of the section, and each of their lordships reached the conclusion that in the words of the Lord President (Lord Clyde): '... The words 'so far as is reasonably practicable' consequently become, in my view, an integral part of the duty imposed and define the ambit of what is made obligatory. If so, it follows that the pursuer has not made out a relevant averment of a breach of the duty under s 29(1) unless he avers that it was reasonably practicable to make the lower bales a secure foothold before the superincumbent bales had been removed by the crane.'

My Lords, as a matter solely of construction of s 29 taken by itself there can be no doubt that there is great force in the views expressed by the First Division, but I have reached the conclusion that this is too narrow a view to take of its true construction. My noble and learned friend, Lord Reid, in his speech has already drawn attention to the great variety of phraseology that has been employed in the drafting of the sections of the Factories Act 1961 and similar legislation. No doubt it would have been perfectly easy so to have drawn the section so as to make it clear that the onus was on the defender to show that it was not reasonably practicable to make the working place safe. But this Act and its several predecessors are notoriously badly drafted, and in my opinion one must approach its true construction bearing in mind the object of the Act itself ...

My Lords, it is not in doubt that the whole object of the Factories Act 1961 is to reinforce the common law obligation of the employer to take care for the safety of his workmen ... My lords, I cannot believe that Parliament intended to impose on the injured workman or, if dead, his widow or other personal representative the obligation to aver with the necessary particularity the manner in which the employer should have employed reasonably practicable means to make and keep the place safe for him. Although the pursuer can nowadays consult experts he is at a great disadvantage compared to the employer. He may have little recollection of the accident, or of course he may have been killed, and his widow be in an even worse state. Then, on the other hand, it is the duty of the employer to make the place safe so far as is reasonably practicable. It is his duty with his experts to consider the state of the place of work in all its circumstances and to take whatever steps he can, so far as reasonably practicable, to make it safe. He must know and be able to give the reasons why he considered it was impracticable for him to make the place safe. If he cannot explain that it can only be because he failed to give it proper consideration, in breach of his bounden duty to the safety of his workmen ... I think that the section requires the occupier to make it one hundred per cent safe (judged of course by a reasonable standard of care), if that is reasonably practicable and, if it is not, to make it as safe so far as is reasonably practicable to a lower percentage. It would, indeed, impose a very heavy burden on the workmen if he and his experts had to set out on such an investigation. In my opinion Parliament intended to impose on the occupier the obligation of averring and proving at the trial that it was not reasonably practicable to make and keep the place of work safe, so that the pursuer's averments cannot be dismissed as irrelevant ...

I would allow this appeal.[15]

JC Smith, 'The Presumption of Innocence,' *Northern Ireland Legal Quarterly* 38 (1987)

The Haphazard Application of Section 101

Prior to *Hunt*, the leading case which established that section 101 imposes a legal burden of proof, and not merely an evidential burden on the defendant, was *Gatland v Metropolitan Police Commissioner* (1968). That was a case under section 140 of the Highways Act 1959 (section 161 of the Highways Act 1980) under which it is an offence: 'If a person, without lawful authority or excuse, deposits any thing whatever on a highway ... '. Lord Parker CJ, giving the judgment of the Divisional Court, stated that the effect of section 101 was that it was for the accused to raise and prove lawful authority or excuse. In *Hunt* Lord Ackner stated that it was accepted that this decision was correct. Similarly in the House of Lords' decision in *Nimmo v Alexander Cowan & Sons Limited*, Lord Pearson said that the express provisions of the Scottish equivalent of section 101 applied to the case of a parent whose child 'without reasonable excuse' failed to attend school regularly. Notwithstanding the fact that Schedule 2 to the Education (Scotland) Act 1946 required the words 'without reasonable excuse' to be included in a complaint, the section still imposed the burden on the parent to prove reasonable excuse.

But there is another section of the Highways Act (section 121(1) of the 1959 Act and sections 137(1) of the 1980 Act) which provides that it is an offence: 'If a person, without lawful authority or excuse, in any way wilfully obstructs ...' In the leading case of *Nagy v Weston* (1965) Lord Parker CJ, not referring to section 101, accepted the submission of counsel that the prosecution had to prove that there was no lawful authority or reasonable excuse. In *Hubbard v Pitt* (1975) Lord Denning MR, not mentioning either *Gatland* or section 101, regarded Lord

---

15. [1967] 3 All ER 187. Lord Wilberforce also delivered a dissenting speech. Lord Guest and Lord Pearson were in favour of allowing the appeal.

Parker's judgment on this point as 'authoritative'; and in the very recent case of *Hirst and Agu v The Chief Constable of the West Yorkshire Police* (1987) the Divisional Court cited it as binding authority, again without referring to Gatland or section 101. But, I have to ask, what is the difference between: 'If a person, without lawful authority or excuse, deposits any thing on a highway ... ' and 'If a person, without lawful authority or excuse, in any way wilfully obstructs ...?'

I can see no relevant difference. If section 101 applies to the one, it surely applies to the other. Of course, the obstruction section is the more important one in practice and its interpretation has serious implications for civil liberties because those taking part in demonstrations or picketing are likely to find themselves charged with an offence under this section. To impose on such persons the burden of proving that every obstruction of the highway which they might have caused was done with lawful authority or excuse would be a grave step. To deduce from this that Parliament intended to exclude the effect of section 101 from the obstruction offence, though not from another offence under the same statute, in respect of which Parliament has used exactly the same language, would seem to be to indulge in fiction of an arbitrary and undesirable kind. Of course, the courts have not done that. They and counsel have behaved as if section 101 did not exist. But section 101 is there, its authority and effect is confirmed by the House of Lords in *Hunt*.

Section 137(1) of the Highways Act is by no means alone in receiving this treatment. The Firearms Act 1968, section 1 provides: 'Subject to any exemption in this Act, it is an offence for a person (a) to have in his possession any firearm'; and section 58(2) provides an exemption in the case of an antique firearm possessed as a curiosity or ornament. Yet in *Burke* (1978) the court thought that, while there was an evidential burden on the appellant, he had satisfied it and that 'it was certainly upon the prosecution in the view of this court to establish that these firearms were not antiques and that they required a certificate'.

Section 12(1) of the Theft Act 1968 makes it an offence to take a vehicle without the consent of the owner or other lawful authority and section 12(6) provides that a person does not commit an offence by anything done in the belief that he has lawful authority to do it or that he would have the owner's consent if the owner knew of his doing it and the circumstances of it. In *Macpherson* (1973) the court expressed the view that subsection (6) creates a defence and that if an issue is raised it is for the prosecution to prove that the defendant had no authority or consent. Under the substituted section 16 of the Offences against the Person Act 1861, a person who, without lawful excuse, makes to another a threat to kill that other commits an offence. In *Cousins* (1982) the court stressed that the onus was on the prosecution to prove the absence of any lawful excuse which had been set up.

Perhaps most striking of all is the treatment of the legislation relating to drinking and driving which makes it an offence to fail, 'without reasonable excuse', to provide a specimen of breath or a laboratory specimen as the case may be. These provisions have been very strictly construed against the defendant. The courts have taken a very narrow view of what is capable of being a reasonable excuse, no doubt because they consider that it is in the interest of public safety on the roads to do so. Yet they seem consistently to have held, without reference to section 101, that the only burden on the defendant is an evidential burden and that the burden of proof of absence of reasonable excuse is on the prosecution. [*Mallows v Harris* (1979); *Anderton v Waring* (1986); *Cotgrave v Cooney* (1987).]

It appears that this provision is overlooked by law reformers and legislators as well as by the courts. Take an important statute like the Criminal Damage Act 1971. This Act is based on the report of the Law Commission on Offences of Damage to Property (Law Com No 29, 1970). The definitions of the offences under the Act in sections 1(1), 1(2) and 2 all begin with the words, 'A person who, without lawful excuse ... '. Section 3 also includes the phrase 'without lawful excuse ... '. This seems quite plainly to fall within the terms of section 101. The sections provide an 'excuse [accompanying] the description of the offence in the enactment creating the offence'. In their Report, the Law Commission wrote: 'We consider that the absence of lawful excuse should be an element of the offence and thus the burden of proving its absence should be upon the prosecution in each case.' They add, in a footnote: 'It is generally accepted that no burden lies on the defence where there is an issue involving a matter of general justification or excuse, unless a statute specifically so provides ... or the common law so requires (eg, where the defence of insanity is raised).'

The Law Commission were writing before the decision in *Edwards* and it appears to me that they must have been thinking in terms of trial on indictment or, if they thought about summary trial, they must have overlooked section 81 of the Magistrates' Courts Act 1952 which was in precisely the same terms as section 101 of the 1980 Act.

If this was an oversight by the Law Commission, then it has been repeated by at least one court. In *Jaggard v Dickinson* (1981) the defendant lived in a house belonging to one Heyfron. One night, making her way home drunk, she went by mistake to the wrong house. Finding it locked she broke in, causing damage. She relied on section 5(2) of the Act which provided that a person has a lawful excuse, for the purposes of the Act, if, at the time of the act alleged to constitute the offence, he believed that the person whom he believed to be entitled to consent to the damage to the property in question would have consented if he had known of the damage and its circumstances. The Magistrates' Court held that the defendant could not rely on this belief because it was a drunken belief. The Divisional Court allowed the defendant's appeal. The point of present interest is that Mustill LJ said: 'It is convenient to refer to the exculpatory provisions of section 5 as if they created a defence whilst recognising that the burden of disproving the facts referred to by the subsection remains on the prosecution.'

No reference was made by the court to section 101 or its predecessor. It does not appear that either party had raised the question of onus of proof and these remarks were not necessary to the decision. Like the Law Commission, Mustill LJ seems to have accepted it as obvious that the principle in *Woolmington* applies. Yet he was dealing with an appeal from a magistrates' court where section 101 expressly applies; and he offers no explanation why it did not apply to this particular provision. The most likely explanation, it seems to me, is that the section was overlooked. Section 101 was cited recently in the House of Lords in *Westminster City Council v Croyalgrange Limited* (1986), but held inapplicable by giving it a remarkably narrow construction. By paragraph 6(1) of Schedule 3 to the Local Government (Miscellaneous Provisions) Act 1982, ' ... no person shall in any area in which this Schedule is in force use any premises as a sex establishment except under and in accordance with the terms of a licence granted under this Schedule by the appropriate authority.' By paragraph 20(1) of the Schedule, 'A person who (a) knowingly uses, or knowingly causes or permits the use of, any premises ... contrary to paragraph 6 above ... shall be guilty of an offence.' The House held that section 101 did not operate to shift to the defendant the burden of proving that he had (or believed he had) a licence. Lord Bridge said: 'Moreover, the reliance on section 101 of the Act of 1980 is quite misconceived. That section places the onus of proof on a defendant who relies for his defence on "any exception, exemption, proviso, excuse or qualification, whether or not it accompanies the description of the offence ... in the enactment creating the offence ...". The exceptions and exemptions under Schedule 3 to the Act qualify the prohibition created by paragraph 6, not the offence created by paragraph 20(1)(a).'

The basis of this decision seems to be that the two paragraphs of the same Schedule to the Act were different 'enactments'. This is a remarkable conclusion, apart from the fact that it seems to ignore the words, 'whether or not [the exception] accompanies the description of the offence'. Moreover, the enactment creating the offence, that is paragraph 20(1), necessarily incorporates by reference paragraph 6 – otherwise paragraph 20(1) would be meaningless. The *Croyalgrange* case does not explain the cases discussed above where words like 'without lawful excuse' were obviously part of the enactment creating the offence. It was just another indication that the section is almost a dead letter in practice.

Parliament itself seems to have no confidence in the effectiveness of section 101 and any equivalent rule of common law – else, why provide in section 47 of the Sexual Offences Act 1956: 'Where in any of the foregoing sections the description of an offence is expressed to be subject to exceptions mentioned in the section, proof of the exception is to lie on the person relying on it?'

Section 101 is supposed to do this job already for summary trials and the common law rule for trial on indictment. Why provide in the Prevention of Crime Act 1953 that it is an offence for a person to have with him an offensive weapon in a public place without lawful authority or excuse 'the proof whereof shall lie on him'? Again, section 101 as interpreted in *Gatland* and the common law do this. Many other examples could be cited.[16]

Glanville Williams, 'The Logic of "Exceptions"', *Cambridge Law Journal* 47 (1988)

Take a statute making it an offence for an employer to fail in his duty to take safety precautions 'so far as reasonably practicable'. Some may think it reasonable to treat the qualifying phrase as an exception, because leaving it out still makes the offence one of failing to take safety precautions, which is an intelligible charge. So why not put the burden on the defendant employer to prove that he took all the safety precautions that were reasonably practicable?

There is a general argument against doing so. It is becoming obvious, is it not, that in trying to distinguish between rules and exceptions, between offences and defences, we are ensnared by words? The courts are in a logical difficulty, though they give no sign of perceiving it. They have to grapple with the practical problems of a distinction that they (and Parliament) assume to exist, but totally ignore this theoretical problem.

I believe that the first person to earn the distinction of addressing himself to the logic of the matter in a legal context was Julius Stone [(1944) 60 LQR at 280]. He pointed out that there is no rational difference between a quality of a class as contained in the definition of the class and a quality of a class as contained in an

---

16. Smith, 'Presumption of Innocence', pp 231-36.

exception to the class. 'Thus,' he said, 'the proposition "All animals have four legs except gorillas", and the proposition "All animals which are not gorillas have four legs", are, so far as their meanings are concerned, identical.' He poured scorn on any attempt to extract a difference of meaning out of the arrangement of the words. If he was right, it follows that everyone who tries to base an argument on a distinction between rules and exceptions drops a logical clanger.

Stone was dealing with the civil law. Putting his point in terms appropriate to the criminal law, it is that there is no intrinsic difference between the elements of an offence and an exception (or defence) to that offence. As was observed at the beginning, all the exceptions (defences) can be stated in negative form as part of offences, instead of as something outside the offences. Our thinking tends to be warped by language: if, instead of talking about an exception to an offence we talked about a modification of it, we might less readily suppose that the exception is something different from the offence.

The logical point may be illustrated by an old squib, written by some English classicist against his German counterparts, and running like this:

The Germans in Greek

Are badly to seek.

All, save only Hermann -

And Hermann's a German!

Does Hermann lack proficiency in Greek or not? All Germans lack it (premise 1), and we know Hermann is a German, so he does lack it. But he is an exception (premise 2); therefore he does not lack it. Which is true? If we are daft enough, we may begin to think that we have two premises, closely related yet yielding contrary conclusions.

The paradox, a puerile one of course, disappears as soon as one realises that an exception modifies the rule. Premise 1 is modified by premise 2, and so should be rewritten 'All Germans except Hermann are poor at Greek'. One can no longer argue from premise 1 in its original unqualified form. Hermann does not belong to the class 'Germans except Hermann'.

The paradox shows that a rule that is subject to an exception is only partly true if it is stated without the exception – which indeed is obvious. By omitting reference to the exception one has omitted a bit of the rule. The exception is, rationally regarded, part and parcel of the rule. Hence looking for the line between a rule and an exception is, to use the proverbial simile, like looking in a dark room for a black cat that isn't there. There are no characteristic features of an exception: 'exceptions' are merely linguistic constructs. Since they lack any specific definition, the negative of an element of an offence can be regarded as an exception, and the negative of an exception can be regarded as an element of the offence ... The argument so far is that there are no exceptions as self-subsisting concepts. An exception distinct from a rule is inconceivable, just as the Cheshire cat's smile is inconceivable apart from its face.

But then there is a further point. It is not merely a question of being unable to define exceptions. Parliament could define exceptions for us: it could say that such and such shall be exceptions to the rule, and as lawyers we would then have to think of them that way, if a question involving them ever arose. But obeying Parliament would not get us out of the injustice of using a rule about exceptions to shift the burden of proof.

Julius Stone, it must be said, did not see this. Having discovered that it is quite arbitrary to try to spell out exceptions from the arrangement of the words of a law, he proposed to get over the difficulty by looking for exceptions by the test of policy; we can then place the burden of proving exceptions, so discovered, on the defendant to a civil action. This will not do. The defendant will still be condemned on a cause of action that has not been proved against him. And the same objection holds for the criminal law. Neither in the civil nor in the criminal law can a distinction between rules and exceptions properly be used in allocating the burden of proof.

To show this, and in order to avoid the ambiguity and question-begging tendency of the word 'offence', let me speak instead of the 'offence package'. The offence package consists of the offence elements and the negative of defences (exceptions); and it is an indivisible whole. The defendant cannot be convicted unless he committed the offence package – that is to say, committed the offence and lacked a defence. If a bit is missing he is not guilty and will be acquitted of the offence charged. This is perfectly clear law.

Now, on the question of proof, if the legislator decrees that the persuasive burden in respect of a defence (however defined) rests on the defendant, he is decreeing that, failing proof of the defence, the defendant can be convicted without proof of the offence package. The defendant can be convicted notwithstanding that there is evidence in favour of the defence and the defence has not been disproved. That is the effect of the enactment, even though the legislator supposes himself to be motivated by the highest considerations of public policy. And I do not believe that any considerations of public policy can justify it ...

[The three Law Lords who gave full statements of reasons in *Hunt*] held that the implication of a reverse onus can be based not only on linguistic grounds (the wording of the legislation) but on general ideas of policy. In fact, the lords thought that policy has overriding importance. It can *produce* a reverse onus without any linguistic grounds in the statute, and it can *negative* a reverse onus even in respect of a statutory exception ...

This embrace of policy ... raises afresh the question whether the decision is compatible with *Woolmington*. Is a policy implication made by the judges properly called a 'statutory exception'? Viscount Simon in *Mancini* (1942), it will be recalled, interpreted *Woolmington* as allowing a reverse onus where this is 'specially dealt with by statute'. Is a policy implication by the judges, made without a word to support it in the statute, aptly described as being 'specially dealt with by statute'? When Parliament expressly reverses the burden of proof, the responsibility for any consequent injustice lies with Parliament; when the judges do it with only pretended statutory authority, the responsibility lies with them.

A particular objection to allowing the judges a roving commission in terms of policy is that it makes decisions hard to predict. Lord Griffiths confessed to the bothersome questions inherent in the law as he was proclaiming it to be. He said that 'the real difficulty lies in determining upon whom Parliament intended to place the burden of proof when the statute has not expressly so provided' – thus begging the question whether Parliament had an intention to depart from the ordinary rule that the burden lies on the prosecution if it did not say so. The 'real difficulty' in which the judges find themselves results entirely from their abandonment of the clear rule, thought to have been established by *Woolmington*, that a statute does not reverse the burden of proof in the absence of express words or, theoretically, necessary implication (using this phrase in its proper legal sense). It is highly unlikely that if Parliament were minded to reverse the burden of proof in a criminal case it would leave its intention to be gathered from implication, whether of the 'necessary' variety or not. In practice, and very properly, Parliament uses express words for this purpose. (The Misuse of Drugs Act, which was being considered in *Hunt*, contained several provisions in which the burden of proof was expressly reversed; and this fact should in itself have been sufficient to dispose of the argument that other provisions could carry a reverse burden by implication. *Expressio unius est exclusio alterius.*)

As has just been observed, the three lords did not propose an automatic rule that all statutory exceptions from liability should produce a reverse onus. They evidently considered that even the wording of a provision in terms of exception does not justify a reverse onus unless considerations of policy speak the same way. And policy considerations can justify a reverse onus even in respect of what would normally be regarded as the elements of the offence.

The latter proposition appears to be the explanation of what might otherwise be thought to be certain inconsistencies in the opinions. While Lord Griffiths concurred with the other lords in holding that the enactment before them only created an offence, without any question of an exception, he also cited with approval earlier decisions of the Court of Appeal that an offence of doing something without a licence created an implied exception relating to the possession of a licence, the burden of proof being on the defendant. There is no satisfactory linguistic distinction between the legislative wording in these cases and that under consideration in *Hunt*, but Lord Griffiths saw a distinction in point of policy. The reason why he thought that the burden of proving a licence rightly lay on the defendant was that if the defendant had a licence it would be simple for him to produce it.

To the same effect, both Lord Griffiths and Lord Ackner approved the decision of the lords in a civil case, *Nimmo v Alexander Cowan & Sons Ltd*. This decision, to which the three lords attached decisive importance, turned on the following provision of the Factories Act: 'There shall, so far as reasonably practicable, be provided and maintained safe means of access to every place at which any person has at any time to work ...'

A majority in *Nimmo's* case held that these words imposed upon an employer, when sued for damages arising from breach of section, the burden of proving that it was not reasonably practicable to provide safe means of access, if that was his defence. Here again it is hard to see how these words could reasonably have been read as creating an exception from liability. On the contrary, they defined the scope of the duty, just as much as the words of the enactment considered in Hunt. But the lords in *Nimmo's* case saw reasons of policy for putting the persuasive burden on the employer, and Lords Griffiths and Ackner accepted the decision. Lord Griffiths summed it up by saying: 'Their lordships were in agreement that if the linguistic construction of the statute did not clearly indicate upon whom the burden should lie the court should look to other considerations to determine the intention of Parliament such as the mischief at which the Act was aimed and practical considerations affecting the burden of proof and, in particular, the ease or difficulty that the respective parties would encounter in discharging the burden.'

So here we have it. Where statutory offences are concerned, the principle of *Woolmington* (which Viscount Simon said was 'of general application in all charges under the criminal law') ceases to operate. Instead, the courts can shift the burden to the defendant whenever 'practical considerations' dictate, which means that they can do so whenever they deem it politic. Even when a statute expressly shifts the burden in respect of some issues, the courts can find reasons of policy for shifting it on others as well. This is judicial law-making run riot. No mention is made of the policy (I would say the imperative principle) of not convicting persons who are not proved to be guilty; but then the lords did not appear to understand that that principle is involved.

Lord Griffiths' generalisation applies only when 'the linguistic construction did not clearly indicate upon whom the burden should lie'. But he evidently did not think that the inclusion of a particular item in the description of the offence was a clear indication that the burden of proof should lie on the prosecution. In Nimmo's case, although the words 'so far as reasonably practicable' appeared in the description of the offence, the lords threw the burden of proof of this issue on the defendant.

As regards 'the mischief at which the Act was aimed', which Lord Griffiths took as a relevant consideration, did he mean that if the perceived mischief is very serious the defendant must bear the burden of justifying or excusing himself, or did he mean that if the mischief is very great and if, therefore, the offence is a serious one, the burden of disproving the defence should be left with the prosecution? Apparently the latter. And in weighing the 'mischief', does one look at the mischief involved in what is alleged to have been done in the particular case, or at some average mischief that may be expected in cases of the type covered by the statute, or again does one consider the maximum mischief that may be expected in any circumstances? We do not know.

Ease of proof as affecting the burden of proof

The position of the three lords was that in a criminal case statutory words can be held, on account of 'practical considerations', to impose persuasive burdens on the defendant in respect of any issues, notwithstanding that such words as a matter of linguistic construction merely create an offence. The practical consideration to which they attached particular importance was the question whether it would be hard for the prosecution to prove the issue and easy for the defendant to disprove it.

The three lords were, of course, aware of the distinction between evidential and persuasive burdens, but had they really grasped the point that arguments for the first should not automatically be treated as arguments for the second? That it is easy for the defendant to give evidence on an issue, and relatively difficult for the prosecution, may be an excellent reason for placing an evidential burden upon the defendant. It is a very poor reason for telling the jury, at the end of the day, that the defendant is to be convicted if he has not established his version of the issue. This matter appears nowhere in the lords' opinions. They treat the burden of proof as though it were a purely technical affair, and do not seriously consider its possible impact upon the fate of individual human beings.

The difficulties experienced by the courts with a rule referring to ease of proof are illustrated by the split of opinion in *Hunt* between the Court of Appeal and the Appeal Committee. The former held that the burden should be on the defendant because sometimes he could more easily discharge it than could the prosecution: for instance, when there was evidence that the defendant possessed the substance in question and he refused to surrender it for examination. This was a remarkable position to take, because (as the lords pointed out) in the case at bar the boot was on the other foot; it was the prosecution that possessed the substance in question and could easily have performed the required test. So which party can most easily establish the issue depends on the circumstances.

In, say, a licence case, where a question arises as to ease of proof, what question is the trial judge supposed to ask himself? Perhaps it is this: 'Do I find that on the balance of probability the defendant can (if innocent) satisfy the jury of his innocence on the balance of probability, whereas the balance of probability is that the prosecution cannot satisfy the jury beyond reasonable doubt that he is guilty, even if he is guilty?' It would be an extraordinary question to ask, even if the judge is merely communing with himself. And how can the judge answer the question without hearing evidence? As soon as the evidence is heard it will become obvious that the licensing authority has pretty good evidence that the defendant has no licence, because otherwise the authority would not have brought the charge. The only sensible course is to stick to the simple rule that the prosecution carry the burden of establishing all the elements of the offence including the negative of defences. This is not to say that the defendant should not sometimes carry an evidential burden.[17]

STANDARDS OF PROOF

In criminal cases the formulas traditionally favoured are that the prosecution must 'satisfy the jury so that they are sure' of the defendant's guilt, or that the jury must be satisfied 'beyond reasonable doubt' that the prosecution has proved its case.

Walters v The Queen (1969, Privy Council)

Lord Diplock: ... It is the duty of each individual juror to make up his own mind as to whether the evidence that the defendant committed the offence with which he is charged is so strong as to convince him personally of the defendant's guilt. Inevitably, because of differences of temperament or experience some jurors will take more convincing than others. That is why there is safety in numbers. And shared responsibility and the opportunity for discussion after retiring serves to counteract individual idiosyncrasies.

By the time he sums up the judge at the trial has had an opportunity of observing the jurors. In their Lordships' view it is best left to his discretion to choose the most appropriate set of words in which to make *that* jury understand that they must not return a verdict against a defendant unless they are sure of his guilt ... Their Lordships would deprecate any attempt to lay down some precise formula or to draw fine distinctions between one set of words and another. It is the effect of the summing-up as a whole that matters.[18]

Ferguson v The Queen (1979, Privy Council)

Lord Scarman: ... Though the law requires no particular formula, judges are wise, as a general rule, to adopt one.

The time-honoured formula is that the jury must be satisfied beyond reasonable doubt. [A]ttempts to substitute other expressions have never prospered. It is generally sufficient and safe to direct a jury that they must be satisfied beyond reasonable doubt so that they feel sure of the defendant's guilt. Nevertheless, other words will suffice, so long as the message is clear.[19]

Where there is a legal burden on a defendant in a criminal case in respect of any issue, that burden will be discharged by proof on the balance of probabilities – the civil standard.

---

17. Williams, *'Logic of "Exceptions"'*, pp 276-80, 286-90.
18. [1969] 2 AC 26.
19. [1979] 1 All ER 877.

R v Carr-Briant (1943, Court of Criminal Appeal)

Humphreys J read the judgment of the court (Viscount Caldecote CJ, Humphreys and Lewis JJ): ... What is the burden resting on a plaintiff or defendant in civil proceedings can, we think, best be stated in the words of the classic pronouncement on the subject by Willes J in *Cooper v Slade* (1856). That learned judge referred to an ancient authority in support of what he termed, 'the elementary proposition that in civil cases the preponderance of probability may constitute sufficient ground for a verdict'. The authority in question was the judgment of Dyer CJ and a majority of the Justices of the Common Pleas in *Newis v Lark* (1571), decided in the reign of Queen Elizabeth. The report contains this passage: 'Where the matter is so far gone that the parties are at issue ... so that the jury is to give a verdict one way or other, there, if the matter is doubtful, they may found their verdict upon that which appears the most probable and by the same reason that which is most probable shall be good evidence.'

In our judgment, in any case where, either by statute or at common law, some matter is presumed against an accused person 'unless the contrary is proved', the jury should be directed that it is for them to decide whether the contrary is proved, that the burden of proof required is less than that required at the hands of the prosecution in proving the case beyond a reasonable doubt, and that the burden may be discharged by evidence satisfying the jury of the probability of that which the accused is called upon to establish.[20]

The criminal courts have produced many decisions which attempt to clarify the criminal standard of proof as a result of the need for judges to instruct the jury correctly on the burden and standard in summing up. Because very few civil cases are heard with a jury, the opportunity to define the civil standard and show in what respects it differs from that applied in criminal cases has not often arisen. An attempt sometimes referred to is that of Denning J, as he then was, in 1947.

Miller v Minister of Pensions (1947, King's Bench Division)

Denning J: ... The first point of law in the present appeal is whether the tribunal properly directed itself as to the burden of proof. The proper direction is covered by decisions of this court. It is as follows.

1   In cases falling under art 4(2) and art 4(3) of the Royal Warrant Concerning Retiring Pay, Pensions, etc, 1943 (which are generally cases where the man was passed fit at the commencement of his service, but is later afflicted by a disease which leads to his death or discharge) there is a compelling presumption in the man's favour which must prevail unless the evidence proves beyond reasonable doubt that the disease was not attributable to or aggravated by war service, and for that purpose the evidence must reach the same degree of cogency as is required in a criminal case before an accused person is found guilty. That degree is well settled. It need not reach certainty, but it must carry a high degree of probability. Proof beyond reasonable doubt does not mean proof beyond the shadow of a doubt. The law would fail to protect the community if it admitted fanciful possibilities to deflect the course of justice. If the evidence is so strong against a man as to leave only a remote possibility in his favour which can be dismissed with the sentence 'of course it is possible, but not in the least probable', the case is proved beyond reasonable doubt, but nothing short of that will suffice.

---

20. [1943] KB 607.

2   In cases falling under art 4(2) and art 4(4) (which are generally cases where the man was fit on his discharge, but incapacitated later by a disease) there is no compelling presumption in his favour, and the case must be decided according to the preponderance of probability. If at the end of the case the evidence turns the scale definitely one way or the other, the tribunal must decide accordingly, but if the evidence is so evenly balanced that the tribunal is unable to come to a determinate conclusion one way or the other, then the man must be given the benefit of the doubt. This means that the case must be decided in favour of the man unless the evidence against him reaches the same degree of cogency as is required to discharge a burden in a civil case. That degree is well settled. It must carry a reasonable degree of probability, but not so high as is required in a criminal case. If the evidence is such that the tribunal can say: 'We think it more probable than not,' the burden is discharged, but, if the probabilities are equal, it is not.[21]

Where an allegation is made in civil proceedings of reprehensible conduct, including allegations of what amounts in effect to the commission of a serious criminal offence, the question has sometimes been considered whether the standard of proof required is sufficiently expressed by 'proof on the balance of probabilities'. The courts have tended to cope with this in two ways. One approach has been to say that although the standard is proof 'on the balance of probabilities' in all civil cases, there may be degrees of probability within that standard. Another approach has been to emphasise not degrees of proof, but the weight of evidence required to satisfy a court that a particular allegation has been proved. Varieties of emphasis can be seen in the following sample of cases.

Bater v Bater (1951, Court of Appeal)

APPEAL from Mr Commissioner Grazebrook, KC.

The appellant wife petitioned for divorce on the grounds of the alleged cruelty of the respondent, her husband ...

Tolstoy for the wife: The commissioner in his judgment said: 'That is the evidence, and in order to succeed the wife has to satisfy me that there has been injury to life, limb, or health, bodily or mentally, or reasonable apprehension of it, and she has to prove her case beyond reasonable doubt.' In that last sentence, it is submitted, the commissioner misdirected himself, since the phrase 'beyond reasonable doubt' was to denote the standard of proof applicable in a criminal case ...

Denning LJ: The difference of opinion which has been evoked about the standard of proof in recent cases may well turn out to be more a matter of words than anything else. It is of course true that by our law a higher standard of proof is required in criminal cases than in civil cases. But this is subject to the qualification that there is no absolute standard in either case. In the criminal cases the charge must be proved beyond reasonable doubt, but there may be degrees of proof within that standard.

As Best CJ and many other great judges have said, 'In proportion as the crime is enormous, so ought the proof to be clear'. So also in civil cases, the case may be proved by a preponderance of probability, but there may be degrees of probability within that standard. The degree depends on the subject matter. A civil court, when considering a charge of fraud, will naturally require for itself a

---

21. [1947] 2 All ER 372.

higher degree of probability than that which it would require when asking if negligence is established. It does not adopt so high a degree as a criminal court, even when it is considering a charge of a criminal nature; but still it does require a degree of probability which is commensurate with the occasion. Likewise, a divorce court should require a degree of probability which is proportionate to the subject matter.

I do not think that the matter can be better put than it was by Lord Stowell in *Loveden v Loveden* (1810): 'The only general rule that can be laid down upon the subject is, that the circumstances must be such as would lead the guarded discretion of a reasonable and just man to the conclusion.' The degree of probability which a reasonable and just man would require to come to a conclusion – and likewise the degree of doubt which would prevent him from coming to it – depends on the conclusion to which he is required to come. It would depend on whether it was a criminal case or a civil case, what the charge was, and what the consequences might be; and if he were left in real and substantial doubt on the particular matter, he would hold the charge not to be established: he would not be satisfied about it.

But what is a real and substantial doubt? It is only another way of saying a reasonable doubt; and a reasonable doubt is simply that degree of doubt which would prevent a reasonable and just man from coming to the conclusion. So the phrase 'reasonable doubt' takes the matter no further. It does not say that the degree of probability must be as high as 99 per cent or as low as 51 per cent. The degree required must depend on the mind of the reasonable and just man who is considering the particular subject matter. In some cases 51 per cent would be enough, but not in others. When this is realized, the phrase 'reasonable doubt' can be used just as aptly in a civil case or a divorce case as in a criminal case ... The only difference is that, because of our high regard for the liberty of the individual, a doubt may be regarded as reasonable in the criminal courts which would not be so in the civil courts. I agree therefore with my brothers that the use of the phrase 'reasonable doubt' by the commissioner in this case was not a misdirection ...

If, however, the commissioner had put the case higher and said that the case had to be proved with the same strictness as a crime is proved in a criminal court, then he would, I think, have misdirected himself ... It would be adopting too high a standard. The divorce court is a civil court, not a criminal court, and it should not adopt the rules and standards of the criminal court. I agree that the appeal should be dismissed.[22]

Hornal v Neuberger Products Ltd (1957, Court of Appeal)

Denning LJ: The question in this case is whether Mr Neuberger orally represented to the plaintiff that a certain capstan lathe had been 'Soag reconditioned'. I should have thought it was a simple question of fact for the judge to decide on the evidence, but it has become so mixed up with questions of law that the case took many days in the court below and over two days before us ... The judge seems to have found it difficult to make up his mind whether Mr Neuberger made that representation [that it was Soag reconditioned] or not. The judge said that his decision depended on the standard of proof which was to apply. If he was to apply the standard in civil cases – the balance of probability – he would hold that the representation was made by Mr Neuberger: but if he was to apply the

---

22. [1951] P 35.

standard in criminal cases – proof beyond reasonable doubt – he would hold that the representation was not made.

Such being the judge's state of mind, he considered first whether there was a contractual warranty. On that issue the civil standard of proof clearly applied. He found on the balance of probabilities that Mr Neuberger did say that the machine had been Soag reconditioned, that Mr Neuberger made it in order to persuade Mr Hornal to enter into the transaction, and that Mr Hornal relied upon it: but he found that it was not a contractual warranty because it was not so intended. I do not think we can disturb that finding ...

Thus having disposed of the warranty the judge turned to consider whether Mr Neuberger was guilty of fraud. If Mr Neuberger did in fact represent that the machine had been Soag reconditioned, he was clearly guilty of fraudulent misrepresentation, because he knew it was not true. He had got £300 from his German supplier because it had not been reconditioned. So the only question was whether Mr Neuberger made the representation or not. It was there that the judge ran into difficulty – about the standard of proof. He said: 'If I have to be satisfied beyond all reasonable doubt, I should not be so satisfied in regard to the statement that it was Soag reconditioned. I have come to the conclusion on the preponderance of probability that the statement was made, but in my view no jury would dream of convicting a defendant of a fraud based on that statement, and if I had to consider whether, sitting as a magistrate trying a case of false pretences, I should convict Mr Neuberger of making this statement, I have no hesitation in saying I should not dream of doing so.'

In setting himself this problem the judge showed an uncommon nicety of approach. I must say that, if I was sitting as a judge alone, and I was satisfied that the statement was made, that would be enough for me, whether the claim was put in warranty or on fraud. I think it would bring the law into contempt if a judge were to say that on the issue of warranty he finds the statement was made, and that on the issue of fraud he finds it was not made.

Nevertheless, the judge having set the problem to himself, he answered it, I think, correctly. He reviewed all the cases and held rightly that the standard of proof depends on the nature of the issue. The more serious the allegation the higher the degree of probability that is required: but it need not, in a civil case, reach the very high standard required by the criminal law. Take this very case. If Mr Neuberger did represent that the machine was Soag reconditioned he did very wrong because he knew it was untrue. His moral guilt is just as great whatever the form of the action, no matter whether in warranty or in fraud. He should be judged by the same standard in either case.

I have already expressed my views on this subject in *Bater v Bater* and I need not repeat them here ...

Hodson LJ: The county court judge, having reached the conclusion, on the basis of a balance of probability, that a fraudulent statement had been made, found himself unable to find that fraud had been proved beyond all reasonable doubt. Thus he posed himself the question: 'In a civil action are criminal standards of proof necessary in considering what is or may be a crime?' This question, after a review of the authorities, he answered in the negative.

The comparative dearth of express authority on this topic is not surprising. No responsible counsel undertakes to prove a serious accusation without admitting that cogent evidence is required, and judges approach serious accusations in the same way without necessarily considering in every case whether or not there is a criminal issue involved. For example, in the ordinary case arising from a collision between two motor cars involving charges of negligence, I have never heard of a judge applying the criminal standard of proof, on the ground that his judgment might involve the finding of one of the parties guilty of a criminal offence.

The judge took great pains to consider the cases in which the question he posed had been considered. I do not propose to follow him in their review, agreeing as I do with his conclusion ...

Notwithstanding the existence of some cases where the point appears to have been argued and decided in a contrary sense, I think the true view, and that most strongly supported by authority, is that which the judge took, namely, that in a civil case the balance of probability standard is correct.

Morris LJ: After a very full hearing which extended over many days, the judge delivered a judgment in the course of which he examined and analysed all the evidence. The plaintiff had become aware that the defendants possessed a Herbert No 4 capstan lathe. The plaintiff, accompanied by his engineer, went to see it, and had an interview with Mr Neuberger at which others were present. There was a discussion about the machine. There was bargaining about its price. The plaintiff was shown the gears. The power was turned on. The plaintiff thought that the machine was fit for immediate use and that it would avail him for some work of his that he had in mind. The plaintiff as a result acquired the machine. The acquisition was not effected by direct purchase but by the assisting introduction of a hire-purchase company. The plaintiff affirmed and Mr Neuberger denied that in the course of the discussion Mr Neuberger had said that the machine had been 'Soag reconditioned'. The significance of the phrase in question was well understood by those concerned. It was first of all a question of fact whether Mr Neuberger had made the alleged statement. The judge held that he had. On that finding the question arose whether what Mr Neuberger had said had contractual effect. Being an affirmation made during negotiations for a sale, it would not have been surprising if it had been held that the statement had contractual quality. But the judge made a correct approach in law when he considered the totality of the evidence so as to decide whether contractual intention existed. There was much oral evidence to be considered: there was correspondence which, either by reason of what it contained or by reason of what it did not contain, had some evidential value. The judge had no hesitation in holding that the statement of Mr Neuberger was not contractual. He held that neither the plaintiff nor Mr Neuberger had thought it to be. 'It was simply a matter of talking about the machine.' Although wrong statements made when someone is about to buy ought not readily to be held to be beyond the frontiers of contract, it seems to me that the judge approached the issue with discrimination. He appears to have applied the correct tests, and, accordingly, I do not think that his conclusion should be displaced.

It is not in dispute that if Mr Neuberger made a representation that the machine was Soag reconditioned he knew that the representation was false. Accordingly, if the representation was made, then, although there was no warranty, there was an actionable misrepresentation. But here a question arises as to whether the judge misdirected himself when deciding the issue as to whether the two words 'Soag reconditioned' were or were not spoken. He has said that if as to this he ought to be satisfied in the way in which a court or a jury would have to be satisfied before convicting in a criminal case, then in this case he was not so satisfied, but he was satisfied if he was entitled to decide the matter as issues in civil actions are decided, that is, according to the balance of probabilities. The precision of this revealed judicial heart-searching is impeccable from the point of view of its logical nicety. The question of fact which the judge had to decide was simply whether Mr Neuberger spoke the two words in question. If he did, the words might have been a warranty or they might have been a representation, which in this case would be actionable because fraudulent. It would be strange if different standards of proof as to the speaking of the two words could be applicable according as to what civil legal rights followed.

In a criminal case a jury must be directed that the onus is all the time upon the prosecution and that before they convict they must feel sure of the accused's guilt. Authoritative guidance in regard to directing juries in criminal cases is to be found in the judgment of Lord Goddard CJ in *Regina v Hepworth and Fearnley*, and in other cases. It has, however, been emphasized that what is vital is not the mere using of some particular formula of words but the effect of a summing-up in giving true guidance as to the right approach.

It is, I think, clear from the authorities that a difference of approach in civil cases has been recognized. Many judicial utterances show this. The phrase 'balance of probabilities' is often employed as a convenient phrase to express the basis upon which civil issues are decided. It may well be that no clear-cut logical reconciliation can be formulated in regard to the authorities on these topics. But perhaps they illustrate that 'the life of the law is not logic but experience.' In some criminal cases liberty may be involved; in some it may not. In some civil cases the issues may involve questions of reputation which can transcend in importance even questions of personal liberty. Good name in man or woman is 'the immediate jewel of their souls.'

But in truth no real mischief results from an acceptance of the fact that there is some difference of approach in civil actions. Particularly is this so if the words which are used to define that approach are the servants but not the masters of meaning. Though no court and no jury would give less careful attention to issues lacking gravity than to those marked by it, the very elements of gravity become a part of the whole range of circumstances which have to be weighed in the scale when deciding as to the balance of probabilities. This view was denoted by Denning LJ when in his judgment in *Bater v Bater* he spoke of a 'degree of probability which is commensurate with the occasion' and of 'a degree of probability which is proportionate to the subject matter'.

In English law the citizen is regarded as being a free man of good repute. Issues may be raised in a civil action which affect character and reputation, and these will not be forgotten by judges and juries when considering the probabilities in regard to whatever misconduct is alleged. There will be reluctance to rob any man of his good name: there will also be reluctance to make any man pay what is not due or to make any man liable who is not or not liable who is. A court will not be deterred from a conclusion because of regret at its consequences: a court must arrive at such conclusion as is directed by the weight and preponderance of the evidence.

In my judgment, the judge did not misdirect himself in approaching the case on the basis of the preponderance of probability in deciding that Mr Neuberger had stated that the machine was Soag reconditioned ...[23]

In re Dellow's Will Trusts (1964, Chancery Division)

Ungoed-Thomas J: This is a very sad question arising out of tragic and depressing circumstances. I am asked to decide whether or not Daisy Ethel Dellow

---

23. [1957] 1 QB 247.

feloniously killed her husband, Harold Dellow. The tragedy of their deaths occurred on December 31 1957 at their home in Devon. The husband by his will left all he had to his wife with a provision that if her death preceded his he gave the property over to others. His wife similarly made a will in favour of the husband if he were alive at her death and failing that she left her property to others.

I have decided that, in accordance with the presumption raised by section 184 of the Law of Property Act 1925 the husband, as the older of the two, died first. The result of that is that the husband's will in favour of the wife would take effect, unless she feloniously killed him. But if she did so kill him, then it is clear that neither she nor anybody claiming through her could claim his estate, and the gift to her in the husband's will would not take effect. A passage in *Theobald on Wills* (1963, 12th edn), para 385, states that since the passing of the Forfeiture Act 1870 the provisions of which I need not refer to, 'it has been held that it is against public policy for a person who is guilty of feloniously killing another to take any benefit in that other person's estate. And this principle applies to a case of manslaughter as well as one of murder. It applies to an intestacy as well as to a will. But it does not apply if the killer is insane. If there is no evidence as to the killer's state of mind, the killing is presumed to be felonious.' In this case there is clearly no substantial evidence of insanity within the legal meaning of that term and no case is made out before me on that ground.

It is, then, established that the wife killed the husband? It is conceded that, in a case of this kind before me in the Chancery Division dealing with the devolution of property, the standard of proof required is not so severe as that required by the criminal law. The standard of proof was considered in *Hornal v Neuberger Products Ltd*, where Morris LJ stated: 'Though no court and no jury would give less careful attention to issues lacking gravity than to those marked by it, the very elements of gravity become a part of the whole range of circumstances which have to be weighed in the scale when deciding as to the balance of probabilities.'

It seems to me that in civil cases it is not so much that a different standard of proof is required in different circumstances varying according to the gravity of the issue, but, as Morris LJ says, the gravity of the issue becomes part of the circumstances which the court has to take into consideration in deciding whether or not the burden of proof has been discharged. The more serious the allegation the more cogent is the evidence required to overcome the unlikelihood of what is alleged and thus to prove it. This is perhaps a somewhat academic distinction and the practical result is stated by Denning LJ: 'The more serious the allegation the higher the degree of probability that is required: but it need not, in a civil case, reach the very high standard required by the criminal law.' In this case the issue is whether or not the wife feloniously killed the husband. There can hardly be a graver issue than that, and its gravity weighs very heavily against establishing that such a killing took place, even for the purposes of deciding a civil issue ...[24]

In re G (1987, Family Division)

SUMMONS: On 15 August 1986 the custody of a girl, born on 22 October 1983, was granted to the father by justices to be supervised by the probation service. The mother was granted defined access arrangements which included alternate

---

24. [1964] 1 All ER 771.

weekend staying access. On 2 February 1987 the father obtained an order *ex parte*, requiring the mother to return the child forthwith and on 4 February 1987, Judge Mark Smith confirmed the order at an *inter partes* hearing. On 5 February 1987 a place of safety order was issued and the child was taken into the interim care of the local authority, who issued wardship proceedings. By an interim order Judge Counsell confirmed that the child should remain in the interim care of the local authority, gave interim access to the father and to the mother and invited the Official Solicitor to act as guardian *ad litem*.

Sheldon J: ... [I]n general terms, the issues which I have had to resolve are: (1) whether Mr G is the ward's father; (2) whether the child has been subject to any form of sexual abuse and, if so, whether its perpetrator has been the father; and (3) what plan is to be made for her future upbringing ...

I should at once make plain that there is no evidence which would justify the prosecution of Mr G for any form of sexual abuse or improper behaviour with his daughter; the available evidence falls far short of the standard of proof beyond reasonable doubt that would be needed to lead to a conviction in criminal proceedings, as those would be.

In the present context, however, that is not an end of the matter. In wardship proceedings, as these proceedings are, although alleged wrongdoing by an individual may be an issue, the predominant consideration is the welfare of the child and not the behaviour of any particular adult. They are also civil proceedings.

I agree therefore with Waite J in *In re W (Child Abuse: Evidence)* (1987), (as indeed I have been invited to by Mrs Matthews appearing on behalf of Mr G) that in general terms the standard of proof to be applied in such proceedings as these is that based on the balance of probabilities. On the other hand, having regard to the diversity of issues that might be raised in such proceedings, I also take the view, as was expressed by Denning LJ, in *Bater v Bater* (1951), that the 'degree of probability' required in any particular context may vary and must be 'commensurate with the occasion' or 'proportionate to the subject matter'. Thus in my opinion, in such proceedings as the present, a higher degree of probability is required to satisfy the court that the father has been guilty of some sexual misconduct with his daughter than would be needed to justify the conclusion that the child has been the victim of some such behaviour of whatever nature and whoever may have been its perpetrator.

In the latter context, indeed, I am of the opinion that the gravity of the matter is such from the child's point of view that any tilt in the balance suggesting that she has been the victim of sexual abuse would justify a finding to that effect. In my view, indeed, there may also be circumstances in which the application of a 'standard of proof' as that phrase is commonly understood, is inapt to describe the method by which the court should approach the particular problem; as, for example, where the suspicion of sexual abuse or other wrong-doing, although incapable of formal proof, is such as to lead to the conclusion that it would be an unacceptable risk to the child's welfare to leave him in his previous environment; or (more likely in the case of older children) where, although the court may be satisfied that no sexual abuse has taken place, the very fact that it has been alleged by a child against a parent suggests that in the child's interests, some change in, or control over the existing regime is required.

So also, as has been suggested in the present case, if the child has been the subject of sexual abuse, even if the father cannot be identified as the offender, his character and behaviour, taken in conjunction with all the other circumstances, may lead to the conclusion that it would be an unacceptable risk to her welfare to return her to his care ...

In all the circumstances, however, even applying a more stringent test than a mere 'balance of probabilities', I have been driven to the conclusion, without considering it necessary to spell it out in greater detail, that Mr G has been guilty of an over-familiar and sexually inappropriate relationship with her, amounting in the present context to sexual abuse, which could bode ill for the future and which has created the 'particularly vulnerable' little girl described by Dr Gaye. Nor, in my judgment, is there any evidence to justify the conclusion that anyone but Mr G could be held responsible for that state of affairs ...[25]

---

25. [1987] 1 WLR 1461.

CHAPTER 3

COMPETENCE AND COMPELLABILITY

Inability to testify has always been regarded as the exception rather than the rule. When the modern law of evidence was beginning to develop in the 18th century the exception was a wide one whose rationale was probably twofold: a desire to keep people away from a situation where they might be tempted to commit perjury, and the view that certain types of people were so unreliable that any testimony from them would be worthless. Those excluded from testimony were the parties to civil actions and any other person with a financial interest in the outcome of the proceedings; the accused in criminal cases; certain persons with criminal convictions; and many people who would not, or could not, take a Christian oath before testifying. This last category was likely to include children, who often could not satisfy the court that they understood the nature and significance of an oath. Subject to some exceptions, a witness who was competent was generally compellable.[1] For the last two centuries the tendency has been to expand the capacity to testify while maintaining a few instances where a competent witness is not compellable. Three classes of witness require special consideration:

- Defendants in criminal proceedings.
- Spouses of defendants in criminal proceedings.
- Children.

DEFENDANTS IN CRIMINAL PROCEEDINGS

Accused persons as a general class were not allowed to give evidence on their own behalf until the Criminal Evidence Act 1898. It is a mistake, however, to state that they were always unable to testify prior to this Act. In the decades prior to the Act statutes were sometimes passed which created new offences and which specifically allowed prisoners charged under the statute to testify in their own defence. This gave rise to some curious anomalies which in the end helped to ease the path of the 1898 Act.[2] Under that Act prosecuting counsel could not comment on the failure of an accused person to testify, but comments could be made by counsel for a co-accused and by the judge. That restriction on

---

1. *Ex parte Fernandez* (1861) 10 CBNS 3. 'Every person in the kingdom except the sovereign may be called upon and is bound to give evidence to the best of his knowledge upon any question of fact material and relevant to an issue tried in any of the Queen's courts, unless he can shew some exception in his favour ... ' *per* Willes J, 39.

2. The Criminal Law Amendment Act 1885 produced particularly blatant anomalies. This Act created a number of sexual offences, mainly against women. A person charged with any of these was allowed by the statute to give evidence in his own defence. But a person charged with rape, a common law offence, was incompetent to testify. A highly experienced criminal practitioner and Treasury Counsel at the Central Criminal Court, Sir Harry Poland, described the law as 'absolutely grotesque in some cases. If an accused person is charged with an indecent assault he is a competent witness, but if he is charged with a common assault he is not, so that his competency as a witness depends upon what part of the body he is charged with assaulting' (*Parl Deb* 3rd series, vol 300, col 911, 3 August 1885; (1896) Times, 12 November, p 4).

prosecuting counsel's right to comment on silence has now been abolished by Schedule II of the Criminal Justice and Public Order Act 1994. Where a prisoner did testify, the evidential status of his testimony in relation to a co-accused was for a while a matter of some argument.

The Criminal Justice and Public Order Act 1994 has permitted inferences to be drawn from a defendant's silence at trial; prior to the Act judges had a duty to warn juries where a defendant had exercised his right to silence at trial that they were not entitled to infer guilt from silence. This innovation has now been the subject of interpretation by the courts: See *R v Cowan* below. Some assistance may possibly be derived from *Murray v DPP* (1992), a case dealing with a similar statutory provision in Northern Ireland.

Criminal Evidence Act 1898 s 1

Every person charged with an offence shall be a competent witness for the defence at every stage of the proceedings, whether the person so charged is charged solely or jointly with any other person. Provided as follows:

(a)   A person so charged shall not be called as a witness in pursuance of this Act except upon his own application ...

R v Wickham (1971, Court of Appeal)

In a case involving several defendants which resulted from a fight in a gambling club at Ramsgate there was a conflict of interest between one of the defendants, Wickham, and two others, named Ferrara and Bean. Neither Ferrara nor Bean went into the witness-box to support their case, which had involved, *inter alia*, allegations of violent behaviour by Wickham. On appeal Ferrara and Bean argued that counsel for Wickham should not have been allowed to comment in his speech to the jury on the fact that they had chosen not to give evidence.

Fenton Atkinson LJ: ... The only point [on] which the single judge gave leave to these two appellants on conviction was this: that Mr Flack, who was appearing for Wickham, and Mr Beckman, who was appearing for Stisi and Grais, announced their intention, before speeches began, of commenting in their final speeches on the failure of Ferrara and Bean to give evidence. Nobody could find any authority as to whether they could or could not do this. It was pressed upon the learned deputy chairman that he had, at any rate, a discretion to prevent comment being made, but he decided that he had no discretion to prevent such comment, although he suggested clearly to counsel concerned that they might on second thoughts think it unnecessary from the point of view of their clients and possible prejudice, and he indicated that, if he had a discretion, he would have stopped them from doing that which they wished to do, but he concluded that he could not do it. Counsel insisted that they thought this course necessary in the interests of their clients, there still being this conflict between Wickham on the one hand and Ferrara and Bean on the other.

In the view of this court, the learned deputy chairman was quite right. Counsel were entitled, in our view, to comment. The Criminal Evidence Act 1898 restricts the prosecution from making such comment, but says nothing to restrict counsel for co-accused, and it is perhaps important to notice that when one looks at section 1(f)(iii), where the right is given to the co-accused to cross-examine about character any other person charged with the same offence, in that instance the court has no discretion to prevent such cross-examination where evidence has been given against a co-accused. No authority has been discovered by anyone ...

It seems right to this court that whereas there is a fetter on the prosecution, a co-accused ought to be free through his counsel to put his case as he in his discretion thinks fit.

It is interesting perhaps to look at the case of *Kennedy and Browne*, a very famous murder case, *The Times*, May 23 1927, when the defendants appeared at the Central Criminal Court charged with the murder of Police Constable Gutteridge in Essex. Both men had been convicted and there was an appeal. Mr Powell was appearing for Kennedy, who had a number of previous convictions, and his complaint to this court was this: that his client had been put in an impossible position because Mr Lever, who was appearing for Browne, had told him in plain terms that, if Kennedy was called as a witness and gave evidence that Browne had committed the murder, he would be bound to cross-examine Kennedy as to his bad record, but, alternatively, if Kennedy did not give evidence, he would take advantage of the legal position and comment in no measured terms on Kennedy's absence from the witness-box. When the case came to the Court of Criminal Appeal presided over by the then Lord Chief Justice (Lord Hewart), Mr Powell drew attention to the appalling position in which his client had been placed in that regard. It seems clear that, reading the report of that case from *The Times* newspaper, neither Avory J, who tried the case nor the learned judges of the Court of Appeal thought there was anything wrong or that Mr Lever should not have had the right to take the alternative course of commenting on the failure of Browne to give evidence. In fact, when it came to the point, counsel, Mr Lever, made very vigorous comment, perhaps more vigorous than one would expect to hear in a court today, and said that Kennedy had 'taken all the advantage of a coward's screen by the panel of the dock', but there was nothing in that comment which seemed to draw any disfavour from Avory J, who in fact reinforced it himself by commenting on the failure of that co-accused to give evidence.

That case, so far as it goes, does seem to us to be an authority which supports the right of counsel to comment on the failure of a co-accused to give evidence and we can find nothing in statute or authority to limit his right to do so. In our opinion, there is no discretion in the judge to intervene, although of course he always has the last word and no doubt can make very forceful comment in a case where he thinks it right and draw the jury's attention to the undoubted right of an accused not to give evidence, and if he thinks that counsel has gone rather too far or has been unfair, he can deal with that satisfactorily in the course of his summing-up. The appeals against convictions fail.

We are dealing of course here with a case where there was a clear conflict as between Wickham and the two co-accused. In a case where there is in fact no conflict at all, responsible counsel would no doubt feel that there was no justification for making comment of that kind ...[3]

R v Paul (1920, Court of Criminal Appeal)

APPLICATIONS for leave to appeal against conviction and sentence.

The appellants, Paul and McFarlane, were charged at the Central Criminal Court jointly with three other persons with breaking and entering a warehouse and stealing therein divers furs of the value of 3000*l*. A number of men broke into the warehouse and took away the furs in a motor lorry. The two appellants were recognized by police officers who were on the watch as being among the men

---

3.   55 Cr App R 199.

concerned in the robbery. The defence set up by the two appellants was an alibi, and evidence was given in support of that defence.

Near the end of the trial the recorder told one of the prisoners, named Goldberg, that he was not bound to give evidence upon oath unless he wished, but that if he wished to go into the witness-box and give evidence he could do so. Goldberg thereupon went into the witness-box, and, after having been sworn, said that he pleaded guilty, and had nothing more to say. Goldberg was then cross-examined by counsel for the prosecution, and in the course of the cross-examination said that the two appellants were present at the robbery; that they, in fact, arranged it; that they sold the stolen furs; and that they shared the proceeds among the men concerned in the robbery ... The judgment of the court (Earl of Reading CJ, Bray and Avory JJ) was delivered by –

Earl of Reading CJ: The main point raised in this appeal is that counsel for the prosecution ought not to have been allowed to cross-examine Goldberg after he had pleaded guilty, and that the cross-examination having been allowed, the conviction is vitiated, and the appeal ought to be allowed. The argument is based upon s 1 of the Criminal Evidence Act 1898. It is said that although that Act makes a prisoner a competent witness for the defence, if the prisoner goes into the witness-box and says that he is guilty he cannot be cross-examined by the prosecution as the issue is then dead. That contention is, however, based upon a fallacy. When a prisoner goes into the witness-box to give evidence for the defence and has been sworn he is in the same position as an ordinary witness, and therefore subject to cross-examination. It is immaterial whether he stands mute or whether he gives evidence for the defence or for the prosecution. It is not what he says in the witness-box that subjects him to cross-examination, but the fact that he is called as a witness for the defence. As soon as a prisoner goes into the witness-box as a witness for the defence and is sworn counsel for the prosecution is entitled to cross-examine him. It has also been contended that counsel for the prosecution is not entitled to cross-examine a prisoner called as a witness for the defence so as to incriminate a prisoner charged jointly with him. That contention is a novel one; no case has been cited in support of it, and it is also contrary to the usual practice, and in the opinion of the court it entirely fails ...[4]

R v Rudd (1948, Court of Criminal Appeal)

Humphreys J: The applicant was convicted at Birmingham City Quarter Sessions before the deputy recorder of receiving stolen property knowing it to have been stolen. It is quite unnecessary to deal with the facts of the case in any detail because it is admitted that there was ample evidence to go to the jury and the grounds of appeal do not challenge that fact.

We are asked to give leave to appeal against conviction on three grounds. The first, which was the ground suggested by the applicant himself in his original notice of appeal, was that the learned judge in summing-up did not refer to the fact that a statement made by the applicant's co-defendant Powell in the absence of the applicant was not admissible against the applicant. To that objection there are two conclusive answers. The first is that the deputy recorder did refer to the matter, for he told the jury that a statement made by one prisoner in the absence of the other was not admissible against the other. The real gravamen of that attack on the summing-up is that the deputy recorder said this only once and did not repeat it. The second answer is that, inasmuch as Powell gave evidence on

---

4.   [1920] 2 KB 183.

oath and repeated all that he said in his statement, it would not have made much difference if the learned deputy recorder had referred to the matter many times.

I now turn to the second ground, which is a further ground settled by counsel since the adjournment of this case a week ago. It is put in this way: 'The learned deputy recorder never directed the jury that the sworn evidence of Powell should not be used in evidence against me in accordance with the decision of the Court of Criminal Appeal in *Meredith and Others* (1943), and failed to direct them at all as to how they should regard it.' It is an astonishing thing for this court to be told that a learned judge was guilty of misdirection in failing to direct the jury that the sworn evidence given in the case was not evidence against one of the parties being tried. Ever since this court was established it has been the invariable rule to state the law in the same way – that, while a statement made in the absence of the accused person by one of his co-defendants cannot be evidence against him, if a co-defendant goes into the witness-box and gives evidence in the course of a joint trial, then what he says becomes evidence for all the purposes of the case including the purpose of being evidence against his co-defendant. That is the law as we have always understood it, and there is ample authority to that effect, and most assuredly *Meredith and Others* (*supra*) said nothing to the contrary ...[5]

Criminal Justice and Public Order Act 1994

35 (1) At the trial of any person who has attained the age of fourteen years for an offence, subsections (2) and (3) below apply unless –

(a) the accused's guilt is not in issue; or

(b) it appears to the court that the physical or mental condition of the accused makes it undesirable for him to give evidence;

but subsection (2) below does not apply if, at the conclusion of the evidence for the prosecution, his legal representative informs the court that the accused will give evidence or, where he is unrepresented, the court ascertains from him that he will give evidence.

(2) Where this subsection applies, the court shall, at the conclusion of the evidence for the prosecution, satisfy itself (in the case of proceedings on indictment, in the presence of the jury) that the accused is aware that the stage has been reached at which evidence can be given for the defence and that he can, if he wishes, give evidence and that, if he chooses not to give evidence, or having been sworn, without good cause refuses to answer any question, it will be permissible for the court or jury to draw such inferences as appear proper from his failure to give evidence or his refusal, without good cause, to answer any question.

(3) Where this subsection applies, the court or jury, in determining whether the accused is guilty of the offence charged, may draw such inferences as appear proper from the failure of the accused to give evidence or his refusal, without good cause, to answer any question.

(4) This section does not render the accused compellable to give evidence on his own behalf, and he shall accordingly not be guilty of contempt of court by reason of a failure to do so.

(5) For the purposes of this section a person who, having been sworn, refuses to answer any question shall be taken to do so without good cause unless–

---

5. 32 Cr App R 138.

(a) he is entitled to refuse to answer the question by virtue of any enactment, whenever passed or made, or on the ground of privilege; or

(b) the court in the exercise of its general discretion excuses him from answering it.

(6) Where the age of any person is material for the purpose of subsection (1) above, his age shall for those purposes be taken to be that which appears to the court to be his age.

(7) This section applies–

(a) in relation to proceedings on indictment for an offence, only if the person charged with the offence is arraigned on or after the commencement of this section;

(b) in relation to proceedings in a magistrates' court, only if the time when the court begins to receive evidence in the proceedings falls after the commencement of this section.

Murray v DPP (1994, House of Lords)

Article 4(4) of the Criminal Evidence (Northern Ireland) Order 1988 provided as follows:

> The court or jury, in determining whether the accused is guilty of the offence charged, may – (a) draw such inferences from the refusal [to give evidence on his own behalf] as appear proper ...

Lord Mustill: ... [W]e approach the question of the inferences to be drawn from the silence of the accused on the assumption that by the time is reached at which he must decide whether to testify or remain silent the prosecutor has erected a case which, absent rebuttal, the fact-finder may (but will not necessarily) accept as proved. At this stage the trial is in a state of balance. The fact-finder waits to see whether in relation to each essential ingredient of the offence the direct evidence, which it is at least possible to believe should in the event be believed, and whether inferences that might be drawn from such evidence should actually be drawn. Usually, the most important of the events for which the fact-finder is keeping his judgment in suspense will be the evidence of the accused himself, for most prosecutions depend upon witnesses who speak directly to the participation of the defendant, who knows very well where the truth lies. So also with many of the inferences which the prosecutor seeks to draw from facts which are directly proven. If in such circumstances the defendant did not go on oath to say that the witnesses who have spoken to his actions are untruthful or unreliable, or that an inference which appears on its face to be plausible is in reality unsound for reasons within his personal knowledge, the fact-finder may suspect that the defendant does not tell his story because he has no story to tell, or none which will stand up to scrutiny; and this suspicion may be sufficient to convert a provable prosecution case into one which is actually proved. This is not of course because a silent defendant is presumed to be guilty, or because silence converts a case which is too weak to call for an answer into one which justifies a conviction. Rather, the fact-finder is entitled as a matter of common sense to draw his own conclusions if a defendant who is faced with evidence which does call for an answer fails to come forward and provide it.

So also if the defendant seeks to outflank the case for the prosecution by means of a 'positive' defence – as for example where he replies in relation to a charge of murder that although he did kill the deceased he acted under provocation. If he does not give evidence in support of this allegation there will in very many cases be a legitimate inference that the defence is untrue.

It is, however, equally a matter of common sense that even where the prosecution has established a *prima facie* case in the sense indicated above it is not in every situation that an adverse inference can be drawn from silence, the more so because in all but the simplest case the permissible inferences may have to be considered separately in relation to each individual issue. Everything depends on the nature of the issue, the weight of the evidence adduced by the prosecution upon it ... and the extent to which the defendant should in the nature of things be able to give his own account of the particular matter in question. It is impossible to generalise, for dependent upon circumstances the failure of the defendant to give evidence may found no inference at all, or one which is for all practical purposes fatal ...

Lord Slynn of Hadley: ... Since article 4 of the Order follows closely the wording of clause 5 of the draft Bill proposed by the Criminal Law Revision Committee [11th Report of the Criminal Law Revision Committee: Evidence (General) (1972)], it is permissible to see what was the mischief which the statute was intended to remedy ...

The Criminal Law Revision Committee itself said in paragraph 109 of their report: 'How far the judge can properly go in commenting on the failure of the accused to give evidence, and in particular in inviting the jury to draw adverse inferences against the accused from his failure to do so, is not altogether clear.'

They continued, at paragraph 110: 'In our opinion the present law and practice are much too favourable to the defence ... As to what may properly be included in a comment, we have no doubt that the same kinds of adverse inferences, such as common sense dictates, should be allowed to be drawn from the accused's failure to give evidence as those which we have proposed should be allowed to be drawn from his failure to mention, when interrogated, a fact on which he intends to rely at his trial. In fact the argument for allowing this seems even stronger in the case of failure to give evidence. We would stress that our proposals depend on there being a prima facie case against the accused. Failure to give evidence may be of little or no significance if there is no case against him or only a weak one. But the stronger the case is, the more significant will be his failure to give evidence.'

The committee thus considered that the law was too favourable to the accused and that there was in any event doubt as to its application. It is in my view clear that the 1988 Order intended to change the law and practice and to lay down new rules as to the comments which could be made and as to the inferences which could be drawn when a person failed to mention particular facts when questioned or charged, to explain the state of objects or to give evidence at his trial ...

The accused cannot be compelled to give evidence but he must risk the consequences if he does not do so. Those consequences are not simply, as the defendant contends, that specific inferences may be drawn from specific facts. They include in a proper case the drawing of an inference that the accused is guilty of the events with which he is charged.

This does not mean that the court can conclude simply because the accused does not give evidence that he is guilty. In the first place the prosecutor must establish a *prima facie* case – a case for him to answer. In the second place in determining whether the accused is guilty the judge or jury can draw only 'such inferences from the refusal as appear proper'. As Lord Diplock said in *Haw Tua Tau v Public Prosecutor* (1982): 'What inferences are proper to be drawn from an accused's refusal to give evidence depends upon the circumstances of the particular case, and is a question to be decided by applying ordinary common sense.'

There must thus be some basis derived from the circumstances which justify the inference.

If there is no *prima facie* case shown by the prosecution there is no case to answer. Equally, if parts of the prosecution case had so little evidential value that they called for no answer, a failure to deal with those specific matters cannot justify an inference of guilt.

On the other hand, if aspects of the evidence taken alone or in combination with other facts clearly call for an explanation which the accused ought to be in a position to give, if an explanation exists, then a failure to give any explanation may as a matter of common sense allow the drawing of an inference that there is no explanation and that the accused is guilty ...[6]

R v Cowan (1995, Court of Appeal)

Lord Taylor of Gosforth CJ read the following judgment of the court. These three appeals raise important questions as to the proper interpretation and implementation of section 35 of the Criminal Justice and Public Order Act 1994 ...

It is clear that the section alters and was intended by Parliament to alter the law and practice applicable when a defendant in a criminal trial does not give evidence. The issues raised are (1) whether the discretion to draw inferences from silence under section 35(3) should be open in the generality of cases or only exceptionally and (2) if it is to apply in a jury trial, what directions should the judge give?

For all the appellants, it is argued that section 35 either breaches or verges on breaching long established principles. Although, therefore, it is conceded that some effect must be given to the enactment, it should be applied only very exceptionally and not in the general run of cases. Mr Mansfield, supported by Mr Hurst, submits that the section constitutes an infringement of the defendant's right of silence. By permitting a court or jury to draw an adverse inference should the defendant remain silent at trial, it is submitted that his free choice is inhibited.

It should be made clear that the right of silence remains. It is not abolished by the section; on the contrary, subsection (4) expressly preserves it. As to inhibitions affecting a defendant's decision to testify or not, some existed before the Act of 1994. On the one hand, a defendant whose case involved an attack on the character of a prosecution witness could well be inhibited from giving evidence by fear of' cross-examination as to his own record. On the other hand, in certain cases, judges were entitled to comment on the defendant's failure to testify: *Reg v Martinez-Tobon* (1994). Arguably, this put pressure on a defendant to give evidence. Even in a case calling only for the classic direction in *Reg v Bathurst* (1968) a defendant might be inhibited from remaining silent for fear the jury would hold it against him that he chose to leave the prosecution evidence uncontradicted.

It is further argued that the section alters the burden of proof or 'waters it down' to use Mr Mansfield's phrase. The requirement that the defendant give evidence on pain of an adverse inference being drawn is said to put a burden on him to testify if he wishes to avoid conviction.

In our view that argument is misconceived. First, the prosecution have to establish a *prima facie* case before any question of the defendant testifying is

---

6.   [1994] 1 WLR 1.

raised. Secondly, section 38(3) of the Act of 1994 is in the following terms: 'A person shall not ... be convicted of an offence solely on an inference drawn from such a failure or refusal as is mentioned in ... section 35(3) ...' Thus the court or jury is prohibited from convicting solely because of an inference drawn from the defendant's silence. Thirdly the burden of proving guilt to the required standard remains on the prosecution throughout. The effect of section 35 is that the court or jury may regard the inference from failure to testify as, in effect, a further evidential factor in support of the prosecution case. It cannot be the only factor to justify a conviction and the totality of the evidence must prove guilt beyond reasonable doubt.

We therefore reject the two premises relied upon by Mr Mansfield to support his submission that section 35 should only be invoked in exceptional cases. In any event, whatever the jurisprudential merits of the two premises, the plain words of the section simply do not justify confining its operation to exceptional cases. Section 35(1) deals with exceptional situations in which subsections (2) and (3) are not to be invoked. Otherwise the section is in terms of general application. Indeed, subsection (2) is in mandatory terms. In cases other than those in subsection (1) 'the court shall satisfy itself' etc.

It is true that the operative subsection (3) as to the finding of the court or verdict of the jury is in permissive rather than mandatory terms.

Accordingly, the judge has a discretion as to whether and in what terms he should advise a jury for or against drawing inferences. In what circumstances, then, should the court or jury be prepared to draw an adverse inference? Mr Mansfield's answer is: 'only exceptionally where there is no reasonable possibility of an innocent explanation for the defendant's silence.' He suggested a number of possible reasons for silence at trial which may be consistent with innocence. They were (1) a weak case barely surviving a submission of no case; (2) other defence evidence contradicting prosecution evidence; (3) if the defendant is nervous, inarticulate or unlikely to perform well; (4) if the defendant's medical condition is abnormal although not within section 35(1); (5) fear, duress or the protection of others; (6) previous convictions of the defendant where he is liable to be cross-examined on them; (7) a 'mixed situation' – ie, where the Act of 1994 was not in force at the time of the defendant's arrest or interviews but was in force at the time of the trial. If any of these reasons or excuses exist or may do so, it is submitted the court should not draw, or the jury should be directed not to draw, an adverse inference. Moreover, Mr Mansfield suggests such reasons or excuses could properly be advanced by defending counsel without the need for evidence.

The breadth of these propositions is patently inconsistent with the scheme and plain words of section 35. To use the inevitable cliché, they would drive a coach and horses through the statutory provisions. Mr Mansfield's approach frankly was that section 35 is so at variance with established principle, that its operation should be reduced and marginalised as far as possible. We cannot agree.

In particular, we should deal specifically with two of the suggested 'good reasons.' First, the general proposition that a previous criminal record upon which a defendant could be cross-examined (if he has attacked prosecution witnesses) is a good reason for directing a jury that they should not hold his silence against him, would lead to a bizarre result. A defendant with convictions would be in a more privileged position than one with a clean record. The former could avoid submitting himself to cross-examination with impunity: the latter could not. We reject that proposition.

Secondly, in what he calls 'a mixed situation', Mr Mansfield argues that where the Act of 1994 was not in force at the time of arrest or interview, the defendant may have remained silent then, without realising that his silence later at trial could he held against him. Had he realised that, he might have given his story in interview and left his counsel at trial to submit he had already given his account and could not add to it. However, apart from the unreality of such a scenario, subsection (7)(a) clearly contemplates that proper inferences from silence at trial can be drawn in just such a situation.

We accept that apart from the mandatory exceptions in section 35(1), it will be open to a court to decline to draw an adverse inference from silence at trial and for a judge to direct or advise a jury against drawing such inference if the circumstances of the case justify such a course. But in our view there would need either to be some evidential basis for doing so or some exceptional factors in the case making that a fair course to take. It must be stressed that the inferences permitted by the section are only such 'as appear proper'. The use of that phrase was no doubt intended to leave a broad discretion to a trial judge to decide in all the circumstances whether any proper inference is capable of being drawn by the jury. If not he should tell them so; otherwise it is for the jury to decide whether in fact an inference should properly be drawn.

By way of guidance, a specimen direction has been suggested by the Judicial Studies Board in the following terms:

> The defendant has not given evidence. That is his right. But, as he has been told, the law is that you may draw such inferences as appear proper from his failure to do so. Failure to give evidence on its own cannot prove guilt but depending on the circumstances, you may hold his failure against him when deciding whether he is guilty. [There is evidence before you on the basis of which the defendant's advocate invites you not to hold it against the defendant that he has not given evidence before you namely ... If you think that because of this evidence you should not hold it against the defendant that he has not given evidence, do not do so.] But if the evidence he relies on presents no adequate explanation from his absence from the witness box then you may hold his failure to give evidence against him. You do not have to do so. What proper inferences can you draw from the defendant's decision not to give evidence before you? If you conclude that there is a case for him to answer, you may think that the defendant would have gone into the witness box to give you an explanation for or an answer to the case against him. If the only sensible explanation for his decision not to give evidence is that he has no answer to the case against him or none that could have stood up to cross-examination then it would be open to you to hold against him his failure to give evidence. It is for you to decide whether it is fair to do so. (The words in square brackets are to be used only where there is *evidence*.)

We consider that the specimen direction is in general terms a sound guide. It may be necessary to adapt or add to it in the particular circumstances of an individual case. But there are certain essentials which we would highlight. (1) The judge will have told the jury that the burden of proof remains upon the prosecution throughout and what the required standard is. (2) It is necessary for the judge to make clear to the jury that the defendant is entitled to remain silent. That is his right and his choice. The right of silence remains. (3) An inference from failure to give evidence cannot on its own prove guilt. That is expressly stated in section 38(3) of the Act. (4) Therefore, the jury must be satisfied that the prosecution have established a case to answer before drawing any inferences from silence. Of course, the judge must have thought so or the question whether the defendant was to give evidence would not have arisen. But the jury may not believe the witnesses whose evidence the judge considered sufficient to raise a prima facie case. It must therefore be made clear to them that they must find there to be a case to answer on the prosecution evidence before drawing an adverse inference from the defendant's silence. (5) If, despite any evidence relied upon to explain his silence or in the absence of any such evidence, the jury conclude the silence can only sensibly be attributed to the defendant's having no answer or none that would stand up to cross-examination, they may draw an adverse inference.

It is not possible to anticipate all the circumstances in which a judge might think it right to direct or advise a jury against drawing an adverse inference. Nor would it be wise even to give examples as each case must turn on its own facts. As Kelly LJ said in *Reg v McLernon* (1990) (a Northern Ireland case concerning provisions of article 4 of the Criminal Evidence (Northern Ireland) Order 1988 (SI No 1987 (NI20)), which are in terms similar to but stronger than those of section 35 of the Act of 1994), at p 102: 'the court has then a complete discretion as to whether inferences should be drawn or not. In these circumstances it is a matter for the court in any criminal case (1) to decide whether to draw inferences or not; and (2) if it decides to draw inferences what their nature, extent and degree of adversity, if any, may be. It would be improper and indeed quite unwise for any court to set out the bounds of either steps (1) or (2). Their application will depend on factors peculiar to the individual case.'

Kelly LJ was considering a trial without a jury, but we regard his remarks as applicable equally to the directions or advice a judge needs to give in his summing up to a jury ...

We wish to stress, moreover, that this court will not lightly interfere with a judge's exercise of discretion to direct or advise the jury as to the drawing of inferences from silence and as to the nature, extent and degree of such inferences. He is in the best position to have the feel of the case and so long as he gives the jury adequate directions of law as indicated above and leaves the decision to them, this court will be slow to substitute its view for his.

Finally, we wish to make it clear that the rule against advocates giving evidence dressed up as a submission applies in this context. It cannot be proper for a defence advocate to give to the jury reasons for his client's silence at trial in the absence of evidence to support such reasons ...[7]

The position of an accused person as witness for the prosecution has given rise to some difficulties. Of course, so long as two defendants are in the dock together, the prosecution cannot call one to give evidence in support of its case against the other – see s 1 of the 1898 Act – though, as has been shown above, if one defendant chooses to testify in his own defence the prosecution can take advantage of that to elicit from him in cross-examination evidence which may incriminate his co-accused. But sometimes persons may have been partners in the commission of a particular crime and the prosecution may wish to arrange things so that one of the partners in the crime is able, if he wishes, to give evidence against his accomplices. Some device must then be adopted which will in effect ensure that the accomplice giving evidence for the Crown is not in the dock with the others at the time of their trial.

---

7.   [1995] 3 WLR 818.

R v Pipe (1966, Court of Appeal)

The appellant was convicted of housebreaking and larceny. A Mrs Harrison's bungalow had been broken into and a safe and its contents were stolen. The safe was later found dumped in a pond with the back ripped open. Among the prosecution's witnesses was a man named Swan.

The Lord Chief Justice: ... In addition, the prosecution called a witness called Swan and in evidence he said, as was admitted in fact, that that evening the appellant had come round with his car. He then said the appellant opened the boot of the car, and at that point Swan was warned that he need not incriminate himself and, accordingly, when he was asked what he saw in the boot of the car, he said: 'I decline to answer that question.' He further declined to answer questions on what he then did, whether he and the appellant had left together in the car, but he did say that he had – at any rate this was the inference from what he said – shown the police where the safe was dumped in the pond.

The appellant then gave evidence and denied that he had ever been to Mrs Harrison's bungalow on the night in question. He said that he had gone to the Aldreds' House, that from there he had gone to Swan's house, and that he had stayed for about half an hour after some discussion on the brakes ...

There is no doubt that there was overwhelming evidence against the appellant. The point upon which leave to appeal was given by the learned chairman concerned the admissibility of the evidence of Swan, evidence which was highly prejudicial because no jury could conceivably fail to fill in the gaps in the evidence, and particularly because they were invited by the prosecution to fill in those gaps. It is true that the chairman, in summing up, tried to belittle the evidence and say that it was no real evidence against this appellant and that anyhow it would require corroboration, but quite clearly the evidence was such that no jury could conceivably put out of their mind.

Now the position in regard to Swan was this: he had been called by the prosecution before the committing justices, and there, having been warned more than once that he need not incriminate himself, he gave evidence and a deposition was taken. In that deposition he described how the appellant had called at his house, that in the boot of the car was Mrs Harrison's safe, that they had taken the safe into a shed in the back garden and hacked open the back with an axe, that then they put the safe back into the boot of the car and both had driven to Blunderstone and pushed the safe into a pond. It was a very frank admission of his part in the matter. By the beginning of the appellant's trial on May 16, an information had been laid against Swan, and it was in those circumstances that counsel for the defendant submitted at the trial that Swan, being a person charged and against whom criminal proceedings were to begin the very next day, should not be allowed to be called. There was considerable discussion on the matter and finally the chairman ruled that Swan, despite the fact that he had been charged, was a competent witness and that there were no grounds in his discretion for excluding the evidence. It was in those circumstances that Swan was called, and having by then been charged and been told again that he need not incriminate himself, chose to say nothing in answer to many of the questions.

In the judgment of this court, the course taken here was wholly irregular. It may well be, and indeed it is admitted, that in strict law Swan was a competent witness, but for years now it has been the recognised practice that an accomplice who has been charged, either jointly charged in the indictment with his co-accused or in the indictment though not under a joint charge, or indeed has been charged though not brought to the state of an indictment being brought against him, shall not be called by the prosecution, except in limited circumstances. Those circumstances are set out correctly in *Archbold*, in paragraph 1297 of the current edition, where it is said that where it is proposed to call an accomplice at the trial, it is the practice (a) to omit him from the indictment or (b) take his plea of guilty on arraignment or before calling him either (c) to offer no evidence and permit his acquittal or (d) to enter a *nolle prosequi*.

Mr Ryman for the prosecution has explained how it came about that Swan was not dealt with before he gave evidence, the reason being that there were difficulties in the case being adjourned in that the defence had a witness or witnesses who would not be available at a later stage. Nevertheless, this court is quite satisfied that if the case had to go on, and the prosecution were still minded to call Swan, they must have let it be known that in no event would proceedings be continued against him. In the judgment of this court, it is one thing to call for the prosecution an accomplice, a witness whose evidence is suspect, and about whom the jury must be warned in the recognised way. It is quite another to call a man who is not only an accomplice, but is an accomplice against whom proceedings have been brought which have not been concluded. There is in this case an added reason for making his evidence suspect. In the judgment of this court, this well-recognised rule of practice is one which must be observed, and, accordingly, in the circumstances of this case there is no alternative but to quash the conviction.[8]

R v Turner (1975, Court of Appeal)

Lawton LJ: ... There can be no doubt that at common law an accomplice who gave evidence for the Crown in the expectation of getting a pardon for doing so was a competent witness. The two most persuasive authorities in English law say just that. In *Rudd* (1775) the Court of King's Bench had to consider an application for bail made by a woman who had given King's evidence and who claimed that in consequence she was entitled to be released on bail pending the grant of the pardon which she submitted she was entitled to as of right. Lord Mansfield CJ adjudged that hers was not one of the three types of cases in which pardons could be claimed as of right (that is, pardons promised by proclamation or given under statute or earned by the ancient procedure of approvement). He continued as follows: 'There is besides a practice, which indeed does not give a legal right; and that is where accomplices having made a full and fair confession of the whole truth, are in consequence thereof admitted evidence for the Crown and that evidence is afterwards made use of to convict the other offenders. If in that case they act fairly and openly, and discover the whole truth, though they are not entitled as of right to a pardon, yet the usage, lenity and the practice of the courts is to stop the prosecution against them and they have an equitable title to a recommendation for the King's mercy.'

Blackstone wrote to the same effect; see *Commentaries*, 23rd edn (1854), Vol 4 at p 440. It is manifest that in the eighteenth century the courts did not consider an accomplice to be incompetent to give evidence because any inducement held out to him to do so was still operating on his mind when he was in the witness-box. Blackstone considered that an accomplice could not expect to receive his pardon unless he gave his evidence 'without prevarication or fraud'. The nineteenth century brought about no change in the competence of accomplices to give evidence even though the prospect of immunity from prosecution was before

---

8. (1966) 51 Cr App R 17.

them ... The contribution of the nineteenth century to this topic was the rule of practice that judges should warn juries of the dangers of convicting on the uncorroborated evidence of accomplices. In this century that practice became a rule of law.

It is against that background that the case of *Pipe* should be considered. There is nothing in either the arguments or the judgment itself to indicate that the court thought it was changing a rule of law as to the competency of accomplices to give evidence which had been followed ever since the seventeenth century. The facts of that case must be closely examined. Pipe was being tried on an indictment charging him with housebreaking and larceny. He was alleged to have stolen a safe and its contents. A man named Swan was called to prove that he had helped Pipe to break open the safe. Swan, however, before Pipe's trial had begun had himself been charged with complicity in Pipe's crime in relation to the safe. The form of the charge is not stated in the report. He was not indicted with Pipe. It was intended to try him later. The court adjudged that Swan should not have been called in these circumstances ...

In our judgment *Pipe* is limited to the circumstances set out in *Archbold*. Its *ratio decidendi* is confined to a case in which an accomplice, who has been charged, but not tried, is required to give evidence of his own offence in order to secure the conviction of another accused. *Pipe* on its facts was clearly a right decision. The same result could have been achieved by adjudging that the trial judge should have exercised his discretion to exclude Swan's evidence on the ground that there was an obvious and powerful inducement for him to ingratiate himself with the prosecution and the court and that the existence of this inducement made it desirable in the interests of justice to exclude it ... To have reached the decision on this basis would, we think, have been more in line with the earlier authorities. Lord Parker CJ in *Pipe* seems, however, to have viewed the admission of Swan's evidence in the circumstances of that case as more than a wrong exercise of discretion. He described what happened as being 'wholly irregular'. It does not follow, in our judgment, that in all cases calling a witness who can benefit from giving evidence is 'wholly irregular'. To hold so would be absurd. Examples are provided by the prosecution witness who hopes to get a reward which has been offered 'for information leading to a conviction', or even an order for compensation or whose claim for damages may be helped by a conviction ...[9]

SPOUSES OF DEFENDANTS IN CRIMINAL PROCEEDINGS

Police and Criminal Evidence Act 1984

80 (1) In any proceedings the wife or husband of the accused shall be competent to give evidence –

(a) subject to subsection (4) below, for the prosecution; and

(b) on behalf of the accused or any person jointly charged with the accused.

(2) In any proceedings the wife or husband of the accused shall, subject to subsection (4) below, be compellable to give evidence on behalf of the accused.

---

9.   60 Cr App R 80.

(3) In any proceedings the wife or husband of the accused shall, subject to subsection (4) below, be compellable to give evidence for the prosecution or on behalf of any person jointly charged with the accused if and only if –

(a) the offence charged involves an assault on, or injury or a threat of injury to, the wife or husband of the accused or a person who was at the material time under the age of sixteen; or

(b) the offence charged is a sexual offence alleged to have been committed in respect of a person who was at the material time under that age; or

(c) the offence charged consists of attempting or conspiring to commit, or of aiding, abetting, counselling, procuring or inciting the commission of, an offence falling within paragraph (a) or (b) above.

(4) Where a husband and wife are jointly charged with an offence neither spouse shall at the trial be competent or compellable by virtue of subsection (1)(a), (2) or (3) above to give evidence in respect of that offence unless that spouse is not, or is no longer, liable to be convicted of that offence at the trial as a result of pleading guilty or for any other reason.

(5) In any proceedings a person who has been but is no longer married to the accused shall be competent and compellable to give evidence as if that person and the accused had never been married.

(6) Where in any proceedings the age of any person at any time is material for the purpose of subsection (3) above, his age at the material time shall for the purposes of that provision be deemed to be or to have been that which appears to the court to be or to have been his age at that time.

(7) In subsection (3)(b) above 'sexual offence' means an offence under the Sexual Offences Act 1956, the Indecency with Children Act 1960, the Sexual Offences Act 1967, section 54 of the Criminal Law Act 1977 or the Protection of Children Act 1978.

(8) The failure of the wife or husband of the accused to give evidence shall not be made the subject of any comment by the prosecution.

(9) Section (1)(d) of the Criminal Evidence Act 1898 (communications between husband and wife) and section 43(1) of the Matrimonial Causes Act 1965 (evidence as to marital intercourse) shall cease to have effect.

CHILDREN

Civil cases

The first question that will arise is whether the child is competent to give sworn evidence. The test is the one which used to govern both civil and criminal cases and which was laid down in *R v Hayes* (1977): Does the child understand *the solemnity of the occasion* and *the special duty to tell the truth*, over and above the ordinary social duty to do so? A knowledge of the nature of a divine sanction is not necessary. Suppose the child does not fulfil these requirements. The court must then turn to the Children Act 1989.

Children Act 1989

96 (1) Subsection (2) applies where a child who is called as a witness in any civil proceedings does not, in the opinion of the court, understand the nature of an oath.

(2) The child's evidence may be heard by the court if, in its opinion –

(a) he understands that it is his duty to speak the truth and;

(b) he has sufficient understanding to justify his evidence being heard.

[A 'child' is a person under the age of 18: s 105.]

Criminal cases

The current law is contained in s 33A of the Criminal Justice Act 1988 as amended.

Criminal Justice Act 1988

33A (1) A child's evidence in criminal proceedings shall be given unsworn.

(2) A deposition of a child's unsworn evidence may be taken for the purpose of criminal proceedings as if that evidence had been given on oath.

(2A) A child's evidence shall be received unless it appears to the court that the child is incapable of giving intelligible testimony.

(3) In this section 'child' means a person under fourteen years of age.

R v Hampshire (1995, Court of Appeal)

Auld J: ... In our view, the effect of the recent statutory changes has been to remove from the judge any duty to conduct a preliminary investigation of a child's competence, but to retain his power to do so if he considers it necessary, say because the child is very young or has difficulty in expression or understanding. Where there has been an application under section 32A of the Act of 1988 to rely on video recorded evidence, the judge's pre-trial view of the recording, if the interview has been properly conducted, should normally enable him to form a view as to the child's competence. Where it has left him in doubt, or where the child's evidence-in-chief is not to be given by a video recording and his or her competence as a witness is questionable, he should conduct a preliminary investigation into the matter. Whether or not he conducts such a preliminary investigation, he has the same duty as in the case of an adult witness, namely to exclude or direct disregard of the evidence, if and when he concludes that the child is not competent ...

In our view, the preliminary investigation of a child, if there is one, should be conducted by the judge: see *Reg v N* (1992). It is a matter of his perception of the child's understanding demonstrated in the course of ordinary discourse. It is not an issue to be resolved by him in response to an adversarial examination and cross-examination by counsel ...

[A] judge who considers it necessary to investigate a child's competence to give evidence in addition to or without the benefit of an earlier view of a videotaped interview under section 32A of the Act of 1988 should do so in open court in the presence of the defendant because it is part of the trial, but need not do so in the presence of the jury. The jury's function is to assess the child's evidence, including its weight, from the evidence he or she gives on the facts of the case after the child has been found competent to give it. The exercise of determining competence is not a necessary aid to that function ...

However, even though a judge is no longer bound to investigate a child's competence to give evidence (unless he has reason to doubt it), he may find it appropriate to remind the child, in the presence of the defendant and the jury, of the importance of telling the truth. A softly worded and spoken reminder of the sort suggested by the Pigot Committee in paragraph 5.15 of its report would do: 'Tell us all you can remember of what happened. Don't make anything up or leave anything out. This is very important.'...[10]

10. 2 Cr App R 319.

CHAPTER 4

HEARSAY: THE SCOPE OF THE RULE

The rule against hearsay has been stated as follows: 'An assertion other than one made by a person while giving oral evidence in the proceedings is inadmissible as evidence of any fact asserted.' This statement, originally in *Cross on Evidence*, was approved by Lord Havers in *Sharp* (1988). It is important to notice that the rule against hearsay excludes an item of evidence only if the purpose of adducing that evidence is to establish the truth of the matter asserted. It follows that in relation to any item of evidence which you suspect may be caught by the rule, you need first to ask: 'What is the job of proof that this item of evidence is being put forward to do?' In other words, to apply the law you need first to think about relevancy.[1] It may be helpful to remember this principle if you think of the rule against hearsay as a rule about use rather than as a rule of exclusion.[2]

The modern justification for the rule was given by Lord Bridge in *Blastland* (1985):

> Hearsay evidence is not excluded because it has no logically probative value. Given that the subject matter of the hearsay is relevant to some issue in the trial, it may clearly be potentially probative. The rationale of excluding it as inadmissible, rooted as it is in the system of trial by jury, is a recognition of the great difficulty, even more acute for a juror than for a trained judicial mind, of assessing what, if any, weight can properly be given to a statement by a person whom the jury have not seen or heard and which has not been subject to any test of reliability by cross-examination.

HEARSAY AS A RULE OF USE

Sparks v R (1964, Privy Council)

The appellant was arraigned before the Supreme Court of Bermuda on a charge of indecently assaulting a small girl who was just under the age of four.

The mother's evidence before the examining magistrate included the following passage: 'I lifted up her dress and I found blood on her body. I do not recall Wendy Sue saying anything to me at that time. But she did say that I should have looked the other way; I do not know what she meant. Then I asked her who took her out of the car. I asked this and she said that she did not know. I then asked her what did the person look like, and she said that it was a coloured boy. She did not say anything more after that.'

---

1. Hearsay is defined for the purposes of the Civil Evidence Act 1995 as 'a statement made otherwise than by a person while giving oral evidence in the proceedings which is tendered as evidence of the matters stated': s 1.

2. See further Philip McNamara, 'The Canons of Evidence – Rules of Exclusion or Rules of Use?' (1986) 10 *Adelaide L Rev* 341. The subject of hearsay in criminal proceedings is dealt with in the Law Commission's Consultative Paper No 138. This provides a clear exposition of law, discussion of justifications given for the rule, criticisms, and proposals for reform.

At the trial evidence as to what the girl had said and her statement that 'it was a coloured boy' was held to be inadmissible. On behalf of the appellant, who was not coloured but white, it was submitted before the Board that the statement should have been held to be admissible.

Lord Morris of Borth-y-Gest: ... The defence submitted at the trial that the mother should be permitted to recount what the girl had said to her. The alleged utterance was made very shortly after the girl was restored to her mother. That was probably within $1^1/_2$ hours of the time when the girl left the motor car. The words, if spoken, were probably spoken at the earliest opportunity for the making of a complaint to the mother, who was the person to whom it would be natural to voice a complaint ... The mother would clearly be giving hearsay evidence if she were permitted to state what her girl had said to her. It becomes necessary, therefore, to examine the contentions which have been advanced in support of the admissibility of the evidence. It was said that 'it was manifestly unjust for the jury to be left throughout the whole trial with the impression that the child could not give any clue to the identity of her assailant'. The cause of justice is, however, best served by adherence to rules which have long been recognised and settled. If the girl had made a remark to her mother (not in the presence of the appellant) to the effect that it was the appellant who had assaulted her and if the girl was not to be a witness at the trial, evidence as to what she had said would be the merest hearsay. In such circumstances it would be the defence who would wish to challenge a contention, if advanced, that it would be 'manifestly unjust' for the jury not to know that the girl had given a clue to the identity of her assailant. If it is said that hearsay evidence should freely be admitted and that there should be concentration in any particular case upon deciding as to its value or weight it is sufficient to say that our law has not been evolved upon such lines but is firmly based upon the view that it is wiser and better that hearsay should be excluded save in certain well-defined and rather exceptional circumstances'.[3]

R v McLean (1967, Court of Appeal)

Appeal against conviction

According to a Mrs Roberts, employed by a car-hire firm at Liverpool, on 24 May 1966 the appellant, using the name of Robert Coakley, completed a hire agreement for an Austin 1100 car, registration no HKB138D.

On Friday 27 May 1966 at about 11 am William Gomery, a 65 year old man, was walking in Brunswick Road, Liverpool, taking the money of his employers to the bank, when he was attacked from behind by two men wearing green overalls and beret-type hats, and they snatched from him an envelope containing £40 in cash and some cheques. He thought they got into an 1100 car, driven off apparently by a third man. Mr Gomery made a mental note of the car's registration number, and not more than three minutes later he dictated something, he could not say what, to a Mr Cope, who thereupon wrote down the number HKB138D on a card; but Mr Gomery did not himself see what Mr Cope wrote down, and was therefore in no position to say that the note which Mr Cope made was an accurate note.

---

3. [1964] AC 964. The appeal was allowed on other grounds.

Mr Cope himself had earlier seen two men standing on a corner of the road, but he saw no car. Mr Gomery himself could not remember the car's number.

Edmund Davies LJ: With the utmost reluctance, which is shared by all three members of this court, this appeal against conviction is allowed.

On January 16 1967 at the Liverpool Crown Court the appellant John McLean was convicted of robbery with aggravation and sentenced to four years' imprisonment ...

The crucial defect in this case arises in relation to the evidence given by Mr Cope, Mr Cope being called to say (in effect): 'I wrote down on a piece of paper – here is the paper – what Mr Gomery told me was the number of the car. It was HKB138D.' We confess that we have strained to find some means whereby the testimony of Mr Cope might be regarded as properly admitted in this case, for it is difficult to see that justice is done by its exclusion. But we are bound to apply the law as we find it ...

[I]t seems to us that for Mr Cope to be allowed to say that what he was told by Mr Gomery was that the car involved was HKB138D is a contravention of the hearsay rule when that remark is adduced as evidence that the car involved in the robbery was in fact HKB138D, and so we hold ...[4]

R v Turner (1975, Court of Appeal)

In this case one of the defendants, Donald Barrett, appealed against his conviction for robbery. He argued that the trial judge had wrongly excluded evidence to the effect that a man called Saunders, who did not give evidence at the trial, had told the police that he, and not Barrett, had been involved in the robbery in question. The appeal was dismissed.

Milmo J: This court is of the opinion that the ruling of the learned judge in refusing to admit in evidence the statement made to a third party by a person not himself called as a witness in the trial was clearly correct.

Assuming for the present purpose that it was relevant to prove that Saunders had been one of the robbers at Ilford, the defence would have been entitled to call witnesses to prove the fact of their own knowledge, such as people who had actually seen him at the bank. They could have called Saunders himself. No such evidence was called and evidence of what Saunders said to a third party was not probative of anything. It would have been hearsay evidence which did not come within any of the well-settled exceptions to the general rule that hearsay evidence is not admissible. That the categories of these exceptions is now closed and cannot be added to without legislation was made clear by Lord Reid in his speech in *Myers v Director of Public Prosecutions* (1965), a case in which it had been sought to extend the exceptions to the ban on the reception of hearsay in evidence ... Lord Reid said: '... The common law must be developed to meet the changing economic conditions and habits of thought, and I would not be deterred by expressions of opinion in this House in old cases. But there are limits to what we can or should do. If we are to extend the law it must be by the development and application of fundamental principles. We cannot introduce arbitrary conditions or limitations: that must be left to legislation.'

[Counsel for Barrett] cited a number of authorities which he contended supported his argument that evidence of what Saunders was alleged to have said to the police was admissible ...

---

4. 52 Cr App R 80.

This court does not find in any of these cases any authority for the proposition advanced in this case that hearsay evidence is admissible in a criminal case to show that a third party who has not been called as a witness in the case has admitted committing the offence charged. The idea, which may be gaining prevalence in some quarters, that in a criminal trial the defence is entitled to adduce hearsay evidence to establish facts, which if proved would be relevant and would assist the defence, is wholly erroneous.[5]

Subramaniam v Public Prosecutor (1956, Privy Council)

Their Lordships' reasons for allowing the appeal were delivered by –

Mr LMD De Silva: This is an appeal, by special leave, from a judgment of the Supreme Court of the Federation of Malaya dismissing an appeal against a conviction in the High Court of Johore Bahru whereby the appellant was found guilty of being in possession on April 29 1955 of 20 rounds of ammunition contrary to regulation 4(1)(b) of the Emergency Regulations 1951 and sentenced to death ...

It was common ground that on April 29 1955 at a place in the Rengam District in the State of Johore, the appellant was found in a wounded condition by certain members of the security forces; that when he was searched there was found around his waist a leather belt with three pouches containing 20 live rounds of ammunition; no weapon of any description was found upon him or in the immediate vicinity.

The defence put forward on behalf of the appellant was that he had been captured by terrorists, that at all material times he was acting under duress, and that at the time of his capture by the security forces he had formed the intention to surrender, with which intention he had come to the place where he was found ...

The appellant gave evidence in defence. He called witnesses to give evidence as to his character and to support his story as to how he had been occupied for some months before his capture by the terrorists. The appellant described his capture ...

He then described how he was forced to accompany the terrorists, one of whom walked in front and two behind, who told him he was being taken to their leader. At this stage an intervention by the trial judge is recorded thus: '*Court*: I tell Murugason hearsay evidence is not admissible and all the conversation with bandits is not admissible unless they are called.'

Murugason was counsel assigned to defend the appellant.

In ruling out peremptorily the evidence of conversation between the terrorists and the appellant the trial judge was in error. Evidence of a statement made to a witness by a person who is not himself called as a witness may or may not be hearsay. It is hearsay and inadmissible when the object of the evidence is to establish the truth of what is contained in the statement. It is not hearsay and is admissible when it is proposed to establish by the evidence, not the truth of the statement, but the fact that it was made. The fact that the statement was made, quite apart from its truth, is frequently relevant in considering the mental state and conduct thereafter of the witness or of some other person in whose presence the statement was made. In the case before their Lordships statements could have been made to the appellant by the terrorists, which, whether true or not, if

---

5.   60 Cr App R 80.

they had been believed by the appellant, might reasonably have induced in him an apprehension of instant death if he failed to conform to their wishes ...[6]

Mawaz Khan v The Queen (1967, Privy Council)

The judgment of their Lordships was delivered by –

Lord Hodson: This is an appeal from a judgment of the Supreme Court of Hong Kong (Hogan CJ, Rigby and Briggs JJ) dated August 23 1965 dismissing the appeals of both appellants against their conviction for murder by the Supreme Court sitting in its criminal jurisdiction with a jury, on May 5 1965. Both were sentenced to death: each made statements, but neither gave evidence in the witness-box.

The main ground of appeal is that the learned trial judge erred in ruling that a statement made by one accused person in the absence of the other could be used for any purpose or in any way against the other. To admit such a statement would, it is said, violate the 'hearsay' rule.

Before considering the facts of this case it is convenient to state what is meant by the 'hearsay' rule, for contravention of the rule makes evidence inadmissible.

The accepted textbooks on the law of evidence are at one in saying that such statements are inadmissible to prove truth of the matters stated. *Wigmore on Evidence* (3rd edn, vol 6, page 178) puts the matter clearly in this way: 'The prohibition of the hearsay rule, then, does not apply to all words or utterances merely as such. If this fundamental principle is clearly realised, its application is a comparatively simple matter. The hearsay rule excludes extrajudicial utterances only when offered for a special purpose, namely, as assertions to evidence the truth of the matter asserted.'

The rule has been stated to the same effect by their Lordships in *Subramaniam v Public Prosecutor* ...

[C]ircumstantial evidence connected both appellants with the scene of the crime, but the Crown relied strongly upon the fact that each of the appellants had in his respective statement sought to set up a joint alibi which was demonstrated to be false.

Each of the appellants separately told the police that they were at a place called the Ocean Club on the night in question and endeavoured to explain their injuries as having been sustained in a fight between them and as having no connection with the killing of the deceased. Many of the details of their statements were contradicted by the evidence of the witnesses. The statement of each appellant was used against him, the judge directing the jury: 'A statement which is made by an accused person in the absence of the other is not evidence against the other: it is evidence against the maker of the statement but against him only.'

No complaint was made of this direction, but the learned judge went on to say: 'The Crown's case here is not that these statements are true and that what one says ought to be considered as evidence of what actually happened. What the Crown says is that these statements have been shown to be a tissue of lies and that they disclose an attempt to fabricate a joint story. Now, members of the jury, if you come to that conclusion then the fabrication of a joint story would be evidence against both. It would be evidence that they had co-operated after the alleged crime.'

---

6.   [1956] 1 WLR 965.

It was submitted that the direction of the learned judge that a statement made by one accused person in the absence of the other is not evidence against that other was nullified by the further direction that the jury were entitled to compare the statements and if they came to the conclusion that they were false that would be evidence that they had co-operated after the alleged crime and jointly concocted the story out of a sense of guilt.

Their Lordships are of opinion that this submission, which appealed to one member of the Court of Appeal and no doubt impressed the Chief Justice and Rigby AJ, when they made reference to the importance of the question involved, ought not to be sustained.

Their Lordships agree with Hogan CJ and Rigby AJ in accepting the generality of the proposition maintained by the text writers and to be found in *Subramaniam's* case that a statement is not hearsay and is admissible when it is proposed to establish by the evidence, not the truth of the statement, but the fact that it was made. Not only therefore can the statements of each appellant be used against each appellant individually, as the learned judge directed, but they can without any breach of the hearsay rule be used, not for the purpose of establishing the truth of the assertions contained therein, but for the purpose of asking the jury to hold the assertions false and to draw inferences from their falsity.

The statements were relevant as tending to show that the makers were acting in concert and that such action indicated a common guilt. This is a factor to be taken into account in conjunction with the circumstantial evidence to which reference has been made in determining the guilt or innocence of the accused persons ...

Their Lordships are of opinion that there was no misdirection of the jury and will accordingly humbly advise Her Majesty that the appeal be dismissed.[7]

Woodhouse v Hall (1980, Divisional Court)

Donaldson LJ: This is a prosecutor's appeal by case stated against the dismissal of a charge against the defendant under section 33 of the Sexual Offences Act 1956. The charge was that between and including November 18 and 22 1977 at Wanstead Sauna in Wanstead, London, she acted in the management of a brothel at those premises contrary to that section.

The question of the admissibility of certain evidence was raised at the beginning of the hearing, and, in consequence, the case does not find facts but sets out the evidence which the prosecution sought to adduce to prove the charge, and which, as was admitted, they could only prove if two police officers gave evidence of a conversation.

The prosecution case, so far as relevant, was this. The premises consisted of a reception area, a sauna room, a solarium, an exercise gymnasium, showers and cubicles for changing and massage. The defendant was the manageress of the establishment. Two other women were also employed there with her from time to time, so that there were always two women on the premises at any one time. During the period referred to in the information four police officers kept observation and also entered the premises in the guise of customers. They used the sauna, the gymnasium and the showers. They were massaged by the defendant and by the two other women.

Then I get to the crucial matter upon which the prosecution relied, the evidence of the police officers 'that while being massaged they had been offered

---

7.   [1967] 1 AC 454.

masturbation under the name "hand relief" by the defendant and also by the other two women, such offers having been on some occasions unsolicited and on others in response to questions from the officer concerned, and that the price quoted for "hand relief" was £6 and for "topless hand relief" £10.' Then the prosecution case goes on to allege 'that such offers were made when the defendant or other woman making the offer was alone with one of the police officers, so that when made by one of the other women the defendant was neither present nor within earshot' and 'that none of the officers had accepted any such offer, each making some excuse'. It appeared that the other two women, not unnaturally, were not to be called as witnesses for the prosecution.

The justices ruled that the evidence of the police officers as to the offers made by the two other women were inadmissible unless the women themselves gave evidence as to what they had said. The prosecution accepted that in the absence of the evidence of the police officers, they could not establish that this was a brothel, namely an establishment at which two or more women were offering sexual services. The question is whether the evidence was rightly excluded.

I suspect that the justices were misled by *Subramaniam's* case and thought that this was a hearsay case, because they may have thought that they had to be satisfied as to the truth of what the ladies said or were alleged to have said in the sense they had to satisfy themselves that the words were not a joke but were meant seriously and something of that sort. But this is not a matter of truth or falsity. It is a matter of what was really said – the quality of the words, the message being transmitted.

That arises in every case where the words themselves are a relevant fact. The quality of the words has to be assessed, but that is quite different from the situation where the words are evidence of some other matter. Then their truth and accuracy has to be assessed and they are hearsay.

There is no question here of the hearsay rule arising at all. The relevant issue was, did these ladies make these offers? The offers were oral and the police officers were entitled to give evidence of them. The evidence, in my judgment, was wrongly excluded and should have been admitted ...[8]

R v Rice (1963, Court of Criminal Appeal)

The appellant and another man, Moore, were convicted on two counts of conspiracy to steal motor cars and to obtain log books by false pretences. The case for the Crown was supported by a mass of evidence. Amongst other things it was alleged that in furtherance of the conspiracy Rice had made a journey to Manchester by air. As appears from the judgment, evidential problems arose at trial in connection with an airline ticket which was produced to establish this. The trial judge's treatment of the ticket was subsequently the basis of Rice's unsuccessful appeal against conviction. The ticket was for two seats on a flight from London to Manchester in the names of 'Rice and Moore' for 10 May 1961. Rice said he had never flown to Manchester and knew nothing of the ticket or how it had come to be booked.

Winn J: ... Subsequently, after objection and discussion, that ticket was produced in evidence by the airline representative whose function it was to deal with flight tickets returned after use. The court has no doubt that the ticket and the fact of the presence of that ticket in the file or other place where tickets used by

---

8.   72 Cr App R 39.

passengers would in the ordinary course be found, were facts which were in logic relevant to the issue whether or not there flew on those flights two men either of whom was a Mr Rice or a Mr Moore.

The relevance of that ticket in logic and its legal admissibility as a piece of real evidence both stem from the same root, *viz*, the balance of probability recognised by common sense and common knowledge that an air ticket which has been used on a flight and which has a name upon it has more likely than not been used by a man of that name or by one of two men whose names are upon it.

A comparable document would be a passport, which is more likely on the whole to be in the possession of the person to whom it was issued than that of anyone having no right to it.

It is, however, essential, whether for the purposes of logical reasoning or for a consideration of the evidentiary effect in law of any such document to distinguish clearly between its relevance and its probative significance: the document must not be treated as speaking its contents for what it might say could only be hearsay. Thus a passport cannot say, 'my bearer is X', nor the air ticket, 'I was issued to Y'.

Counsel for the Crown clearly appreciated and accepted this distinction when he said during the discussion of the objection to the admission of the ticket in evidence: 'It is not for one moment suggested that the point of this evidence is to prove that Rice or Moore or any particular person took this ticket up ... it is evidence that this ticket was used for two persons on that particular flight to Manchester ... it must be a relevant matter from which the jury can draw such inference as they think proper.'

In ruling upon the objection the recorder said: 'Hoather [a co-defendant] in his evidence said that about a week before he actually opened up in Manchester, which he puts, I think, as May 16, he flew to Manchester and flew there in company with Rice. It appears now, *scilicet* from the ticket, that on May 10, not exactly a week before as Hoather said, but within 24 hours of it, two people did fly to Manchester at the time that Hoather says he flew there and one of them is called Rice. It goes no further than that and I propose to allow this evidence.'

The court thinks that it would have been more accurate had the recorder said that the production of the ticket from the place where used tickets would properly be kept was a fact from which the jury might infer that probably two people had flown on the particular flight and that it might or might not seem to them by applying their common knowledge of such matters that the passengers bore the surnames which were written on the ticket.

It is plain that the latter inference was not one to be readily accepted in a case where it was not suggested that Moore, whose name was on the ticket, had actually flown; indeed it is obvious that *pro tanto* the potential inference was excluded. Nevertheless it remained open for partial acceptance in respect of Rice.

When summing up on this matter the recorder gave a direction which afforded complete protection to Moore against any adverse effect from the introduction into evidence of this ticket ...

So far as Rice was concerned the ticket was treated differently and assumed importance from the direction given that the jury might, if they saw fit, regard it as a corroboration of Hoather's evidence that Rice flew with him to Manchester and that Rice booked the ticket.

In one passage the recorder put it thus: 'In considering Rice's connection with Northern Auto Agency if Hoather is believed – and that is for you – ... if Hoather is believed [Rice] was behind the whole thing. But, of course, it would be dangerous ... to accept that evidence unless you find it corroborated, and you may think that ... there is no evidence independent of Hoather's that Rice was behind it beyond the explanation which you might regard as corroboration – and it is entirely for you to say whether you accept it or not ... that on May 10 he flew to Manchester and back.' The court finds no misdirection in that passage; indeed it put well the issue: did Rice fly to Manchester with Hoather? The matter was also referred to in an earlier passage in the following somewhat less appropriate terms: '... Hoather having said that he went to Manchester for a man called Rice, who booked the tickets ... you then find on May 10 a man called Rice, whoever he may have been, did book tickets upon the morning flight for Manchester and return. You may find that that evidence supports what Hoather says about the matter. It is simply evidence that on that date, or before that date, May 10, a man called Rice, whoever he may be, booked these air passages.'

The court doubts whether the air ticket could constitute admissible evidence that the booking was effected either by Rice or even by any man of that name but it does not think that for relevant purposes the distinction between the booking of the ticket and the use of it was material with regard either to the case against Rice or to his defence ... [9]

Ratten v The Queen (1972, Privy Council)

The reasons for their Lordships' decision were delivered by –

Lord Wilberforce: The appellant was convicted, on August 20 1970, after a trial before Winneke CJ and a jury, of the murder of his wife. His application to the Full Court of the Supreme Court of Victoria for leave to appeal was dismissed on September 16 1970. By special leave he now appeals to the Board.

The appellant lived with his wife, the deceased, and three young children in Echuca, a small country town in the State of Victoria. The deceased was eight months pregnant. The appellant, for over a year, had been carrying on a liaison with another woman and it was suggested by the prosecution, though not admitted by the appellant, that his relations with her had reached a critical state.

The death of the deceased took place in the kitchen of her house on May 7 1970 as the result of a gunshot wound. The evidence established the times of certain events as follows:

(i) At 1.09 pm, the appellant's father S R Ratten telephoned to the appellant from Melbourne; the call was a trunk call and so was timed and the time recorded. It lasted 2.9 minutes. The conversation was perfectly normal: Mr S R Ratten heard the voice of the deceased woman in the background apparently making comments of a normal character.

(ii) At about 1.15 pm a telephone call was made from the house and answered at the local exchange. The facts regarding this call are critical and will be examined later.

(iii) At about 1.20 pm a police officer, calling from the local police station, telephoned the appellant's house and spoke to the appellant. By this time the appellant's wife had been shot. Thus the shooting of the deceased, from which she died almost immediately, must have taken place between 1.12 pm and about 1.20 pm.

---

9. [1963] 1 QB 857.

The death of the deceased was caused by a wound from a shotgun held by the appellant. The appellant's account was that the discharge was accidental and occurred while he was cleaning his gun ...

It is clear that ... there was a *prima facie* case against the appellant, and the case against him would depend on whether the prosecution could satisfy the jury, on this circumstantial evidence, that the killing was deliberate or whether the jury would accept his account of an accident.

It was relevant and important to inquire what was the action of the appellant immediately after the shooting. His evidence, which he first gave in a signed statement to the police on May 8 1970, was that he immediately telephoned for an ambulance and that shortly afterwards the police telephoned him upon which he asked them to come immediately. He denied that any telephone call had been made by his wife, and also denied that he had telephoned for the police. It should be added that he gave evidence from the witness-box at the trial, maintaining his account of events.

In these circumstances, and in order to rebut the appellant's account, the prosecution sought to introduce evidence from a telephonist at the local exchange as to the call made from the house at about 1.15 pm.

The evidence as given by the telephonist ... was as follows:

' ... I plugged into a number at Echuca, 1494 and I said – I opened the speak key and I said to the person: "Number please", and the reply I got was: "Get me the police please." I kept the speak key open as the person was hysterical.'

His Honour – 'You what?'

Witness – 'I kept the speak key open as the person was in an hysterical state [later, the witness added that the person sobbed] and I connected the call to Echuca 41 which is the police station. As I was connecting the call the person gave her address as 59 Mitchell Street.'

The witness then said that the caller hung up but that she (the witness) after consulting her superior spoke to the police and told them that they were wanted at 59 Mitchell Street. It was in consequence of this that, as narrated above, the police telephoned to the house at about 1.20 pm and spoke to the accused. Echuca 1494 was the number of the appellant's house.

There were a number of matters to be considered as to the evidence relating to this telephone call. The first, and probably the most critical, was whether it was made by the deceased woman at all ...

The next question related to the further facts sought to be proved concerning the telephone call. The objection taken against this evidence was that it was hearsay and that it did not come within any of the recognised exceptions to the rule against hearsay evidence.

In their Lordships' opinion the evidence was not hearsay evidence and was admissible as evidence of fact relevant to an issue.

The mere fact that evidence of a witness includes evidence as to words spoken by another person who is not called, is no objection to its admissibility. Words spoken are facts just as much as any other action by a human being. If the speaking of the words is a relevant fact, a witness may give evidence that they were spoken. A question of hearsay only arises when the words spoken are relied on 'testimonially', ie as establishing some fact narrated by the words. Authority is hardly needed for this proposition, but their Lordships will restate what was said in the judgment of the Board in *Subramaniam v Public Prosecutor* (1956): 'Evidence of a statement made to a witness by a person who is not himself called as a witness may or may not be hearsay. It is hearsay and inadmissible when the object of the evidence is to establish the truth of what is contained in the statement. It is not hearsay and is admissible when it is proposed to establish by the evidence, not the truth of the statement, but the fact that it was made.'

A fuller statement of the same principle is provided by Dean Wigmore in his work on *Evidence* § 1766. He emphasises, as their Lordships would emphasise, that the test of admissibility, in the case last mentioned, is relevance to an issue.

The evidence relating to the act of telephoning by the deceased was, in their Lordship's view, factual and relevant. It can be analysed into the following elements.

(1)   At about 1.15 pm the number Echuca 1494 rang. I plugged into that number.

(2)   I opened the speak key and said: 'Number please.'

(3)   A female voice answered.

(4)   The voice was hysterical and sobbed.

(5)   The voice said: 'Get me the police please.'

The factual items numbered (1)–(3) were relevant in order to show that, contrary to the evidence of the appellant, a call was made, only some 3-5 minutes before the fatal shooting, by a woman. It not being suggested that there was anybody in the house other than the appellant, his wife and small children, this woman, the caller, could only have been the deceased. Items (4) and (5) were relevant as possibly showing (if the jury thought fit to draw the inference) that the deceased woman was at this time in a state of emotion or fear (*cf Aveson v Lord Kinnaird* (1805) *per* Lord Ellenborough CJ). They were relevant and necessary evidence in order to explain and complete the fact of the call being made. A telephone call is a composite act, made up of manual operations together with the utterance of words (*cf McGregor v Stokes* (1952) and remarks of Salmond J therein quoted). To confine the evidence to the first would be to deprive the act of most of its significance. The act had content when it was known that the call was made in a state of emotion. The knowledge that the caller desired the police to be called helped to indicate the nature of the emotion – anxiety or fear at an existing or impending emergency. It was a matter for the jury to decide what light (if any) this evidence, in the absence of any explanation from the appellant, who was in the house, threw upon what situation was occurring, or developing at the time.

If then, this evidence had been presented in this way, as evidence purely of relevant facts, its admissibility could hardly have been plausibly challenged. But the appellant submits that in fact this was not so. It is said that the evidence was tendered and admitted as evidence of an assertion by the deceased that she was being attacked by the accused, and that it was, so far, hearsay evidence, being put forward as evidence of the truth of facts asserted by his statement. It is claimed that the Chief Justice so presented the evidence to the jury and that, therefore, its admissibility, as hearsay, may be challenged.

Their Lordships, as already stated, do not consider that there is any hearsay element in the evidence, nor in their opinion was it so presented by the trial judge ...[10]

---

10.   [1972] AC 378.

R v Lydon (1987, Court of Appeal)

Woolf LJ read the judgment of the court: After a trial lasting three days at the Crown Court in Oxford, the appellant was found guilty of one offence of taking a conveyance without authority, in respect of which he was sentenced to 12 months' imprisonment, and one offence of robbery, in respect of which he was sentenced to seven years' imprisonment concurrent ...

He now appeals against conviction by leave of the single judge.

The robbery took place on July 31 1985 and was of a post office at Crowmarsh Gifford in Oxfordshire. The sum taken was £1,700. The robbery was carried out by two men, one of whom was the appellant's co-accused Fernandez who pleaded guilty.

The only issue at the trial was whether or not the appellant was the second man.

The other count related to the car used for the robbery, which was taken from the Neasden area of London on the same morning as the robbery.

There was substantial identification evidence incriminating the appellant by a customer who had been in the post office at the time of the robbery, by a part-time assistant who was working in the post office, and by the taxi driver who drove two men from a pub at Nettlebed to Neasden. His description of one of the men fitted the description of the appellant's co-accused, and he identified the appellant on an identification parade. However in relation to each identification there were points which could be made to undermine the identification. A description was also given by two women who were outside the post office, one of whom took the number of the car used for the robbery which was later found abandoned on the Nettlebed road.

The principal ground of appeal relates to the evidence which was put before the jury notwithstanding an objection made by Mr Grunwald on behalf of the appellant, that the evidence was hearsay and in any event more prejudicial than it was probative.

The evidence was as to the discovery of a gun on the grass verge, 12 inches from the edge of the road which would have been used by the getaway car when travelling towards Nettlebed and about a mile from where the robbery took place. The gun was in four pieces. Immediately in the vicinity of it was found two pieces of rolled up paper which had written upon them 'Sean rules' and 'Sean rules 85'. The gun had broken into four pieces. On the surface of the broken gun barrel there was a heavy smear of blue ink on the inside which, according to the forensic evidence, was similar in appearance and dye composition to that on the pieces of paper, so that the ink could have originated from the same pen. However the gun was black and silver, whereas Mr Ham, who only saw part of the barrel of the gun and who was the only witness at the scene to give a description, said that it was dark brown in colour and had a makeshift look about it.

The appellant gave evidence on his own behalf, and it was his case, supported by witnesses, that at the time of the offence he was in Neasden.

Mr Grunwald on behalf of the appellant contended that, apart from the writing on the paper referring to 'Sean'. there was nothing to connect the accused with the gun and he submitted that the references to 'Sean' were hearsay and in any event, bearing in mind that there are a great many people who are are called Sean, the evidence was highly prejudicial. He accepted that the decision of this court in *Rice* (1963) was some support for the ruling of the learned recorder, since in that case this court upheld the use of an air ticket to establish that Rice flew from London to Manchester on a particular day. However he submitted that that decision had been overruled by implication by the House of Lords in *Myers v Director of Public Prosecutions* (1964).

He drew the court's attention to a decision of the Supreme Court of Australia, *Romeo* (1982), in which Cox J examined in detail the English and Australian decisions, and expressed the view that the decision of this court was inconsistent with the reasoning of the majority of the House of Lords in *Myers v DPP* (*supra*).

In *Rice* Winn J, in giving the judgment of this court ... drew a distinction between the relevance and probative significance of the ticket as distinct from its contents, since 'what it might say could only be hearsay', and Cox J recognised this distinction in his judgment. He said: 'Sometimes it is possible to avoid the hearsay rule by showing that a statement made in a document is being used as an original and independent fact – for instance, that a person who made use of the document had certain information in his possession at a relevant time – and not as evidence of the facts stated. It is always important, therefore, whenever an objection is taken on hearsay grounds, to ascertain for precisely what purpose the evidence is being tendered. It may be hearsay for one purpose and not, and therefore admissible, for another.'

However he went on to say with some justification: 'It is clear that the airline ticket in *Rice*, in the absence of any other evidence, was being put forward as proof of the truth of the statement implicit in it, namely, that a man named Rice flew from London to Manchester on the flight mentioned in the ticket.'

However, whether or not the case of *Rice* is still good law, the decision of the learned recorder in this case can be supported on the approach adopted by Cox J. The reference to Sean could be regarded as no more than a statement of fact involving no assertion as to the truth of the contents of the document.

The most important issue with which the jury were faced was whether they could be satisfied that the identification evidence was accurate. That identification evidence was supported by the fact that the appellant admittedly came from Neasden, and it was from Neasden that the car was taken which was used on the robbery, and it was to Neasden that the taxi driver took a man who he identified as the appellant. The appellant's name was Sean, and if the jury were satisfied that the gun was used on the robbery and that the pieces of paper were linked to the gun, then the reference to Sean on the paper could be a further fact which would fit in with the appellant being the person who committed the robbery.

In dealing with the distinction between writing which is admissible and which is not admissible in these circumstances, *Cross on Evidence* (6th edn at p 464) states: 'In these cases it seems that the writing when properly admissible at all, is relevant not as an assertion of the state of facts but as itself a fact which affords circumstantial evidence upon the basis of which the jury may draw an inference as it may from any other relevant circumstance of the case.'

The inference that the jury could draw from the words written on the piece of paper is that the paper had been in the possession of someone who wished to write 'Sean rules', and that person would presumably either be named Sean himself or at least be associated with such a person, and thus it creates an inferential link with the appellant. By itself it could not possibly satisfy the jury that the appellant was the other robber, but it could be circumstantial evidence which could help to satisfy the jury that the Crown's case was correct.

This approach to the probative value and relevance of the evidence can be readily illustrated by examples where it could not be suggested that the evidence was inadmissible as being hearsay. If instead of the word 'Sean' appearing on the paper the paper had blood upon it and could be linked to the gun by other evidence, or the gun also had blood upon it, and both samples were of the same blood group as that of the appellant, or again if the gun was proved to have been used in the robbery, the samples could provide evidence which the jury could perfectly properly be asked to take into account, albeit that the appellant's blood group was one which was extremely common. The rarity of the blood group would only go to the weight of the evidence and not its admissibility.

Similarly, if the gun had been wrapped in a local paper normally only circulating in Neasden, that again, having regard to the fact that the appellant admittedly came from Neasden, would have been relevant circumstantial evidence. If there had been written on the pieces of paper the appellant's full name, then clearly that would have been much stronger circumstantial evidence, but, although the name 'Sean' may be fairly common, it is still material to which the jury could have regard.

In the view of this court therefore, the learned recorder was entitled to rule as he did, since the evidence was not unduly prejudicial ...[11]

IMPLIED HEARSAY

Words can be used for purposes other than the making of assertions. For example, they can be used to ask questions, to give orders or to greet somebody. There are also occasions when to utter a form of words is to perform an act. Such occasions may be governed by a religious or social convention, as when words are uttered as part of a ceremony of baptism or of launching a new ship. Further, the law may say that the utterance or words in certain circumstances amounts to an act, as where words are uttered by way of contractual offer or acceptance. For all apparently non-assertive utterances it is possible to make inferences about surrounding circumstances. Because of this it is tempting to say that the utterance, though not an express assertion, is an *implied* one as to the circumstances which may be inferred. Thus if I am overheard asking Gerald if his cat has had kittens yet, the person who overheard my question might infer that someone called Gerald has a cat, and a lawyer might argue that the question operates as an implied assertion of the fact. This could mean that an out-of-court utterance which doesn't look like an assertion, and which was not intended to operate as such, is still caught by the rule against hearsay.

The House of Lords in *R v Kearley* (1992) made it clear that, in principle, the hearsay rule affected implied as well as express assertions. The Court of Appeal had taken the same line in *R v Harry* (1988), but as their main authority the Lords relied on a much earlier decision of the Court of Exchequer Chamber (a pre-Judicature Act civil appellate court) in *Wright v Doe d Tatham* (1837); in particular, on the judgment of Parke B in that case. As can be seen below, Parke B thought that even *non-spoken conduct* which might give rise to inferences could be caught by the rule against hearsay, and although this part of his judgment was not relied on in *Kearley*, it seems likely that in an appropriate case it could be cited and adopted as at least persuasive authority. For these reasons the scope of the application of the rule against hearsay is in some respects most

---

11. 85 Cr App R 221.

unclear, as JR Spencer's note shows. Would *Ratten* (see above) now be decided in the same way on the hearsay point? Would *Lydon* (see above)?

R v Harry (1988, Court of Appeal)

Lawton LJ: On December 6 1985 in the Crown Court at Southwark, after a trial before His Honour Judge Butler, this appellant, Deryck Harry, was convicted and sentenced as follows: on count 2, of possessing a controlled drug, four months' imprisonment; on count 5, supplying a controlled drug, 12 months' imprisonment; on count 7, to which he pleaded guilty, possessing a controlled drug, one month's imprisonment, all sentences to run concurrently.

The appeal is directed to the convictions on counts 2 and 5. The points raised on behalf of the appellant reveal, somewhat strikingly, what many members of the public would regard as the absurdities of the law of evidence. The absurdities arise from the technicalities of the hearsay rule. But, as was said in *Director of Public Prosecutions v Myers* (1964), the hearsay rule is part of our law, and until such time as changes are made by Parliament, it is the duty of the courts to apply it.

The indictment charged the appellant in counts 1 and 2 with being in possession of a controlled drug jointly with a man called Bhupinda Parmar. Count 1 charged them with being in joint possession of cocaine with intent to supply. The amount charged in the indictment was 53.8 gms of cocaine.

Count 2 charged them with being in joint possession of the same amount of cocaine, but this time there was no allegation that they were in possession with intent to supply.

Count 5 charged the appellant with supplying a controlled drug to a number of people, including Bhupinda Parmar.

It was undisputed evidence that on June 19 1984 the appellant, Parmar, and a young woman called Garcia, together with a man called Doyin spent the day together in Parmar's rented fourth floor flat in Chelsea. Parmar had been in possession of the flat for a fortnight. It was undisputed that on June 19 1984 the appellant, Parmar, the woman, and the other man, Doyin, had all been there using cocaine at various times. According to Parmar at the trial, the appellant left the flat between 6.30 and 7 pm. He returned a short time later, and in the flat some kind of disturbance arose. One of Parmar's neighbours, alarmed by the noise, telephoned the police to complain.

Shortly before 8 pm police officers arrived at Parmar's flat to investigate the complaint. Whilst they were there, the man Doyin jumped out of the window. As the jump was from the fourth floor, he was very seriously injured. He was not subsequently charged with any offence.

As a result of this incident the police, who had merely come to investigate the disturbance, started questioning the appellant, Parmar, and the woman. In the course of that questioning, Parmar admitted to the police that he had been taking cocaine and was, to use the colloquial expression, 'high.' These police officers then noticed some white powder on the carpet and commenced a search of the flat. In the toilet brush holder in the bathroom they found 53.8 gms of cocaine wrapped in a plastic bag. It was that 53.8 gms of cocaine which was the subject matter of counts 1 and 2. They also found in the flat various articles which the courts have come to recognise as the equipment used by drug dealers. Subsequent analysis of that equipment revealed that it all bore traces of cocaine.

After the search of the flat was completed the appellant and Parmar were both arrested. When the appellant was searched he was found to be in possession of

458 mg of cocaine. That was the amount which was the subject matter of count 7 of the indictment.

On interview, the appellant admitted taking drugs to the flat and giving them to his friends to use. It was that admission which was the basis for count 5 of the indictment. He further admitted trying to hide incriminating evidence when the police arrived. He alleged in his interview that the police had said his co-accused Parmar was 'a big coke dealer', whereas 'I only deal in small amounts'.

The prosecution's case against him on counts 2 and 5 appears that both he and Parmar had been in joint possession and control over a pool of drugs from which either could draw at will.

After the police had completed their search and had taken the appellant and Parmar to the police station, other police officers stayed behind in the flat to complete the investigation. Whilst they were in the flat that evening the telephone kept ringing. One police officer that night answered the telephone every time it rang. There were seven telephone calls between approximately 8.45 pm and 1 am the next morning. They were all telephone calls asking for a man called Sasha who it was admitted at the trial was Parmar, or a man called Peter, and the inquirers were asking questions, the effect of which was that they wanted to know whether any cocaine or other drugs were available for sale. For the purposes of this judgment I refer to two of those telephone calls in some detail. I refer to one in which a man asked for Sasha. The police officer explained that he was out; and he went on to say that he was called Peter. The caller asked if it would be all right to come round, and the police officer said it would be. The caller then asked if he could get two Gs if he came round. Presumably, that is two grammes. The police officer said yes, and the man said he would be round within a half-hour. He did not come.

Another call to which I will refer in detail was from a man who sounded like an Arab. His English was far from clear. He asked for Sasha and upon being told that he was out, began to talk continually about 'the stuff' he had bought the night before, complaining that it had been of poor quality and he was not happy. He wanted to know if Sasha had brought in any good quality, to which the police officer said yes and asked the caller if he was going to come round. The caller said he would within an hour.

The following day the police were in the flat again in the evening, and more calls of a similar kind were received. At the trial the prosecution decided that they would not seek to rely upon the fact that these 20 or so telephone calls had been made on June 19 and 20.

The appellant was represented by Mr Glossop. Mr Glossop wanted to cross-examine the police officers giving evidence to bring out the facts about the telephone calls. The prosecution, and counsel defending Parmar, objected. There was a long discussion before the trial judge as to whether or not Mr Glossop was to be allowed to cross-examine about these telephone calls. The argument put forward, as one would expect from Parmar's counsel, was that these telephone calls amounted in law to hearsay. In the end, after listening to the submissions of counsel, in order to be as helpful as possible the judge ruled that Mr Glossop, on behalf of the appellant, should be allowed to ask the police whether, whilst they were in the flat, there had been a number of telephone calls and whether any of the callers had asked to speak to the appellant. Mr Glossop was not satisfied with that, but of course he had to accept the judge's ruling. He did ask the questions which the judge had ruled that he could ask ...

[On appeal] Mr Glossop submitted that the evidence was admissible to show the purpose for which the flat was being used. It was the prosecution's case, as I have already recounted, that the flat was a centre of drug dealing by both the appellant and Parmar. It was also the appellant's case that it was a centre for drug dealing. The only difference between the prosecution's case and the appellant's case was that, according to the appellant, only Parmar was dealing in drugs from the premises, and he sought to rely upon the telephone calls as showing the purpose for which the flat used ...

[T]here was never any dispute that the premises were being used for the purposes of drug dealing. The issue between the appellant and the Crown was: by whom were they being used for drug dealing?

Mr Glossop, on behalf of the appellant, wanted to rely upon the telephone calls to show that they were being used by Sasha – that is Parmar – for the purposes of drug dealing. The only benefit he could get from the calls was by reference to their contents in which most of them referred to Sasha. He was seeking to rely upon the contents of the telephone calls, not to prove their purpose but to establish his case that it was Parmar and not he who was doing the drug dealing on the premises.

This is a borderline case between what is admissible and what is inadmissible. It is one in which we have to apply the principles laid down by the Judicial Committee of the Privy Council in the case of *Ratten v R* (1972). In a well-known passage Lord Wilberforce said: 'The mere fact that evidence of a witness includes evidence as to words spoken by another person, who is not called, is no objection to its admissibility. Words spoken are facts just as much as any other action by a human being. If the speaking of the words is a relevant fact, a witness may give evidence that they were spoken. A question of hearsay only arises when the words spoken are relied on "testimonially", ie as establishing some fact narrated by the words.'

[Counsel for the Crown] has pointed out that the purpose of Mr Glossop's cross-examination was to show that Parmar, not the appellant, was the one who was running what everyone at the trial admitted was a drug dealing business. He could only do that by relying on the words used by the people who telephoned. In other words, in Lord Wilberforce's phrase, he was proposing to rely on the evidence testimonially and not for any other purpose.

In this court with admirable frankness, Mr Glossop has accepted that that was the reason why he wanted these facts brought out.

In our judgment the decision taken by the judge in ruling the cross-examination to be inadmissible was right ...[12]

Wright v Doe d Tatham (1837, Court of Exchequer Chamber)

On an issue raising the question whether or not a testator had, during any part of his life, possessed ordinary powers of understanding, letters were produced in evidence, written at various periods, and sent to the testator by persons acquainted with him, and since deceased, in which the writers addressed him as an intelligent man. Held, in the Exchequer Chamber, that such letters were not admissible unless connected in evidence with some act done by the testator.

Parke B [After stating the contents of the record]: The question for us to decide is, whether all or any of the three rejected letters were admissible evidence, on the issue raised in this case, for the purpose of shewing that Mr *Marsden* was, from his majority in 1779 to and at the time of the making of the alleged will and

---

12. 86 Cr App R 105.

codicil in 1822 and 1825, a person of sane mind and memory, and capable of making a will?

It is contended, on the part of the learned counsel for the plaintiff in error, that all were, on two grounds:

First, that each of the three letters was evidence of an act done by the writers of them *towards* the testator, as being a competent person; and that such acts done were admissible evidence on this issue *proprio vigore*, without any act of recognition, or any act done thereupon by him.

Secondly, that in each of the three cases mentioned in the bill of exceptions, or at least in one of them, there was sufficient evidence of an act done by the testator, with reference to those letters respectively, to render their contents admissible evidence by way of explaining that act upon the principle laid down by the Court of King's Bench (6 *Nevile and Manning*, 146). I am of opinion, upon a careful consideration of the case, and the arguments on both sides, at this bar, that none of the three letters were admissible, either on one ground or the other. It will be convenient, and facilitate the arrival at a just conclusion, to keep these two questions entirely distinct from each other.

First, then, were all or any of these letters admissible on the issue in the cause as acts done by the writers, assuming, for the sake of argument, that there was no proof of any act done by the testator upon or relating to these letters or any of them – that is, would such letters or any of them be evidence of the testator's competence at the time of writing them, if sent to the testator's house and not opened or read by him?

Indeed this question is just the same as if the letters had been intercepted before their arrival at his house; for, in so far as the writing and sending the letters by their respective writers were acts done by them towards the testator, those acts would in the two supposed cases be actually complete. It is argued that the letters would be admissible because they are evidence of the *treatment* of the testator *as* a competent person by individuals acquainted with his habits and personal character, not using the word *treatment* in a sense involving any *conduct* of the testator himself; that they are more than mere statements to a third person indicating an opinion of his competence by those persons; they are acts done *towards* the testator by them, which would not have been done if he had been incompetent, and from which, therefore, a legitimate inference may, it is argued, be derived that he was so.

Each of the three letters, no doubt, indicates that in the opinion of the writer the testator was a rational person. He is spoken of in respectful terms in all. Mr *Ellershaw* describes him as possessing hospitality and benevolent politeness; and Mr *Marton* addresses him as competent to do business to the limited extent to which his letter calls upon him to act; and there is no question but that, if any one of those writers had been living, his evidence, founded on personal observation, that the testator possessed the qualities which justified the opinion expressed or implied in his letters, would be admissible on this issue. But the point to be determined is, whether *these letters* are admissible as proof that *he did possess these qualities*?

I am of opinion that, according to the established principles of the law of evidence, the letters are all inadmissible for such a purpose. One great principle in this law is, that all facts which are relevant to the issue may be proved; another is, that all such facts as have not been admitted by the party against whom they are offered, or someone under whom he claims, ought to be proved under the sanction of an oath (or its equivalent introduced by statute, a solemn affirmation), either on the trial of the issue or some other issue involving the same question between the same parties or those to whom they are privy. To this rule certain exceptions have been recognised; some from very early times, on the ground of necessity or convenience; such as the proof of the quality and intention of acts by declarations accompanying them; of pedigrees, and of public rights by the statement of deceased persons presumably well acquainted with the subject, as inhabitants of the district in the one case, or relations within certain limits in the other. Such also is the proof of possession by entries of deceased stewards or receivers charging themselves, or of facts of a public nature by public documents; within none of which exceptions is it contended that the present case can be classed.

That the three letters were each written by the persons whose names they bear, and sent, at some time before they were found, to the testator's house, no doubt are *facts*, and those facts are proved on oath; and the letters are without doubt admissible on an issue in which the fact of sending such letters by those persons, and within that limit of time, is relevant to the matter in dispute; as, for instance, on a feigned issue to try the question whether such letters were sent to the testator's house, or on any issue in which it is the material question whether such letters or any of them had been sent. Verbal declarations of the same parties are also *facts*, and in like manner admissible under the same circumstances; and so would letters or declarations to third persons [be] upon the like supposition.

But the question is, whether the contents of these letters are evidence of the *fact to be proved upon this issue* – that is, the actual existence of the qualities which the testator is, in those letters, by implication, stated to possess: and those letters may be considered in this respect to be on the same footing as if they had contained a direct and positive statement that he was competent. *For this purpose* they are mere hearsay evidence, statements of the writers, not on oath, of the truth of the matter in question, with this addition, that they have acted upon the statements on the faith of their being true, by their sending the letters to the testator. That the so acting cannot give sufficient sanction for the truth of the statement is perfectly plain; for it is clear that, if the same statements had been made by parol or in writing to a third person, that would have been insufficient; and this is conceded by the learned counsel for the plaintiff in error. Yet in both cases there has been an acting on the belief of the truth, by making the statement, or writing and sending a letter *to* a third person; and what difference can it possibly make that this is an acting of the same nature by writing and sending the letter *to* the testator? It is admitted, and most properly, that you have no right to use in evidence the fact of writing and sending a letter to a third person containing a statement of competence, on the ground that it affords an inference that such an act would not have been done unless the statement was true, or believed to be true, although such an inference no doubt would be raised in the conduct of the ordinary affairs of life, if the statement were made by a man of veracity. But it cannot be raised in a judicial inquiry; and, if such an argument were admissible, it would lead to the indiscriminate admission of hearsay evidence of all manner of facts.

Further, it is clear that an acting to a much greater extent and degree upon such statements to a third person would not make the statements admissible. For example, if a wager to a large amount had been made as to the matter in issue by two persons, the payment of that wager, however large the sum, would not be admissible to prove the truth of the matter in issue. You would not have had any right to present it to the jury as raising an inference of the truth of the fact, on the ground that otherwise the bet would not have been paid. It is, after all, nothing but the *mere statement* of that fact, with strong evidence of the belief of it by the party making it. Could it make any difference that the wager was between the third person and one of the parties to the suit? Certainly not. The payment by other underwriters on the same policy to the plaintiff could not be given in evidence to prove that the subject insured had been lost. Yet there is an act done, a payment strongly attesting the truth of the statement, which it implies, that there had been a loss. To illustrate this point still further, let us suppose a third person had betted a wager with Mr *Marsden* that he could not solve some mathematical problem, the solution of which required a high degree of capacity; would payment of that wager to Mr *Marsden's* banker be admissible evidence that he possessed that capacity? The answer is certain; it would not. It would be evidence of the fact of competence given by a third party not upon oath.

Let us suppose the parties who wrote these letters to have stated the matter therein contained, that is, their knowledge of his personal qualities and capacity for business, on oath before a magistrate, or in some judicial proceeding to which the plaintiff and defendant were not parties. No one could contend that such statement would be admissible on this issue; and yet there would have been an act done on the faith of the statement being true, and a very solemn one, which would raise in the ordinary conduct of affairs a strong belief in the truth of the statement, if the writers were faith-worthy. The acting in this case is of much less importance, and certainly is not equal to the sanction of an extrajudicial oath.

Many other instances of a similar nature, by way of illustration, were suggested by the learned counsel for the defendant in error, which, on the most cursory consideration, any one would at once declare to be inadmissible in evidence. Others were supposed on the part of the plaintiff in error, which, at first sight, have the appearance of being mere facts, and therefore admissible, though on further consideration they are open to precisely the same objection. Of the first description are the supposed cases of a letter by a third person to any one demanding a debt, which may be said to be a treatment of him *as a debtor*, being offered as proof that the debt was really due; a note, congratulating him on his high state of bodily vigour, being supposed as evidence of his being in good health; both of which are manifestly at first sight objectionable. To the latter class belong the supposed conduct of the family or relations of a testator, taking the same precautions in his absence as if he were a lunatic; his election, in his absence, to some high and responsible office; the conduct of a physician who permitted a will to be executed by a sick testator; the conduct of a deceased captain on a question of seaworthiness, who, after examining every part of the vessel, embarked in it with his family; all these, when deliberately considered, are, with reference to the matter in issue in each case, mere instances of hearsay evidence, mere statements, not on oath, but implied in or vouched by the actual conduct of persons by whose acts the litigant parties are not to be bound.

The conclusion at which I have arrived is, that proof of a particular fact, which is not of itself a matter in issue, but which is relevant only by implying a statement or opinion of a third person on the matter in issue, is inadmissible in all cases where such a statement or opinion not on oath would be of itself inadmissible; and, therefore, in this case the letters which are offered only to prove the competence of the testator, that is, the truth of the implied statements therein contained, were properly rejected, as the mere statement or opinion of the writer would certainly have been inadmissible ...[13]

---

13. 7 A & E 313, 112 ER 488.

Stephen Guest, 'The Scope of the Hearsay Rule', *Law Quarterly Review* 101 (1985)

... The conclusion is that any possible extension to the hearsay rule in order to accommodate the cases, particularly Parke B's examples in *Wright v Tatham*, would have to omit qualification in relation to rules or conventions of speech. The reformulation of Cross's rule would then have to be as follows: 'Conduct (including stating) other than that of a person while giving oral evidence in the proceedings is inadmissible as evidence of any state of mind to be inferred from that conduct.' But this would be a ridiculously wide rule! Take the following example. A, who has a knife, is observed to follow B in a stealthy manner. Coming quickly up behind B he yells, 'I intend to kill you, B', and then delivers a mortal wound. The report of A's statement offered as evidence of his state of mind in his trial for murder is clearly hearsay (although admissible *via* the *res gestae* exception to it). Now compare this with a report of A's being observed to do precisely the same thing but in the absence of his yelling out, 'I intend to kill you, B'. The report of A's behaviour is then offered as evidence of his state of mind, the court being asked to infer from A's behaviour that he has an intention to kill.

This cannot be hearsay. Nevertheless if we follow the logic of the cases (such as the sea-captain case), once stating is seen to be just one of the types of conduct from which states of mind can be inferred the hearsay rule becomes too wide. The argument is thus a *reductio ad absurdum*. The absurdity that this conduct falls under the above extension to the hearsay rule shows that the extension to the hearsay rule is absurd ...[14]

R v Kearley (1992, House of Lords)

The accused was arrested at 11 Perth Close, Christchurch, where drugs were discovered. In the hours following the arrest, police officers (in the absence of the accused) answered 15 telephone calls. Ten of those calls asked for 'Chippie' (a name by which other evidence proved the accused to be known) and asked for drugs. There were also nine persons who called in person at the premises and asked for 'Chippie'; seven of them indicated that they wished to purchase drugs. At the trial of the accused on a charge, *inter alia*, of being in possession of drugs with intent to supply, the police officers were allowed to give evidence of those calls including evidence of what was said by the callers. With one irrelevant exception, the callers themselves did not give evidence. The accused was convicted. The question was whether the evidence given by the police officers as to the calls was admissible.

The certified question before the House was as follows: 'Whether evidence may be adduced at a trial of words spoken (namely a request for drugs to be supplied by the defendant), not spoken in the presence or hearing of the defendant, by a person not called as a witness, for the purpose not of establishing the truth of any fact narrated by the words, but of inviting the jury to draw an inference from the fact that the words were spoken (namely that the defendant was a supplier of drugs).'

---

14. Guest, 'Scope of Hearsay Rule', p 400.

The appeal was allowed (Lord Griffiths and Lord Browne-Wilkinson dissenting).

Lord Griffiths: ... [I]t is said that evidence of what was said by those who telephoned or called at the flat asking to be supplied with drugs was evidence of no more than their belief or opinion that they could obtain drugs from the appellant and on the authority of *Wright v Doe d Tatham* to be treated as inadmissible hearsay.

I cannot accept this submission. It is of course true that it is almost certain that the customers did believe that they could obtain drugs from the appellant, otherwise they would not have telephoned or visited his premises. But why did all these people believe they could obtain drugs from the appellant? The obvious inference is that the appellant had established a market as a drug dealer by supplying or offering to supply drugs and was thus attracting customers. There are of course other possible explanations, such as mistaken belief or even a deliberate attempt to frame the appellant, but there are very few factual situations from which different inferences cannot be drawn and it is for the jury to decide which inference they believe they can safely draw.

The evidence is offered not for the purpose of inviting the jury to draw the inference that the customers believed they could obtain drugs but to prove as a fact that the telephone callers and visitors were acting as customers or potential customers, which was a circumstance from which the jury could if so minded draw the inference that the appellant was trading as a drug dealer, or to put it in the language of the indictment that he was in possession of drugs with intent to supply them to others.

The requests for drugs made by the callers were not hearsay as generally understood, namely an out-of-court narrative description of facts which have to be proved in evidence. The callers were neither describing the appellant as a drug dealer nor stating their opinion that he was a drug dealer. They were calling him up or visiting him as customers, a fact revealed by the words they used in requesting drugs from him ...

I would be prepared to answer the certified question in the affirmative. It is true that the question as drafted refers to only one customer and the strength of the evidence lies in the fact that there were so many customers. But in order to be able to establish so many customers as to constitute a market in the drugs created by the dealer it is necessary to introduce evidence of the number of individual customers who collectively can be regarded as a market. If the evidence of each individual customer is held to be inadmissible it is obviously impossible ever to give evidence of a market. If there had been only one or two calls made to the premises offering to buy drugs they would carry little weight; they might be the result of mistake or even malice, but as the number of calls increases so these possibilities recede till the point is reached when any man of sense will be confident that any inference other than that the accused was a dealer can be safely rejected. A judge always has power to refuse to admit any evidence whose prejudicial value outweighs its probative value and if in the circumstances of this case it had been wished to adduce no more than one or possibly two calls I feel confident that a judge would have exercised his discretion to exclude such evidence.

Lord Bridge of Harwich: ... The first question then is whether the fact of the request for drugs having been made is in itself relevant to the issue whether the defendant was a supplier. The fact that words were spoken may be relevant for various purposes, but most commonly they will be so when they reveal the state of mind of either the speaker or the person to whom the words were spoken when that state of mind is itself in issue or is relevant to a matter in issue. The state of mind of the person making the request for drugs is of no relevance at all to the question whether the defendant is a supplier. The sole possible relevance of the words spoken is that by manifesting the speaker's belief that the defendant is a supplier they impliedly assert that fact. This is most clearly exemplified by two of the requests made to police officers in the instant case by callers requesting drugs from the defendant where the speaker asked for a supply of his 'usual amount'. The speaker was impliedly asserting that he had been supplied by the defendant with drugs in the past. If the speaker had expressly said to the police officer that the defendant had supplied him with drugs in the past, this would clearly have been inadmissible as hearsay. When the only relevance of the words spoken lies in their implied assertion that the defendant is a supplier of drugs, must this equally be excluded as hearsay? This, I believe, is the central question on which this appeal turns. Is a distinction to be drawn for the purposes of the hearsay rule between express and implied assertions? If the words coupled with any associated action of a person not called as a witness are relevant solely as impliedly asserting a relevant fact, may evidence of those words and associated actions be given notwithstanding that an express assertion by that person of the same fact would only have been admissible if he had been called as a witness? Unless we can answer that question in the affirmative, I think we are bound to answer the certified question in the negative.

The answer to the question given by the English authorities is clear and unequivocal. In *Wright v Doe d Tatham* (1837) letters written to a deceased testator by persons who could not be called to give evidence which clearly implied the writers' belief in the addressee's sanity were held unanimously by the Court of King's Bench, in a single judgment delivered by Lord Denman CJ, and by the six judges in the Exchequer Chamber to be, *per se*, inadmissible as hearsay on the issue of the testator's testamentary capacity. It is instructive for present purposes to note part of the argument of Sir Frederick Pollock, counsel for the plaintiff in error in the Exchequer Chamber, where he said: 'Suppose a testator were proved to have received a great number of letters from learned and intelligent persons, consulting him on points of science or policy; that those persons were shewn to have been well acquainted with him, and, in some instances, to have written to him repeatedly on the same subjects; can it be said that the sending of such letters, even though not proved to have been acknowledged or acted upon, would, in the ordinary course of life, produce no effect on a reasonable mind? The question being, not whether the testator was of sound understanding at a particular moment, but what the general state of his mind was throughout his life. If letters had been written to him in a foreign language, with an apparent view to correspondence, by a person who knew him, would no inference arise as to his knowledge of the language? The present evidence is precisely the same in character, though perhaps not calculated to produce so strong an effect.'

This argument closely mirrors that advanced here that the quantity and quality of the evidence of what speakers or writers have said or written which implies their belief in a certain state of facts is so cogent as to be self-authenticating and should be received on that ground. But the argument was emphatically rejected ...

In the instant case, even if we enlarge the certified question to take account of the fact that the requests for drugs of which police officers gave evidence were made either by telephone calls or personal calls to the defendant's house, we get no further. I accept the proposition that, if an action is of itself relevant to an issue, the words which accompany and explain the action may be given in evidence, whether or not they would be relevant independently. But here the mere fact of the calls being made to the defendant's house was by itself of no relevance whatever, so we are back to the bare issue as to whether the implied assertion involved in the request for drugs should be excluded as hearsay. As English law presently stands, I am clearly of the opinion that it should.

The next question is whether, if evidence from a police officer that he heard one person, in the absence of the defendant, requesting a supply of drugs from the defendant is inadmissible to prove the defendant's intent to supply on the ground that it is hearsay, the evidence becomes admissible if the prosecution are in a position to tender evidence relating to a plurality of such requests made at the same place and on the same day. I know of no principle which can be applied to render evidence of many such requests admissible, if the evidence of each one, considered separately, would not be. Of course I appreciate the probative force of a plurality of requests. But the probative force of hearsay evidence in particular circumstances has never afforded a ground for disregarding the hearsay rule ...

Lord Ackner: ... Each of those requests was, of course, evidence of the state of mind of the person making the request. He wished to be supplied with drugs and thought that the appellant would so supply him. It was not evidence of the fact that the appellant had supplied or could or would supply the person making the request. But the state of mind of the person making the request was not an issue at the trial; accordingly evidence of his request was irrelevant and therefore inadmissible. If the prosecution had sought to call any of the persons who made such requests, merely to give evidence of the making of the requests, in order to establish their appetite for drugs and their belief that such appetite would be satisfied by the appellant, such evidence could not have been properly admitted. Indeed, Miss Goddard QC for the Crown essentially conceded this. The evidence of the requests were, she submits, not being tendered in order to establish that the person making the request believed that the appellant was a supplier of drugs. She accepted that the state of mind of the person or persons making the request was irrelevant. That must include not only his or their beliefs but his or their appetites for the drug, the 'potential market' referred to by my noble and learned friend Lord Browne-Wilkinson in his speech, which I have had the privilege of reading in draft. Miss Goddard maintained that the evidence of the request for drugs to be supplied by the appellant tended to show that the premises at which the request was made were *being used* as a source of supply of drugs and that the supplier (ie that person who *had been* supplying the drugs) was the appellant.

The certified question confines itself to a single request. Miss Goddard accepts that a single request would not provide evidence either that the premises were being used as a source of supply of drugs or that the appellant was the supplier. It could only be evidence of the state of mind of the person making the request. I can see no basis in logic or principle for validly contending that an additional request or requests would fundamentally alter the situation. The request or requests, in terms which I have described, and which were so referred to by the learned judge in his summing-up, contain neither an express nor an implied assertion that the person making the inquiry has either obtained drugs from the premises, or from the appellant in the past, or has been told by the appellant (or his duly authorised agent) that he, the appellant, would satisfy his requirements (the 'potential market') for drugs if he phoned or called at the premises. Indeed the request or requests do not contain any factual assertion. They ask a question of the appellant: will you supply me with drugs? – thus by inference suggesting that they believed the appellant would supply what they requested.

Thus my reply to the certified question would simply be as follows. An oral request or requests for drugs to be supplied by the defendant, not spoken in his presence or in his hearing, could only be evidence of the state of mind of the person or persons making the request, and since his or their state of mind was not a relevant issue at the trial, evidence of such a request or requests, however given, would be irrelevant and therefore inadmissible. The jury would not be entitled to infer from the fact that the request(s) was made that the appellant was a supplier of drugs.

It will be apparent from what I have already stated that the application of the hearsay rule does not, on the facts so far recited, fall for consideration. The evidence is not admissible because it is irrelevant. It is as simple as that. But in case I have been guilty of oversimplification, let me consider the position upon the assumption that the very nature of the request or requests carries with it a permissible implication that the appellant was a supplier of drugs. It is only in such a situation that the request, spoken not in the appellant's presence or hearing and by a person not called as a witness, that the rule against the admission of hearsay evidence falls to be considered. As was made abundantly clear by the judge in his summing-up, there was no impediment to the prosecution calling the persons who made the inquiries. The prosecution had decided to rely not on their direct evidence but upon recollection of the police officers to whom they allegedly spoke.

Because the precise scope of the rule against hearsay is in some respects a matter of controversy, there are a variety of formulations of the rule. In the current edition of *Cross on Evidence* (7th edn, 1990) p 42 the rule is thus stated: 'an assertion other than one made by a person while giving oral evidence in the proceedings is inadmissible *as evidence of any fact asserted.*' (Cross's emphasis.)

This formulation was approved in your Lordships' House in *R v Sharp* ...

Such being the law, Miss Goddard frankly concedes that if the inquirer had said in the course of making his request, 'I would like my usual supply of amphetamine at the price which I paid you last week', or words to that effect, then, although the inquirer could have been called to give evidence of the fact that he had in the past purchased from the appellant his requirements of amphetamine and had made his call at the appellant's house for a further supply on the occasion when he met and spoke to the police, the hearsay rule prevents the prosecution from calling police officers to recount the conversation which I have described. This is for the simple reason that the request made in the form set out above contains an express assertion that the premises at which the request was being made were being used as a source of supply of drugs and the supplier was the appellant.

If, contrary to the view which I have expressed above, the simple request or requests for drugs to be supplied by the appellant, as recounted by the police, contains in substance, but only by implication, the same assertion, then I can find neither authority nor principle to suggest that the hearsay rule should not be equally applicable and exclude such evidence. What is sought to be done is to use the oral assertion, even though it may be an implied assertion, as evidence of the truth of the proposition asserted. That the proposition is asserted by way of necessary implication rather than expressly cannot, to my mind, make any difference ...

Professor Cross in his book *Evidence* (5th edn, 1979) p 479 stated that a further reason justifying the hearsay rule was the danger that hearsay evidence might be concocted. He dismissed this as 'simply one aspect of the great pathological dread of manufactured evidence which beset English lawyers of the late eighteenth and early nineteenth centuries.' Some recent appeals, well known to your Lordships, regretfully demonstrate that currently that anxiety, rather than being unnecessarily morbid, is fully justified.

I too would allow this appeal.

Lord Oliver of Aylmerton: ... [T]he question which presents itself in the instant appeal can be expressed thus: was the evidence of the police officers being tendered simply as evidence of the fact of the conversation or was it introduced 'testimonially' in order to demonstrate the truth either of something that was said or something that was implicit in or to be inferred from something that was said?

Miss Goddard QC, for the Crown, has submitted that the evidence admitted by the judge of what was said by the callers did not fall foul of the hearsay rule at all. It was not tendered as hearsay evidence but simply as probative of the fact that calls were made on the day in question either at or to the house and that the callers were seeking to purchase drugs from 'Chippie'. There was independent evidence of the presence of drugs at the premises and the fact that there were calls at or to the house by persons seeking drugs was relevant, simply as a fact, as tending to show that the accused had an intent to supply, the contents of the conversations being admissible as material explaining the making of the calls. Mr de Navarro QC, for the appellant, contends that this submission simply fails to analyse both the true purpose and the effect of the evidence tendered. The fact that callers asked for drugs in the absence of the appellant, there being no evidence of any reaction by him to their requests, cannot possibly, it is said, go any distance at all towards showing what had to be proved, that is to say, that the appellant had an intention to supply drugs. It proved no more than that the callers made the calls in the belief, which the jury were invited to infer from the words spoken, that the appellant had drugs and was willing to supply them. That belief, no grounds being stated or capable of being investigated, was being tendered as evidence that the fact believed was true and in the form in which it was tendered could not have been admitted even if the callers had themselves given evidence. So, it is said, the jury were being invited to draw a double inference, that is to say, first, an inference that what the callers were saying was, in effect, 'Chippie has drugs and intends to supply them', and, secondly, an inference that, because the caller believed this to be the case, it was therefore true. Thus this was evidence which, standing alone and without supplementary information indicating the grounds of the caller's belief, could not have been admitted even if given directly by the caller; and, tendered as it was through the mouth of the police officer who heard the statement, it was in any event hearsay and thus inadmissible.

My Lords, to any ordinary layman asked to consider the matter, one might think that the resort of a large number of persons to 11 Perth Close, all asking for 'Chippie', all carrying sums of cash and all asking to be supplied with drugs, would be as clear an indication as he could reasonably expect to have that 11 Perth Close was a place at which drugs were available; and if he were to be asked whether or not this showed also that 'Chippie' was dealing in drugs, I cannot help feeling that his answer would be, 'Of course it does'. But so simple – perhaps, one might say, so attractively common sense – a layman's approach is not necessarily a reliable guide in a criminal trial. I have in mind Parke B's observation in *Wright v Doe d Tatham* (1837) that, although an inference from a statement that an act would not have been done unless the statement were true, or at least believed to be true, 'no doubt would be raised in the conduct of the ordinary affairs of life, if the statement were made by a man of veracity ... it cannot be raised in a judicial inquiry ... ' Indeed, even accepting the layman's immediate impression, if one goes on to ask, 'Why do you say, "Of course"?' the matter becomes a little more complex. The answer to that question has to be, 'Because, of course, they would not go and ask for drugs unless they expected to get them'. But then if one asks, 'Well, why did they expect to get them?' even the layman is compelled into an area of speculation. They expected to get them either because they had got them before or because they had been told, rightly or wrongly, or had heard or thought or guessed that there was somebody called 'Chippie' at 11 Perth Close who supplied drugs. So, straight away, even the layman is, on analysis, compelled to accept that his instinctive 'of course' rests upon a process of deductive reasoning which starts from an assumption about the state of mind or belief of a number of previously unknown individuals of whom the only known facts are that they telephoned or called at 11 Perth Close and made offers to purchase drugs.

Now, if we translate that inquiry into the context of a criminal trial in which the accused, by pleading not guilty, is saying to the prosecution, as he is entitled to do: 'I challenge you to prove, by relevant and admissible evidence, that I was in possession of the drugs found at 11 Perth Close with intent to supply them', we have to start with the terms of the charge and ask ourselves whether and to what extent the evidence of a police officer that he heard a number of callers to or at the premises asking for drugs goes any way at all towards establishing that the accused, one of the three residents at the premises, was intending to supply drugs.

The first inquiry must be: is it relevant evidence? For nothing that is not relevant is admissible. 'Relevant' cannot, I think, be better defined than in art 1 of *Stephen's Digest of the Law of Evidence* (12th edn, 1936) p 4, that is to say that the word means that : 'any two facts to which it is applied are so related to each other that according to the common course of events one either taken by itself or in connection with other facts proves or renders probable the past, present or future existence or non-existence of the other.'

To put it, perhaps more succinctly, a fact to be relevant must be probative, and if one asks whether the fact that a large number of persons called at the premises seeking to purchase from 'Chippie' renders probable the existence of a person at the premises called 'Chippie' who is willing to supply drugs, the answer can, I think, only be in the affirmative. But the difficulty here is that it is only the combination of the facts (a) that persons called, (b) that they asked for 'Chippie' and (c) that they requested drugs which renders the evidence relevant. The mere fact that people telephoned or called, in itself, is irrelevant, for it neither proves nor renders probable any other fact. In order to render evidence of the calls relevant and therefore admissible there has to be added the additional element of what the callers said, and it is here that the difficulty arises. What was said – in each case a request for drugs – is, of course, probative of the state of mind of the caller. But the state of mind of the caller is not the fact in issue and is, in itself, irrelevant, for it is not probative of anything other than its own existence. It becomes relevant only if and so far as the existence of other facts can be inferred from it. So far as concerns anything in issue at the trial, what the caller said and the state of mind which that fact evinces becomes relevant and probative of the fact in issue (namely the intent of the appellant) only if, or because, (i) what was said amounts to a statement, by necessary implication, that the appellant has in the past supplied drugs to the speaker (as in two cases in which requests were made for 'the usual') or (ii) it imports the belief or opinion of the speaker that the appellant has drugs and is willing to supply them. And here, as it seems to me, we are directly up against the hearsay rule which forms one of the major established exceptions to the admissibility of relevant evidence. Clearly if, at the trial, the prosecution had sought to adduce evidence from a witness to the effect that the appellant had, in the past, supplied him with quantities of drugs, that evidence would have been both relevant and admissible; but equally clearly, if it had been sought to introduce the evidence of a police constable to the effect that a person not called as a witness had told him, in a conversation in a public house, that the appellant had supplied drugs, that would have been inadmissible hearsay evidence and so objectionable. It cannot, it is cogently argued, make any difference that exactly the same evidence is introduced in an indirect way by way of evidence from a witness that he has overheard a request by some other person for 'the usual', from which the jury is to be asked to infer that which cannot be proved by evidence of that other person's direct assertion. Equally if, at the trial, the prosecution had sought to adduce evidence from a witness not that drugs had been supplied but that it was his opinion or belief that drugs had been or would be supplied, that evidence would be inadmissible as amounting to no more than a statement of belief or opinion unsupported by facts upon which the belief is grounded. *A fortiori*, it is argued, that same inadmissible belief or opinion cannot be introduced by inference from the reported statement of someone who is not even called as a witness. Thus, it is said, in seeking to introduce the evidence of the police officers of what callers said, the Crown faces the difficulty that it has to contend that by combining two inadmissible items of evidence – that is to say the evidence of the calls (which are, standing alone, inadmissible because irrelevant) and the evidence of what was said by the callers (which might be relevant but is inadmissible because hearsay) – it can produce a single item of admissible evidence ...

Suppose ... a case in which the issue is whether premises are being used for the retailing of goods in breach of a covenant in a lease. Quite clearly evidence by a witness of a conversation in a public house with another person not called to give evidence, who told him that he either believed goods to be sold on the premises or that he had himself purchased goods there, would be inadmissible as evidence of the fact in issue. Such a conversation becomes no more admissible as evidence of the fact if the witness narrates that it took place, not in a public house, but in the street outside the premises where the maker of the statement was standing carrying a shopping bag. I cannot, for my part, follow why it should be said to become any more admissible by evidence that the maker of the statement evinced his belief by knocking at the door and asking to purchase goods. On the other hand, evidence that persons employed on the premises were offering goods for sale would obviously fall into quite a different category ...

Clearly the existence of a body of potential customers provides the *opportunity* to the accused (and, indeed, to anyone else who knows of their existence) to supply their requirements if he has the wish or intention to do so. But in what way does it establish that intention? The fact that potential customers make statements indicative of their existence as potential customers demonstrates no more than their desire to be supplied by anyone minded to supply them, which would, on this analysis, include also the police officers who intercept the calls. The general proposition that any statement indicating that the maker of the statement is a potential customer of an accused person for the purpose of purchasing drugs is admissible as evidence of the accused's intent to supply is manifestly insupportable. But it is said ... that what renders such evidence admissible in the instant case is that the statements were made on the occasion of visits to or calls at the premises where the accused lived. The visits or calls, irrelevant in themselves, were invested with a relevance as 'acts' of the persons concerned by the contemporaneous words which, though inadmissible as hearsay if they stood alone as proof of the veracity of the belief which they indicate, are nevertheless admissible as 'explaining' the state of mind of the caller in performing the act of making the call or visiting the premises. From that combination of words and acts it is said that it is permissible to infer that the accused had dealt in and was dealing in drugs; that is to say, that he was known to the callers as a drug dealer, which is what I take to be intended in the reference to 'an established market'. To my mind, this reasoning is fallacious in that it mistakes the real purpose of the evidence by investing the acts of the callers in calling or visiting the premises with an entirely false significance, so that they become merely a peg on which to hang the statement. The issue to which the evidence is directed is not ... the use which was being made of the accused's house. It is the intention or state of mind of the accused and it is, on analysis, the content of the statement and that alone from which the jury is invited to infer that intention. The fact that it was made in the course of a telephone call or at the front door of the house – the circumstance which, it is said, the statement is admissible to 'explain' – adds nothing at all. One can illustrate this with a simple example. Suppose that the evidence of a police officer was that he was in a café in the neighbourhood of the accused's house when he overheard a number of conversations in which the speakers indicated that they had assembled there with the intention of going on to visit the accused in order to buy drugs from him. Such statements would no doubt explain the 'acts' of the speakers in being present at the café, but I can see no possible basis upon which they could be admitted as evidence of the accused's intention except by reliance upon the manifestly insupportable proposition to which I have referred. How can it make any difference that the words were spoken not at a nearby café but at the front door of the house? In neither case does the place where the words were spoken or the means by which they were communicated have any significance at all apart from the words themselves. To say that they are admitted in order to 'explain' an act which is, in itself, without any significance is merely to conceal the true purpose of their admission. Their significance lies not in where or how they were spoken but in the fact that they were spoken at all.

The critical point of divergence – and I agree that it is a narrow point – is perhaps most clearly encapsulated in the proposition that if the callers had themselves been called to give evidence at the trial and if their evidence had consisted solely and exclusively of a statement that, on the relevant day, they had called at the house and asked to be supplied with drugs, that evidence must have been admitted. I have not felt able to accept this, for I cannot see how that evidence, standing alone, could have any possible relevance to any issue at the trial. It neither supports nor detracts from the existence of the intention which is in issue. It can do so only if and to the extent that it is treated as a demonstration not merely of the caller's hope, but of his belief or opinion, that 'Chippie' is a supplier of drugs. Introduced for that purpose it would, in my view, be manifestly inadmissible and the judge would, it seems to me, be bound to direct the jury to ignore it.

Accordingly, I for my part feel compelled to answer the certified question in the negative.

That question, however, has been framed in such a way as to relate to a request made by a single caller. Can it make any difference that in fact the evidence submitted related to a large number of callers and requests made within a matter of a few hours? To put it another way, can a substantial number of items of evidence, each inadmissible individually, acquire by association with one another a quality of cumulative admissibility which they do not possess individually? I find it impossible to see how they can. If, as I believe is the correct analysis, the evidence relating to each caller demonstrates no more than that caller's individual and inadmissible belief, the cumulative beliefs of a number of callers could demonstrate no more than the existence of a common reputation which, in any event, would be inadmissible in evidence save on an issue of pedigree or of public right.

Lord Browne-Wilkinson: ... I accept that the opinions or beliefs of the callers were irrelevant and as such inadmissible. But in my judgment the calls prove more than the opinions or beliefs of the callers.

The evidence was, in my judgment, relevant because it showed that there were people resorting to the premises for the purpose of obtaining drugs from 'Chippie'. Although evidence of the existence of such would-be buyers is not, in itself, conclusive, the existence of a substantial body of potential customers provides some evidence which a jury could take into account in deciding whether the accused had an intent to supply. The existence of a contemporaneous potential market to buy drugs from 'Chippie', by itself, shows that there was an opportunity for the accused to supply drugs.

In order to eliminate, for the purpose of considering relevance only, the complication that the purpose of the callers can only be demonstrated by the words the callers use, I will seek to demonstrate the position by reference to a case where no such recourse is necessary. Suppose a shop which has a sole proprietor and sells only coffee. Say the issue is whether the proprietor had an intent to supply coffee. On a particular day there was a long queue of persons at the door of the shop waiting for it to open. Evidence of the existence of the queue would surely be admissible towards proving an intent to supply. The presence of potential purchasers is circumstantial evidence from which a jury can draw the inference that the shopkeeper was going to supply coffee. There can be no supply without persons to whom supply is made: if the existence of such persons is shown, that provides evidence of the opportunity for supply.

Mr de Navarro submitted, and the majority of your Lordships accept, that on analysis the only effect of such evidence is to prove a belief in the minds of members of the queue that the shopkeeper will supply coffee. But although that is one of the matters which may be inferred from the existence of the queue, in my judgment it is not the only matter which can be inferred. The existence of the queue is a fact from which a jury could draw any one or more of a number of inferences, *viz*: (1) the existence of potential buyers of coffee on that day from that shop; (2) the belief of the members of the queue that the proprietor will sell coffee; (3) the fact that some at least of the members of the queue are running short of coffee; (4) the opinion of some at least of the members of the queue that the proprietor sells good coffee etc. Inferences (3) and (4) are wholly irrelevant to the issue. Inference (2), though bearing on the issue, is irrelevant because it is mere belief. But the existence of irrelevant inferences which could be drawn does not mean that the evidence is not probative in support of inference (1), although a judge would no doubt be careful as the judge was in this case to caution the jury against drawing the wrong inferences.

In my view Mr de Navarro's analysis seeks to eliminate the probative fact (that people were seeking to buy drugs) by concentrating on the reasons why they were seeking to buy drugs. The reasons for a third party doing an act will, normally, be irrelevant and inadmissible. Any action involving human activity necessarily implies that the human being had reasons and beliefs on which his action was based. But the fact that his action (*viz* asking for drugs or queuing for coffee) is capable of raising an inadmissible inference of irrelevant fact does not mean that evidence of that action cannot be admitted with a view to proving a relevant fact.

In my view therefore the fact that there were a number of people seeking to buy drugs was legally relevant and admissible as showing that there was a market to which the accused could sell, even though such evidence was also capable of giving rise to an impermissible secondary inference, *viz* that the callers believed 'Chippie' supplied drugs. If the callers had themselves given evidence at the trial and said only that on the relevant day they had made a call for the purpose of obtaining drugs from 'Chippie', I can see no ground on which such evidence could have been excluded as being irrelevant ...

In considering relevance, I have so far assumed that it can be proved (a) that calls were made and (b) that the purpose of the calls was to acquire drugs from 'Chippie'. Unless both (a) and (b) are proved, the calls do not satisfy the requirements of relevance. Telephone or personal calls, in the absence of proof of the purpose of the calls, are evidence of nothing. The only evidence of the purpose of the calls was the police officers' account of what the callers said. Is such evidence inadmissible on the grounds that it breaches the hearsay rule? ...

One of the classic examples of evidence which does not fall within the hearsay rule is a statement by a third party accompanying and explaining his acts, sometimes called verbal acts. Such evidence is admitted not to prove the truth of what the third party said but to explain the acts of the third party.

This approach has been adopted so as to permit a recipient of a telephone call to give evidence of what was said to him by the caller. The most important authority on this is the decision of the Privy Council in *Ratten v R* (1971) ...

It will be found that in each case the crucial question is: for what purpose is the evidence tendered? As I have stated, the evidence if tendered as evidence of the existence of a market willing to purchase drugs from 'Chippie' at the premises is factual and relevant. The majority of your Lordships apparently either do not accept that the availability of such a market is relevant or regard the evidence of the calls as being evidence only of the beliefs or opinions of the callers. In the present case, there is no doubt that evidence of the beliefs or opinions of the callers is not admissible. But in some cases evidence is admissible. Such a case was *Wright v Doe d Tatham* (1837).

In that case, the issue was whether a testator had the capacity to make a will. It was common ground that witnesses could have been called to give evidence of their own opinions or beliefs as to his competence. However, it was sought to put in evidence letters written to the testator by persons who had died on the grounds that the contents of those letters inferentially showed the beliefs of the writers that the testator had capacity. The very large number of judges who considered the case were all of the view that the letters were not admissible unless the testator was shown to have adopted or understood them. On that latter point the judges were sharply divided. The grounds of the decision were that the letters were inadmissible as being hearsay in that they constituted an attempt to prove from the contents of the letters an implied assertion as to the writers' view of the capacity of the testator, ie the letters were being introduced testimonially as evidence of the truth of the inference to be drawn from their contents. If, as your Lordships consider, the evidence of the callers in the present case is evidence only of the callers' beliefs, *Wright v Doe d Tatham* is unnecessary to bolster that view because, in any event in the present case, evidence of the callers' belief is irrelevant. If, on the other hand, I am correct in thinking that the calls show an admissible fact, ie the existence of a potential market, the case is not in point. The letters in *Wright v Doe d Tatham* were being tendered testimonially to prove the belief of the writers: the calls in this case are being tendered to prove a relevant fact and not the belief of the callers. Accordingly, the hearsay rule does not apply.

That this is a valid distinction is shown by the words of Parke B: 'That the three letters were each of them written by the persons whose names they bear, and sent, at some time before they were found, to the testator's house, no doubt are facts, and those facts are proved on oath; and the letters are without doubt admissible on an issue in which the fact of sending such letters by those persons, and within that limit of time, is relevant to the matter in dispute ... Verbal declarations of the same parties are also facts, and in like manner admissible under the same circumstances; and so would letters or declarations to third persons upon the like supposition. But the question is, whether the contents of these letters are evidence of the facts to be proved upon this issue – that is, the actual existence of the qualities which the testator is, in those letters, by implication, stated to possess: and those letters may be considered in this respect to be on the same footing as if they contained a direct and positive statement that he was competent. For this purpose they are mere hearsay evidence ...'

In my judgment the opening words of that passage show that Parke B would have adopted the same view as the Privy Council in *Ratten v R* if the sending of a letter and its contents had itself been a circumstantial fact from which an inference (other than an inference as to the writers' opinions) could be drawn ...

I must now revert to the certified question before this House and consider the case on the basis that there was only one caller. Would evidence of his call alone be admissible? In my judgment the reasoning which has led me to the view that evidence of multiple calls is both relevant and admissible applies also to one call alone: the caller is a potential customer. But a single call would have little probative value in showing the existence of a market. The possible prejudice to the accused by the jury drawing the wrong inference would be so great that I would expect a judge in his discretion to exclude it. I would modify the question so as to make it clear that the inference to be drawn by the jury is to be drawn not from the words used by the callers but from the fact that there were callers who (from the words used) were shown to be seeking to acquire drugs.

For these reasons, my Lords, I can find no reason why the evidence of multiple calls should not have been admitted. For myself I would have dismissed the appeal and answered the certified question (as amended) in the affirmative. In the event, I can only express the view that there may well be a good case for the legislature to review the hearsay rule in criminal law. In cases such as the present it hampers effective prosecution by excluding evidence which your Lordships all agree is highly probative and, since it comes from the unprompted actions of the callers, is very creditworthy. The hearsay rule can also operate to the detriment of the accused, as the decision in *R v Harry* and *R v Blastland* both show. A review of the operation of the hearsay rule in criminal cases is long overdue.[15]

---

15. [1992] 2 All ER 345.

JR Spencer, 'Hearsay, Relevance and Implied Assertion', *Cambridge Law Journal* 52 (1993)

In a hutch in 'Chippie' Kearley's garden in Christchurch, the police found amphetamines instead of rabbits. The drug squad said that while they were searching the property, seven people called at the door asking to buy drugs, and eleven others telephoned to ask if 'Chippie' had any drugs for sale. Kearley was prosecuted for possessing controlled drugs with intent to supply and, not surprisingly, police witnesses gave evidence of the visits and 'phone calls to help establish the intent. In a judgment which certainly deserves full marks for effort – the five speeches cover 50 pages – the House of Lords held by a majority that this evidence was legally inadmissible. So the conviction was quashed: *R v Kearley* (1992).

Lord Griffiths and Lord Browne-Wilkinson dissented. Said Lord Griffiths: ' ... as a matter of common sense it is difficult to think of much more convincing evidence of his activity as a drug dealer than customers constantly ringing his house to buy drugs and a stream of customers beating a path to his door for the same purpose ... In my view the criminal law of evidence should be developed along common sense lines readily comprehensible to the men and women who comprise the jury ... I believe that most laymen if told that the criminal law of evidence forbade them even to consider such evidence as we are debating in this appeal would reply, "The law is an ass".'

In the light of this, what reasons could have induced the majority (Lords Bridge, Ackner and Oliver) to decide that the evidence should not have been heard?

The first was that it was hearsay. In so deciding, the House finally resolved a long debated point: does the hearsay rule extend beyond statements intended as assertive, and include what are usually referred to as 'implied assertions'? To prove X has body odour, clearly you may not call Y to say Z says he has: but can you do so by getting Y to say he saw Z walk away from X with a clothes-peg on his nose? Though commentators (like *Archbold* (1992) para 11-5) have seen this as a difficult point on which the authorities conflict, the majority in Kearley thought the law was already clear, and that implied assertions come within the ambit of the rule. Though the callers did not expressly say, '"Chippie" deals in drugs', their words and acts – said their Lordships – were proved as impliedly asserting this: and therefore should have been rejected as hearsay. (Lord Griffiths and Lord Browne-Wilkinson, dissenting, thought otherwise: the evidence was admissible to show that Kearley had a market for his drugs, rather than because it contained implied assertions).

By giving the hearsay rule a wide interpretation this case goes against the main thrust of the modern case-law which, backed up by various pieces of legislation, limits the rule by making more and more exceptions to it. These exceptions, what is more, have been mainly designed to let in hearsay evidence of direct assertions; like statements that potential witnesses have made to the police. These are usually thought to be more dangerous than implied assertions, for a number of obvious reasons. They are more likely to be detailed and circumstantial (and hence likely to carry more weight, even if false); they are more likely to contain distortions as the result of suggestive questioning; and they are more likely to contain lies, because it is usually easier to tell a lie than to act one. Indeed, a number of jurisdictions that keep the hearsay rule have thought it sensible to limit it to express assertions – as do the Federal Rules of Evidence in the USA, as Lord Bridge mentions in his speech. So this decision extends a previously contracting rule into an area where there seems to be less need for it: and with important practical implications, because it thereby renders debatable quite a lot of evidence which previously everyone would almost certainly have assumed to be admissible. For example, to support the evidence of P that D uttered a threat to shoot him, can the prosecution now lead evidence that the other drinkers in the bar immediately fled? The decision spells more arguments about admissible evidence at trial, and more appeals on evidential technicalities.

The second reason the majority gave for suppressing this evidence was that they thought it was irrelevant. What the callers said showed their intent to buy – but that, said the majority, did not prove that Kearley had the intention to sell. As Lord Oliver put it, 'Can one, for instance, legitimately infer an intention to make a gift to charity from evidence of calls made by collectors seeking donations?' The answer to this, surely, is that it all depends on what you mean by 'prove'. The behaviour of the would-be buyers does not prove it conclusively, but it tends to suggest it – which is all we normally mean in the law of evidence by 'prove' – because people are more likely to try to buy a product from someone who makes a habit of selling it than from someone who does not. Buyers of drugs, unlike charity collectors, do not usually go systematically down a street, knocking at every door. If only one buyer calls at a given house that may be due to a hoax, a frame-up, or an error: but the more who do, the less likely such explanations are.

The third factor underlying the decision seems to have been an uneasy feeling that evidence of 'phone calls from anonymous people is easy to invent ... The difficulty with this as a reason for holding evidence inadmissible, however, is that it applies to so much else; it is as easy for bent policemen to plant drugs (or other cogent clues) as to fabricate 'phone-calls about them.

Underlying the speeches of the majority is the idea that if the exclusionary rules of evidence are an affront to common sense, so much the worse for common sense: what is apparently irrational is justified by the need to be fair to defendants. As Lord Oliver said at the end of his speech, the hearsay rule 'has been evolved and applied over many years in the interests of fairness to persons accused of crime and if it is now to be modified that should, in my opinion, be done only by the legislature.'

This attitude needs challenging. The hearsay rule works against defendants as well as for them. In Kearley the House of Lords approved Harry (1986), where on similar facts the defence were not allowed to prove the 'phone-calls, which were made to someone else, so suggesting that the drug dealer in residence was someone other than Harry. Furthermore, a major exception to the hearsay rule is confessions. In other words, we reject D's out-of-court statements about the offence if he said that he was innocent, but let them in if he said that he was guilty. The cynical rationale for this is that what a person admits against himself is likely to be true: but yet, as the House of Lords affirmed in Blastland (1986), D is not allowed to prove a confession made by X that he, and not D, committed the crime for which D is now on trial. The truth, surely, is that the hearsay rule in its present form shuts out relevant evidence in such a way as to help the courts acquit the guilty, and to convict the innocent, with pretty much an even hand.

In recent years, Parliament has made three attempts to reform the hearsay rule in criminal proceedings, each one more muddled than the last. Which makes it all the more depressing that the courts, when given the chance to knock some sense into it, refuse.'[16]

---

16. JR Spencer, 'Hearsay, Relevance and Implied Assertion', *Cambridge Law Journal* 52 (1993) pp 40-42.

CHAPTER 5

HEARSAY EXCEPTIONS

The rule against receiving hearsay evidence may be inapplicable for several reasons.

- The tribunal or the proceedings may not be governed by the strict rules of evidence.
- A common law exception may apply.
- A statutory exception may apply.

The first of these reasons can be dealt with shortly. Much of the administration of justice takes place not in the courts of law, but in administrative tribunals or before arbitrators. In many of the proceedings,

> either the formal rules of evidence do not officially apply, but nevertheless exert an influence on the proceedings; or the tribunal is guided but not bound by the rules of evidence; or they exert a shadowy influence on the ways of thought and styles of argument. It is not uncommon for a barrister to arrive at a tribunal dealing with wrongful dismissal or welfare matters unsure whether all or any of the strict rules of evidence will be applied. In many of these arenas something close to a system of free proof operates a great deal of the time.[1]

Even where the tribunal is a court of law, hearsay evidence may be admissible in interlocutory proceedings.

Common law exceptions are of importance only in criminal trials. Statutory exceptions have made significant inroads in criminal proceedings and the Civil Evidence Act 1995 has abolished the rule against hearsay in civil proceedings.

COMMON LAW EXCEPTIONS

The main common law exceptions are:

- *Res gestae* statements.
- Statements of deceased persons.
- Confessions and informal admissions.

Res gestae statements

The expression *res gestae* may be loosely translated as 'events occurring' or 'things happening'. If a statement is said to be part of the *res gestae*, what is meant is that it is an out-of-court statement which is so closely associated with the circumstances in which it is made that it is likely to be more reliable than other evidence of out-of-court assertions and so may safely be admitted. The psychology lying behind this notion may be suspect but that, historically, is the rationale for this cluster of exceptions. Having said that, it might also be better

---

1. William Twining, 'What is the Law of Evidence?' in *idem Rethinking Evidence: Exploratory Essays* (Oxford: Basil Blackwell, 1990), p 198.

to forget the rationale altogether and regard the four exceptions listed below as standing independently. The reason for this is that many examination candidates assume that the 'excited utterance' conditions have somehow got to apply in the other three cases as well. This is not so.

Excited utterances

These will generally be the spontaneous exclamations of the victim of an offence or of an observer.

R v Andrews (1987, House of Lords)

The accused was charged with aggravated burglary and murder. The case for the Crown was that he, with an accomplice named O'Neill, had attacked a man named Morrow in his flat with knives and had stolen property there. Morrow, bleeding profusely from a deep stomach wound, went downstairs to the flat below for assistance within minutes of the attack. The police and ambulance were immediately telephoned, and, again within a matter of minutes, the police arrived and were followed shortly afterwards by the ambulance. When the police arrived one of them asked Morrow how he had received his injuries. He replied by giving information which pointed to O'Neill and to Andrews. Morrow later died from his injuries. O'Neill pleaded guilty to manslaughter and subsequently gave evidence for the Crown against Andrews. The question arose whether Morrow's answer to the policeman's questions was admissible as part of the *res gestae*. The trial judge held that it was, saying that he was satisfied that there was no possibility in the circumstances of any concoction or fabrication of the identification. It was argued, *inter alia*, for the defence that Morrow's answer was inadmissible because for the exception to apply the statement had to form part of the criminal act for which the accused was being tried. The House of Lords rejected this argument and upheld the ruling of the trial judge. In delivering the sole speech, Lord Ackner explained how this particular *res gestae* exception was to be applied:

Lord Ackner: My Lords, may I therefore summarise the position which confronts the trial judge when faced in a criminal case with an application under the *res gestae* doctrine to admit evidence of the statements, with a view to establishing the truth of some fact thus narrated, such evidence being truly categorised as 'hearsay evidence'?

1   The primary question which the judge must ask himself is: can the possibility of concoction or distortion be disregarded?

2   To answer that question the judge must first consider the circumstances in which the particular statement was made, in order to satisfy himself that the event was so unusual or startling or dramatic as to dominate the thoughts of the victim, so that his utterance was an instinctive reaction to that event, thus giving no real opportunity for reasoned reflection. In such a situation the judge would be entitled to conclude that the involvement or the pressure of the event would exclude the possibility of concoction or distortion, provided that the statement was made in conditions of approximate but not exact contemporaneity.

3   In order for the statement to be sufficiently 'spontaneous' it must be so closely associated with the event which has excited the statement, that it can be fairly stated that the mind of the declarant was still dominated by the event. Thus

the judge must be satisfied that the event, which provided the trigger mechanism for the statement, was still operative. The fact that the statement was made in answer to a question is but one factor to consider under this heading.

4   Quite apart from the time factor, there may be special features in the case, which relate to the possibility of concoction or distortion. In the instant appeal the defence relied upon evidence to support the contention that the deceased had a motive of his own to fabricate or concoct; namely, a malice which resided in him against O'Neill and the appellant because, so he believed, O'Neill had attacked and damaged his house and was accompanied by the appellant, who ran away on a previous occasion. The judge must be satisfied that the circumstances were such that having regard to the special feature of malice, there was no possibility of any concoction or distortion to the advantage of the maker or the disadvantage of the accused.

5   As to the possibility of error in the facts narrated in the statement, if only the ordinary fallibility of human recollection is relied upon, this goes to the weight to be attached to and not to the admissibility of the statement and is therefore a matter for the jury. However, here again there may be special features that may give rise to the possibility of error. In the instant case there was evidence that the deceased had drunk to excess, well over double the permitted limit for driving a motor car. Another example would be where the identification was made in circumstances of particular difficulty or where the declarant suffered from defective eyesight. In such circumstances the trial judge must consider whether he can exclude the possibility of error ...

Where the trial judge has properly directed himself as to the correct approach to the evidence and there is material to entitle him to reach the conclusions which he did reach, then his decision is final, in the sense that it will not be interfered with on appeal. Of course, having ruled the statement admissible the judge must ... make it clear to the jury that it is for them to decide what was said and to be sure that the witnesses were not mistaken in what they believed had been said to them. Further, they must be satisfied that the declarant did not concoct or distort to his advantage or the disadvantage of the accused the statement relied upon and where there is material to raise the issue, that he was not activated by any malice or ill-will. Further, where there are special features that bear on the possibility of mistake then the jury's attention must be invited to those matters ...[2]

Statements relating to the maker's contemporaneous state of mind or emotion

A statement in this category may have clear relevancy. For example, a statement by the accused showing antipathy to a deceased person may be relied upon to establish a motive for murder.[3] But relevancy may be more problematic. This has been particularly so where the state of mind or emotion relied upon is an intention to do a particular act in the future. Not surprisingly, different facts have given rise to different inferences.

---

2.   [1987] AC 281.
3.   For a case where the earlier statement of a victim was held relevant and admissible on this basis see *R v Gilfoyle*, (1995) Times, 31 October.

R v Buckley (1873, Chester Spring Assizes)

James Buckley, gardener, was indicted for the wilful murder of a policeman named James Green, at Morton, on 24 February 1873 ...

It seemed from the evidence adduced that the prisoner, who lived in a small cottage some distance away from other houses, was a man who, for many years past, had borne an excellent character, but that in the previous year he had been prosecuted and convicted for larceny, mainly by the testimony of the deceased man Green, who had seen him commit the offence. After his imprisonment for such theft, the prisoner had been heard to mutter threats of vengeance against Green for the part he had taken in prosecuting him. On 24 February 1873 in consequence of certain information given, Green, who was then on duty as police constable, met his inspector and made a certain statement to him, no one else being present at the time.

It was most important for the prosecution to get this statement before the court, inasmuch as the whole of the evidence for the Crown was circumstantial in its character, and as in fact Green had told the inspector that he was going that night, *viz* 24 February, to watch the prisoner, and as the deceased was never seen alive after this conversation, excepting by a person who saw him a short time after dark that evening, on the road in what might be the direction of the prisoner's cottage; and as the body of Green was not found until two days afterwards, when it was discovered in the canal some distance off, and was covered with wounds.

The following evidence was given leading up to the statement in question.

Inspector Joseph Hulme, of Sandbach, said: I knew the deceased man, James Green; he had been in our police force about five years. I last saw him alive on Monday, the 24th of February 1873 at 11.30 in the morning. If a constable was going on a particular duty he should report to me, if convenient. He might, in case of emergency, act without so doing. Green did make a report to me on that occasion of his intended duty that night. That report was verbal.

By **Bowen QC** [for the defence] – The meeting was quite accidental, and we had a general conversation. Constables do report at times to me what they are going to do in their own district: – not always in writing. Green was one of those constables who possessed a little more confidence and had a little more latitude given him than others.

By **Giffard QC** [for the prosecution] – Each man had a conference point, and I met Green going to the place of meeting half-an-hour before the time.

By **the judge [Lush J]** – Prisoner's house was in Green's beat; Green's duty was day and night duty on 24th of February; from eleven to three in the day, and from nine to two at night.

Giffard QC – I propose to ask the question what the report was.

Bowen QC objected.

The judge – I think it is admissible.

Bowen QC, submitted that under the circumstances the report was not admissible, on the ground, amongst others, that it was mere gossip.

The judge thought that the statement made by the deceased man was quite admissible, but went to the other court to consult with Mr Justice Mellor on the point. After an absence of some minutes the learned judge returned, and said that his learned brother had no doubt at all of its admissibility, and the statement was therefore received in evidence; and was, that the deceased had had private information that the prisoner was at his old game of thieving again, and that therefore the deceased intended to watch his movements that night. Witness said to the deceased, 'I will send a man to assist you about nine o'clock'; and the deceased replied, 'That will be too late, I will go about dusk, myself'.

After a trial which lasted two days, the jury found a verdict of not guilty.[4]

R v Moghal (1977, Court of Appeal)

Moghal and his mistress, Sadiga, were jointly charged with the murder of Rashid. An order was made for separate trials and Sadiga was tried first. Her defence was that Moghal had been solely responsible. She was acquitted. Then Moghal was tried. His defence was that Sadiga had been solely responsible. The question arose whether, in order to support this, evidence could be given of Sadiga's state of mind and feeling at times before and after the killing. The killing took place on 30 October 1975. Evidence was available that at a family conference in March 1975 Sadiga had declared her intention to kill Rashid and had prophesied his death within months. There was also available evidence of a confession made by Sadiga to police who had investigated the crime. The Court of Appeal upheld the trial judge's decision to exclude the evidence of her confession on the basis that what Sadiga told the police about her previous (murderous) state of mind was hearsay. But the court disapproved of the judge's preliminary view that what she had said at the family conference was inadmissible also.

Scarman LJ [delivering the judgment of the court]: We accept ... that the state of mind and feeling of Sadiga before and at the time of the killing were relevant facts. Evidence of her state of mind and feeling at these times was, therefore, admissible. The judge refused to allow police evidence as to what she said to them after the event, on the ground that what she said of her prior state of mind was hearsay. He referred to Sir Rupert Cross's well known book on *Evidence* (4th edn), 197, 510, where it is said that the condition precedent to the admissibility of such statements is that they should relate to the maker's contemporaneous state of mind or emotion. Contemporaneousness is, as Professor Rupert Cross comments, a question of degree. But we are clear that what Sadiga said to policemen investigating the crime was far too long after the event to be admitted as evidence in Moghal's trial of the state of her mind and feelings before and at the time of the killing.

The tape-recording of the family conference is, however, a very different matter. It records what she said at the family conference of her then state of mind and feeling. Being contemporaneous, these statements are admissible: for we accept ... that her state of mind at that time was relevant to the appellant's defence.[5]

Note: The evidence of what was said at the family conference was not held admissible because it was thought to be contemporaneous with the *murder*. It is the state of mind and the utterance that expresses it that have to be contemporaneous, not the state of mind and the action (in this case murder) under investigation. This exception should not be confused with 'excited utterances' in the sort of situation illustrated by *Andrews*. The court thought that

---

4.   13 Cox CC 293.

5.   65 Cr App R 56.

Sadiga's state of animosity towards Rashid in March was relevant to Moghal's defence that it was she, and not he, who had killed Rashid in October. It does not, of course, follow that in every case in the future where a statement of intention is made seven months before the crime under investigation it will be regarded as relevant evidence. Previous decisions do not generally determine relevancy – see Chapter One.

R v Wainwright (1875, Central Criminal Court)

Two brothers were tried for the murder of a woman named Harriet Lane. Evidence was available from the person who had last seen Harriet Lane on the afternoon of 11 September 1874, when the deceased had left her lodgings. After that date Harriet Lane was not seen alive again, and that was the date alleged by the prosecution to be the date of the murder. The witness was ready to say that she had been with Harriet that afternoon and that when they parted Harriet said she was going to 115 Whitechapel Road. That was the address of the premises occupied by one of the accused. The prosecution appears to have argued that this statement of intention was admissible as part of the act of leaving. They appear, therefore, to have relied upon a different hearsay exception – see (iv) below. But it could be argued that the words of the Lord Chief Justice [Cockburn], who excluded evidence of what Harriet had said as hearsay, are relevant to this exception also.

> **The Lord Chief Justice**: It was no part of the act of leaving, but only an incidental remark. It was only a statement of intention which might or might not have been carried out. She would have gone away under any circumstances. You may get the fact that on leaving she made the statement, but you must not go beyond it.[6]

R v Thomson (1912, Court of Criminal Appeal)

The accused was charged with using an instrument upon a woman for the purpose of procuring a miscarriage. The woman died before trial but not as a result of the operation. The defence was that the accused had done nothing and that the woman had performed the operation upon herself.

> At the trial counsel for the accused proposed to ask one of the witnesses for the prosecution in cross-examination whether the deceased woman had made in the month of February 1912 a statement that she intended to perform an operation upon herself in order to procure miscarriage, and on March 29, a statement that she had performed such an operation upon herself. The learned judge ruled that this evidence was inadmissible and that these questions could not be asked. The accused was found guilty and sentenced to three years' penal servitude.

> The accused appealed upon the ground (among others) that the learned judge was wrong in law in refusing to admit the evidence as to statements made by the deceased woman.

> **Sturges**, for the appellant. The statements made by the deceased woman that she intended to perform and that she had performed upon herself the operation which the appellant was charged with having performed were admissible in evidence on behalf of the accused. His defence was that he had not done anything to the woman, but that she had used an instrument upon herself. When

---

6.   13 Cox CC 171.

a prisoner properly sets up a defence he ought to be permitted to prove it by any relevant evidence which he can adduce, and this evidence was of vital importance to his defence. In *Reg v Edwards* (1872) a statement made by a murdered woman a week before the murder was admitted in evidence, and that case is a direct authority in favour of the appellant.

[**Lord Alverstone CJ** referred to *Reg v Gloster* (1888).] The ruling of Charles J in that case was only the *dictum* of a single judge. The accused is entitled to adduce any evidence which will prove his defence whether it is admissible according to the strict rules of evidence or not. [He also referred to *Reg v Bedingfield* (1879).]

RD Muir (Travers Humphreys with him), for the prosecution. This evidence, being merely hearsay, was clearly inadmissible. If the contention of the appellant were right, all the learning, arguments, and decisions as to statements being admissible in evidence as part of the *res gestae* or as dying declarations would have been quite superfluous. This is simply a question as to admissibility of evidence, and the rule is the same whether the prosecution or the defence seeks to give the evidence. If this kind of hearsay evidence were admissible for the defence, it would be equally admissible for the prosecution. It is clear from the authorities that it is not admissible: *Reg v Wainwright* (1875).

[He was stopped by the court.]

Sturges replied.

The judgment of the court (Lord Alverstone CJ, Darling and Avory JJ) was delivered by–

Lord Alverstone CJ: This point is one of importance and at first appeared to be difficult. Counsel for the appellant was not allowed in cross-examination to put questions to a witness for the prosecution as to what the deceased woman had told her some time before the miscarriage as to her intentions and also a few days before her death as to what she had done. If put in a popular way, the argument for the appellant, that what the woman had said she had done to herself ought to be admissible for the defence, might be attractive; but upon consideration it is seen to be a dangerous argument, and in the opinion of the court, the rejection of evidence of that kind is much more in favour of the accused than of the prosecution. If such evidence is admissible for one side it must also be admissible for the other.

In our opinion there is no principle upon which this evidence is admissible any more than any other hearsay evidence. If it were admissible, then all those decisions in which it was considered whether statements were admissible in evidence as dying declarations, or as part of the *res gestae*, or as admissions against pecuniary or proprietary interest, would have been unnecessary. The only ground upon which it has been suggested in argument that such evidence ought to be admitted is that since the Criminal Evidence Act 1898 and the Criminal Appeal Act 1907 a new rule of evidence has been introduced under which anything must be admitted in evidence which will help the accused to prove his defence. There is a decision of a great authority, Charles J, against that contention. In *Reg v Gloster* the prisoner was charged with having caused the death of a woman by an illegal operation, and it was sought to give in evidence statements made by the woman a few days after the operation as to who had caused the injuries from which she died. Charles J refused to admit the evidence ... In this case it cannot be argued that the statements were admissible as part of the *res gestae*; the statements sought to be proved were not made at the time when anything was being done to the woman.

In our opinion the ruling of the learned judge in rejecting this evidence was correct and this appeal must be dismissed.[7]

Note: This case is often referred to in connection with the exception under consideration. But, as the report shows, the defence tried to argue for admissibility on a much broader basis. *Buckley* does not appear to have been cited. *Wainwright* was but, as noted above, it is not clear that in that case the court had this particular exception clearly in mind.

Statements relating to the maker's physical sensations

The statement must be approximately contemporaneous with the sensations, and may not be used to prove what caused them.

R v Gloster (1888, Central Criminal Court)

The prisoner was indicted for the murder of a woman. The case for the Crown was that he had performed upon her an operation for the purpose of procuring an abortion which had resulted in her death. Before she died, the woman made a number of oral statements in the absence of the prisoner as to her bodily condition, her sufferings, and as to the person who had caused them. These oral statements were tendered as evidence by counsel for the prosecution.

Charles J: Mr Poland proposes to ask the witness what the deceased said as to her bodily condition and what had been done to her. My judgment is this: that the statements must be confined to contemporaneous symptoms, and nothing in the nature of a narrative is admissible as to who caused them, or how they were caused.[8]

R v Black (1922, Court of Criminal Appeal)

Application for leave to appeal against conviction for murder.

The appellant was convicted at the Cornwall Assizes, at Bodmin, on the 2nd February 1922 before Rowlatt J, of the wilful murder of his wife, and was sentenced to death.

JL Pratt for the appellant ... contended that the conviction was against the evidence, as no motive for the crime had been suggested, and the course of the deceased's illness was consistent with her having suffered from gastritis only up to the date when Black left home, and with arsenic having subsequently accidentally found its way into the body, eg as an impurity in food and medicine. Gastritis was admittedly prevalent in the neighbourhood at the time. Mrs. Black's doctor treated her throughout for gastritis; a witness for the prosecution admitted that the deceased was suffering from indigestion, sickness, and diarrhoea two days before the alleged purchase of arsenic by Black. The Crown experts admitted that the minute quantity of arsenic found in the body was consistent with the administration of arsenic in medicinal doses, or with accidental administration of one-third grain of arsenic the day after Black left home.

Hearsay evidence was wrongly admitted: (1) The doctor who attended the deceased gave evidence of (a) complaints by the deceased of vomiting and diarrhoea, although he never saw signs of either trouble; (b) of her statements

---

7.   [1912] 3 KB 19.
8.   16 Cox CC 471.

about what she had done on the day preceding and the morning of her illness; (c) of enquiries made by the doctor whether other members of the household were affected, and the result of such enquiries. (2) Neighbours gave evidence that although they never saw any vomiting [the] deceased complained to them that she suffered from it, and in particular stated that the medicine had caused her great pain and vomiting after Black had given it to her.

This evidence was sought to be justified (a) as statements by the deceased of her bodily feelings and symptoms, and (b) as being made in the presence of Black. Statements about bodily feelings must be confined to contemporaneous symptoms. Any narrative of past symptoms or statements about the cause of symptoms is inadmissible.

[**Salter J**: Surely 'contemporaneous' cannot be confined to feelings experienced at the actual moment when the patient is speaking; it must include such statements as 'Yesterday I had a pain after meals'.]

This class of evidence has all the vices of hearsay, and must be confined within the narrowest limits if admitted at all ...

Holman Gregory KC (with him Harold Murphy) for the Crown. The question of motive was immaterial. There was a false statement about the purchase of the arsenic. The jury had all the evidence before them, and their finding was justified. The evidence objected to consisted of statements made in the accused's presence. *Johnson*, 2 C & K 354: 1847 ...

Avory J after reviewing the facts, continued: The criticism addressed to the admissibility of the evidence is really the only point that requires consideration. With regard to the statements made by the deceased about her past symptoms, the court is clearly of opinion that these statements were all admissible. If it had appeared that these were statements made behind the back of the appellant it would have required grave consideration whether they could have been admitted, but the court is satisfied that they were made in his presence in such circumstances as to require some answer or comment from him, and that the absence of any such comment was evidence from which the jury might draw inferences ... [9]

Statements relating to the maker's performance of an act

R v McCay (1990, Court of Appeal)

Russell LJ: ... On 4 April 1988 in a public house in Grove Park, south-east London, a man was attacked and a beer glass thrust in his face, causing him serious injuries. The attack was witnessed by the licensee, Mr Paul Beach. The assailant left the premises. Some 12 weeks later on 27 June 1988 Mr Beach was invited to attend an identification parade. The appellant was alleged to have been the attacker and he agreed to attend the parade, which was held at the Brixton police station. What is called the identification suite at Brixton police station consists of two parallel rooms divided by a two-way mirror. The suspect and volunteers, each numbered, are in one room, whilst the witness, a police inspector and a solicitor representing the suspect are in the other. The witness can see those on parade, but those on parade cannot see anyone in the viewing room. The system is also soundproofed so that those on the parade cannot hear what is said in the viewing room.

---

9. 16 Cr App R 118.

The appellant occupied position number 8. There being no physical contact between anyone on the parade and the witness, Mr Beach was invited to make his identification by indicating verbally the number of the person whom he identified. This he did by saying, 'It is number 8'. No complaint as to the conduct of the parade was made either by the appellant or by his solicitor.

The trial of the appellant, who was charged with wounding with intent to cause grievous bodily harm, took place in the Crown Court at Inner London Sessions before Judge Fabyan Evans and a jury on 12 September 1988. On the second day of the proceedings Mr Beach was called to give evidence, nearly three months after the identification parade. The witness was asked if he attended the parade and there made an identification. He answered affirmatively. When asked if he could recall the number of the person whom he had identified, he told the court that he could not remember the number. So far as we are aware, the witness was not shown his witness statement before going into the witness box. That statement is dated 27 June 1988, the same day as the identification parade, and refers in terms to the identification as being of a man bearing a number 8 at the parade. Had Mr Beach been shown that statement before he went into the witness box perhaps the problem that ensued would not have arisen.

Inspector Murfin, who had conducted the parade, was the next witness. He told the court that the appellant occupied position number 8 and was then asked what the identifying witness told him as he made his identification. Objection was taken to the question by counsel for the appellant on the ground that, if the inspector told the jury that the witness had said, 'It is number 8', such testimony would be hearsay and inadmissible. The trial judge overruled the objection and the evidence was admitted. In due course the jury convicted the appellant. There was no other evidence of identification and the sole ground of appeal is that inadmissible evidence was adduced, that amounting to a material irregularity in the trial.

We say at once that in our judgment the evidence was properly admitted ...

We are satisfied ... that the admissibility of the words, 'It is number 8', can be fully justified, albeit spoken by the witness in the absence of the appellant, because the contemporary statement accompanied a relevant act and was necessary to explain that relevant act. The statement was not relevant as to the identity of the assailant, but it was relevant as to the identification of the suspect by the witness. Whether that identification assisted the jury was a matter for them. In asserting that the man whom the witness thought was the assailant was numbered 8 on the parade, Mr Beach was doing no more that explaining his physical and intellectual activity in making the identification at the material time.

Counsel for the appellant was constrained to acknowledge that if the words, 'It is number 8', had been accompanied by some physical touching of the appellant by Mr Beach (the normal procedure adopted in the old style identification parades) he could not have objected to Insp Murfin giving evidence of what he heard from the witness. The reason for this concession was that the words would then accompany a physical act, whereas no such physical act was part of the identification process employed in the instant case. We consider this to be a distinction without a difference. In our judgment the procedure of looking at the suspect through the mirror, employing the physical activity of seeing coupled with the intellectual activity of recognising are together sufficient to amount to a relevant act in respect of which accompanying words are admissible. As Grove J said long ago in *Howe v Malkin* (1878): ' ... though you cannot give in evidence a declaration *per se*, yet when there is an act accompanied by a statement which is so mixed up with it as to become part of the *res gestae*, evidence of such statement may be given [in evidence].'

In our view, whether the true analysis of the statement is that it was original evidence or whether it was admissible as an exception to the hearsay rule, the judge came to a proper decision ...

Statements by deceased persons

The law, though archaic, is not particularly complicated and can be found in any of the standard books. Reference to the law reports is unlikely to be needed, though for the sake of convenience an extract from *Higham v Ridgway* is set out below.

There are five categories. Only the first two seem to attract the attention of examiners, largely because the other three will in practice usually be covered by a statutory exception.

- Dying declarations.
- Statements against pecuniary or proprietary interest. (See *Higham v Ridgway*.)
- Statements in the course of duty.
- Statements as to public or general rights.
- Statements as to pedigree.

Higham v Ridgway (1808, Court of King's Bench)

In litigation concerning real property it was necessary to prove the date of birth of a man named William Fowden junior who had died some years before the trial of the action. It was sought to do this by producing the records of a male midwife who had also died before trial.

Lord Ellenborough CJ: ... The question is, Whether the books of a man-midwife, attending upon a woman at the time of her delivery, and making charges for such his attendance, which he thereby acknowledges to have been paid, are evidence of the time of the birth of the son, as noted in those entries? That the books would be evidence in themselves, as regarding this event of the birth and other similar events in the course of his attendance on his patients, at the several times when they took place, I am by no means prepared to say. Nor is my opinion in this case formed with reference to the declarations of parents, &c received in evidence, as to the birth or time of the birth of their children. But I think the evidence here was properly admitted, upon the broad principle on which receivers' books have been admitted; namely, that the entry made was in prejudice of the party making it. In the case of the receiver, he charges himself to account for so much to his employer. In this case the party repelled by his entry a claim which he would otherwise have had upon the other for work performed, and medicines furnished to the wife; and the period of her delivery is the time for which the former charge is made; the date of which is the 22nd of *April*; when, it appears by other evidence, that the man-midwife was in fact attending at the house of *Wm Fowden*. If this entry had been produced when the party was making a claim for his attendance, it would have been evidence against him, that his claim was satisfied. It is idle to say that the word *paid* only shall be admitted in evidence without context, which explains to what it refers: we must therefore look to the rest of the entry, to see what the demand was, which he thereby admitted to be discharged. By the reference to the ledger, the entry there is virtually incorporated with and made a part of the other entry, of which it is explanatory ...

[Grose, Le Blanc and Bayley JJ delivered concurring judgments. See also *R v Rogers* [1995] 1 Cr App R 374.]

Confessions

Confessions by persons accused in criminal cases are dealt with separately in Chapter Seven because of the substantial body of statutory law and practice which affects this topic.

STATUTORY EXCEPTIONS

Criminal Justice Act 1988

23(1) Subject –

    (a) to subsection (4) below;

    (b) to paragraph 1A of Schedule 2 to the Criminal Appeal Act 1968 (evidence given orally at original trial to be given orally at retrial); and

    (c) to section 69 of the Police and Criminal Evidence Act 1984 (evidence from computer records),

a statement made by a person in a document shall be admissible in criminal proceedings as evidence of any fact of which direct oral evidence by him would be admissible if –

    (i) the requirements of one of the paragraphs of subsection (2) below are satisfied; or

    (ii) the requirements of subsection (3) below are satisfied.

(2) The requirements mentioned in subsection (1)(i) above are –

    (a) that the person who made the statement is dead or by reason of his bodily or mental condition unfit to attend as a witness;

    (b) that –

        (i) the person who made the statement is outside the United Kingdom; and

        (ii) it is not reasonably practicable to secure his attendance; or

    (c) that all reasonable steps have been taken to find the person who made the statement, but that he cannot be found.

(3) The requirements mentioned in subsection (1)(ii) above are –

    (a) that the statement was made to a police officer or some other person charged with the duty of investigating offences or charging offenders; and

    (b) that the person who made it does not give oral evidence through fear or because he is kept out of the way.

(4) Subsection (1) above does not render admissible a confession made by an accused person that would not be admissible under section 76 of the Police and Criminal Evidence Act 1984.

R v Acton Justices, ex p McMullen and Others (1990, Divisional Court)

Watkins LJ: These applications were heard together by us since they involved somewhat like issues arising out of proceedings under section 6(1) of the Magistrates' Courts Act 1980 (old style committals). The applicants Christopher McMullen, David Burke, and Raymond Canning on January 19 1990 appeared in such proceedings at the Acton Magistrates' Court on charges of aggravated burglary, violent disorder, malicious wounding and criminal damage. One of the Crown's witnesses was a victim, a Mrs Ethel Woodruff, of a very serious assault. Her evidence is of importance. She describes, though she does not identify anyone, certain features about her attacker or attackers. She did not attend the hearing of the proceedings. The justices accepted that she was not present to give oral evidence through fear and ruled that the statement she had made to the police was admissible in evidence under section 23(3)(b) of the Criminal Justice Act 1988 ...

Before turning to the submissions made by counsel for the applicants in both applications and counsel for the Crown, a few general observations need, I think, to be made about the in some part novel provisions contained in Part II of the the 1988 Act wherein the sections I have referred to lie. Part II is headed 'Documentary Evidence in Criminal Proceedings'. The origins of some of the provisions are in section 13 of the Criminal Justice Act 1925. The purpose of Part II is to stipulate the conditions governing the admissibility and admission to evidence of a statement made by a witness, so obviating the necessity for the maker of the statement to give oral evidence of its contents.

The effect of the conditions, generally speaking, is to cause the court first to decide whether the statement in question is admissible, having regard to the conditions for admissibility in section 23. If the statement is thus ruled admissible the court has to decide under section 25 (this does not apply to committal proceedings) having regard to the matters within subsection (2) of section 23 whether the statement nevertheless ought to be admitted or under section 26 (this clearly does apply to committal proceedings; note the reference to 'any proceedings' in the section) having regard to the matters within subsection (3) of section 23 whether nevertheless the statement ought not in the interest of justice to be admitted. Whatever else may be seen to present difficulties for the court in these provisions there is no doubt in my view that the dual test – admissibility and whether to admit – which has to be applied before a statement is admitted and read to the court will in many circumstances call for the most careful and scrupulous exercise of judgment and discretion. Moreover I am in no doubt that the criminal standard of proof must be applied to subsections (2) and (3) ...

The grounds which the applicants rely upon are that a constrained and not a liberal construction should be placed upon the wording of section 23(3)(b). A constrained construction imposes the requirements that before a statement can be adduced as evidence of any facts those seeking to adduce it must satisfy the court that the maker of the statement is in fear of giving oral evidence and that such fear is due to attempts made since the making of the statement to place the maker in fear. That construction, it is maintained, should apply regardless as to whether the proceedings are in the magistrates' court or in the Crown Court ...

The submissions of Mr Georghiades [defence counsel] were concentrated upon section 23(3)(b) and I quote again that provision: 'that the person who made it does not give oral evidence through fear or because he is kept out of the way.' It is apparent, I think, that Parliament has thereby let loose one or two potentially unruly horses which the courts will have to be vigilant to control ...

[T]he words of the provision are in my judgment plain and call to be read disjunctively. There really are, therefore, two unruly horses, one named 'fear' and the other 'kept out of the way.' Fear of what and whether that is relevant is a matter for the court's consideration in the given circumstances; likewise, if that is relied on, the fact that and the reason why a witness is kept out of the way. Whilst the burden placed on the court may in some cases be an onerous one when this provision is relied upon, the constraints upon admission in section 26 properly regarded afford, it seems to me, adequate protection for a defendant ...

Mr Campbell-Tiech [another defence counsel] in his submissions concentrated more upon the test to be applied in relation to fear. The fear specified must, he said, be genuine and based on reasonable grounds. In that he was supported by Mr Evans [counsel for the Crown]. A test of fear is objective not subjective, he maintained.

Despite the fact that Mr Evans supported Mr Campbell-Tiech as to reasonable grounds, I do not agree with that test. It is not helpful in this context to speak of the objective or subjective approach and wholly inappropriate in my view to introduce the concept of reasonable grounds. It will be sufficient that the court on the evidence is sure that the witness is in fear as a consequence of the commission of the material offence or of something said or done subsequently in relation to that offence and the possibility of the witness testifying as to it ...[10]

R v Ashford Magistrates' Court, ex p Hilden (1992, Divisional Court)

The applicant was charged with committing grievous bodily harm against his girlfriend. At the committal in the magistrates' court the girl went into the witness box but gave evasive answers when questioned on behalf of the prosecution. The examining magistrate concluded from her demeanour and responses that she was refusing to answer questions out of fear. The prosecution applied for the witness statement to be admitted in evidence under s 23 of the Criminal Justice Act 1988. The magistrate admitted it and the applicant was subsequently committed for trial. He applied for judicial review on the basis that the statement had been improperly admitted.

McCowan LJ: ... Appearing for the applicant before this court, Mr French has made three submissions. The first of those turns upon the words in section 23(3)(b), 'the person who made it does not give oral evidence through fear or because he is kept out of the way.' In this case there is no suggestion that she was kept out of the way. The important words therefore are 'does not give oral evidence through fear.'

Mr French submits that for section 26 to bite (as he puts it), the court must have before it a witness that does not utter a single word of evidence. He says that oral evidence starts immediately after the taking of the oath. Indeed, he went so far as to submit that this section is aimed at covering those who will not come into court at all; they may not have been kept out of the way, they may have arrived at the court building, but they will not come into court and in fact do not come into court. Once they come into court and take the oath, anything they say thereafter, be it only their name and address, amounts to oral evidence.

---

10.   92 Cr App R 98.

He sought also to get some support from the words in section 26(ii) 'if the person making it does not attend to give oral evidence'. For my part, I cannot see how that assists him. If anything, I should have thought it was against him. Those words 'does not attend to give oral evidence' do not appear in section 23. What is said there is 'does not give oral evidence through fear or because he is kept out of the way'. Those words are clearly disjunctive. It is one or the other. In the present case the question is: did this witness give oral evidence?

I cannot accept the submission that she must literally utter not one word, that she must stand there completely mute in order that section 26 can have any effect. In my judgment, what it means is that she must not have given evidence of significant relevance to the case.

Mr Hillen, appearing for the prosecution before us drew our attention to definitions of 'evidence' in two very well-known textbooks. *Cross on Evidence* (7th edn, 1990) at p 42 defines testimony as 'the statement of a witness in court offered as evidence of the truth of that which is stated'. *Phipson on Evidence* (14th edn) at para 1-03 says: 'In a real sense evidence is that which may be placed before the court in order that it may decide the issue of fact.'

Those definitions are saying in another and perhaps more elegant way what I am saying, namely that before there is oral evidence in the context of this section, there must be evidence of significant relevance to the case.

Looking back at this young woman's deposition, I note in particular these phrases: 'I do not remember where I was on Friday 1st May 1992 ...'. 'I do not know who that is in the photos. I have no comment as to whether I have any injuries like that or have had any injuries like that ...'. 'I do not have to say nothing. Again no comment as to why I don't want to tell the court why I have ever had injuries like that ...'. 'I do not now live at 65 Cranford Road, Ashford. I do not know if I was there on the 28th June ...'. 'I cannot remember what happened. It was a long time ago.'

In my judgment, she clearly gave no evidence of significant relevance to the case. Put another way, in no real sense did the evidence which she placed before the court go to decide the issues of fact in the case. Accordingly, I for my part would reject Mr French's first submission.

His second submission turns upon the words 'through fear'. He submits in effect that either the witness has actually to say, 'I am not giving evidence through fear', or there has to be evidence from a witness, presumably a police officer, to say that he has seen the witness outside the court and has concluded that she was in fear. This ties in with his argument that the section is to cover those who will not come into court; and since the witness has not come into the court, it is perfectly permissible, he submits, for a police officer to say, 'I have seen her outside and she was shaking with fear'.

I cannot for my part understand how that is better evidence than a magistrate seeing the witness and forming her own view that the witness is shaking with fear. I see nothing in the section which requires that the witness herself should say, 'I am not giving evidence through fear'. I have already recounted the affidavit of the magistrate which makes it clear that in this case she formed a clear view that the reason why the witness was not giving oral evidence was because she was fearful of doing so.

Mr French points out that the criminal standards of proof must be applied. He is right about that. It is apparent from the affidavit of the magistrate she appreciated that, and she made it clear that she was sure that the witness was not giving evidence as a result of fear.

I have no doubt that it is open to magistrates to be satisfied of that fact, namely that the evidence is not being given through fear, by reason of the demeanour of the witness. Accordingly, I reject Mr French's second submission ...

Popplewell J: I agree with the result proposed by McCowan LJ but, as I have arrived at the same conclusions by a somewhat different route, I propose to express my own views in relation to the interpretation of section 23 of the Criminal Justice Act 1988. McCowan LJ has already set out the section with which we are concerned.

In my judgment, it is capable of two interpretations. First is the interpretation which Mr French puts on it, that is that the person who made the statement does not give (in my words) any oral evidence through fear, that is to say that he or she is prevented from going into the witness-box through fear. I do not accede to the submission made by Mr Hillen that the phrase 'oral evidence' must mean some material oral evidence. The Act quotes no support for such an interpretation. It seems to me that once the witness has gone into the witness box, taken the oath and given any evidence, that constitutes oral evidence.

The other interpretation is to remove the word 'any' and insert the word 'some'. That is to say, if a person starts giving oral evidence (even material oral evidence) without fear but is prevented from giving further oral evidence through fear, that is a person who can properly be categorised as a person who does not give oral evidence through fear.

Both those interpretations seem to me to be possible and there being in my judgment an ambiguity, the question which then arises is which interpretation is to be preferred ...

It seems to me there is no logic in the submission made by Mr French as to his interpretation. Why should a witness who is terrified during the course of giving evidence be treated differently from a witness terrified before giving evidence? It is by no means uncommon for a witness to dry up during the course of giving evidence. If a threat inducing fear is made during the trial, there seems to be no logical reason for treating its effect differently from a threat made before trial. Common sense requires that Mr French's submissions, admirably made, should be rejected. He makes a submission that will cause difficulties in dealing with evidence at trial. Those difficulties in my judgment are easily and readily overcome by the provisions of section 26 which provide that a statement will not be admitted unless the court is of the opinion that it is in the interests of justice. The anxieties which he expresses in my judgment are non-existent given the power of the court under section 26. I entirely agree with what McCowan LJ said about the other submissions made, and I agree with the conclusion that this application must be dismissed.[11]

Neill v North Antrim Magistrates' Court (1992, House of Lords)

Two witnesses to a robbery gave written statements to the police identifying the appellant and the other accused persons as participants. These were tendered to the magistrates at the preliminary inquiry, but the appellant's solicitor requested that the witnesses should attend and give oral evidence. The magistrate, having heard evidence from a police officer, admitted the statements pursuant to the relevant Northern Ireland legislation on the ground that the witnesses had refused to give evidence through fear. The police officer

---

11. 96 Cr App R 92.

had testified that on the previous day the mothers of the witnesses had told him that their sons were afraid to come to court because of threats made against them. The officer added that the mothers had come to court and had confirmed that their sons were afraid to attend. The statements were admitted, and the appellant and the other accused were committed for trial. The appellant applied for judicial review, contending that the statements should not have been admitted. The Divisional Court upheld that contention but refused to quash the committal. The appellant appealed to the House of Lords. The sole speech was delivered by Lord Mustill.

Lord Mustill: ... I turn to the present appeal. Plainly, the first step must be to decide whether the evidence of the two boys was admissible under art 3 of the 1988 order. It is convenient to approach this by way of the ruling given by Kenneth Jones J at a trial at the Central Criminal Court, reported as *R v O'Loughlin* (1988). The report is deceptive at first glance; although the ruling was not reported until 1988, it was in fact given in 1986 before the significant change in the law effected by s 23 of the Criminal Justice Act 1988, a change which appears to have been made to counteract the effect of the ruling (see *Cross on Evidence* (7th edn, 1990) p 630). At the material time the governing provision was s 13(3) of the Criminal Justice Act 1925, which provided that depositions would be read in evidence at a trial if the witness was 'proved at the trial by the oath of a credible witness ... to be kept out of the way by means of the procurement of the accused or on his behalf'. Two important witnesses refused to come to this country to give evidence because they were frightened for themselves and their families. Evidence was given by police officers of conversations with the witnesses, who had spoken of their fear and of threats made to them. The learned judge declined to admit the depositions of the witnesses, on these grounds: (i) the officers' evidence of what the witnesses had told them about threats was hearsay and hence inadmissible; (ii) even if admissible the evidence did not show that the threats were uttered by 'the accused or on his behalf'; and (iii), in the circumstances of the case, when the only evidence against the accused was that of the two witnesses, it should be excluded in the exercise of the discretion conferred by s 78(1) of the Police and Criminal Evidence Act 1984.

On the principal point which it decided *R v O'Loughlin* has been overtaken by s 23 of the 1988 Act (and the kindred provisions of art 3 of the 1988 order), which permits the use of documents in criminal proceedings upon proof that the maker does not give evidence through fear or because he is kept out of the way. The requirements are disjunctive, and it is now sufficient to prove that the witness is absent through fear: see *R v Acton Justices, ex p McMullen* (1990), a case on documentary evidence in committal proceedings. What the case does not decide is that the evidence of the officers about the witnesses' complaints was inadmissible. It would have been surprising to find any such decision for it would entail that the learned judge had quite overlooked the long-established law that a person's declaration of his contemporaneous state of mind is admissible to prove the existence of that state of mind: see *R v Blastland* (1985) and *Cross on Evidence* (7th edn, 1990) p 666 ff, and the cases there cited. In fact, however, Kenneth Jones J said no such thing. On the contrary, he distinguished between the officers' evidence of what the witnesses had said about their fear and what they had said about the reason for their fear. As to the former he observed: ' ... that, of course, is evidence which can be given ... ' I agree, and pause only to remark that the evidence must be, not that the witnesses were afraid (for that is an inference to be drawn by the court), but that they said they *were* afraid and (if it be the case) that their demeanour was consistent with what they had said.

Secondly, *R v O'Loughlin* decides that the fact of the witness being absent through fear must be proved by admissible evidence. Again I agree, and do not consider that the difference in the language of the more recent legislation has altered the position in this respect.

Finally, *R v O'Loughlin* is a reminder that, even if the requirements of s 23 of the English Criminal Justice Act 1988 (corresponding to art 3 of the 1988 order) are satisfied, the courts must ask themselves whether it is in the interests of justice to admit the statement (see now s 26 of the 1988 Act and art 6 of the 1988 order).

I return to the present appeal. For the reasons stated, I consider that if the police officers' evidence had been that the two young men had spoken to them directly of their fear, their witness statements would have been potentially admissible under art 3. I say 'potentially' because even on a committal, as distinct from a trial, the court will be cautious about admitting in evidence, and founding a decision upon, documentary evidence of identification (or, as in the case of one of the two young men, recognition) where this is the principal element in the prosecution's case.

In the event, however, the officers gave no such evidence, but merely recounted what the mothers had been told by their sons. Whatever may be the intellectual justification of the exception to the hearsay rule which enables the court to receive first-hand hearsay as to state of mind, I feel no doubt that it cannot be stretched to embrace what is essentially a third-hand account of the witness's apprehensions. Accordingly, in agreement with the Divisional Court I would hold that the witness statements of the two young men should not have been admitted in evidence ...[12]

Criminal Justice Act 1988

24(1) Subject –

    (a) to subsection (3) and (4) below;

    (b) to paragraph 1A of Schedule 2 to the Criminal Appeal Act 1968; and

    (c) to section 69 of the Police and Criminal Evidence Act 1984,

    a statement in a document shall be admissible in criminal proceedings as evidence of any fact of which oral evidence would be admissible, if the following conditions are satisfied –

        (i)   the document was created or received by a person in the course of a trade, business, profession or other occupation, or as the holder of a paid or unpaid office; and

        (ii) the information contained in the document was supplied by a person (whether or not the maker of the statement) who had, or may reasonably be supposed to have had, personal knowledge of the matter dealt with.

  (2) Subsection (1) above applies whether the information contained in the document was supplied directly or indirectly but, if it was supplied indirectly, only if each person through whom it was supplied received it –

    (a) in the course of a trade, business, profession or other occupation; or

    (b) as the holder of a paid or unpaid office.

---

12. [1992] 4 All ER 846.

(3) Subsection (1) above does not render admissible a confession made by an accused person that would not be admissible under section 76 of the Police and Criminal Evidence Act 1984.

(4) A statement prepared otherwise than in accordance with section 3 of the Criminal Justice (International Cooperation) Act 1990 or an order under paragraph 6 of Schedule 13 to this Act or under section 30 or 31 below for the purposes –

(a) of pending or contemplating criminal proceedings; or

(b) of a criminal investigation,

shall not be admissible by virtue of subsection (1) above unless –

(i) the requirements of one of the paragraphs of subsection (2) of section 23 above are satisfied; or

(ii) the requirements of subsection (3) of that section are satisfied; or

(iii) the person who made the statement cannot reasonably be expected (having regard to the time which has elapsed since he made the statement and to all the circumstances) to have any recollection of the matters dealt with in the statement.

25 (1) If, having regard to all the circumstances –

(a) the Crown Court –

(i) on a trial on indictment;

(ii) on an appeal from a magistrates' court; or

(iii) on the hearing of an application under section 6 of the Criminal Justice Act 1987 (applications for dismissal of charges of fraud transferred from magistrates' court to Crown Court); or

(b) the Criminal Division of the Court of Appeal; or

(c) a magistrates' court on a trial of an information,

is of the opinion that in the interests of justice a statement which is admissible by virtue of section 23 or 24 above nevertheless ought not to be admitted, it may direct that the statement shall not be admitted.

(2) Without prejudice to the generality of subsection (1) above, it shall be the duty of the court to have regard –

(a) to the nature and source of the document containing the statement and to whether or not, having regard to its nature and source and to any other circumstances that appear to the court to be relevant, it is likely that the document is authentic;

(b) to the extent to which the statement appears to supply evidence which would otherwise not be readily available;

(c) to the relevance of the evidence that it appears to supply to any issue which is likely to have to be determined in the proceedings; and

(d) to any risk, having regard in particular to whether it is likely to be possible to controvert the statement if the person making it does not attend to give oral evidence in the proceedings, that its admission or exclusion will result in unfairness to the accused or, if there is more than one, to any of them.

26 Where a statement which is admissible in criminal proceedings by virtue of section 23 or 24 above appears to the court to have been prepared, otherwise than in accordance with section 3 of the Criminal Justice (International

Cooperation) Act 1990 or an order under paragraph 6 of Schedule 13 to this Act or under section 30 or 31 below, for the purposes –

(a) of pending or contemplated criminal proceedings; or

(b) of a criminal investigation,

the statement shall not be given in evidence in any criminal proceedings without the leave of the court, and the court shall not give leave unless it is of the opinion that the statement ought to be admitted in the interests of justice; and in considering whether its admission would be in the interests of justice, it shall be the duty of the court to have regard –

(i)   to the contents of the statement;

(ii) to any risk, having regard in particular to whether it is likely to be possible to controvert the statement if the person making it does not attend to give oral evidence in the proceedings, that its admission or exclusion will result in unfairness to the accused or, if there is more than one, to any of them; and

(iii) to any other circumstances that appear to the court to be relevant.

R v Cole (1990, Court of Appeal)

Ralph Gibson LJ [delivering the judgment of the court]: ... The nature of the discretion to be exercised by the court under ss 25 and 26 of the 1988 Act, and the matters to which in exercising that discretion the court is required to have regard, have been laid down by Parliament and, in the view of this court, are clearly expressed. There will be difficulty in applying those provisions to the facts of particular cases.

The overall purpose of the provisions was to widen the power of the court to admit documentary hearsay evidence while ensuring that the accused received a fair trial. In judging how to achieve the fairness of the trial a balance must on occasions be struck between the interests of the public in enabling the prosecution case to be properly presented and the interests of a particular defendant in not being put in a disadvantageous position, for example by the death or illness of a witness. The public of course also has a direct interest in the proper protection of the individual accused. The point of balance, as directed by Parliament, is set out in the sections.

It is not of course the case that these provisions are available only to enable the prosecution to put evidence before the court. A defendant also may wish to make use of the provisions, in order to get before the jury documentary evidence which would not otherwise be admissible.

Next, some comment on the structure of these sections is necessary. By s 25, if, having regard to all the circumstances, the court is of opinion that a statement, admissible by virtue of s 23 or s 24, 'in the interests of justice ought not to be admitted', it may direct that it be not admitted. The court is then, in considering that question, directed to have regard to the list of matters set out in s 25(2). They include 'any risk' of unfairness caused by admission or exclusion of the statement 'having regard in particular to whether it is likely to be possible to controvert the statement if the person making it does not attend'. In short, the court must be made to hold the opinion that the statement ought not to be admitted.

By contrast under s 26, which deals with documents prepared for purpose of criminal proceedings or investigation, when a statement is admissible in criminal proceedings by virtue of s 23 or s 24, and was prepared for the purposes of criminal proceedings, the statement shall not be given in evidence unless the court is of opinion that the statement *'ought to be admitted in the interests of justice'*. The matters to which the court must have regard ... include ... 'any risk' of unfairness caused by admission or exclusion having regard to the possibility of controverting the statement. Again, in short, the court is not to admit the statement unless made to hold the opinion that in the interests of justice it *'ought to be admitted'*. The emphasis is the other way round.

The first submission of counsel for the appellant was that the words 'whether it is likely to be possible to controvert the statement if the person making it does not attend' contemplate only, and should not be restricted to, the possibility of controverting the statement by cross-examination directed to witnesses to be called for the prosecution.

We reject that submission. We see no reason to imply any such restriction on the plain meaning of the words. The meaning of 'controvert' includes that of 'dispute' or 'contradict'. The court is entitled, in our judgment, to have regard to such information as it has at the time that the application is made which shows 'whether it is likely to be possible to controvert the statement' in the absence of the ability to cross-examine the maker. The court cannot require to be told whether the accused intends to give evidence or to call witnesses, but the court is not required, in our judgment, to assess the possibility of controverting the statement upon the basis that the accused will not give evidence or call witnesses known to be available to him. The decision by an accused whether or not to give evidence or to call witnesses is to be made by him by reference to the admissible evidence put before the court; and the accused has no right, as we think, for the purposes of this provision, to be treated as having no possibility of controverting the statement because of his right not to give evidence or to call witnesses. If Parliament had intended the question to be considered on that basis, express words would, we think, have been used to make the intention clear.

This question, however, is only one part of a complex balancing exercise which the court must perform. For example, the fact that the court concludes that it is likely to be possible for the accused to controvert the statement if the person making it cannot be cross-examined does not mean that the court will therefore necessarily be of opinion that admission of the statement will not result in unfairness to the accused or that the statement ought not to be admitted in the interests of justice.

The court must consider the contents of the statement, as explained in *R v Blithing* (1983), where the court was concerned with s 13(3) of the 1925 Act; the statement may leave relevant questions unanswered and appear to provide evidence of greater certainty than is warranted having regard to the absence of those answers. As Lord Griffiths observed in *Scott v R* (1989) after reference to a need for proper warnings when a statement is admitted: 'It is the quality of the evidence in the deposition that is the crucial factor that should determine the exercise of the discretion. By way of example, if the deposition contains evidence of identification that is so weak that a judge in the absence of corroborative evidence would withdraw the case from the jury, then, if there is no corroborative evidence, the judge should exercise his discretion to refuse to admit the deposition for it would be unsafe to allow the jury to convict on it.'

Thus the weight to be attached to the inability to cross-examine and the magnitude of any consequential risk that admission of the statement will result in unfairness to the accused, will depend in part on the court's assessment of the quality of the evidence shown by the contents of the statement. Each case, as is obvious, must turn on its own facts. The court should, we accept, consider whether, as was the court's view in *R v Blithing*, the inability to probe a statement by cross-examination of the maker of it must be regarded as having such consequences, having regard to the terms and substance of the statement in the light of the issues in the case, that for that reason the statement should be excluded.

In considering a submission to that effect the court is entitled, and in our view required, to consider how far any potential unfairness, arising from the inability to cross-examine on the particular statement, may be effectively counter-balanced by the sort of warning and explanation in the summing-up described by Lord Griffiths and in fact given by the judge in this case. The court will also, for example, consider whether, having regard to other evidence available to the prosecution, the interests of justice will be properly served by excluding the statement ...[13]

R v Foxley (1995, Court of Appeal)

The defendant was charged with corruption. The question arose whether certain documents obtained from abroad were admissible at his trial under s 24 of the Criminal Justice Act 1988.

Roch LJ: Having satisfied ourselves that the correct formalities for obtaining the documents from abroad had been observed by the Crown Prosecution Service, we now turn to the ground of appeal based on section 24 of the Criminal Justice Act 1988. Section 24(1) of that Act provides that a statement in a document shall be admissible in criminal proceedings as evidence of any fact of which direct oral evidence would be admissible if certain conditions are satisfied. Those conditions are (1) that the document was created or received by a person in the course of a trade, business, profession or other occupation, or as the holder of a paid or unpaid office, and (2) the information contained in the documents was supplied by a person (whether or not the maker of the statement) who had, or may reasonably be supposed to have had, personal knowledge of the matters dealt with ...

The appellant's counsel makes these observations about these documents; namely that no witness spoke to them nor to the transaction reflected by the document. The documents were not directed to or seen by the appellant. There was no evidence from the creator of the document either as to the purpose for which it was created or that the maker had personal knowledge of the contents or that it was created in the course of a trade or business. There was no evidence as to where the document had been kept, although each document was many years old. Thus cross-examination as to the documents or the transactions they purported to reflect was impossible. Further, it was impossible for the appellant to have dealt with them in evidence had he chosen to give evidence.

The result, submits counsel for the appellant, is that the conditions required by section 24 have not been satisfied. It has not been proved that the documents were created or received by a person in the course of a trade or business. It cannot be said that a document which effects a corrupt payment is a document created in the course of a trade or business because this must mean in the legitimate course of a trade or business. Next, the information in the document was not proved to have been supplied by a person with personal knowledge of its contents. The two conditions set out in section 24(1) must be proved by evidence adduced by the prosecution, it is submitted by counsel for the

---

13.   [1990] 2 All ER 108.

appellant, relying upon the cases of *Minors and Harper* (1989) and *Bedi and Bedi* (1992) ...

A reading of section 24 must be made in the light of the provisions of section 23 of the 1988 Act, which makes admissible in criminal proceedings a statement made by a person in a document as evidence of any fact of which direct oral evidence by him would be admissible if one of the requirements of section 23(2) are satisfied (these all relate to the unavailability of the person who made the statement) or the requirements of section 23(3) are satisfied: namely, that the statement was given to a person under a duty to investigate offences and that the maker of the statement does not give oral evidence through fear or because he is being kept out of the way. It may be that direct evidence of the requirements of subsections (2) and (3) are required, although this may not always need to be oral evidence. In the normal case it probably will be oral evidence, see *Case* (1991) ...

Section 24 deals with the statements in a document and makes such statements admissible of any fact of which direct oral evidence would be admissible if two conditions are satisfied. The wording of condition (ii) demonstrates that Parliament anticipated that courts would draw inferences as to the personal knowledge of the person supplying the information of the matters dealt with. The purpose of section 24 is to enable the document to speak for itself; the safeguard being the two conditions and the other statutory provisions applicable, for example in the case of a statement made for the purpose of a criminal investigation, one of the requirements of section 23(2) or the requirements of section 23(3) have to be fulfilled. In *Cole* (1990), speaking of sections 23 to 26 of the 1988 Act, Ralph Gibson LJ said: 'The overall purpose of the provisions was to widen the power of the court to admit documentary hearsay evidence while ensuring that the accused receives a fair trial.'

With regard to section 24, we would suggest that Parliament's intention would be defeated if oral evidence was to be required in every case from a person who was either the creator or keeper of the document, or the supplier of the information contained in the document ...

In this case, these documents were being adduced in evidence by the Crown as copies of the documents which effected payment by the three manufacturing companies to the three intermediaries. These were not documents in which the creator of the documents recorded that another had told him that such a payment had been made. These documents were copies of the payments themselves. The documents had been produced by the appropriate authorities in Italy, Germany and Norway responding to letters of requests for assistance addressed to them by the prosecuting authorities in the United Kingdom and the court was entitled to infer that these documents had been obtained from the three manufacturing companies by the appropriate authorities acting within the laws of their respective countries.

This, it seems to us, is the answer to the crucial question in this appeal. Is direct oral evidence required either from the officer of the appropriate authority in the foreign country that he has seized the documents in accordance with the laws of his country or from an officer of the company that these were indeed documents from his company created in the course of business containing information supplied by a person who had or may reasonably be supposed to have had personal knowledge of the matters dealt with? In our judgment such direct evidence is not essential, although it will often be desirable to have such evidence. The court may, as Parliament clearly intended, draw inferences from the documents themselves and from the method or route by which the documents have been produced before the court.

In this case the judge could infer that each of the manufacturing companies had an obligation to keep proper records and accounts; and that payments made by the companies would have to be made by documents of which copies would be kept for the purposes of the company's accounts. The documents effecting these payments were documents created in the course of the company's business. The fact that the payments were corrupt would not prevent the documents for effecting payment (still less copies kept for accounting purposes) being documents created in the course of the company's business. The company's book-keepers and accountants and the revenue authority would already look upon them as such. It was reasonable for the court to infer that these were all documents created by the company's officers in the course of business. The information contained in the document was that money had been paid by means of the originals to one of the intermediaries. That must have been information within the personal knowledge of the creator of the document, whether that was the accounts clerk who prepared the document or, more probably, the officer of the company who signed it. Again, in our judgment, the trial judge was entitled to infer this from the documents themselves ...[14]

Criminal Justice Act 1988

27   Where a statement contained in a document is admissible as evidence in criminal proceedings, it may be proved –

(a) by the production of that document; or

(b) (whether or not that document is still in existence) by the production of a copy of that document, or of the material part of it, authenticated in such manner as the court may approve; and it is immaterial for the purposes of this subsection how many removes there are between a copy and the original.

28(1) Nothing in this Part of this Act shall prejudice –

(a) the admissibility of a statement not made by a person while giving oral evidence in court which is admissible otherwise than by virtue of this Part of this Act; or

(b) any power of a court to exclude at its discretion a statement admissible by virtue of this Part of this Act.

(2)   Schedule 2 to this Act shall have effect for the purpose of supplementing this Part of this Act.

SCHEDULE 2

DOCUMENTARY EVIDENCE – SUPPLEMENTARY

1   Where a statement is admitted as evidence in criminal proceedings by virtue of Part II of this Act –

(a) any evidence which, if the person making the statement had been called as a witness, would have been admissible as relevant to his credibility as a witness shall be admissible for that purpose in those proceedings;

(b) evidence may, with the leave of the court, be given of any matter which, if that person had been called as a witness, could have been put to him in cross-examination as relevant to his credibility as a witness but which evidence could not have been adduced by the cross-examining party; and

(c) evidence tending to prove that that person, when before or after making the statement, made (whether orally or not) some other statement which

---

14.   [1995] 2 Cr App R 523.

is inconsistent with it shall be admissible for the purpose of showing that he has contradicted himself ...

3   In estimating the weight, if any, to be attached to such a statement regard shall be had to all the circumstances from which any inference can reasonably be drawn as to its accuracy or otherwise.

4   Without prejudice to the generality of any enactment conferring power to make them –

(a) Crown Court Rules;

(b) Criminal Appeal Rules; and

(c) rules under section 144 of the Magistrates' Courts Act 1980,

may make such provision as appears to the authority making any of them to be necessary or expedient for the purposes of Part II of this Act.

5(1) In Part II of this Act –

'document' means anything in which information of any description is recorded;

'copy', in relation to a document, means anything onto which information recorded in the document has been copied, by whatever means and whether directly or indirectly; and

'statement' means any representation of fact, however made ...

6.   In Part II of this Act 'confession' has the meaning assigned to it by section 82 of the Police and Criminal Evidence Act 1984.

Police and Criminal Evidence Act 1984

69(1) In any proceedings, a statement in a document produced by a computer shall not be admissible as evidence of any fact stated therein unless it is shown –

(a) that there are no reasonable grounds for believing that the statement is inaccurate because of improper use of the computer;

(b) that at all material times the computer was operating properly, or if not, that any respect in which it was not operating properly or was out of operation was not such as to affect the production of the document or the accuracy of its contents; and

(c) that any relevant conditions specified in rules of court under subsection (2) are satisfied.

Civil Evidence Act 1995

Admissibility of hearsay evidence

1 (1) In civil proceedings evidence shall not be excluded on the ground that it is hearsay.

(2)   In this Act –

(a) 'hearsay' means a statement made otherwise than by a person while giving oral evidence in the proceedings which is tendered as evidence of the matters stated; and

(b) references to hearsay include hearsay of whatever degree.

(3)   Nothing in this Act affects the admissibility of evidence admissible apart from this section.

(4) The provisions of sections 2 to 6 (safeguards and supplementary provisions relating to hearsay evidence) do not apply in relation to hearsay evidence admissible apart from this section, notwithstanding that it may also be admissible by virtue of this section.

Safeguards in relation to hearsay evidence

2 (1) A party proposing to adduce hearsay evidence in civil proceedings shall, subject to the following provisions of this section, give to the other party or parties to the proceedings –

(a) such notice (if any) of that fact; and

(b) on request, such particulars of or relating to the evidence,

as is reasonable and practicable in the circumstances for the purpose of enabling him or them to deal with any matters arising from its being hearsay.

(2) Provision may be made by rules of court –

(a) specifying classes of proceedings or evidence in relation to which subsection (1) does not apply; and

(b) as to the manner in which (including the time within which) the duties imposed by that subsection are to be complied with in the cases where it does apply.

(3) Subsection (1) may also be excluded by agreement of the parties; and compliance with the duty to give notice may in any case be waived by the person to whom notice is required to be given.

(4) A failure to comply with subsection (1), or with rules under subsection (2)(b), does not affect the admissibility of the evidence but may be taken into account by the court –

(a) in considering the exercise of its powers with respect to the course of proceedings and costs; and

(b) as a matter adversely affecting the weight to be given to the evidence in accordance with section 4.

3 Rules of court may provide that where a party to civil proceedings adduces hearsay evidence of a statement made by a person and does not call that person as a witness, any other party to the proceedings may, with the leave of the court, call that person as a witness and cross-examine him on the statement as if he had been called by the first-mentioned party and as if the hearsay statement were his evidence in chief.

4 (1) In estimating the weight (if any) to be given to hearsay evidence in civil proceedings the court shall have regard to any circumstances from which any inference can reasonably be drawn as to the reliability or otherwise of the evidence.

(2) Regard may be had, in particular, to the following –

(a) whether it would have been reasonable and practicable for the party by whom the evidence was adduced to have produced the maker of the original statement as a witness;

(b) whether the original statement was made contemporaneously with the occurrence or existence of the matters stated;

(c) whether the evidence involves multiple hearsay;

(d) whether any person involved had any motive to conceal or misrepresent matters;

(e) whether the original statement was an edited account, or was made in collaboration with another or for a particular purpose;

(f) whether the circumstances in which the evidence is adduced as hearsay are such as to suggest an attempt to prevent proper evaluation of its weight.

Supplementary provisions as to hearsay evidence

5 (1) Hearsay evidence shall not be admitted in civil proceedings if or to the extent that it is shown to consist of, or to be proved by means of, a statement made by a person who at the time he made the statement was not competent as a witness.

For this purpose 'not competent as a witness' means suffering from such mental or physical infirmity, or lack of understanding, as would render a person incompetent as a witness in civil proceedings; but a child shall be treated as competent as a witness if he satisfies the requirements of section 96(2)(a) and (b) of the Children Act 1989 (conditions for reception of unsworn evidence of child).

(2) Where in civil proceedings hearsay evidence is adduced and the maker of the original statement, or of any statement relied upon to prove another statement, is not called as a witness –

(a) evidence which if he had been so called would be admissible for the purpose of attacking or supporting his credibility as a witness is admissible for that purpose in the proceedings; and

(b) evidence tending to prove that, whether before or after he made the statement, he made any other statement inconsistent with it is admissible for the purpose of showing that he had contradicted himself.

Provided that evidence may not be given of any matter of which, if he had been called as a witness and had denied that matter in cross-examination, evidence could not have been adduced by the cross-examining party.

6 (1) Subject as follows, the provisions of this Act as to hearsay evidence in civil proceedings apply equally (but with any necessary modifications) in relation to a previous statement made by a person called as a witness in the proceedings.

(2) A party who has called or intends to call a person as a witness in civil proceedings may not in those proceedings adduce evidence of a previous statement made by that person, except –

(a) with the leave of the court; or

(b) for the purpose of rebutting a suggestion that his evidence has been fabricated.

This shall not be construed as preventing a witness statement (that is, a written statement of oral evidence which a party to the proceedings intends to lead) from being adopted by a witness in giving evidence or treated as evidence.

(3) Where in the case of civil proceedings section 3, 4 or 5 of the Criminal Procedure Act 1865 applies, which make provision as to –

(a) how far a witness may be discredited by the party producing him;

(b) the proof of contradictory statements made by a witness; and

(c) cross-examination as to previous statements in writing,

this Act does not authorise the adducing of evidence of a previous inconsistent or contradictory statement otherwise than in accordance with those sections.

This is without prejudice to any provision made by rules of court under section 3 above (power to call witness for cross-examination on hearsay statement).

(4) Nothing in this Act affects any of the rules of law as to the circumstances in which, where a person called as a witness in civil proceedings is cross-examined on a document used by him to refresh his memory, that document may be made evidence in the proceedings.

(5) Nothing in this section shall be construed as preventing a statement of any description referred to above from being admissible by virtue of section 1 as evidence of the matters stated.

7(1) The common law rule effectively preserved by section 9(1) and (2)(a) of the Civil Evidence Act 1968 (admissibility of admissions adverse to a party) is superseded by the provisions of this Act.

(2) The common law rules effectively preserved by section 9(1) and (2)(b) to (d) of the Civil Evidence Act 1968, that is, any rule of law whereby in civil proceedings –

(a) published works dealing with matters of a public nature (for example, histories, scientific works, dictionaries and maps) are admissible as evidence of facts of a public nature stated in them;

(b) public documents (for example, public registers, and returns made under public authority with respect to matters of public interest) are admissible as evidence of facts stated in them; or

(c) records (for example, the records of certain courts, treaties, Crown grants, pardons and commissions) are admissible as evidence of facts stated in them,

shall continue to have effect.

(3) The common law rules effectively preserved by section 9(3) and (4) of the Civil Evidence Act 1968, that is, any rule of law whereby in civil proceedings –

(a) evidence of a person's reputation is admissible for the purpose of proving his good or bad character; or

(b) evidence of reputation or family tradition is admissible –

(i) for the purpose of proving or disproving pedigree or the existence of a marriage; or

(ii) for the purpose of proving or disproving the existence of any public or general right or of identifying any person or thing,

shall continue to have effect in so far as they authorise the court to treat such evidence as proving or disproving that matter.

Where any such rule applies, reputation or family tradition shall be treated for the purposes of this Act as a fact and not as a statement or multiplicity of statements about the matter in question.

(4) The words in which a rule of law mentioned in this section is described are intended only to identify the rule and shall not be construed as altering it in any way.

Other matters

8 (1) Where a statement contained in a document is admissible as evidence in civil proceedings, it may be proved –

(a) by the production of that document; or

(b) whether or not that document is still in existence, by the production of a copy of that document or of the material part of it,

authenticated in such manner as the court may approve.

(2) It is immaterial for this purpose how many removes there are between a copy and the original.

9 (1) A document which is shown to form part of the records of a business or public authority may be received in evidence in civil proceedings without further proof.

(2) A document shall be taken to form part of the records of a business or public authority if there is produced to the court a certificate to that effect signed by an officer of the business or authority to which the records belong.

For this purpose –

(a) a document purporting to be a certificate signed by an officer of a business or public authority shall be deemed to have been duly given by such an officer and signed by him; and

(b) a certificate shall be treated as signed by a person if it purports to bear a facsimile of his signature.

(3) The absence of an entry in the records of a business or public authority may be proved in civil proceedings by affidavit of an officer of the business or authority to which the records belong.

(4) In this section –

'records' means records in whatever form;

'business' includes any activity regularly carried on over a period of time, whether for profit or not, by any body (whether corporate or not) or by an individual;

'officer' includes any person occupying a responsible position in relation to the relevant activities of the business or public authority or in relation to its records; and

'public authority' includes any public or statutory undertaking, any government department and any person holding office under Her Majesty.

(5) The court may, having regard to the circumstances of the case, direct that all or any of the above provisions of this section do not apply in relation to a particular document or record, or description of documents or records.

[...]

General

11 In this Act 'civil proceedings' means civil proceedings, before any tribunal, in relation to which the strict rules of evidence apply, whether as a matter of law or by agreement of the parties.

References to 'the court' and 'rules of court' shall be construed accordingly.

12 (1) Any power to make rules of court regulating the practice or procedure of the court in relation to civil proceedings includes power to make such provision as may be necessary or expedient for carrying into effect the provisions of this Act.

(2) Any rules of court made for the purposes of this Act as it applies in relation to proceedings in the High Court apply, except in so far as their operation is excluded by agreement, to arbitration proceedings to which this Act applies, subject to such modifications as may be appropriate.

Any question arising as to what modifications are appropriate shall be determined, in default of agreement, by the arbitrator or umpire, as the case may be.

13   In this Act –

'civil proceedings' has the meaning given by section 11 and 'court' and 'rules of court' shall be construed in accordance with that section;

'document' means anything in which information of any description is recorded, and 'copy', in relation to a document, means anything onto which information recorded in the document has been copied, by whatever means and whether directly or indirectly;

'hearsay' shall be construed in accordance with section 1(2);

'oral evidence' includes evidence which, by reason of a defect of speech or hearing, a person called as a witness gives in writing or by signs;

'the original statement', in relation to hearsay evidence, means the underlying statement (if any) by –

(a) in the case of evidence of fact, a person having personal knowledge of that fact; or

(b) in the case of evidence of opinion, the person whose opinion it is; and

(c) 'statement' means any representation of fact or opinion, however made.

[...]

SCHEDULE 1

CONSEQUENTIAL AMENDMENTS

[...]

Police and Criminal Evidence Act 1984 (c 60)

9 (1) The Police and Criminal Evidence Act 1984 is amended as follows.

(2)   In section 72(1) (interpretation of provisions relating to documentary evidence), for the definition of 'copy' and 'statement' substitute –

'"copy", in relation to a document, means anything onto which information recorded in the document has been copied, by whatever means and whether directly or indirectly, and "statement" means any representation of fact, however made; and'.

(3)   In section 118(1) (general interpretation), in the definition of 'document', for 'has the same meaning as in Part I of the Civil Evidence Act 1968' substitute 'means anything in which information of any description is recorded'.

[...]

Criminal Justice Act 1988 (c 33)

12   In Schedule 2 to the Criminal Justice Act 1988 (supplementary provisions as to documentary evidence), for paragraph 5 (application of interpretation provisions) substitute –

'5 (1) In Part II of this Act –

"document" means anything in which information of any description is recorded:

"copy", in relation to a document, means anything onto which information recorded in the document has been copied, by whatever means and whether directly or indirectly; and

"statement" means any representation of fact, however made.

(2) For the purposes of Part II of this Act evidence which, by reason of a defect of speech or hearing, a person called as a witness gives in writing or by signs shall be treated as given orally.'

[...]

SCHEDULE 2

REPEALS

Chapter	Short title	Extent of repeal
1938 c 28	Evidence Act 1938	Sections 1 and 2. Section 6(1) except the words from 'Proceedings' to 'references'. Section 6(2)(b).
1968 c 64	Civil Evidence Act 1968	Part I.
1971 c 33	Armed Forces Act 1971	Section 26.
1972 c 30	Civil Evidence Act 1972	Section 1. Section 2(1) and (2). In section 2(3)(b), the words from 'by virtue of section 2' to 'out-of-court statements'. In section 3(1), the words 'Part I of the Civil Evidence Act 1968 or'. In section 6(3), the words ' 1 and', in both places where they occur.

CHAPTER 6

HAZARDOUS EVIDENCE

All evidence, without exception, is hazardous. There are several reasons for this.

The first is that all evidence emerges as a result of some sort of selection. One kind may be loosely described as 'natural selection'. Not all the evidence that is relevant to a particular inquiry will have survived. Witnesses may have died; documents may have been destroyed; the physical features of a building may have been altered. Another sort of selection is 'human selection'. In any investigation someone has to gather the evidence that has survived. But to gather effectively you have to be intelligent enough to recognise what may be significant, and honest enough to do the job without preconceived ideas of what the outcome of the investigation should be. Natural selection and human frailty between them ensure that no jury ever sees more than a part of the whole picture, and that part may be a very small, misleading one.[1]

Another reason for the hazardous nature of evidence is that too much has to be taken on trust. It is not always appreciated that the only direct experience upon which a tribunal of fact can depend in a legal inquiry is its perception of witnesses testifying in the witness-box, and perhaps also the perceptions which it experiences from its own examination of an item of real evidence. In relation to a testifying witness two difficulties arise. The first comes from uncertainty as to whether the witness can trust the evidence of his own senses. He may believe that he saw the defendant stab the victim, but what guarantee has he that things were not otherwise? The second difficulty comes from the fact that the jury has to rely on the witness for an insight into what happened on the occasion under investigation. But all the jury can perceive is the witness in the box giving evidence. What is their justification for inferring from the witness's testimony that the defendant did in fact stab the victim?

A third reason for the hazardous nature of evidence is that, save for some items of real evidence, it is presented through the medium of language. But language is notoriously ambiguous. 'Words ... may be easily misunderstood by a dull man. They may easily be misconstrued by a knave. What was spoken metaphorically may be apprehended literally. What was spoken ludicrously may be apprehended seriously. A particle, a tense, a mood, an emphasis, may make the whole difference between guilt and innocence.'[2] But more than this, the adversary system adopted in our courts tends to perpetuate ambiguity. One of the earliest lessons learned by a student of advocacy is how to avoid giving a witness whom he is cross-examining a chance to explain his testimony. Closed, leading questions which require a 'yes' or 'no' answer are recommended. These may be good trial tactics, but they are ill-designed for the recovery of truth.[3]

---

1. *Cf* EH Carr, 'The Historian and His Facts', in *What is History?* 2nd edn, RW Davies (ed) (Penguin Books, 1987).

2. Lord Macaulay, *The History of England from the Accession of James II* (London: Longmans, Green, and Co, 1880) vol 2, chap 5, p 161.

3. See, eg Marcus Stone, *Cross-Examination in Criminal Trials* (London: Butterworths, 1988), p 107; Andy Boon, *Advocacy* (London: Cavendish Publishing Limited, 1993), pp 113-14. Cf Jenny McEwan, *Evidence and the Adversarial Process: the Modern Law* (Oxford: Blackwell Business, 1992), pp 16-19.

Politicians and lawyers have generally turned a blind eye to these fundamental defects. Attempts to make verdicts a little more reliable have been made only erratically, and on a piecemeal basis. This chapter deals with attempts that have been made:

- to remove the hazards involved in the selection by police and prosecuting authorities of evidence to be used against defendants in criminal trials;
- to control the way in which juries think about evidence which at various times has been thought to be particularly unreliable.

From the first of these there developed a duty on the prosecution to disclose to the defence matters which come to light during their investigations and which might assist the defence case. The second kind of attempts gave rise to law which compelled judges to warn juries in a particular way when they had to consider certain types of evidence, or evidence from certain types of witnesses.

The prosecution's duty of disclosure

In 1981 the Attorney General issued guidelines to improve the existing practice of disclosure by the Crown. But these guidelines do not have the force of law. The law of disclosure is that laid down by the judge, in decided cases, and today the guidelines fail to reflect the law in a number of important respects. Their value as a set of instructions to prosecutors has thus largely been eroded by important new developments. For the status of the guidelines and a summary of the current law on disclosure, see *Brown* (1995) below.

Mandatory warnings to the jury

In the 18th century, when the beginnings of our modern law of evidence can be perceived, both prosecution and defence were often unrepresented by counsel, and the judge played a much larger part in criminal cases than he did in the 19th century and later. In particular, judges had a greater control over juries' deliberations. Summings-up could contain much more of the judge's opinion than would now be thought proper. Where it appeared that a deliberation was likely to be short the jury would often not leave the jury-box, and this could provide an opportunity for informal dialogue with the judge about the evidence. Even if a jury returned a verdict with which the judge disagreed, he could persuade them to reconsider.

In time this informal procedure gave way to a system more like the one we are used to today, though there was one major difference: until 1898 there was no general right for a defendant to testify in his own defence. Prosecution and defence came increasingly to be represented by counsel, possibly because of an increase in the size of the Bar, and the judge's control over the jury's deliberations slackened. But because jurors were free to weigh the evidence without judicial intervention, it became more necessary to warn them during summing-up about the weight to be attached to certain types of witness and testimony, and of the danger in convicting on the basis of such evidence without some independent support. Warnings were thought to be necessary in three main cases: those involving the evidence of children, of accomplices, and of complainants in cases where a sexual crime was alleged.

For a long time the manner in which a warning was given, and even whether a warning was given at all, was a matter solely for the trial judge's discretion. But when the Court of Criminal Appeal was set up in 1907, discretionary practices tended to develop into rigid rules of law. Before very long a highly complex law of corroboration had developed. Eventually it was thought to be so unsatisfactory that Parliament very largely abolished it in the Criminal Justice Act 1988 s 34(2) and in the Criminal Justice and Public Order Act 1994 s 32.

Alongside the strict law of corroboration there had also developed a less formal body of law about warnings that should be given to a jury where a witness might be unreliable even though he did not fall within the limited classes to which corroboration law applied. Thus it was held that an informal warning should be given where witnesses had a purpose of their own to serve in giving evidence, or suffered from mental disorder.[4] This body of law remains unaffected by the statutory provisions abolishing most of the old corroboration law. But it is unlikely now to have an independent existence. In *Makanjuola* (1995) the Court of Appeal emphasised the wide discretion now possessed by trial judges to adapt warnings about the testimony of any particular witness to the circumstances of the case. It is possible that the old, less formal law may be *suggestive* in considering whether a judge should now give any warning to the jury. What is clear is that if he decides in his discretion to give a warning, the exercise of that discretion will only exceptionally be reviewed by the Court of Appeal. *Makanjuola* has also been helpful in killing the notion that the old law about corroboration might still apply once the judge had decided to give a discretionary warning.

There remains one type of evidence where a warning is required which is still governed by a rule-based rather than a discretionary system. Identification evidence which falls within the principles set out in *Turnbull* (1977) and subsequent cases must be the subject of a particular type of judicial warning in the summing-up.

Code D of the current (1995) Codes of Practice made under the Police and Criminal Evidence Act 1984 is likely to be relevant in any problem involving identification. The whole of the Code is important, and you should pay special attention to Annex A (identification parades) and Annex D (showing photographs).

If there has been a breach of the Code, you must be able to advise on the likely consequences. Remember the following:

* What allows the court to look at the provisions of the Code, and what makes them relevant. See s 67(11) of the of the Police and Criminal Evidence Act 1984.

* If the quality of the identification evidence is poor and there is no other evidence to support it, the jury should be directed to acquit: *Turnbull* (1977). Thus the code-breach may so weaken the identification evidence that a submission of no case to answer will be successful.

---

4. *Beck* [1982] 1 WLR 461; *Spencer* [1987] AC 128. See The Law Commission, *Corroboration of Evidence in Criminal Trials* (1991, Cm 1620), Appendix C.

- The evidence may be excluded under s 78 of PACE 1984.

Finally, you should note that there remain two cases where a conviction cannot be secured without corroboration: see the Treason Act 1795 s 1 and the Perjury Act 1911 s 13. In these cases the old law about what amounts to corroboration will apply.

THE PROSECUTION'S DUTY OF DISCLOSURE

In 1981 the Attorney General issued guidelines which covered amongst other subjects, the prosecution's duty to disclose unused material to the defence. This covered, for example, all witness statements and documents not included in the committal bundles served on the defence and the unedited versions of any edited statements included in the committal bundles. The status of the guidelines and their interaction with the common law as it had been developed since 1981 was the subject of discussion in *Brown* (1995). In *Turner* (1995) Lord Taylor CJ stated principles governing the situation arising where the defence request details relating to an informant.

R v Brown **(1995, Court of Appeal)**

Steyn LJ: ...

The Attorney General's guidelines

The guidelines were issued in 1981. The Attorney General's objective was no doubt to improve the existing practice of disclosure by the Crown. That was a laudable objective. But the Attorney General was not trying to make law, and it was certainly beyond his power to do so ...

In fairness to the Attorney General at the time, and to his successors, it must be acknowledged that the guidelines were not issued on the basis that the guidelines established the law. But unfortunately some misunderstood the function of the guidelines. Surprisingly, this misunderstanding extended to the Royal Commission on Criminal Justice. The report (Cm 2263) states at p 91, n 22: 'The guidelines, although not statutory, to all intents and purposes have the force of law.'

That is plainly wrong. The guidelines are mainly a set of instructions to Crown Prosecution Service lawyers and prosecuting counsel ...

Judged simply as a set of instructions to prosecutors, the guidelines would be unobjectionable if they exactly matched the contours of the common law duty of non-disclosure. If they set higher standards of disclosure than the common law, that would equally be unobjectionable. But if the guidelines, judged by the standards of today, reduce the common law duties of the Crown and thus abridge the common law rights of a defendant, they must be *pro tanto* unlawful.

That is not to say that the guidelines have not served a useful purpose in the past. They improved the consistency in decision-making of prosecutors and set minimum standards of fairness at a time when there was a conspicuous lack of clarity about the common law duty of disclosure. But today the guidelines do not conform to the requirements of the law of disclosure in a number of critically important respects. First, the judgment in *Ward* established that it is for the court, not prosecuting counsel, to decide on disputed questions as to disclosable materials and on any asserted legal ground to withhold production of relevant material ... [T]here is no hint in the guidelines of the primacy of the court in deciding on issues of disclosure. On the contrary, paragraphs 7 to 9 of the guidelines indicate that it is for prosecuting counsel to determine doubtful cases and not for the judge. Paragraph 13 provides that only if the defendant is unrepresented should the judge 'be consulted' in a doubtful case. *Ward* (1993) is a landmark case precisely because it extended the rule of law, of which the courts must be the arbiter, to this important branch of law. Secondly, the guidelines are not an exhaustive statement of the Crown's common law duty of disclosure: *Ward* (*supra*). To that extent, too, the guidelines are out of date. Thirdly, the guidelines were drafted before major developments in the field of public interest immunity. Again, in paragraph 6 the guidelines are cast in the form of a prosecutor's discretion. That discretion applies when: '6(v) The statement is, to a greater or lesser extent, "sensitive" and for this reason it is not in the public interest to disclose it.'

Much of what is listed as 'sensitive material' is no doubt covered by public interest immunity. But not everything so listed is covered by public interest immunity. Thus paragraph 6(v)(g) lists as sensitive material the case where: 'It contains details of private delicacy to the maker and/or might create risk of domestic strife.'

Such trivial grounds could not possibly support a legal objection to the production of documents which are relevant and may exculpate a defendant ... The concept of sensitivity *simpliciter* surely has no place in this particular corner of the law. Subject to statutory exceptions, such as section 9 of the Interception of Communications Act 1985, the focus should be on the question whether there is a legal objection to disclosure rooted in the preservation of the public interest as balanced against the interests of the defendant.

These remarks about the *Attorney General's Guidelines* are not intended to be exhaustive of divergences between the guidelines and the common law. However, they show that the value of the guidelines as a set of instructions to prosecutors has largely been eroded by major legal developments, and it is in the public interest that this reality should be squarely faced and addressed. Only in this way can progress be made in this important area of the law.

The common law duty of disclosure

It is to the common law that the criminal justice system must turn to provide the framework of the rules which govern disclosure by the Crown. It is, however, necessary to place the common law rules in their proper context. The objective of the criminal justice system is the control of crime, but in a civilised society that objective cannot be pursued in disregard of other values. That everybody who comes before our courts is entitled to a fair trial is axiomatic. Lord Wilberforce stated in *Raymond v Honey* (1983) that the right of every citizen to unimpeded access to a court is a basic right. Similarly, the right of every accused to a fair trial is a basic or fundamental right. That means that under our unwritten constitution those rights are regarded as deserving of special attention by the courts. However, in our adversarial system, in which the police and prosecution control the investigatory process, an accused's right to fair disclosure is an inseparable part of his right to a fair trial. That is the framework in which the development of common law rules about disclosure by the Crown must be seen.

The first question is to determine the extent of the Crown's duty of disclosure. In *Keane* (1994), the Lord Chief Justice adopted the test suggested by Jowitt J in *Melvin and Dingle*, December 20, 1993, unreported. The learned judge said: 'I would judge to be material in the realm of disclosure that which can be seen on a sensible appraisal by the prosecution: (1) to be relevant or possibly relevant to an issue in the case; (2) to raise or possibly raise a new issue whose existence is not apparent from the evidence the prosecution proposes to use; (3) to hold out a real (as opposed to fanciful) prospect of providing a lead on evidence which goes to (1) or (2).'

That is a test which we would also adopt. It might be helpful, however, if we added a few comments under two headings. In the first place the phrase 'an issue in the case' must not be construed in the fairly narrow way in which it is used in a civil case. It must be given a broad interpretation. This distinction results in an important difference in the duty to give discovery in a civil case and the duty of disclosure of the Crown in a criminal case. In a civil case a party is not entitled to discovery in respect of the credit of a party or a witness: *Ballantine (George) and Sons Ltd v FER Dixon and Sons Ltd* (1974). However, in a criminal case, the Crown is under a duty to give disclosure of significant material which may affect the credibility of a prosecution witness. Three examples will be sufficient. It is the principal reason for the rule that the Crown is obliged to disclose previous statements of prosecution witnesses ... Another example is the disclosability of a request for a reward by a prosecution witness: *Taylor*, June 11 1993, unreported; *Rasheed, The Times*, May 20 1994. The most important illustration is, however, the rule that the prosecution is obliged to disclose previous convictions of a prosecution witness. In an important judgment in *Wilson v Police* (1992), the Court of Appeal of New Zealand considered what convictions of a prosecution witness must be disclosed. Giving the judgment of the court Cooke P held: 'As to the kind of conviction within the scope of the duty, the test must be whether a reasonable jury or other tribunal of fact could regard it as tending to shake confidence in the reliability of the witness.'

That test may be capable of being applied to other collateral material which could affect the credibility of a prosecution witness.

That brings us to the second observation which we wish to make about Jowitt J's formulation of the duty of disclosure. Usually the material will be in documentary form and it does not matter whether it is a statement, a report, a memorandum, a note or any other kind of document. What matters is the relevance of the information contained in it. Sometimes relevant information may be received orally by the police. It is certainly good practice to make a written record of such information which would then be disclosable: see the Director of Public Prosecution's Guidance to Chief Constables on Disclosure of Unused Material, August 1992, paragraph 9. Conceivably cases can arise where there is no written record of the relevant information; for example, oral information that a witness who purported to identify an attacker by the colour of his clothes is partly colour-blind. Counsel concedes on behalf of the Crown Prosecution Service that in principle the duty of disclosure applies equally to written and oral statements. In our judgment that concession was rightly made ...

Finally, there is the important subject of public interest immunity in criminal proceedings. This branch of the law is not yet fully developed. It is, however, better that the law should be developed on a case by case basis in the context of an intense focus on particular practical problems ... For the present purposes it is sufficient to state four propositions which are now clearly established. First, it is for the court to rule on the question of immunity and that necessarily involves the court studying the material for which immunity is claimed. Secondly, the judge must always perform a balancing exercise, taking into account the public interest and the interests of the defendant. Thirdly, in *Keane (supra)*, the Lord Chief Justice explained how this balancing exercise is to be reconciled with a defendant's fundamental right to a fair trial: 'If the disputed material may prove the defendant's innocence or avoid a miscarriage of justice, then the balance comes down resoundingly in favour of disclosing it.'

Fourthly, even if the trial judge initially decided against disclosure, he is under a continuous duty, in the light of the way in which the trial develops, to keep that decision under review. Prosecuting counsel, as a minister of justice, must inform himself fully about the content of any disputed material so that he is in a position to invite the judge to reassess the situation if the previous denial of the material arguably becomes untenable in the light of developments in the trial ...[5]

R v Turner (1995, Court of Appeal)

Lord Taylor CJ: ... Coming to the balancing exercise which the learned judge has to conduct on such an application, we refer again to *Keane* (1994), where the principles are set out. [T]he judgment states: 'If the disputed material may prove the defendant's innocence or avoid a miscarriage of justice, then the balance comes down resoundingly in favour of disclosing it.'

[T]he judgment continues: '... when the court is seized of the material, the judge has to perform the balancing exercise by having regard on the one hand to the weight of the public interest in non-disclosure. On the other hand, he must consider the importance of the documents to the issues of interest to the defence, present and potential, so far as they have been disclosed to him or he can foresee them.'

Since *Ward* (1993) there has been an increasing tendency for defendants to seek disclosure of informants' names and roles, alleging that those details are essential to the defence. Defences that the accused has been set up, and duress, which used at one time to be rare, have multiplied. We wish to alert judges to the need to scrutinise applications for disclosure of details about informants with very great care. They will need to be astute to see that assertions of a need to know such details, because they are essential to the running of the defence, are justified. If they are not so justified, then the judge will need to adopt a robust approach in declining to order disclosure. Clearly, there is a distinction between cases in which the circumstances raise no reasonable possibility that information about the informant will bear upon the issues and cases where it will. Again, there will be cases where the informant is an informant and no more; other cases where he may have participated in the events constituting, surrounding, or following the crime. Even when the informant has participated, the judge will need to consider whether his role so impinges on an issue of interest to the defence, present or potential, as to make disclosure necessary ...

It is sufficient for us to say that in this case we are satisfied that the information concerning the informant showed a participation in the events concerning this crime which, coupled with the way in which the defence was raised from the very first moment by the defendant when he said that he was being set up, gave rise to the need for the defence to be aware of the identity of the informant and his role in this matter. We, therefore, conclude that if one applies the principle which has been quoted from *Keane* to the facts of the present case, there could only be one answer to the question as to whether the details concerning the informer were so important to the issues of interest to the defence, present or

---

5.   [1995] 1 Cr App R 191.

potential, that the balance which the learned judge had to strike came down firmly in favour of disclosure ...[6]

DISCRETIONARY WARNINGS TO THE JURY

In *Beck* (1982) the Court of Appeal acknowledged the existence, quite apart from the law then governing corroboration, of an 'obligation upon a judge to advise a jury to proceed with caution where there is material to suggest that a witness's evidence may be tainted by an improper motive'. As to the strength of the advice, the court said that it 'must vary according to the facts of the case'. Examples of evidence that might support the testimony of a witness in respect of whom such a warning has been given can be found in earlier cases where a *Beck* warning was given, and also in cases decided under the old corroboration law. But it should be remembered that the latter are only illustrative and that the strict rules of corroboration no longer apply: see *Makanjuola* (1995).

R v Lillyman (1896, Court for Crown Cases Reserved)

The defendant was charged with a number of sexual offences against a servant girl aged between 13 and 16 years. The complainant was called as a witness and gave evidence of the acts complained of, alleging that they had been without her consent. The prosecution also tendered evidence of a complaint made by her to her mistress, in the absence of the accused, very shortly after the commission of the acts. The question arose whether it was proper to ask about the details of what had been said by the complainant.

Hawkins J [delivering the judgment of the court]: It is necessary, in the first place, to have a clear understanding as to the principles upon which evidence of such a complaint, not on oath, nor made in the presence of the prisoner, nor forming part of the *res gestae*, can be admitted. It clearly is not admissible as evidence of the facts complained of: those facts must therefore be established, if at all, upon oath by the prosecutrix or other credible witness, and strictly speaking, evidence of them ought to be given before evidence of the complaint is admitted. The complaint can only be used as evidence of the consistency of the conduct of the prosecutrix with the story told by her in the witness-box, and as being inconsistent with her consent to that of which she complains.

It is too late now to make serious objection to the admissibility of evidence of the fact that a complaint was made, provided it was made as speedily after the acts complained of as could reasonably be expected.

We proceed to consider the second objection, which is, that the evidence of complaint should be limited to the fact that *a complaint* was made without giving any of the particulars of it. No authority binding upon us was cited during the argument, either in support of or against this objection. We must therefore determine the matter upon principle. That the *general usage* has been substantially to limit the evidence of the complaint to proof that the woman made a complaint of something done to her, and that she mentioned in connection with it the name of a particular person, cannot be denied; but it is equally true that judges of great experience have dissented from this limitation,

---

6.   [1995] 2 Cr App R 94.

and of those who have adopted the usage none have ever carefully discussed or satisfactorily expressed the grounds upon which their views have been based ...

After very careful consideration we have arrived at the conclusion that we are bound by no authority to support the existing usage of limiting evidence of the complaint to the bare fact that a complaint was made, and that reason and good sense are against our doing so. The evidence is admissible only upon the ground that it was a complaint of that which is charged against the prisoner, and can be legitimately used only for the purpose of enabling the jury to judge for themselves whether the conduct of the woman was consistent with her testimony on oath given in the witness-box negativing her consent, and affirming that the acts complained of were against her will, and in accordance with the conduct they would expect in a truthful woman under the circumstances detailed by her. The jury, and they only, are the persons to be satisfied whether the woman's conduct was so consistent or not. Without proof of her condition, demeanour, and verbal expressions, all of which are of vital importance in the consideration of that question, how is it possible for them satisfactorily to determine it? ...

It has been sometimes urged that to allow the particulars of the complaint would be calculated to prejudice the interests of the accused, and that the jury would be apt to treat the complaint as evidence of the facts complained of. Of course, if it were so left to the jury they would naturally so treat it. But it never could be legally so left; and we think it is the duty of the judge to impress upon the jury in every case that they are not entitled to make use of the complaint as any evidence whatever of those facts, or for any other purpose than that we have stated ...[7]

R v Osborne (1905, Court for Crown Cases Reserved)

The questions of law for the court were: (1) Whether the fact that a statement made by a prosecutrix to a third person immediately after the alleged indecent assault was in answer to a question from such person prevented such statement being given in evidence in accordance with the rule laid down in R v Lillyman (1896). (2) If such a statement could be given in evidence, although it was in answer to a question, did the fact that the offence charged was one where the consent of the prosecutrix was immaterial render such statement inadmissible? (3) Could such a statement be given in evidence when the prosecutrix did not state that the act charged was done against her will? ...

The judgment of the court (Lord Alverstone CJ, Kennedy, Ridley, Channel, and Phillimore JJ) was read by –

Ridley J: In this case the prisoner Osborne was tried at the Worcestershire Quarter Sessions on an indictment containing two counts: the first for indecent assault, and the second for common assault on Keziah Parkes, a girl twelve years old. It appeared that Keziah Parkes, along with a younger sister and another girl named Mary Moule, of a similar age, went to a shop kept by the prisoner for the purpose of buying chips. Two of the girls – namely, Moule and the younger sister – went out of the shop on an errand, and during their absence the alleged assault was committed by him on Keziah. She then left the shop, and on her way home met Mary Moule with her sister coming back to the shop. Mary Moule was called at the trial, and was asked when she met Keziah Parkes in the street, 'Did you speak to her?' Moule replied, 'Yes; I asked her why she did not stop for me'. The next question put to the witness was, 'What did she say?' Objection was then

7. [1896] 2 QB 167.

taken for the prisoner that the witness's answer was not admissible in evidence, but the chairman admitted the evidence. The girl's answer was as follows: 'Because she did not like the prisoner and would not go near him again, as he unbuttoned her drawers. That was all she said.' The prisoner was convicted, and the point raised for our decision is whether this ruling was right. It was contended for the prisoner that the evidence was inadmissible – first, because the answer made by the girl was not a complaint, but a statement or conversation, having been made in answer to a question; and, secondly, because, as Keziah Parkes was under the age of thirteen, her consent was not material to the charge ... It appears to us that the mere fact that the statement is made in answer to a question in such cases is not of itself sufficient to make it inadmissible as a complaint. Questions of a suggestive or leading character will, indeed, have that effect, and will render it inadmissible; but a question such as this, put by the mother or other person, 'What is the matter?' or 'Why are you crying?' will not do so. These are natural questions which a person in charge will be likely to put; on the other hand, if she were asked 'Did So-and-so' (naming the prisoner) 'assault you? ... Did he do this and that to you?' then the result would be different, and the statement ought to be rejected. In each case the decision on the character of the question put, as well as other circumstances, such as the relationship of the questioner to the complainant, must be left to the discretion of the presiding judge. If the circumstances indicate that but for the questioning there probably would have been no voluntary complaint, the answer is inadmissible. If the question merely anticipates a statement which the complainant was about to make, it is not rendered inadmissible by the fact that the questioner happens to speak first. In this particular case, we think that the chairman of quarter sessions acted rightly, and that the putting of this particular question did not render the statement inadmissible.

Upon the second point it was contended that, although under the decision of *Reg v Lillyman* the particulars of a complaint made may, in some circumstances, be given in evidence on a charge of rape, that ruling does not extend to a charge of criminal knowledge or indecent assault, where, as in the present case, consent is not legally material ... By the judgment in *Reg v Lillyman* it was decided that the complaint was admissible, not as evidence of the facts complained of, nor as being a part of the *res gestae* (which it was not), but as evidence of the consistency of the conduct of the prosecutrix with the story told by her in the witness-box, and as being inconsistent with her consent to that of which she complains. Mr Marchant [for the prisoner] argued upon this that the reasons so given were one only, and that the consistency of the complaint with the story given by the prosecutrix was material only so far as the latter alleged non-consent. If, however, that argument were sound, the words in question might have been omitted from the sentence, and it would have been sufficient to say that the complaint was admissible only and solely because it negatived consent ... [I]t appears to us that, in accordance with principle, such complaints are admissible, not merely as negativing consent, but because they are consistent with the story of the prosecutrix. In all ordinary cases, indeed, the principle must be observed which rejects statements made by any one in the prisoner's absence. Charges of this kind form an exceptional class, and in them such statements ought, under proper safeguards, to be admitted. Their consistency with the story told is, from the very nature of such cases, of special importance. Did the woman make a complaint at once? If so, that is consistent with her story. Did she not do so? That is inconsistent. And in either case the matter is important for the jury.

It is in accordance with this view that in early times it was incumbent on the woman who brought an appeal of rape to prove that while the offence was recent she raised 'hue and cry' in the neighbouring towns, and shewed her injuries and clothing to men, and that the appellee might raise as a defence the denial that she had raised the hue and cry ... A further weighty authority for the existence of this exception to an acknowledged general rule is to be found in *Hale's Pleas of the Crown*, vol i 633, where it is stated that the party ravished is to give evidence on oath; and her credibility must be left to the jury: 'For instance, if the witness be of good fame, if she presently discovered the offence, made pursuit after the offender, shewed circumstances and signs of the injury ... these and the like are concurring evidences to give greater probability to her testimony, when proved by others as well as herself. But on the other hand, if she concealed the injury for any considerable time after she had opportunity to complain ... and she had made no outcry when the fact was supposed to be done, when and where it is probable she might be heard by others; these and the like circumstances carry a strong presumption, that her testimony is false or feigned.' We think these words may be adopted as stating the law accurately, and they indicate that these complaints are to be admitted, not only because they bear on the question of consent, but also because they bear on the probability of her testimony in a case in which, without such or other corroboration, reliance might not be placed on her testimony ...

We are, at the same time, not insensible of the great importance of carefully observing the proper limits within which such evidence should be given. It is only to cases of this kind that the authorities on which our judgment rests apply; and our judgment also is to them restricted. It applies only where there is a complaint not elicited by questions of a leading and inducing or intimidating character, and only when it is made at the first opportunity after the offence which reasonably offers itself. Within such bounds, we think the evidence should be put before the jury, the judge being careful to inform the jury that the statement is not evidence of the facts complained of, and must not be regarded by them, if believed, as other than corroborative of the complainant's credibility, and, when consent is in issue, of the absence of consent. For these reasons we think the conviction should be affirmed.[8]

R v Lucas (1981, Court of Appeal)

Lord Lane CJ: ... There is, without doubt, some confusion in the authorities as to the extent to which lies may in some circumstances provide corroboration and it was this confusion which probably and understandably led the judge astray in the present case. In our judgment the position is as follows. Statements made out of court, for example, statements to the police, which are proved or admitted to be false may in certain circumstances amount to corroboration ... It accords with good sense that a lie told by a defendant about a material issue may show that the liar knew if he told the truth he would be sealing his fate ...

To be capable of amounting to corroboration the lie told out of court must first of all be deliberate. Secondly, it must relate to a material issue. Thirdly, the motive for the lie must be realisation of guilt and a fear of the truth. The jury should in appropriate cases be reminded that people sometimes lie, for example, in an attempt to bolster up a just cause, or out of shame or out of a wish to conceal disgraceful behaviour from their family. Fourthly, the statement must be clearly shown to be a lie by evidence other than that of the accomplice who is to be corroborated, that is to say by admission or by evidence from an independent witness.

8.   [1905] 1 KB 551.

As a matter of good sense it is difficult to see why, subject to the same safeguards, lies proved to have been told in court by a defendant should not equally be capable of providing corroboration ...

Providing that the lies told in court fulfil the four criteria which we have set out above, we are unable to see why they should not be available for the jury to consider in just the same way as lies told out of court ...[9]

R v Goodway (1993, Court of Appeal)

The appellant was convicted of murder. Identification had been a major issue at the trial, the appellant bearing a striking resemblance to another man called Chapman who was said by the defence to have been responsible for the commission of the offence, and not the appellant.

Lord Taylor CJ: ... The third, and in our view the most substantial, ground of appeal relates to the lies admittedly told by the appellant in the police interviews when he falsely denied ever getting close to either victim. The prosecution, we are told, relied on the lies as support for other evidence of the appellant's guilt. That evidence included blood on his clothes, but it also included identification evidence. Accordingly, the learned judge gave a *Turnbull* direction to the jury in impeccable terms (see *R v Turnbull* (1976)). Towards the end of it he said: 'Finally, is there other evidence to support the witness's identification?' After making clear that the failure of the appellant to testify could not be regarded as supporting evidence, the learned judge went on to say: 'What you have are the answers that he gave to the police in those very long and, dare I say it, sometimes rather dreary interviews ... You consider his answers that he gave and I will remind you of them (not every one of them but the substance of them), and you give them the weight you think they deserve.'

In three subsequent passages, the learned judge referred to those assertions in the interviews which the prosecution relied upon as lies. Nowhere, however, did he give any direction as to how the jury should approach the lies told by an accused.

It is well established that where lies told by the defendant are relied on by the Crown, or may be relied upon by the jury as corroboration, where that is required, or as support for identification evidence, the judge should give a direction along the lines indicated in *R v Lucas* (1981). That is to the effect that the lie must be deliberate and must relate to the material issue. The jury must be satisfied that there is no innocent motive for the lie and should be reminded that people sometimes lie, for example, in an attempt to bolster up a just cause, or out of shame, or out of a wish to conceal disgraceful behaviour. In regard to corroboration, the lie must be established by evidence other than that of the witness who is to be corroborated ...

In the present case the appellant's lies were relied upon by the Crown as support of the identification evidence and the summing up in the passages quoted encouraged the jury so to regard them. Accordingly, even on the limited basis established by *R v Turnbull* and the other authorities cited above, this was a case in which a *Lucas* direction was required. Mr Marshall-Andrews [for the appellant] submits that on that basis (which he calls his narrow proposition), the summing up was defective in a material respect and the court should therefore allow the appeal.

---

9.   [1981] QB 720.

In our judgment, he is right. We consider the omission of a *Lucas* direction was a material misdirection and in view of the conflicting evidence of identification and the strikingly similar appearance of the appellant and Chapman, this is not a case in which it would be appropriate to apply the proviso. This appeal must therefore be allowed.

However, Mr Marshall-Andrews goes further and contends for a broader proposition. He submits that a *Lucas* direction should be given wherever lies are relied upon by the Crown, or might be used by the jury to support evidence of guilt as opposed to merely reflecting on the appellant's credibility. In *Broadhurst v R* (1964) Lord Devlin, giving the advice of the Privy Council, said: 'It is very important that a jury should be carefully directed on the effect of a conclusion, if they reach it, that the accused is lying. There is a natural tendency for a jury to think that if an accused is lying, it must be because he is guilty and accordingly to convict him without more ado. It is the duty of the judge to make it clear to them that this is not so. Save in one respect, a case in which an accused gives untruthful evidence is no different from one in which he gives no evidence at all. In either case the burden remains on the prosecution to prove the guilt of the accused. But if on the proved facts two inferences may be drawn about the accused's conduct or state of mind, his untruthfulness is a factor which the jury can properly take into account as strengthening the inference of guilt. What strength it adds depends of course on all the circumstances and especially on whether there are reasons other than guilt that might account for untruthfulness. That is the sort of direction which it is at least desirable to give to a jury.'

... [I]n *R v Dehar* (1969), after citing the above passage from *Broadhurst v R*, North P went on as follows: 'We think that it follows from the cases which we have cited, that where lies constitute an important element in the chain of proof put forward by the Crown a clear direction from the trial judge is necessary. We do not say that in every case in which lies are put forward in aid of the Crown case to reinforce the other evidence it is always necessary for the trial judge to give any specific form of direction. How far a direction is necessary will depend upon circumstances. There may be ... cases where the rejection of the explanation given by the accused almost necessarily leaves the jury with no choice but to convict as a matter of logic.'

R v Dehar was followed in a number of other New Zealand cases ...

In *R v Sharp* (1993) whilst confining the strict legal requirements of a direction on lies to cases of corroboration or identification, Stuart-Smith LJ went on to say: 'Such a direction is however now commonly given and a specimen direction appears in the Judicial Studies Board guidance.' In our view, there is no reason in principle or logic for drawing a distinction between corroboration and identification cases and any other case in which lies may be relied upon in support of prosecution evidence. Accordingly, we consider Mr Marshall-Andrews' broader proposition is sound and that a *Lucas* direction should be given, save where it is otiose as indicated in *R v Dehar*, whenever lies are, or may be, relied upon as supporting evidence of the defendant's guilt ...[10]

R v Cheema (1994, Court of Appeal)

This case was concerned with the old law or corroboration. It established that a formal corroboration warning was not required where evidence from one

---

10. [1993] 4 All ER 894.

defendant supported the prosecution case against a co-defendant. However, the court noted that a less formal warning would be appropriate in such a case.

Lord Taylor CJ: ... The effect of this considerable body of case law is to show that in recent years time and again the court has reiterated that although a warning in suitable terms as to the danger of a co-defendant having an axe to grind is desirable, there is no rule of law or practice requiring a full corroboration directive ...

Accordingly, in our judgment, what is required when one defendant implicates another in evidence is simply to warn the jury of what may very often be obvious – namely that the defendant witness may have a purpose of his own to serve. That is precisely what the learned judge did in the present case. He said: 'Let me turn to co-defendant's evidence. Over the years one has one's shorthand ways of referring to it and "axes to grind" is the way I always think of this one. If you decide that the evidence of one defendant has damaged the other defendant's case, you must examine that evidence with particular care for the witness, in saying what he or she did, may have been paying more regard to his or her own interests in protecting himself or herself, than to speaking the truth. Do bear that in mind when deciding whether or not you feel able to accept what one defendant has said about another...'[11]

R v Makanjuola (1995, Court of Appeal)

Lord Taylor of Gosforth CJ: These two applications for leave to appeal raise important issues about the effect of s 32 of the Criminal Justice and Public Order Act 1994. In each case the applicant was convicted of an indecent assault on a young girl. In each it has been argued that the trial judge should have given the jury a full direction in accordance with established corroboration rules not withstanding the provisions of s 32.

On 9 May, having heard both applications together, we refused them. We now give our reasons ...

It was argued for both applicants that although the requirement to do so is abrogated by sub-s (1), the judge should still in his discretion warn the jury that it is dangerous to convict on the uncorroborated evidence of a complainant in a sexual case or of an accomplice. The underlying rationale of the corroboration rules developed in case law was that accomplices may well have purposes of their own to serve and complainants about sexual offences may lie or fantasize for unascertainable reasons or no reason at all. That rationale, it is argued, cannot evaporate overnight. So the traditional warnings to juries should continue. The statute removes the requirement to give them but the judge is still free to do so and he should.

If that were right, Parliament would have enacted s 32(1) in vain: practice would continue unchanged. It is clear that the judge does have a discretion to warn the jury if he thinks it necessary, but the use of the word 'merely' in the subsection shows that Parliament does not envisage such a warning being given just because a witness complains of a sexual offence or is an alleged accomplice.

It is further submitted that if the judge does decide a warning is necessary, he should give the jury the full old-style direction on corroboration. That means using the phrase 'dangerous to convict on the uncorroborated evidence', explaining the meaning of corroboration, identifying what evidence under the old rules is capable of being corroboration, what evidence is not so capable, and

---

11. [1994] 1 All ER 639.

the respective roles of judge and jury in this bipartite quest … It was, in our judgment, partly to escape from this tortuous exercise, which juries have found more bewildering than illuminating, that Parliament enacted s 32 …

Given that the requirement of a corroboration direction is abrogated in the terms of s 32(1), we have been invited to give guidance as to the circumstances in which, as a matter of discretion, a judge ought in summing up to a jury to urge caution in regard to a particular witness and the terms in which that should be done. The circumstances and evidence in criminal cases are infinitely variable and it is impossible to categorise how a judge should deal with them. But it is clear that to carry on giving 'discretionary' warnings generally and in the same terms as were previously obligatory would be contrary to the policy and purpose of the 1994 Act. Whether, as a matter of discretion, a judge should give any warning and if so its strength and terms must depend upon the content and manner of the witness's evidence, the circumstances of the case and the issues raised. The judge will often consider that no special warning is required at all. Where, however, the witness has been shown to be unreliable, he or she may consider it necessary to urge caution. In a more extreme case, if the witness is shown to have lied, to have made previous false complaints, or to bear the defendant some grudge, a stronger warning may be thought appropriate and the judge may suggest it would be wise to look for some supporting material before acting on the impugned witness's evidence. We stress that these observations are merely illustrative of some, not all, of the factors which judges may take into account in measuring where a witness stands in the scale of reliability and what response they should make at that level in their directions to the jury. We also stress that judges are not required to conform to any formula and this court would be slow to interfere with the exercise of discretion by a trial judge who has the advantage of assessing the manner of a witness's evidence as well as its content.

To summarise:

(1) Section 32(1) abrogates the requirement to give a corroboration direction in respect of an alleged accomplice or a complainant of a sexual offence simply because a witness falls into one of those categories.

(2) It is a matter for the judge's discretion what, if any, warning he considers appropriate in respect of such a witness, as indeed in respect of any other witness in whatever type of case . Whether he chooses to give a warning and in what terms will depend on the circumstances of the case, the issues raised and the content and quality of the witness's evidence.

(3) In some cases, it may be appropriate for the judge to warn the jury to exercise caution before acting upon the unsupported evidence of a witness. This will not be so simply because the witness is a complainant of a sexual offence nor will it necessarily be so because a witness is alleged to be an accomplice. There will need to be an evidential basis for suggesting that the evidence of the witness may be unreliable. An evidential basis does not include mere suggestions by cross-examining counsel.

(4) If any question arises as to whether the judge should give a special warning in respect of a witness, it is desirable that the question be resolved by discussion with counsel in the absence of the jury before final speeches.

(5) Where the judge does decide to give some warning in respect of a witness, it will be appropriate to do so as part of the judge's review of the evidence and his comments as to how the jury should evaluate it rather than as a set-piece legal direction.

(6) Where some warning is required, it will be for the judge to decide the strength and terms of the warning. It does not have to be invested with the whole florid regime of the old corroboration rules.

(7) It follows that we emphatically disagree with the tentative submission made by the editors of *Archbold*. Attempts to re-impose the straitjacket of the old corroboration rules are strongly to be deprecated.

(8) Finally, this court will be disinclined to interfere with a trial judge's exercise of his discretion save in a case where that exercise is unreasonable in the *Wednesbury* sense (see *Associated Provincial Picture Houses Ltd v Wednesbury Corpn* (1947)).[12]

IDENTIFICATION

R v Turnbull (1977, Court of Appeal)

On this occasion the Court of Appeal considered three different appeals together because they raised similar identification problems. The guidelines laid down are known by reference to the first-named of these appellants in the report. In fact, Mr Turnbull got no benefit from the decision because his appeal was dismissed. But the appeals in the other cases were allowed.

Lord Widgery CJ: ... Each of these appeals raises problems relating to evidence of visual identification in criminal cases. Such evidence can bring about miscarriages of justice and has done so in a few cases in recent years. The number of such cases, although small compared with the number in which evidence of visual identification is known to be satisfactory, necessitates steps being taken by the courts, including this court, to reduce that number as far as is possible. In our judgment the danger of miscarriages of justice occurring can be much reduced if trial judges sum up to juries in the way indicated in this judgment.

First, whenever the case against an accused depends wholly or substantially on the correctness of one or more identifications of the accused which the defence alleges to be mistaken, the judge should warn the jury of the special need for caution before convicting the accused in reliance on the correctness of the identification or identifications. In addition he should instruct them as to the reason for the need for such a warning and should make some reference to the possibility that a mistaken witness can be a convincing one and that a number of such witnesses can all be mistaken. Provided this is done in clear terms the judge need not use any particular form of words.

Secondly, the judge should direct the jury to examine closely the circumstances in which the identification by each witness came to be made. How long did the witness have the accused under observation? At what distance? In what light? Was the observation impeded in any way, as for example by passing traffic or a press of people? Had the witness ever seen the accused before? How often? If only occasionally, had he any special reason for remembering the accused? How long elapsed between the original observation and the subsequent identification to the police? Was there any material discrepancy between the description of the accused given to the police by the witness when first seen by them and his actual appearance? If in any case, whether it is being dealt with summarily or on

---

12. [1995] 3 All ER 730.

indictment, the prosecution have reason to believe that there is such a material discrepancy they should supply the accused or his legal advisers with particulars of the description the police were first given. In all cases if the accused asks to be given particulars of such descriptions, the prosecution should supply them. Finally, he should remind the jury of any specific weaknesses which had appeared in the identification evidence.

Recognition may be more reliable than identification of a stranger; but even when the witness is purporting to recognise someone whom he knows, the jury should be reminded that mistakes in recognition of close relatives and friends are sometimes made.

All these matters go to the quality of the identification evidence. If the quality is good and remains good at the close of the accused's case, the danger of a mistaken identification is lessened; but the poorer the quality, the greater the danger.

In our judgment when the quality is good, as for example when the identification is made after a long period of observation, or in satisfactory conditions by a relative, a neighbour, a close friend, a workmate and the like, the jury can safely be left to assess the value of the identifying evidence even though there is no other evidence to support it: provided always, however, that an adequate warning has been given about the special need for caution ...

When, in the judgment of the trial judge, the quality of the identifying evidence depends solely on a fleeting glance or on a longer observation made in difficult conditions, the situation is very different. The judge should then withdraw the case from the jury and direct an acquittal unless there is other evidence which goes to support the correctness of the identification ...

The trial judge should identify to the jury the evidence which he adjudges is capable of supporting the evidence of identification. If there is any evidence or circumstances which the jury might think was supporting when it did not have this quality, the judge should say so ...

Care should be taken by the judge when directing the jury about the support for an identification which may be derived from the fact that they have rejected an alibi. False alibis may be put forward for many reasons: an accused, for example, who has only his own truthful evidence to rely on may stupidly fabricate an alibi and get lying witnesses to support it out of fear that his own evidence will not be enough. Further, alibi witnesses can make genuine mistakes about dates and occasions like any other witnesses can. It is only when the jury is satisfied that the sole reason for the fabrication was to deceive them and there is no other explanation for it being put forward can fabrication provide any support for identification evidence. The jury should be reminded that proving the accused has told lies about where he was at the material time does not by itself prove that he was where the identifying witness says he was ...

A failure to follow these guidelines is likely to result in a conviction being quashed and will do so if in the judgment of this court on all the evidence the verdict is either unsatisfactory or unsafe ...[13]

---

13. [1977] QB 224. The importance in identification cases of giving the *Turnbull* warning has been frequently stated. It applies to recognition as well as to 'pure identification cases'. The cases in which the warning can be entirely dispensed with must be wholly exceptional, even where the defence is not based on the witness's honest mistake. See *Shand v The Queen* [1996] 1 WLR 67.

R v Christie (1914, House of Lords)

The respondent was convicted at the Middlesex sessions upon a charge of indecently assaulting a boy aged five.

At the trial the boy's mother was called and stated that on 25 July 1913 her boy went out to play in the fields at 10 o'clock in the morning and returned at 10.30; that he came back screaming and with his dress disarranged; that she took him across the fields and had a conversation with a man who was working there, and that the prisoner was fetched back. Asked whether the little boy said anything in the hearing of the prisoner, she replied, 'Yes'.

Counsel for the respondent objected to the evidence of what the little boy said and the mother was ordered to stand down until after the little boy had been called.

The little boy gave his evidence without being sworn, in accordance with s 30 of the Children Act 1908. He described the assault and identified the prisoner in court. He was asked no questions as to any previous identification and he was not cross-examined. The mother was then recalled and was again asked whether the little boy said anything in the prisoner's presence. Counsel for the respondent repeated his objection ...

The deputy chairman overruled the objection.

The mother then said that as she and her son were going towards the prisoner he said, 'That is the man, mum'; that a police constable who was on the spot asked him, 'Which man?', and made him go right up to the man and identify him; that the little boy said, 'That is the old man, mum, who' – and then he described what the prisoner did to him; that the prisoner replied, 'I am innocent'. She was not cross-examined.

The police constable was called and confirmed the mother's story. He said that the little boy went up to the prisoner and touched him on the sleeve and said, 'That is the man', describing the nature of the assault, and that the prisoner replied, 'I am innocent'. He was cross-examined, but his evidence on this point was not affected.

In the House of Lords one of the questions considered was how far the evidence of what the boy had said and done in the field could be admitted as evidence of a previous identification. This was not the main point of the appeal; counsel for Christie conceded in argument that if the statement had been limited to identification it might have been admissible. Later he said, 'If this were a mere question of identification it would not be unreasonable that someone should prove that the accuser had identified the prisoner before, but this statement goes far beyond that.' On the question of admissibility as evidence of identification various opinions were expressed. They are of some interest because of the use made of *Christie* by the defence in the more recent case of *Osbourne & Virtue* (1973). Broadly speaking, there were three different opinions.

(1) The whole of what the boy said outside the court could be given in evidence by another witness because it amounted to the fact of identification.

(2) It was improper to give such evidence without first having evidence from the boy to this effect.

(3) There was no objection to admitting the brief utterance, 'That is the man', as part of the identification, but the rest of the statement went beyond what was permissible for that purpose.

The extracts here are confined to those parts of the speeches dealing with identification.

Viscount Haldane LC: My Lords, I have had the advantage of considering the opinions which three of your Lordships are about to express. For the special reasons given by my noble and learned friends Lord Atkinson and Lord Reading I agree that the judgment of the Court of Criminal Appeal quashing the conviction should be affirmed. But the important question is not the minor one as to whether the particular direction given by the deputy chairman to the jury was open to exception on the special grounds, but whether the general law laid down in the case as to the statement of the boy alleged to have been indecently assaulted was rightly laid down. In the opinions about to be delivered by Lord Atkinson, Lord Moulton and Lord Reading the true view of the law appears to me to be expressed. The only point on which I desire to guard myself is the admissibility of the statement in question as evidence of identification. For the boy gave evidence at the trial, and if his evidence was required for the identification of the prisoner that evidence ought, in my opinion, to have been his direct evidence in the witness-box and not evidence of what he said elsewhere. On this point I share the doubt which I understand is to be expressed by my noble and learned friend Lord Moulton. Had the boy, after he had identified the accused in the dock, been asked if he had identified the accused in the field as the man who assaulted him, and answered affirmatively, then that fact might also have been proved by the policeman and the mother who saw the identification. Its relevancy is to shew that the boy was able to identify at the time and to exclude the idea that the identification of the prisoner in the dock was an afterthought or a mistake. But beyond the mere fact of such identification the examination ought not to have proceeded. Subject to this observation I concur in the judgments about to be delivered.

Lord Atkinson: ... [I]t cannot, I think, be open to doubt that if the boy had said nothing more, as he touched the sleeve of the coat of the accused, than, 'That is the man', the statement was so closely connected with the act which it accompanied, expressing, indeed, as it did, in words little if anything more than would have been implied by the gesture *simpliciter*, that it should have been admitted as part of the very act of identification itself. It is on the admissibility of the further statement made in answer to the question of the constable that the controversy arises. On the whole, I am of opinion, though not without some doubt, that this statement only amplifies what is implied by the words, 'That is the man', plus the act of touching him.

A charge had been made against the accused of the offence committed on the boy. The words, 'That is the man', must mean: 'That is the man who has done to me the thing of which he is accused.' To give the details of the charge is merely to expand, and express in words what is implied under the circumstances in the act of identification. I think, therefore, that the entire statement was admissible on these grounds, even although the boy was not asked at the trial anything about the former identification. The boy had in his evidence at the trial distinctly identified the accused. If on another occasion he had in the presence of others identified him, then the evidence of these eye witnesses is quite as truly primary evidence of what acts took place in their presence as would be the boy's evidence of what he did, and what expressions accompanied his act. It would, I think, have been more regular and proper to have examined the boy himself as to what he did on the first occasion, but the omission to do so, while the bystanders were examined on the point, does not, I think, violate the rule that the best evidence must be given. His evidence of what he did was no better in that sense than was their evidence as to what they saw him do ...

My Lords, I have been requested by my noble and learned friend Lord Parker to express his concurrence in this judgment.

Lord Moulton: ... Speaking for myself, I have great difficulty in seeing how this evidence is admissible on the ground that it is part of the evidence of identification. To prove identification of the prisoner by a person, who is, I shall assume, an adult, it is necessary to call that person as a witness. Identification is an act of the mind, and the primary evidence of what was passing in the mind of a man is his own testimony, where it can be obtained. It would be very dangerous to allow evidence to be given of a man's words and actions, in order to shew by this extrinsic evidence that he identified the prisoner, if he was capable of being called as a witness and was not called to prove by direct evidence that he had thus identified him. Such a mode of proving identification would, in my opinion, be to use secondary evidence where primary evidence was obtainable, and this is contrary to the spirit of the English rules of evidence ...

Lord Reading: ... No objection was raised by Mr Dickens, for the respondent, to the admission of the first part of the statement, namely, 'That is the man'. It implied that Christie was the man designated by the boy as the person who had committed the offence, and meant little, if anything, more than the act of touching the sleeve of Christie or pointing to him. The importance is as to the admission of the additional words, describing the various acts done by Christie. These were not necessary to complete the identification or to explain it. There was no dispute that in the presence of his mother and the police constable the boy designated Christie as the man who had committed the offence. According to the constable's evidence the additional statement was made in answer to his question to the boy, 'What did he do to you?' (Question 138.) At the trial, and before the statement was admitted, the boy identified Christie in court, and was not cross-examined. The additional statement was not required by the prosecution for the purpose of proving the act of identification by the boy. The statement cannot, in my judgment, be admitted as evidence of the state of the boy's mind when in the act of identifying Christie, as that would amount to allowing another person to give in evidence the boy's state of mind, when he was not asked, and had not said anything about it in his statement to the court.

If the prosecution required the evidence as part of the act of identification it should have been given by the boy before the prosecution closed their case. In my judgment it would be a dangerous extension of the law regulating the admissibility of evidence if your Lordships were to allow proof of statements made, narrating or describing the events constituting the offence, on the ground that they form part of or explain the act of identification, more particularly when such evidence is not necessary to prove the act, and is not given by the person who made the statement. I have found no case in which any such statement has been admitted ...

I have been requested by Lord Dunedin to say that he concurs in this judgment.[14]

R v Osbourne & Virtue (1973, Court of Appeal)

The defendants were charged with robbery. They appealed against conviction, *inter alia*, because the trial judge permitted a police inspector to give evidence that witnesses had identified the defendants at an identification parade. At trial those witnesses failed to give evidence of their earlier identifications, one of

---

14. [1914] AC 545.

them saying that she could not remember picking anyone out on an earlier occasion.

Lawton LJ [giving the judgment of the court]: ... After the interrogation the two defendants were put up for identification on an identification parade. It is necessary to say something about what happened at that parade. The two defendants had a solicitor's representative present at the parade. The parade, it would appear, was carried out strictly in accordance with the regulations relating to identification parades. No criticism of any kind has been made about the way in which the parade was conducted. Members of the staff at the South Suburban Co-operative Store attended the identification parade. A number, indeed I think the majority, failed to pick out anybody, which was not surprising, as some of the gunmen were wearing masks. Others picked out the wrong person. That again in the experience of this court in this class of case is not unusual. A few, including Mrs Brookes and Mrs Head, picked out one or more. So far as Mrs Head was concerned, the evidence at the trial clearly established that when she attended the identification parade she was in a very upset and distressed condition, which was not to be wondered at as she had been standing near her manager when he was gunned down. At one stage of the parade she nearly fainted. Unfortunately the trial did not take place until seven and a half months after the identification parade so there was a long interval of time before the two ladies whom I have mentioned went into the witness-box and were called upon once again to identify the men whom they had seen for only for moments when they were escaping from the Co-operative Store. But to return to the sequence of events immediately after the identification parade. No doubt because of the identifications made at it (which included identifications by Mrs Brookes and Mrs Head) the two defendants were duly cautioned and then charged. No further point arises with regard to the procedure carried out by the police.

At the trial, it is necessary to refer to the events at the trial, Mrs Brookes gave evidence on the first day, and she was asked in the witness-box, as all identifying witnesses are asked, whether she could pick out the man in the dock whom she had identified at the identification parade seven and a half months before. According to the summing-up, she gave this answer: she said that she did not remember that she had picked out anyone on the last parade – which may have been a somewhat surprising answer in all the circumstances – but that was what she said.

When Mrs Head was in the witness-box, according both to the summing-up and a note taken by one of the prosecuting counsel, which has been accepted in this court as an accurate note, she was very nervous, her hands were shaking, and at one stage she became emotional. According to the note which counsel made in his notebook, her voice shook when she gave some important answers. I think that it is right that I should read some extracts from counsel's note. She said that she had picked out the defendant Virtue, but a few moments later she corrected that and said, 'I didn't pick the fair man out' – that was the defendant Virtue – 'I recognised him but didn't point the finger. On another parade I spoke to the officer. I pointed to a man.' She said that she had spoken to the police inspector in charge of the parade and pointed to someone. Then she went on to say, 'I don't think the man I picked out is here today'. A moment or two later in her evidence she said again, 'The man I picked out, I don't think he is in the dock today'. She also said in cross-examination, 'I do not see anybody else here whom I recognise'. She was a very unsatisfactory witness, not because she wanted to prevaricate or be difficult, but because she was in an emotional state. When the trial judge came to sum up the case to the jury he reminded them in the clearest possible terms of the weaknesses in her evidence and left them in no doubt at all that virtually no weight of any kind should be attached to what she said in so far as she purported to identify any of the men then in the dock. That being so, on any view of this case, if the issue before this court had been whether the verdict was unsafe or unsatisfactory, it could not have been adjudged that, because of Mrs Head's evidence, it was. But that does not reflect the point which has been made by the defendant Osbourne.

That point arises in this way. After Mrs Brookes and Mrs Head had given evidence, then, as has been common for many years, the officer in charge of the parade, Chief Inspector Stevenson, was called to give evidence, and he was asked by prosecuting counsel whom Mrs Brookes and Mrs Head had pointed out. Thereupon counsel defending the defendant Osbourne objected, and the basis of his objection was that the evidence of Chief Inspector Stevenson would contradict the evidence which had been given by the two ladies. The trial judge rejected that objection and admitted the evidence. The objection has been repeated in this court ...

Now I turn to the point which was taken on behalf of the defendant Osbourne about the admissibility of Chief Inspector Stevenson's evidence. It is right that I should stress that the point was that such evidence was inadmissible. Its weight was another matter altogether and, as I have pointed out already, the trial judge advised the jury to attach little, if any, weight to Mrs Head's evidence of identification. He reminded the jury of Mrs Brookes' lapse of memory. It was strenuously argued before the trial judge and equally strenuously argued before us, that such evidence was not admissible at all and that its wrongful admission made the conviction unsafe. An analogy was drawn between the situation which arose in this case with those two ladies and the situation which can arise in the witness-box when a witness for the prosecution gives evidence which the Crown does not like. Our attention was drawn to the Criminal Law Procedure Act 1865. The situation envisaged by section 3 of the Act of 1865 did not arise in this case at all because nobody suggested that those two ladies were acting in the way envisaged by that Act, namely, adversely, or, to use the modern term, hostilely, but it was said that the trial judge allowed the prosecution to call evidence to contradict them, which is not admissible.

We do not agree that Chief Inspector Stevenson's evidence contradicted their evidence. All that Mrs Brookes had said was that she did not remember, and, as I have already indicated, that is very understandable after a delay of seven and a half months. She had, however, done something. Within four days of the robbery she had attended an identification parade. She had been told in the presence and hearing of the defendant Osbourne, as is the usual practice, what she was to do, namely, point out anybody whom she had seen at the time of the raid. She did point somebody out and it was the defendant Osbourne. One asks oneself as a matter of common sense why, when a witness has forgotten what she did, evidence should not be given by another witness with a better memory to establish what, in fact, she did when the events were fresh in her mind. Much the same situation arises with regard to Mrs Head. She said in the witness-box that she had picked somebody out. She did not think that the man she had picked out was in the court, but that again is understandable because appearances can change after seven and a half months, and if the experience of this court is anything to go by, accused persons often look much smarter in the dock than they do when they are first arrested. This court can see no reason at all in principle why evidence of that kind should not be admitted.

It was submitted that the admission of that evidence was contrary to a decision of the House of Lords in *Rex v Christie* (1914). That case has long been regarded as a difficult one to understand because the speeches of their Lordships were not directed to the same points, but this can be got from the speeches: that evidence of identification other than identification in the witness-box is admissible. All that the prosecution were seeking to do was to establish the fact of identification at the identification parades held on November 20. This court can see no reason why that evidence should not have been admitted. The court is fortified in that view by a passage in the judgment of Sachs LJ which appears in *Reg v Richardson* (1971), which was a very different case from the present case, but the principle enunciated by Sachs LJ is applicable. Sachs LJ said: 'The courts, however, must take care not to deprive themselves by new, artificial rules of practice of the best chances of learning the truth. The courts are under no compulsion unnecessarily to follow on a matter of practice the lure of the rules of logic in order to produce unreasonable results which would hinder the course of justice.'

It is pertinent to point out that in 1914 when the House of Lords came to consider *Rex v Christie* the modern practice of identity parades did not exist. The whole object of identification parades is for the protection of the suspect, and what happens at those parades is highly relevant to the establishment of the truth. It would be wrong, in the judgment of this court, to set up artificial rules of evidence, which hinder the administration of justice. The evidence was admissible ...[15]

R v Cook (1987, Court of Appeal)

The defendant was charged with robbery and indecent assault. He appealed against conviction on the ground that the trial judge erred in allowing the jury to see a photofit picture which had been made of the assailant by the victim with the assistance of a police officer.

Watkins LJ [giving the judgment of the court]: It is submitted that the judge was wrong to allow counsel for the prosecution to refer in opening to the photofit and was wrong to allow it to be introduced into evidence whilst Miss Tanswell was giving evidence-in-chief. This, he argues, constituted a material irregularity which should cause us to quash the convictions. A photofit is, he asserts, a self-serving previously consistent statement. Unlike what is said at an identification parade it does not constitute an exception to the rule against hearsay. Exceptions to the rule can only be made by statute. A photofit is not, he argues, a photograph or even similar to a photograph. It is no more than an attempted description of someone ...

We begin by stating what upon authority is in our judgment beyond dispute, namely, that Miss Tanswell when in the witness-box could have been permitted to see the photofit which she had observed being composed for the purpose of refreshing her memory ...

Using a photofit for the purpose of refreshing memory may be regarded as a step in the right direction but it cannot of itself have the effect of rendering the photofit admissible so as to enable the jury to see it. If either the hearsay rule or rule against the admission of a previous consistent statement is applicable to this situation, the evidence of photofit being, as must be acknowledged, no exception to these rules there would be no reason in our view why the submission made on

---

15. [1973] QB 678.

the appellant's behalf should not succeed. But we question whether either of those rules apply to evidence of a photofit.

The rule against hearsay is described in *Cross on Evidence*, 6th edn (1985), p 453 as one of the oldest, most complex and most confusing of the exclusion rules of evidence. The author quotes Lord Reid as having said in *Myers v Director of Public Prosecutions* (1965): 'It is difficult to make any general statement about the law of hearsay evidence which is entirely accurate.'

We agree with all that. What, however, is clear is that what was said by a prospective witness to a police officer in the absence of a defendant is hearsay and cannot, therefore, be admissible as evidence. But, admissibility of a photofit is not dependent upon a recital by a witness when giving evidence of what that person said to the police officer composing it. So that aspect of hearsay need no further be considered.

The rule is said to apply not only to assertions made orally, but to those made in writing or by conduct. Never, so far as we know, has it been held to apply to this comparatively modern form of evidence; namely, the sketch made by the police officer to accord with the witness's recollection of a suspect's physical characteristics and mode of dress and the even more modern photofit compiled from an identical source. Both are manifestations of the seeing eye, translations of vision on to paper through the medium of a police officer's skill of drawing or composing on to which a witness does not possess. The police officer is merely doing what the witness could do if possessing the requisite skill. When drawing or composing he is akin to a camera without, of course, being able to match in clarity the photograph of a person or scene which a camera automatically produces.

There is no doubt that a photograph taken, for example, of a suspect during the commission of an offence is admissible. In a bigamy case, namely, *Reg v Tolson* (1864), Willes J said: 'The photograph was admissible because it is only a visible representation of the image or impression made upon the minds of the witnesses by the sight of the person or the object it represents; and it therefore is, in reality, only another species of the evidence which persons give of identity, when they speak merely from memory.'

That ruling has never since been doubted and is applied with regularity to photographs, including those taken nowadays automatically in banks during a robbery. Such photographs are invaluable aids to identification of criminals. It has never been suggested of them that they are subject to the rule against hearsay.

We regard the production of the sketch or photofit by a police officer making a graphic representation of a witness's memory as another form of the camera at work, albeit imperfectly and not produced contemporaneously with the material incident but soon or fairly soon afterwards. As we perceive it the photofit is not a statement in writing made in the absence of a defendant or anything resembling it in the sense that this very old rule against hearsay has ever been expressed to embrace. It is we think *sui generis*, that is to say, the only one of its kind. It is a thing apart, the admissibility to evidence of which would not be in breach of the hearsay rule.

Seeing that we do not regard the photofit as a statement at all it cannot come within the description of an earlier consistent statement which, save in exceptional circumstances, cannot ever be admissible in evidence. The true position is in our view that the photograph, the sketch and the photofit are in a class of evidence of their own to which neither the rule against hearsay nor the rule against the admission of an earlier consistent statement applies ...[16]

R v Lamb (1979, Court of Appeal)

The defendant was charged with wounding with intent to do grievous bodily harm. He alleged an alibi and said that he had been wrongly identified. He appealed against conviction. His main argument was that the production of photographs, including his own, from criminal records as part of the prosecution case rendered the jury's verdict unsafe and unsatisfactory.

Lawton LJ [giving the judgment of the court]: ... In due course the appellant appeared before the justices and those defending him decided that they would ask for a committal under section 2 of the Criminal Justice Act 1967. As a result, the prosecution had to call all their evidence before the justices. The lawyers who were prosecuting decided to put in as an exhibit the album of photographs which contained the photograph which had been picked out by Skinner and Gibbins. The justices committed the appellant for trial.

At the trial, the Crown was represented by Mr Shorrock of counsel and the defence were represented by Mr Conrad. Mr Shorrock had before him, of course, the depositions and the exhibits. He was of the opinion that it should be part of the prosecution's case to produce the album of photographs to the jury and to show them the photograph which had been picked out by Skinner and Gibbins. The reason he took this course was, so he told us, that it was part of the prosecution's case that it was a very striking coincidence that Skinner and Gibbins had both picked out the same photograph, from a total of 900.

Before the trial, Mr Conrad did not make any suggestion to Mr Shorrock that the album of photographs should not be produced and shown to the jury, nor did he, at the stage when it was produced by one of the witnesses for the Crown, make any objection to its production. It was produced and shown to the jury. The recollection of Mr Shorrock was that the way in which it was done, was to hold up the album at the page containing the photograph of the appellant. It must have been clear to the jury, when they were shown it, what kind of photograph it was. It could not have been clearer to any intelligent member of the jury that it was a photograph which had been taken of someone who had been convicted of an offence. It had all the characteristics of such a photograph and all the other photographs on the same page were of the same kind. It was an album of photographs of local villains. That was the situation at the end of the prosecution's case ...

In our judgment, the production of the photographs as part of the prosecution's case and without anything being said or done by the defence, calling for or justifying production of these photographs, was an irregularity which should not have occurred. It is not, I think, overstating the case to say that it was equivalent to the prosecution leading, as part of their case, the fact that the accused had a criminal record ...

Before we announce the order which we will be making, we wish to say a few words about the practice which has been revealed in this case. Before the Home Office Circular of 1978, it was a practice at the Bar when prosecuting counsel knew that photographs had been shown to witnesses for the purposes of discovering whom the police should interview about an alleged offence, and a

---

16. [1987] QB 417.

suspect identified by a photograph was later put on trial, for the defence to be told that that is what had been done. The defence were then left to decide whether they wished the jury to know that the photographs had been used.

It is the experience of the members of this court that in general experienced counsel for the defence took care to ensure that the jury were not told that the photographs had been used, because they were conscious of the danger which would arise from the inferences the jury were likely to draw about the existence of a criminal record.

We understand ... that since the publication of the Home Office Circular no 109 of 1978, prosecuting counsel from time to time do produce photographs as part of their case. That modern practice was what was followed by Mr Shorrock in this case. There may be exceptional cases in which the production of photographs as part of the prosecution's case is proper. An example is provided by the case where a crime has been committed; likely witnesses are shown photographs; they identify a photograph as being that of the criminal; a suspect so identified is then arrested and on arrest refuses to co-operate in any way and in particular refuses to be put on an identification parade. In those circumstances, the prosecution may only be able to get their case going by revealing the fact that the witness was able to pick out the defendant from photographs.

But in such cases such as this one, in our judgment, photographs should not be produced or referred to by the prosecution as part of their case. The defence should be informed that photographs have been shown to one or more of the witnesses, whom the prosecution propose to call. The old practice should follow, that the defence should be left to decide for themselves whether any reference will be made to the fact that photographs have been seen by those who purport to pick out the defendant on an identification parade.

In all the circumstances of this case, the appeal will be allowed and the conviction will be quashed.[17]

---

17. 71 Cr App R 198.

CHAPTER 7

CONFESSIONS AND IMPROPERLY OBTAINED EVIDENCE

One of the most important of defence counsel's objectives at trial is to ensure that as little of the prosecution evidence as possible reaches the jury – unless, of course, it happens to favour the defendant. We have already seen several ways of achieving this. It may be possible to argue that an item of evidence is irrelevant, and so inadmissible. Even if the evidence is relevant, it may be argued that it should be excluded under the rule against hearsay or for some other legal reason. In this chapter we come to two important statutory weapons in the defence's armoury. These are ss 76 and 78 of the Police and Criminal Evidence Act 1984, which deal respectively with confessions and with a discretion to exclude for reasons of fairness evidence on which the prosecution proposes to rely. As will shortly appear, these sections are very often relied on in the alternative – it was decided in *R v Mason* (1988) that s 78 applies to confessions just as much as to any other evidence – and the cases, therefore, cannot be read on the basis that one group is relevant to s 76 and another to s 78. Some overlap should therefore be expected in what follows.

One important warning needs to be given. In reading cases where evidence has been excluded under either section, but particularly under s 78, you are not reading precedents which will have to be followed in later cases. Remember that no situation is ever exactly repeated, that defendants are not all alike, and that the effect of acts or omissions by the police is likely to vary greatly from case to case. The decisions which have been selected are merely intended to give some idea of the ways in which the courts have behaved. Knowledge of the decisions is no substitute for rigorous thought about the facts of your own particular case, including the nature of your particular defendant, and the struggle to work out a satisfactory argument which would bring *those* facts within the scope of either s 76 or 78. In *R v Jelen and Katz* (1990) Auld J, delivering the judgment of the Court of Appeal, stated:

> [W]e observe first that the decision of a judge whether or not to exclude evidence under section 78 of the 1984 Act is made as a result of the exercise by him of a discretion based upon the particular circumstances of the case and upon his assessment of the adverse effect, if any, it would have on the fairness of the proceedings. The circumstances of each case are almost always different, and judges may well take different views in proper exercise of their discretion even where the circumstances are similar. This is not an apt field for hard case law and well-founded distinctions between cases.

As appears immediately below, subsection (2)(b) of s 76 – probably the provision in that section most frequently relied on – has the effect of requiring the court to attend to the particular circumstances of the individual defendant who relies upon the provision.

Police and Criminal Evidence Act 1984

76 (1) In any proceedings a confession made by an accused person may be given in evidence against him in so far as it is relevant to any matter in issue in the proceedings and is not excluded by the court in pursuance of this section.

(2) If, in any proceedings where the prosecution proposes to give in evidence a confession made by an accused person, it is represented to the court that the confession was or may have been obtained –

(a) by oppression of the person who made it; or

(b) in consequence of anything said or done which was likely, in the circumstances at the time, to render unreliable any confession which might be made by him in consequence thereof,

the court shall not allow the confession to be given in evidence against him except in so far as the prosecution proves to the court beyond reasonable doubt that the confession (notwithstanding that it may be true) was not obtained as aforesaid.

(3) In any proceedings where the prosecution proposes to give in evidence a confession made by an accused person, the court may of its own motion require the prosecution, as a condition of allowing it to do so, to prove that the confession was not obtained as mentioned in subsection (2) above.

(4) The fact that a confession is wholly or partly excluded in pursuance of this section shall not affect the admissibility in evidence –

(a) of any facts discovered as a result of the confession; or

(b) where the confession is relevant as showing that the accused speaks, writes or expresses himself in a particular way, of so much of the confession as is necessary to show that he does so.

(5) Evidence that a fact to which this subsection applies was discovered as a result of a statement made by an accused person shall not be admissible unless evidence of how it was discovered is given by him or on his behalf.

(6) Subsection (5) above applies –

(a) to any fact discovered as a result of a confession which is wholly excluded in pursuance of this section; and

(b) to any fact discovered as a result of a confession which is partly so excluded, if the fact is discovered as a result of the excluded part of the confession.

(7) Nothing in Part VII of this Act shall prejudice the admissibility of a confession made by an accused person.

(8) In this section 'oppression' includes torture, inhuman or degrading treatment, and the use or threat of violence (whether or not amounting to torture).

78 (1) In any proceedings the court may refuse to allow evidence on which the prosecution proposes to rely to be given if it appears to the court that, having regard to all the circumstances, including the circumstances in which the evidence was obtained, the admission of the evidence would have such an adverse effect on the fairness of the proceedings that the court ought not to admit it.

(2) Nothing in this section shall prejudice any rule of law requiring a court to exclude evidence.

82 (1) In this Part of this Act –

'confession', includes any statement wholly or partly adverse to the person who made it, whether made to a person in authority or not and whether made in words or otherwise;

(3) Nothing in this Part of this Act shall prejudice any power of a court to exclude evidence (whether by preventing questions from being put or otherwise) at its discretion.

What is a confession? The answer appears in s 82(1) of PACE 1984 and has been discussed in several cases.

R v Sat-Bhambra (1989, Court of Appeal)

In this case the court had to consider the admissibility of a number of tape-recorded interviews between customs officers and the accused. The question arose whether what was said in the interviews amounted to confessions at all.

The Lord Chief Justice: ... First, were the answers given by the appellant upon the interviews properly to be described as a confession or confessions? Section 82(1) of the Act defines confession as follows: '"confession," includes any statement wholly or partly adverse to the person who made it, whether made to a person in authority or not and whether made in words or otherwise.'

His answers upon the interviews, the tapes of which the jury heard, were, as his counsel described, exculpatory. Their principal damaging effect was to demonstrate that the appellant was evasive and prevaricating and that many of the statements which he made proved eventually to be false.

This question therefore arises: can a statement be described as wholly or partly adverse to the person making it, when it is intended by the maker to be wholly exculpatory and appears to be so on its face, but becomes damaging at the trial because, for example, its contents can by then be shown to be evasive or false or inconsistent with the maker's evidence on oath?

The words 'wholly or partly' are no doubt included in order to emphasise the views of the House of Lords in *Customs and Excise Commissioners v Harz and Power* (1967), and do not help to solve the problem. The words of the section do seem *prima facie* to be speaking of statements adverse on the face of them. The section is aimed at excluding confessions obtained by words or deeds likely to render them unreliable, ie admissions or partial admissions contrary to the interests of the defendant and welcome to the interrogator. They can hardly have been aimed at statements containing nothing which the interrogator wished the defendant to say and nothing apparently adverse to the defendant's interests. If the contentions of the appellant in the present case are correct, it would mean that the statement, 'I had nothing to do with it', might in due course become a 'confession', which would be surprising, with or without section 82(1).

We are inclined to the view that purely exculpatory statements are not within the meaning of section 82(1). We are supported in this view by the learned author of *Cross on Evidence*, 6th edn p 544. The same view is taken by *Andrews and Hirst on Criminal Evidence*, paragraph 19.04. They cite the words of Lord Widgery CJ in *Pearce* (1979), where he says: 'A denial does not become an admission because it is inconsistent with another denial.'

In so far as they express a contrary view we respectfully dissent from the views of the Supreme Court of Canada in *Piche v R* (1970), and of Chief Justice Warren in *Miranda v Arizona* (1966), where he said that such statements 'are incriminating in any meaningful sense of the word'.

However in the light of what we have to say hereafter, we do not need to come to any firm conclusion on this aspect of the case nor upon the further question of whether the appellant's voluntary ingestion of a daonil tablet could amount to 'something done' which was likely to render unreliable any confession.[1]

---

1.   88 Cr App R 55.

R v Park (1994, Court of Appeal)

The accused and a co-accused had been stopped in a motor car by police who had noticed that the car had a defective rear light and that the occupants were not wearing seat-belts. The police then saw a quantity of goods in the car. A conversation took place between one of the officers and the accused, as a result of which the officers came to suspect that the goods had been stolen. The question arose whether the conversation had contained any confessions by the accused. The prosecution relied on a later conversation as well which is not reproduced here, but the first conversation is quoted to show that what is said may be adverse to an accused person because it makes him appear to be prevaricating, but may still not amount to a confession because the speaker was intending to exculpate himself.

Kennedy LJ: ... [The trial judge] held that the questions and answers at the roadside did not amount to either an interview or a confession. Was the judge entitled so to decide? In order to answer that question it is necessary to look first at the contents of the roadside conversation, secondly at the judge's findings of fact in relation to Police Constable Lamb, and thirdly at those authorities to which our attention has been invited and which throw some light on the issues with which we are confronted.

As to the content of the roadside conversation, at p 2F of the transcript it is recorded thus:

'Question: Is this your car?

Answer: No, it's my father's. I'm just borrowing it.'

The Road Traffic offences were then pointed out and the officer noticed in the rear of the car on the back seat some electrical goods.

'Question: Are these yours? (indicating a stereo system and some cassette tapes).

Answer: Yes.

Question: Do you know what make this stereo system is?

Answer: No, I can't remember.'

The officer then asked how the damage to the car ignition system, which he had spotted, had occurred and the defendant is reported to have replied:

'I don't know. I've only borrowed the car.

Question: Why do you have all these tapes and CDs in the back?

Answer: I had an argument with my father. I've moved out. I'm moving in with my friend over there and I'm putting all my gear in his place.

Question: Your father's given you the car?

Answer: Only borrowing it.

Question: Is everything in the car yours?

Answer: Yes.

Question: What do you have in the boot?

Answer: Nothing much.'

At this stage, having previously given no cause for apprehension by the officer, the appellant, according to the officer, appeared nervous and the officer asked him to open the boot, which he did, and in the boot was the video recorder, two television sets, a black suitcase and other items of property. The officer asked:

'Question: Whose is this?

Answer: Oh, it's mine.

Question: Where from?

Answer: I'm moving it out of my father's address.

Question: What make is the video?

Answer: I don't know. Sanyo, I think.

Question: What about the television?

Answer: They're both Sanyo as well, I think.

Question: You don't seem very sure.

Answer: It's all mine.

Question: What's in the briefcase?

Answer: Tools.

Question: What is your friend's name?

Answer: Graham.

Question: Do you know his last name?

Answer: No, I haven't known him very long.

Question: But you are staying with him?

Answer: Yes.

Question: Are you sure this video and television etc are yours?

Answer: Oh yes, they're mine.'

There then followed a conversation between the two police officers, one of them having been with the co-accused, Noon, and having spoken to that officer Police Constable Lamb returned to the appellant and said:

'In the car is some jewellery. Whose is that?

Answer: Mine; no, his.

Question: What do you mean?

Answer: It's his, his girlfriend Janet was with us earlier in the car and it's hers, or that's what he told me.

Question: Is the jewellery the only thing in car that's his?

Answer: Yes.

Question: Have you been together all day?

Answer: Yes

Question: Where have you been?

Answer: To the pub, just out.'

At this stage Constable Lamb considered what he had been told and he decided he was not satisfied and said to the appellant: 'I am arresting you on suspicion of theft of the car and the property in it', and he cautioned him. He asked him: 'Do you understand?', to which the appellant said: 'Yes, sure.' He was then asked to empty his pockets and among the property was a large roll of English money. The officer asked: 'Where is this from?' Answer: 'It's mine. I won it on the horses today.'

There was then a conversation about how much there was and where it had come from, and he was told he was also under arrest for suspected theft of the money. Then both he and his co-accused were taken to West Drayton police station ...

The next matter to which we turn, in the light of the evidence, is the allegation that this conversation amounted to a confession. Both in this interview, and more particularly in the later interview, the appellant at times is alleged to have admitted ownership of certain items, although by no means all of them, that were found in the car ...

In the current edition of *Archbold* (1993) ... it is said that section 82(1) was not aimed at statements which the maker intended to be exculpatory and which were exculpatory on their face, but which could later be shown to be false or inconsistent with the maker's evidence on oath. It seems to us that that is precisely the situation here in relation not only to the answers in which the appellant denied ownership of certain items but also in relation to those answers where he accepted ownership of certain items, and accordingly, in our judgment, neither the conversation at the roadside nor, when we come to it, the conversation in the police station yard amounted to a confession ...[2]

R v Sharp (1988, House of Lords)

Detectives were called to a house which had been recently burgled. As they drove towards the scene, they saw the defendant running in the opposite direction. They were suspicious and followed him. They saw him get into a car parked in a lay-by. The defendant then appeared to see them; he drove off at high speed and the officers lost him. Three days later the defendant went voluntarily to the police and was interviewed. He said that he had been in the area at the time of the burglary and that he had heard a burglar alarm. But he gave innocent explanations for his presence and he said that he had not known that the car following him contained police officers.

Lord Havers: My Lords, the question certified for your Lordships' decision is in the following form: 'Where a statement made to a police officer out of court by a defendant contains both admissions and self-exculpatory parts do the exculpatory parts constitute evidence of the truth of the facts alleged therein?'

... In his summing-up the judge treated the defendant's statement as a 'mixed statement', that is, a statement that is in part admission and in part exculpatory. He directed the jury that they were entitled to regard that part of the defendant's account in which he said he was in the area at the time of the burglary as an admission and therefore evidence of the fact that he was there, but that the other parts of the statement which explained his reason for being there were exculpatory and therefore were not evidence of the facts related ...

I accept the definition of the hearsay rule in *Cross on Evidence*, 6th edn (1985), p 38: 'an assertion other than one made by a person while giving oral evidence in the proceedings is inadmissible as *evidence of any fact asserted*.' The rule is so firmly entrenched that the reasons for its adoption are of little more than historical interest but I suspect that the principal reason that led judges to adopt it many years ago was the fear that juries might give undue weight to evidence the truth of which could not be tested by cross-examination, and possibly also the risk of an account becoming distorted as it was passed from one person to another. It is the application of this rule that has led the courts to hold that an exculpatory or, as it is sometimes called, a self-serving statement made by the accused to a third party, usually the police, is not admissible as evidence of the truth of the facts it asserts.

---

2.   99 Cr App R 270.

Evidence contained in a confession is however an exception to the hearsay rule and is admissible. The justification for the adoption of the exception was presumably that, provided the accused had not been subjected to any improper pressure, it was so unlikely that he would confess to any crime he had not committed that it was safe to rely upon the truth of what he said. This exception became extended to include not only a full confession to the crime but also a partial confession in which the accused admitted some matter that required to be established if the crime alleged was to be proved against him and is now recognised in statutory form in the Police and Criminal Evidence Act 1984 in which confessions are defined by section 82(1) ...

The difference in the authorities centres upon the status to be attached to those parts of a mixed statement that excuse or explain an admission and are intended to show that the admission does not bear the inference of guilt it might otherwise attract: for example, 'I admit that I stabbed him but he was about to shoot me', or, as in this appeal, 'I admit I was at the scene of the burglary but I was looking for something that had fallen off my car'. All the authorities agree that it would be unfair to admit the admission without admitting the explanation and the only question is how best to help the jury evaluate the accused's statement. The view expressed in *Duncan* (1981), is that the whole statement should be left to the jury as evidence of the facts but that attention should be drawn, when appropriate, to the different weight they might think it right to attach to the admission as opposed to the explanation or excuses. The other view, which I might refer to as the 'purist' approach, is that, as an exculpatory statement is never evidence of the facts it relates, the jury should be directed that the excuse or explanation is only admitted to show the context in which the admission was made and they must not regard the excuse or explanation as evidence of its truth ...

My Lords, the weight of authority and common sense leads me to prefer the direction to the jury formulated in *Duncan*, to an attempt to deal differently with the different parts of a mixed statement. How can a jury fairly evaluate the facts in the admission unless they can evaluate the facts in the excuse or explanation? It is only if the jury think that the facts set out by way of excuse or explanation might be true that any doubt is cast on the admission, and it is surely only because the excuse or explanation might be true that it is thought fair that it should be considered by the jury. I agree with Lawton LJ that a jury will make little of a direction that attempts to draw a distinction between evidence which is evidence of facts and evidence in the same statement which whilst not being evidence of facts is nevertheless evidentiary material of which they may make use in evaluating evidence which is evidence of the facts. One only has to write out the foregoing sentence to see the confusion it engenders.

I cannot improve upon the language of Lord Lane CJ in *Duncan* and will not attempt to do so. It is in my opinion rightly decided and should be followed.

I would therefore dismiss the appeal and answer the certified question in the affirmative but amend it by substituting for the words 'a police officer' the words 'a person', to make it clear that this exception is of general application and not limited to statements to the police.[3]

[The other Law Lords agreed]

---

3. 86 Cr App R 274.

R v Gunewardene (1951, Court of Criminal Appeal)

In this case the court considered the position where one accused person makes an out-of-court statement which implicates a co-accused.

Lord Goddard CJ: ... We now turn to the second of the main questions argued on behalf of the appellant. As we have said, there is no doubt that the statement made by the prisoner Hanson incriminated the appellant in a high degree. This is a matter of very frequent occurrence where two or more prisoners are charged with complicity in the same offence. This state of affairs is no doubt a ground upon which the judge can be asked to exercise his discretion and order a separate trial, but no such application was made in the present case. If no separate trial is ordered it is the duty of the judge to impress on the jury that the statement of one prisoner not made on oath in the course of the trial is not evidence against the other and must be entirely disregarded ... But it would be impossible to lay down that where two prisoners are being tried together counsel for the prosecution is bound, in putting in the statement of one prisoner, to select certain passages and leave out others ...

If we were to lay down that the statement of one prisoner could never be read in full because it might implicate, or did implicate, the other, it is obvious that very difficult and inconvenient situations might arise. It not infrequently happens that a prisoner, in making a statement, though admitting his or her guilt up to a certain extent, puts greater blame upon the co-prisoner, or is asserting that certain of his or her actions were really innocent and it was the conduct of the co-prisoner that gave them a sinister appearance or led to the belief that the prisoner making the statement was implicated in the crime. In such a case that prisoner would have a right to have the whole statement read and could, with good reason, complain if the prosecution picked out certain passages and left out others.[4]

Since a confession may be made 'in words or otherwise' it is possible that the silence of a person who has an allegation put to him will amount to a confession of the truth of that allegation. An example of this in a civil context can be seen in *Bessela v Stern* (1877).

In a criminal context it was formerly not possible to infer anything adverse to a defendant from his silence in the face of police questioning because suspects had a right to remain silent in such a situation. The right to silence remains, but now if it is exercised adverse inferences may be drawn.

Criminal Justice and Public Order Act 1994

34 (1) Where, in any proceedings against a person for an offence, evidence is given that the accused –

    (a) at any time before he was charged with an offence, on being questioned under caution by a constable trying to discover whether or by whom the offence had been committed, failed to mention any fact relied on in his defence in those proceedings; or

    (b) on being charged with the offence or officially informed that he might be prosecuted for it, failed to mention any such fact,

---

4.   [1951] 2 KB 610. And see also *Lobban v The Queen* [1995] 1 WLR 877.

being a fact which in the circumstances existing at the time the accused could reasonably have been expected to mention when so questioned, charged or informed, as the case may be, subsection (2) below applies.

(2) Where this subsection applies –

(a) a magistrates' court, in deciding whether to grant an application for dismissal made by the accused under section 6 of the Magistrates' Court Act 1980 (application for dismissal of charge in course of proceedings with a view to transfer for trial);

(b) a judge in deciding whether to grant an application made by the accused under –

(i) section 6 of the Criminal Justice Act 1987 (application for dismissal of charge of serious fraud in respect of which notice of transfer has been given under section 4 of that Act); or

(ii) paragraph 5 of Schedule 6 to the Criminal Justice Act 1991 (application for dismissal of charge of violent or sexual offence involving child in respect of which notice of transfer has been given under section 53 of that Act);

(c) the court, in determining whether there is a case to answer; and

(d) the court or jury, in determining whether the accused is guilty of the offence charged,

may draw such inferences from the failure as appear proper.

(3) Subject to any directions by the court, evidence tending to establish the failure may be given before or after evidence tending to establish the fact which the accused is alleged to have failed to mention.

(4) This section applies in relation to questioning by persons (other than constables) charged with the duty of investigating offences or charging offenders as it applies in relation to questioning by constables; and in subsection (1) above 'officially informed' means informed by a constable or any such person.

(5) This section does not –

(a) prejudice the admissibility in evidence of the silence or other reaction of the accused in the face of anything said in his presence relating to the conduct in respect of which he is charged, in so far as evidence thereof would be admissible apart from this section; or

(b) preclude the drawing of any inference from any such silence or other reaction of the accused which could properly be drawn apart from this section.

(6) This section does not apply in relation to a failure to mention a fact if the failure occurred before the commencement of this section.

(7) In relation to any time before the commencement of section 44 of this Act, this section shall have effect as if the reference in subsection (2)(a) to the grant of an application for dismissal was a reference to the committal of the accused for trial.[5]

---

5. Similarly, by ss 35-37 inferences may be drawn from the accused's failure to give evidence at trial; failure to account for objects, substances or marks; and failure to account for presence at a particular place. By s 62(10) of the Police and Criminal Evidence Act 1984, inferences may also be drawn from failure to provide intimate samples.

If for some reason a confession is not excluded under s 76, it may still be excluded by virtue of the discretion contained in s 78.

R v Mason (1988, Court of Appeal)

The accused was convicted of arson, the case for the prosecution being that he had set fire to a car belonging to his former girlfriend's father. He made a confession, but its admissibility was challenged because of the way in which it had been obtained.

Watkins LJ: ... When the police came to the scene there was a lot of broken glass, as they discovered, about the place near the car. It was soon found that an inflammable liquid had been used, probably a combination of petrol and paint thinners. About 12 hours or so later the police paid a visit to the appellant. He denied having been involved in setting fire to the car. On July 10 he was arrested. Be it noted that upon arrest the police had in their possession no evidence at all to associate him with the cause of the fire. Before arrest one or more police officers decided to invent evidence and to acquaint the appellant of that so-called evidence as though it was genuinely possessed. What they decided to do was to tell the appellant that a fingerprint of his had been found in a very telling place. As to that Detective Constable Gunton said: 'Detective Constable Walton and I set out deliberately to make the defendant believe we had a fingerprint on some glass fragments from the bottle that was used to perpetrate this crime. I agreed with the detective constable to this play-acting and it was a trick. The bottle, or the fragments of it, had not even been sent for fingerprint testing at that stage. We set about "conning" the defendant. We had a suspicion, but only suspicion, against him and we realised that we needed more proof ... I felt the only way to get the truth from him was to do this.'

Having been told by these police officers, falsely, that a fingerprint of his had been found on a fragment of glass from the bottle, the appellant saw his solicitor and told him his version of what had happened. The solicitor asked DC Gunton to confirm the fact, as the police were asserting, that they had found a fingerprint upon a fragment of glass at the scene of the crime. He confirmed to the solicitor that that was so. That was a deliberate falsehood. When giving evidence DC Gunton said as to this: 'My motive ... was because if the defendant had had nothing to do with this glass bottle there was no way he would produce a confession. If he ... knew very well he had handled ... the bottle and had been active in the preparation, of course, he would begin to doubt himself and whether or not he was going to be discovered.'

The solicitor, influenced by what he had been told by the police as to the fingerprint, advised the appellant to answer their questions and to give his explanation of any involvement he had had in the incident. What he told the police as a consequence of that was that he was not present when the car was set alight. He had asked a friend, whom he refused to name, if he would do it. This was because Mr Askew had been threatening him, and setting fire to his car would frighten Mr Askew away from repeating conduct of that kind. The only involvement which he (the appellant) had in the incident was to fill the bottles which were used, one with petrol and the other with paint thinners. That was done at his home. The bottles were then taken away by the friend and the fire started.

The appellant did not give evidence at the trial. Before the end of the prosecution case and when the confession – because that is what it amounted to – was sought to be put in evidence by counsel for the prosecution, objection to its admissibility was made by counsel for the appellant. The judge heard argument in the absence of the jury and heard some evidence from the police as to how the confession had been obtained. He decided that the confession was, in his discretion, admissible. He was referred in the course of argument to sections 76 and 78 of the Police and Criminal Evidence Act 1984. He gave a ruling at the conclusion of the argument and then said he would allow the prosecution to adduce that evidence. He dealt with what he believed to be the effects of section 76 and 78, and went on to say (page 11E of the transcript), with the provisions of section 78 in mind: 'I have no doubt that this defendant was well aware of his right to remain silent and could have remained silent, with his solicitor being present, had he so chosen that alternative. But he did not choose that alternative; he chose to give the interview, listen to the questions and decide individually which questions he was going to answer. In fact he answered all of them. I see nothing wrong in his doing that which adversely affects the fairness of the proceedings.'

It is contended here by Mr Knox for the appellant that the judge exercised his discretion wrongly. Mr Lowden, who also appeared in the court below for the prosecution, has argued that the judge undoubtedly had a discretion and that in exercising it he took account of all matters which it was necessary for him to take into account and did not give thought to any impermissible matter in coming to his conclusion. Mr Lowden has also submitted that there is no authority for the proposition that section 78 of the Act refers to confessions and admissions, seeing that they are especially dealt with in section 76.

Section 76, so far as relevant, states: ... [He set out the provisions.]

It is to be observed of those provisions that whilst a confession made by an accused person may generally speaking be given in evidence (subsection (1)), the court is obliged to rule out that confession if it finds to exist any one or more of the circumstances referred to in subsection (2).

Section 78(1) states: ... [He set out the provisions.]

It is submitted that when a comparison is made between the provisions of those two sections and reference made to *R v Sang* (1979), it was not the intention of Parliament that section 78 be understood as though the word 'evidence' includes evidence of confessions and admissions. We see no reason whatsoever to put that, in our view, extremely strained construction upon the plain words used in this section. In our judgment on a proper construction of it the word 'evidence' includes all evidence which may be introduced by the prosecution into a trial. Thus it is that regardless as to whether the admissibility of a confession falls to be considered under section 76(2), a trial judge has a discretion to deal with the admissibility of a confession under section 78 ...

It is obvious from the undisputed evidence that the police practised a deceit not only upon the appellant, which is bad enough, but also upon the solicitor whose duty it was to advise him. In effect, they hoodwinked both solicitor and client. That was a most reprehensible thing to do. It is not however because we regard as misbehaviour of a most serious kind conduct of that nature that we have come to the decision soon to be made plain. This is not the place to discipline the police. That has been made clear here on a number of previous occasions. We are concerned with the application of the proper law. The law is, as I have already said, that a trial judge has a discretion to be exercised of course upon right principles to reject admissible evidence in the interests of a defendant having a fair trial. The judge in the present case appreciated that, as the quotation from his ruling shows. So the only question to be answered by this court is whether, having regard to the way the police have behaved, the judge exercised that discretion correctly. In our judgment he did not. He omitted a vital factor from his consideration, namely the deceit practised upon the appellant's solicitor. If he had included that in his consideration of the matter we have not the slightest doubt that he would have been driven to an opposite conclusion, namely that the confession be ruled out and the jury not permitted therefore to hear of it. If that had been done, an acquittal would have followed for there was no other evidence in the possession of the prosecution.

For those reasons we have no alternative but to quash this conviction.

Before parting from this case, despite what I have said about the role of the court in relation to disciplining the police, we think we ought to say that we hope never again to hear of deceit such as this being practised upon an accused person, and more particularly possibly on a solicitor whose duty it is to advise him, unfettered by false information from the police.[6]

Examination candidates sometimes assume too readily that any police impropriety amounts to oppression. Attention should be paid to the partial definition in subsection (8) and to two cases where the meaning of 'oppression' was discussed by the Court of Appeal.

R v Fulling (1987, Court of Appeal)

Lord Lane CJ read the following judgment of the court: On 6 August 1986 in the Crown Court at Leeds before Judge Hurwitz and a jury, the appellant was convicted by a majority verdict of 10 to 2 of obtaining property by deception. She faced a further similar count, the trial of which was adjourned. No sentence has yet been passed. She appeals against conviction by leave of the single judge.

The facts which gave rise to the charge were these. In September 1981 the appellant claimed some £5,665 from her insurers in respect of what she claimed was a burglary at her flat in Leeds. The insurance company in July 1982 paid her £5,212 in settlement of the claim.

Many months later a man called Turnpenny, an acknowledged criminal, gave the police a mass of information about the activities of other criminals, which resulted in a large number of people being arrested, among them being the appellant. Turnpenny gave evidence that the appellant had told him that her 'burglary' was bogus; that a man named Maddon had committed it; that she knew the whereabouts of the stolen property. She gave him to understand that the idea of the bogus burglary had been initiated by one Drewery with whom the appellant had been living and with whom she was infatuated. Turnpenny conceded that he had good reason for wishing to harm Drewery.

As a result of this information the appellant was arrested in the early hours of Friday 12 July 1985. Drewery was arrested at the same time. She was interviewed twice on that day, but exercised her right to say nothing despite persistent questioning by the police. She was interviewed again on the following day, Saturday. The interview was split into two, with a break in between, according to the police of 50 minutes, according to her of about 5 or 10 minutes.

The police witnesses describe how, after initially refusing to answer questions, her attitude started to change. One of the officers, Detective Sergeant Beech, said: 'You've obviously got a lot on your mind, are you finding it difficult?' 'Yes.' 'Would I be right in saying that you want to talk about this but every bone in your body is telling you you shouldn't?' 'Something like that', was the reply. Then came the break already described.

6. 86 Cr App R 349.

When the interview was resumed, in answer to questions from the officer she admitted a number of offences. Amongst them was the setting up of the bogus burglary: 'I approached a man in a pub because I was short of money and asked him if he would break in for me.' She admitted obtaining the money from her insurers. She said that she had spent some of it on a holiday for herself and Drewery. She expressed her sorrow at having committed the offences and said she felt relieved that she had confessed. She sought, it should be added, to exculpate Drewery.

Thus there were two legs to the prosecution case: Turnpenny's evidence and the police account of her confession. The only corroboration of the former was the latter. The prosecution concede that, if the confession goes, then the appeal should be allowed. They would not seek to rely on Turnpenny's uncorroborated evidence. The only issue in the appeal is whether or not the confession was properly obtained.

A submission was made to the judge that the confession should be ruled inadmissible by virtue of the provisions of section 76 of the Police and Criminal Evidence Act 1984 ...

It was represented to the judge that the confession was or might have been obtained by oppression of the appellant within the meaning of subsection (2)(a).

The appellant's evidence on the *voir dire* as to her reason for making the confession was this. After the break in the final interview one of the police officers, Detective Constable Holliday, told her that Drewery, her lover, had been having for the last three years or so an affair with a woman called Christine Judge. Now Christine Judge was one of the many people who had been arrested as a result of Turnpenny's disclosures. She was in the next cell to the appellant and, said the appellant, Detective Constable Holliday told her so. These revelations, said the appellant, so distressed her that she 'just couldn't stand being in the cells any longer.' Then later in her evidence she said: 'As soon as the matter about Christine came out, Detective Constable Holliday left the room and my head was swimming. I felt numb and after a while I said to Detective Sergeant Beech, "Is it true?" and he said, "Ronnie shouldn't have said that, he gets a bit carried away. Look, Ruth, why don't you make a statement?" '

She said that she knew Drewery had in 1982 had an affair with a woman called Christine. She had before the interview noticed that the cell next door to hers had the name Christine Judge on its door, but said she did not realise that this was the same Christine until the police told her. After she had made her confession she had shouted to Christine to ask her if what the police had told her was true. Up to that point she said she was not particularly expressing her distress, but once she had spoken to Christine she just cried and cried. Later in cross-examination she said, 'I agreed to a statement being taken; it was the only way I was going to be released from the cells', but she conceded that she was not suggesting that she had been offered bail in return for a statement. The officers denied that they had made to her any such revelation as she suggested.

The basis of the submission to the judge was that the information given to her by the police about Christine amounted to oppression, and that the confession was, or might have been, obtained thereby, and that the prosecution had failed to discharge the burden of proving beyond reasonable doubt that the confession was not so obtained.

In his ruling on the matter the judge declined to make any express finding of fact as to whether the appellant or the police were correct in their account of events. He was prepared to assume for the purposes of argument that the appellant's version of events was the true one and to judge the matter on that basis ...

The material part of the ruling runs: 'Bearing in mind that whatever happens to a person who is arrested and questioned is by its very nature oppressive, I am quite satisfied that in section 76(2)(a) of the Police and Criminal Evidence Act, the word oppression means something above and beyond that which is inherently oppressive in police custody and must import some impropriety, some oppression actively applied in an improper manner by the police. I do not find that what was done in this case can be so defined and, in those circumstances, I am satisfied that oppression cannot be made out on the evidence I have heard in the context required by the statutory provision. I go on to add simply this, that I have not addressed my mind as to whether or not I believe the police or the defendant on this issue because my ruling is based exclusively upon the basis that, even if I wholly believed the defendant, I do not regard oppression as having been made out. In those circumstances, her confession – if that is the proper term for it – the interview in which she confessed, I rule to be admissible.'

... [Counsel for the appellant] submits to us that on the strength of those decisions the basis of the judge's ruling was wrong; in particular when he held that the word 'oppression' means something above and beyond that which is inherently oppressive in police custody and must import some impropriety, some oppression actively applied in an improper manner by the police ...

The point is one of statutory construction. The wording of the Act of 1984 does not follow the wording of earlier rules or decisions, nor is it expressed to be a consolidating Act, nor yet to be declaratory of the common law. The preamble runs: 'An Act to make further provision in relation to the powers and duties of the police, persons in police detention, criminal evidence, police discipline and complaints against the police; to provide for arrangements for obtaining the views of the community on policing and for a rank of deputy chief constable; to amend the law relating to the Police Federation and Police Forces and Police Cadets in Scotland; and for connected purposes.'

It is a codifying Act, and therefore the principles set out in *Bank of England v. Vagliano Brothers* (1891) apply. Lord Herschell, having pointed out that the Bills of Exchange Act 1882 which was under consideration was intended to be a codifying Act, said, at pp 144-145: 'I think the proper course is in the first instance to examine the language of the statute and to ask what is the natural meaning, uninfluenced by any considerations derived from the previous state of the law, and not to start with inquiring how the law previously stood, and then, assuming that it was probably intended to leave it unaltered, to see if the words of the enactment will bear an interpretation in conformity with this view. If a statute, intended to embody in a code a particular branch of the law, is to be treated in this fashion, it appears to me that its utility will be almost entirely destroyed, and the very object with which it was enacted will be frustrated. The purpose of such a statute surely was that on any point specifically dealt with by it, the law should be ascertained by interpreting the language used instead of, as before, by roaming over a vast number of authorities in order to discover what the law was, extracting it by a minute critical examination of the prior decisions, dependent upon a knowledge of the exact effect even of an obsolete proceeding such as a demurrer to evidence.'

... Section 76(2) of the Act of 1984 distinguishes between two different ways in which a confession may be rendered inadmissible: (a) where it has been obtained by oppression; (b) where it has been made in consequence of anything said or done which was likely in the circumstances to render unreliable any confession which might be made by the defendant in consequence thereof. Paragraph (b) is wider than the old formulation, namely that the confession must be shown to be voluntary in the sense that it was not obtained by fear of prejudice or hope of advantage, excited or held out by a person in authority. It is wide enough to cover some of the circumstances which under the earlier rule were embraced by what seems to us to be the artificially wide definition of oppression in *Reg v Prager* (1972).

This in turn leads us to believe that 'oppression' in section 76(2)(a) should be given its ordinary dictionary meaning. The *Oxford English Dictionary* as its third definition of the word runs as follows: 'Exercise of authority or power in a burdensome, harsh, or wrongful manner; unjust or cruel treatment of subjects, inferiors, etc; the imposition of unreasonable or unjust burdens.' One of the quotations given under that paragraph runs as follows: 'There is not a word in our language which expresses more detestable wickedness than oppression.'

We find it hard to envisage any circumstances in which such oppression would not entail some impropriety on the part of the interrogator. We do not think that the judge was wrong in using that test. What, however, is abundantly clear is that a confession may be invalidated under section 76(2)(b) where there is no suspicion of impropriety. No reliance was placed on the words of section 76(2)(b) either before the judge at trial or before this court. Even if there had been such reliance, we do not consider that the policeman's remark was likely to make unreliable any confession of the appellant's own criminal activities, and she expressly exonerated – or tried to exonerate – her unfaithful lover.

In those circumstances, in the judgment of this court, the judge was correct to reject the submission made to him under section 76 of the Act of 1984. The appeal is accordingly dismissed.[7]

R v Paris (1993, Court of Appeal)

Paris, Abdullahi and Miller were convicted of the murder of a woman named Lynette White. An important item of prosecution evidence was an alleged confession by Miller. It was argued for Miller that this evidence should have been excluded on the basis that it had been obtained by oppression.

The Lord Chief Justice: ... Miller was arrested on December 7 in London. He was taken to Cardiff and over five days, between December 7 and 11, he was interviewed for some 13 hours. All of the interviews were tape-recorded, and in total there were 19 tapes. Although a solicitor was engaged from the start, he was not allowed to be present during the first two interviews on December 7. From the third interview on December 8 onwards he was present. On tapes 1, 2, 6 and 7, the interviewing officers were Detective Constables Greenwood and Seaford. On all the other tapes the interviewing officers were Detective Constable Evans and Murray, save for 16 and 17 when Detective Constable Toogood replaced Detective Constable Murray.

In summary, Miller denied both participation and presence at the scene on tapes 1 to 7. On 8 and 9 he began to accept he was present. Thereafter he was pressed to say who had stabbed Lynette and eventually to admit that he did. Having denied involvement well over 300 times, he was finally persuaded to make three admissions on which the prosecution particularly relied, in addition to his admission to being present. The first of those was on tape 18, where page 7 of the transcript records him as saying, 'Paris went crazy so I started stabbing.' Miller was speaking very fast at that point and the word 'I' is by no means clear. It was

---

7.   [1987] QB 426.

certainly not taken up by the officers at the time as an admission that he had stabbed Lynette.

Secondly, towards the end of tape 18 the officers put it to Miller that he was drugged and may have stabbed Lynette without knowing what he was doing. Thus at page 81 of the transcript Detective Constable Murray said: 'OK, OK at least we can now say we've got it right, because even if you can't say yes I did, or no I didn't. You were so blocked up you didn't know what you were doing.'

At page 84 Miller said, 'That's what I say, I don't know. I might have done, I might have done.' Thirdly, on tape 19 at page 52 of the transcript the appellant said after a period of pressure, 'I just stabbed her, not stabbed her just fucking thumped her in the face, I mean'.

Mr Mansfield, who did not appear in the court below, submits that the interviews were oppressive and the whole course of questioning was such as to render Miller's admission unreliable. He relies on section 76(2) of the Police and Criminal Evidence Act 1984. ...

Three points on that section require emphasis. First, the issue having been raised by the defence, the burden of proving beyond reasonable doubt that neither (2)(a) nor (2)(b) applied was on the Crown. Secondly, what matters is how the confession was obtained, not whether or not it may have been true. Thirdly, unless the prosecution discharged the burden of proof, the judge was bound as a matter of law to exclude the admissions. His decision was not discretionary.

As to the meaning of 'oppression', we refer to *Fulling* (1987) ...

We have read the transcripts of the tapes and have heard a number of them played in open court. It became clear that the two pairs of officers employed different methods. Greenwood and Seaford were tough and confrontational. Evans and Murray were milder in manner, aiming to gain the appellant's confidence and persuade him to accept their version of the facts.

We are bound to say that on hearing tape 7, each member of this court was horrified. Miller was bullied and hectored. The officers, particularly Detective Constable Greenwood, were not questioning him so much as shouting at him what they wanted him to say. Short of physical violence, it is hard to conceive of a more hostile and intimidating approach by officers to a suspect. It is impossible to convey on the printed page the pace, force and menace of the officer's delivery, but a short passage may give something of the flavour:

Stephen Wayne Miller: 'I wasn't there.'

DC Greenwood: 'How you can ever ...?'

Stephen Wayne Miller: 'I wasn't there.'

DC Greenwood: 'How you ... I just don't know how you can sit there, I ... '

Stephen Wayne Miller: 'I wasn't ... '

DC Greenwood: 'Really don't.'

Stephen Wayne Miller: 'I was not there. I was not there.'

DC Greenwood: 'Seeing that girl, your girlfriend, in that room that night like she was. I just don't know how you can sit there and say it.'

Stephen Wayne Miller: 'I wasn't there.'

DC Greenwood: 'You were there that night.'

Stephen Wayne Miller: 'I was not there.'

DC Greenwood: 'Together with all the others, you were there that night.'

Stephen Wayne Miller:	'I was not there, I'll tell you already ... '
DC Greenwood:	'And you sit there and say that.'
Stephen Wayne Miller:	'They can lock me up for 50 billion years, I said I was not there.'
DC Greenwood:	'Cause you don't wanna be there.'
Stephen Wayne Miller:	'I was not there.'
DC Greenwood:	'You don't wanna be there because if ... '
Stephen Wayne Miller:	'I was not there.'
DC Greenwood:	'As soon as you say that you're there you know you're involved.'
Stephen Wayne Miller:	'I was not there.'
DC Greenwood:	'You know you were involved in it.'
Stephen Wayne Miller:	'I was not involved and I wasn't there.'
DC Greenwood:	'Yes, you were there.'
Stephen Wayne Miller:	'I was not there.'
DC Greenwood:	'You were there, that's why Leanne is coming up now ... '
Stephen Wayne Miller:	'No.'
DC Greenwood:	' 'Cause her conscience is ...'
Stephen Wayne Miller:	'I was not there.'
DC Greenwood:	'She can't sleep at night ... '
Stephen Wayne Miller:	'No. I was not there.'
DC Greenwood:	'To say you were there that night ... '
Stephen Wayne Miller:	'I was not there.'
DC Greenwood:	'Looking over her body seeing she was like ... '
Stephen Wayne Miller:	'I was not there.'
DC Greenwood:	'With her head like she had and you have got the audacity to sit there and say nothing at all about it.'
Stephen Wayne Miller:	'I was not there.'
DC Greenwood:	'You know damn well you were there.'
Stephen Wayne Miller:	'I was not there.'

and so on for many pages.

We have no doubt that this was oppression within the meaning of section 76(2). [Counsel for the Crown] submits that Miller stood his ground and made no admission in that interview despite what he concedes was bad behaviour by the officers. Moreover, his solicitor was present to look after his interests. In our view, although we do not know what instructions he had, the solicitor appears to have been gravely at fault for sitting passively through this travesty of an interview. We are told he was called to give evidence at the first trial but not the second, and he agreed in evidence, having heard the tapes played, that he ought to have intervened.

As to Miller standing his ground, it is significant that in the very next interview (tape 8) within an hour after the bullying, he was persuaded by insidious questioning to concede that under the effect of drugs, it was possible he was there and did not remember it clearly. Thus at tape 8, page 32, he said: 'I am just ... I am just certain that I wasn't there that's all, I am, I am certain I wasn't there but it could ... it could happen, it could have happened.'

Once he opened that chink, the officers kept up the questioning to open it further. Of course, it is perfectly legitimate for officers to pursue their interrogation of a suspect with a view to eliciting his account or gaining admissions. They are not required to give up after the first denial or even after a number of denials. But here, after the oppression in tape 7, Mr Mansfield complains that the other officers were also guilty of a less blatant form of oppression. They made it clear to Miller on many occasions that they would go on questioning until they 'got it right.' By that they clearly meant, until Miller agreed with the version they were putting.

Mr Mansfield submits that additional pressure was applied by telling the appellant he was talking drivel and rubbish and telling him his alibi was blown away. The alibi had never been totally water-tight, but so far as it went, it was not, on the police information, blown away. The prosecution's version of events was said to be supported by a number of witnesses, which it was not ... Miller was threatened with the prospect of a life sentence more than once. Much of the interviewing was taken up, not with questions put to the appellant but with the officers putting detailed descriptions of what they believed had happened and what role Miller may have played. Thus, they persistently suggested he was 'stoned' due to the effects of cocaine so as to persuade him that he might have been present even though he had no clear recollection of it. Having gained admissions by this approach, the officers then insisted that the appellant must know and tell them every detail of what occurred at the scene, eg which way Lynette fell, where the body was in the room, who came in, at what stage and so on. It is submitted that Miller was in effect brain-washed over these thirteen hours into repeating back to the officers facts they had asserted many times to him.

It is clear on listening to the tapes that for extended periods Miller was crying and sobbing, yet he was not given any respite. It is true that after some of the interviews concluded, he was asked if he wanted a break and he expressed willingness to continue. The context was that he was being led to believe the officers were seeking to eliminate him from participation in the attack and he wanted to get to the end of the questioning.

The solicitor in attendance did intervene during the last tape (tape 19, p 15). He said he had asked to be allowed to take instructions from Miller between tapes 18 and 19, since fresh matters had been raised. Presumably, the fresh matters were the officer's ultimate assertions that Miller had not only been present but had himself stabbed the deceased. The solicitor's request had not been met and he renewed it. The officers fobbed him off by refusing to interrupt the interview but promising to inform the custody officer of his request. They never did.

Having considered the tenor and length of these interviews taken as a whole we are of the opinion that they would have been oppressive and confessions obtained in consequence of them would have been unreliable, even with a suspect of normal mental capacity. In fact, there was evidence on the *voir dire* from Dr Gudjonsson, called on behalf of Miller, that he was on the borderline of mental handicap with an IQ of 75, a mental age of 11 and a reading age of eight.

It is fair to the learned judge to say that, although he was invited to listen to part of tape 7, it was played only up to page 17 of the transcript. The bullying and shouting was from page 20 onward. Why the most important part was not played to the learned judge has not been explained to us. Had he heard the rest of it, as we did, we do not believe he would have ruled as he did.

In the upshot, it is sufficient to say that in our judgment the Crown did not and could not discharge the burden upon them to prove beyond reasonable doubt that the confessions were not obtained by oppression or by interviews which were likely to render them unreliable. Accordingly, in our view these interviews ought not to have been admitted in evidence ...

Before parting with this case, we should comment on the apparent failure of the provisions in the Police and Criminal Evidence Act 1984 to prevent evidence obtained by oppression and impropriety from being admitted. In our judgment, the circumstances of this case do not indicate flaws in those provisions. They do indicate a combination of human errors.

First, the police officers adopted techniques of interrogation which were wholly contrary to the spirit and in many instances the letter of the codes laid down under the Act. In our view, those responsible for police training and discipline must take all necessary steps to see that guidelines are followed.

Secondly, although we did not hear what his instructions were, the solicitor who sat in on the interviews, seems to have done that and little else. Guidelines for solicitors on 'advising a suspect in the police station' were first published by the Law Society in 1985 with a second and third editions in 1988 and 1991. The current edition provided under paragraph 6 as follows, *inter alia*:

> 6.3.2   you may need to intervene if the questions are: ... (c) oppressive, threatening or insulting;
>
> 6.3.3   you should intervene if the officer is not asking questions but only making his/her own comments ...
>
> 6.4.1   if questions are improper or improperly put, you should intervene and be prepared to explain your objections ...
>
> 6.4.2   if improprieties remain uncorrected or continue, advise the suspect of his/her right to remain silent.

It is of the first importance that a solicitor fulfilling the exacting duty of assisting a suspect during interviews should follow the guidelines and discharge his function responsibly and courageously. Otherwise, his presence may actually render disservice. We can only assume that in the present case the officers took the view that unless and until the solicitor intervened, they could not be criticised for going too far. If that is so, they were wholly wrong.

Finally, it is most regrettable that the worst example of the police excesses (tape 7) was not played in full to the learned judge before he ruled on admissibility.

Despite this combination of errors, it must be pointed out that the records of timings and the tape recordings of the interviews required by the Act have enabled this court to review what took place and, albeit belatedly, to allow these appeals. At the conclusion, we now direct the learned registrar to send copies of tape 7 to the Chief Inspector of Constabulary, to the Director of Public Prosecutions and to The Chairman of the Royal Commission on Criminal Justice.[8]

For either subsection (2)(a) or (2)(b) to apply it must be shown that the matters complained of did in fact cause the confession to be made. It is particularly important to remember this when considering subsection (2)(b) because a confession that may very well be unreliable is not covered by that subsection unless it was made as a result of something 'said or done' by a person other than the suspect.

---

8.   97 Cr App R 99.

R v Goldenberg (1989, Court of Appeal)

Neill LJ read the judgment of the court: On September 8 1987 at the Crown Court at Snaresbrook, the appellant, Meir Goldenberg, was convicted following a trial lasting eight days on an indictment charging him together with two other men with conspiracy to supply diamorphine ...

The second ground of appeal concerned the interview which took place at Boreham Wood police station on June 16 1987. At the trial counsel for the appellant sought to exclude evidence about this interview on the basis that it was unreliable. It was also argued at one stage that this evidence was not relevant and that its prejudicial effect outweighed its probative value.

The judge rejected these arguments in the following ruling: 'Mr Pownall relies in substance on the basis that the evidence may be unreliable under section 76 of the Police and Criminal Evidence Act. He submitted initially that such evidence was not relevant and that its prejudicial value in any event outweighed its probative value. He did not pursue that ultimately, and rightly so, as the evidence in my view is obviously relevant and highly probative. Its only prejudicial value is that that follows all admissions. I have to decide therefore the sole issue as to its reliability. Mr Pownall says that it may be unreliable because, on the face of it, the admissions in the interview are an attempt to get bail and, secondly, that as Mr Goldenberg was a heroin addict and as he had been in custody for some weeks, it might be expected that he would do or say anything, however false, to get bail, presumably thus to be able to feed his addiction. The earlier admissions by Mr Goldenberg seem to me highly relevant. He accepted in those earlier admissions following shortly after his arrest that in substance he had acquired heroin in order to sell that on through his co-defendants but at that early stage was not prepared to go into any further details. In these admissions he goes into some further detail but seems to limit those details, suggesting that he can only provide the fullness of them if and when granted bail. It seems to me, therefore, that this confession is perfectly consistent and follows on from his previous confessions. Bail may well have been in his mind, as indeed other motives may well have been, but there is nothing that I can see which suggests in any way that this confession is in any way unreliable. There is no evidence before me that he was suffering from heroin addiction at the time or shortly before June 16 but even if he had been, my view of the admissibility of this interview remains the same. I can see nothing, even in those circumstances, which would in any way render the admission or the interview in any way unreliable. Of course, it is for the prosecution to satisfy me that the admissions in the interview are not unreliable and for the reasons that I have given they have done so. In my view, therefore, this interview (and the admissions contained in it) is admissible.'

In this court, though counsel did not abandon his submission that the evidence was more prejudicial than probative, the argument against the admissibility of evidence about the June 16 interview was put in two principal ways: (a) that the judge should have ruled against the admissibility of the evidence in accordance with section 76(2)(b) of the Police and Criminal Evidence Act 1984 ('the 1984 Act') and (b) that, in the alternative, the judge should have excluded the evidence in accordance with section 78 of the 1984 Act ...

The submission based on section 78 of the 1984 Act can be dealt with quite shortly. It will be seen that by this section the court is given a discretion to exclude evidence in certain circumstances. It does not appear however that in the present case any submission was made to the judge at the trial to the effect that the evidence should be excluded in accordance with section 78. In these circumstances it does not appear to us that it would be right for this court to give effect to a submission which depends on the failure of a judge to exclude evidence by a discretion which at his trial he was not asked to exercise.

We turn therefore to the argument based on section 76 of the 1984 Act. Here, if the argument is well founded, the exclusion of the evidence is mandatory and in any event it is clear that the point was fully canvassed before the judge.

It was submitted on behalf of the appellant that the words 'said or done' in the phrase 'in consequence of anything said or done' could include what was said or done by the appellant himself.

He had requested the interview and his motive, it was said, was to obtain bail or alternatively, as one of the police officers said in the course of the trial, to obtain credit for helping the police. It was also submitted, though without great force, that the confession was unreliable because of the words used by Detective Sergeant Leader at the outset of the interview which might have led the appellant to think that anything he said would be 'off the record', or at any rate would not be used against him in the present proceedings. It is to be noted that this alternative submission was not advanced at the trial.

It is important to remember that in the present case there was an application on behalf of the appellant that the evidence should not be admitted. The case therefore fell within section 76(2) of the 1984 Act rather than within section 76(3), under which the court may, of its own motion, require the prosecution to prove the reliability of a confession.

It follows therefore that if criticism is now to be made of the judge's ruling, it is necessary to bear in mind the arguments addressed to him at the trial. Thus the obligation on the court under section 76(2) arises where 'it is represented to the court that the confession was or may have been obtained in consequence of anything said or done which was likely, in the circumstances existing at the time, to render unreliable any confession which might be made by him in consequence thereof'.

In the present case it is clear that no reliance was placed at the trial on anything said or done by Detective Sergeant Leader at the start of the interview. The argument was based on what was said or done by the appellant himself and on his state of mind. It is in that context that the judge's ruling has to be considered. It is also to be noted that on the *voir dire* the appellant himself did not give evidence.

It was submitted on behalf of the appellant that in a case to which section 76(2)(b) of the 1984 Act applied, the court was concerned with the objective reliability of the confession and not merely with the conduct of any police officer or other person to whom the confession was made. Accordingly the court might have to look at what was said or done by the person making the confession, because the confession might have been made 'in consequence' of what he himself had said or done and his words or actions might indicate that this confession was or might be unreliable.

In our judgment the words 'said or done' in section 76(2)(b) of the 1984 Act do not extend so as to include anything said or done by the person making the confession. It is clear from the wording of the section and the use of the words 'in consequence' that a causal link must be shown between what was said or done and the subsequent confession.

In our view it necessarily follows that 'anything said or done' is limited to something external to the person making the confession and to something which is likely to have some influence on him.

In the circumstances of the present case we are satisfied that on the proper construction of section 76(2)(b) the judge's ruling as to the admissibility of evidence relating to the June 16 interview was correct. We are therefore satisfied that the judge was right to rule against the submission that the prejudicial effect of this evidence outweighed its probative value. We therefore reject the second ground of appeal. Accordingly for these reasons the appeal against conviction must be dismissed.[9]

R v McGovern (1991, Court of Appeal)

The appellant had been convicted of manslaughter by reason of diminished responsibility. The prosecution had relied on evidence of a confession.

Farquharson LJ: ... Whilst she was at the police station, two interviews took place. One was at 3.20 pm on November 17, when she was on her own and the second was in the morning of the following day, but on this occasion in the presence of the solicitor who had been summoned on her behalf. The contents of both those interviews amounted to confessions on the part of the appellant and of her complicity in the homicide. We are told that apart from these two interviews and the statements made therein there was virtually no other evidence against the appellant implicating her in the crime. It was submitted by Mr Clegg at the trial before His Honour Judge Lowery QC that the evidence in relation to the first interview should not be admitted to the jury under the provisions of the Police and Criminal Evidence Act 1984. This submission was rejected by the learned judge. The trial proceeded. The appellant was not called to give evidence but medical evidence was called on her behalf. In the result she succeeded in proving diminished responsibility. That is the explanation of why the jury convicted her of manslaughter. Before us, Mr Clegg submits that the learned judge was wrong to admit the evidence of that first interview. His submission is based on the admitted facts that the police officers responsible for the custody of the appellant and for the conduct of the interviews were in breach of section 58 of the Police and Criminal Evidence Act 1984 and certain Codes of Conduct made thereunder. Section 58(1) provides that a person who is in police detention 'shall be entitled, if he so requests, to consult a solicitor privately at any time.' On her arrival at the police station the appellant had requested access to a solicitor, but this was unlawfully refused. It is not suggested that the police had any grounds for delaying access. The refusal was unlawful, as I have stated, and is agreed by the Crown to be unlawful. So far as the first interview was concerned, no contemporaneous note was taken and when a note of the interview was made subsequently it was not thereafter given to the appellant to read and sign. Furthermore, no record was made in the interviewing officer's notebook of the reason why no contemporaneous note was taken. These omissions were in breach of Code C, paragraphs 11.3, 12.12 and 11.6. We assume for the purposes of this appeal that the police were not, at any stage, acting in bad faith.

These breaches are, of course, important features of the case. In the case of *Samuel* (1988), Hodgson J described the right of access to a solicitor as one of the most important and fundamental rights of a citizen. While in the case of *Walsh* (1990), 163, Saville J said that 'the main object of section 58 of the Act and indeed of the Codes of Practice is to achieve fairness – to an accused or suspected person so as, among other things, to preserve and protect his legal rights.' The learned judge went on to say that it follows that if there are significant and substantial breaches

---

9. 88 Cr App R 285.

of section 58 or of the provisions of the Code then *prima facie* at least the standards of fairness set by Parliament have not been met. It is clear that not every breach of the statute or of the Codes results in unfairness to a detained person. It must depend on all the circumstances of the particular case. Mr Clegg submits in the present appeal that the effect of these admitted breaches should have caused the trial judge to have excluded the evidence of the first interview either under the provisions of section 76(2) of the Act or of section 78 ...

It will be observed that unless the prosecution prove to the necessary standard that the confession was not so obtained, the court has a mandatory duty to exclude it. Before the trial judge, Mr Clegg submitted that the prosecution had failed to prove the absence of oppression, but the learned judge rejected that submission. He ruled that there was no evidence of oppression before him. Mr Clegg, before us, tacitly accepts that ruling of the learned judge and he has not sought to renew his argument under the provisions of paragraph (a) of subsection (2). He does, however, rely, primarily now, on the provisions of paragraph (b). He submits that there are four grounds for saying that the confession was made in consequence of things said or done which were likely in the circumstances existing at the time to render the confession unreliable. These grounds are, first, the fact that the appellant was unlawfully denied access to a solicitor; secondly, the breach of the Code of Conduct by the police in relation to the notes of the interview; thirdly, the appellant was peculiarly vulnerable; and, fourthly, the physical condition of the appellant at the time of the interview. While it appears that grounds three and four, thus described, are hardly within the rubric of 'anything said or done', they do form the background upon which the submission is made that the confession was unreliable. It is really the absence of the solicitor which is Mr Clegg's main ground of criticism. The importance of this feature is underlined by the course the interview took. The appellant, when reminded of the caution, said she did not understand what the officer was saying. The words of the caution were then spelt out in the usual form and the appellant then said she did understand it. At the interview which took place the following day when those same words were recited, she denied comprehension and the caution had to be explained to her again in ordinary language. Returning now to the first interview, the police asked her to account for her movements on November 16. She proceeded to tell lies to them, saying that she had been with her mother all day until she was taken home in the evening. She was told that she had been seen by a neighbour at Charlton Avenue and to that she replied that she was confused. It is apparent from the following questions that were being put that the police were anxious to establish the whereabouts of Helen and whether she was alive or dead.

Under repeated questions designed to get an answer to that inquiry the appellant began to cry, saying that she did not know where Helen was. As more questions were asked, she began weeping heavily and gradually admitted that she was present at the house at the time Helen was assaulted, that there had been a fight but, as she put it, 'it was an accident'. After further questions, she finally admitted to stabbing Helen. The interviewing officer, Detective Sergeant Snow, who was apparently unaware that the appellant had been denied the services of a solicitor, then made enquiries about one being summoned. By that time – and to use his words – 'the appellant was weeping uncontrollably'. Mr Clegg submits that if a solicitor had been present he or she would never have allowed the appellant to be questioned when she was in such an emotional state. Indeed, when a solicitor arrived at the police station later that evening it was agreed that the appellant was in no fit state to be further questioned. Mr Clegg further points out that the appellant, who was six months' pregnant at the time, had been vomiting in her cell before the interview took place. At the trial a psychologist had described her as borderline subnormal with an IQ of 73. The psychologist compared her mentally with a child of 10.

Mr Bevan, on behalf of the Crown, submits that the prosecution has satisfied the burden laid on it by section 76. He submits that one has to look at the effect of the admitted breaches upon the girl and then determine whether her response to questions demonstrated that the confession was unreliable. When she was asked to explain her movements on the day of Helen's death, the appellant gave an account in some detail which in substance was quite untrue. The judge, having heard the psychologist's evidence and looking at the evidence of the girl's own statements, described the appellant as streetwise.

In the more formal second interview, when her solicitor was present, she gave a long and coherent account of what she said was her part in the attack upon Helen. It was a much more detailed and comprehensive description than she had given at the interview the day before. Counsel claims that the judge can properly take those factors into account when considering the effect upon the appellant of the breaches which are complained of and which are admitted. It must be remembered that while the psychologist had rated her as nearly subnormal she was, in fact, a woman at that time of 19 years of age, the mother of a child, carrying another, and has lived as the wife of Watkinson for some years.

Having considered these conflicting arguments and submissions, this court is clearly of the view that even if the confession given at the first interview was true, as it was later admitted to be, it was made in consequence of her being denied access to a solicitor and is for that reason in the circumstances likely to be unreliable. It follows that the prosecution has not in our judgment proved otherwise. We think Mr Clegg is right, that if a solicitor had been present at the time this mentally backward and emotionally upset young woman was being questioned, the interview would have been halted on the very basis that her responses would be unreliable. It seems that the interview was held quickly and without the formalities prescribed by the Code of Conduct because the police were anxious to discover the missing girl, but this heightened the risk of the confession being unreliable.

This view of the court is underlined by the evidence of Detective Sergeant Snow given to the learned judge at the trial on the *voir dire*. Amongst other answers he gave to the questions put to him were these: 'I conduct most of my interviews with a solicitor present. That is because it is not fair without a solicitor ... If we had used or made contemporary notes we would have got nowhere. That's my experience ... The appellant was questioned as a suspect for murder.'

The officer went on to say that he did not believe that they had done anything outside the spirit of the Police and Criminal Evidence Act 1984. He said that a contemporary note would have slowed the interview down or prevented them from recovering the body. He said that she had been at the prison – meaning the police station – for eight hours before he had spoken to her. He did not think that anyone had spoken to her before. He could not say why he did not take a contemporaneous note but said that he chose not to. In a later section of his evidence he made these observations: 'The lady' – meaning the prisoner – 'didn't understand all the questions. She didn't even know why she was in the police station. In the last part of the interview she was crying; she was clearly upset; she was crying heavily. Yes, I carried on questioning her. She was not offered a break to compose herself, not even a glass of water. I never offered her a solicitor until she confessed.' I say at once, in fairness to the officer, that he was unaware that she had been refused one. Finally, he said that the appellant seemed confused and he did not ask her to sign anything. Later she did, in fact, ask for a solicitor.

The second interview, to which I have already made reference, took place the following day in compliance with the provisions of the Code. The appellant, in the presence of her solicitor, made a full confession. Mr Bevan seeks to rely upon that second interview on the grounds that it was not tarnished by the shortcomings of the first. He submitted that the interview was entirely voluntary and that in no sense throughout the interview had the appellant been overborne. She had the advantage of a solicitor to advise her whom she previously consulted for a period of about half an hour before that second interview had taken place. She was in no sense under stress emotionally and there had, of course, been the delay between the two interviews so that she could compose herself.

Mr Clegg, however, argues, correctly in our view, that if the first interview is inadmissible where the appellant has made admissions she may not otherwise have done, then the subsequent confession was a direct consequence of the first. Moreover, the appellant's solicitor was not informed, as he tells us, that the appellant had been wrongfully denied access when she was brought to the police station. If the solicitor had known that she would have realised immediately that the first confession was suspect and in all probability would not have allowed the second interview to have taken place.

We are of the view that the earlier breaches of the Act and of the Code renders the contents of the second interview inadmissible also. One cannot refrain from emphasising that when an accused person has made a series of admissions as to his or her complicity in a crime at a first interview, the very fact that those admissions have been made are likely to have an effect upon her during the course of the second interview. If, accordingly, it be held, as it is held here, that the first interview was in breach of the rules and in breach of section 58, it seems to us that the subsequent interview must be similarly tainted.[10]

R v Delaney (1989, Court of Appeal)

The appellant had been convicted of indecently assaulting a child at a trial where evidence had been given of a confession.

The Lord Chief Justice: ... The assault took place on October 17 1986 in Hastings. It was some 12 days later, on October 29, that this appellant was interviewed by the police, first of all, at the place where he was living and then later at the police station. He was questioned about his movements on October 17. He was then 17 years of age. The evidence before the court from an educational psychologist was that he, the appellant, was educationally subnormal, with an intelligence quotient of about 80. His personality, according to the psychologist, was such that when being interviewed as a suspect he would be subject to quick emotional arousal which might lead him to wish to rid himself of the interview by bringing it to an end as rapidly as possible.

These were circumstances in which, *par excellence*, any interrogation should have been conducted with meticulous care and with meticulous observance of the rules of fairness, whether those rules were by virtue of common law or by statute or otherwise. Unhappily, that is not what happened. After a lengthy interview at the police station lasting for about an hour and a half, the appellant eventually said that it was he who had assaulted the little girl. He followed up that admission with further admissions at further interviews which took place. That initial admission and what followed was in effect the whole basis of the

---

10. 92 Cr App R 228.

prosecution case. Without it and without the further admissions, the case against the appellant was non-existent. There is no dispute about that.

The learned judge was called upon to rule whether the confession should be admitted in evidence. It was submitted that by virtue of section 76 of the Police and Criminal Evidence Act 1984 it was his duty to reject it and that by virtue of section 78 of the Police and Criminal Evidence Act 1984 in his discretion he ought to have rejected it.

In a ruling which is as clear and succinct as one comes to expect from Judge Gower, he ruled that the confessions should be admitted. It is the appellant's contention, advanced before this court by Mr Hunt, that that ruling should have been otherwise.

In order to decide those questions one must examine the facts of the interview with some care. The first interview, of about an hour and a half at the police station, consisted until the very end of a series of denials by the appellant that he had anything to do with the assault upon this little girl. Detective Constable Kitchen and Detective Constable Miller were the two officers. It is clear from what they said at the trial that they had come to the conclusion that the appellant was indeed the person who had committed this offence. Even on their own account, it is plain that they were at pains to minimise the gravity of the offence when questioning this youth. They were at pains to suggest that the real requirement of the offender in the circumstances was psychiatric help. One of the expressions they used was: 'People would be looking for ways of helping you with any problem that you might have.' In short, they were making it clear that this was a case, in their view, more for the attention of doctors than the attention of judges. So much was apparent from the evidence of the officers themselves.

However, and this was a matter which exercised the judge particularly, that note of evidence was not made up until the following morning, the interview having taken place in the early afternoon of the previous day. The note was then made up the following morning by Detective Constable Kitchen dictating it to a typist. That note emerged as a statement some 12 days later. It occupied three and a half pages, during the course of which the appellant was stoutly denying his guilt. At the end of the 90 minutes, Detective Constable Kitchen said: 'We don't think that there is any doubt that you are the person responsible,' to which the appellant is reported to have replied: 'You know it is me, don't you, but I am finding it very hard to talk about it.' Thereupon, Detective Constable Miller said: 'Come on, let's get it off your chest. Let's get it sorted out once and for all,' to which the appellant replied: 'You know it was me, don't you?' Detective Constable Kitchen said: 'Does that mean you are actually admitting it?' The appellant said: 'Yes.' Then, for the first time, the officer began to record the interview.

The matter which exercised the judge particularly was the way in which the officers had disregarded the terms of the Codes of Practice which were made under section 66 of the Police and Criminal Evidence Act 1984. The material parts of that Code in the present circumstances are to be found at C.11.3. It reads, so far as is material, as follows:

(a) An accurate record must be made of each interview with a person suspected of an offence, whether or not the interview takes place at a police station.

(b) If the interview takes place in the police station or other premises –

...

(ii) the record must be made during the course of the interview, unless in the investigating officer's view this would not be practicable or would interfere with the conduct of the interview, and must constitute either a verbatim record of what has been said or, failing this, an account of the interview which adequately and accurately summarises it.

11.4 If an interview record is not made during the course of the interview it must be made as soon as practicable after its completion.

The officers' assertion that it was not practicable to make a verbatim record was described by the judge as being the sheerest nonsense, a comment with which this court entirely agrees. That flagrant breach of the Code, as the judge correctly described it, was the starting point of the submission made to the judge by counsel for the appellant that the confessions should be rejected. But the mere fact that there has been a breach of the Codes of Practice does not of itself mean that evidence has to be rejected. It is no part of the duty of the court to rule a statement inadmissible simply in order to punish the police for failure to observe the Codes of Practice ...

By failing to make a contemporaneous note, or indeed any note, as soon as practicable, the officers deprived the court of what was, in all likelihood, the most cogent evidence as to what did indeed happen during these interviews and what did induce the appellant to confess. To use the words of Mr Hunt to the court this morning, the judge and the prosecution were *pro tanto* disabled by the omission of the officers to act in accordance with the Codes of Practice, disabled from having the full knowledge upon which the judge could base his decision. The judge of course is entitled to ask himself why the officers broke the rules. Was it mere laziness or was it something more devious? Was it perhaps a desire to conceal from the court the full truth of the suggestions they had held out to the defendant? These are matters which may well tip the scales in favour of the defendant in these circumstances and make it impossible for the judge to say that he is satisfied beyond reasonable doubt, and so require him to reject the evidence.

In this case, even on their own account, the officers, as the judge found, said things which could well be regarded as improper persuasion to the defendant to admit guilt; for example, the references to the need for psychiatric help and the assertion that if such an offender admitted what he had done people would go out of their way to help him. Detective Constable Kitchen agreed that he had deliberately sought to play down the seriousness of the assault because he had the feeling that the defendant was the man responsible and he, Detective Constable Kitchen, did not want to frighten the appellant away from confessing his guilt. He seems to have overlooked the possibility that he might, by the same token, be encouraging a false confession.

Mr Hunt seeks to derive assistance from what was said in *Fulling* (1987) where in the judgment there are set out a number of examples of what, prior to the 1984 Act, were properly described as oppression, but since the 1984 Act may well fall within the terms not of oppression but of section 76(2)(b) of the Act, the part of the Act which we are now considering.

The judge considered these matters, but he came to the conclusion that the defendant, when he made his admissions, did not think that the effect of the admissions would be to enable him to go home. He thought, rightly, that the probability was that it would lead him to being kept in custody and not granted bail. It was for those reasons that the judge came to the conclusion, despite the flagrant and serious breaches of the code, that the confession was not obtained in the consequence of anything said or done likely to render unreliable any confession made by the defendant.

We hesitate to criticise that conclusion, coming as it does from this particular judge, a judge who had, moreover, seen and heard both the appellant and the police officers, which of course we have not. However, it seems to us that Mr Hunt's submission is correct; namely, that it was not so much the question of immediate release which was exercising the mind of the appellant at interview. The evidence from the psychologist was that this man was poorly equipped to cope with sustained interrogation and the longer the pressure was imposed upon him the more confused he was likely to be in his own mind. He would experience what we have already described, the heightened sense of arousal from which he would want to escape. As the judge said, the appellant was under no illusions about the possibility of immediate release were he to confess; but what the officers, even on their own account of the interview, had been stressing was that in the long run treatment was required rather than punishment. We think that it was this long-term prospect, as Mr Hunt has rightly described it, to which the judge paid insufficient attention. The appellant may have felt it was easier to get away from the unpleasant state of arousal by making these confessions, particularly in the light of the suggestion that what was required was treatment rather than prison ...

Had the learned judge paid the attention which we think he should have paid to the long-term expectations of the appellant rather than to the prospects of immediate release, and had he paid attention to the fact that the breaches of the code deprived the court of the knowledge which should have been available to it, namely of precisely what was said by these officers in the vital interview, the judge would, and we think should, have ruled against the admission of these confessions, particularly so against the background of the appellant's age, his subnormal mentality and the behaviour of the police and what they had admittedly said to him ...[11]

R v Crampton (1991, Court of Appeal)

The appellant, who was a heroin addict, was convicted of a conspiracy to supply heroin. The prosecution relied on admissions made in interviews.

Stuart-Smith LJ: ... He did not dispute the records of interview and admitted understanding and intending to give the answers. He said that he had vomited bile at the beginning of the first interview but did not ask to stop. He felt a bit sick from withdrawing but thought he had better get it over with. He said he did not spend any money on drugs and did not sell them. He said he was confused and wanted to protect [his co-accused], and wanted to get out of the police station. He did not know why he had given some of the answers. The confession was the subject of a trial within a trial. It was submitted to the learned judge that he should not admit the confession because of the provisions of section 76(2) of the Police and Criminal Evidence Act ...

In the alternative it was submitted that in the exercise of his discretion the learned judge should not have permitted the evidence to be given under the discretion conferred by section 78 of that Act. It is submitted by [counsel for the appellant] that the confession was likely to be unreliable because the appellant might say anything with a view to getting out of the police station and getting more drugs, and that in those circumstances what he said was likely to be unreliable.

---

11. 88 Cr App R 338.

The factual basis upon which [counsel for the appellant] founds that submission is to be found in paragraph 2 of his notice of appeal. He submits, first of all, that the appellant was a heroin addict at the time of his arrest. That was known to the police. The police for reasons of their own – and he does not criticise them for this but merely points out that it was nothing to do with the appellant – did not interview him for nearly 19 hours. The police relied upon their own judgment to determine whether he was withdrawing or not and – I add to that – whether he was fit to be interviewed. The police failed to secure the attendance of a doctor, before interviewing the appellant, to determine his condition. That is perfectly correct. The doctor did not see him until after the interview. The police agreed that they would not have interviewed the appellant if they had known that he was withdrawing. It is right to say that that is what the police officers said.

The appellant gave evidence that he was withdrawing at the time of his interviews and his complaint of withdrawing was recorded in the custody record immediately after the conclusion of the first interview and by the doctor thereafter. Next, the evidence of both doctors called was that an addict would start to withdraw at the earliest after eight hours and the latest by 15 hours after his last fix so that by 19 hours he would have been suffering from symptoms of withdrawal. Both doctors credited the appellant's symptoms of withdrawal and he was given medication to alleviate it. Finally, the police and doctors both agreed that an addict withdrawing would or might be unreliable in what he said in view of his desire for a further fix. That last statement may have to be looked at a little more closely.

The court has considered the case of *Goldenberg* (1989), in which questions of admissibility of confessions where a drug addict may have been suffering symptoms of withdrawal were considered. In that case it is plain that it was the appellant himself who requested the interview with the police. The court held that there was nothing said or done other than by the appellant himself and that the case therefore did not fall within section 76(2) (b) at all.

[Counsel for the appellant] submits that case is distinguishable from the present because in this case it was the police who conducted the interview at their own convenience and not at the request of the appellant. That is perfectly true; but nevertheless it seems to us that it is in fact doubtful whether the mere holding of an interview at a time when the appellant is withdrawing from the symptoms of heroin addiction is something which is done within the meaning of section 76(2). However, for the purpose of this appeal we are content to assume that it is. The reason why we say it is doubtful is because the words of the subsection seem to postulate some words spoken by the police or acts done by them which were likely to induce unreliable confessions. The word 'unreliable', in our judgment, means 'cannot be relied upon as being the truth'. What the provision of subsection 2(b) is concerned with is the nature and quality of the words spoken or the things done by the police which are likely to, in the circumstances existing at the time, render the confession unreliable in the sense that it is not true. It is quite plain that if those acts and words are of such a quality, whether or not the confession is in fact true, it is inadmissible. That becomes clear when one reads the following words of subsection (3). It is the likelihood of the confession being unreliable in the sense of being untrue that is being considered in subsection (3).

In our judgment, the learned judge was right to reject the submission that was made to him. It is plain that the experienced officers, who dealt with drug addicts, considered that he was fit to be interviewed. More important perhaps, Dr Koppell said that when he saw the appellant he considered that he was then fit to be interviewed. It follows *a fortiori* that the appellant would have been fit at the time of his interview, which occurred earlier. [Counsel for the appellant] makes the point that that answer given by Dr Koppell was some eight months after the event. He was not asked about it at the time and therefore that answer is not reliable. In our judgment, the learned judge was perfectly entitled to accept that evidence, as he plainly did. He accepted the doctor's evidence as reliable, based upon the symptoms that the doctor saw when he examined the appellant after the interview. It is clear from the evidence that when Dr Koppell did examine the appellant there were no serious symptoms at all. Indeed there were no symptoms other than a raised pulse, which may have been attributable to stress or excitement at being in the police station.

The medical opinion is to be found at p 35G of the summing-up. It was said: 'A patient suffering from withdrawal symptoms can be manipulative and tell lies; he can do anything to get more drugs or to get rid of the symptoms. At the same time, he can be perfectly lucid. When he is manipulative, he might pretend his symptoms are worse than they are to get more drugs or substitute medication. He might say that he is suffering from a pain he has not really got, but normally there is no mental confusion and the addict's intelligence is working normally during the withdrawal – they know that they are telling lies.'

The appellant's own evidence about why he confessed is of interest. He was reminded that he had said he was feeling all right at the beginning of the interview. At p 42A he said this: 'In fact, I was feeling a bit sick. I'd been in custody for 14 or 15 hours and I was withdrawing from heroin, but I thought I might as well get it over and out of the way. I understood what I was saying and I understood what was going on.'

A little later he said that his answers were designed to protect Joe, that is Mr Vieira. He said: 'Joe was selling gear; I knew it later. I was trying to protect him. I knew that he had a little bit of form.' That is a previous record.

Finally, he said this: 'I understood all the questions. The answers I gave I intended to give. Withdrawal makes you confused. My answers were confused at the interview. I wanted to get on the streets again. When I gave the answers in the interview I understood how serious my admissions were, how serious was the charge I was being charged with, but I wanted to get out and to help Joe. Mainly I wanted to get out.'

In re-examination he said in the interview: 'I gave all the answers, I understood what I was saying. So far as my answers were concerned about dealing, the answers were not true. I was sick and I was slightly confused. I was concerned about the flat.'

There is no mention there of any desire to get the interview over quickly because he required another fix, which, as I understand it, is the basis upon which it is suggested that he might have been motivated to tell lies.

The high-watermark of the appellant's case, if I can put it like that, is that the police themselves said that they would not have interviewed the appellant if they had known he was withdrawing. [Counsel for the appellant] submits that that view should take precedence; yet at the same time, and in the same breath, he says that the police were not medically qualified and were not therefore competent to make the judgment they did that he was fit to be interviewed.

In our judgment, the position is this. Whether or not someone who is a drug addict is fit to be interviewed, in the sense that his answers can be relied upon as being truthful, is a matter for judgment of those present at the time. It is interesting to observe what a note to the Code of Practice says on this point. I am reading the note C: 9B of the Code of Practice where it says this: 'It is important to remember that a person who appears to be drunk or behaving abnormally may be suffering from illness or the effect of drugs or may have sustained injury (particularly head injury) which is not apparent, and that someone needing or addicted to certain drugs may experience harmful effects within a short time of being deprived of their supply. Police should therefore always call the police surgeon when in any doubt, and act with all due speed.'

That of course is concerned mainly with the condition of the defendant in the police station and the need to call a doctor in the event that the police are in doubt as to whether or not he is well. Nevertheless, it has relevance, in our judgment, in relation to the question of interview. The position here, as it seems to us, is this. If the police had summoned the doctor, Dr Koppell, and he had seen the appellant before the interview, the doctor would have certified that he was fit to be interviewed. That is the evidence that he effectively gave and the evidence that the judge accepted. It is then for the judge at the trial within the trial to decide whether the assessment of those present at the time was correct. The mere fact that someone is withdrawing, and may have a motive for making a confession, does not mean the confession is necessarily unreliable. In the case of *Rennie* (1982), a case which was before the Police and Criminal Evidence Act 1984 – nevertheless the observations of the Lord Chief Justice at p 212 are, in our judgment, relevant – the learned judge said this: 'Very few confessions are inspired solely by remorse. Often the motives of an accused are mixed and include a hope that an early admission may lead to an earlier release or a lighter sentence. If it were the law that the mere presence of such a motive, even if prompted by something said or done by a person in authority, led inexorably to the exclusion of a confession, nearly every confession would be rendered inadmissible. This is not the law. In some cases the hope may be self-generated. If so, it is irrelevant, even if it provides the dominant motive for making the confession. In such a case the confession will not have been obtained by anything said or done by a person in authority. More commonly the presence of such a hope will, in part at least, owe its origin to something said or done by such a person. There can be few prisoners who are being firmly but fairly questioned in a police station to whom it does not occur that they might be able to bring both their interrogation and their detention to an earlier end by confession.'

In our judgment, those words are in point here. We can see no reason upon the evidence in this case to conclude that the learned judge came to the wrong conclusion on the facts before him, either on the application under section 76(2), if indeed it was applicable, or in the exercise of his discretion under section 78. For those reasons the appeal will be dismissed.[12]

An argument often used in connection with both ss 76 and 78 is that the challenged item of evidence was obtained by breach of the defendant's right to legal advice.

Police and Criminal Evidence Act 1984

58 (1) A person arrested and held in custody in a police station or other premises shall be entitled, if he so requests, to consult a solicitor privately at any time.

(2) Subject to subsection (3) below, a request under subsection (1) above and the time at which it was made shall be recorded in the custody record.

---

12. 92 Cr App R 372.

(3) Such a request need not be recorded in the custody record of a person who makes it at a time while he is at a court after being charged with an offence.

(4) If a person makes such a request, he must be permitted to consult a solicitor as soon as is practicable except to the extent that delay is permitted by this section.

(5) In any case he must be permitted to consult a solicitor within 36 hours from the relevant time, as defined in section 41(2) above.

(6) Delay in compliance with a request is only permitted –

(a) in the case of a person who is in police detention for a serious arrestable offence; and

(b) if an officer of at least the rank of superintendent authorises it.

(7) An officer may give an authorisation under subsection (6) above orally or in writing but, if he gives it orally, he shall confirm it in writing as soon as practicable.

(8) An officer may only authorise delay where he has reasonable grounds for believing that the exercise of the right conferred by subsection (1) above at the time when the person detained desires to exercise it –

(a) will lead to interference with or harm to evidence connected with a serious arrestable offence or interference with or physical injury to other persons; or

(b) will lead to the alerting of other persons suspected of having committed such an offence but not yet arrested for it; or

(c) will hinder the recovery of any property obtained as a result of such an offence.

(9) If delay is authorised –

(a) the detained person shall be told the reason for it; and

(b) the reason shall be noted on his custody record.

(10) The duties imposed by subsection (9) above shall be performed as soon as is practicable.

(11) There may be no further delay in permitting the exercise of the right conferred by subsection (1) above once the reason for authorising delay ceases to subsist.

...

116 (1) This section has effect for determining whether an offence is a serious arrestable offence for the purposes of this Act.

(2) The following arrestable offences are always serious –

(a) an offence (whether at common law or under any enactment) specified in Part I of Schedule 5 to this Act; and

(b) an offence under an enactment specified in Part II of that Schedule.

(3) Subject to subsections (4) and (5) below, any other arrestable offence is serious only if its commission –

(a) has led to any of the consequences specified in subsection (6) below; or

(b) is intended or is likely to lead to any of those consequences.

(4) An arrestable offence which consists of making a threat is serious if carrying out the threat would be likely to lead to any of the consequences specified in subsection (6) below.

...

(6)   The consequences mentioned in subsections (3) and (4) above are

(a) serious harm to the security of the State or to public order;

(b) serious interference with the administration of justice or with the investigation of offences or of a particular offence;

(c) the death of any person;

(d) serious injury to any person;

(e) substantial financial gain to any person; and

(f) serious financial loss to any person.

(7)   Loss is serious for the purposes of this section if, having regard to all the circumstances, it is serious for the person who suffers it.

(8)   In this section 'injury' includes any disease and any impairment of a person's physical or mental condition.

SCHEDULE 5

SERIOUS ARRESTABLE OFFENCES

Part I

Offences mentioned in section 116(2)(a)

1   Treason.

2   Murder.

3   Manslaughter.

4   Rape.

5   Kidnapping.

6   Incest with a girl under the age of 13.

7   Buggery with –

(a) a boy under the age of 16; or

(b) a person who has not consented.

8   Indecent assault which constitutes an act of gross indecency.

R v Samuel (1988, Court of Appeal)

The appellant was arrested for armed robbery. Access to a solicitor was denied in reliance on the exceptions in s 58 of PACE. In the absence of a solicitor, the appellant made some admissions. The Court of Appeal concluded that access had been wrongly denied and that the evidence should have been excluded.

Hodgson J [delivering the judgment of the court]: It is undesirable to attempt any general guidance as to the way in which a judge's discretion under section 78 or his inherent powers should be exercised. Circumstances vary infinitely. [Counsel for the Crown] has made the extreme submission that, in the absence of impropriety, the discretion should never be exercised to exclude admissible evidence. We have no hesitation in rejecting that submission, although the propriety or otherwise of the way in which the evidence was obtained is something which a court is, in terms, enjoined by the section to take into account.

The Court of Appeal is always reluctant to interfere with the exercise of a judge's discretion but the position is different where there was no discretion to exercise on the judge's ruling and all the court has is an indication of how the judge would have exercised it ...

In this case the appellant was denied improperly one of the most important and fundamental rights of a citizen. The trial judge fell into error in not so holding. If he had arrived at correct decisions on the two points argued before him he might well have concluded that the refusal of access and consequent unlawful interview compelled him to find that the admission of evidence as to the final interview would have 'such an adverse effect on the fairness of the proceedings' that he ought not to admit it ...[13]

R v Canale (1990, Court of Appeal)

The appellant was charged with conspiracy to rob. The prosecution relied on admissions in interviews.

Lord Lane CJ: ... This argument before this court has been confined, at the invitation of the court, merely to the question of breaches, or possible breaches, of the Police and Criminal Evidence Act 1984.

The way in which the matter is put by counsel for the appellant is this. First of all he draws attention to s 67(11) of the 1984 Act ...

A number of breaches of the 1984 Act and the *Code of Practice for the Detention, Treatment and Questioning of Persons by Police Officers* (Code C) issued by the Secretary of State under s 66 of the 1984 Act are alleged. First of all, s 40 of the 1984 Act and s 128(8) of the Magistrates' Court Act 1980 (as inserted by s 48(b) of the 1984 Act) set out requirements as to periodical review of a person who is detained in custody. Those reviews have to be carried out first of all after six hours of detention has taken place, and subsequently thereafter every nine hours. No such reviews took place in the case of the appellant, and indeed no review took place until 48 hours after the initial detention had taken place.

It is submitted by counsel that that was a prejudice to the appellant because if those reviews had taken place it might have revealed that there had been other breaches of the 1984 Act, and it might have revealed that this man should have been charged with the offence at a stage earlier than that at which he was in fact charged.

We say immediately that, although we deplore the fact that these plain and admitted breaches of the review parts of the 1984 Act took place, yet nevertheless we do not think they acted in the upshot in a way which was prejudicial to the appellant.

What was much more worrying to us, and indeed has occupied much more time in this hearing, is the series of rules which appear in Code C in para 11. The material part of those rules read as follows:

> 11.3(a) An accurate record must be made of each interview with a person suspected of an offence, whether or not the interview takes place at a police station. (b) If the interview takes place in the police station or other premises [it did in this case take place at a police station]: (i) the record must state the place of the interview, the time it begins and ends, the time the record is made (if different), any breaks in the interview and the names of all those present; and must be made on the forms provided for the purpose or in the officer's pocket book or in accordance with the code of practice for the tape recording the police interviews with suspects; (ii) the record must be made during the course of the interview, unless in the investigating officer's view this would not be practicable or would interfere with the conduct of the

---

13. [1988] QB 615.

interview, and must constitute either a verbatim record of what has been said or, failing this, an account of the interview which adequately and accurately summarises it.

Taking the four interviews which took place between the police and the appellant with regard to this particular matter ... interviews 1 and 3 were not contemporaneously recorded. That is admitted. It is further admitted that that was a breach of para 11.3(b)(ii).

The reasons given by the two officers, Sgt Eames on the one hand and Det Con Clark on the other hand, for not recording the interview contemporaneously were contained in two initials which appeared in each of the two officers' documents, namely 'BW'. 'BW', the officers said, was short for 'best way'. In the officers' view the reason for failing to record the interview contemporaneously was that the best way was not to record the interview contemporaneously, which of course is not a reason at all. In the view of this court, it demonstrates a lamentable attitude towards the 1984 Act and the code made thereunder.

The rule which obliges the officers to set out the reason is para 11.6 which reads: 'If an interview record is not completed in the course of the interview the reason must be recorded in the officer's pocket book.'

A further breach, again admitted, took place of the requirement to which I have already referred, namely that the record must be made on the forms provided for this purpose, or in the officer's pocket book. The record made subsequently was not made on the forms provided. The record was made on an incident report form. It was not made in the officer's pocket book. The officers were asked: 'Why did you not make the record in your pocket book?' Sgt Eames's reply was that he had left his pocket book in his suit at home when he had changed his clothes. Det Con Clark's reason was that he had joined the Flying Squad only a week or two previously, and had not been issued with a pocket book, evidence which was put into considerable doubt by further testimony with regard to the issue of pocket books to officers of the Flying Squad.

There you have a situation where the rules set out pursuant to the 1984 Act, to which the court is enjoined by s 67(11) to pay attention when deciding matters of admissibility or otherwise, were flagrantly breached.

This case is the latest of a number of decisions emphasising the importance of the 1984 Act. If, which we find it hard to believe, police officers still do not appreciate the importance of that Act and the accompanying Codes, then it is time that they did. The Codes of Practice, and in particular Code C relating to interviews and questioning of suspects, are particularly important.

In the instant case the police officers seem to have displayed a disregard of those rules and, in light of the initials 'BW', and what they stood for, we feel compelled to say that that was a cynical disregard of the rules ...

As this court recently emphasised in *R v Keenan* (1989), the importance of the rules relating to contemporaneous noting of interviews can scarcely be over-emphasised. The object is twofold: not merely is it to ensure, so far as possible, that the suspect's remarks are accurately recorded and that he has an opportunity when he goes through the contemporaneous record afterwards of checking each answer and initialling each answer, but likewise it is a protection for the police, to ensure, so far as possible, that it cannot be suggested that they induced the suspect to confess by improper approaches or improper promises. If the contemporaneous note is not made, then each of those two laudable objects is apt to be stultified.

That is exemplified by what happened in this case, because on the *voir dire*, and eventually in evidence, as already indicated, the appellant was saying that he had been induced by certain promises on behalf of the police to make the admissions which started off the whole of this process, namely the admissions in interview 1, not contemporaneously recorded. Furthermore the interview, not contemporaneously recorded, and eventually put on to the wrong form by the officers, was not, as it should have been, shown to the appellant for him to check it, and for him to say whether he thought it was accurate or not.

So, when it came to the judge's task of deciding whether under s 76 or s 78 of the 1984 Act he should reject the statements as inadmissible, the judge was deprived of the very evidence which would have enabled him to come to a more certain conclusion as to what he should do with regard to the submissions, because he was deprived of that contemporaneous note which should have been made.

It was particularly important in this case, because up to the point of the first interview the appellant, who, it should be mentioned, was, perhaps like the other defendants, a man who had served in the Paratroop Regiment and therefore was perhaps not in the same category as some weak-minded defendant faced by a police interview, was stoutly denying that he had anything to do with the conspiracies or robberies at all. Somehow that *volte-face*, because *volte-face* it was, had to be explained. As I say, the judge, and once the statements were admitted, eventually the jury, had to decide those matters without the evidence which should have been available to them ...

[I]n our judgment the first interview was fatally flawed by the breaches of para 11.3(b) of Code C. It is true, as we have said, that thereafter there were two contemporaneously recorded interviews containing admissions, but the admissibility of those interviews depends in its turn on whether the admissions in the first interview were proved to be properly obtained or not. Thus the initial breaches, in our judgment, affected the whole series of purported admissions.

The fact that the most important evidence in the shape of a contemporaneous note was not available to the judge on the *voir dire* was sufficient to bring the case within the provisions of s 78(1) of the 1984 Act ...

We think that if the judge had appreciated the gravity of the breach of the interview rules in section 11 in Code C he would, and should, have acted under that s 78(1) to rule out the evidence of the admissions from the case. As it was, although he described the review breaches as serious, he did not seem to take the same view of the breaches of section 11 in Code C. In our view they were flagrant breaches. They were, one regrets to have to say, deliberate breaches and cynical breaches. In those circumstances the judge, had he directed his mind to the matters, which he should have done, would and should have come to the conclusion that s 78 applied.

We think that in those circumstances the interviews should have been ruled out of evidence ...[14]

R v Alladice (1988, Court of Appeal)

The appellant was convicted of robbery. The prosecution relied on admissions. It was argued that evidence of the admissions should have been excluded because the appellant had been improperly denied access to a solicitor. The

---

14. 91 Cr App R 1.

Court of Appeal agreed with the submission and held that there had been a breach of section 58. But that was not the end of the matter.

The Lord Chief Justice: ... The breach of section 58 and of paragraph C.6.3 of the Code is however not the end of the matter. There is no express sanction contained in section 58 or elsewhere for any such breach. Such a breach is no doubt one of the matters which the court has to consider under sections 76 and 78 of the Act.

Section 76(2) of the Act provides as follows [He read the subsection.] ...

It is not suggested that there was any oppression in the present case.

There remains the question under sub-paragraph (b) whether the confession may have been obtained in consequence of the breach of section 58, and if so whether that was likely in all the circumstances to render the confession unreliable.

We very much doubt whether it can be said that the confession may have been obtained as a result of the refusal of access to a solicitor. Even assuming that that may have been the case, there is no reason to believe that that fact was likely in all the circumstances to render a confession unreliable. We do not consider that the judge was obliged to rule the evidence inadmissible under section 76.

That leaves section 78 ...

If the police have acted in bad faith, the court will have little difficulty in ruling any confession inadmissible under section 78, if not under section 76. If the police, albeit in good faith, have nevertheless fallen foul of section 58, it is still necessary for the court to decide whether to admit the evidence would adversely affect the fairness of the proceedings, and would do so to such an extent that the confession ought to be excluded. No doubt in many cases it will, and it behoves the police to use their powers of delaying access to a solicitor only with great circumspection. It is not possible to say in advance what would or would not be fair ...

The judge in the instant case decided that the authorisation of delay was properly given, and consequently did not have to consider the question whether section 78 was applicable in the light of a breach of section 58.

What the appellant himself said in evidence was that he was well able to cope with the interviews; that he had been given the appropriate caution before each of them; that he had understood the caution and was aware of his rights. Indeed he asserts that he had said nothing at all after the first four (innocuous) questions, and what had been written down by the interviewing officer was nothing that he said but had been invented by the writer. His reason for wanting a solicitor was to have some sort of check on the conduct of the police during the interview.

The judge rejected the allegations that the police had invented the admissions. He found as a fact that the interviews had been conducted properly. He concluded that the only difference the presence of a solicitor would have made would have been to provide additional advice as to the appellant's right to say nothing, a right which he knew and understood and indeed at times during the interview exercised.

It may seldom happen that a defendant is so forthcoming about his attitude towards the presence of a legal adviser. That candour does however simplify the task of deciding whether the admission of the evidence 'would have such an adverse effect on the fairness of the proceedings' that it should not have been admitted. Had the solicitor been present, his advice would have added nothing to the knowledge of his rights which the appellant already had. The police, as the judge found, had acted with propriety at the interviews and therefore the solicitor's presence would not have improved the appellant's case in that respect.

This is therefore a case where a clear breach of section 58 nevertheless does not require the court to rule inadmissible subsequent statements made by the defendant ...[15]

Breaches of the Codes of Practice are frequently relied on in submissions under ss 76 and 78. The statutory background appears below.

Police and Criminal Evidence Act 1984

66   The Secretary of State shall issue Codes of Practice in connection with –

(a) the exercise by police officers of statutory powers –

(i)   to search a person without first arresting him; or

(ii) to search a vehicle without making an arrest;

(b) the detention, treatment, questioning and identification of persons by police officers;

(c) search of premises by police officers; and

(d) the seizure of property found by police officers on persons or premises.

67 (1) When the Secretary of State proposes to issue a Code of Practice to which this section applies, he shall prepare and publish a draft of that Code, shall consider any representations made to him about the draft and may modify the draft accordingly.

(2)   This section applies to a Code of Practice under section 60 or 66 above.

(3)   The Secretary of State shall lay before both Houses of Parliament a draft of any Code of Practice prepared by him under this section.

(4)   When the Secretary of State has laid the draft of a Code before Parliament, he may bring the Code into operation by order made by statutory instrument.

(5)   No order under subsection (4) above shall have effect until approved by a resolution of each House of Parliament.

...

(8)   A police officer shall be liable to disciplinary proceedings for a failure to comply with any provision of such a Code, unless such proceedings are precluded by section 104 below.

(9)   Persons other than police officers who are charged with the duty of investigating offences or charging offenders shall in the discharge of that duty have regard to any relevant provision of such a Code.

(10) A failure on the part –

(a) of a police officer to comply with any provision of such a Code; or

(b) of any person other than a police officer who is charged with the duty of investigating offences or charging offenders to have regard to any relevant provision of such a Code in the discharge of that duty,

shall not of itself render him liable to any criminal or civil proceedings.

---

15. 87 Cr App R 380. It is important not to overstate the significance of this decision. It is *not* authority for the proposition that suspects with previous convictions cannot rely on a breach of s 58 because they already know their rights. The case is no more than the application, in highly unusual circumstances, of the basic principle that there must be a causal link between the matter complained of and the confession. Remember the fallacy of *post hoc ergo propter hoc*. (Chapter One, note 15.)

(11) In all criminal or civil proceedings any such Code shall be admissible in evidence; and if any provision of such a Code appears to the court or tribunal conducting the proceedings to be relevant to any question arising in the proceedings it shall be taken into account in determining that question ...

R v Christou (1992, Court of Appeal)

Lord Taylor of Gosforth CJ: ... In our view, although [Code C] extends beyond the treatment of those in detention, what is clear is that it was intended to protect suspects who are vulnerable to abuse or pressure from police officers or who may believe themselves to be so. Frequently, the suspect will be a detainee. But the Code will also apply where a suspect, not in detention, is being questioned about an offence by a police officer acting as a police officer for the purpose of obtaining evidence. In that situation, the officer and the suspect are not on equal terms. The officer is perceived to be in a position of authority; the suspect may be intimidated or undermined ...[16]

R v Smurthwaite & Gill (1994, Court of Appeal)

Lord Taylor CJ: ... In our judgment, section 78 has not altered the substantive rule of law that entrapment or the use of an *agent provocateur* does not *per se* afford a defence in law to a criminal charge. A purely evidential provision in a statute, which does not even mention entrapment or *agent provocateur*, cannot, in our view, have altered a substantive rule of law enunciated so recently by the House of Lords. Had Parliament intended to alter the substantive law, it would have done so in clear terms.

However, that is not to say that entrapment, *agent provocateur*, or the use of a trick are irrelevant to the application of section 78. The right approach to the 1984 Act, a codifying Act, is that stated in *Fulling* (1987) following the principles laid down in *Bank of England v Vagliano* (1891). That is simply to examine the language of the relevant provision in its natural meaning and not to strain for an interpretation which either reasserts or alters the pre-existing law. Viewed in that way, the phrase emphasised by Mr Worsley clearly permits the court to have regard to 'the circumstances in which the evidence was obtained' and to exclude it, but only if it 'would have such an adverse effect on the fairness of the proceedings that the court ought not to admit it'. Thus, the fact that the evidence has been obtained by entrapment, or by *agent provocateur*, or by a trick does not of itself require the judge to exclude it. If, however, he considers that in all the circumstances the obtaining of the evidence in that way would have the adverse effect described in the statute, then he will exclude it ... 'Fairness of the proceedings' involves a consideration not only of fairness to the accused but also, as has been said before, of fairness to the public.

In exercising his discretion whether to admit the evidence of an undercover officer, some, but not an exhaustive list, of the factors that the judge may take into account are as follows: Was the officer acting as an *agent provocateur* in the sense that he was enticing the defendant to commit an offence he would not otherwise have committed? What was the nature of any entrapment? Does the evidence consist of admissions to a completed offence, or does it consist of the actual commission of an offence? How active or passive was the officer's role in obtaining the evidence? Is there an unassailable record of what occurred, or is it

---

16. [1992] 1 QB 979, 991.

strongly corroborated? In *Christou and Wright* (1992) this court held that discussions between suspects and undercover officers, not overtly acting as police officers were not within the ambit of the Codes under the 1984 Act. However, officers should not use their undercover pose to question suspects so as to circumvent the Code. In *Bryce* (1992) the court held that the undercover officer had done just that. Accordingly, a further consideration for the judge in deciding whether to admit an undercover officer's evidence, is whether he has abused his role to ask questions which ought properly to have been asked as a police officer and in accordance with the Codes.

Beyond mentioning the considerations set out above, it is not possible to give more general guidance as to how a judge should exercise his discretion under section 78 in this field since each case must be determined on its own facts ...[17]

17. (1994) 98 Cr App R 437, 440.

CHAPTER 8

SIMILAR FACT EVIDENCE

Similar fact evidence has a reputation for being an impenetrable subject. Quite often students who have coped well with other parts of an evidence course reach the examination still feeling that they don't know what it's about or how it works. They are aware of a few slogans – 'striking similarity', 'positive probative value' – but helplessness tends to set in when they are confronted by a problem question.

There are several reasons for this difficulty. One is that the very name of the topic – 'similar fact evidence' – is misleading because it is quite possible to encounter cases under this head which do not, strictly speaking, deal with similar facts at all. For example, this subject is generally taken to include cases where the accused is found in possession of incriminating material. There may also be cases where the circumstances surrounding the similar fact evidence are relevant independently of the similarity. PB Carter has given the example of a person charged with theft where the prosecution allege that he knew the key to a combination lock. Evidence of the fact that he had previously stolen the victim's diary containing a record of that key would be admissible, not to show that the accused was in the habit of stealing, but to show that he knew the key.[1]

Another reason for difficulty is that this topic cannot be learned by reading masses of cases and trying to summarise them in an elaborate structure of rules, subrules and exceptions. This topic is not, essentially, one of law at all: it concerns instead facts and problems of proof. Although it was not always so, it is now the case that with this topic facts and principles come first, and other decided cases a long way after.[2]

The key to understanding is to realise that the law relating to similar fact evidence developed from the need to ensure that juries reached correct decisions. If evidence of significant probative value is kept from a jury, it is likely that the strength of the prosecution case will not be fully appreciated, and this may lead to wrongful acquittal. But there is also the danger of misdecision if the jury hears too much evidence: if a jury hears evidence that has some probative value but not as much as the jury is likely to think it has, this may lead to a wrongful conviction. Similarly, if the jury hears evidence which, though relevant and probative, is likely to lead to a dim view being taken of the defendant's general character, there is a danger of conviction for the wrong reasons.

In every case it is necessary to try to assess the probative value of the disputed item of evidence, and to weigh this value against any danger there may be that the jury will go astray in their use of the evidence in question. It is this misuse, or abuse, of evidence by the jury that is referred to when lawyers talk about the 'prejudicial effect' of an item of similar fact evidence. In a sense,

---

1. PB Carter, 'Forbidden Reasoning Permissible: Similar Facts after *Boardman*' (1985) 48 MLR 29, 30.
2. See *Butler* (1987) 84 Cr App R 12, 18.

all sound prosecution evidence is 'prejudicial' to the accused because it makes a conviction more likely. But the 'prejudice' with which we are here concerned is the *improper* prejudice that may arise because of misuse or abuse of the evidence in question. The higher the probative value of a piece of evidence, the less will be the danger of misuse or abuse. The reason for this is that although such evidence may still provide some opportunity for the jury to convict for the wrong reason, it is more likely to persuade them to convict for the right reason: realisation of the strength of the case against the accused.

This principle is illustrated by the approach taken by courts to cases that involve admissibility of evidence about what are literally similar facts. When Charlie is charged with burglary of a tobacconist's shop, the jury is not allowed to know of his 27 previous convictions for breaking into other tobacconists' shops. The reason for this is that the jurors might say, 'Well, it's obvious. He's always doing this. He must be guilty'. They might even say, 'This chap needs putting away; he's a public nuisance. The easiest way to achieve this is to find him guilty on this charge. Don't let's waste time thinking about the evidence'. The fact that Charlie has burgled tobacconists' shops on at least 27 previous occasions is not irrelevant; a person with that history is more likely than someone without it to have committed the particular burglary with which the court is concerned. But that doesn't go very far towards proving that Charlie, as opposed to anyone else, committed the crime in question. It is thought, however, that juries would be unlikely to appreciate this, so the information is kept from them.

But now suppose rather more. When Charlie committed his previous burglaries he wrote on every occasion on one of the shop walls five lines from Homer's *Odyssey* in the original Greek and in sequence. A piece of writing which fits this pattern was found on a wall of the premises to which the present charge relates. At once the probative value of Charlie's previous history increases greatly because it puts Charlie in a very much narrower range of potential burglars – almost certainly in a class of one. But, you may object, someone could have framed him. This is true. But similar fact evidence, like any other evidence, does not have to be conclusive to be admitted. No evidence given in court can be conclusive. The testimony of someone claiming to be an eye-witness is not conclusive, for the witness may be mistaken or be committing perjury. The defendant's own confession is not conclusive, as recent cases have all too clearly shown.

In both the stories about Charlie we were relying for the relevancy of the previous history on an assumption that people tend to follow patterns of previous behaviour. But the first pattern was one followed by quite a large number of persons, and so did not point at all clearly to Charlie as having been the burglar on the occasion in question. Yet the second pattern was so peculiar to Charlie that it would defy belief to suggest that there might have been someone else operating in the same way.

I have gone into what must appear a rather obvious comparison because I want to show how we can set about assessing the probative worth of an item of evidence. Such an assessment depends not on law, but on a mixture of logic and general experience. What has already been said in Chapter One about relevancy is of vital importance here. To argue effectively, you need to clarify those basic assumptions about the way things are in the world which have to be true if a particular piece of information is to be relevant at all. If you need to attack the admissibility of a piece of similar fact evidence, the best approach may often be to attack the generalisation upon which your opponent must rely to establish its relevancy. (What unexpressed generalisations can you find, for example, in the case of *Butler* in 1987?)

It should come as no surprise to find that the 'similar fact' problem was first discussed as part of the question of relevancy.[3]

R v Dossett (Oxford Assizes, 1846)

ARSON. The prisoner was indicted for having, on 29 March 1846, feloniously set fire to a rick of wheat straw, the property of William Cox.

It appeared that the rick was set on fire by the prisoner's having fired a gun very near to it; and it was proposed on the part of the prosecution to go into evidence to shew that the rick had been on fire on 28 March, and that the prisoner was then close to it with a gun in his hand.

J Jefferys Williams, for the prisoner: I submit that this evidence is not admissible. It is seeking to prove one felony by another; and it is in effect asking the jury to infer that the prisoner set fire to the rick on the 29th, because he did so on the 28th. The firing of the rick on the 28th, if wilfully done, was a distinct felony.

Maule J: Although the evidence offered may be proof of another felony, that circumstance does not render it inadmissible, if the evidence be otherwise receivable. In many cases it is an important question whether a thing was done accidentally or wilfully. If a person were charged with having wilfully poisoned another, and it were a question whether he knew a certain white powder to be poison, evidence would be admissible to shew that he knew what the powder was because he administered it to another person, who had died, although that might be proof of a distinct felony. In the cases of uttering forged banknotes knowing them to be forged, the proofs of other utterings are all proofs of distinct felonies. I shall receive the evidence.[4]

1860 saw the beginnings of an attempt to lay down a list of exceptions to a general rule excluding evidence of similar facts. In *R v Winslow* counsel for the defence submitted that:

The cases in which other felonies prior or subsequent to the particular act charged have been admitted in evidence range themselves under one of the following heads–

1   Where the several felonies are all parts of one entire transaction.

2   In an exceptional class of cases where guilty knowledge must be proved.

3   Where the other felonies are the direct acts of the accused, and tend to show malice in the particular act itself, and as against the individual prosecuting.'[5]

But there is no indication that the judges were prepared to accept such a formulation. Cases that would now be seen to give rise to a 'similar fact'

---

3.   Julius Stone, 'The Rule of Exclusion of Similar Fact Evidence: England' (1932) 46 HLR 954.

4.   2 Car & K 306, 175 ER 126.

5.   8 Cox CC 397, 399.

problem continued to be argued on the basis of relevancy alone, though after about 1850 there was an increasing tendency to cite precedents for the admissibility of evidence and for judges to make decisions on analogies.

The general reluctance to become involved in rule-based law on this subject can be seen from the arguments that were presented to the court in the leading case of *Makin v Attorney General for New South Wales* (1894).

For the appellants it was argued that the general rule was to confine the testimony strictly to direct evidence of the commission of the particular act charged. Evidence of similar acts committed, or supposed to have been committed, by the same person on other occasions was to be excluded, not because it was wholly irrelevant but because it was 'inconvenient and dangerous'. To admit such evidence would be likely to take the accused by surprise and to confuse and unduly prejudice the jury.

The respondents did indeed argue that it was 'the general and not the exceptional rule of law to admit such evidence to rebut defence of accident, and to shew existence of motive and a systematic course of conduct'. But it was made clear that this was only part of a general principle that evidence was admissible of any acts or doings of the persons accused, 'if such acts or doings are so connected with the transaction under charge or are of a character so similar thereto as to lead to a reasonable inference that the prisoner committed the act charged, or at the least that such act if committed was wilful and not accidental'. The opinion of the Judicial Committee of the Privy Council was delivered by the Lord Chancellor, Lord Herschell. It contained a passage which has been quoted on innumerable occasions since then.

Makin v Attorney General for New South Wales (1894, Privy Council)

The Lord Chancellor: The appellants in this case were tried and found guilty at the Sydney Gaol Delivery held at Darlinghurst of the murder of the infant child of one Amber Murray. The learned judge before whom the case was tried deferred passing sentence until after the argument of the special case which he stated for the opinion of the Supreme Court of New South Wales.

The points reserved by the learned judge were: first, that his honour was wrong in admitting evidence of the finding of other bodies than the body of the child alleged to be Horace Amber Murray; secondly, that his honour was wrong in admitting the evidence of Florence Risby, Mary Stacey, Agnes Todd, Agnes Ward and Mrs Sutherland [to the effect that they had entrusted other children to the prisoners, which children had never been seen again] ...

Special leave was granted to appeal to this Board from the judgment of the Supreme Court of New South Wales ...

The question which their Lordships had to determine was the admissibility of the evidence relating to the finding of other bodies, and to the fact that other children had been entrusted to the appellants.

In their Lordships' opinion the principles which must govern the decision of the case are clear, though the application of them is by no means free from difficulty. It is undoubtedly not competent for the prosecution to adduce evidence tending to shew that the accused has been guilty of criminal acts other than those covered by the indictment, for the purpose of leading to the conclusion that the accused is a person likely from his criminal conduct or character to have committed the offence for which he is being tried. On the other hand, the mere fact that the evidence adduced tends to shew the commission of other crimes does not render it inadmissible if it be relevant to an issue before the jury, and it may be so relevant if it bears upon the question whether the acts alleged to constitute the crime charged in the indictment were designed or accidental, or to rebut a defence which would otherwise be open to the accused. The statement of these general principles is easy, but it is obvious that it may often be very difficult to draw the line and to decide whether a particular piece of evidence is on the one side or the other.

The principles which their Lordships have indicated appear to be on the whole consistent with the current of authority bearing on the point, though it cannot be denied that the decisions have not always been completely in accord ...

Their Lordships do not think it necessary to enter upon a detailed examination of the evidence in the present case. The prisoners had alleged that they had received only one child to nurse; that they received 10s a week whilst it was under their care, and that after a few weeks it was given back to the parents. When the infant with whose murder the appellants were charged was received from the mother she stated that she had a child for them to adopt. Mrs Makin said that she would take the child, and Makin said that they would bring it up as their own and educate it, and that he would take it because Mrs Makin had lost a child of her own two years old. Makin said that he did not want any clothing; they had plenty of their own. The mother said that she did not mind his getting £3 premium so long as he took care of the child. The representation was that the prisoners were willing to take the child on payment of the small sum of £3, inasmuch as they desired to adopt it as their own.

Under these circumstances their Lordships cannot see that it was irrelevant to the issue to be tried by the jury that several other infants had been received from their mothers on like representations, and upon payment of a sum inadequate for the support of the child for more than a very limited period, or that the bodies of infants had been found buried in a similar manner in the gardens of several houses occupied by the prisoners.[6]

For the next 80 years similar fact evidence developed as a commentary on Lord Herschell's statement of principles, which was treated almost as a legislative enactment. The problems of this approach have been highlighted by CR Williams.

CR Williams, 'The Problem of Similar Fact Evidence', *Dalhousie Law Journal* 5 (1979)

[I]f Lord Herschell's formulation is examined it will be seen to contain an internal logical contradiction which would appear to render it unworkable. The first sentence states a rule of exclusion. The second sentence states a rule of inclusion, but a rule of such width as to render the rule of exclusion of no effect. It is not possible to say that evidence of a particular class is inadmissible, and then to say that such evidence is admissible 'if it be relevant to an issue before the jury'. To be admissible any item of evidence must be relevant to an issue before the jury. If evidence relevant to an issue before the jury is to be admissible notwithstanding the exclusionary rule, then the exclusionary rule is of no effect.

Broadly, three approaches have been adopted to the problem of giving a workable meaning to Lord Herschell's formulation.

---

6. [1894] AC 57.

1 A Rule of Exclusion With Exceptions

The first approach is to state that there is a general rule requiring the exclusion of similar fact evidence. This rule is stated in the first sentence of Lord Herschell's formulation. To this rule of exclusion, however, there are a number of exceptions. It is to the class of exceptions that the second sentence of Lord Herschell's formulation refers. The two exceptions mentioned (cases where evidence bears upon the question whether the acts alleged to constitute the crime charged in the indictment were designed or accidental, and cases where the evidence rebuts a defence which would otherwise be open to the accused) were not intended to be exhaustive of the classes of case where relevant similar fact evidence may be admitted. It is now recognised that there are other classes of case where such evidence may be admissible, and further classes may be developed [*Thompson v The King* (1918); *Harris v DPP* (1952); *MacDonald v Canada Kelp Co Ltd* (1973); *R v Schell and Paquette* (1977)] The most commonly listed classes of exception are: 1) To Prove Identity, 2) To Prove Knowledge or Intent, 3) To Rebut a Defence of Mistake or Involuntary Conduct, 4) To Establish System, 5) To Rebut a Defence of Innocent Association.

Such an understanding of Lord Herschell's formulation has often been adopted by the courts [eg *R v Bond* (1906); *Harris v DPP* (1952); *R v Horwood* (1969)], and it is the approach taken in many of the textbooks on evidence. The difficulty with this approach is that it tends to encourage an overly simplistic view of the question of the admissibility of similar fact evidence. When faced with a particular case its adherents often simply ask whether the case fits neatly within one of the established categories. If it does the evidence will usually be admitted; it it does not the evidence will usually be rejected. It is submitted that if such a procedure is adopted, the true factors which ought to determine whether an item of similar fact evidence is to be admitted or rejected are being largely ignored.

2 Relevance Via Propensity and Relevance Other than Via Propensity

This second approach treats as crucial the distinction between evidence which is relevant only as establishing a propensity or disposition on the part of the accused to commit acts similar in nature to those acts constituting the subject matter of the crime charged, and evidence which possesses a relevance other than by establishing such a propensity or disposition. The words 'propensity' and 'disposition' are here treated as equivalents. If the evidence is relevant only via propensity it is excluded by the first sentence of Lord Herschell's formulation. If the evidence possesses a relevance other than via propensity it is admissible as falling within the second sentence of Lord Herschell's formulation.

If the evidence possesses a relevance other than via propensity it is admissible notwithstanding the fact that it also possesses a relevance via propensity. Indeed, by definition similar fact evidence will always possess some relevance via propensity. In this context what Wigmore termed the doctrine of 'multiple admissibility' is applicable. He wrote: '... *when an evidentiary fact is offered for one purpose, and becomes admissible by satisfying all the rules applicable to it in that capacity, it is not inadmissible because it does not satisfy the rules applicable to it in some other capacity and because the jury might improperly consider it in the latter capacity*' [*Wigmore on Evidence* (3rd edn Boston: Little Brown and Co, 1940) Volume 1 at 300].

It is only if the evidence possesses no substantial relevance other than via propensity that it is inadmissible as falling within the first limb of Lord Herschell's formulation.

The expressions 'relevance via propensity' and 'relevance other than via propensity' require explanation. Assume that the accused is charged with burglary. Evidence that the accused on some previous occasion broke into another house is, without more, inadmissible. It is inadmissible because it shows no more than that the accused has a propensity for dishonesty, or, at most, a propensity for burglary. Assume however that at the scene of the second burglary an article left by the burglar is found. Assume further, that it is established that this article was taken from the first house which was burgled. When the facts are changed in this way, evidence that the accused committed the first burglary becomes relevant in a quite different way to show he committed the second burglary. The evidence now possesses a relevance other than via propensity. The evidence is relevant in the same sort of way as evidence that a wallet honestly acquired and belonging to the accused was discovered at the scene of the second burglary.

The evidence does, of course, still possess a relevance via propensity; it tends to show that the accused has a propensity for burglary. This latter relevance may constitute a reason for its exclusion by the trial judge in the exercise of his discretion. Because of the risk that prejudicial evidence may be admissible as possessing some slight relevance other than via propensity, proponents of this interpretation of Lord Herschell's formulation place considerable emphasis on the discretion which, in English law at least, the trial judge has to reject legally admissible evidence.

The difficulty with an approach based upon the distinction between relevance via propensity and other relevance, is that in many cases undoubtedly admissible similar fact evidence derives its only relevance from an argument via propensity. A particularly clear illustration is the case of *R v Straffen* (1952). The accused was charged with the murder by manual strangulation of two girls at Bath. He was found unfit to plead by reason of insanity, and committed to Broadmoor Institution. A year later the accused escaped, and was at liberty for a period of approximately four hours. During the period the accused was at large a small girl, Linda Bowyer, was murdered by strangulation. The accused was seen near the place where the body was found, but there were other passers-by who might have committed the crime. When questioned by the police the accused admitted killing the two girls at Bath, but denied he was responsible for the murder of Linda Bowyer.

The accused was tried for the murder of Linda Bowyer. The trial judge admitted evidence of the statements made by the accused to the police, and also evidence of the circumstances surrounding the killing of the little girls at Bath. The following points of similarity existed between the two earlier killings and the killing of Linda Bowyer: (1) in each case the victim was a young girl, (2) each of the children was killed by manual strangulation, (3) in no case was there any attempt at sexual interference or any apparent motive for the crime, (4) in none of the cases was there any evidence of a struggle, and (5) in no case was any attempt made to conceal the body although that could easily have been done.

The accused was convicted, and appealed to the Court of Criminal Appeal. The court dismissed the appeal, holding that the similar fact evidence had been properly admitted admitted. Delivering the judgment of the court Slade J stated: 'In the opinion of the court that evidence was rightly admitted, not for the purpose of showing ... that the appellant was "a professional strangler", but to show that he strangled Linda Bowyer; in other words, for the purpose of identifying the murderer of Linda Bowyer as being the same individual as the person who had murdered the other two little girls in precisely the same way.'

Clearly the decision of the court was correct. The evidence was of the highest possible probative value, and it would have been absurd to have held it inadmissible. The sole relevance of the evidence was, however, via propensity. The similar fact evidence established that the accused possessed a propensity of the most unusual kind: he was a strangler of small girls, in peculiar circumstances, and for no apparent motive. The unusual nature of the propensity gave the evidence its great probative value and rendered it admissible.

R v Straffen is in no way highly unusual in this regard. In many cases the only relevance of undoubtedly admissible similar fact evidence is by virtue of an argument via propensity. [Other leading cases in which the similar fact evidence was relevant solely via propensity include *R v Ball* (1911); *Thompson v The King* (1918); *O'Leary v The King* (1946); *R v Drysdale* (1969); *R v Morris* (1969); *R v Bird* (1970); *R v McDonald* (1974); *DPP v Boardman* (1975).]

A modified form of the present approach recognises that there are many cases where evidence relevant solely via propensity is admissible, but nonetheless insists on the importance of the distinction. Those adopting this approach maintain that evidence relevant solely via propensity is *prima facie* inadmissible, but may be admissible if it is of exceptional probative value. This argument was elaborated in an influential essay in Cowen and Carter's *Essays on the Law of Evidence* ['The Admissibility of Evidence of Similar Facts: A Re-Examination' in Zelman Cowen and PB Carter, *Essays on the Law of Evidence* (Oxford: Clarendon Press, 1956) at 106.] The authors summarised the position regarding the admissibility of similar fact evidence as follows:

> *Rule 1.* Evidence of similar facts which is relevant via propensity is inadmissible unless it is exceptional.

> *Rule 2.* Such evidence is exceptional and therefore admissible provided:

> (i) it has very great real probative value upon any issue upon which the jury is likely to use it; and

> (ii) its admission is not unnecessary (ie the issue upon which it is tendered can reasonably be regarded as a real one in the circumstances of the case).

> *Rule 3.* Evidence of similar facts which has substantial relevance otherwise than via propensity (even if as well as via propensity) is admissible provided it is sufficiently relevant.

> *Rule 4.* In criminal cases the judge has a discretion to exclude evidence admissible under any of the foregoing rules if their strict application would operate unfairly against the accused.

> *NB*: It should be remembered that:

> (a) Evidence which is relevant via propensity is a much wider category than has often been supposed.

> (b) Rule 2 means (obviously) that *not all* evidence the primary relevance of which is via propensity is excluded.

> (c) The nature of the issue to which the evidence is relevant (eg that it is to show system, to prove intent) does not control its admissibility. The nature of the issue *may*, however, affect the strength of the probative value of the similar fact evidence and thus indirectly influence its admissibility.

The approach taken by Cowen and Carter is certainly more satisfactory than others considered thus far. However, having accepted the probative value or weight as a vital factor, it is difficult to see why the authors nonetheless insist upon the primary significance of the distinction between relevance via propensity and relevance other than via propensity.

3 An Approach Based Upon a Comparison of Probative Value and Risk of Prejudice

The third approach, and the one argued for in the present article, treats the balance between probative value and the risk of prejudice as the key to determining the admissibility of similar fact evidence. It is submitted that the question of whether the evidence derives its relevance from an argument via propensity or from an argument other than via propensity ought properly to be regarded as largely incidental.

This approach involves treating Lord Herschell's formulation not as containing two conflicting rules, one of exclusion and one of inclusion, but rather as referring to two competing principles. [On the distinction between rules and principles, see RM Dworkin, *Taking Rights Seriously* (London: Duckworth, 1977), chs 2 and 3]. The first sentence refers to the principle that evidence which shows the accused to be of bad character or disposition is not admissible to establish his guilt of the crime charged. The second sentence refers to the principle that relevant evidence which does not fall within a recognised rule of exclusion ought to be admitted.

The rationale behind the principle of exclusion embodied in the first sentence of Lord Herschell's formulation is the risk of prejudice inherent in evidence of this sort. The term 'prejudice' is here used in the sense adopted by Wigmore, ie

(1) The over-strong tendency to believe the defendant guilty of the charge merely because he is a likely person to do such acts;

(2) the tendency to condemn, not because he is believed guilty of the present charge, but because he has escaped unpunished from other offences; both of these represent the principle of Undue Prejudice.

What Lord Herschell's formulation requires is that these two competing factors, the probative value of the evidence and the risk of prejudice, be weighed one against the other. If the risk of prejudice is great, and the probative value small by comparison, the evidence should be rejected. If the probative value is great, and the risk of prejudice slight by comparison, the evidence should be admitted.

The problem of estimating the probative value of evidence is one which has received surprisingly little attention. Relevance and weight are generally treated as matters of common sense or experience both by judges and by academic commentators. In this way, the difficulties associated with what is in fact the key concept in the law of evidence are largely glossed over. It is, of course, impossible to ever estimate the probative value of evidence with any degree of exactitude. The degree of relevance possessed by an item of evidence is obviously dependent upon an almost infinite number of variables. In the present context the key variables appear to be the nature of the similar fact evidence itself, the issues in contest in the case and the other evidence presented in the case.

Equally it is extremely difficult to assess, even in a very approximate fashion, the extent of the risk of an item of evidence being misused by a jury so as to result in prejudice to the accused. However, the risk of prejudice is quite clearly the rationale for the exclusionary aspect of the similar fact rule. This being so, the difficulty in estimating potential for prejudice in no way removes the necessity for attempting some such estimate when determining whether a given item of similar fact evidence ought to be admitted.

The present approach does not involve complete rejection of the process of categorization which is the essence of the first approach discussed. The traditional categories in fact group together types of situation in which similar fact evidence is likely to possess a high degree of probative value. They do so, however, in an imprecise and haphazard way, and they have been accorded far greater significance than they ought to possess.[7]

Although basic questions of relevancy and weight were never completely forgotten during this period, from time to time they tended to become obscured by a structure of rules and categories thrown up by members of the Court of Criminal Appeal who were in a hurry and who looked to *stare decisis* for quick fixes. But in 1974 a case now seen as a landmark came before the House of Lords, and once again the emphasis was firmly placed on the relevancy and weight of evidence rather than on supposed rules of law.

DPP v Boardman (1975, House of Lords)

The appellant was tried on three counts. The offences were alleged to have been committed against boys at a small English language school in Cambridge of which the appellant, then aged about 45, was headmaster. Count 1 charged the appellant with having, on a day in October or November 1972, committed buggery with S, a boy then aged 16. Count 2 charged the appellant with having on a day in January 1973 incited H, who was then aged 17, to commit buggery with him. A conviction on a third count in relation to another boy was subsequently quashed by the Court of Appeal.

The trial judge ruled, among other things, that the evidence on count 2 was admissible in relation to count 1, and vice versa. In due course the appellant was convicted on all three counts. The Court of Appeal upheld the convictions on counts 1 and 2, but certified that a point of law of general public importance arose, namely, '[Where], on a charge involving an allegation of homosexual conduct there is evidence that the accused person is a man whose homosexual proclivities take a particular form, that evidence is thereby admissible although it tends to show that the accused has been guilty of criminal acts other than those charged'.

In the House of Lords the appellant's main contention was that the trial judge's ruling about the mutual admissibility of evidence on counts 1 and 2 had been wrong. The Crown did not argue that homosexuality as such was ever sufficient of itself to justify the admission of similar fact evidence. But the trial judge's ruling was supported by contending that the evidence of the two boys, S and H, showed several striking similarities in the appellant's behaviour; such as waking the boys in the middle of the night, taking them to his sitting room, and his request that the boys should bugger him rather than vice versa.

Lord Morris of Borth-y-Gest: My Lords, the well-known words of Lord Herschell LC in delivering the judgments of the Privy Council in *Makin v Attorney General for New South Wales* (1894) have always been accepted as expressing cardinal principles. On the one hand, it is clear that the prosecution cannot adduce evidence which tends to show that an accused person has been guilty of criminal acts other than those with which he is charged for the purpose of leading to the

---

7.   CR Williams, 'Problem of Similar Fact Evidence', *Dalhousie Law Journal* 5 (1979) pp 283-90.

conclusion that he is one who is likely from his criminal conduct or character to have committed the criminal acts with which he is charged. On the other hand, there may be evidence which is relevant to an issue in a criminal case and which is admissible even though it tends to show that an accused person has committed other crimes.

The line separating exclusion and admission will often, as Lord Herschell said, be difficult to draw. In some cases a ruling will be sought from the judge at the time when certain evidence is tendered. The judge will then have to decide whether a particular piece of evidence is on the one side or the other and whether in the words of Lord du Parcq in *Noor Mohamed v The King* (1949) quoted by Viscount Simon in *Harris v Director of Public Prosecutions* (1952) the evidence which is it proposed to adduce is sufficiently substantial having regard to the purpose to which it is professedly directed to make it desirable in the interest of justice that it should be admitted. But at whatever stage a judge gives a ruling he must exercise his judgment and his discretion having in mind both the requirements of fairness and also the requirements of justice. The first limb of what was said by Lord Herschell LC in *Makin's* case was said by Viscount Sankey LC in *Maxwell v Director of Public Prosecutions* (1935) to express ' ... one of the most deeply rooted and jealously guarded principles of our criminal law ... '. Judges can be trusted not to allow so fundamental a principle to be eroded. On the other hand, there are occasions and situations in which in the interests of justice certain evidence should be tendered and is admissible in spite of the fact that it may or will tend to show guilt in the accused of some offence other than that with which he is charged. In the second limb of what he said in *Makin's* case Lord Herschell gave certain examples. In his speech in *Harris v Director of Public Prosecutions* (1952) Viscount Simon pointed out ... that it would be an error to attempt to draw up a closed list of the sorts of cases in which the principle operates. Just as a closed list need not be contemplated, so also, where what is important is the application of principle, the use of labels or definitive descriptions cannot be either comprehensive or restrictive. While there may be many more reasons why what is called 'similar fact' evidence is admissible there are some cases where words used by Hallett J are apt. In *Reg v Robinson* (1953): 'If a jury are prejudiced by some rule of law from taking the view that something is a coincidence which is against all the probabilities if the accused person is innocent, then it would seem to be a doctrine of law which prevents a jury from using what looks like ordinary common sense.'

But as Viscount Simon pointed out in *Harris v Director of Public Prosecutions* (1952) evidence of other occurrences which merely tend to deepen suspicion does not go to prove guilt: so evidence of 'similar facts' should be excluded unless such evidence has a really material bearing on the issues to be decided. I think that it follows from this that, to be admissible, evidence must be related to something more than isolated instances of the same kind of offence ...

The certified point of law requires some examination. If the question is raised whether there is a special rule in cases where there is a charge involving an allegation of homosexual conduct the answer must be that there is no special rule. But in such cases there may be, depending upon the particular facts, room for the application of the principle to which I have been referring. [*Viz* that there are cases in which evidence of certain acts becomes admissible because of their striking similarity to other acts being investigated and because of their resulting probative force.] The word 'thereby' in the certified point of law seems to raise a question whether there is a rule which gives automatic admissibility to evidence where proclivities take a particular form. There is no such specific rule which would automatically give admissibility. But there may be cases where a judge, having both limbs of Lord Herschell LC's famous proposition ... in mind, considers that the interests of justice (of which the interests of fairness form so fundamental a component) make it proper that he should permit a jury when considering the evidence on a charge concerning one fact or set of facts also to consider the evidence concerning another fact or set of facts if between the two there is such a close or striking similarity or such an underlying unity that probative force could fairly be yielded ...

The learned judge left the matter fairly to the jury. He mentioned the possibility of two people conspiring together and he examined the question whether there were or were not any indications that S and H had conspired together. That was important because one question which the jury may have wished to consider was whether it was against all the probabilities, if the appellant was innocent, that two boys, unless they had collaborated, would tell stories having considerable features of similarity. In dealing with the similarity of the kind of behaviour spoken to by S and H the learned judge concentrated, and perhaps unduly so, on that feature of it which showed that the request and desire was that it was the youngster who was to play the active part and the appellant the passive part. But another feature of rather striking similarity lay in the evidence concerning the nocturnal dormitory visits of the appellant ...

In the course which he took the learned judge acted, in my view, within legal principle and in so far as the matter depended upon his exercise of discretion I do not consider that his exercise of it was unjustified.

I would dismiss the appeal.

Lord Wilberforce: ... Whether in the field of sexual conduct or otherwise, there is no general or automatic answer to be given to the question whether evidence of facts similar to those the subject of a particular charge ought to be admitted. In each case it is necessary to estimate (i) whether, and if so how strongly, the evidence as to other facts tends to support, ie, to make it more credible, the evidence given as to the fact in question; (ii) whether such evidence, if given, is likely to be prejudicial to the accused. But these elements involve questions of degree.

It falls to the judge, in the first place by way of preliminary ruling, and indeed on an application for separate trials if such is made (see the opinion of my noble and learned friend Lord Cross of Chelsea), to estimate the respective and relative weight of these two factors and only to allow the evidence to be put before the jury if he is satisfied that the answer to the first question is clearly positive, and, on the assumption, which is likely, that the second question must be similarly answered, that on a combination of the two the interests of justice clearly require that the evidence be admitted.

Questions of this kind arise in a number of different contexts and have, correspondingly, to be resolved in different ways. I think that it is desirable to confine ourselves to the present set of facts, and to situations of a similar character. In my understanding we are not here concerned with cases of 'system' or 'underlying unity' ... words whose vagueness is liable to result in their misapplication, nor with a case involving proof of identity, or an alibi, nor, even, is this a case where evidence is adduced to rebut a particular defence. It is sometimes said that evidence of 'similar facts' may be called to rebut a defence of innocent association, a proposition which I regard with suspicion since it seems a specious manner of outflanking the exclusionary rule. But we need not consider the validity or scope of this proposition. The Court of Appeal dealt with the case on the basis, submitted by the appellant's counsel, that no defence of innocent association was set up; in my own opinion we should take the same course.

This is simply a case where evidence of facts similar in character to those forming the subject of the charge is sought to be given in support of the evidence on that charge. Though the case was one in which separate charges relating to different complainants were tried jointly, the principle must be the same as would arise if there were only one charge relating to one complainant. If the appellant were being tried on a charge relating to S, could not the prosecution call H as a witness to give evidence about acts relating to H? The judge should apply as strict a rule in the one case as in the other. If, as I believe, the general rule is that such evidence cannot be allowed, it requires exceptional circumstances to justify the admission. This House should not, in my opinion, encourage erosion of the general rule.

We can dispose at once of the suggestion that there is a special rule or principle applicable to sexual, or to homosexual, offences. This suggestion had support at one time – eminent support from Lord Sumner in *Thompson v The King* (1918) – but is now certainly obsolete: see *per* Lord Reid and the other learned Lords in *Reg v Kilbourne* (1973). Evidence that an offence of a sexual character was committed by A against B cannot be supported by evidence that an offence of a sexual character was committed by A against C, or against C, D and E.

The question certified suggests that the contrary may be true if the offences take a 'particular form'. I do not know what this means: all sexual activity has some form or other and varieties are not unlimited: how particular must it be for a special rule to apply? The general salutary rule of exclusion must not be eroded through so vague an epithet. The danger of it being so is indeed well shown in the present case for the judge excluded the (similar fact) evidence of one boy because it showed 'normal' homosexual acts while admitting the (similar fact) evidence of another boy because the homosexual acts assumed a different, and, in his view, 'abnormal', pattern. Distinctions such as this, rightly called fine distinctions by the judge, lend an unattractive unreality to the law.

If the evidence was to be received, then, it must be on some general principle not confined to sexual offences. There are obvious difficulties in the way of formulating any such rule in such a manner as, on the one hand, to enable clear guidance to be given to juries, and, on the other hand, to avoid undue rigidity.

The prevailing formulation is to be found in the judgment of the Court of Criminal Appeal in *Rex v Sims* (1946) where it was said: 'The evidence of each man was that the accused invited him into the house and there committed the acts charged. The acts they describe bear a striking similarity. That is a special feature sufficient in itself to justify the admissibility of the evidence ... The probative force of all the acts together is much greater than one alone; for, whereas the jury might think that one man might be telling an untruth, three or four are hardly likely to tell the same untruth unless they were conspiring together. If there is nothing to suggest a conspiracy their evidence would seem to be overwhelming.'

Sims has not received universal approbation or uniform commentary but I think that it must be taken that this passage has received at least the general approval of this House in *Reg v Kilbourne* (1973). For my part, since the statement is evidently related to the facts of that particular case, I should deprecate its literal use in other cases. It is certainly neither clear nor comprehensive. A suitable adaptation, and, if necessary, expansion, should be allowed to judges in order to suit the facts involved. The basic principle must be that the admission of similar fact evidence (of the kind now in question) is exceptional and requires a strong degree of probative force. This probative force is derived, if at all, from the circumstance that the facts testified to by the several witnesses bear to each other such a striking similarity that they must, when judged by experience and common sense, either all be true, or have arisen from a cause common to the witnesses or from pure coincidence. The jury may, therefore, properly be asked to judge whether the right conclusion is that all are true, so that each story is supported by the other(s).

I have used the words 'a cause common to the witnesses' to include not only (as in *Rex v Sims*) the possibility that the witnesses may have invented a story in concert but also the possibility that a similar story may have arisen by a process of infection from media of publicity or simply from fashion. In the sexual field, and in others, this may be a real possibility: something much more than mere similarity and absence of proved conspiracy is needed if this evidence is to be allowed. This is well illustrated by *Reg v Kilbourne* (1973) where the judge excluded '*intra* group' evidence because of the possibility, as it appeared to him, of collaboration between boys who knew each other well. This is, in my respectful opinion, the right course rather than to admit the evidence unless a case of collaboration or concoction is made out.

If this test is to be applied fairly, much depends in the first place upon the experience and common sense of the judge. As was said by Lord Simon of Glaisdale in *Reg v Kilbourne* in judging whether one fact is probative of another, experience plays as large a place as logic. And in matters of experience it is for the judge to keep close to current mores. What is striking in one age is normal in another: the perversions of yesterday may be the routine or the fashion of tomorrow. The ultimate test has to be applied by the jury using similar qualities of experience and common sense after fair presentation of the dangers either way of admission or of rejection. Finally, whether the judge has properly used and stated the ingredients of experience and common sense may be reviewed by the Court of Appeal.

The present case is, to my mind, right on the borderline ...

These matters lie largely within the field of the judge's discretion, and of the jury's task; the Court of Appeal has reviewed the whole matter in a careful judgment. I do not think that there is anything which justifies the interference of this House. But I confess to some fear that the case, if regarded as an example, may be setting the standard of 'striking similarity' too low ...

I would dismiss the appeal.

Lord Hailsham of St Marylebone: ... In all these cases it is for the judge to ensure as a matter of law in the first place, and as a matter of discretion where the matter is free, that a properly instructed jury, applying their minds to the facts, can come to the conclusion that they are satisfied so that they are sure that to treat the matter as pure coincidence by reason of the 'nexus', 'pattern', 'system', 'striking resemblances' or whatever phrase is used is 'an affront to common sense': *Reg v Kilbourne* (1973). In this the ordinary rules of logic and common sense prevail, whether the case is one of burglary and the burglar has left some 'signature' as the mark of his presence, or false pretences and the pretences alleged have too many common characteristics to have happened coincidentally, or whether the dispute is one of identity and the accused in a series of offences has some notable physical features or behavioural or psychological characteristics or, as in some cases, is in possession of incriminating articles, like a jemmy, a set of skeleton keys or, in abortion cases, the apparatus of the abortionist. Attempts to codify the rules of common sense are to be resisted. The first rule in Makin is designed to exclude a particular kind of inference being drawn which might upset the presumption of innocence by introducing more heat than light. When that is the only purpose for which the evidence is being tendered, it should be excluded altogether, as in *Reg v Horwood* (1970). Where the purpose is an inference of another kind, subject to the judge's overriding discretion to exclude, the evidence is admissible, if in fact the evidence be logically probative. Even then it is for the jury to assess its weight, which may be greater or less according as to how far it accords with other evidence, and according as to how that other evidence may be conclusive.

There are two further points of a general character that I would add. The 'striking resemblances' or 'unusual features', or whatever phrase is considered appropriate, to ignore which would affront common sense, may either be in the objective facts, as for instance in *Rex v Smith* (1915) or *Reg v Straffen* (1952), or may constitute a striking similarity in the accounts by witnesses of disputed transactions. For instance, whilst it would certainly not be enough to identify the culprit in a series of burglaries that he climbed in through a ground floor window, the fact that he left the same humorous limerick on the walls of the sitting room, or an esoteric symbol written in lipstick on the mirror, might well be enough. In a sex case, to adopt an example given in argument in the Court of Appeal, whilst a repeated homosexual act by itself might be quite insufficient to admit the evidence as confirmatory of identity or design, the fact that it was alleged to have been performed wearing the ceremonial head-dress of a Red Indian chief or other eccentric garb might well in appropriate circumstances suffice ... [Lord Hailsham agreed that the appeal should be dismissed]

Lord Cross of Chelsea: My Lords, on the hearing of a criminal charge the prosecution is not as a general rule allowed to adduce evidence that the accused has done acts other than those with which he is charged in order to show that he is the sort of person who would be likely to have committed the offence in question. As my noble and learned friend, Lord Simon of Glaisdale, pointed out in the recent case of *Reg v Kilbourne*, the reason for this general rule is not that the law regards such evidence as inherently irrelevant but that it is believed that if it were generally admitted jurors would in many cases think that it was more relevant than it was, so that, as it is put, its prejudicial effect would outweigh its probative value. Circumstances, however, may arise in which such evidence is so very relevant that to exclude it would be an affront to common sense. Take, for example, *Reg v Straffen*. There a young girl was found strangled. It was a most unusual murder for there had been no attempt to assault her sexually or to conceal the body though this might easily have been done. The accused, who had just escaped from Broadmoor and was in the neighbourhood at the time of the crime, had previously committed two murders of young girls, each of which had the same peculiar features. It would, indeed, have been a most extraordinary coincidence if this third murder had been committed by someone else and though an ultra-cautious jury might still have acquitted him it would have been absurd for the law to have prevented the evidence of the other murders being put before them although it was simply evidence to show that Straffen was a man likely to commit a murder of that particular kind. As Viscount Simon said in *Harris v Director of Public Prosecutions* (1952), it is not possible to compile an exhaustive list of the sort of cases in which 'similar fact' evidence – to use a compendious phrase – is admissible. The question must always be whether the similar fact evidence taken together with the other evidence would do no more than raise or strengthen a suspicion that the accused committed the offence with which he is charged or would point so strongly to his guilt that only an ultra-cautious jury, if they accepted it as true, would acquit in face of it. In the end – although the admissibility of such evidence is a question of law, not of discretion – the question as I see it must be one of degree ...

... When in a case of this sort the prosecution wishes to adduce 'similar fact' evidence which the defence says is inadmissible, the question whether it is admissible ought, if possible, to be decided in the absence of the jury at the outset of the trial and if it is decided that the evidence is inadmissible and the accused is being charged in the same indictment with offences against the other men the charges relating to the different persons ought to be tried separately. If they are tried together the judge will, of course, have to tell the jury that in considering whether the accused is guilty of the offence alleged against him by A they must put out of mind the fact – which they know – that B and C are making similar allegations against him. But, as the Court of Criminal Appeal said in *Rex v Sims* (1946), it is asking too much of any jury to tell them to perform mental gymnastics of this sort. If the charges are tried together it is inevitable that the jurors will be influenced, consciously or unconsciously, by the fact that the accused is being charged not with a single offence against one person but with three separate offences against three persons. It is said, I know, that to order separate trials in all these cases would be highly inconvenient. If and so far as this is true it is a reason for doubting the wisdom of the general rule excluding similar fact evidence. But so long as there is that general rule the courts ought to strive to give effect to it loyally and not, while paying lip service to it, in effect let in the inadmissible evidence by trying all the charges together ...

In *Reg v Kilbourne* my noble and learned friend, Lord Reid, expressed the view ... that in a case of this sort 'similar fact' evidence could only be admitted if it showed that the accused was pursuing what could be 'loosely called a system' and that two instances would not be enough to constitute a system. I naturally hesitate to differ from my noble and learned friend but I am not myself prepared to draw a line of this sort. On the other hand, I think that when you have so few as two instances you need to proceed with great caution. It is by no means unheard of for a boy to accuse a schoolmaster falsely of having made homosexual advances to him. If two boys make accusations of that sort at about the same time independently of one another then no doubt the ordinary man would tend to think that there was 'probably something in it'. But it is just this instinctive reaction of the ordinary man which the general rule is intended to counter and I think that one needs to find very striking peculiarities common to the two stories to justify the admission of one to support the other. The feature in the two stories upon which attention was concentrated in the courts below is that both youths said that the appellant suggested not that he should bugger them but that they should bugger him. This was said to be an 'unusual' suggestion. If I thought that the outcome of this appeal depended on whether such a suggestion was in fact 'unusual' I would be in favour of allowing it. It is no doubt unusual for a middle-aged man to yield to the urge to commit buggery or to try to commit buggery with youths or young men but whether it is unusual for such a middle-aged man to wish to play the pathic rather than the active role I have no idea whatever and I am not prepared, in the absence of any evidence on the point, to make any assumption one way or the other. As I see it, however, the point is not whether what the appellant is said to have suggested would be, as coming from a middle-aged active homosexual, in itself particularly unusual but whether it would be unlikely that two youths who were saying untruly that the appellant had made homosexual advances to them would have put such a suggestion into his mouth. In one passage in his summing-up the judge touched on this aspect of the matter and said that the jury might think it more likely that if their stories were untrue S and H would have said that the appellant wished to bugger or did bugger them than that he wished them to bugger or induce them to bugger him. There is, I think, force in that observation, but I do not think that this similarity standing alone would be sufficient to warrant the admission of the evidence. My noble and learned friends, Lord Morris of Borth-y-Gest, Lord Hailsham of St Marylebone and Lord Salmon, point, however, to other features common to the two stories which, it may be said, two liars concocting false stories independently of one another would have been unlikely to hit upon and, although I must say that I regard this as very much a borderline case, I am not prepared to dissent from their view that the 'similar fact' evidence was admissible here and that the appeal should be dismissed.

[Lord Salmon also delivered a speech dismissing the appeal.][8]

Even now some preferred to grasp at a shadow rather than the substance, and for a time it seemed that 'striking similarity' or some other formula would be employed as a substitute for thought. Nevertheless, leading cases since Boardman have re-emphasised the principle that the admissibility of 'similar fact' evidence depends on relevancy and weight, and the fact that these are not matters for which prescription can be made in advance by legal rules.

R v Scarrot (1978, Court of Appeal)

Appeal against conviction

The defendant, Ernest Theodore Scarrot, was convicted in April 1976 at Bristol Crown Court, before Judge Vowden and a jury of one count of buggery, a count of attempted buggery and eight counts of indecent assault on eight boys. He appealed against his conviction on the grounds, *inter alia*, that, the judge erred in law in failing to sever the indictment and to order separate trials in relation to each boy; that he was wrong in law and in fact in holding that the evidence in relation to each boy was capable of corroborating the evidence of each of the other boys in that it was similar fact evidence; and that the verdicts were unsafe or unsatisfactory.

The judgment of the court to dismiss the appeal was given by –

Scarman LJ: ... To be admissible, the evidence by its striking similarity has to reveal an underlying link between the matters with which it deals and the allegations against the defendant upon the count under consideration. Subject to one comment, which really goes only to choice of language, we would respectfully accept the way in which the general principle was put by Lord Salmon in *Reg v Boardman* (1975). Lord Salmon puts the general principle as follows: '... whether or not evidence is relevant and admissible against an accused is solely a question of law. The test must be: is the evidence capable of tending to persuade a reasonable jury of the accused's guilt on some ground other than his bad character and disposition to commit the sort of crime with which he is charged? In the case of an alleged homosexual offence, just as in the case of an alleged burglary, evidence which proves merely that the accused has committed crimes in the past and is therefore disposed to commit the crime charged is clearly inadmissible. It has, however, never been doubted that if the crime charged is committed in a uniquely or strikingly similar manner to other crimes committed

---

8. [1975] AC 421.

by the accused the manner in which the other crimes were committed may be evidence upon which a jury could reasonably conclude that the accused was guilty of the crime charged. The similarity would have to be so unique or striking that common sense makes it inexplicable on the basis of coincidence. I would stress that the question as to whether the evidence is capable of being so regarded by a reasonable jury is a question of law. There no easy way out by leaving it to the jury to see how they decide it.'

Thus, the admissibility of similar fact evidence, even when it is adduced as it is in this case as corroboration of direct evidence, does not depend upon whether it is capable of corroborating the evidence of the victim or accomplice; it depends upon its positive probative value. Its corroborative capability is a consequence of its probative value and not vice versa; for, if the evidence be admissible, it follows that it is capable of corroborating ... I now come to the one comment which this court would make on the statement of general principle made by Lord Salmon. Hallowed though by now the phrase 'strikingly similar' is (it was used by Lord Goddard CJ in *Rex v Sims* (1946) and has now received the accolade of use in the House of Lords in *Boardman*) it is no more than a label. Like all labels it can mislead; it is a possible passport to error. It is, we repeat, only a label and it is not to be confused with the substance of the law which it labels. We think that Lord Widgery CJ had the danger of a label in mind when, in a very different class of case, he made a comment on the passage from Lord Salmon's speech which we have quoted. In *Reg v Rance* (1975) Lord Widgery CJ ... said: 'It seems to us that one must be careful not to attach too much importance to Lord Salmon's vivid phrase "uniquely or strikingly similar". The gist of what is being said both by Lord Cross and by Lord Salmon is that evidence is admissible as similar fact evidence if, but only if, it goes beyond showing a tendency to commit crimes of this kind and is positively probative in regard to the crime now charged. That, we think, is the test which we have to apply on the question of the correctness or otherwise of the admission of the similar fact evidence in this case.'

Positive probative value is what the law requires, if similar fact evidence is to be admissible. Such probative value is not provided by the mere repetition of similar facts; there has to be some feature or features in the evidence sought to be adduced which provides a link – an underlying link as it has been called in some of the cases. The existence of such a link is not to be inferred from mere similarity of facts which are themselves so commonplace that they can provide no sure ground for saying that they point to the commission by the accused of the offence under consideration ...

We have had our attention drawn ... to a number of recent cases, of which there are short reports available. It is very difficult to determine why or how the court reached the decision that it did in these cases. This is not a criticism either of the reports, or of the judgments under report; it is merely an illustration of how, upon a question such as this, ultimately the task of judgment is to assess the evidence, and, in this class of case, the degree of similarity. That must be a matter for judgment upon the particular circumstances of each case.

We therefore have to consider in this appeal whether the evidence sought to be adduced by the Crown does reveal similarities which may be described as striking, or, as we prefer to put it, which may be described as giving to the evidence positive probative value. We must bear in mind that our decision must proceed not upon an attempt to categorise the law under a vivid or unforgettable label, but upon the basis of seeking out the substance of the law and seeing whether, the law being in substance what it is, the evidence sought to be adduced possesses the necessary degree of probative value. At the end of the day it appears to us that what has to be determined is whether the similar fact evidence sought to be adduced possesses, logically considered, a probative value sufficiently positive to assist the court to determine whether or not the offence charged against the accused was committed by him ...

... Plainly some matters, some circumstances, may be so distant in time or place from the commission of an offence as not to be properly considered when deciding whether the subject matter or similar fact evidence displays striking similarities with the offence charged. On the other hand, equally plainly, one cannot isolate, as a sort of laboratory specimen, the bare bones of a criminal offence from its surrounding circumstances and say that it is only within the confines of that specimen, microscopically considered, that admissibility is to be determined. Indeed, in one of the most famous cases of all dealing with similar fact evidence, the brides in the bath case, *Rex v Smith* (1915), the court had regard to the facts that the accused man married the women, and that he insured their lives. Some surrounding circumstances have to be considered in order to understand either the offence charged or the nature of the similar fact evidence which it is sought to adduce and in each case it must be a matter of judgment where the line is drawn. One cannot draw an inflexible line as a rule of law ...

That is not, however, quite the end of the appeal. I have referred already to the fact that [counsel for the appellant] did submit both before arraignment and later, at the end of the prosecution's case, that there was a real danger that the evidence of these boys was tainted by conspiracy or ganging up – the 'group' point as it is called. The judge had to consider this point first before arraignment, when the only material available to him was that contained in the depositions. He had to form a judgment at that stage as to whether it was, in all the circumstances, safe in the interests of justice to allow the trial to proceed upon a multi-count indictment. Clearly there was a suggestion that some, or perhaps all, of these boys might have been party to a ganging up organised by the older brother of Peter B. He took the view that the matter could be dealt with by him in summing up, that whether or not there was such a ganging up should be considered by the jury. It was of course a matter for his discretion as to whether to accede to the application to sever the indictment or not and, in our judgment, he cannot be said to have erred in the exercise of his discretion in taking the view that in all the circumstances of this case the matter could properly be left to the jury, always assuming, as in the event occurred, that there was a full and proper direction and warning. There is therefore nothing in this point in our judgment ...[9]

R v Lunt (1986, Court of Appeal)

The judgment of the court was delivered by –

Neill LJ: ... On May 31 1985 a chequebook and a cheque card belonging to Mrs Susan Trow were stolen. At the subsequent trial of the appellant and other defendants it was alleged by the Crown that the appellant received the stolen chequebook and card and then passed them to his co-defendants, Samantha Bevis and Alyson Foreman, with instructions that they should forge cheques in the chequebook and use them to obtain goods for the appellant.

It was further alleged that in the period between Saturday June 15 1985 and Tuesday June 18 the appellant, together with the two women, went to a number of shops and other premises in towns in Dorset and elsewhere and paid for

---

9.   [1978] 1 QB 1016.

goods and services by means of the forged cheques. The offences covered by counts 4 and 5, which related to a shop at Winton in Bournemouth, comprised, it was said, a single incident in a series of similar offences ...

Shortly before the trial the Crown served on the appellant a notice of additional evidence which included a statement from Samantha Bevis. In her statement Samantha Bevis dealt not only with the occasion when a forged cheque was used for the purpose of obtaining goods from Flicks Video Library at Winton (the occasion covered by counts 4 and 5) but also with numerous other occasions between June 15 and June 18 1985 when no less than 24 forged cheques from Mrs Trow's chequebook were used for the purpose of obtaining goods and services.

At the outset of the trial it was submitted on behalf of the appellant that the evidence of Samantha Bevis relating to dealings with the cheques from the chequebook was inadmissible except in so far as it was confined to the offences alleged in counts 4 and 5. After hearing argument the judge rejected this submission ...

In this court counsel for the appellant advanced three submissions: (1) that the evidence of Samantha Bevis relating to the passing of the 24 other cheques was not 'similar fact' evidence, because it had no feature of true probative value which inculpated the appellant. Her evidence, it was said, was merely a narration of similar events; (2) that even if the evidence had some probative value, such value was plainly outweighed by its prejudicial effect; accordingly, the judge should have excluded the evidence as inadmissible; (3) that in any event this evidence should have been excluded because 'similar fact' evidence from an accomplice alone, in the absence of any other supporting evidence, is not permitted, because of the risk of concoction.

We can deal with the first two submissions together. It was argued on behalf of the applicant that 'similar fact' evidence is not admitted, unless there is some unusual feature which is common both to the events which form the subject matter of the relevant charge or charges and to the events which are covered by the 'similar fact' evidence. In a case such as the present, said counsel, 'similar fact 'evidence would have been admissible if, for example, a number of the shopkeepers had been called to prove that on each occasion the presenter of the cheque had been accompanied by a one-legged man. But the facts disclosed in the statement by Samantha Bevis about dealings with the other cheques had no unusual features, and the evidence about them was therefore inadmissible.

The basic rule as to the circumstances in which 'similar fact' evidence may be adduced was stated by Lord Herschell LC in *Makin v Att Gen for NSW* ...

Lord Herschell's words must now be read in the light of later authorities, including in particular *DPP v Kilbourne* (1973) and *Boardman v DPP* (1974) ...

Having considered these authorities, we would venture to suggest that the following guidelines can be collected from them: (1) As a general rule the prosecution may not adduce evidence tending to show that the accused has been guilty of criminal acts other than those charged against him, or that the accused has a propensity to commit crimes of the kind charged. (2) Notwithstanding the general rule, however, evidence is admissible as 'similar fact' evidence if, but only if, it goes beyond showing a tendency to commit crimes of the kind charged and is positively probative in regard to the crime charged: see *Rance* (1975), *Scarrott* (1977). (3) In order to decide whether the evidence is positively probative in regard to the crime charged it is first necessary to identify the issue to which the evidence is directed. Thus the evidence may be put forward, for example, to support an identification (where unusual points of similarity of appearance or method can be relevant and positively probative), or to prove intention, or to rebut a possible defence of accident or innocent association. In these several examples the answer to the question of what is positively probative may vary. (4) Once the issue has been identified the question will be: will the 'similar fact' evidence be positively probative, in the sense of assisting the jury to reach a conclusion on that issue on some ground other than the accused's bad character or disposition to commit the sort of crime with which he is charged? ... (5) If the evidence is positively probative in the foregoing sense the judge will nevertheless have a discretion to exclude it if it 'would probably have a prejudicial influence on the minds of the jury which would be out of proportion to its true evidential value': see *R v Sang* (1979).

We turn to the facts of the present case. The case for the prosecution was that the appellant was the organiser, who used Samantha Bevis and Alyson Foreman to go into shops and other premises to obtain goods by means of forged cheques. The case for the appellant was that, though he accompanied the two girls on a number of occasions, he took no part in their illegal use of the cheques. Plainly, therefore, the appellant raised an issue to which the term 'innocent association' can be conveniently applied.

To resolve this issue in relation to counts 4 and 5 it was, in our view, of assistance to the jury to hear evidence from Samantha Bevis of the part which the appellant had allegedly played in the other transactions over the same weekend. The 'similar fact' evidence was positively probative and, though it was prejudicial, the judge was fully entitled to admit it ...

[The Court of Appeal also rejected the third submission.][10]

DPP v P (1991, House of Lords)

Lord Mackay of Clashfern LC: My Lords, on 26 January 1988 the defendant was convicted in the Crown Court of two counts of rape and eight counts of incest. The indictment charged him with four offences of rape and four offences of incest in respect of each of two daughters, B and S. These were specimen counts. The defendant was convicted in the case of each girl on the first count of rape and all the counts of incest. He was acquitted of the later charges of rape. At the outset of the trial application was made on behalf of the defendant that the counts relating to the girl B should be tried separately from those relating to the girl S. The trial judge refused that application and the trial proceeded upon all the counts. The defendant appealed to the Court of Appeal (Criminal Division) against the judge's refusal. The Court of Appeal (Criminal Division) allowed the appeal and quashed the conviction.

The appellant, the Director of Public Prosecutions, applied for a certificate that a point of law of general public importance was involved in this decision and for leave to appeal to this House. The Court of Appeal granted these applications and certified the following questions for the House:

> 1 Where a father or stepfather is charged with sexually abusing a young daughter of the family, is evidence that he also similarly abused other young children of the family admissible (assuming there to be no collusion) in support of such charge in the absence of any other 'striking similarities'?

---

10. 85 Cr App R 241.

2 Where a defendant is charged with sexual offences against more than one child or young person, is it necessary in the absence of 'striking similarities' for the charges to be tried separately?

In giving the judgment of the court Lord Lane CJ after quoting from well-known passages in the speeches in this House in *Reg v Boardman* (1975), said: 'The way in which this doctrine has developed has led, it seems, to courts requiring some feature of similarity beyond what has been described as the paederast's or the incestuous father's 'stock in trade', before one victim's evidence can be properly admitted upon the trial of another: see for example *Reg v Inder* (1977), and more recently *Reg v Brooks* (1990).'

After examining the features upon which the judge had founded as allowing the evidence of one girl to be properly admitted upon the trial of the counts relating to the other, Lord Lane CJ concluded that they could not properly be described in the light of the authorities to which he referred as unusual features such as to make the account given by one girl more credible because those features are mirrored by the statement of the other. He went on: 'We have searched the committal papers to see whether there might be other matters which amounted to striking similarities between the girls' account of their father's behaviour towards them. Such incidents as we have been able to find do not, for one reason or another, fulfil the necessary requirements and were no doubt for that reason rejected by the prosecution as a possible ground for their arguments. It follows that there were, in the circumstances of this particular case, and in the light of the authorities as they now stand, no grounds for saying that the evidence of one girl was admissible so far as the other was concerned.'

The court therefore felt compelled to allow the appeal and quash the conviction. Lord Lane CJ added: 'However, the prosecution might like to consider whether the time has not come for the House of Lords to be asked to look again at this branch of the law. We have said enough to indicate that it is an area which is difficult to understand and even more difficult to apply in practice. Mr Mansfield suggested, not without some force, that it is almost a lottery whether separate trials will be ordered or not. It seems to us absurd that counsel and judge should be spending time searching through committal papers, which may in the upshot not represent the evidence actually given, searching for 'striking similarities' such as to justify allowing the jury to hear the evidence of that which they would naturally and rightly consider themselves entitled to know, namely that the defendant is charged with abusing not merely one but two or more of his young daughters. We see force in the suggestion adumbrated in the argument before us that where the father has allegedly shown himself to be someone prepared to abuse sexually girls who are no more than children, in this case under the age of 13, girls who are moreover his own children, and to use his position of power over them in their own home to achieve those ends, this might provide a sufficient hallmark to render the evidence of one girl admissible in the case of the other where the danger of collusion can be discounted. In the current state of decided cases we are, we think, inhibited from so deciding.'

It is apparent that the particular difficulty which arose in this case is the development of the authorities in this area of the law requiring some feature of similarity beyond what has been described as the paederast's or the incestuous father's stock in trade before one victim's evidence can be properly admitted upon the trial of another that inhibited the Court of Appeal from deciding as otherwise they would have done. The question in this appeal therefore is whether this development is a sound one or not ...

As this matter has been left in *Reg v Boardman* I am of opinion that it is not appropriate to single out 'striking similarity' as an essential element in every case in allowing evidence of an offence against one victim to be heard in connection with an allegation against another. Obviously, in cases where the identity of the offender is in issue, evidence of a character sufficiently special reasonably to identify the perpetrator is required and the discussion which follows in Lord Salmon's speech on the passage which I have quoted indicates that he had that type of case in mind.

From all that was said by the House in *Reg v Boardman* I would deduce the essential feature of evidence which is to be admitted is that its probative force in support of the allegation that an accused person committed a crime is sufficiently great to make it just to admit the evidence, notwithstanding that it is prejudicial to the accused in tending to show that he was guilty of another crime. Such probative force may be derived from striking similarities in the evidence about the manner in which the crime was committed and the authorities provide illustrations of that of which *Reg v Straffen* and *Rex v Smith*, provide notable examples. But restricting the circumstances in which there is sufficient probative force to overcome prejudice of evidence relating to another crime to cases in which there is some striking similarity between them is to restrict the operation of the principle in a way which gives too much effect to a particular manner of stating it, and is not justified in principle ... Once the principle is recognised, that what has to be assessed is the probative force of the evidence in question, the infinite variety of circumstances in which the question arises demonstrates that there is no single manner in which this can be achieved. Whether the evidence has sufficient probative value to outweigh its prejudicial effect must in each case be a question of degree.

The view that some feature of similarity beyond what has been described as the paederast's or the incestuous father's stock in trade before one victim's evidence can be properly admitted upon the trial of another seems to have been stated for the first time in those terms in *Reg v Inder* (1977). Although that case also contains a reference to a warning not to attach too much importance to Lord Salmon's vivid phrase 'uniquely or strikingly similar' I think in the context this is what has occurred. This trend has been followed in later cases ... In so far as these decisions required, as an essential feature, a similarity beyond the stock in trade I consider they fall to be overruled.

In the present case the evidence of both girls describes a prolonged course of conduct in relation to each of them. In relation to each of them force was used. There was a general domination of the girls with threats against them unless they observed silence and a domination of the wife which inhibited her intervention. The defendant seemed to have an obsession for keeping the girls to himself, for himself. The younger took on the role of the elder daughter when the elder daughter left home. There was also evidence that the defendant was involved in regard to payment for the abortions in respect of both girls. In my view these circumstances taken together gave strong probative force to the evidence of each of the girls in relation to the incidents involving the other, and was certainly sufficient to make it just to admit that evidence, notwithstanding its prejudicial effect. This was clearly the view taken by the Court of Appeal and they would have given effect to it were it not for the line of authority in the Court of Appeal to which I have referred ...

When a question of the kind raised in this case arises I consider that the judge must first decide whether there is material upon which the jury would be entitled to conclude that the evidence of one victim, about what occurred to that victim, is so related to the evidence given by another victim, about what happened to that victim, that the evidence of the first victim provides strong enough support for the evidence of the second victim to make it just to admit it notwithstanding the prejudicial effect of admitting the evidence. This relationship, from which support is derived, may take many forms and while these forms may include 'striking similarity' in the manner in which the crime is committed, consisting of unusual characteristics in its execution the necessary relationship is by no means confined to such circumstances. Relationships in time and circumstances other than these may well be important relationships in this connection. Where the identity of the perpetrator is in issue, and evidence of this kind is important in that connection, obviously something in the nature of what has been called in the course of the argument a signature or other special feature will be necessary. To transpose this requirement to other situations where the question is whether a crime has been committed, rather than who did commit it, is to impose unnecessary and improper restrictions upon the application of the principle.

For the reasons which I have given, I am of the opinion that there was sufficient connection between the circumstances spoken of by the two girls in the present case for their testimonies mutually to support each other, that the appeal should be allowed, and the conviction restored.

I would answer the first question posed by the Court of Appeal by saying that the evidence referred to is admissible if the similarity is sufficiently strong, or there is other sufficient relationship between the events described in the evidence of the other young children of the family, and the abuse charged, that the evidence, if accepted, would so strongly support the truth of that charge that it is fair to admit it notwithstanding its prejudicial effect. It follows that the answer to the second question is no, provided there is a relationship between the offences of the kind I have just described ...

[The other Law Lords agreed with Lord MacKay's speech.][11]

How should an examination candidate use cases in dealing with a similar fact point? Use them as you would if you were arguing a case in court. They don't come first, but they can provide a useful boost for your argument.

You will begin with an argument about relevancy. In that argument you will refer to the overriding principle: if the disputed testimony has greater danger of prejudice than probative weight, it ought not to go in. At this stage your argument will be confined to the facts, and it may by itself be enough. If the judge seems reluctant to accept your submission you may be able to push him in the right direction by drawing his attention to a decided case if it is very much in point. But a case will be only an illustration of the basic principle. It should not be treated as a 'precedent' which has to be 'followed'. Never try to play a game of snap based on the comparison of features in a particular problem with those in earlier decided cases.

It follows that earlier cases should be read for their reasoning rather than for their results. They should be read critically, too, because you do not have to

---

11. [1991] 2 AC 447. On the problem of collusion, see *R v H* [1995] 2 All ER 865, HL.

look very far before coming across modes of approach which must be treated at least cautiously in the light of later developments. A good example of this sort of thing is Lord Hailsham's reference to the 'inadmissible chain of reasoning' in *Boardman*,[12] or references in some pre-*DPP v P* cases to *an independent* discretion to exclude similar fact evidence on the ground that it would be more prejudicial than probative. Too much damage has already been done by attempts to classify similar fact cases and I do not wish to do any more. Remember the warning of Sir Ralph Kilner Brown in *R v Butler* (1987): 'Within the well-established principles every case is one to be decided on its own particular circumstances.'[13]

The cases that follow are presented as examples of reasoning with facts. For this reason I have presented them chronologically. In reading them, I suggest that at least these questions should be asked: What sort of evidence can count as similar fact evidence? To what issues was the similar fact evidence in question relevant? How was it relevant? How great was the risk of prejudice?

R v Ball (1911, House of Lords)

Lord Loreburn LC: My Lords, in this case two persons, a brother and a sister, were indicted for incest in July 1910 and September 1910. Certain evidence, which was obviously admissible, was given to establish that at all events there was ample opportunity for this offence, and that there were circumstances which, to say the least, were very suggestive of incest. Also these two persons lived together and occupied the same bedroom and the same bed. Further evidence was then tendered to shew that these persons had previously carnally known each other and had a child in 1908. The object was to establish that they had a guilty passion towards each other, and that therefore the proper inference from their occupying the same bedroom and the same bed was an inference of guilt, or – which is the same thing in another way – that the defence of innocent living together as brother and sister ought to fail.

My Lords, the law on this subject is stated in the judgment of Lord Chancellor Herschell in *Makin v Attorney General for New South Wales*; it is well-known and I need not repeat it – the question is only of applying it. In accordance with the law laid down in that case, and which is daily applied in the Divorce Courts, I consider that this evidence was clearly admissible on the issue that this crime was committed – not to prove the *mens rea*, as Darling J considered, but to establish the guilty relations between the parties and the existence of a sexual passion between them as elements in proving that they had illicit connection in fact on or between the dates charged. Their passion for each other was as much evidence as was their presence together in bed of the fact that when there they had guilty relations with each other.

My Lords, I agree that courts ought to be very careful to preserve the time-honoured law of England, that you cannot convict a man of one crime by proving that he had committed some other crime; that, and all other safeguards of our criminal law, will be jealously guarded; but here I think the evidence went directly to prove the actual crime for which these parties were indicted.[14]

---

12. [1975] AC 421, 453.
13. See n 2.
14. [1911] AC 47. The other Law Lords agreed.

R v Taylor (1923, Court of Criminal Appeal)

Appeal against conviction and sentence by leave of the court on 16 April

Applicant was convicted at the Warwick Assizes on 12 March 1923 before Bailhache J, of shopbreaking, and sentenced to 21 months' imprisonment with hard labour.

CK Tatham for the appellant: ... I submit that evidence was wrongly admitted, there was an inadequate summing-up, and there were other irregularities which make the trial so unsatisfactory that the conviction should not stand. There was no evidence that any instrument was used to break open the shop, and nothing was stolen, yet evidence was given of the finding at appellant's house of an alleged jemmy, which was inadmissible, as there was no connection between what appellant was alleged to have done and the instrument ...

The Lord Chief Justice: In this case a police officer gave evidence that at about midnight he saw appellant and another man outside a refreshment shop, heard the door forced open, and saw the appellant and the other man run out. Being arrested, appellant denied any attempt to commit an offence, and said that the affair was a drunken escapade, that he and the other man had been drinking and, playing football with a cabbage stalk, had charged one another against the door and broken it open. There were no marks of any kind on the door and nothing was stolen. It is conceded on the part of the prosecution that there were some irregularities at the trial, but said that those irregularities do not matter, and that under the proviso to s 4 of the Criminal Appeal Act the conviction ought to stand. The court cannot take that view. Although appellant was arrested on the spot, and there were no marks to suggest that an instrument had been used, evidence was given of an alleged jemmy having been afterwards found in his house. He was questioned by the police about the jemmy eight days after his arrest, and evidence was given of that questioning. There are other matters also which make the trial unsatisfactory.[15]

R v Mortimer (1936, Court of Criminal Appeal)

Appeal against conviction

The appellant was convicted at Hampshire Assizes on 27 November 1935 of the murder of a woman named Phyllis Mary Doreen Oakes and was sentenced by Finlay J to death.

The case for the prosecution was that at about 9.25 am on the morning of 8 August 1935 the appellant knocked down Miss Oakes when she was riding her bicycle by deliberately driving a motor car at her. Evidence was called to show that at about 6.30 pm and 7.15 pm, respectively, on 7 August the appellant had knocked down two other women cyclists in a similar way, and had stopped his car to assault them. Evidence was also given that at about 3.30 pm on 8 August he had knocked down another women cyclist and stolen her handbag, and that he had subsequently driven straight at three different parties of police officers who had tried to stop the car. Objection was taken to the tendering of the above evidence, but was overruled.

---

15. 17 Cr App R 109.

The Lord Chief Justice: ... It appears to us that it was of crucial importance to show that what was done in relation to Miss Oakes was deliberately and intentionally done. If the defence was to be, as indeed it proved to be in one of its aspects, that what was done amounted to no more than manslaughter, it was manifestly fundamental to establish the guilty intent of the prisoner either to kill or, at any rate, to cause grievous bodily harm. It seems to us that the evidence which was admitted ... was of the very kind which in such a case was proper to be admitted. Undoubtedly where such evidence is offered great responsibility lies upon the judge, and ... in view of the strong prejudice that would necessarily be created in the minds of the jury by the evidence of this class, which shows that the prisoner has been guilty on another occasion of a similar offence, the greatest care ought to be taken to reject such evidence unless it is plainly necessary to prove something which is really in issue. In our opinion, this evidence satisfies that test; it was plainly necessary to prove something which was really in issue; namely, the intent with which the prisoner did the act, if he was the person who did it.[16]

Noor Mohamed v R (1949, Privy Council)

Lord du Parcq: The appellant was tried before the Supreme Court of British Guiana on a charge of murdering a woman commonly known, and referred to during the trial, as Ayesha. The jury found him guilty, and he was sentenced to death. Evidence was admitted at the trial to which objection was taken by the appellant's counsel on the ground that it tended to show that the appellant had murdered another woman, his wife Gooriah. It was said on behalf of the appellant that the evidence ought to be excluded as being prejudicial to him and irrelevant. For the Crown it was contended, on grounds which will be necessary to state later in this judgment, that the circumstances attending the two deaths made evidence concerning the earlier of them relevant to the charge. It was properly conceded at their Lordships' Board on behalf of the Crown that, if the evidence were found to have been wrongly admitted, it would follow, according to the settled principles by which their Lordships are guided in criminal cases, that the appeal must be allowed.

The evidence which related directly to the charge of murdering Ayesha may be summarized as follows. The appellant's wife Gooriah died May 17 1944. At some time in that year Ayesha had left her husband and gone to live with him. They lived together as man and wife, and there was evidence that in the year 1945 they went through a ceremony of marriage according to the rites of the Mahomedan religion, although Ayesha's husband was still living. After the first few weeks of their union, their life together had not been happy. It was said that the appellant had often beaten Ayesha and had sometimes driven her from his house. On one occasion she had lived apart from him for two weeks, though she seems to have continued to feel affection for him, and to have been anxious to return to him. The earlier quarrels were due to the fact that the appellant suspected and accused her of infidelity. Later, he made a different charge against her. On a day in August 1946 a neighbour named Mildred James, who employed Ayesha to do some dress-making, witnessed an assault on her by the appellant. She tried to rescue Ayesha, whereupon the appellant said, according to the witness, 'Through this woman people got to say I kill my first wife. She must go away.' Ayesha refused to go, and the appellant was alleged to have threatened her with the words, 'If you can't go alive you got to go dead'. There was also evidence of a quarrel and a threat by the appellant to kill Ayesha on the night of September 16

---

16. 25 Cr App R 150.

1946. On the morning of the following day, Ayesha died of poisoning by potassium cyanide. It must here be stated that the appellant is a goldsmith by trade and used a solution of potassium cyanide in the ordinary course of his business. He kept it in a press or cupboard. This cupboard was usually locked, but the padlock in use was defective, and it was not difficult to force the cupboard door. Potassium cyanide is a poison which acts quickly, and causes loss of consciousness in a few seconds.

Ayesha was said to have been seen alive at or after 9 o'clock in the morning of September 17. A witness called for the Crown swore that he had then seen her go with the appellant into the house in which they lived. The evidence was inconsistent with statements made by the appellant. According to him, his daughter, a child of fourteen, had awakened him shortly before 9.30 am from a sleep which followed a drinking bout, and had told him that Ayesha 'was frothing'. He said that he had found the woman unconscious. After some delay, he had reported this to a chemist in the neighbourhood. It appeared that he had told this chemist that he had gone to fetch a doctor, but had not found him at home. He was advised to take his 'wife' to hospital, and did so between 9 and 10 am. The appellant, at the request of the assistant dispenser there, had produced a sheet on which Ayesha had vomited. There was a stain on it which the appellant said smelled like gold solution. The assistant dispenser said he could smell nothing. Ayesha was given a stimulant by the assistant dispenser, and the appellant was advised to take her to the doctor. At 11 o'clock the appellant arrived at a doctor's surgery, bringing with him what the doctor found to be the dead body of Ayesha. A post-mortem examination showed without doubt that death was due to cyanide poisoning. It also indicated that there had been some exaggeration in some of the evidence as to the more recent assaults on Ayesha by the appellant, since, although some 'bruise blood' was found near the right kidney, there were no external signs of violence. This evidence having been given, the question was argued, in the absence of the jury, whether evidence tendered as to the death of Gooriah should be admitted. The learned judge, after an elaborate argument, decided to admit it. At this stage the defence had put forward no theory as to the manner in which the poison had been taken by, or administered to, Ayesha. Later, in his final address to the jury, counsel for the defence suggested that the facts were consistent with suicide ...

Their Lordships do not find it necessary to set out in any detail the evidence relating to Gooriah's death. It is sufficient to quote in full para 7 of the respondent's case which is as follows:

The prosecution then called a great deal of evidence relating to Gooriah's death, including evidence of the following facts:

(1) The appellant believed Gooriah to be unfaithful and had used to beat her.

(2) The appellant had said of Gooriah to Ayesha's husband, 'Buddy ah got a mind to poison this bitch.'

(3) Gooriah on the day of her death, May 17 1944, went to the nearby house of the appellant's brother-in-law, carrying a piece of folded white paper wrapped in her hand. She had had toothache and the appellant was overheard to say to her, 'You must drink this; it will do you good.'

(4) Shortly after a boy ran for the appellant shouting, 'Pawah Gooriah dead.' The appellant went to the house and summoned Dr Besson, who was passing.

(5) The accused went to the window and called a boy to bring him a paper, similar to that which Gooriah had had in her hand, from the yard. The boy

brought the paper which the appellant handed to Dr Besson saying it smelt of cyanide. The doctor found that the paper had no substance on it and had no smell. A little later the appellant brought the doctor an enamel cup saying, 'This cup smells of cyanide'. The cup was empty and had no smell.

(6) Gooriah died, and Dr Besson's examination showed her death to be consistent with potassium cyanide poisoning. On analysis 2 grains of potassium cyanide were found in Gooriah's stomach. Dr Besson stated that her death was caused by cyanide poisoning.

Their Lordships now turn to the important question of law raised by this appeal ... The first comment to be made on the evidence under review is that it plainly tended to show that the appellant had been guilty of a criminal act which was not the act with which he was charged ...

The second principle stated in *Makin's* case was that 'the mere fact that the evidence adduced tends to show the commission of other crimes does not render it inadmissible if it be relevant to an issue before the jury, and it may be so relevant if it bears upon the question whether the acts alleged to constitute the crime charged in the indictment were designed or accidental, or to rebut a defence which would otherwise be open to the accused'. The statement of this latter principle has given rise to some discussion. A plea of not guilty puts everything in issue which is a necessary ingredient of the offence charged, and if the Crown were permitted, ostensibly in order to strengthen the evidence of a fact which was not denied and, perhaps, could not be the subject of rational dispute, to adduce evidence of a previous crime, it is manifest that the protection afforded by the 'jealously guarded' principle first enunciated would be gravely impaired. This aspect of the matter was considered by the House of Lords in *Thompson v The King* (1918). Their Lordships need not allude to the facts of that case. It is enough to say that the evidence there admitted was held to be relevant as one of the indicia by which the accused man's identity with the person who had committed the crime could be established ... In the words of Lord Atkinson, it rebutted the defence of an alibi which otherwise would have been open. Nothing of the kind can be suggested in the present case. The value of the case for the present purpose is that Lord Sumner dealt particularly with the difficulty to which their Lordships have referred, and stated his conclusions as follows: 'Before an issue can be said to be raised, which would permit the introduction of such evidence so obviously prejudicial to the accused, it must have been raised in substance if not in so many words, and the issue so raised must be one to which the prejudicial evidence is relevant. The mere theory that a plea of not guilty puts everything material in issue is not enough for this purpose. The prosecution cannot credit the accused with fancy defences in order to rebut them at the outset with some damning piece of prejudice.'

Their Lordships respectfully agree with what they conceive to be the spirit and intention of Lord Sumner's words, and wish to say nothing to detract from their value. On principle, however, and with due regard to subsequent authority, their Lordships think that one qualification of the rule laid down by Lord Sumner must be admitted. An accused person need set up no defence other than a general denial of the crime alleged. The plea of not guilty may be equivalent to saying, 'Let the prosecution prove its case, if it can', and having said so much the accused may take refuge in silence. In such a case it may appear (for instance) that the facts and circumstances of the particular offence charged are consistent with innocent intention, whereas further evidence, which incidentally shows that the accused has committed one or more other offences, may tend to prove that they are consistent only with a guilty intent. The prosecution could not be said, in their Lordships' opinion, to be 'crediting the accused with a fancy defence' if they sought to adduce such evidence. It is right to add, however, that in all such cases the judge ought to consider whether the evidence which it is proposed to adduce is sufficiently substantial, having regard to the purpose to which it is professedly directed, to make it desirable in the interest of justice that it should be admitted. If, so far as that purpose is concerned, it can in the circumstances of the case have only trifling weight, the judge will be right to exclude it. To say this is not to confuse weight with admissibility. The distinction is plain, but cases must occur in which it would be unjust to admit evidence of a character gravely prejudicial to the accused even though there may be some tenuous ground for holding it technically admissible. The decision must then be left to the discretion and the sense of fairness of the judge.

Their Lordships have considered with care the question whether the evidence now in question can be said to be relevant to any issue in the case. They have asked themselves, adopting the language of Lord Sumner in Thompson's case, 'What exactly does this purport to prove?' At the trial the learned counsel for the Crown, when submitting that the evidence should be admitted, referred to the possible defences of accident and suicide. In his address to the jury he said, according to the note, that the evidence was led 'to meet the defence of suicide', and pointed out that the circumstances surrounding the death of the two women 'followed a similar pattern'. At their Lordships' bar it was submitted that this similarity of circumstances would lead to the inference that the appellant administered poison to Ayesha with felonious intent.

There can be little doubt that the manner of Ayesha's death, even without the evidence as to the death of Gooriah, would arouse suspicion against the appellant in the mind of a reasonable man. The facts proved as to the death of of Gooriah would certainly tend to deepen that suspicion, and might well tilt the balance against the accused in the estimation of a jury. It by no means follows that this evidence ought to be admitted. If an examination of it shows that it is impressive just because it appears to demonstrate, in the words of Lord Herschell in *Makin's* case, 'that the accused is a person likely from his criminal conduct or character to have committed the offence for which he is being tried', and if it is otherwise of no real substance, then it was certainly wrongly admitted. After fully considering all the facts which, if accepted, it revealed, their Lordships are not satisfied that its admission can be justified on any of the grounds which have been suggested or on any other ground. Assuming that it is consistent with the evidence relating to the death of Ayesha that she took her own life, or that she took poison accidentally (one of which assumptions must be made for the purpose of the Crown's argument at the trial) there is nothing in the circumstances of Gooriah's death to negative these possible views. Even if the appellant deliberately caused Gooriah to take poison (an assumption not lightly to be made, since he was never charged with having murdered her) it does not follow that Ayesha may not have committed suicide. As to the argument for similarity of circumstances, it seems on analysis to amount to no more than this, that if the appellant murdered one woman because he was jealous of her, it is probable that he murdered another for the same reason. If the appellant were proved to have administered poison to Ayesha in circumstances consistent with accident, then proof that he had previously administered poison to Gooriah in similar circumstances might well have been admissible. There was, however, no direct evidence in either case that the appellant had administered the poison. It is true that in the case of Gooriah there was evidence from which it might be inferred that he persuaded her to take the poison by a trick, but this evidence cannot properly be used to found an inference that a similar trick was used to deceive Ayesha, and so to fill a gap in the available evidence. The evidence which was properly adduced as to Ayesha shows her to have been acquainted, as it were, it may be supposed, [like] most of the inhabitants of the village in which the appellant lived, with the fact that suspicion rested on him in respect of Gooriah's death, and the theory that Ayesha was deceived into taking poison by a similar ruse to that which is supposed to have succeeded with Gooriah seems to their Lordships to rest on an improbable surmise. The effect of the admission of the impugned evidence may well have been that the jury came to the conclusion that the appellant was guilty of the murder of Gooriah, with which he had never been charged, and having thus adjudged him a murderer, were satisfied with something short of conclusive proof that he had murdered Ayesha. In these circumstances the verdict cannot stand ...[17]

Harris v DPP (1952, House of Lords)
Appeal from the Court of Criminal Appeal

Viscount Simon stated the facts as follows: This was an appeal from a decision of the Court of Criminal Appeal which came before the House of Lords in consequence of a certificate given by the Attorney General that the decision involved a point of law of exceptional public importance and that it was desirable in the public interest that a further appeal should be brought.

The appellant was a member of the City of Bradford Police Force. He was tried at the Leeds Autumn Assizes in November 1951 before Pearson J, on an indictment containing eight counts charging him with officebreaking and larceny on a series of dates in May, June and July 1951 by breaking into and entering the premises of a company of fruit and vegetable merchants situated in an enclosed and extensive Bradford market and stealing therefrom various sums of money. In every case the stolen money was only a part of the amount that the thief, whoever he was, might have taken; in every case the same means of access was used; and in every case the theft occurred in a period during part of which the appellant was on duty in uniform in the course of patrolling the market, and apparently at an hour when most of the gates to the market were closed to the general public. But, on the first seven of these occasions, there was no further evidence to associate the appellant specifically with the thefts. On the eighth occasion, however, which was between 6 and 7 am on Sunday morning, July 22, the appellant, who was on a solitary duty in the market as before, was found to be just outside the premises by the two detective officers who had rushed to the spot on hearing, in the quarters where they were secretly waiting, the ringing of a bell actuated, without the knowledge of the appellant, by the thief's weight when he stepped on the floor of the shop. On this occasion, marked money which had been placed in the till had been abstracted, but it was not found on the appellant when he was arrested. It had been concealed in a coal-bin, not far away from where he was when he [was] first seen. The two detectives were well-known to the appellant and might have been expected to be at once recognized by him, but when they entered the market, one by climbing over a gate and the other by opening it with some difficulty, though they were in the appellant's view at no great distance, he contended that he had not recognized them at first as members of the police force and so had not moved to join them; he said he thought that they were market-men entering the area for some innocent purpose. By the time the two detectives had reached the premises he had disappeared from view and a little later came running up to join them. The time which

---

17. [1949] AC 182.

elapsed between their first sight of him and his return was just sufficient to have enabled him to have reached the coal-bin and come back.

Before the appellant was arraigned and in the absence of the jury, his counsel asked for the severance of the indictment and urged that the charge contained in the eighth count should be tried first and separately. Pearson J applied section 5 (3) of the Indictments Act 1915 and ruled that there was no good reason for ordering a separate trial on the eighth count and that the case fell within rule 3 of the Sch I to the Act, since the charges formed part of a series of offences of the same or a similar character.

The appellant was acquitted on the first seven counts and convicted on the eighth. The Court of Criminal Appeal dismissed his appeal.

Burton QC and **Rudolph Lyons** for the appellant: The grounds for the appeal are (1) that the judge wrongly refused the application of the defence for a separate trial of the eighth count; (2) that he was wrong in holding that the evidence relating to the first seven counts was admissible on the eighth; and (3) that he was wrong in leaving the first seven counts to the jury. The second is the substantial ground ...

Viscount Simon: ... In my opinion, the principle laid down by Lord Herschell LC in *Makin's* case remains the proper principle to apply, and I see no reason for modifying it. Makin's case was a decision of the Judicial Committee of the Privy Council, but it was unanimously approved by the House of Lords in *R v Ball*, and has been constantly relied on ever since. It is, I think, an error to attempt to draw up a closed list of the sort of cases in which the principle operates: such a list only provides instances of its general application, whereas what really matters is the principle itself and its proper application to the particular circumstances of the charge that is being tried. It is the application that may sometimes be difficult, and the particular case now before the House illustrates that difficulty ...

The substance of the matter appears to me to be that the prosecution may adduce all proper evidence which tends to prove the charge. I do not understand Lord Herschell's words to mean that the prosecution must withhold such evidence until after the accused has set up a specific defence which calls for rebuttal. Where, for instance, *mens rea* is an essential element in guilt, and the facts of the occurrence which is the subject of the charge, standing by themselves, would be consistent with mere accident, there would be nothing wrong in the prosecution seeking to establish the true situation by offering, as part of its case in the first instance, evidence of similar action by the accused at another time which would go to show that he intended to do what he did on the occasion charged and was thus acting criminally. *R v Mortimer* is a good example of this. What Lord Sumner meant when he denied the right of the prosecution to 'credit the accused with fancy defences' (in *Thompson v The King* (1918)) was that the evidence of similar facts involving the accused ought not to be dragged in to his prejudice without reasonable cause ...

It is, of course, clear that evidence of 'similar facts' cannot in any case be admissible to support an accusation against the accused unless they are connected in some relevant way with the accused and with his participation in the crime (see Lord Sumner in *Thompson v The King*). It is the fact that he was involved in the other occurrences which may negative the inference of accident or establish his *mens rea* by showing 'system'. Or, again, the other occurrences may sometimes assist to prove his identity, as, for instance, in *Perkins v Jeffery* (1915). But evidence of the other occurrences which merely tend to deepen suspicion does not go to prove guilt. This is the ground, as it seems to me, on which the Judicial Committee of the Privy Council allowed the appeal in *Noor*

Mohamed v The King. The Board there took the view that the evidence as to the previous death of the accused's wife was not relevant to prove the charge against him of murdering another woman, and if it was not relevant it was at the same time highly prejudicial ...

It must always be remembered that every case is decided on its own facts, and expressions used, or even principles stated, when the court is considering particular facts, cannot always be applied as if they were absolute rules applicable in all circumstances.

Applying the above general propositions to the case before us, it appears to me that the only difficulty arises from the form of the summing-up. The judge, having decided that the eight counts should be tried together, did not warn the jury that the evidence called in support of the earlier counts did not in itself provide confirmation of the last charge. Yet, if the eighth count had been the only charge to be tried, it is difficult to see how the fact that there had been similar thefts of the same pattern before would confirm the allegation that the appellant was the thief on July 22. The eighth count raised two issues: (1) Was the money stolen on July 22? (2) Is it proved that it was the appellant who stole it? Previous events could not confirm (1), which indeed was proved beyond dispute. As for (2), the accused denied that he was the thief and the fact that someone perpetrated the earlier thefts when the accused may have been somewhere in the market does not provide material confirmation of his identity as the thief on the last occasion. The case against him on July 22 depended on the facts of that date. Yet the jury may well have been swayed, however illogically, in reaching its verdict on the eighth count by the earlier evidence. It should have been warned of this danger, especially as *R v Sims* (1946) shows that on an indictment containing several counts evidence may be given which supports only some of them ... One of the grounds stated in the appellant's notice of appeal to the Court of Criminal Appeal was that the judge failed to direct the jury that it was its duty to consider each count separately and not to be influenced in its decision upon the eighth count by the evidence of the earlier thefts. The judge did indeed, in his summing-up, go through each count separately, but he treated the evidence as cumulative and told the jury that the main question was whether it was satisfied that the appellant 'stole the money' without pointing out that the relevant considerations might be somewhat different on the different counts. True it is that the jury by its verdict distinguished between them, but the fact remains that it was not directed to consider what part of the evidence was properly of weight in deciding its verdict on the eighth count ...

My Lords, my noble and learned friend, Lord Porter, who is unable to be present today, authorizes me to say that he agrees in all respects with this opinion.

Lord Oaksey: My Lords, I agree with the principles stated by the noble Viscount on the Woolsack as to the admissibility of evidence, but I find myself unable to agree with your Lordships' application of those principles to the facts of the case. I agree with your Lordships that the discretion of Pearson J to try the eight counts all together ought not to be disturbed. As I understand it your Lordships are of the opinion that the evidence on counts 1 to 7 was relevant on the eighth count but so slightly relevant that it should have been excluded by the judge. I agree with the principle that the judge at the trial has a discretion to exclude evidence which though strictly speaking admissible is only slightly relevant and if it relates to former offences by the accused may have a prejudicial effect out of proportion to its relevance, but I do not agree that that principle is applicable to the facts of this case and I am of the opinion that the summing-up of Pearson J and the judgment of the Court of Criminal Appeal were right.

There is, in my opinion, no question of general importance in this appeal. The only question is: Do the facts which were proved as to the thefts referred to in counts 1 to 7 tend so slightly to implicate the accused in the crime in July on which he was charged in the eighth count that they ought to have been excluded?

The facts on the eight occasions were undoubtedly similar: the premises were the same; the method of entry to the premises was the same; the money taken was less than the money on the premises; the accused might have broken into the premises while on duty as a police constable when money was stolen; and when he was on leave no thefts took place. The only difference in the July facts was that the accused was proved then to be close by the premises directly after the alarm was given in circumstances of suspicion.

It is, in my opinion, important to observe that there was no direct evidence that the accused broke in and committed the theft in July. The evidence, of course, was much more cogent than the evidence in May and June, but it was not conclusive and was really only a much stronger case of opportunity. It is true that the admission of the evidence of the facts of May and June involves the suggestion that the accused committed crimes other than the particular crime on which *ex hypothesi* he was being tried, and if the only relevance of the facts as to counts 1 to 7 was that he had committed crimes on those occasions, I should agree that the evidence of such facts would be inadmissible. But that is not the only relevance of these facts. Their relevance consists and consists only, in my opinion, in the similarities which existed between the facts of May and June, and the facts of July. It is one thing to prove that the accused has committed a number of different crimes on different occasions; it may be a totally different thing to adduce evidence which tends to show that he has committed the same sort of offence in the same circumstances on several occasions. I do not understand your Lordships to hold that the evidence of what happened in July was inadmissible or should have been excluded on any of the counts 1 to 7 and, if that is so, it could, in my opinion, only be because of the same similarities in the evidence, from which it might be inferred that the accused stole the money on the first seven occasions although there was no direct evidence that he was in fact present when the money was stolen on any one of these occasions. The question may be tested in this way: can it be said that no jury could reasonably find that one person committed all eight thefts? In my opinion, the same similarity must be equally relevant whether it is adduced on one count or on the others ...

The issue to which the evidence in question was, in my opinion, relevant was whether the accused was near the premises in July for an innocent purpose or not.

For these reasons I agree with the judgment of the Court of Criminal Appeal.

Lord Morton of Henryton: My Lords, I agree with the speech which has been delivered by my noble and learned friend on the Woolsack. I desire only to add that, in my view, evidence as to the thefts which occurred on the first seven occasions was not admissible for the purpose of the trial of the appellant on the eighth count, because the appellant was not proved to have been near the shop, or even in the market, at the time when these thefts occurred. It is, however, clear that the judge invited the jury to take that evidence into account when considering the eighth count. In making these observations, I do not regard myself as differing in any way from the speech with which I have just expressed my agreement. I make them only for the purpose of explaining why I cannot accept the views which have just been expressed by my noble and learned friend, Lord Oaksey.

Lord Tucker: My Lords, for the reasons which have been stated by my noble and learned friend on the Woolsack, I concur in the motion which he has proposed.

I agree with my noble and learned friend, Lord Morton of Henryton, that the evidence with regard to the first seven occasions was irrelevant to the charge on the eighth count, but was left to the jury as relevant.

Appeal allowed.[18]

R v Brown, Smith & Others (1963, Court of Criminal Appeal)

The appellants were convicted at East Sussex Quarter Sessions on 8 January 1963 of shopbreaking and larceny. The appellant Smith pleaded guilty to an earlier offence of a similar nature.

The following statement of facts is taken, in substance, from the judgment.

The joint offence was alleged to have been committed by all four appellants on 12 November 1962 at East Grinstead. The appellant Smith pleaded guilty to having five days before, on 7 November at Hailsham, broken and entered a shop and stolen some transistor radios and the sum of nearly £50 in cash.

The Hailsham offence, which was committed on 7 November 1962, by Smith alone, was perpetrated somewhere shortly after one o'clock in the luncheon break when the shopkeeper was out. According to the evidence, entry must have been effected by means of a key unlocking the front door, there being no signs of forcing at all. The evidence in relation to the East Grinstead offence, with which all four appellants were charged, was that it was committed on 12 November, when some person or persons broke and entered a shop between one o'clock and two o'clock when the shopkeeper was away at lunch, and stole £8 in notes, a raincoat and an overcoat. Again it is clear that that entry was effected by unlocking the shop door.

Edmund Davies J [after stating the facts as set out above]: Counsel for the appellants applied for separate trials on the first count relating to shopbreaking and larceny at East Grinstead. The application was resisted by counsel for the Crown, who said that in any event as against Smith he proposed to introduce the evidence of the Hailsham offence, albeit Smith had pleaded guilty to it, as establishing a nexus between Smith and the East Grinstead offence. Ultimately, the learned judge, despite the protests of the defence counsel, decided to have all four men tried jointly on the first count relating to East Grinstead and furthermore, again despite the protests of defence counsel, allowed evidence to be given against Smith on his activities at Hailsham five days before, the criminal character of which he had admitted by his plea of guilty ...

As against Smith there was adduced evidence relating to the Hailsham incident to which reference has been made. How does learned counsel for the Crown seek to justify the adducing of that testimony despite defence counsel's protests? He concedes that the general principle is that a person cannot be implicated in one criminal offence by saying that he has on other occasions committed criminal offences, even similar criminal offences, and therefore, being criminally disposed, is likely to have committed the offence charged. That fundamental

---

18. [1952] AC 694.

principle is of course accepted by Mr McCowan [Counsel for the Crown], but he draws attention to the various exceptions which have cropped up in our law where evidence of other offences of a similar character has been admitted for one reason or another, either to anticipate and destroy a defence or by way of rebuttal to destroy a defence raised, such as that the person acted in mistake or that the whole thing was an accident, or similar disclaimers of any criminal intention or activity at all. He has drawn our attention to the fact that there are cases ... in which evidence of other offences committed has been given to establish the identity of the perpetrator of the crime which is investigated by the court ... He concedes that some kind of nexus must be established by the Crown between the offence charged and the other offences sought to be relied upon ...

What is the hallmark of the Hailsham crime which goes to show that Smith was also involved in the East Grinstead crime? The first two matters relied upon by Mr McCowan, so far from establishing a nexus, seem to me to operate in precisely the opposite direction. He says, first of all, that the two offences were merely five days apart in point of time. Five days is a long time; if they had been committed within half an hour of each other and in the same locality, there might be something in the point, but it seems to me this point has no value at all. Then he says: look at the proximity of the places where these offences were committed. Well, let us look at it. East Grinstead is twenty miles away from Hailsham, and both shops are on the main London-Eastbourne Road. I make the same comment about that alleged nexus as I did about the first, twenty miles is a long distance. I personally can attach no value to that at all. Both offences were committed in the lunch-hour when the shopkeeper was away, Mr McCowan says, and lastly he says both offences were perpetrated by the criminal gaining access by using a skeleton key to open the mortice lock on each door. There are no idiosyncratic features about those matters at all. That is the way in which thousands upon thousands of criminal entries are effected into shop premises in the lunch-hour when the shopkeeper is away.

This court is unanimous in thinking that there were no peculiar features linking the East Grinstead offence with the earlier Hailsham offence which could justify the admission of the earlier offence as evidence to support the implication of Smith in relation to the latter. I put an example in the course of argument. Supposing that a person charged with housebreaking was found with a piece of celluloid in his possession, and supposing it was found that he had used celluloid as a means of gaining access to 100 houses on previous occasions, could it possibly be said that that fact was any reason why the 100 other offences should be used to establish the identity of the accused as the perpetrator of the offence charged? The question has only to be asked to answer itself. Were the court to approve of what was done in this case it would mean the annihilation of the fundamental rule, that criminal propensity as such can never be adduced in order to establish the guilt of a person of the offence charged.[19]

[The sole judgment was that of Edmund Davies J]]

R v Lewis (1982, Court of Appeal)

Application for leave to appeal against conviction

On 24 July 1981, at the Crown Court at Worcester (Judge Lee) the applicant was convicted on four counts of indecent assault and two counts of indecency with a

---

19. 47 Cr App R 204.

child. He was sentenced to concurrent terms of three months' imprisonment suspended for two years.

The following facts are taken from the judgment.

At the material time Mrs Layland was separated from her husband and was living in Droitwich with twin 10 year old daughters, Cecilia and Kerry, who were the subject matter of the alleged offences, and a 14 year old son, Andrew. A relationship developed between the applicant and Mrs Layland and he moved into her home, where, as he put it, he sought to establish himself as a 'father figure' for the children.

Although there were six counts in the indictment, these involved only four incidents because two of them involved both the twins and the involvement of each was included in a separate count. The incidents can be summarised as follows.

(a) The urination incident. The twins were having a bath when, as the prosecution alleged, the applicant entered the bathroom, urinated in the lavatory and then shook his penis at them causing a small quantity of urine to strike them. The applicant's case was that whilst he was using the lavatory, the twins splashed him and that when he had finished and washing his hands he held his penis under his shirt and pointed it at them saying: 'You would not like that, would you, if I did it to you?' In an interview with the police he admitted that he shook his penis at the twins, but said that his gesture 'was only in fun'.

(b) The masturbation incident. The prosecution alleged that the applicant, when naked, masturbated himself in the presence of the twins in circumstances in which they could not fail to see what was going on and that he continued to do so in the face of their obvious embarrassment and distress. The applicant denied that this incident ever occurred, although it was corroborated by the evidence of the boy Andrew. He fully accepted that on occasion he was naked in the presence of the children, but this was because he believed that children should be taught not to be ashamed of their bodies.

(c) The towelling incident. This concerned only Cecilia. The prosecution alleged that the applicant indecently assaulted her by persistently rubbing between her legs with a towel when drying her after she had had a bath, notwithstanding her protest and the fact that at the age of 10 she was quite capable of drying herself. The applicant admitted drying Cecilia, but said that he did not dry between her legs. As he put it, 'I never dried between her legs, not horizontally. Possibly the towel touched between her legs while I was drying them vertically'.

(d) The fondling incident. This concerned only Kerry. The prosecution alleged that the applicant indecently assaulted Kerry by fondling her chest when 'cuddling' her in bed. The applicant admitted that Kerry would sometimes come into bed with him and he would give her a cuddle. However, he said that it was simply a gesture of affection and was part of the father image which he was trying to cultivate. So far as fondling her chest was concerned, he said that his hand may have straying there but that it was without significance.

Donaldson LJ: ... The suggested ground of appeal is that the learned judge wrongly admitted evidence that he had in his possession documents, magazines, letters and posters obtained from the Paedophilic Society, that in interviews with the police the applicant referred to himself as a paedophile, expressing the view that all love and affection is sexually motivated, whilst drawing a sharp distinction between being a paedophile and being a molester of children and that he asked Mrs Layland whether she could live with a paedophile ...

In the instant appeal we are not concerned with evidence tending to show that the applicant has been guilty of criminal acts other than those covered by the indictment. However, we are concerned with evidence which could lead the jury to conclude that the applicant was likely, or more likely, to have committed the offences for which he was being tried. The principles stated by Lord Herschell are therefore applicable and we are faced with the difficulty of drawing the line.

Mr Wood [Counsel for the appellant] concedes, as he must, that such evidence is admissible in order to rebut a defence of accident or innocent association, where that is the only defence in issue. But that will not always be the case. There may, as here, be more than one count and the defence may be a complete denial of the facts alleged in respect of one count, a defence of accident for another and of innocent association for a third. Furthermore, a situation can arise in which, although the defence is a complete denial, justice requires that consideration be given to the possibility of accident or innocence if the denial be not accepted.

In the instant appeal there was a complete denial of the masturbation incident and there was, on the facts of that incident, no possibility of a defence of accident or that his actions, if proved, could bear an innocent explanation. However in the case of the other three incidents issues of accident and an innocent explanation of whatever occurred quite clearly arose and had to be considered by the jury. In our judgment neither the fact that the paedophilic evidence was inadmissible in the context of the masturbation count nor that there was some degree of denial of the basic facts in the case of the other counts rendered it inadmissible in the context of the other counts.

This leaves the question of whether, in the exercise of his discretion, the judge should have excluded the evidence. Clearly it could have had an unduly prejudicial effect if its true impact and significance was not most carefully explained to the jury. But this the judge did. Having pointed out that the jury were not concerned to approve or disapprove of the applicant's views, he said: 'You are entitled to consider his opinions as expressed in the past, the letter; you are entitled to consider his statements to the police and decide what he then meant by those statements which may or may not be the same as what he now says he meant. You are entitled to refer to the documents which you have seen or you have heard about. What you are not entitled to do, members of the jury, is to assume that in any way – if you come to the conclusion he does hold these opinions or he makes these statements or he possesses this sort of literature – that evidence goes to prove these charges of itself. It does not. If there is no adequate evidence that the alleged events occurred, you acquit him, whatever opinion he holds. But if you are satisfied on the evidence that the events which the prosecution allege did occur, then his attitudes, his opinions, his literature, his letters may be relevant in considering the effect first of all of what he said to the police and what it then meant and in considering whether matters which you are satisfied did occur were accidental or innocent. "I may have casually touched her chest", or he rubbed it for minutes. Whether accident or innocent, were they deliberate and with a sexual purpose? Do you follow what I am saying? The fact that a man has certain views, the fact that a man is an admitted homosexual for instance, does not mean if he is accused of it that he has necessarily committed a homosexual act with a boy. But if what he does with a boy is something which really needs explanation, then you are entitled to see whether his explanation is innocent or otherwise or the explanation for what he did.' Again at the end of the summing-up, the judge came back to the same point saying: 'I have not referred to this literature we have seen in any detail. There is little contest about the general nature of Magpie. It is written pursuing a theme that contact and sexual contact and sexual behaviour between adults and children whether homosexual, heterosexual or lesbian is not merely justifiable but beneficial and the age of consent is too high, and things of that sort, but I have pointed out they must not be used as a substitute or addition to evidence to prove facts of the incident. They cannot do that. They can only be used in consideration of what the defendant meant by what he said to the police and what he has said to Mrs Layland and in considering his innocent explanations of facts which you find proved.' In our judgment, the summing-up was full, fair and balanced and the application for leave to appeal against conviction should be refused.[20]

PB Carter, 'Forbidden Reasoning Permissible: Similar Fact Evidence a Decade after *Boardman*', *Modern Law Review* 48 (1985)

A fiction that has died hard in the law of evidence is that similar fact evidence, the only relevance of which involves ascribing a propensity to the accused, or, as it can now be said, rests upon the forbidden reasoning, is always inadmissible. The longevity of this fiction was greatly helped by several devices which mitigated the rigidity of its mandate. Similar fact evidence was said to be nevertheless admissible for the purpose of proving a particular issue, such as identity or *mens rea*. The plausibility of singling out for special treatment evidence going to this latter issue was often heightened by the ambiguity of the defence of accident which has been referred to above. Again, sometimes a dubious distinction was drawn between evidence tending to show propensity and that tending to show system, the latter being admissible; whereas in fact evidence of system has usually been simply evidence of propensity to behave regularly and consistently (ie systematically) in a particular way. At other times reliance was placed upon a supposed distinction between defences of complete denial and defences of innocent explanation or innocent association. The logical and practical shortcomings of this supposed distinction were succinctly pointed out by Lord Cross in *R v Boardman*: 'If I am charged with a sexual offence why should it make a difference to the admissibility or non-admissibility of similar fact evidence whether my case is that the meeting at which the offence is said to have been committed never took place or that I committed no offence in the course of it? In each case I am saying that my accuser is lying.' In the same case Lord Wilberforce drew attention to the dangers inherent in this dubious distinction: 'It is sometimes said that the evidence of similar facts may be called to rebut a defence of innocent association, a proposition which I regard with suspicion since it seems a specious manner of outflanking the exclusionary rule.'

Since the *Boardman* decision, or more particularly, having regard to what was said by several of their Lordships in that case, it is now accepted – albeit intermittently – that similar fact evidence, although only substantially relevant on the basis of propensity type reasoning, will be admitted provided its likely prejudicial effect is sufficiently underpinned by its true probative worth. It is no

---

20. 76 Cr App R 33.

longer necessary for a judge to seek out a specific escape route from a supposedly inflexible rule of exclusion. The rationality of this change of approach cannot be gainsaid. Its effect is to constitute a second and separate justification for the reception of similar fact evidence. The evidence is received not because it has substantial relevance without involving resort to the forbidden reasoning, but rather because such resort is in the circumstances exceptionally warranted. It is, however, important to understand some of the implications of this new approach and to be aware of potential dangers.

When considering the admissibility of similar fact evidence which lacks substantial relevance otherwise than by resort to the forbidden reasoning, a judge must first make his own assessment of its true probative worth. He must assess the weight of the disputed evidence, and in doing this he is performing a function of a type usually reserved for a jury or trier of fact. It is to be noted that he (unlike a jury) must usually make his assessment before there has been an opportunity for the evidence to be tested by cross-examination. The judge's second task is of a different order. He must form a view as to the effect which the evidence is in fact likely to have upon the minds of the jurypersons. It is to be emphasised that what is involved here is not an exercise in logic but rather a prognostic evaluation of likely jury reactions. Finally the judge must compare what are not altogether comparable. He must decide whether the true probative worth (a euphemism for judicial assessment of probative worth) of the evidence fully measures up to its prejudicial effect (ie the judge's conjecture as to what its effect is in the circumstances in fact likely to be upon the jury). Obviously this new approach will often impose a formidable task upon the judge. Moreover it can be seen as representing a shift, albeit an indirect and insidious one, away from trial by jury. Not only is the judge always involved in a preliminary, and in the event of exclusion controlling, assessment of weight, but also his decision to admit might in some cases be seen by an astute juror as a signal that the evidence is reliable. It is far from being the present writer's suggestion that these implications of the new approach warrant its rejection. They do, however, perhaps indicate a danger which must be guarded against. That danger is, in short, that prejudicial propensity evidence is liable to be too readily admitted and that appellate courts will be unduly reluctant to intervene. It would be a bold judge who would claim that in assessing true probative worth he is himself totally free from the influence of the sort of prejudice to which it is feared the jury might fall victim. However, having regard to the flexible nature of the rule, an appeal court may be reluctant to intervene for the same sort of reasons as warrant reluctance to disturb the exercise of discretion by a trial judge. It is, therefore, important to remember that the new approach posits the application by the judge of a rule of law, not the exercise of a discretion. The distinction between a flexible rule of law and a discretion is no mere pedantry. It is a distinction that can be crucial in terms of appellate control. The forbidden reasoning is in the great majority of cases forbidden for very good cause – the protection of an accused against being convicted on his record of a crime which he did not commit. It is only in the clearest case that true probative value should be seen as adequately underpinning possible prejudicial effect. It is obviously preferable for a multiplicity of reasons that justice be done at the trial without resort to appeal. It is, therefore, especially incumbent upon the judge to be constantly mindful of the words of Kennedy J in *R v Bond* (1906) in the Court for Crown Cases Reserved nearly eighty years ago: 'Nothing can so certainly be counted upon to make a prejudice against an accused upon his trial as the disclosure to the jury of other misconduct of a kind similar to that which is the subject of the indictment, and, indeed, when the crime alleged is one of revolting character ... and the hearer is a person who has not been trained to think judicially, the prejudice must sometimes be almost insurmountable.'

This present encapsulated disquisition upon the perennial problem of the admissibility of similar fact evidence has been provoked by the recent Court of Appeal case of *R v Lewis* (1983) ...

[In this case] the Court of Appeal was apparently unwilling to accept that the reception of evidence, which is likely to cause the jury to have resort to the forbidden reasoning, is only to be justified if, either it has additionally substantial relevance which does not involve this type of reasoning, or its true probative value (even on the basis of the forbidden reasoning) so clearly outweighs its prejudicial content that, in the words of Lord Cross in the *Boardman* case, its exclusion would be 'an affront to common sense'. In *R v Lewis* there was undoubtedly a serious risk that the disputed evidence would cause the jury to have resort to the forbidden reasoning, and indeed the evidence would seem to have no substantial relevance in any other way. It can scarcely be denied that the reception of the evidence could be highly prejudicial to the accused, and yet its probative worth might well not be commensurate with this.

Instead of accepting that the reception of propensity evidence – that is evidence likely to involve the forbidden reasoning – depends upon the true probative value/prejudicial content equation, the Court of Appeal reverted to the atavistic view that the admissibility of such evidence depends almost exclusively upon the nature of the issue upon which the evidence bears. More specifically the court relied upon the distinction between the issue raised by a defence of 'innocent association' or of 'accident' and that raised by a complete denial, the assumption being that the evidence of the applicant's interest in, and thus predisposition towards, paedophilia was admissible upon the former issues but not upon the latter issue ...

If different issues are raised by different counts in an indictment, the holding that the admissibility of a piece of evidence depends upon the nature of the issue to which it is relevant could clearly present a court with a dilemma ... [I]t is totally unrealistic to suppose that even the most lucid and meticulous trial judge can ensure that a jury will only use damning evidence of this type when considering one count and will refrain from using it when considering another count, or ensure that when considering a particular count a jury will have regard to such evidence in relation to one issue but will disregard it in relation to a supposedly different issue. As Lord Cross said in *R v Boardman*: 'It is asking too much of any jury to tell them to perform mental gymnastics of this sort.'[21]

There is a statutory provision in the Theft Act 1968 which allows for the admission of something like similar fact evidence. It has been narrowly construed and little used; evidence which it makes admissible may be excluded in the judge's discretion.[22]

Theft Act 1968

27(3) Where a person is being proceeded against for handling stolen goods (but not for any offence other than handling stolen goods), then at any stage of the

---

21. PB Carter, 'Forbidden Reasoning Permissible: Similar Fact Evidence a Decade after Boardman', *Modern Law Review* 48 (1985) pp 35-41.

22. *Hacker* [1994] 1 WLR 1659.

proceedings, if evidence has been given of his having or arranging to have in his possession the goods the subject of the charge, or of his undertaking or assisting in, or arranging to undertake or assist in, their retention, removal, disposal or realisation, the following evidence shall be admissible for the purpose of proving that he knew or believed the goods to be stolen goods–

(a) evidence that he has had in his possession, or has undertaken or assisted in the retention, removal, disposal or realisation of, stolen goods from any theft taking place not earlier than twelve months before the offence charged; and

(b) (provided that seven days notice in writing has been given to him of the intention to prove the conviction) evidence that he has within the five years preceding the date of the offence charged been convicted of theft or of handling stolen goods.

CHAPTER 9

THE CHARACTER OF THE ACCUSED

Most problems in this area concern cross-examination under the Criminal Evidence Act 1898. But sometimes the defence may wish to give evidence of the accused's good character in order to establish the improbability of his having committed the offence with which he is charged. It is not always appreciated that there are limitations on the sort of evidence that can be adduced for this purpose.

R v Rowton (1865, Court for Crown Cases Reserved)[1]

Cockburn CJ: This case turns upon the admissibility of an answer given by a witness who was called to rebut evidence of good character which had been given in favour of the prisoner, and who was asked what was the prisoner's general character for decency and morality. The answer was in these terms: 'I know nothing of the neighbourhood's opinion, because I was only a boy at school when I knew him; but my opinion, and the opinion of my brothers who were also pupils of his, is that his character is that of a man capable of the grossest indecency and the most flagrant immorality.' The chief question for us is whether that answer was proper to be left to the consideration of the jury. I am of opinion that it was not, and that the conviction cannot stand.

There are two questions to be decided. The first is whether, when evidence of good character has been given in favour of a prisoner, evidence of his general bad character can be called in reply. I am clearly of the opinion that it can be ...

Assuming, then, that evidence was receivable to rebut the evidence of good character, the second question is, was the answer which was given in this case, in reply to a perfectly legitimate question, such an answer as could be properly left to the jury? Now, in determining this point, it is necessary to consider what is the meaning of evidence of character. Does it mean evidence of general reputation or evidence of disposition? I am of opinion that it means evidence of general reputation. What you want to get at is the tendency and disposition of the man's mind towards committing or abstaining from committing the class of crime with which he stands charged; but no one has ever heard the question, what is the tendency and disposition of the prisoner's mind?, put directly. The only way of getting at it is by giving evidence of his general character founded on his general reputation in the neighbourhood in which he lives. That, in my opinion, is the sense in which the word 'character' is to be taken, when evidence of character is spoken of. The fact that a man has an unblemished reputation leads to the presumption that he is incapable of committing the crime for which he is being tried. We are not now considering whether it is desirable that the law of England should be altered – whether it is expedient to import the practice of other countries and go into the prisoner's antecedents for the purpose of showing that he is likely to commit the crime with which he is charged, or, stopping short of that, whether it would be wise to allow the prisoner to go into facts for the purpose of showing that he is incapable of committing the crime charged against

---

1. In the report that follows references to the Chief Justice of England are to Cockburn CJ, the Chief Justice of the Court of Queen's Bench. Erle CJ was Chief Justice of the Court of Common Pleas. The other judges before whom the case was argued were: Pollock CB, Williams J, Willes J, Channell B, Byles J, Blackburn J, Keating J, Piggott B and Shee J.

him. It is quite clear that, as the law now stands, the prisoner cannot give evidence of particular facts, although one fact would weigh more than the opinion of all his friends and neighbours. So too, evidence of antecedent bad conduct would form equally good ground for inferring the prisoner's guilt, yet it is quite clear evidence of that kind is inadmissible. The allowing of evidence of good character has arisen from the fairness of our laws, and is an anomalous exception to the general rule. It is quite true that evidence of character is most cogent, when it is preceded by a statement shewing that the witness has had opportunities of acquiring information upon the subject beyond what the man's neighbours in general would have; and in practice the admission of such statements is often carried beyond the letter of the law in favour of the prisoner. It is, moreover, most essential that a witness who comes forward to give a man a good character should himself have a good opinion of him; for otherwise he would only be deceiving the jury; and so the strict rule is often exceeded. But, when we consider what, in the strict interpretation of the law, is the limit of such evidence, in my judgment it must be restricted to the man's general reputation, and must not extend to the individual opinion of the witness. Some time back, I put this question – suppose a witness is called who says that he knows nothing of the general character of the accused, but that he has had abundant opportunities of forming an individual opinion as to his honesty or the particular moral quality that may be in question in the particular case. Surely, if such evidence were objected to, it would be inadmissible.

If that be the true doctrine as to the inadmissibility of evidence to character in favour of the prisoner, the next question is, within what limits must the rebutting evidence be confined? I think that that evidence must be of the same character and confined within the same limits – that, as the prisoner can only give evidence of general good character, so the evidence called to rebut it must be evidence of the same general description, shewing that the evidence which has been given in favour of the prisoner is not true, but that the man's general reputation is bad. In this case the witness disclaims all knowledge of the general reputation of the accused. I take his meaning to be this: 'I know nothing of the opinion of those with whom the man has in the ordinary occupations of life been brought into contact. I knew him; and so did two brothers of mine, when we were at school; and in my opinion his disposition' (for that is the sense in which the word 'character' is used by the witness) 'is such, that he is capable of committing the class of offences with which he stands charged.' I am strongly of opinion that that answer was not admissible. As, when a witness is called to speak to the character of the accused, he cannot say, 'I know nothing of his general character, but I have had an opportunity of forming an opinion as to his disposition, and I consider him incapable of committing this offence': so here, when the witness declared that he knew nothing of the general character of the accused, but that in his opinion the prisoner's disposition was such as to make it likely that he would commit the offence in question – applying the same principle – the answer was inadmissible. But, if an objectionable answer is given to an unobjectionable question, the judge who presides at the trial should stop the answer before it is completed, or, if that is impossible, should tell the jury that they must withdraw it from their consideration; and then the answer would not prejudice the case. Here, however, it was not so. The learned judge expressly left the answer to the jury, and directed them to take it into account and balance it against the evidence of character given in favour of the prisoner. That being so, the answer became a part of the case, and cannot be treated as an objectionable answer inadvertently given to an unexceptionable question. I beg in conclusion that it may be understood that I do not offer any opinion as to what the law should be, or what evidence of character should be admissible, either in favour of the prisoner, or in reply on the part of the prosecution. I find it uniformly laid down in the text books that the evidence to character must be general evidence of reputation; and, dealing with the law as I find it, my opinion is that the answer given in this case was inadmissible, and that the conviction ought not to stand.

Erle CJ: I concur with the Chief Justice of England on many points of the judgment that he has just delivered. The admissibility of evidence of character for the prisoner stands on peculiar grounds. The question of admissibility of evidence that the good character given to the prisoner is undeserved is now brought for the first time before us for adjudication. The progress of our law should be adapted to the interests of society; and the rules relating to the admissibility of evidence should be regulated by attending carefully to the interests of truth. If the prisoner, having a bad character, misleads the court by calling witnesses to say that he has a good one, in the interests of truth and justice the false impression should be removed; and I quite agree with the Chief Justice of the Queen's Bench upon the first question, that evidence was admissible in this case to rebut the good character given to the prisoner. With respect to the second question, I agree that evidence of individual facts is to be excluded; but whether the answer given by the witness in this case is in the nature of an individual fact or not I do not stop to inquire, because a question of very general importance has been raised; and, with reference to that question, I am of opinion that the answer, understood as evidence of disposition, is admissible.

Now, what is the principle on which evidence of character is admitted? It seems to me that such evidence is admissible for the purpose of shewing the disposition of the party accused, and basing thereon a presumption that he did not commit the crime imputed to him. Disposition cannot be ascertained directly; it is only to be ascertained by the opinion formed concerning the man, which must be founded either on personal experience, or on the expression of opinion by others, whose opinion again ought to be founded on their personal experience. The question between us is, whether the court is at liberty to receive a statement of the disposition of a prisoner, founded on personal experience of the witness, who attends to give evidence and state that estimate which long personal knowledge of and acquaintance with the prisoner has enabled him to form. I think that each source of evidence is admissible. You may give in evidence the general rumour prevalent in the prisoner's neighbourhood, and, according to my experience, you may have also the personal judgment of those who are capable of forming a more real, substantial, guiding opinion than that which is to be gathered from general rumour. I never saw a witness examined to character without an inquiry being made into his personal means of knowledge of that character. The evidence goes to the jury depending entirely upon the personal experience of the witness who has offered his testimony. Suppose a witness to character were to say, 'This man has been in my employ for twenty years. I have had experience of his conduct; but I have never heard a human being express an opinion of him in my life. For my own part, I have always regarded him with the highest esteem and respect, and have had abundant experience that he is one of the worthiest men in the world.' The principle the Lord Chief Justice has laid down would exclude this evidence; and that is the point where I differ from him. To my mind personal experience gives cogency to the evidence; whereas such a statement as, 'I have heard some persons speak well of him', or, 'I have heard general report in favour of the prisoner', has a very slight effect in comparison. Again, to the proposition that general character is alone admissible the answer is that it is impossible to get at it. There is no such thing as general character; it is the general inference supposed to arise from hearing a number of separate and disinterested statements in favour of the prisoner. But I think that the notion that general character is alone admissible is not accurate. It would be wholly inadmissible to ask a witness what individual he has ever heard give his opinion of a particular fact connected with the man. I attach considerable weight to this distinction, because, in my opinion, the best character is that which is the least talked of ...

[T]he practice is to stop a witness when he refers to particular facts only, but to leave him at liberty to give his opinion founded on those facts. In this particular case the question was, 'What was the character of the prisoner?', and, if the answer had been, 'I knew him when I was a pupil, and I say that his character is bad', and it had stopped there, it would in my opinion have been unobjectionable. It was a statement of personal experience; and the witness gave his answer according to the general inference which he had drawn from that experience. But the witness added a specific fact: the opinion of his brothers. Strictly, that specific fact was not admissible; but, in a grave case involving a very important question, I cannot rest my decision on the particular answer. On the general principle which I have stated, I think that both questions ought to be answered in the affirmative, and that the conviction should stand.

Cockburn CJ: I would not for a moment make any attempt at a reply on anything that has fallen from the Chief Justice of the Common Pleas. I am only anxious not to be misunderstood in the judgment I have pronounced. So far from excluding, I admit that negative evidence, such as 'I never heard anything against the character of the man', is the most cogent evidence of a man's good character and reputation, because a man's character is not talked about till there is some fault to be found with it. It is the best evidence of his character that he is not talked about at all; and in that sense such evidence is admissible.

Martin B: With respect to the second question, I concur with the Chief Justice of the Queen's Bench. In my judgment the answer of the witness to the question put to him was not general evidence of character, but was an answer that related to particular facts known to himself and his brothers; and I think that the learned judge was wrong in allowing such evidence to go to the jury ...

Willes J: I am of opinion that upon both questions the ruling of the judge was right ... I entirely agree with the Chief Justice of *England*, that it is a mistake to suppose that, because the prisoner only can raise the question of character, it is therefore a collateral issue. It is not. Such evidence is admissible, because it renders it less probable that what the prosecution has averred is true. It is strictly relevant to the issue; but it is not admissible upon the part of the prosecution, because ... if the prosecution were allowed to go into such evidence, we should have the whole life of the prisoner ripped up, and, as has been witnessed elsewhere, upon a trial for murder you might begin by shewing that when a boy at school the prisoner had robbed an orchard, and so on through the whole of his life; and the result would be that the man on his trial might be overwhelmed by prejudice, instead of being convicted on that affirmative evidence which the law of this country requires. The evidence is relevant to the issue, but is excluded for reasons of policy and humanity; because, although by admitting it you might arrive at justice in one case out of a hundred, you would probably do injustice in the other ninety-nine. There are cases in which it is allowable to go into the prisoner's antecedents, as for the purpose of shewing that he has had opportunity of committing the offence, or that in a particular instance his act could not have been accidental. But these cases only establish the principle that a relevant fact which incidentally casts a slur upon a prisoner is not thereby rendered inadmissible, when it is part of the direct evidence of the case. The ultimate fact to be arrived at by such evidence is that the prisoner's character, in the sense of the particular disposition which nature or education may have given him, is good and not evil. You can, no doubt, go into the question of reputation, and inquire as to the opinion of others concerning the man. But I apprehend that his disposition is the principal matter to be inquired into, and that his reputation is merely accessory and admissible only as evidence of disposition; and, when it is stated that general evidence is alone admissible, that, in my opinion, does not mean merely general evidence of the opinion of others as to the prisoner's character, but general evidence of the disposition of the man. Evidence of particular facts is excluded, because a robber may do acts of generosity; and the proof of such acts is therefore irrelevant to the question of whether he was likely to have committed a particular act of robbery ... Evidence of character is, however, admissible on the part of the prisoner, not only in the sense of what people in general think of him, which is mere rumour, but also in the sense of what is known of him generally in the judgment of the particular witness, which judgment is superior in quality and value to mere rumour. Numerous cases may be put in which a man may have no general character in the sense of any reputation or rumour about him at all, and yet may have a good disposition. For instance, he may be of a shy, retiring disposition, and known only to a few; or again, he may be a person of the vilest character and disposition, and yet only his intimates may be able to testify that this is the case. One man may deserve that character without having acquired it, which another man may have acquired without deserving it. In such cases the value of the judgment of the man's intimates upon his character becomes manifest. In ordinary life, when we want to know the character of a servant, we apply to his master. A servant may be known to none but the members of his master's family: so the character of a child is only known to its parents and teachers, and the character of a man of business to those with whom he deals. I apprehend that there is nothing to prevent a man of business from calling every person with whom he has dealt for years, and asking each in succession whether he was a person, according to the witness's observation, of an honest and just character; and such evidence would be of the highest value. But if a witness to character were to say that the man has got a good character in the parish, it might be that he has gained it because he has gone through the parish offices with decency; and the witness may have had no opportunity of judging of the man's real character and disposition. According to the experience of mankind one would ordinarily rely rather on the information and judgment of a man's intimates than on general report; and why not in a court of law? ...

If, then, such evidence may be admitted upon the part of the prisoner, the evidence admissible to rebut it must be at least as extensive. The evidence in this particular case was of a very particular character, because the prisoner was charged with an offence which would not only be committed in secret, if it were committed at all, but would be likely to be kept secret by the persons who were subjected to it. Such being the case, in order to ascertain the prisoner's character for morality and decency, the persons of whom you would inquire would be those who had been within the reach of his influence – persons who would not be likely to communicate his conduct to the neighbourhood or to one another. Here there was called a person who had been at the prisoner's school, and who stated that, according to his opinion, formed on his experience, the prisoner was capable of the grossest indecency and the most flagrant immorality. I understand this witness to say, 'I have been at that man's school; and, having been there, I can say from what I know and what I have learnt from my brothers who were there also, that his character is most immoral and indecent.' It appears to me that that evidence of the man's character comes within the scope of the principle I have been referring to, and ought to have been admitted, if any evidence of the prisoner's bad character is to be admitted at all. Had I tried the case, although I certainly should have endeavoured to persuade the counsel for the prosecution not to attempt that which was unusual, yet in administering the law according to the custom of England and the usage and practice which have prevailed, if he had insisted on offering the evidence, I should have admitted it, and have fallen into the same mistake which, as appears from the judgment of the majority of the court, the learned judge who had to deal with the case has done.

Cockburn CJ: I am desired by my brother Byles to say that, though he takes no part in the judgment, not having heard the whole of the argument, he entirely concurs with the view of the majority of the judges on both points.

The other learned judges concurred in the judgment delivered by the Lord Chief Justice of England.

Conviction quashed.[2]

R v Redgrave (1981, Court of Appeal)

The defendant was charged with an offence involving homosexual activity in a public lavatory. As part of his defence he wished to adduce evidence, which included love letters, Valentine cards and photographs, to show that he had been very actively involved in relationships with women. The trial judge held this evidence inadmissible. The defendant was convicted and appealed.

Lawton LJ: ... In our judgment the defendant is bound by the same rules as the prosecution. He can call evidence to show that he did not commit the acts which are alleged against him, but he is not allowed, by reference to particular facts, to call evidence that he is of a disposition which makes it unlikely that he would have committed the offence charged.

That this is the common law of England is shown clearly by the decision in *Rowton* (1865) Le & Ca 520. In the course of his judgment in that case Cockburn CJ said at p 530: 'It is quite clear that, as the law now stands, the prisoner cannot give evidence of particular facts, although one fact would weigh more than the opinion of all his friends and neighbours.' That is what the appellant was trying to do in this case. He was trying, by his evidence about his relations with particular women and by the production of these letters and photographs, to show that he had had intimate heterosexual relationships with the writers of the letters and the girls in the photographs, and he was relying on those particular facts to show that he had not got a disposition to behave in the sort of way which the prosecution alleged.

The problem in this case is whether there is any exception in law to the general proposition laid down by Cockburn CJ nearly 120 years ago. The Court of Crown Cases Reserved in *Rowton* (*supra*), made up of no less than 12 judges, came to the conclusion, with two dissensions, that when a defendant wishes to show that he has not got a disposition to commit the kind of offence with which he is charged, he is limited in what he can say. In 1866 he could call evidence to show that his general reputation made it unlikely that he would commit the kind of offence with which he was charged. He could do that by calling people who knew him, but beyond that he could not go.

It follows therefore, so it seems to us, that in this case, although disposition to commit the kind of offence charged was relevant, the law is as decided in *Rowton*

2.　Le & Ca 520, 169 ER 1497.

(*supra*), *viz* that the defendant could do no more than say, or call witnesses to prove, that he was not by general repute the kind of young man who would have behaved in the kind of way that the Crown alleged.

The circumstances of this case show the undesirability of the law going further. Giving evidence and producing documents of this kind would be so easy for somebody who was putting a false defence forward. Clearly it would have been undesirable for this young man to have given evidence that he has had sexual intercourse with a number of named women who were not in court; and it would also not be in the public interest that he should be allowed to subpoena young women to give evidence on oath that they had had sexual intercourse with him. These are the sort of factors which no doubt before 1866 were taken into account by the judges when, during the seventeenth, eighteenth and early part of the nineteenth century, they formulated the rules dealing with evidence.

It seems to us that it is in the public interest generally that evidence of this kind should be limited as laid down in *Rowton* (*supra*). But it is not for us to consider whether the law is a good law or a bad law, unjust or fair law. We are here to apply the law.

It was brought to our attention by [Counsel for the appellant] that nowadays, as a matter of practice in this class of case, defendants are often allowed to say that they are happily married and having a normal sexual relationship with their wives. We are not seeking to stop defending counsel putting that kind of information before a jury. It has long been the practice for judges to allow some relaxation of the law of evidence on behalf of defendants. Had this young man been a married man, or alternatively, had he confined his relationship to one girl, it might not have been all that objectionable for him to have given evidence in general terms that his relationship with his wife or the girl was satisfactory. That would have been an indulgence on the part of the court. It would not have been his right to have said it. Until such time as Parliament amends the law of evidence, it is the duty of this court, and of judges, to keep to the rules, and the rules are clear.[3]

Where evidence of good character is given, its significance must be explained to the jury.

R v Vye (1993, Court of Appeal)

The Lord Chief Justice read the judgment of the court: These three appeals are all based upon criticisms of the learned judges' directions in regard to good character. At one time these issues would not have been regarded even as arguable in this court.

The trial judge was understood to have a broad discretion to comment on the defendant's good character or not as he thought fit. The principle applied by this court was that the judge had no obligation to give directions on good character or even to remind the jury of it (*Aberg* (1948), *Smith* (1971)).

Since about 1989, however, there has been a dramatic change. This court has been inundated with appeals based upon the judge's alleged misdirection or failure to give any direction to the jury about good character. Save in one respect, clear principles have not emerged and Mr Martin Wilson QC on behalf of the Crown in these appeals described the present situation as 'something of a lottery.' After drawing our attention to all the relevant authorities reported and

---

3.   74 Cr App R 10.

unreported since 1989, Mr Wilson submitted that this court should now give clear guidance as to the relevant principles.

Before considering the authorities, it is helpful to say something of the historical background. The defendant was entitled to adduce evidence of his good character long before the law treated him as a competent witness in his own defence. Such evidence was allowed, '... to be submitted to the jury, to induce them to say whether they think it likely that a person with such a character would have committed the offence' (*Stannard* (1837) 7 C & P 673).

Once the defendant became able to give evidence, a further consideration in regard to good character was introduced. Thus in *Bellis* (1966), that consideration was encapsulated by Widgery J as follows: 'Although there is ... no formal or standard direction in these terms, this court does not take the view that possession of a good character is a matter which primarily goes to credibility.'

In *Bryant and Oxley* (1978) the defendant, a man of good character, elected not to give evidence. In his direction to the jury, the judge appeared to suggest that good character was relevant only to credibility. In this court that approach was said to be 'too restrictive'. Good character was relevant 'primarily to the issue of credibility'. Nevertheless, juries 'should' be directed that it was capable of general significance of the kind suggested in the passage quoted from *Stannard*. However, notwithstanding the omission of a *Stannard* direction, the verdict was found neither unsafe nor unsatisfactory.

In February 1989, in *Berrada* (1990) this court considered, amongst other grounds, an alleged misdirection about good character. The defendant had given evidence. Waterhouse J, giving the judgment of the court, said at page 134: 'In the judgment of this court, the appellant was entitled to have put to the jury from the judge herself a correct direction about the relevance of his previous good character to his credibility. That is a conventional direction and it is regrettable that it did not appear in the summing-up in this case. It would have been proper also (but was not obligatory) for the judge to refer to the fact that the previous good character of the appellant might be thought by them to be one relevant factor when they were considering whether he was the kind of man who was likely to have behaved in the way that the prosecution alleged ... We have no doubt, however, that the modern practice is that, if good character is raised by a defendant, it should be dealt with in the summing-up. Moreover when it is dealt with the direction should be fair and balanced, stressing its relevance primarily to a defendant's credibility.'

That decision, therefore, confirmed that, whatever the position may have been previously, it is now an established principle that, where a defendant of good character has given evidence, it is no longer sufficient for the judge to comment in general terms. He is required to direct the jury about the relevance of good character to the credibility of the defendant. Conventionally this has come to be described as the 'first limb' of a character direction. The passage quoted also stated that the judge was entitled, but not obliged, to refer to the possible relevance of good character to the question whether the defendant was likely to have behaved as alleged by the Crown. That (in effect the *Stannard* direction) is the 'second limb'.

Leaving aside cases involving more that one defendant where one is of good character and one is not, virtually all the numerous decisions since Berrada have reiterated that the first limb direction is necessary whenever the defendant has given evidence. This has been held to be so even when, on his own admission, he has told lies in interview with the police (*Kabariti* (1991)).

Accordingly, we turn to the three problems which seem presently to be unresolved on the authorities. They are:

(a) Whether a first limb direction needs to be given in a case where the defendant does not give evidence but has made statements to the police or others.

(b) Whether the second limb direction should now be regarded as discretionary or obligatory; and

(c) What course the judge should take in a joint trial where one defendant is of good character but another is not.

(a) Defendant of good character not giving evidence

There are authorities suggesting there is a discretion whether a first limb direction should be given in relation to answers to the police in interview which are relied upon in support of the defence ...

In our judgment, when the defendant has not given evidence at trial but relies on exculpatory statements made to the police or others, the judge should direct the jury to have regard to the defendant's good character when considering the credibility of those statements. He will, of course, be entitled to make observations about the way the jury should approach such exculpatory statements in contrast to evidence given on oath (see *Duncan* (1981)), but when the jury is considering the truthfulness of any such statements, it would be logical for them to take good character into account, just as they would in regard to a defendant's evidence.

Clearly, if a defendant of good character does not give evidence and has given no pre-trial answers or statements, no issue as to his credibility arises and a first limb direction is not required.

(b) The second limb direction

The relevant authorities as to the judge's duty with regard to the second limb are confusing. On a number of occasions it has been said that the second limb direction is 'discretionary' or 'not obligatory' ...

Nevertheless, despite these repeated statements, in a number of recent cases this court has held omission of such a direction to be inappropriate ...

Having considered those cases, we have been unable to discern any principle or consistent pattern as to when a second limb direction should be given and when it need not. Neither the nature of the crime, its gravity, the age of the defendant, whether he is merely of no previous convictions or of positively good character nor the nature of his defence would seem to have provided clear guidance as to whether this court would regard a second limb direction as entirely discretionary, desirable, important or necessary.

We have considered the whole spectrum of the situations likely to face the trial judge. At one extreme there is the case of an employee who has been entrusted with large sums of money over many years by his employer and, having carried out his duties impeccably, is finally charged with stealing from the till. There a second limb direction is obviously relevant and necessary. At the other extreme is a case such as *Richens* where the defendant, charged with murder, admits manslaughter. It might be thought that in such a case a second limb direction would be little help to the jury. The defendant's argument that he has never stooped to murder before would be countered by the fact that he never stooped to manslaughter before either. Nevertheless, there might well be a residual argument that what was in issue was intent and he had never shown any intent to use murderous violence in the past.

We have reached the conclusion that the time has come to give some clear guidance to trial judges as to how they should approach this matter. It cannot be satisfactory for uncertainty to persist so that judges do not know whether this court, proceeding on a case by case basis, will hold that a second limb direction should or need not have been given. Our conclusion is that such a direction should be given where a defendant is of good character.

Does the need for a second limb direction still exist when the defendant has not given evidence? ...

We can see no logical ground for distinguishing in regard to a second limb direction between cases where the defendant has given evidence and cases where he has not.

Having stated the general rule, however, we recognise it must be for the trial judge in each case to decide how he tailors his direction to the particular circumstances. He would probably wish to indicate, as is commonly done, that good character cannot amount to a defence. In cases such as that of the long serving employee exemplified above, he may wish to emphasise the second limb direction more than in the average case. By contrast, he may wish in a case such as the murder/manslaughter example given above, to stress the very limited help the jury may feel they can get from the absence of any propensity to violence in the defendant's history. Provided that the judge indicates to the jury the two respects in which good character may be relevant, ie credibility and propensity, this court will be slow to criticise any qualifying remarks he may make based on the facts of the individual case.

(c) Two or more defendants of good and bad character

This situation clearly creates difficulties for the trial judge in summing up ...

In our judgment a defendant A of good character is entitled to have the judge direct the jury as to its relevance in his case even if he is jointly tried with a defendant B of bad character. This leaves the question as to what, if anything, the judge should say about the latter. In some cases the judge may think it best to grasp the nettle in his summing-up and tell the jury they must try the case on the evidence: there has been no evidence about B's character; they must not speculate and must not take the absence of information as to B's character as any evidence against B. In other cases the judge may, however, think it best to say nothing about the absence of evidence as to B's character. What course he takes must depend upon the circumstances of the individual case; for example, how great an issue has been made of character during the evidence and speeches.

The question has been raised ... whether defendants of disparate characters might require separate trials. However, in our judgment, the possibility of separate trials is a matter for the judge and is to be decided in accordance with well-established principles. Problems such as statements of one defendant being inadmissible against another, the possibility of cross-examination of one defendant adversely on behalf of another and disparate characters are to be considered and weighed on a case by case basis. There can certainly be no rule in favour of separate trials for defendants of good and bad character. Generally, those jointly indicted should be jointly tried.

To summarise, in our judgment the following principles are to be applied:

(1) A direction as to the relevance of his good character to a defendant's credibility is to be given where he has testified or made pre-trial answers or statements.

(2) A direction as to the relevance of his good character to the likelihood of his having committed the offence charged is to be given, whether or not he has testified, or made pre-trial answers or statements.

(3) Where defendant A of good character is jointly tried with defendant B of bad character, (1) and (2) still apply.[4]

R v Cain (1994, Court of Appeal)

Judge J: On 1 April 1992 in the Crown Court at Harrow before Judge Levy QC and a jury this appellant was convicted of affray. He was sentenced to two months' imprisonment. At the same time the jury returned a verdict of guilty on the same affray against a co-defendant named Wayne Hylton and a verdict of not guilty in the case of another co-defendant, Lizette Hylton. The appellant now appeals against conviction with leave of the single judge.

The only issue in the appeal concerns the way in which the judge directed the jury on the issue of character and previous convictions.

The material facts can be summarised shortly. On 29 June 1991 a social worker, Desmond Coke, was attacked by a group of men. Mr Coke was responsible for organising and distributing kit for local football teams. Earlier that same evening he had, for perfectly good reason, been unable to supply football kit to the appellant and Wayne Hylton. He also said that he would take the kit to the home of Mrs Hylton later that night. He was on his way in his van when he was attacked. The gang included Wayne Hylton and the appellant, who were identified by Mr Coke as two of those who were carrying bottles. Mr Coke was knocked to the ground. The attack on him continued as he lay there.

Later he saw Mrs Hylton at the scene. As she was acquitted by the jury we do not propose to say anything further about the part she was alleged to have played in the incident, but it is not in dispute that she was heard to order the attackers to stop what they were doing.

It was, therefore, an unpleasant incident of public violence, which created fear in those who witnessed it. Mr Coke needed stitches in a head wound and suffered bruising to his chest and feet.

The first defendant on the indictment was Lizette Hylton. After the close of the prosecution case she gave evidence about the facts and the part that she had played in the incident. She also emphasised her positive good character, which was amply supported by character witnesses. The second defendant was her son, Wayne Hylton. He also gave evidence about his involvement in this incident. Nothing at all was said to the jury about his character. The third defendant was the present appellant. He gave evidence which, put briefly, denied any criminal participation in the incident. His account was that Mr Coke had started the fight and that he, the appellant, had intervened when he saw that Mrs Hylton had been pushed to the ground. In effect, he was not acting unlawfully because he only did what he did in self-defence and, indeed, in defence of Mrs Hylton. By their verdict the jury must have rejected his account.

The appellant also volunteered evidence to the jury that he had previous convictions for theft and possession of cannabis. Counsel appearing for him on the appeal cannot now recall why this evidence was put before the jury. There had been a sustained attack on the creditworthiness of Mr Coke, but as far as counsel could recollect, the judge had not given any warning to him that he was at risk of putting his client's character before the jury. It is also possible that

---

4.   97 Cr App R 134.

because there were no convictions for any offences of violence the jury might have been persuaded to take a favourable view of the absence of any known propensity to violence. In any event, however, the appellant's previous convictions were before the jury.

When the evidence was concluded the judge faced the problem of how to leave the issue of character of each defendant to the jury, when the evidence relating to the character of each was different: with the first defendant, positive good character; with the second defendant, no evidence whatever either way; with the third defendant, the appellant, previous convictions. The problem was compounded by the fact that at the time when the case was heard the principles relating to the question of character were unclear ...

When the judge summed up the case to the jury he reminded them of Mrs Hylton's good character. He directed them as follows: 'A good character affects the position in two ways. It adds to the credibility of the evidence; [it makes it] more likely she is telling you the truth and, members of the jury, it is also less likely that a person of her background, of her character, would have behaved in the manner alleged by the prosecution. That does not mean to say that she has not.'

When setting out Mrs Hylton's account of the incident he ended it by saying: 'Well, members of the jury, no doubt, as I said, when you consider her evidence you will take very seriously indeed the fact that she is of previous good character.'

When the judge referred to the evidence of Wayne Hylton he said nothing at all about his character. When he came to deal with the appellant's evidence, he said: 'He has had paid employment with Sun Star, and he is 21. He has had a spot of trouble with the police before ... '

Since the conclusion of this trial the decision of the Court of Appeal in *R v Vye* ... has clarified the principles which apply, not only when the defendant of good character is tried on his own, but also when he is jointly tried with a defendant of bad character ...

In view of these principles, therefore, the judge in the present case was correct when he referred to Mrs Hylton's good character and its possible relevance to her credibility and propensity to commit the crime alleged. She was entitled to such a direction. Furthermore, the judge had a discretion whether to say anything at all to the jury about Wayne Hylton's character. He chose not to do so, and his decision is not open to criticism.

However, as the passage from the judgment shows, the observations in *R v Vye* about the co-defendant of 'bad character' did not extend to cases where there was positive evidence on the subject, and in particular did not suggest that the defendant whose previous convictions were put before the jury should be treated in the same way as the defendant about whose character there was no evidence either way. In other words, it was not dealing with the problem which arises in the present case, where there was positive evidence before the jury that the co-defendant had previous criminal convictions.

The decision in *R v Vye* underlines that in a joint trial the defendant of good character is 'entitled' to the benefit of a direction 'as to its relevance', both to credibility and to propensity. In the absence of directions about the possible relevance of evidence of the co-defendant's previous convictions, the jury may assume that they are relevant to the same issues and, in particular, to propensity to commit crime and, therefore, to guilt.

In our judgment that risk should be avoided by directions about the limited relevance of the evidence of previous convictions and the way in which it should be approached. The requirement for appropriate directions about character therefore applies equally to the defendant with previous convictions as it does to the defendant of good character. The precise terms of the directions will be decided by the judge on his analysis of the issues in the individual case.

It follows that in the present case the judge's reference to the appellant's previous convictions was incomplete ...

[However], notwithstanding the judge's omission to give appropriate directions to the jury about the appellant's previous convictions, we have concluded that this was immaterial to the outcome of the case and that no miscarriage of justice actually occurred. Accordingly, this appeal will be dismissed.[5]

Where the accused has a bad character the prosecution may be able to use this fact to support their case under the principles governing similar fact evidence. In most of these cases the evidence will be adduced as part of the prosecution case and the question of admissibility will not be affected by the decision of the defendant to testify or to remain silent. But the way in which the defence is conducted will affect the operation of the statutory power of the prosecution to cross-examine the defendant about his previous misconduct or the operation of the common law power to call witnesses to rebut evidence called by the defendant of his good character.

Where similar fact evidence has not been called as part of the prosecution case but where, because of the way the defence is run, the prosecution subsequently wish to adduce evidence of the accused's previous misconduct, two situations must be distinguished. Where the accused himself testifies, the 1898 Act applies. But where he does not, even though other defence witnesses may, the position is governed by common law.

Criminal Evidence Act 1898 s 1 (as amended)

...

 (e) A person charged and being a witness in pursuance of this Act may be asked any question in cross-examination notwithstanding that it would tend to criminate him as to the offence charged;

 (f) A person charged and called as a witness in pursuance of this Act shall not be asked, and if asked shall not be required to answer, any question tending to show that he has committed or been convicted of or been charged with any offence other that that wherewith he is then charged, or is of bad character, unless –

  (i) the proof that he has committed or been convicted of such other offence is admissible evidence to show that he is guilty of the offence wherewith he is then charged; or

  (ii) he has personally or by his advocate asked questions of the witnesses for the prosecution with a view to establish his own good character, or has given evidence of his good character, or the nature or conduct of the defence is such as to involve imputations on the character of the prosecutor or the witnesses for the prosecution or the deceased victim of the alleged crime; or

---

5. [1994] 2 All ER 398.

(iii) he has given evidence against any other person charged in the same proceedings.

R v Butterwasser (1948, Court of Criminal Appeal)

Appeal against conviction

The appellant was convicted at the Central Criminal Court of wounding with intent to do grievous bodily harm and was sentenced to three years penal servitude.

At the trial the evidence for the prosecution was given by the prosecutor and his wife, who deposed that on 21 March 1947 in Shaftesbury Avenue, the appellant slashed the prosecutor in the face with a razor. The appellant's counsel in cross-examination attacked the character of the prosecutor and his wife, putting to them a number of previous convictions including convictions of offences of violence, which they admitted, and thereby suggesting that it was really the prosecutor who attacked the appellant. The appellant was not called to give evidence and thereupon, with leave of the court, a police officer was called for the prosecution and read out a record of the appellant's previous convictions. The police officer had not been present on the occasion of any one of those convictions and had no personal knowledge of them, but had been supplied with a list of them by Scotland Yard.

The appellant appealed.

Lord Goddard CJ: We have to consider whether what was done in this case was in accordance with law. When it became clear that the appellant's counsel, after having attacked the witnesses for the prosecution, was not going to call the appellant, the prosecution sought and were allowed to give evidence-in-chief of the prisoner's bad character. A police officer was called, who testified to the prisoner's previous convictions and general character. In the opinion of the court, that was a course which cannot possibly be allowed as the law is at present. It is elementary law that ever since it became the practice, as it has been for the last one hundred and fifty or two hundred years, of allowing a prisoner to call evidence of good character, or where he has put questions to witnesses for the Crown and obtained or attempted to obtain admissions from them that he is a man of good character; in other words, where the prisoner himself puts his character in issue, evidence in rebuttal can be given by the prosecution to show that he is in fact a man of bad character. Evidence of character nowadays is very loosely given and received, and it would be as well if all courts paid attention to a well-known case in the Court of Crown Cases Reserved, *Reg v Rowton* ... in which a court of twelve judges laid down the principles which should govern the giving of evidence of character and of evidence in rebuttal of bad character. It was pointed out that the evidence must be evidence of general reputation and not dependent upon particular acts or actions. But however that may be, there is no case to be found in the books – and it is certainly contrary to what all the present members of the court have understood during the whole of the time they have been in the profession – that where the prisoner does not put his own character in issue, but has merely attacked the witnesses for the prosecution, evidence can be called for the prosecution to prove that the prisoner is a man of bad character. It is, of course, permissible, where a prisoner takes advantage of the Act of 1898, which made prisoners competent witnesses on their trial in all cases, and goes into the witness-box and attacks the witnesses for the prosecution, to cross-examine him with regard to convictions and matters of character; and no doubt if a conviction is put to him and he denies it, the provisions of [the Criminal Procedure Act 1865] would apply and the conviction would be proved against him. But it is admitted that there is no authority, and I do not see on what principle it could be said, that if a man does not go into the box and put his own character in issue, he can have evidence given against him of previous bad character when all that he has done is to attack the witnesses for the prosecution. The reason is that by attacking the witnesses for the prosecution and suggesting they are unreliable, he is not putting his character in issue; he is putting their character in issue. And the reason why, if he gives evidence, he can be cross-examined if he attacks the witnesses for the prosecution is that the statute says he can. It seems to the court, therefore, that it is impossible to say that because the prisoner in this case attacked the witnesses for the prosecution but did not himself give evidence, evidence of his bad character was admissible. In those circumstances, the learned recorder should have declined to allow the evidence to be given, and therefore inadmissible evidence on a most vital point was admitted in this case ...

Since there are certain cases in which evidence of a prisoner's bad character can be given, I will deal with the second ground of appeal shortly. It is said that, even assuming that the evidence of bad character was admissible, it could not be proved in the way it was proved in this case. In this case a police officer was called, who did not pretend that he knew the prisoner; all he could say was that according to the records at Scotland Yard, this man had so many convictions against him, and so on. That evidence would be quite properly admissible – and it is received in almost every criminal trial – after verdict. What happens after verdict is very different from what happens before verdict. After verdict, there is no longer an issue between the Crown and the prisoner. The issue has been determined by the verdict of the jury and there is no more room for evidence except to inform the mind of the court as to what the prisoner's previous history has been for the purpose of enabling the court, if the court desires to hear it, to assess the proper sentence ... It seems to us that there is no pretence for saying that, if it becomes admissible and relevant, as it may do in a certain limited class of cases, to prove that the prisoner was of bad character, you can call a witness to give evidence other than that which is strictly evidence according to the well-known rules which govern the giving of evidence in English courts. It must be evidence to which a person can swear of his own knowledge, and the evidence of a police officer who knows the prisoner and his habits, and has seen him in the streets, is, no doubt, very proper evidence; but an officer, who may be the proper person to come and tell the court after conviction, 'I have here a list of the prisoner's convictions', is not a person who can give evidence where it is a matter which must be proved according to legal evidence.[6]

For the sake of convenience, and despite some overlapping, the operation of provisos (e) and (f) can be dealt with under the following heads:

- the relation between proviso (e), and the opening words of proviso (f), and proviso (f)(i);
- s 1(f)(ii);
- s 1(f)(iii);
- cross-examination of a co-accused generally.

---

6.   [1948] KB 4.

THE RELATION BETWEEN PROVISO (e), THE OPENING WORDS OF PROVISO (f), AND PROVISO (f)(i)

The relation between provisos (e) and (f) is a stock topic for essay questions in examinations. Candidates should be familiar with the discussion (*obiter*) of this question by the House of Lords in *Jones v DPP* (1961) and by Lord Lane CJ (arguably as part of the ratio) in *Anderson* (1988). Note should also be taken of what was said to be the scope of provisos (e) and (f) in *Maxwell v DPP* (1935).

In studying the opening words of s 1(f) the following points should be specifically noted:

- Questions under s 1(f) must be relevant, and questions about previous acquittals will be so only rarely (*Maxwell v DPP* (1935)).

- Even where a s 1(f) condition is satisfied, cross-examination will not always automatically follow; save in relation to s 1(f)(iii), it can be excluded in the judge's discretion (*Stirland v DPP* (1944)).

- 'Charged' means 'accused before a court' (*Stirland v DPP* (1944)).

Note in connection with the scope of s 1(f)(i) that cross-examination about another offence is restricted to cases where the prosecution wish to prove that the accused has committed or been convicted of that offence; cross-examination about occasions when the accused was acquitted is not permitted (*Cokar* (1960)). In practice, the operation of s 1(f)(i) gives rise to few difficulties. Its most likely use is to enable prosecuting counsel to cross-examine the accused about similar fact evidence that has already been admitted as part of the prosecution case. Sometimes, however, reference for the first time to previous misconduct is necessary in cross-examination because the defendant gives evidence that takes the prosecution by surprise. That was the case in *Anderson* (1988) and appears to have been the case in *Jones v DPP* (1961).

Maxwell v DPP (1935, House of Lords)

Viscount Sankey LC: My Lords, the appellant, William Maxwell, was convicted at Leeds Assize of the manslaughter of a woman called May Holliday, also of using on her an instrument with intent to procure miscarriage. In effect he was found guilty of causing a woman's death by performing on her an illegal operation. He was sentenced to twenty months' imprisonment with hard labour. He appealed from conviction to the Court of Criminal Appeal, who dismissed the appeal. From their decision he has now appealed to your Lordships' House ... The question is whether it was permissible in the particular facts of the case, under the Criminal Evidence Act 1898 s 1 proviso (f) for the prosecution to ask the prisoner whether on a previous occasion he had been charged with a similar offence, the charge having been tried and having resulted in an acquittal ...

It must first of all be stated that it has been admitted throughout that the prisoner, in saying that he had lived a good, clean, moral life, had put his character in issue, and had in the words of the proviso (f)(ii) 'given evidence of his good character.' The first question here is, What consequences follow from that?

When Parliament by the Act of 1898 effected a change in the general law and made the prisoner in every case a competent witness, it was in an evident difficulty, and it pursued the familiar English system of compromise. It was clear that if you allowed a prisoner to go into the witness-box, it was impossible to allow him to be treated as an ordinary witness. Had that been permitted, a prisoner who went into the box to give evidence on oath could have been asked about any previous conviction, with the result that an old offender would seldom, if ever, have been acquitted ... Some middle way, therefore, had to be discovered, and the result was that a certain amount of protection was accorded to a prisoner who gave evidence on his own behalf. As it has been expressed, he was presented with a shield, and it was provided that he was not to be asked, and that, if he was asked, he should not be required to answer, any question tending to show that he had committed, or been convicted of, or been charged with, any offence other than that wherewith he was then charged, or was a bad character. Apart, however, from this protection, he was placed in the position of an ordinary witness in an ordinary civil case. The laws of evidence were not otherwise altered by the Criminal Evidence Act 1898 and the prisoner who was a witness in his own case could not be asked questions which were irrelevant or had nothing to do with the issue which the court was endeavouring to decide. As has already been pointed out, the prisoner in the present case threw away his shield and, therefore, the learned counsel for the prosecution was entitled to ask him, and he could be required to answer, any question tending to show that he had committed or been convicted of or been charged with an offence, but subject to the consideration that the question asked him must be one which was relevant and admissible in the case of an ordinary witness. The Act does not in terms say that in any case a prisoner may be asked or required to answer questions falling within proviso (f), or impose any such affirmative or absolute burden upon him. I think this conclusion is confirmed by a study of the words of the statute. In s 1 proviso (e), it has been enacted that a witness may be cross-examined in respect of the offence charged, and cannot refuse to answer questions directly relevant to the offence on the grounds that they tend to incriminate him: thus if he denies the offence, he may be cross-examined to refute the denial. These are matters directly relevant to the charge on which he is being tried. Proviso (f), however, is dealing with matters outside, and not directly relevant to, the particular offence charged; such matters, to be admissible at all, must in general fall under two main classes: one is the class of evidence which goes to show not that the prisoner did the acts charged, but that, if he did these acts, he did them as part of a system or intentionally, so as to refute a defence that if he did them he did them innocently or inadvertently, as for instance in *Makin v Attorney General for New South Wales* (1894), where the charge was one of murder; another illustration of such cases is *Rex v Bond* (1906). This rule applies to cases where guilty knowledge or design or intention is of the essence of the offence.

The other main class is where it is sought to show that the prisoner is not a person to be believed on his oath, which is generally attempted by what is called cross-examination to credit. Closely allied with this latter type of question is the rule that, if the prisoner by himself or his witnesses seeks to give evidence of his own good character, for the purpose of showing that it is unlikely that he committed the offence charged, he raises by way of defence an issue as to his good character, so that he may fairly be cross-examined on that issue, just as any witness called by him to prove his good character may be cross-examined to show the contrary. All these matters are dealt with in proviso (f). The substantive part of that proviso is negative in form and as such is universal and is absolute unless the exceptions come into play. Then come the three exceptions: but it does not follow that when the absolute prohibition is superseded by a permission, that the permission is as absolute as the prohibition. When it is sought to justify a question it must not only be brought within the terms of the permission, but also must be capable of justification according to the general rules of evidence and in particular must satisfy the test of relevance. Exception (i) deals with the former of the two main classes of evidence referred to above, that is, evidence falling within the rule that where issues of intention or design are involved in the charge or defence, the prisoner may be asked questions relevant to these matters, even though he has himself raised no question of his good character. Exceptions (ii) and (iii) come into play where the prisoner by himself or his witnesses has put his character in issue, or has attacked the character of others. Dealing with exceptions (i) and (ii), it is clear that the test of relevance is wider in (ii) than in (i); in the latter, proof that the prisoner has committed or been convicted of some other offence can only be admitted if it goes to show that he was guilty of the offence charged. In the former (exception (ii)), the questions permissible must be relevant to the issue of his own good character and if not so relevant cannot be admissible. But it seems clear that the mere fact of a charge cannot in general be evidence of bad character or be regarded otherwise than as a misfortune. It seems to be contended on behalf of the respondent that a charge was *per se* such evidence that the man charged, even though acquitted, must thereafter remain under a cloud, however innocent. I find it impossible to accept any such view. The mere fact that a man has been charged with an offence is no proof that he committed the offence. Such a fact is, therefore, irrelevant; it neither goes to show that the prisoner did the acts for which he is actually being tried nor does it go to his credibility as a witness. Such questions must, therefore, be excluded on the principle which is fundamental in the law of evidence as conceived in this country, especially in criminal cases, because, if allowed, they are likely to lead the minds of the jury astray into false issues; not merely do they tend to introduce suspicion as if it were evidence, but they tend to distract the jury from the true issue – namely, whether the prisoner in fact committed the offence on which he is actually standing his trial. It is of the utmost importance for a fair trial that the evidence should be *prima facie* limited to matters relating to the transaction which forms the subject of the indictment and that any departure from these matters should be strictly confined.

It does not result from this conclusion that the word 'charged' in proviso (f) is otiose: it is clearly not so as regards the prohibition; and when the exceptions come into play there may still be cases in which a prisoner may be asked about a charge as a step in cross-examination leading to a question whether he was convicted on the charge, or in order to elicit some evidence as to statements made or evidence given by the prisoner in the course of the trial on a charge which failed, which tend to throw doubt on the evidence which he is actually giving, though cases of this last class must be rare and the cross-examination permissible only with great safeguards.

Again, a man charged with an offence against the person may perhaps be asked whether he had uttered threats against the person attacked because he was angry with him for bringing a charge which turned out to be unfounded. Other probabilities may be imagined ...

But these instances all involve the crucial test of relevance. And in general no question whether a prisoner has been convicted or charged or acquitted should be asked or, if asked, allowed by the judge, who has a discretion under proviso (f), unless it helps to elucidate the particular issue which the jury is investigating, or goes to credibility; that is, tends to show that he is not to be believed on his oath; indeed the question whether a man has been convicted, charged or acquitted ought not to be admitted, even if it goes to credibility, if there is any risk of the jury being misled into thinking that it goes not to credibility but to the probability of his having committed the offence of which he is charged ...[7]

Stirland v DPP (1944, House of Lords)

Viscount Simon LC: ... The appellant clearly put his character in issue in the course of the trial, and that more than once. It will be observed that the questions by counsel for the prosecution were not put in order to suggest a previous conviction or even a previous charge (if by 'charge' is meant a criminal proceeding), but they insinuated that the appellant had left his previous employment under suspicion, whether well or ill-founded, of dishonesty ... Before your Lordships it was contended that this cross-examination was wholly inadmissible as tending to suggest that the appellant had been guilty of a crime other than that with which he was charged and as being irrelevant to the question of his guilt in respect of the crime for which he was being tried ...

... This House has laid down in *Maxwell v Director of Public Prosecutions* that, while para (f) of this section absolutely prohibits any question of this kind there indicated being put to the accused in the witness-box unless one or other of the conditions (i), (ii) or (iii) is satisfied, it does not follow that such questions are in all circumstances justified whenever one or other of the conditions is fulfilled ...

Atkinson J, in delivering the judgment of the Court of Criminal Appeal in the present case, thought that there was nothing in the trial which conflicted with the decision in *Maxwell's* case largely because the appellant swore that he had never in his life 'been charged with any offence whatever'. Therefore, argued Atkinson J, cross-examination about the alleged suspicious circumstances in which the appellant left the bank was relevant and admissible to disprove his denial that he had ever been 'charged'. I should agree with the learned judge that, if an accused person, in the witness-box makes a statement of fact which the prosecution does not accept, he is liable to be cross-examined on the statement with a view of showing that it is not true, and this applies to a statement as to the accused's past record where he puts his character in issue just as much as to a statement on any other matter. But this is all subject, as explained below, to the judge's discretion to disallow any question which in the circumstances he thinks to be unfair. It is necessary, however, to guard against a possible confusion in the use of the word 'charged'. In para (f) of s 1 of the Act of 1898 the word appears five times and it is plain that its meaning in the section is 'accused before a court' and not merely 'suspected or accused without prosecution'. When the appellant denied that he had ever been 'charged', he may fairly be understood to use the word in the sense it bears in the statute and to mean that he had never previously been brought before a criminal court. Questions whether his former employer had suspected him of forgery were not, therefore, any challenge to the veracity of what he had said. Neither were they relevant as going to disprove good character. The most virtuous may be suspected, and an unproved accusation proves nothing against the accused, but the questions, while irrelevant both to the charge which was being tried and to the issue of good character, were calculated to injure the appellant in the eyes of the jury by suggesting that he had been in trouble before, and were, therefore, not fair to him. They should not have been put, and, if put, should have been disallowed. It must not be forgotten that the judge presiding at a criminal trial has a discretion (as Lord Sankey said in *Maxwell's* case) to disallow questions addressed to the accused in cross-examination if he considers that such questions, having regard to the issues

---

7.   [1935] AC 309. The other Law Lords agreed.

before the jury and to the risk of the jury being misled as to what those issues really are, would be unfair, and the judge's disallowance cannot be challenged on appeal. A question whether the accused, who has put his character in issue, was not suspected of a previous crime of which he was never charged in court, or, if charged, was acquitted, is an example of a case where the judge should intervene. It is true that a miscarriage of justice may arise from the acquittal of the guilty no less than from the conviction of the innocent, but when *Maxwell's* case decided that where the prosecution had enough evidence to indict a man for a crime, but not enough to convict, no questions can be asked about that incident in a later trial at which he puts his character in issue, how can mere suspicion alleged to have been entertained by his previous employer on an earlier occasion be a legitimate topic for cross-examination to credit?

There is perhaps some vagueness in the use of the term 'good character' in this connexion. Does it refer to the good reputation which a man may bear in his own circle, or does it refer to the man's real disposition as distinct from what his friends and neighbours may think of him? In *Reg v Rowton* on a re-hearing before the full court, it was held by the majority that evidence for or against a prisoner's good character must be confined to the prisoner's general reputation, but Erle CJ and Willes J thought that the meaning of the phrase extended to include actual moral disposition as known to an individual witness, though no evidence could be given of concrete examples of conduct. In the later case of *Rex v Dunkley* (1927), the question was further discussed in the light of the language of the section, but not explicitly decided. I am disposed to think that in para (f) (where the word 'character' occurs four times) both conceptions are combined ...

... It is no disproof of good character that a man has been suspected or accused of a previous crime. Such questions as, 'Were you suspected?', or, 'Were you accused?', are inadmissible because they are irrelevant to the issue of character, and can only be asked if the accused has sworn expressly to the contrary ...

... It has been said more than once that a judge when trying a case should not wait for objection to be taken to the admissibility of the evidence, but should stop such questions himself: see *Rex v Ellis* (1910). If that be the judge's duty, it can hardly be fatal to an appeal founded on the admission of an improper question that counsel failed at the time to raise the matter. No doubt, as was said in the same case, the court must be careful in allowing an appeal on the ground of reception of inadmissible evidence when no objection has been made at the trial by the prisoner's counsel. The failure of counsel to object may have a bearing on the question whether the accused was really prejudiced. It is not a proper use of counsel's discretion to raise no objection at the time in order to preserve a ground of objection for a possible appeal, but where, as here, the reception or rejection of a question involves a principle of exceptional public importance, it would be unfortunate if the failure of counsel to object at the trial should lead to a possible miscarriage of justice. There is nothing in the Act of 1898 to suggest that such an objection is necessarily invalid unless taken at the time, and in other branches of the law the right to object on appeal that evidence was inadmissible is not necessarily forfeited by the failure to object when the evidence was given. The object of British law, whether civil or criminal, is to secure, as far as possible, that justice is done according to law, and, if there is substantial reason for allowing a criminal appeal, the objection that the point now taken was not taken by counsel at the trial is not necessarily conclusive ...[8]

---

8. [1944] AC 315. The other Law Lords agreed.

R v Cokar (1960, Court of Criminal Appeal)

The appellant, Jottai Cokar, a native of West Africa and a man of poor intelligence, was charged at County of London Sessions on 9 February 1960 with entering the dwelling-house of one James Ballantyne by night on 14 January 1960 with intent to steal.

The evidence was that at about midnight on 14 January he climbed through the open window of the house in Portland Grove, London, SW8, into a room in which Ballantyne was sleeping. Shortly afterwards Ballantyne woke up and found the appellant asleep in an armchair before the fire with his, Ballantyne's, coat over him. The appellant had apparently made no attempt to steal anything and there was loose money in the room which had not been touched. The defence put forward on behalf of the appellant was that he had entered the room to sleep because he was not feeling well, and had not intended to steal anything.

The prosecution sought to show that the appellant knew that it was no offence to be found on private premises for an innocent purpose, such as sleeping, and the deputy-chairman, FH Cassels, Esq, in spite of objection by the defence, permitted questions to be put to the appellant in cross-examination as to a previous occasion when he had been found on private premises and charged with entering the premises with intent. On that occasion he had been acquitted. The appellant was convicted and sentenced to 18 months' imprisonment. He appealed against conviction on the ground, *inter alia*, that cross-examination in relation to the previous proceedings in which he had been acquitted had been prejudicial and contrary to s 1(f) of the Criminal Evidence Act 1898.

Lord Parker CJ: This is in some ways a curious case. The appellant, a native of West Africa, was convicted at the County of London Sessions of entering a dwelling-house by night with intent to steal, and he was sentenced to 18 months' imprisonment. From that conviction he appeals to this court by leave of the court. [His Lordship stated the facts and continued:] The sole issue was: Had the appellant entered that night with intent to steal?

The appellant was a man of poor intelligence. He was cross-examined, and the answers he gave were very unsatisfactory and not by any means always to the point. The suggestion which the prosecution sought to make was that he, the appellant, knew that it was no offence if he was just found sleeping on the premises. Again, the answers were: 'I do not know', and answers of that sort, and ultimately leave was sought to cross-examine the appellant as to a previous occasion on which he had been found on private premises and had been charged. In fact he had been acquitted, but it was sought to introduce this evidence to show that on the occasion of the previous charge he must have learned that to be on premises for an innocent purpose, such as sleeping, was in law no offence. The questions were allowed and the appellant was ultimately convicted.

Whether or not those questions should have been allowed depends on the true interpretation of section 1 of the Criminal Evidence Act 1898 and, in particular, proviso (f) ... [T]he sole question is whether the questions became admissible by reason of the first exception, contained in paragraph (i) of proviso (f) ... That, as is well known, is directed to the common class of case where evidence of previous convictions is admissible to show system, and matters of that sort. It is to be observed that the exception deals only with the case where proof that the accused has 'committed or been convicted' of another offence is admissible evidence. There is no reference in the exception to being 'charged' and, accordingly, it seems to this court that the prohibition against any of the matters in the first part of the proviso (f) is only lifted when it is sought to prove that the accused has committed or been convicted of the other offence. Provided that proof of that other offence is admissible evidence, it would be clearly proper as leading up to proof of conviction to say to the prisoner: 'Were you charged?' and, if the answer is, 'Yes', 'Were you convicted?'; but it seems to this court quite impossible, under exception (i), to question a man in regard to a charge in respect of which he was acquitted.

Reference has been made to *Maxwell v Director of Public Prosecutions*, and, in particular, to a passage in the speech of Viscount Sankey LC, where he said: 'It does not result from this conclusion that the word "charged" in proviso (f) is otiose: it is clearly not so as regards the prohibition; and when the exceptions come into play, there may still be cases in which a prisoner may be asked about a charge as a step in cross-examination leading to a question whether he was convicted on the charge.' Pausing there, if exception (i) came into play and it was sought to prove that the accused had been convicted of the previous offence, it would be perfectly possible leading up to that to ask him in the first place whether he had been charged. Viscount Sankey continued: 'or in order to elicit some evidence as to statements made or evidence given by the prisoner in the course of the trial on a charge which failed, which tend to throw doubt on the evidence which he is actually giving, though cases of this last class must be rare and the cross-examination permissible only with great safeguards.' The court has not found it altogether easy to understand what Viscount Sankey was referring to in that last passage, but it might well cover the case where the prohibition has been lifted by the prisoner putting his character in issue. True, he could not then be asked about the charge resulting in acquittal as negativing good character, because as has been said, such a charge or acquittal is merely a misfortune and does not tend to show bad character. But, the prohibition having been removed, it would be possible then to refer to a charge on which the prisoner had been acquitted in order to bring up evidence as to statements made at that trial which tended to conflict with the evidence which he was giving in the current trial. Read in that way, this court does not think that *Maxwell's* case is in any way a proposition for the fact that questions may be put in regard to a charge resulting in an acquittal when the sole ground for removing the prohibition is exception (i), namely, proof that he has been charged and convicted of another offence.

In these circumstances, the court feels that cross-examination in this case on the lines referred to was wrongly allowed ...[9]

Jones v DPP (1962, House of Lords)

The appellant was convicted of the murder of a young girl. Some three months before his trial on the charge of murder he had been convicted of raping a different girl. There was a remarkable feature common to both cases. When the police first interviewed the appellant in the course of their inquiries into murder, the appellant accounted for his movements on the evening of the day when the murder victim had been last seen alive by stating that he had visited his sister-in-law. Later the appellant admitted that this was false. His explanation for producing a false alibi was that he had had trouble with the

---

9.　[1960] 2 QB 207.

police in the past and did not want to be in trouble with them again. The defence did not specify further, though it appears to have been accepted in the House of Lords that his reference was in fact to a much earlier, and wholly unrelated, matter. For the false alibi he substituted the account which he later gave in evidence at the murder trial; namely, that he spent the latter part of the evening in question with a prostitute. This new account included details of his wife's stormy reaction to his late return home and her conversation with him on the two following days. When the appellant had been earlier tried on the rape charge, the account of his movements on the evening when that offence had been committed, and of his wife's reaction, had been almost exactly the same as his account of the evening when the murder victim had last been seen alive. The main issue in the Court of Criminal Appeal and the House of Lords was whether it had been proper to cross-examine the appellant in the murder trial about the two similar explanations which he had given concerning his movements on the respective evenings, with a view showing that the similarities between them were so remarkable as to render the evidence incredible . The speeches in the House of Lords show a difference of opinion. The majority thought that cross-examination had not 'tended to show' to the jury anything new, and thus had not been forbidden under s 1(f). On this point Lord Denning and Lord Devlin dissented. The majority further held that had the cross-examination come within proviso (f), it would not have been made admissible by virtue of proviso (e). On this point Lord Denning dissented; the position of Lord Devlin is unclear.

The 'tending to show' point

Majority view

Viscount Simonds: ... I return to the second question. Here it is common ground that the challenged questions must be regarded not in isolation but in relation to the evidence that had already been given: see *Rex v Ellis* (1910). So regarded they do not appear to me to tend to show to the jury anything that had not been shown before. I will not analyse the evidence. That, too, has been done by my noble and learned friend. As to the meaning of the words 'tend to show' I see no difficulty. It is not the intention of the question that matters but the effect of the question and, presumably, the possible answer. Nor is the word 'show' in its context ambiguous. Primarily it may mean a visual demonstration, but in relation to the giving of oral evidence it can only mean 'make known'. The issue, then, is whether the challenged questions made known anything to the jury which they did not know before ...

Lord Reid: ... So I turn to proviso (f). It is an absolute prohibition of certain questions unless one or other of the three conditions is satisfied. It says the accused 'shall not be asked, and if asked shall not be required to answer', certain questions. It was suggested that this applies to examination-in-chief as well as to cross-examination. I do not think so. The words 'shall not be required to answer' are quite inappropriate for examination-in-chief. The proviso is obviously intended to protect the accused. It does not prevent him from volunteering evidence, and does not in my view prevent his counsel from asking questions leading to disclosure of a previous conviction or bad character if such disclosure is thought to assist in his defence.

The questions prohibited are those which 'tend to show' certain things. Does this mean tend to prove or tend to suggest? ... What matters is the effect of the questions on the jury. A veiled suggestion of a previous offence may be just as damaging as a definite statement. In my judgment, 'tends to show' means tends to suggest to the jury. But the crucial point in the present case is whether the questions are to be considered in isolation or whether they are to be considered in the light of all that had gone before them at the trial. If the questions or line of questioning have to be considered in isolation I think that the questions with which this appeal is concerned would tend to show at least that the accused had previously been charged with an offence. The jury would be likely to jump to that conclusion, if this was the first they had heard of this matter. But I do not think that the questions ought to be considered in isolation. If the test is the effect the questions would be likely to have on the minds of the jury that necessarily implies that one must have regard to what the jury had already heard. If the jury already knew that the accused had been charged with an offence, a question inferring that he had been charged would add nothing and it would be absurd to prohibit it. If the obvious purpose of this proviso is to protect the accused from possible prejudice, as I think it is, then 'show' must mean 'reveal', because it is only a revelation of something new which could cause such prejudice ...

Lord Morris of Borth-y-Gest: ... The jury were told by the defence that the appellant had had trouble with the police in the past or had been in trouble. This information was vague and was purposely left vague, but it could convey to the jury that the appellant was one with a 'record' and was of bad character and it could also suggest that he had been involved in some police inquiries or some charge. It was brought out by the defence to the jury because the appellant was trying to explain to the jury why it was that ... he put forward his first and admittedly false alibi ... The reference to the trouble was left in an imprecise way, but it would be reasonable for the jury to understand that the appellant had some previous conviction or convictions for some offence or offences at some time or times. If the jury could have supposed that the questions put in cross-examination denoted that the appellant had been involved in some unspecified prior charge then nothing new was being disclosed to them ... I consider, in agreement with the Court of Criminal Appeal, that in the proviso the words 'tend to show' have the meaning of tending to reveal or tending to disclose, and in the circumstances of this case I do not think that objection can be taken to the questions which were put in cross-examination ...

Dissenting views

Lord Denning: My Lords, much of the discussion before your Lordships was directed to the effect of section 1(f) of the Criminal Evidence Act 1898: and if that were the sole paragraph for consideration, I should have thought that counsel for the Crown ought not to have asked the questions he did. My reasons are these:

First: The questions *tended* to show that Jones had previously been charged in a court of law with another offence. True it is that they did not point definitely to that conclusion, but they conveyed that impression, and that is enough. Counsel may not have intended it, but that does not matter. What matters is the impression the questions would have on the jury. The Attorney General said that, if the questions left the matter evenly balanced, so that there was some other conclusion that could equally be drawn, as, for instance, that Jones had not been 'charged' in a court of law but had only been interrogated in a police station, there was no bar to the questions being asked. I cannot agree. If the questions asked by the Crown are capable of conveying two impressions – one objectionable and the other not – then they 'tend to show' each of them: and the questions must be excluded, lest the jury adopt the worse of the two impressions. I do not think it is open to the prosecution to throw out prejudicial hints and insinuations – from which a jury might infer that the man had been charged before – and then escape censure under the cloak of ambiguity.

Second: I think that the questions tended to show that Jones had been charged with an offence, even though he had himself brought out the fact that he had been 'in trouble' before. It is one thing to confess to having been in trouble before. It is quite another to have it emphasised against you with devastating detail. Before these questions were asked by the Crown, all that the jury knew was that at some unspecified time in the near or distant past, this man had been in trouble with the police. After the questions were asked, the jury knew, in addition, that he had been very recently in trouble for an offence on a Friday night which was of so sensational a character that it featured in a newspaper on the following Sunday – in these respects closely similar to the present offence – and that he had been charged in a court of law with that very offence. It seems to me that questions which tend to reveal an offence, thus particularised, are directly within the prohibition in section 1(f) and are not rendered admissible by his own vague disclosure of some other offence. I do not believe the mere fact that he said he had been in trouble before with the police – referring as he did to an entirely different matter many years past – let in this very damaging cross-examination as to recent events.

Lord Devlin: ... The alibi which the accused in this case put forward in the witness-box was the second of those which he had advanced. In statements made to the police he had advanced another alibi, about which it is not necessary to say more than that before the trial he withdrew it and admitted it was false. He had, therefore, to explain at the trial why he had given a false alibi. His explanation was that he had been in trouble with the police; and therefore he did not dare to rely upon the second alibi, which he was putting forward as true, because he could not call a witness to prove it. As it was put in the evidence of his wife: 'he knew he had a previous record and he wanted to fix an alibi because he could not prove where he had been.' She agreed to help him with it because she did not want it known that he was associating with prostitutes. Accordingly, the court held, notwithstanding that the questions by Mr Griffith-Jones suggested that the appellant had either committed or been charged with some offence, that they went no further than the defence itself had already gone and so 'revealed' nothing.

My Lords, in my opinion this is not the correct approach to the question of what should be permitted in cross-examination when the accused has, without putting his whole character in issue, referred to some specific matter. I have already said that in doing so counsel for the defence is in breach of the general prohibition if it is construed without modification. One modification that can be suggested is that counsel for the defence must be permitted to refer to matters that are a necessary part of his defence: this can be justified by the sort of general reasons put forward by Humphreys J in *Rex v Turner* (1944). Another way is to look upon the proviso as a shield available to the defence which it can raise or lower to expose the whole or a part of itself as it chooses. Whichever way it is looked at, it comes to the same thing, for the defence is bound just as much as the prosecution by the ordinary rule that irrelevant matter may not be introduced. So, if the accused is referring to past incidents in his life otherwise than for the purpose of establishing his good character, he must refer to them in order to raise some point that is relevant to his defence. Upon that point, whatever it may be, since he has made it relevant, he can be cross-examined.

The difficulty and danger inherent in the approach adopted by the Court of Criminal Appeal is that it sets no clear limits to the extent of the cross-examination. If cross-examination is permitted because it goes to an issue raised by the defence, the judge knows where he is; he will permit cross-examination that is relevant to that issue and no more. Thus, in the present case counsel could have asked about the nature of the 'trouble' because, if it were shown to be quite trivial, it would be an inadequate excuse for manufacturing a false alibi. If the issue were different, it might be relevant to show the gravity of the trouble instead of its triviality. In other cases, it might be improper to go into the nature of the trouble at all. Relevance affords a clear guide as to what the limit should be; revelation does not. If it means no more than that the accused can be asked to repeat himself, it is at best otiose and at worst objectionable. It would, for example, be objectionable if it were done merely for the purpose of 'rubbing it in'. If the accused can be asked to do more than repeat himself, how much more? When the accused puts his whole character in issue, the door is thrown wide open; but when he puts only a part of it in issue, I can see no satisfactory way of defining a limit except by the test of relevance. I do not think that some vague rule which enables the prosecution to ask what it likes so long as it does not make out the accused's character to be substantially worse than he himself had suggested would be at all a safe guide. If, for instance, in this case the questions had not been relevant to the second alibi, I think it would have been quite wrong, just because the prisoner had mentioned a previous record and trouble with the police, to refer to an incident in the newspaper, thus running the risk that the jury might feel that they ought to pay attention to the newspaper publicity in connection with the earlier offence.

A similar objection applies, in my opinion, to the argument that cross-examination on discreditable matters forming part of the case for the prosecution is justifiable on the ground that it will reveal nothing not already known. What are the limits? If a man is being prosecuted for larceny, the evidence for the prosecution will inevitably tend to show that he is a thief. Does that mean that he can be asked in cross-examination about other matters tending to show that he is a thief on the basis that nothing is thereby being revealed beyond what was already suggested? Obviously not. But then does that mean that if what is suggested is precise, it cannot be added to; but that if it is vague and general, the details can be filled in? In *Rex v Chitson* (1909) and *Rex v Kennaway* (1917) evidence of conversations with the accused was admitted against him, notwithstanding that in those conversations he had admitted to some discreditable incident in the past. How much of the prisoner's bad character must that sort of thing be taken to reveal? I see no satisfactory basis for cross-examination except the one I hold to be correct; namely, that he can be cross-examined on the issue to which the evidence relates and upon nothing more ...

Scope of proviso (f)

Majority view

Viscount Simonds: ... The first and more important [question] is whether, even if the questions that were asked tended to show that the appellant had committed or been convicted of or charged with any other offence than that wherewith he was then charged (see section 1(f) of the Act), yet they were admissible on the ground that they were relevant to an issue in the case in that they tended to criminate him as to the offence charged ...

My Lords, in my opinion, the answer to the first question depends first and last upon the construction of section 1 of the Act, and particularly of provisos (e) and (f), and, pressed as I am by the difficulties which some of your Lordships foresee may arise from it, I see no answer to the view expressed by my noble and learned friends, Lord Reid and Lord Morris of Borth-y-Gest. It appears to me that no language could be plainer than that by which the Act, for the first time making an accused person a competent witness on his trial, provides first what questions he may be asked and then what questions he may not be asked. I do not understand upon what canon of construction it can be said that the second proviso is in some way subordinate to the first. On the contrary, as if to make it clear that the first proviso is not generally paramount, there are particular qualifications introduced in the second proviso. I must reject the implied inclusion of another qualification, which, if it had been intended, could well have been stated. Here, if ever, the maxim *'expressio unius, exclusio alterius'* is applicable. It is not necessary for me to suggest in what language any further qualification might be expressed, but I am not satisfied that relevancy to an issue in the trial would, without further explanation, be a sufficiently clear test.

Upon this part of the case I am so fully in agreement with the reasoning and conclusions of my noble and learned friends, Lord Reid and Lord Morris of Borth-y-Gest, that I cannot usefully add anything further ...

Lord Reid: ... It is well established that the 1898 Act has no application to evidence given by any person other than the accused: where it was competent before the Act for a witness to prove or refer to a previous conviction of the accused, that is still competent. What the Act does is to alter the old rules as regards the accused. It might merely have provided that the accused should be a competent witness; then the ordinary rules would have applied to him. But it goes on to afford to him protection which the ordinary rules would not give him: it expressly prohibits certain kinds of question being put to him. That must mean questions which would be competent and relevant under the ordinary rules, because there was no need to prohibit any question which would in any event have been excluded by the ordinary rules. So what must now be considered is what kinds of question, which would have been competent and relevant under the ordinary rules of evidence, does the Act prohibit ...

The Act deals specifically with three kinds of questions: (1) those which would tend to criminate the accused as to the offence charged, (2) those tending to show that he has committed or been convicted of or been charged with some other offence, and (3) those tending to show that he is of bad character. The first class is permitted; the second and third classes are prohibited unless one or other of the subparagraphs of proviso (f) applies. Rightly or wrongly the Act assumes that these classes are exclusive of each other, that a question which falls within the second class cannot also fall within the first class, for otherwise the same question might be prohibited by proviso (f) but allowed by proviso (e).

This raises at once the question what is the proper construction of the words in proviso (e), 'tend to criminate him, as to the offence charged'. Those words could mean 'tend to convince or persuade the jury that he is guilty', or they could have the narrower meaning – 'tend to connect him with the commission of the offence charged'. If they have the former meaning, there is at once an insoluble conflict between provisos (e) and (f). No line of questioning could be relevant unless it (or the answers to it) might tend to persuade the jury of the guilt of the accused. It is only permissible to bring in previous convictions or bad character if they are so relevant, so, unless proviso (f) is to be deprived of all content, it must prohibit some questions which would tend to criminate the accused of the offence charged if those words are used in the wider sense. But if they have the narrower meaning, there is no such conflict. So the structure of the Act shows that they must have the narrower meaning ...

Lord Morris of Borth-y-Gest: ... It is to be observed that paragraph (e) of section 1 relates to questions which tend to criminate as to the 'offence charged', while paragraph (f) relates to questions which tend to show some other offence or to show bad character. All questions put to witnesses must satisfy the test of relevance and this applies to questions put in cross-examination to an accused. If, however, questions are proposed which can be regarded as relevant, but which tend to show that he has committed or been convicted of or has been charged with some offence other than that wherewith he is then charged or is of bad character, such questions can only be put and can only be allowed if they qualify within the permitting provisions of proviso (f) ... There is a contrast between proviso (e) and proviso (f). Proviso (e) shows that an accused person who avails himself of his opportunity to give evidence 'may be asked' questions in cross-examination although they would tend 'to criminate him as to the offence charged'. That denotes questions on matters directly relevant to the charge. Then proviso (f) gives the accused person a 'shield'. He 'shall not be asked' certain questions unless certain conditions apply. Proviso (e) permits questions to be asked: the corollary is that they must be answered. Proviso (f) does not say that certain questions may be asked; it says that certain questions may not be asked. This means that even if the questions are relevant and have to do with the issue before the court they cannot be asked unless covered by the permitting provisions of proviso (f) ...

Dissenting views

Lord Denning: ... In my judgment, the questions were admissible under section 1(e), which says that a person charged 'may be asked any question in cross-examination notwithstanding that it would tend to criminate him as to the offence charged'. As to this subsection, Viscount Sankey LC, speaking for all in this House in *Maxwell's* case, said that under section 1(e), 'a witness may be cross-examined in respect of the offence charged, and cannot refuse to answer questions directly relevant to the offence on the ground that they tend to incriminate him: thus if he denies the offence, he may be cross-examined to refute the denial'. I would add that, if he gives an explanation in an attempt to exculpate himself, he may be cross-examined to refute his explanation. And nonetheless so because it tends incidentally to show that he had previously been charged with another offence.

Let me first say why I think in this case the questions were directly relevant to the offence charged. They were directly relevant because they tended to refute an explanation which the accused man had given. He had given a detailed explanation of his movements on the crucial weekend, and so forth, all in an attempt to exculpate himself. The prosecution sought to show that this explanation was false: and I think it was of direct relevance for them to do so. From the very earliest times, long before an accused man could give evidence on his own behalf, the law has recognised that, in considering whether a man is guilty of the crime charged against him, one of the most relevant matters is this: What explanation did he give when he was asked about it? Was that explanation true or not? If he gives a true explanation, it tells in his favour. If he gives a false explanation, it tells against him. The prosecution have, therefore, always been entitled, as part of their own case, to give evidence of any explanation given by the accused and of its truth or falsity ...

Now, suppose the man does this further thing which Jones did here. He discards the story that he went to his sister-in-law's house and puts forward a different story. He says that he went up to London and was with a prostitute, but he does not identify her. So the prostitute cannot be called to falsify his story. Nevertheless the prosecution can falsify it by other means, if they have it available. They can call such evidence as part of their own case, even though it tends incidentally to show that he was guilty of another offence. For instance, they could prove that his fingerprints were on the window of a house that was broken into at Yateley that night. '... The mere fact that the evidence adduced tends to show the commission of the other crimes does not render it inadmissible if it be relevant to an issue before the jury', see *Makin v Attorney General of New South Wales*. Evidence that he had committed burglary would not be admissible to prove that he had committed murder: but evidence that he was at Yateley would be admissible to prove that he was in the vicinity and had recourse to falsehood to explain his whereabouts. The prosecution would be entitled to call this evidence, even though it tended to show that he was guilty of burglary.

Such is the law as it is, and always has been, as to the evidence which can be called for the prosecution. They can, in the first place, give evidence of any explanation given by the accused of his movements and they can, in the second place, give evidence that his explanation is false, even though it tends incidentally to show the commission by him of some other offence. Now, when Parliament in 1898 enabled an accused man to give evidence on his own behalf, they did not cut down evidence of this kind for the prosecution. And when the prosecution gives such evidence, it must be open to the accused man himself to answer it. He must be able to give evidence about it and to be cross-examined upon it. He can be cross-examined as to any explanation he has given and as to its truth or falsity: and he can be cross-examined upon it nonetheless because incidentally it may tend to show that he has been guilty of some other offence ...

... [I]n the present case [the defendant] made his explanation (about his conversations with his wife, and so forth) for the first time at the trial when he went into the witness-box to give evidence on his own behalf. But this cannot give him any protection from a cross-examination to which he would otherwise be exposed. His explanation is not made sacrosanct, it is not made incapable of challenge, simply because he gives it at the trial instead of at an earlier stage. The prosecution are entitled to expose its falsity, no matter whether he gives it at the trial or beforehand. And they are not precluded from doing so merely because the exposure of it tends to show that he has been guilty of some other offence or is of bad character ...

Lord Devlin: My Lords, I would dismiss this appeal on the short ground that the questions objected to were relevant to an issue in the case upon which the appellant had testified in chief. It is not disputed that the issue to which the questions related was a relevant one. It concerned the identification of the appellant as being at the material time at the scene of the crime. He testified that at the material time he was with a prostitute in the West End and he supported this alibi by giving evidence of a conversation which he had with his wife about it a day or two later. The purpose of the questions objected to was to obtain from the appellant an admission (which was given) that when he was being questioned about his movements in relation to another incident some weeks earlier he had set up the same alibi and had supported it with an account of a conversation with his wife in almost identical terms; the prosecution suggested that these similarities showed the whole story of the alibi to be an invented one ...

... [T]he Act of 1898 was enacted four years after the statement of principle in *Makin v Attorney General for New South Wales*, and I find it difficult to believe that the words in the proviso were not enacted with that principle in mind. If that is so, their effect should not be limited to the subordinate part of the principle. *Makin's* case is so often cited as the authority for the admission of evidence relating to system, design or intent, that it is sometimes forgotten that the rule itself is much wider. That type of evidence is given only as an illustration of the general rule contained in the words I have already cited that 'the mere fact that evidence adduced tends to show the commission of other crimes does not render it inadmissible if it be relevant to an issue before the jury'. So construed, proviso (f) takes a natural place in the law of evidence. The prohibition covers only offences and not discreditable acts falling short of offences; and it covers offences only if they are not 'admissible evidence to show that he is guilty of the offence wherewith he is then charged.' In short, the rule in *Makin's* case covers both evidence led against the accused and evidence sought to be obtained from him in cross-examination; proviso (f) shuts out nothing that is relevant to the issue, but gives complete protection to the accused against attacks on his reputation and credit unless he throws his hat into the ring ...[10]

R v Anderson (1988, Court of Appeal)

Martina Elizabeth Anderson appealed against her conviction on 11 June 1986 in the Central Criminal Court before Boreham J and a jury on a count of conspiracy to cause explosions likely to endanger life or cause serious damage to property.

Lord Lane CJ: ... The question which she now asks to be considered is simply this: Was the judge correct in acceding to a submission by the prosecution that she could be asked in cross-examination whether she was not 'wanted' by the police in Ireland? ...

The facts are these. As already indicated, she was arrested with the others at the flat at 236 Langside Road. There, at the flat, were found a whole series of incriminating pieces of evidence and fingerprints, the nature of which it is not necessary for us to repeat. Furthermore, other evidence was found in the flat at 17 James Gray Street which also tended to implicate Martina Anderson in the crime which was alleged against her.

This, on the face of it, was, as we indicate, a very powerful series of weapons in the prosecution armoury. She admittedly had on her a number of documents which were forged: passports, driving licences and so on. She herself gave evidence and explained how all these apparently damning items of evidence were not evidence of a conspiracy to plant bombs, as was alleged, but were simply the paraphernalia of another conspiracy; that was a conspiracy to assist men who had escaped from prison in Ireland to get to Scotland and thereafter, if it could be engineered, to make their way to the continent of Europe, probably to Copenhagen. That was the basis of her evidence ...

She was then cross-examined, and almost at the end of the cross-examination a submission was made by counsel for the Crown, in the absence of the jury, that he should be permitted to cross-examine her in order to elicit, if he could, the fact that she was 'wanted' by the police in Northern Ireland. It was not his intention, nor did he find it necessary, to suggest why she was wanted, but for reasons

---

10.   [1962] AC 635.

which will become apparent in a minute that was the only evidence he required from her.

The judge gave very careful consideration to the submission and, not without some hesitation, decided first of all that he was entitled, in law, to accede to that submission and second that it would be proper in the exercise of his discretion, quite apart from the question of law, that he should do so.

The basis on which counsel for the Crown founded this submission was this: it was only when it came to her evidence-in-chief that the prosecution were appraised of the fact that this was to be her defence. There had not been a whisper of this defence beforehand. No one had suspected that she was going to put forward the excuse for these damning pieces of evidence, namely the excuse that she was to act as an escort for escapers from prison. Consequently he suggested that the question which he proposed to ask was admissible as showing that, if she was 'wanted' by the police, first, it would be highly unlikely that she would be selected as a person to escort another person who was 'wanted'; so far from diminishing the risk of detection by having a woman present with the escaper, it would double the risk because two of them would be 'wanted', each of whom might be identified. Second, it was suggested it would be highly unlikely that, if she was 'wanted', she herself would undertake such an expedition when it was likely that she might be spotted and arrested herself.

The way in which the problem can be put is this. A defendant is faced with prosecution evidence which *prima facie* incriminates her of the offence charged. She puts forward in evidence an explanation of that prosecution case which is consistent with her innocence of the offence charged. The prosecution wish to cross-examine her about that explanation. Cross-examination necessarily involves questions which tend to show that she, the defendant, has committed a criminal offence, the nature of which the prosecution neither require nor intend to reveal. Are they allowed, by the terms of s 1 of the Criminal Evidence Act 1898, to ask those questions? ...

Section 1 of the 1898 Act is a nightmare of construction ... Section 1(e) allows the accused person to be asked 'any question in cross-examination notwithstanding that it would tend to criminate him as to the offence charged'. Section 1(f), however, provides that he shall not be asked 'any question tending to show that he has committed or been convicted of or charged with any offence' subject to certain exceptions. Those two provisions are mutually contradictory, at least on the face of them, as has been said more than once by courts over the last 90 years. The reason for that is this: a question which tends to incriminate the defendant as to the offence charged, and so is relevant and admissible under para (e), may very well tend to show, and often does, that the defendant has committed another offence and so is inadmissible under para (f). This problem has been the subject of differing views, and those differing views are exemplified by the opinions of five of their Lordships in *Jones v DPP*.

The facts in that case are, very briefly, that Jones was charged with the murder of a young Girl Guide. He put forward an account of his movements which, to all intents and purposes, was the same, almost word for word, as an account he had put forward some three months earlier when he was charged with an offence of rape committed on another young Girl Guide. Not surprisingly the prosecution wished to cross-examine Jones about this remarkable coincidence with a view to showing that his account was false. The question obviously indicated that he had committed another offence. The Court of Criminal Appeal held that the judge was correct to have allowed the questions because they said that Jones had, in his evidence-in-chief, said that he had 'been in trouble with the police'. Since the words 'tending to show' meant 'revealing', the question asked of the defendant did not 'tend to show' the commission of a crime, because that crime had already been revealed to the jury. In other words, if the revelation regarding a previous conviction has already been made to the jury, the prohibition does not apply.

This was the basis on which the majority in the House of Lords (Viscount Simonds, Lord Reid and Lord Morris, Lord Denning and Lord Devlin dissenting) dismissed the appeal. Their Lordships, however, did not leave the matter there. They ventured on a discussion of the difficulties raised by the section, a discussion which is relevant to the present case. The majority supported the view that para (e) is subordinate to and governed by para (f)(i). Lord Reid's view was that the words of para (e) have two possible interpretations ... They could, first of all, mean 'tend to convince or persuade a jury that he [the defendant] is guilty', or, second, 'tend to connect him [the defendant] with the commission of the offence charged'. If they have the first meaning, the broader meaning, that, in Lord Reid's view, produces the insoluble conflict with para (f) which we mentioned a moment or two ago. If, on the other hand, they have the second meaning, the narrower meaning, there is no such conflict because para (f) could then apply to questions which tend to persuade a jury that the defendant is guilty. That, of course, leaves the residual problem which is not easy to answer, namely how close the connection must be with the offence to bring it within the narrower meaning of para (e).

Lord Denning and Lord Devlin were in the minority and we do not feel it necessary to refer to their speeches save to say that they are interesting interpretations of the 1898 Act. Lord Reid seems to have thought that it was open to the House at some time or other to reconsider the matter if it should be directly raised ...

In the present case there was, in the question, a clear tendency to show that Martina Anderson had committed an offence other than that with which she was charged; obviously so because otherwise she would not be 'wanted' by the police. So in the light of the decision in *Jones v DPP* the question would be admissible in any of the following circumstances; that is, applying the reasoning which we have attempted to set out as explained by the House of Lords: first of all, if there was no tendency to reveal the commission of an offence as in *Jones v DPP*, for example, because the commission of an offence had already (properly) been made known to the jury; second, if the proof of the commission tended to connect the defendant with the offence charged; and, third, if the defendant had given evidence of her own good character.

The third matter can be dealt with very shortly. Counsel for Anderson did persuade the prosecution to concede that the appellant was of good character, apart from being 'wanted' by the police, but that concession was only made after the judge had ruled on the submission and consequently that would not, we are prepared to assume, be a ground for admitting the evidence under s 1(f) of the 1898 Act.

As to the tendency to reveal, Anderson had already revealed that it was likely that she had committed a number of offences in respect of any one of which she might well have been 'wanted' by the police. There was probably a conspiracy to assist the escape of a prisoner, probably forgery of documents, probably conspiracy to forge, possession of firearms and so on, as already set out when we detailed the evidence which she gave before the jury. Thus it was already revealed that she had committed offences, although it might be that she was not yet 'wanted' by the police in respect of them. The jury already knew, therefore, that she had committed a number of offences, and the fact that she was 'wanted' by the police in respect of an unspecified offence, and therefore was probably guilty of committing an unspecified offence,[11] was not, on the reasoning in *Jones v DPP*, in the view of this court, a revelation to the jury.

As to the second point: does evidence which tends to destroy the defendant's innocent explanation of *prima facie* circumstances, connect the defendant with the crime so as to come within Lord Reid's analysis of the meaning of para (e)? We are inclined to think that it may, but we prefer to base our conclusion primarily on the fact that the appellant had already revealed that she had committed crimes.

There is however a different approach which is perhaps less artificial than the reasoning in *Jones v DPP*, if we may say so.

Section 1 of the 1898 Act did nothing to alter the pre-existing law regarding what evidence the prosecution were entitled to adduce in order to prove their case. As Lord Reid said in *Jones v DPP*: 'These words of s 1 of the Act of 1898 have no application to evidence given by any person other than the accused: where it was competent before that Act for a witness to prove or refer to a previous conviction of the accused, that is still competent. What the Act does is to alter the old rules as regards the accused.'

The extent of that pre-existing law had been examined only four years previously in *Makin v AG for New South Wales* (1894). Lord Herschell LC said: 'It is undoubtedly not competent for the prosecution to adduce evidence tending to show that the accused has been guilty of criminal acts other than those covered by the indictment for the purpose of leading to the conclusion that the accused is a person likely from his criminal conduct or character to have committed the offence for which he is being tried. On the other hand, the mere fact that the evidence adduced tends to show the commission of other crimes does not render it inadmissible if it be relevant to an issue before the jury, and it may be so relevant if it bears upon the question whether the acts alleged to constitute the crime charged in the indictment were designed or accidental, or to rebut a defence which would otherwise be open to the accused.'

Thus, if the prosecution know that a particular defence is going to be advanced, they may (subject to the judge's discretion) call evidence to rebut it as part of their own substantive case even if that tends to show the commission of other crimes. The defendant can plainly then be cross-examined about the matter. If the prosecution do not know of the defence in advance, then they may call evidence to rebut it and the defendant can then be recalled, if that is desired, to deal with the rebutting evidence. The judge in the present case, wisely, the evidence not being in dispute, allowed that somewhat laborious process to be short-circuited. The result however was just as much in accordance with authority and the 1898 Act as if the procedure had been carried out *in extenso*.

These considerations strengthen our view that the judge's decision in the present case was correct ...[12]

SECTION 1(f)(ii)

Two questions dominate this topic and asking them is a vital part of trial preparation. The first is whether a s 1(f)(ii) situation has arisen at all. The second

---

11.   What hidden generalisation supports this inference?
12.   [1988] 2 All ER 549.

is how the judicial discretion to disallow cross-examination under this provision should be exercised, given that as a matter of law the defendant has brought himself within its scope. The limited relevancy of such cross-examination must also be understood.

Malindi v The Queen (1966, Privy Council)

Lord Morris of Borth-y-Gest: The appellant was found guilty (a) of conspiring to commit arson and malicious injury to property and (b) of arson ...

By the first count of the indictment against the appellant the charge was of conspiracy with certain named natives to commit arson and malicious damage to property at certain specified places in the Chinyika Native Reserve ... There was an alternative charge of incitement to commit such crimes. The second count charged arson of the Salvation Army Church at the same reserve on the same date. The natives referred to in the first count were Hensiby, Masawi, Lovemore, Sixpence, Ronnie and Nowa.

The issues of fact which in respect of the first count called for investigation and decision at the trial were concerned with the events that took place at certain meetings. The prosecution alleged that after an approach made to the appellant on Friday May 11 1962, there was a meeting at his house on May 12. Certain witnesses (Masawi, Lovemore, Ronnie, Hensiby and Nowa) gave evidence that they met on Friday May 11, and discussed 'taking action' in the Chinyika reserve. With the exception of Ronnie they went to see the appellant. There was evidence that he approved of 'the action' and that he suggested that they should all meet at his house on the following evening (ie Saturday May 12). There was evidence given by seven persons (all of whom were regarded as having been accomplices) that a meeting was held at the appellant's house on the Saturday evening, May 12. There were present Sevenzayi (who was said to be the local secretary of the Zimbabwe African People's Union), Masawi, Lovemore, Ronnie, Nowa and Supa. Another (Hensiby) kept watch outside. Another (Sixpence) arrived at the end of the meeting. Evidence was given by Masawi, Lovemore, Ronnie, Nowa and Supa as to what the appellant said at the meeting. There was evidence that they were formed into groups for the purpose of taking action in regard to acts of burning. The case for the prosecution was that as a sequel to the meeting on May 12, a further meeting took place (this time at a football field in Goromonzi) on May 14. At that further meeting the prosecution alleged that the appellant conspired with those named in the indictment. Evidence in regard to the meeting was given by Masawi, Lovemore, Ronnie, Sixpence, Hensiby and Nowa. There was evidence that at the meeting the appellant assigned acts of burning to particular persons ...

After the appellant was arrested (on June 6 1962) his house was searched by Police Sergeant Carver. A roneoed strike notice was found (exhibit 7) and a red-covered book (exhibit 8) and a brown-covered book (exhibit 9). Exhibit 8 contained notes and essays and exhibit 9 contained the beginning of an autobiography and an essay. Certain extracts from these exhibits were read in evidence as part of the case for the prosecution. One essay dealt with the unjust distribution of land in the country. From exhibit 9 certain passages were read which indicated views that religion was used to maintain exploitation of the African. No objection was taken in regard to the reading of these extracts or to their admissibility and no complaint has been made in this appeal as to such evidence.

... The only point which has been argued in the present appeal relates to certain questions which were put to the appellant when he was cross-examined ...

The evidence-in-chief given by the appellant was short. It is desirable to refer to it. He said:

> 'On May 11 this year when I was leaving my school, Ronnie and Masawi approached. They asked if they could talk to me. I waited until they came where I was. Ronnie told me that there would be a strike in Salisbury the following Monday. I asked him how he knew. He told me that he had got some information. He told me that the youth movement in Goromonzi had decided to take action; so they had sent to ask me if I would join them. I told them I had nothing to do with the youth movement; I was not a youth member. They should go and see the secretary. The following day at about five-thirty pm the secretary in company of ... '

By Maisels J: 'Is that Sevenzayi?' 'Yes, my Lord.'

> 'In company of?' – 'Of Ronnie, Masawi, Nowa, Hensiby, Supa and Sixpence, came to my house. They stood outside my garden, which is just about five yards from my house, and asked if they could talk to me. I invited them into the sitting-room. When we got there Sevenzayi repeated what the boys had said the previous day. I asked him what action he had in mind. He gave us an example, churches, dip tanks, and mealie lands. I told him of the lack of education facilities in Goromonzi. I brought to his knowledge the statement by Mr Nkomo that no member of ZAPU would act without his directions. I told him about the illegality of those activities he had proposed. I suggested that they make a procession and even told them that that, also, would need permission. An argument then ensued which ended when the whole group walked out of my house with some shouts that I was a moderate and a police informer; that if I revealed this to the police it would act upon me. The whole group left. I remained in my house thinking about what had happened. I then decided to write to the regional office and tell them about what had happened. This I did, and posted my letter. I did not receive any reply until I was arrested.'

In substance the evidence of the appellant was that he did not conspire to aid or procure the commission of arson or malicious injury to property but that on the contrary he declined to participate in illegal action. The appellant was then cross-examined and he was asked questions as to his political opinions. In reference to the meeting on the Saturday night (May 12) he said that it dispersed because he disagreed with and disapproved of the wish and desire of others to take part in violent action which was to consist of burnings. Counsel for the prosecution then intimated to the learned judge that he wished to cross-examine the appellant in regard to certain passages in exhibit 8. These were some passages there contained other than those which had been given in evidence (and as to which no question arises) as part of the prosecution case ...

Counsel ... then proceeded to cross-examine the appellant about a passage in an essay in exhibit 8. It had been written on February 8 1961. The passage was one in which the use of violence was commended and was asserted to be necessary ...

... The witness was then asked various questions about another note-book in which he had written and which had not been produced by any prosecution witness (exhibit 10) in which there was a reference to a stand against colonialists and settler regimes and the total evacuation of all foreign peoples in Africa and the entire abolition of capitalism. That was probably written in 1960. He was further asked about another note-book (exhibit 11, which had not been produced as part of the evidence for the prosecution) in which he had written of the time when there would be an end of the oppression of the African by the settlers ...

The appellant appealed to the Federal Supreme Court both against his conviction and against his sentence. The grounds of appeal were framed as follows: '(1) That the court was influenced by essays written by me and produced as evidence against me. (2) That the court was misled by the evidence given by the witnesses which were untruthful. (3) I did not commit the crime.'

The appeal was argued on June 10 and 12 1963 and was dismissed on August 12 1963. The Chief Justice was of opinion that the appeal should be allowed. He considered that the questions which related to the appellant's views on violence were questions tending to show that the appellant was of bad character, that the appellant had not put his character in issue ... and that the questions put in cross-examination were not justifiable; he held also that it could not be said that without the inadmissible evidence the court must have convicted. Quenet FJ referred to the judgment of the learned judge and said that references in it to the writings of the appellant could not be construed as indicating that because the appellant had a bad character he was likely to commit the crimes with which he was charged. He considered that the legitimate probative force of the essays was considerable, and though the cross-examination was allowed on a different basis it was legitimate for the reason that the appellant in his evidence had given evidence of his own good character. Forbes FJ was also of opinion that the appeal should be dismissed. He considered that the appellant had in his evidence put his character in issue with the result that the questions in cross-examination were not excluded ...

The first issue which arises is whether the appellant was asked any question tending to show that he was of 'bad character' and whether he had given evidence of his own 'good character' as those phrases are used in section 303 [of the Criminal Procedure and Evidence Act, Laws of Rhodesia and Nyasaland]. The language of that section is clearly derived from the language of the English Act of 1898 ...

... It was submitted that the cross-examination was in any event legitimate because the appellant had himself given evidence of his own good character. It is said that by his evidence the appellant had put himself forward as a person who was and was regarded by others as being a moderate and a man of peace, and that he had accordingly proclaimed himself as a man of good character. Their Lordships cannot accept this. The matter depends upon an examination of the evidence which the appellant gave in chief ... All that the appellant did was to give a narrative of what he says took place at the meetings in question. He records what he asserted was said at the meetings. He gave his version of events and conversations. He did no more. He did not, independently of his giving his account of what had actually happened and of what had actually been said, assert that he was a man of good character. In their Lordships' view the proposed questions could not be introduced on the basis that he had himself given evidence of his own good character.[13]

Selvey v DPP (1968, House of Lords)

Viscount Dilhorne: My Lords, the appellant was convicted at Nottingham Assizes on March 26 1967 of having committed buggery with a young man named

13. [1967] AC 439.

McLaughlin on January 26 1967. He was sentenced by Stable J to four years' imprisonment.

At one time the appellant and McLaughlin lived in the same lodgings. The appellant moved to another lodging house, and during the afternoon of January 26, after they had met in the street, the appellant and McLaughlin went to the appellant's room and it was there that McLaughlin said the offence was committed.

In the course of his cross-examination by counsel for the appellant, McLaughlin was asked the following questions and gave the following answers:

'Q. Did you then ask Mr Selvey if he would give you a pound? A. No, Sir, I did not ask for any money. Q. Did you tell him that you had been with another man that afternoon and earned a pound? A. No, Sir. Q. Did you not then say to him, "If you give me a pound, you can get on the bed with me"? A. No, Sir. Q. Did you not tell him further that you wanted the pound to buy some clothes? A. No, Sir.'

McLaughlin was then asked if certain photographs of an indecent character which he had said had been shown to him by the appellant were not in fact his. He said that they were not.

Later the following questions were put to him and he gave the following answers:

'Q. I suggest to you, Mr McLaughlin, that nothing of the sort happened in Mr Selvey's room at all. A. Not true, Sir. Q. And that an incident of this nature had taken place earlier that afternoon, with another man? A. Not true. Q. And that because Mr Selvey would not give you a pound, you are blaming him for your condition? A. Not true.'

McLaughlin was examined by a doctor on the afternoon of January 26, shortly after the offence was alleged to have been committed and in the doctor's opinion his condition showed that he had been recently the passive partner in an act of buggery.

The appellant in the course of his evidence-in-chief swore that McLaughlin had asked him for a loan of a pound to buy some clothing, that McLaughlin had said that he was prepared to go on the bed and that he had already earned a pound 'by going with a fellow and having sexual connections'. The appellant said that he had told McLaughlin that he was not interested and he denied that he had committed the offence.

At the end of the appellant's cross-examination, Stable J asked him the following questions:

'You are asking the jury, are you not, to disbelieve this young man, because, as you say, he told you that he had been buggered that day and buggered by somebody else? That is what you have told the jury? A. That is correct. Q. You are asking the jury to disbelieve him because he is that sort of young man? A. Yes.'

Stable J then suggested to counsel for the prosecution that there should be a discussion in the absence of the jury. After the jury had retired, Stable J expressed the view that the appellant's defence had gone further than a denial that anything immoral had happened and had alleged that the incident was a blackmail operation and that it had involved an attack on McLaughlin's character. It was not until after the learned judge expressed this view that counsel for the prosecution applied for leave to put to the appellant his previous convictions. Stable J gave him leave to do so but intimated that he should confine his questions to sexual convictions ...

When the jury returned to the court, Stable J told them that as it had been suggested that the evidence of McLaughlin should not be believed as he was a man of bad character, they were entitled to hear the record of the appellant. He told them then that they would not decide the case 'purely on matters of character' and that they would deal with the case upon the evidence that they had heard but at least they would not go into the jury room having heard what was put to McLaughlin 'without knowing anything about the previous record of the man by whom those charges are now brought' ...

The main ground of the appeal before the Court of Appeal was, as it was before your lordships, that the learned judge was wrong in allowing the appellant to be cross-examined in relation to his previous convictions. It was contended that an accused person might, without losing the protection of the Criminal Evidence Act 1898, ask a prosecution witness all questions that are necessitated by the proper conduct of his defence and that, so long as the nature or conduct of the defence is relevant to an issue upon the facts of the case, the accused does not lose the protection of the Act ...

Mr Jeremy Hutchinson for the appellant contended that the word 'character' in paragraph (f) meant general reputation, and he based his argument on *Reg v Rowton* (1865). In that case it was held that where evidence of good character had been given on behalf of the accused, evidence of his bad character might be given in reply; that the evidence whether for the defence or for the prosecution must be confined to evidence of general reputation; and that the individual opinion of a witness founded upon his own experience and observation was inadmissible.

This argument was first advanced in 1927 in *Rex v Dunkley*. In the course of his judgment in that case Lord Hewart CJ, said, at p 329: '... it is not difficult to suppose that a formidable argument might have been raised on the phrasing of this statute, that the character which is spoken of is the character which is so well known in the vocabulary of the criminal law – namely, the general reputation of the person referred to; in other words, that "character" in that context ... bears the meaning which the term "character" was held to bear, for example, in the case of *R v Rowton*, 10 Cox 25 ... Nevertheless, when one looks at the long line of cases beginning very shortly after the passing of the Criminal Evidence Act 1898 it does not appear that that argument has ever been so much as formulated. It was formulated yesterday. One can only say that it is now too late in the day even to consider that argument, because that argument could not now prevail without revision, and indeed to a great extent the overthrow, of a very long series of decisions.'

In *Stirland v Director of Public Prosecutions* (1944) Viscount Simon LC, posed the question whether character referred to the good reputation which a man may bear in his own circle, or to a man's real disposition as distinct from what his friends and neighbours think of him. He said ... that he was 'disposed to think that in paragraph (f) (where the word "character" occurs four times) both conceptions are combined'.

This passage from his speech in this case was cited by Lord Morris of Borth-y-Gest in *Malindi v The Queen* (1967) and was clearly accepted by their lordships as correct.

What has been considered in this case is not what evidence can or cannot be given to establish a man's character, but whether the nature or conduct of the defence involved the imputations on the character of the witness McLaughlin. In my opinion, the questions put to him and the evidence given by the appellant clearly involved imputations on his character and, if it were right to interpret 'character' in the statute as meaning general reputation, also imputations on his general reputation ...

I propose now to turn to Mr Hutchinson's main contention, that the section did not permit of cross-examination of the accused as to character if it was a necessary part of his answer to the charge. He contended that it was unsatisfactory that the liability of the accused to be subjected to such cross-examination should depend on the exercise by the trial judge of discretion, on his estimation of what was fair and what was not. Mr Caulfield for the respondent contended that, despite the observations in a number of cases, a judge had no discretion to refuse to permit cross-examination of the accused as to character if the conditions prescribed by the section were satisfied.

I propose to consider first the construction and interpretation to be given to the section and then to consider Mr Caulfield's argument as to discretion ...

... [I]t cannot, in my opinion, be said that the questions put to McLaughlin and the appellant's evidence were just a traverse or denial of an issue raised by the prosecution. However necessary it may have been to make those imputations if the appellant was to have any hope of acquittal, they were additional to a denial that the conduct alleged had taken place in the appellant's bedroom ...

... It is apparent that over the years controversy has raged on whether the section permits cross-examination of the accused as to character when the making of the imputations was necessary to enable the accused to establish his defence ...

The cases to which I have referred, some of which it is not possible to reconcile, in my opinion finally establish the following propositions:

(1) The words of the statute must be given their ordinary natural meaning (*Hudson* (1912), *Jenkins* (1945), *Cook* (1959)).

(2) The section permits cross-examination of the accused as to character both when imputations on the character of the prosecutor and his witness are cast to show their unreliability as witnesses independently of the evidence given by them and also when the casting of such imputations is necessary to enable the accused to establish his defence (*Hudson*; *Jenkins*; *Cook*).

(3) In rape cases the accused can allege consent without placing himself in peril of such cross-examination (*Sheean*, (1908), *Turner* (1944)). This may be because such cases are *sui generis* (*per* Devlin J in *Rex v Cook* (1959)), or on the ground that the issue is one raised by the prosecution.

(4) If what is said amounts in reality to no more that a denial of the charge, expressed, it may be, in emphatic language, it should not be regarded as coming within the section (*Rouse* (1904), *Rex v Grout* (1909), *Rex v Jones* (1923), *Clark* (1955)).

Applying these propositions to this case, it is in my opinion clear beyond all doubt that the cross-examination of the accused was permissible under the statute.

I now turn to the question whether a judge has discretion to refuse to permit such cross-examination of the accused even when it is permissible under the section. Mr Caulfield submitted that there was no such discretion and contended that a judge at a criminal trial had no power to exclude evidence which was admissible ...

... Let it suffice for me to say that in my opinion the existence of such a discretion is now clearly established.

Mr Caulfield posed the question, on what principles should such a discretion be exercised. In *Reg v Flynn* (1963) the court said: '... where ... the very nature of the defence necessarily involves an imputation, against a prosecution witness or witnesses, the discretion should, in the opinion of this court, be as a general rule exercised in favour of the accused; that is to say, evidence as to his bad character or criminal record should be excluded. If it were otherwise, it comes to this, that the Act of 1898, the very Act which gave the charter, so to speak, to an accused person to give evidence on oath in the witness-box, would be a mere trap because he would be unable to put forward any defence, no matter how true, which involved an imputation on the character of the prosecutor or any of his witnesses, without running the risk, if he had the misfortune to have a record, of his previous convictions being brought up in court while being tried on a wholly different matter.'

No authority is given for this supposed general rule. In my opinion, the court was wrong in thinking that there was any such rule ...

... It is now so well-established that on a charge of rape the allegation that the woman consented, although involving an imputation on her character, should not expose an accused to cross-examination as to character, that it is possible to say, if the refusal to allow it is a matter of discretion, that there is a general rule that the discretion should be so exercised. Apart from this, there is not, I think, any general rule as to the exercise of discretion. It must depend on the circumstances of each case and the overriding duty of the judge to ensure that a trial is fair.

It is desirable that a warning should be given when it becomes apparent that the defence is taking a course which may expose the accused to such cross-examination. That was not given in this case but the failure to give such a warning would not, in my opinion, justify in this case the allowing of the appeal.

In my opinion the cross-examination of the accused was permissible under the section and it cannot be said the judge exercised his discretion wrongly in allowing it to take place ...

Lord Guest: ... If I had thought that there was no discretion in English law for a judge to disallow admissible evidence, as counsel for the Crown argued, I should have striven hard and long to give a benevolent construction to section 1(f)(ii), which would exclude such cases as *Rouse* (1904), 'liar', *Rex v Rappolt* (1911), 'horrible liar', *Rex v Jones* (1923), 'fabricated evidence', *Rex v Turner* (1944), rape and other sexual offences, *Reg v Brown* (1960), 'self defence'. I cannot believe that Parliament can have intended that in such cases an accused could only put forward such a defence at peril of having his character put before the jury. This would be to defeat the benevolent purposes of the 1898 Act which was for the first time to allow the accused to give evidence on his own behalf in all criminal cases. This would deprive the accused of the advantage of the Act. But I am not persuaded by the Crown's argument and I am satisfied upon a review of all the authorities that in English law such a discretion does exist. It was exercised for the first time in relation to this section in *Watson* (1913). Discretion as such has the general blessing of Lord Moulton in *Rex v Christie* (1914) and thereafter it has been the uniform practice of judges to exercise it in this class of case. Discretion was recognised in this House in *Maxwell v Director of Public Prosecutions* (1935); *Stirland* (1944); *Harris v Director of Public Prosecutions* (1952); and *Jones v Director of Public Prosecutions* (1962). And in the Privy Council in *Noor Mohamed v The King* (1949) and *Kurumah* (1955). In face of this long established practice it is, in my opinion, now too late to say that the judge has no discretion. While I leave to others more versed than I am in English criminal law and practice to discuss the origin of this discretion, I would assume that it springs from the inherent power of the judge to control the trial before him and to see that justice is done in fairness to the accused ...

I find it unnecessary to say much more on the principles upon which discretion should be exercised. The guiding star should be fairness to the accused. This idea is best expressed by Devlin J in *Reg v Cook* (1959). In following this star the fact that the imputation was a necessary part of the accused's defence is a consideration which will no doubt be taken into account by the trial judge. If, however, the accused or his counsel goes beyond developing his defence in order to blacken the character of a prosecution witness, this no doubt will be another factor to be taken into account. If it is suggested that the exercise of this discretion may be whimsical and depend on the individual idiosyncrasies of the judge, this is inevitable where it is a question of discretion; but I am satisfied that this is a lesser risk than attempting to shackle the judge's power within a straitjacket ...

Lord Pearce: My Lords, ever since the Criminal Evidence Act 1898 came into force there has been difficulty and argument about application of the words in section 1(f)(ii): 'nature or conduct of the defence is such as to involve imputations on the character of the prosecutor or the witnesses for the prosecution.'

Two main views have been put forward. One view adopts the literal meaning of the words. The prosecutor is cross-examined to show that he has fabricated the charge for improper reasons. That involves imputations on his character. Therefore, it lets in the previous convictions of the accused. The practical justification, for this view is the 'tit for tat' argument. If the accused is seeking to cast discredit on the prosecution, then the prosecution should be allowed to do likewise. If the accused is seeking to persuade the jury that the prosecutor behaved like a knave, then the jury should know the character of the man who makes these accusations, so that it may judge fairly between them instead of being in the dark as to one of them.

The other view would limit the literal meaning of the words. For it cannot, it is said, have been intended by Parliament to make a man liable to have his previous convictions revealed whenever the essence of his defence necessitates imputations on the character of the prosecutor. This revelation is always damaging and often fatal to a defence. The high-water mark of this argument is the ordinary case of rape. In this the vital issue (as a rule) is whether the woman consented. Consent (as a rule) involves imputations on her character. Therefore, in the ordinary case of rape, the accused cannot defend himself without letting in his previous convictions. The same argument extends in varying lesser degrees to many cases ...

It is argued that ... *Reg v Flynn* (1963) set up something in the nature of a rule as to the exercise of the discretion. But if and in so far as *Reg v Flynn* was purporting to do this, I do not accept it. The considerations which *Reg v Flynn* sets out are, indeed, valid factors to be weighed in the exercise of discretion. At the end of it all, however, the judge must make up his own mind.

In the result, I cannot accept the appellant's proposition that *Rex v Hudson* (1912) and the many cases which have followed it were wrong in their strict construction of section 1(f). Nor can I accept his contention that *Reg v Flynn* laid down a rule by which, except in rare cases, the judge's discretion should be used to produce the more liberal construction.

On the other hand, I cannot accede to the contention of Mr Caulfield for the prosecution that the judge has no discretion and must always apply the strict rule in *Rex v Hudson* in its full rigour. There is an overwhelming mass of distinguished authority that the discretion exists. It is not necessary to consider here whether that discretion has been evolved in relation to section 1(f) from the case of *Rex v Watson* (1913) onwards, or whether it comes, as in my opinion it does, from the inherent power of the courts to secure a fair trial for the accused, or, to use the words of Viscount Simon (1952), 'the duty of a judge when trying a charge of crime to set the essentials of justice above the technical rule if the strict application of the latter would operate unfairly against the accused'.

Moreover, it is good sense. Naturally each side seeks to establish a rule rather than a discretion, provided always that the rule is in his own favour. There is always an attraction in rules, since they are so much easier to apply. It would, for instance, be easier for a judge if he did not have a discretion as to costs in civil suits. Moreover, 'the demon of formalism', in the words of Cardozo J, 'tempts the intellect with the lure of scientific order', especially in cases like section 1(f), where decisions in particular cases are so difficult. But the courts have been right in thinking that the question is whether this attack on the prosecution ought to let in these convictions on the particular facts of the case, and on such a point rules are no substitute for a discretion in producing a fair trial. I appreciate that in the result an accused cannot be certain exactly how far he can go without letting in his convictions. But the many cases in the Court of Criminal Appeal have given some reasonably consistent guidance. And unless there is established a rule that an accused can go to the limits of attack without letting in his convictions, there is no possibility of drawing any clearer line for every case ...[14]

R v Britzman (1983, Court of Appeal)

Lawton LJ: ... On 29 May 1980 two men, posing as water board employees, persuaded a Mrs Mayell, then aged 88, to allow them to enter her house on a council estate at Putney in order to inspect her water system, giving as their excuse for doing so that there was reason to believe the supply to be contaminated. One of them, followed by Mrs Mayell, went into the kitchen and turned on the taps. The other went into another room and broke open and damaged a writing bureau which was locked. Mrs Mayell discovered this shortly after the two men had left. Nothing was missing. Mrs Mayell at once telephoned the police and gave them descriptions of both men. A police officer in a motor car was at once sent to search the area and about 15 minutes after the two men had left Mrs Mayell's house he stopped and arrested the two appellants within the limits of the council estate. Both fitted the descriptions given by Mrs Mayell. It was discovered later that Hall was wearing a wig. On 1 June 1980 they were both put on an identification parade but Mrs Mayell did not pick them out. At the trial it was accepted by the prosecution that without the evidence of what had happened after arrest there would not have been enough to justify a conviction of either appellant.

The prosecution's case was that shortly after arrest on 29 May both appellants were interviewed separately by Det Con Self. Both denied guilt. Britzman said: 'If you think you can prove it, then I'll talk to you.' Hall said: 'You fucking prove something and I'll have it son.'

On 30 May they were both separately interviewed by Det Insp Whyte and Det Con Andrews. Britzman refused to answer any questions. Hall said: 'I won't admit anything until the time is right.' On 1 June Det Insp Whyte, accompanied this time by Det Con Boal, had a long interview with Britzman which both

---

14.   [1970] AC 304.

officers said they had recorded in their notebooks. The recorder reminded the jury of this interview in detail. If Britzman had said what he was alleged to have done, there was strong evidence from which the jury could infer guilt.

It is unnecessary to set out in this judgment all of what was alleged to have been said by Britzman. One part of it illustrates its tone: '*Det Insp Whyte*. Fred, we know you did the one at Putney Park Lane. There's no point in discussing it unless you want to put it on paper. *Britzman*. I might do that. Look, you've been fair with me so far. Let's stop pussy-footing about. We are probably fucked on that old woman, but it's still a bit iffy. *Det Insp Whyte*. Not as far as we are concerned. *Britzman*. It is if we get a jury. *Det Insp Whyte*. So. *Britzman*. It's a chance.'

Later that day, according to Det Con Boal, he heard the two appellants shouting to one another whilst in their cells. Once again, if his evidence was accepted by the jury, guilt could be inferred from what was said. One passage was as follows: '*Hall*. Look, we've only got to sweat this out. They can't keep us here for ever. That old bird won't pick us out. Just keep your mouth shut. We'll be OK. *Britzman*. We'll talk about it if they stick us together. *Hall*. I'll fucking do you if you say anything.'

Britzman's case was that he had not spoken at all to Det Con Self on 29 May or to Det Insp Whyte and Det Con Boal on 1 June nor had he had a shouting match with Hall in the cells as alleged by Det Con Boal. Counsel who appeared for Britzman, and who is an experienced advocate in criminal cases, appreciated that putting his client's case to these police officers in cross-examination, as he had to do, was like walking through a legal minefield, because of the provisions of s 1(f)(ii) of the Criminal Evidence Act 1898. It is clear from the way Britzman gave his evidence that he too knew of these dangers, perhaps because his acquaintance with the criminal courts was longer than that of his counsel.

Any denial that the conversations had taken place at all necessarily meant by implication that the police officers had given false evidence which they had made up in order to get the appellants convicted. On the facts of this case there could be no question of mistake, misunderstanding or confusion. If Det Insp Whyte and Det Con Boal had made up this story, they had conspired together to commit perjury and had committed it. Det Con Self must have committed perjury when giving evidence about the alleged conversation on 29 May and Det Con Boal must have done the same about the cell conversation. The conversation on 1 June about which two officers gave evidence was long and of a kind which could have appeared in a television film script for a crime series.

A defence to a criminal charge which suggests that prosecution witnesses have deliberately made up false evidence in order to secure a conviction must involve imputations on the characters of those witnesses with the consequence that the trial judge may, in the exercise of his discretion, allow prosecuting counsel to cross-examine the defendant about offences of which he has been convicted. In our judgment this is what Parliament intended should happen in most cases. When allegations of the fabrication of evidence are made against prosecution witnesses, as they often are these days, juries are entitled to know about the characters of those making them.

The duty of the judge in such cases to exercise a discretion whether to allow prosecuting counsel to cross-examine a defendant about previous convictions puts defending counsel in a difficulty because some judges, so counsel for Britzman told us and we accept from our own experience when we were at the Bar, will exercise their discretion in favour of the defendant if either he or his counsel avoids making specific allegations of misconduct. This practice has a long history and support for it can be found in *R v Clark* (1955) and *R v Jones* (1923). With such judges a suggestion that a witness is mistaken or had misunderstood usually attracts a favourable exercise of discretion.

Britzman seems to have thought that Mr Recorder Titheridge might be such a judge, because he said in evidence that Det Insp Whyte had been mistaken in thinking that he had said what he was alleged to have done on 1 June. Counsel for Britzman in cross-examination contented himself with suggesting to the officers that the alleged conversations had not taken place at all.

Mr Recorder Titheridge would have none of this delicate forensic language. When prosecuting counsel applied for leave to cross-examine Britzman about his previous convictions he ruled that he could do so. He gave a reasoned ruling, the essence of which is contained in the following passage: 'In my judgment, the delicacy with which cross-examination was conducted on behalf of this defendant cannot hide the basic common-sense position, which is this: there is no room for error or mistake; it must be clear to the jury that the only real issue for their consideration, although, I repeat, it has never been so put to these police officers, that the only real issue for their consideration is whether the statements were made, or in the case of the conversation between the two defendants whether the conversation took place, or whether those officers have made them up. There is simply no other possibility.'

Counsel for Britzman submitted that this ruling was wrong, because the defence amounted in reality to no more than a denial of the charge. In putting his case in that way he adopted what Viscount Dilhorne had said in *Selvey v DPP* (1970).

In our judgment the nature and conduct of the defence did involve imputations on the characters of the three officers, despite the delicacy of Britzman's language and the forensic skill of his counsel. The jury had to decide whether these officers had made up what they alleged had been said. If in any case that is the reality of the position and would be seen by a jury to be so, there is no room for drawing a distinction between a defence which is so conducted as to make specific allegations of fabrication and one in which the allegation arises by way of necessary and reasonable implication. Nor can any distinction be validly drawn between an allegation to commit perjury and one of conspiring to commit perjury; but, when the allegation is one of perjury only, discretion may have to be exercised in favour of the defendant more readily than with a conspiracy allegation, having regard to what was said by Viscount Dilhorne in *Selvey* ...

... In our judgment the learned recorder's ruling was right.

In deciding as we have, we have not overlooked the potentiality of unfairness to defendants with previous convictions which a rigid application of s 1(f)(ii) of the 1898 Act would cause and the difficulties in advising and deciding tactics which defending counsel have. No doubt it was appreciation of the potentiality of unfairness to defendants which led the House of Lords in *Selvey* to reject the Crown's submission in that case that judges have no discretion to refuse leave to cross-examine about previous convictions.

We hope that it will be helpful for both judges and counsel if we set out some guidelines for the exercise of discretion in favour of defendants. First, it should be used if there is nothing more than a denial, however emphatic or offensively made, of an act or even a short series of acts amounting to one incident or in what was said to have been a short interview. Examples are provided by the kind of evidence given in pickpocket cases and where the defendant is alleged to have said: 'Who grassed on me this time?' The position would be different however if there were a denial of evidence of a long period of detailed observation extending over hours and just as in this case ... where there were denials of long conversations.

Second, cross-examination should only be allowed if the judge is sure that there is no possibility of mistake, misunderstanding or confusion and that the jury will inevitably have to decide whether the prosecution witnesses have fabricated evidence. Defendants sometimes make wild allegations when giving evidence. Allowance should be made for the strain of being in the witness-box and the exaggerated use of language which sometimes results from such strain or lack of education or mental instability. Particular care should be used when a defendant is led into making allegations during cross-examination. The defendant who, during cross-examination, is driven to explaining away the evidence by saying it has been made up or planted on him usually convicts himself without having his previous convictions brought out. Finally, there is no need for the prosecution to rely on s 1(f)(ii) if the evidence against a defendant is overwhelming ...[15]

R v Owen (1985, Court of Appeal)

Neill LJ [delivering the judgment of the court]: ... The *cross-examination of the appellant upon his previous convictions*. In order to consider this aspect of the case it is necessary to bear the following points in mind:

(1) When an application is made on behalf of the Crown for leave to cross-examine the accused as to his previous convictions on the basis that the nature or conduct of the defence has been such as to involve imputations on the character of the prosecutor, or the witnesses for the prosecution, the judge at trial has two tasks to perform:

(a) first he must form a judgment as to 'the nature or conduct of the defence' in order to decide whether the condition set out in paragraph (ii) of section (1)(f) of the 1898 Act has been satisfied; and

(b) if he is so satisfied, he must decide whether in the exercise of his discretion he should allow the cross-examination to take place.

(2) In forming a judgment as to the nature and conduct of the defence the judge will have to consider the facts of the individual case. Where explicit allegations of the fabrication of evidence have been made against prosecution witnesses, his task will be easy. But it is clear that in many cases imputations on the character of the witnesses for the prosecution may be made even though no explicit allegation of fabrication is made and even though counsel for the accused has conducted his cross-examination with delicacy and restraint. A challenge to the evidence of a witness, where there can be no question of mistake or misunderstanding or confusion, may well bear the necessary implication that the evidence has been fabricated. If the reality of the position is that the jury will have to decide whether the evidence of the witness whose testimony has been challenged, has been made up, then, in the words of Lawton LJ in *Britzman* (1983), 'there is no room for drawing a distinction between a defence which is so conducted as to make specific allegations of fabrication and one in which the allegation arises by way of necessary and reasonable implication'. See also *Tanner* (1978).

---

15. [1983] 1 All ER 369. The judgment of Lawton LJ was that of the court.

(3) Where the condition set out in paragraph (ii) of section 1(f) of the 1898 Act has been satisfied, the trial judge must weigh the prejudicial effect of the questions to be directed to the accused against the damage done by the attack on the prosecution's witness, and must generally exercise his discretion so as to secure a trial that is fair to the prosecution and the defence: see *Burke* (1985) and *Powell* (1985) where the guidance to this effect given by the Court of Criminal Appeal in *Cook* (1959) was approved.

(4) Cases must occur in which, although the grounds for putting questions to the accused about his previous convictions have been established, the effect of allowing such questions might be fraught with results which would unreasonably outweigh the result of the questions put by the defence and might make a fair trial of the accused almost impossible: see *Burke* (*supra*) and *Powell* (*supra*), approving the observations of Singleton J in *Jenkins* (1945).

(5) In the normal and ordinary case, however, the trial judge may feel that if the credit of the prosecutor or his witnesses has been attacked, it is only fair that the jury should have before them material on which they can form their judgment whether the accused person is any more worthy to be believed than those he has attacked: see *Burke* (*supra*) and *Powell* (*supra*). If imputations on the character of a prosecution witness have been made and if there is a real issue about the conduct of that witness which the jury will inevitably have to settle in order to arrive at their verdict, then, in the words of Devlin J delivering the judgment of the full court in *Cook* (*supra*) at p 143 and p 348 of the respective reports, '... the jury is entitled to know the credit of the man on whose word the witness's character is being impugned'. Devlin J was considering the case of a police officer whose evidence had been attacked, but it seems clear that the same principle is to be applied in the case of any important witness against whom such an imputation has been made and about whose conduct the jury will have to reach a conclusion.

(6) The fact that the accused's convictions are not for offences of dishonesty, but may be for offences bearing a close resemblance to the offences charged, are matters for the judge to take into consideration when exercising his discretion, but they certainly do not oblige the judge to disallow the proposed cross-examination: see *Powell* (*supra*).

(7) An appellate court will not intervene with the exercise by the trial judge of his discretion unless he has erred in principle or there was no material on which he could properly arrive at his decision: see *Selvey v DPP* (1970) and *Powell* (*supra*). The court will not quash a conviction merely because it would have exercised the discretion differently ...[16]

R v Inder (1977, Court of Appeal)

The Lord Chief Justice: In October 1976 at the Central Criminal Court, the appellant stood his trial on an indictment containing seven effective counts. On count 1 he was found guilty of buggery of a boy called Malcolm Ward; on count 2 he was found guilty of indecent assault with the same boy; on count 3 he was found guilty of indecent assault on John Ward; and on count 4 he was acquitted of a similar indecency charge relating to a boy called Errol Bent; on count 5 he was found guilty of indecent assault on David Brennan; on count 6 he was found guilty of indecent assault on John Keeley; and on count 7 there was an acquittal in relation to another of the Ward brothers, Mark Ward, in respect of whom the

---

16. 83 Cr App R 100.

appellant had been charged with a similar offence. He appeals against conviction and substantial sentences of imprisonment which were imposed following those convictions ...

The necessary background of the case was ... that the three Ward brothers, mentioned in the counts to which I have already referred, lived with their mother and father in a house where the appellant at all material times also lived as a kind of lodger. In addition to the boys living in the house, he was friendly with some of the boys in the neighbourhood. He had a very bad record for indecent assault upon small boys before he became known to the Ward family at all. In 1960 he was given four years' imprisonment for indecent assault on boys and in 1968 seven years for similar offences. They must have been grave offences to have attracted penalties of that nature. So one has this man with this record behind him living with this family with these boys.

When the matter came before the learned trial judge, two major points were raised and they were the two major points to which I now address the judgment of this court. First of all, the question arose whether reference could properly be made to the past record of similar offences against the accused in the present trial, and the second major point raised was how far the evidence of individual boys could be treated as corroborating the evidence of the other boys ...

The lead-in, as it were, to the admission of the appellant's past record sprang from the fact that in the case of one boy he said that the boy had faked an indecent assault by taking the appellant's hand and putting it on the boy's privates and then blackmailing the appellant saying that he would tell unless money was given to him and the other boys concerned. That evidence clearly shows an imputation of a bad character against a prosecution witness which would open the door to evidence of the past record of the appellant being admitted if the judge, having regard to the well-known considerations, thought it right and proper to let it in. It must have had a devastating consequence when the judge decided that these past offences were to be disclosed, because one can hardly think of a situation more likely to prejudice the jury than admission of evidence of that kind unless, of course, extreme care was taken to prevent that prejudice from occurring.

The judge decided that the evidence was to be let in on the basis of the attack upon the single prosecution witness, but he did not, as we think he might very well have and, indeed, should have done, bear in mind throughout the rest of the case the serious effect which that admission of evidence might have. In other words, although he was correctly telling the jury in respect of this evidence that they were not to regard that evidence as showing guilt of the accused by reason of his having committed similar offences before, and they were directed that this evidence was to enable them to see what kind of a man it was that was the subject of this attack, yet the judge did not have that important factor constantly in mind and occasionally (one mentions one example only) overstepped the mark and almost invited the jury to use this evidence in the way in which it should not be used.

The particular passage I have in mind from the summing-up is in these terms. He referred to the appellant's recent return from prison and then he went on to say: 'Of course, there was Douglas Inder having the dangers of his recent activities, certainly now in the past, finding himself, you may think, subject to a temptation which would require the very strongest resolve to resist. So almost from the very outset he was finding himself in a situation where there were two small boys sharing the same bed. Time went on and there was something of an argument or discordance between himself and Mrs Ward so he went to stay with Mrs Batts for a short period ...' In that passage one sees the judge accepting the fact that this man had been in prison for similar offences and almost inviting the inference that the same thing might happen again.

We do not feel able to say that the judge was wrong in allowing the evidence of past offences to be admitted, but we do find, having done that, that he did not exercise full caution and ensure during the summing-up that the jury were warned from time to time to use the information for purposes of credit only ...[17]

R v McLeod (1994, Court of Appeal)

The following judgment of the court was delivered.

Stuart-Smith LJ: On 20 September 1988 an armed robbery was carried out against a Securicor van. Four men were involved in the attack: the appellant, Hartgeald McLeod, the applicant, Dennis Ellington, Louis Miles and a man called Wilmot. Wilmot escaped and has not been brought to justice. The other three were convicted at the Central Criminal Court on 11 May 1990. McLeod was sentenced to 18 years' imprisonment for the robbery, 7 years concurrent for having a firearm with intent to commit an indictable offence, and 3 years consecutive for using a firearm to resist arrest, making a total of 21 years. He now appeals against his conviction by leave of the full court and against sentence by leave of the single judge ...

At an interview [McLeod] admitted being one of the robbers but would give no details. There was scientific evidence which showed traces of firearms residues on his motor cycle gloves and hat. The jacket he was wearing at the time of the robbery was found some days later. Fibres linked him to the attack vehicle.

McLeod gave evidence. He said he had nothing to do with the robbery; the police had created a false case against him. He had been with Wilmot on three occasions in the attack vehicle; he did not know it was stolen and he gave an innocent explanation of those occasions. He was elsewhere at the time of the robbery and he called witnesses to support his alibi. The admission in interview was fabricated by the police. Since his defence involved a wholesale attack on the police, Mr Kershen QC, his counsel, anticipating that he would be cross-examined on his previous convictions, asked him briefly about them in examination-in-chief. McLeod expressed a willingness to deal with the details of the convictions if he was asked. In respect of a number of offences McLeod had said he was found guilty, but was not in fact guilty.

In the course of the cross-examination, prosecuting counsel sought leave to cross-examine on the convictions pursuant to the Criminal Evidence Act 1898 s 1(f)(ii). The application was not opposed. He was asked first of all about eight court appearances between 1974 and 1977 when he was convicted of a number of offences of dishonesty, some involving motor cars. No objection is taken to those matters. He was then asked the following questions about four offences, including two for robbery between 1978 and 1982 (for convenience we have numbered them):

(1) 'Q. On 12 June 1978, at the Central Criminal Court, for an offence of robbery, five years' imprisonment. That is the one with Mr Ellington involved as well, is it not? A. Yes.

Q. Was that a robbery of a man, something in the order of £1,200? A. Yes, I think so.

17. 67 Cr App R 143.

Q. And the prosecution allegation was that you got away from the scene of the robbery, was it not? A. Yes, that was.

Q. And you pleaded not guilty, did you not? A. Yes, I did.

Q. What was your defence? A. How do you mean?

Q. What was your defence? Was it an alibi? A. Yes.

Q. Did you give evidence in support of that alibi? A. Yes.

Q. And you were convicted. A. Yes, I was.

(2) Q. On 11 July 1979, at the Central Criminal Court, for an offence of robbery; was that breaking into someone's home and taking £26,000 worth of jewellery and antiques? A. Yes, it was.

Q. The person being locked up in a cupboard under the stairs while it was all going on? A. I don't know. I didn't go into the house.

Q. Four years' imprisonment on a plea of not guilty. A. Yes.

(3) Q. On 26 April 1979, at the Inner London Crown Court, theft of a motor car and driving whilst disqualified; was that stealing a motor vehicle in the Wembley area, parking it in the street for a number of days, and then changing the plates on it to a false registration? A. Yes.

Q. Two years' imprisonment consecutive to the five years as well – correct? A. Correct.

(4) Q. 27 May 1984, at the Acton Crown Court, dishonest handling of a motor car on false plates? A. Wrong.

Q. Dishonestly handling of what, do you say, Mr McLeod? A. It's the right offence; wrong date.

Q. You say it is in 1982, do you? A. Yes.

Q. A Ford motor car with false plates; six months' imprisonment? A. Mm.'

No objection was taken to these questions at the time they were asked. But shortly afterwards Mr Kershen submitted that questions as to the details of the offences should not have been permitted on the basis that it was gravely prejudicial to McLeod. The nature of the objection seems to vary somewhat in respect of each offence. Thus, in respect of some it is said that the detail bears a similarity to what was alleged in the instant case and was therefore unduly prejudicial. Thus, in relation to the robbery in 1978, the fact that the appellant got away and put up a false alibi was said to be similar to his defence in the present case. In respect of the offences relating to motor vehicles in 1979 and 1984, it was said that the fact that cars were taken from the Wembley area and fitted with false plates, and one of the vehicles was a Ford motor car, was said to have similarities to the present case.

In relation to the April 1979 conviction for robbery, it was submitted that it was highly prejudicial to suggest that McLeod had locked the occupant of the house in a cupboard under the stairs. It was, Mr Kershen said, an allegation of wicked and ruthless conduct.

Mr Kershen submitted to the judge and to this court that the authorities show that these questions ought not to have been asked. Since no objection was taken at the time they were asked, and Mr Kershen quite rightly in our view did not invite the judge to discharge the jury, he submits that she should forthwith have told the jury that they should not allow the detail of the convictions to impinge upon their consideration of guilt or innocence and that they did not show a propensity to commit armed robbery. He also submits that the direction which the judge gave in the course of her summing-up, where she did deal with it, was inadequate.

We have not found it easy to distil from Mr Kershen's submission the principle which he contends should guide the courts in allowing or disallowing questions designed to elicit the underlying facts of a previous conviction. But it seems to be that such questions are objectionable if they tend to elicit (a) facts similar to some of those in the instant case, (b) that a similar defence was advanced but rejected on a previous occasion, or (c) that the facts of the case, though in no way similar to those in the instant case, disclose exceptionally vicious, depraved or scandalous behaviour.

In granting leave to appeal, Lord Taylor of Gosforth CJ, in giving the judgment of the court, after saying that the authorities in this court were not as clear as it might be hoped, considered that it was desirable that the court should try and clarify how far prosecuting counsel is entitled to go in cross-examining a defendant who has exposed himself to it. Despite the fact that this court has reviewed the authorities in two cases in 1986, *R v Powell* and *R v Owen*, it must be accepted that the authorities are not always easy to reconcile ...

The starting point is the well-known *dictum* of Viscount Sankey LC in *Maxwell v DPP* (1934): 'But these instances all involve the crucial test of relevance. And in general no question as to whether a prisoner has been convicted or charged or acquitted should be asked or, if asked, allowed by the judge, who has a discretion under proviso (f), unless it helps to elucidate the particular issue which the jury is investigating, or goes to credibility; that is, tends to show that he is not to be believed on his oath; indeed the question whether a man has been convicted, charged or acquitted, even if it goes to credibility, ought not to be admitted, if there is any risk of the jury being misled into thinking that it goes not to credibility but to the probability of his having committed the offence with which he is charged.'

Therein lie the seeds of the problem. If an accused man who has attacked prosecution witnesses has many previous convictions for similar offences, it may be necessary that the jury should understand the character of the person making the allegations; at the same time it is difficult to pretend that such a history does not show a propensity to commit the instant offence. Take the case of a drugs dealer: a very common defence is that drugs were planted by the police, and any admission alleged to have been made, fabricated. If he had a number of previous convictions for supplying or possession with intent to supply drugs, the jury cannot judge the substance of the defence without knowing this, and perhaps also, if it be the case, that the defence advanced on previous occasions was that the drugs were planted. Yet the more the convictions, the worse the character, the greater the propensity to commit the offence ...

For the general principles upon which the discretion should be exercised we cannot improve upon the analysis contained in the judgment of Ackner LJ in *R v Burke* (1986) as supplemented by the observations of Neill LJ in *R v Owen*, to which we have referred. As to the nature of the questions that may properly be put, we consider that the following propositions should be borne in mind.

(1) The primary purpose of the cross-examination as to previous convictions and bad character of the accused is to show that he is not worthy of belief. It is not, and should not be, to show that he has a disposition to commit the type of offence with which he is charged: see *Vickers, Khan* and *Barsoum*. But the mere fact that the offences are of a similar type to that charged or because of their number and type have the incidental effect of suggesting a tendency or

disposition to commit the offence charged will not make them improper: *Powell*, *Owen* and *Selvey*.

(2)   It is undesirable that there should be prolonged or extensive cross-examination in relation to previous offences. This is because it will divert the jury from the principal issue in the case, which is the guilt of the accused on the instant offence, and not the details of the earlier ones. Unless the earlier ones are admissible as similar fact evidence, prosecuting counsel should not seek to probe or emphasise similarities between the underlying facts of previous offences and the instant offence.

(3)   Similarities of defences which have been rejected by juries on previous occasions, for example false alibis or the defence that the incriminating substance has been planted, and whether or not the accused pleaded guilty or was disbelieved having given evidence on oath, may be a legitimate matter for questions. These matters do not show a disposition to commit the offence in question; but they are clearly relevant to credibility.

(4)   Underlying facts that show particularly bad character over and above the bare facts of the case are not necessarily to be excluded. But the judge should be careful to balance the gravity of the attack on the prosecution with the degree of prejudice to the defendant which will result from the disclosure of the facts in question. Details of sexual offences against children are likely to be regarded by the jury as particularly prejudicial to an accused and may well be the reason why in *R v Watts* (1983), the court thought the questions impermissible.

(5)   If objection is to be taken to a particular line of cross-examination about the underlying facts of a previous offence, it should be taken as soon as it is apparent to defence counsel that it is in danger of going too far. There is little point in taking it subsequently, since it will not normally be a ground for discharging the jury.

(6)   While it is the duty of the judge to keep cross-examination within proper bounds, if no objection is taken at the time it will be difficult thereafter to contend that the judge has wrongly exercised his discretion. In any event, this court will not interfere with the exercise of the judge's discretion save on well-established principles.

(7)   In every case where the accused has been cross-examined as to his character and previous offences, the judge must in the summing-up tell the jury that the purpose of the questioning goes only to credit and they should not consider that it shows a propensity to commit the offence they are considering.

Applying these principles to the present case we are quite satisfied that the questions were perfectly proper. They were by no means unduly prolonged or extensive. With regard to offence No 1, there was nothing wrong in asking the appellant about his plea and defence of alibi that was rejected, particularly where, as here, the appellant giving evidence-in-chief persisted in his denial of guilt. There is no substance in the suggestion that he should not have been asked about the victim of offence No 2 being locked under the stairs; even if he had accepted that he had done it, which he did not, it merely showed that this offence was somewhat more ruthless than may normally be the case in a robbery where, by definition, violence or the threat of violence, is used. The circumstances were in any event quite different from the instant case. In our judgment, it is fanciful to contend that the facts elicited in respect of offences Nos 3 and 4, which occurred more than nine and four years before the instant offence, were designed to show a tendency or propensity to commit armed robbery, merely because the use of stolen vehicles with false registration plates is the stock in trade of armed robbery.

Mr Kershen also criticised the judge's direction to the jury on how they should treat the cross-examination in question. He submitted that the judge should have reminded the jury of the detail of the cross-examination and told them not to allow those details to impinge upon their consideration of guilt or innocence. In our judgment, since the detail elicited was not objectionable, there was no need to refer to it. All that was needed was that the judge should tell the jury in clear terms that the cross-examination went solely to the issue of credit and they should not regard it as evidence of a propensity to commit the offences for which the appellant was on trial. The judge's summing-up on this point cannot be faulted ...[18]

Quite apart from the considerations governing the exercise of the judge's discretion to allow cross-examination under s 1(f)(ii), an advocate who wishes to cross-examine a witness about bad character should bear in mind what was said by Sankey LJ in *Hobbs v Tinling* (1929). The provisions of the Rehabilitation of Offenders Act 1974 may be relevant.

Hobbs v Tinling (1929, Court of Appeal)

Sankey LJ: ... A long argument was addressed to us as to the limits and effect of cross-examination as to credit ... An opponent may be cross-examined as to his credit, but he cannot be contradicted upon any point not material to the issue in order to show that his evidence is not to be believed. The Indian Evidence Act (I of 1872), s 153, correctly sums up the English law on the subject, and is as follows: 'When a witness has been asked and has answered any question which is relevant to the inquiry only in so far as it tends to shake his credit by injuring his character, no evidence shall be given to contradict him; but if he answers falsely, he may afterwards be charged with giving false evidence.' The court can always exercise its discretion to decide whether a question as to credit is one which the witness should be compelled to answer, and in my view, again referring to the Indian Evidence Act, s 148, in the exercise of its discretion the court should have regard to the following considerations: '(1) Such questions are proper if they are of such a nature that the truth of the imputation conveyed by them would seriously affect the opinion of the court as to the credibility of the witness on the matter to which he testifies. (2) Such questions are improper if the imputation which they convey relates to matters so remote in time, or of such a character, that the truth of the imputation would not affect, or would affect in a slight degree, the opinion of the court as to the credibility of the witness on the matter to which he testifies. (3) Such questions are improper if there is a great disproportion between the importance of the imputation made against the witness's character and the importance of his evidence.'[19]

Rehabilitation of Offenders Act 1974

1(1) Subject to subsection (2) below, where an individual has been convicted, whether before or after the commencement of this Act, of any offence or offences, and the following conditions are satisfied, that is to say –

---

18.   [1994] 3 All ER 254.
19.   [1929] 2 KB 1.

(a) he did not have imposed on him in respect of that conviction a sentence which is excluded from rehabilitation under this Act; and

(b) he has not had imposed on him in respect of a subsequent conviction during the rehabilitation period applicable to the above-mentioned conviction in accordance with section 6 below a sentence which is excluded from rehabilitation under this Act;

then, from the end of the rehabilitation period so applicable (including, where appropriate, any extension under section 6(4) below of the period originally applicable to the first-mentioned conviction) or, where that rehabilitation period ended before the commencement of this Act, after the commencement of this Act, that individual shall for the purposes of this Act be treated as a rehabilitated person in respect of the first-mentioned conviction and that conviction shall for those purposes be treated as spent ...

4 (1) Subject to sections 7 and 8 below, a person who has become a rehabilitated person for the purposes of this Act in respect of a conviction shall be treated for all purposes in law as a person who has not committed or been charged with or prosecuted for or convicted of or sentenced for the offence or offences which were the subject of that conviction; and, notwithstanding the provisions of any other enactment or rule of law to the contrary, but subject as aforesaid –

(a) no evidence shall be admissible in any proceedings before a judicial authority exercising its jurisdiction or functions in Great Britain to prove that any such person has committed or been charged with or prosecuted for or convicted of or sentenced for any offence which was the subject of a spent conviction; and

(b) a person shall not, in any such proceedings, be asked, and, if asked, shall not be required to answer, any question relating to his past which cannot be answered without acknowledging or referring to a spent conviction or spent convictions or any circumstances ancillary thereto.

...

7(1) ...

(2) Nothing in section 4(1) above shall affect the determination of any issue, or prevent the admission or requirement of any evidence, relating to a person's previous convictions or to circumstances ancillary thereto –

(a) in any criminal proceedings before a court in Great Britain (including any appeal or reference in a criminal matter); ...

Practice Direction

Lord Widgery CJ: At the sitting of the court today I have a practice direction to make on the Rehabilitation of Offenders Act 1974.

1   The effect of s 4(1) of the Rehabilitation of Offenders Act 1974 is that a person who has become a rehabilitated person for the purpose of the Act in respect of a conviction (known as a 'spent' conviction) shall be treated for all purposes in law as a person who has not committed or been charged with or prosecuted for or convicted of or sentenced for the offence or offences which were the subject of that conviction.

2   Section 4(1) of the 1974 Act does not apply however to evidence given in criminal proceedings (s 7(2)(a)). Convictions are often disclosed in such criminal proceedings. When the Bill was before the House of Commons on 28 June 1974 the hope was expressed that the Lord Chief Justice would issue a practice direction for the guidance of the Crown Court with a view to

reducing disclosure of spent convictions to a minimum and securing uniformity of approach.

3   During the trial of a criminal charge reference to previous convictions (and therefore to spent convictions) can arise in a number of ways. The most common is when the character of the accused or a witness is sought to be attacked by reference to his criminal record, but there are, of course, cases where previous convictions are relevant and admissible as, for instance, to prove system.

4   It is not possible to give general directions which will govern all these different situations, but it is recommended that both court and counsel should give effect to the general intention of Parliament by never referring to a spent conviction when such reference can be reasonably avoided. If unnecessary references to spent convictions are eliminated much will have been achieved.

5   After a verdict of guilty the court must be provided with a statement of the defendant's record for the purposes of sentence. The record supplied should contain all previous convictions, but those which are spent should, so far as practicable, be marked as such.

6   No one should refer in open court to a spent conviction without the authority of the judge, which authority should not be given unless the interests of justice so require.

7   When passing sentence the judge should make no reference to a spent conviction unless it is necessary to do so for the purpose of explaining the sentence to be passed.[20]

SECTION 1(f)(iii)

There is no discretion to disallow a co-defendant's application to cross-examine under s 1(f)(iii), so argument in court will usually be confined to the question whether a s 1(f)(iii) situation has arisen. The sole relevancy of cross-examination under this provision is to credit, but the distinction between relevancy to credit and relevancy to guilt can be difficult to maintain: see Roderick Munday's article below (which deals with this problem in relation to s 1(f)(ii) as well).

Murdoch v Taylor (1965, House of Lords)

Murdoch and his co-accused, Lynch, were tried together on an indictment which alleged that they had received three cameras, knowing the same to have been stolen. Both pleaded not guilty. The case for the prosecution was that both Lynch and Murdoch had been involved in an attempt to sell the cameras to a watchmaker named Klein. Murdoch gave evidence in his own defence. In examination-in-chief he stated that he had seen a box in Lynch's possession but had discovered that it contained cameras only when Lynch had called him into Klein's shop after first entering and spending some time there himself. Under cross-examination by counsel for Lynch he asserted that he had had nothing to do with the stolen cameras and that they had been entirely Lynch's responsibility. Counsel for Lynch claimed to be entitled to cross-examine

---

20.   [1975] 2 All ER 1072.

Murdoch about his previous convictions under s 1(f)(iii). The trial judge permitted this and both men were subsequently convicted. Murdoch appealed, arguing (1) that 'has given evidence against' in s 1(f)(iii) imported a hostile intent and went beyond giving evidence which simply tended to support the case for the prosecution or undermine the case for the defence; (2) that answers given in cross-examination were part of the case for the prosecution and not for the defence, and so did not come within the words of s 1(f)(iii); and (3) that even if a s 1(f)(iii) situation had arisen, the judge had a discretion to disallow such cross-examination which he had failed to exercise.

Lord Morris of Borth-y-Gest: ... If an accused becomes a witness his sworn testimony, if admissible, becomes a part of the evidence in the case. What he says in cross-examination is just as much a part of that evidence as is what he says in examination-in-chief. The word 'against' is one that is well understood. It is a clear and robust word. It has more decisiveness than is possessed by such phrases as 'tending to show' or 'such as to involve'. It is a word that needs neither explanation nor translation. It calls for no synonym.

The Act does not call for any investigation as to the motives or wishes which may have prompted the giving of evidence against another person charged with the same offence. It is the nature of the evidence that must be considered. Its character does not change according as to whether it is the product of pained reluctance or of malevolent eagerness. If, while ignoring anything trivial or casual, the positive evidence given by the witness would rationally have to be included in any survey or summary of the evidence in the case which, if accepted, would warrant the conviction of the 'other person charged with the same offence', then the witness would have given evidence against such other person. Such other person would then have that additional testimony against him. From his point of view that testimony would be just as damaging whether given with regret or whether given with relish. Such other person might then wish, in order to defend himself, to show that credence ought not to be attached to the evidence which had been given against him. In such circumstances the Act removes one barrier which would otherwise be in his way.

It may be noted that if A and B are jointly charged with the same offence and if A chooses to give evidence which is purely in defence of himself and is not evidence against B he may be asked questions in cross-examination by B notwithstanding that such questions would tend to incriminate him (A) as to the offence charged. In similar circumstances B would be likewise placed. But questions of the kind denoted by section 1(f) could not be put. No doubt during any such cross-examination a judge would be alert to protect a witness from being cajoled into saying more than it was ever his plan or wish or intention to say.

If an accused person, when giving evidence for the defence, has given evidence against any other person charged with the same offence, the question arises whether the latter needs the permission of the court before putting to the witness any question of the kind denoted in section 1(f). In my judgment he must have liberty to defend himself by such legitimate means as he thinks it wise to employ. This does not, however, mean that the judge has no function to discharge. In the first place it will be for him to rule as a matter of law whether a witness has or has not given evidence against any other person charged with the same offence. In the present case I consider that it could fairly and properly be said that the appellant had given evidence against Lynch. In the second place, it is always for a judge to rule in regard to the relevance of any evidence and therefore in regard to the propriety of any question which it is desired to ask. ...

... In some cases proof that a person has committed or been convicted of some other offence is admissible evidence to show that he is guilty of the offence of which he is then charged. In the circumstances now being considered the purpose of a co-accused person in putting any questions of the kind denoted in section 1(f) must be to discredit someone who has given evidence against him. It is therefore for a judge to rule as to the relevance of any proposed questions ...

The result, in my judgment, is that where it is claimed that an accused person has given evidence against another person charged with the same offence and it is desired to put questions of the kind denoted in section 1(f), intimation of this desire should (in such way as may be appropriate) be given to the court and to counsel concerned. The temporary withdrawal of the jury might become desirable. It will then be for the judge to rule in regard to the matters to which I have referred. If he rules as a matter of law that the proposed questions may be put, then he is not called upon either to give or to withhold any permission to put them.

The present case is concerned only with the situation where it is a co-accused person who desires to put questions to another co-accused who has given evidence against him. Different considerations apply where it is the desire of the prosecution to put questions of the kind denoted in section 1(f) ...

Lord Donovan: ... It is now contended on behalf of Murdoch, first, that he had given no evidence against Lynch within the meaning of proviso (f)(iii). That expression in its context connotes, it is said, only evidence given in examination-in-chief and not evidence given in cross-examination. Alternatively, it refers only to evidence given with a hostile intent against a co-accused so that the test to be applied is subjective and not objective. In the further alternative, it is argued that, whatever be the true meaning of the expression, a trial judge has in all cases a discretion whether or not to allow questions to be put pursuant to proviso (f)(iii) just as he has in relation to proviso (f)(ii) of the section.

Prior to the Act of 1898 coming into force an accused person could not (speaking generally) give evidence in his own defence. The Act begins by enacting by section 1 that: 'Every person charged with an offence ... shall be a competent witness for the defence at every stage of the proceedings ... Then follow a number of provisos, the first of which is: '(a) A person so charged shall not be called as a witness in pursuance of this Act except upon his own application.' An accused person was thus given a new right of defending himself, if he wished, by his own sworn testimony. There is thus some initial impetus, at least, towards the view that when the legislature contemplated that he might give evidence against a co-accused, it was thinking of evidence produced directly by the testimony which the accused chose to give and not testimony which he might have preferred not to give but which was extracted from him under the pressure of cross-examination. Be that as it may, the words of the proviso are, in my opinion, too clear to admit of any such distinction. The object of proviso (f)(iii) is clearly to confer a benefit upon a co-accused. If evidence is given against him by another accused he may show, if he can, by reference to the latter's previous offences that his testimony is not worthy of belief. It is the effect of the evidence upon the jury which is material and which may be lessened or dissipated by invoking the proviso. The effect upon the jury is the same whether the evidence be given in examination-in-chief or in cross-examination; and the desirability of the co-accused being able to meet it by cross-examination as to credit is of the same importance, however the evidence is given. I feel no difficulty in holding that the first of the appellant's contentions must be rejected.

The like considerations also lead me to reject the argument that proviso (f)(iii) refers only to evidence given by one accused against the other with hostile intent. Again, it is the effect of the evidence upon the minds of the jury which matters, not the state of mind of the person who gives it. Were that the test, there would have to be something of the nature of a trial within a trial in order to determine the state of mind of the accused who gave the evidence ... The language of the Act gives no support for the view that this was the intention. In my opinion, the test to be applied in order to determine whether one accused has given evidence against his co-accused is objective and not subjective.

What kind of evidence is contemplated by proviso (f)(iii), that is, what is 'evidence against' a co-accused is perhaps the most difficult part of the case. At one end of the scale is evidence which does no more than contradict something which a co-accused has said without further advancing the prosecution's case in any significant degree. I agree with the view expressed by Winn J in giving judgment in *Stannard* (1965) that this is not the kind of evidence contemplated by proviso (f)(iii). At the other end of the scale is evidence which, if the jury believes it, would establish the co-accused's guilt; for example, in a case of theft: 'I saw him steal the purse', or in a case of assault: 'I saw him strike the blow.' It is this kind of evidence which alone, so the appellant contends, will satisfy the words 'has given evidence against'. Again, I regret I cannot share that view. There may well be evidence which regarded in isolation would be quite innocuous from the co-accused's point of view and, so regarded, could not be regarded as evidence 'against' him. For example, what would be proved if one co-accused said of his co-accused: 'He told me he knew of an easy job and persuaded me to help him'? If such evidence is kept unrelated to anything else it proves nothing criminal. But juries hear the whole of the evidence and they consider particular parts of it, not in isolation but in conjunction with all the other evidence, and part of that other evidence may establish that 'job' meant a housebreaking job. Then the item of evidence I have taken as an example obviously becomes evidence 'against' the accused. If, therefore, the effect of the evidence upon the minds of the jury is to be taken as the test, it cannot be right to regard it in isolation in order to decide whether it is evidence against the co-accused. If Parliament had meant by proviso (f)(iii) to refer to evidence which was by itself conclusive against the co-accused it would have been easy to say so.

The test prescribed by the Court of Criminal Appeal in *Stannard* was whether the evidence in question tended to support the prosecution's case in a material respect or to undermine the defence. I have no substantial quarrel with this definition. I would, however, observe that some danger may lurk in the use of the expression 'tended to'. There will probably be occasions when it could be said that evidence given by one accused 'tended to' support the prosecution's case simply because it differed from the evidence of his co-accused; and the addition of the words 'in a material respect' might not wholly remove the danger. The difficulty is not really one of conception but of expression. I myself would omit the words 'tending to' and simply say that 'evidence against' means evidence which supports the prosecution's case in a material respect or which undermines the defence of the co-accused.

The evidence in the present case was clearly against Lynch in that sense. It was evidence which, if the jury accepted it, put Lynch in sole control and possession of property which according to the rest of the evidence had been stolen the day before, and which Lynch had tried to sell for a price which was a fraction of its real value. Murdoch's evidence thus supported the case of the prosecution in a material respect ...

On the question of discretion, I agree with the Court of Criminal Appeal that a trial judge has no discretion whether to allow an accused person to be cross-examined as to his past criminal offences once he has given evidence against his co-accused. Proviso (f)(iii) in terms confers no such discretion and, in my opinion, none can be implied. It is true that in relation to proviso (f)(ii) such a discretion does exist; that is to say, in the cases where the accused has attempted to establish his own good character or where the nature and conduct of the defence is such as to involve imputations on the character of the prosecutor or of a witness for the prosecution.

But in these cases it will normally, if not invariably, be the prosecution which will want to bring out the accused's bad character – not some co-accused; and in such cases it seems to me quite proper that the court should retain some control of the matter. For its duty is to secure a fair trial and the prejudicial value of evidence establishing the accused's bad character may at times wholly outweigh the value of such evidence as tending to show that he was guilty of the crime alleged.

These considerations lead me to the view that if, in any given case (which I think would be rare), the prosecution sought to avail itself of the provisions of proviso (f)(iii) then here, again, the court should keep control of the matter in the like way. Otherwise, if two accused gave evidence one against the other, but neither wished to cross-examine as to character, the prosecution could step in as of right and reveal the criminal records of both, if both possessed them. I cannot think that Parliament in the Act of 1898 ever intended such an unfair procedure. So far as concerns the prosecution, therefore, the matter should be one for the exercise of the judge's discretion, as it is in the case of proviso (f)(ii). But when it is the co-accused who seeks to exercise the right conferred by proviso (f)(iii) different considerations come into play. He seeks to defend himself; to say to the jury that the man who is giving evidence against him is unworthy of belief; and to support that assertion by proof of bad character. The right to do this cannot, in my opinion, be fettered in any way ...[21]

R v Bruce (1975, Court of Appeal)

Bruce, McGuinness and a number of other youths were acquitted of robbery but convicted of theft, the case for the prosecution being that they had frightened a Mr Lecerf, a passenger in a train in which they were travelling, into giving them money. McGuinness's evidence supported the prosecution case of an agreement to rob. According to him, they had all gone to Hampstead that night to look for a Pakistani to rob; on failing to find one there they had taken the train, at which stage they had found their victim. McGuinness said that he had played no part in carrying out the plan. Bruce in his evidence said that there had never been a plan to rob anyone. The trial judge ruled that thereby he had 'given evidence against' McGuinness, and so had brought himself within s 1(f)(iii).

---

21. [1965] AC 574. Lord Evershed agreed with Lord Donovan. Lord Reid delivered a speech in which he agreed with Lord Donovan on the question of discretion. On the construction of 'against' he said that he found great difficulty in agreeing with the other Law Lords, but did not dissent as he was 'unable to find any satisfactory solution for the problem set by the proviso'. Lord Pearce agreed with Lord Morris and Lord Donovan on the question of construction, but dissented to the extent of holding that the judge should have a discretion whether to allow any cross-examination under this proviso.

Stephenson LJ: ... The peculiarity of that evidence is that it contradicted McGuinness's evidence, undermined part of his defence and damaged his credibility, but it did not contradict his evidence that he took no money; it undermined the case for the prosecution and made it not more but less likely that there was a robbery and that McGuinness would be convicted of the offence with which both were charged. Did Bruce give that evidence 'against' McGuinness? Yes, in the sense that he contradicted McGuinness and said that that part of his defence which agreed with the prosecution that there was a plan to rob a Pakistani was untrue; no, in the sense that he supported McGuinness's defence that he did not rob Mr Lecerf and that he provided McGuinness with a different, and possibly a better, defence to the charge than he himself had put forward.

We cannot help thinking that reading the words of s 1(f)(iii) of the 1898 Act in their context in their ordinary meaning a lawyer and a layman would alike regard Bruce's evidence denying that there was a plan to rob as given more in McGuinness's favour than against him. On balance it exculpates him of robbery and did not incriminate him. We think it right to give words their ordinary meaning, if we can, without adding any gloss to them ... But the cases cited to us at first sight show that a gloss has been put on these words which the court is bound to put on them. In *Murdoch v Taylor* the House of Lords – or certainly a majority of their Lordships – approved with a minor modification the construction put upon the words in *R v Stannard* and held that 'evidence against' means evidence which supports the prosecution's case in a material respect or which undermines the defence of the co-accused: see *per* Lord Donovan. But neither in that case nor in *Stannard's* case ... were there under consideration any facts like those of this unusual conflict. Usually evidence which undermines the defence of another defendant supports the prosecution's case against him. Here the evidence did more to undermine the prosecution's case than to undermine the co-accused's defence.

Counsel for the Crown accepts that McGuinness's defence was in two parts, confession of a plan to rob – and avoidance – by denial of participating in the robbery. But he says that these two parts cannot be separated and evidence which attacks the confession attacks also the avoidance by attacking the credibility of him whose defence it is, and the conflict between their evidence goes to the very root of the case. You cannot undermine part without undermining the whole, and that is enough to make Bruce's evidence evidence given against McGuinness, although it also undermines the case for the prosecution and if believed would result in his acquittal.

We do not overlook the possibility that the evidence of one defendant contradicting that of a co-defendant, even though not itself believed, may nevertheless lead the jury to reject the co-defendant's evidence and accept that of the prosecution witnesses. A fanciful version put forward by one defendant may cause the jury to regard a co-defendant's conflicting version as fanciful also. It may be that in such a case a defendant's evidence would be 'given against' a co-defendant. But in the wholly exceptional circumstances of this case we can see no reason why the rejection of Bruce's version that there was no plan to rob should in any way or to any extent lead to the rejection of McGuinness's story that he took no part in what was going on between the others.

In our judgment, evidence cannot be said to be given against a person charged with the same offence as the witness who gives it if its effect, if believed, is to result not in his conviction but in his acquittal of that offence. The fact that Bruce's evidence undermined McGuinness's defence by supplying him with another does not make it evidence given against him. If and only if such evidence undermines a co-accused's defence so as to make his acquittal less likely, is it given against him. If that puts a gloss on a gloss, the addition is needed to preserve the natural meaning of the subparagraph. Bruce's evidence did not so undermine McGuinness's defence. He should not have been asked questions about his previous convictions ...[22]

R v Varley (1982, Court of Appeal)

Varley and Dibble were jointly charged with robbery and possessing a firearm at the time of the commission of an offence. At trial Dibble's defence was that he had taken part in the robbery with Varley, but had done so only under duress because of threats made against his life by Varley. Varley gave evidence that he had not been present at the commission of the crime at all and that Dibble's testimony was untrue. The trial judge ruled that Varley had thereby brought himself within s 1(f)(iii). Both defendants were convicted. Varley appealed, arguing that a s 1(f)(iii) situation had not arisen; alternatively, if it had, the judge should have ordered separate trials.

Kilner Brown J: ... Now was Dibble's evidence 'against' the appellant? Clearly it was. Was the appellant's testimony evidence 'against' Dibble? That is what this appeal is all about. Fortunately, in the interests of justice, the jury learned of Dibble's criminal history because he was cross-examined about his past convictions. The jury rejected his defence of duress and convicted him of participation in the robbery but acquitted him of possession of the firearm. He was sentenced to a term of 18 months' imprisonment.

The trial reached the stage of cross-examination of Varley by counsel on behalf of Dibble when, knowing the nature of Dibble's case, he applied for leave to put questions as to Varley's previous convictions on the basis that his evidence was evidence against Dibble. He made the application relying on the words of s 1(f)(iii) of the Criminal Evidence Act 1898, citing the case of *Murdoch v Taylor* in which the House of Lords applied and followed the reasoning of the Court of Criminal Appeal in *R v Stannard* ...

The operation of this particular part of the proviso seems to have given rise to no difficulty and no detailed analysis for well over 60 years. No doubt, as Lord Pearce indicated in his speech in *Murdoch v Taylor*, 'the practice and the general view of Bench and Bar alike was that a judge had a discretion whether to give leave to cross-examine under s 1(f)(iii)', and, in difficult cases where it was not easy to determine whether the evidence could be categorised as 'against' or where such questioning could well be unduly prejudicial, a judge would decline to rule that the proposed questions could be put. But this discretionary power was removed from trial judges by the Court of Criminal Appeal in *R v Ellis* (1961), when it was decided that cross-examination of a co-defendant who had given evidence against a person jointly charged with him was a matter of right and not of discretion.

The decision was approved by four of the Lords of Appeal (Lord Pearce dissenting) in *Murdoch's* case. This decision created difficult problems in practice because either to establish or to destroy this right involved, in many cases, an acute analysis of whether or not the evidence which had been given was 'against' the other party charged. It sparked off a whole series of cases which have come before this court and at least the one (*Murdoch's* case) in the House of Lords. The

---

22.   [1975] 1 WLR 1252.

instant case is a very good example of the additional burden placed on the trial judge. The application and the resistance to it occupied many hours of judicial time and took up no less than 57 pages of recorded transcript.

Although the judgment of the Court of Criminal Appeal in *R v Stannard* was undoubtedly meant to have been of assistance to trial judges in their consideration of whether evidence was 'against' or not, in practice, it has in fact added to their burden and it has caused considerable anxiety to other divisions of this court as it did to Lord Reid and was tacitly ignored by Lord Morris in Murdoch's case. What was the nature of the guidance in *R v Stannard*? It was this, approved as amended by Lord Donovan in *Murdoch's* case: '... "evidence against" means evidence which supports the prosecution's case in a material respect or which undermines the defence of the co-accused.' There are three reported cases in the Court of Appeal, Criminal Division, in which this interpretation has been considered and to which we were referred ... Now, putting all the reported cases together, are there established principles which might serve as guidance to trial judges when called on to give rulings in this very difficult area of the law? We venture to think that they are these and, if they are borne in mind, it may not be necessary to investigate all the relevant authorities. (1) If it is established that a person jointly charged has given evidence against the co-defendant that defendant has a right to cross-examine the other as to previous convictions and the trial judge has no discretion to refuse an application. (2) Such evidence may be given either in chief or during cross-examination. (3) It has to be objectively decided whether the evidence either supports the prosecution case in a material respect or undermines the defence of the co-accused. A hostile intent is irrelevant. (4) If consideration has to be given to the undermining of the other's defence care must be taken to see that the evidence clearly undermines the defence. Inconvenience to or inconsistency with the other's defence is not of itself sufficient. (5) Mere denial of participation in a joint venture is not of itself sufficient to rank as evidence against the co-defendant. For the proviso to apply, such denial must lead to the conclusion that if the witness did not participate then it must have been the other who did. (6) Where the one defendant asserts or in due course would assert one view of the joint venture which is directly contradicted by the other such contradiction may be evidence against the co-defendant.

We apply these principles to the facts of this case and particularly the latter two. Here was Dibble going to say, as he did, that he took part in the joint venture because he was forced to do so by Varley. The appellant, Varley, was saying that he was not a participant and had not gone with Dibble and had not forced Dibble to go. His evidence therefore was against Dibble because it amounted to saying that not only was Dibble telling lies but that Dibble would be left as a participant on his own and not acting under duress. In our view, the judge was right to rule that cross-examination as to previous convictions was permissible. This ground of appeal is rejected.

The other ground put forward was that the judge wrongly exercised his discretion by refusing to separate trials. We recognise that there may well be occasions where there has been a successful application to cross-examine a co-defendant on his convictions and the trial judge, in his duty to ensure a fair trial, may properly exercise a discretion to order separate trials. We have in mind the situation where the effect of such cross-examination is such as to create such undue prejudice that a fair trial is impossible. But that is not this case. The truth of the matter is that this was a case where two experienced criminals metaphorically cut each other's throats in the course of their respective defences.

If separate trials had been ordered, one or other or both might have succeeded in preventing a just result. This ground of appeal is also rejected and the appeal against conviction is dismissed ...[23]

Roderick Munday, 'The Paradox of Cross-Examination to Credit', *Cambridge Law Journal* 53 (1994)

What exactly renders cross-examination relevant?

Although fundamental to criminal proceedings, the question as to which properties lend evidence of bad character its particular relevance is rarely given systematic treatment. The response the question commonly evokes is that relevance tends to turn on the particular facts of any given case. The relativity of relevance cannot be disputed. Nor can the fact that the live issues in the trial, as they crystallise, do ultimately dictate the broad shape of what is relevant. Nevertheless, a number of principles do underpin the courts' appreciation of what is relevant in the context of cross-examination relating to character. First, there is a broad initial proposition that, putatively, all past criminal offending and bad character has a bearing on a defendant's creditworthiness. The *rationale* of this proposition was perhaps put as compellingly as it can be in a New Hampshire decision: 'What a person is often determines whether he should be believed. When a defendant voluntarily testifies in a criminal case, he asks the jury to accept his word. No sufficient reason appears why the jury should not be informed what sort of person is asking them to take his word. In transactions of everyday life this is probably the first thing that they would wish to know. So it seems to us in a real sense that when a defendant goes on to a stand, "he takes his character with him ...". Lack of trustworthiness may be evinced by his abiding and repeated contempt for laws which he is legally and morally bound to obey ... though the violations are not concerned solely with crimes involving "dishonesty and false statement"' [*State v Duke*, 123 A 2d 745, 746 (NH 1956)].

As has been mentioned elsewhere, this thesis, which arguably proceeds upon a model of human character and behaviour that psychologists abandoned en masse in the late 1920s, is not beyond dispute. Nevertheless, the bedrock assumption that criminality, generally understood, and low moral standards are sufficiently linked with a tendency to tell untruths under oath in the witness-box is then shot through with exceptions and traversed by qualifying principles which variously purport to circumscribe or to focus cross-examination on bad character.

The most important qualification is that such evidence must only be directed to credit, not to issue. This assumes that a crisp distinction can be drawn between any evidence that will assist the tribunal of fact to decide whether the defendant is likely to be truthful when testifying and evidence which is plainly directed to showing that the defendant is likely to be guilty of the offence charged. As Cross once observed, this is pretty much a distinction without a difference. [*An Attempt to Update the Law of Evidence* (Jerusalem, 1974), p 21.] Any direction to a jury, that they may only use their knowledge of the defendant's criminal record to help gauge his credibility and that they are forbidden to treat it as evidence that the defendant is the kind of person who commits offences generally or any particular

23.   [1982] 2 All ER 519.

type of offence, demands unusual analytical temerity. Justice Holmes laid bare the fragility of the underlying reasoning in the last century in *Gertz v Fitchburg Railway Company:* 'When it is proved that a witness has been convicted of a crime the only ground for disbelieving him which such proof affords is the general readiness to do evil which the conviction may be supposed to show. It is from that general disposition alone that the jury is asked to infer a readiness to lie in a particular case, and then that he has lied in fact. The evidence has no tendency to prove that he was mistaken, but only that he has perjured himself, and it reaches that conclusion solely through the general proposition that he is a bad character and unworthy of credit' [137 Mass. 76, 78 (1884)].

The law runs considerable risks for the sake of a broadbrush stroke proposition, which looks geared to help the jury to be satisfied with far less proof than they would otherwise demand for conviction and which enables them to seek comfort from the possibility of error in the fact that, after all, the defendant is a bad person.

Conscious that not all bad character, no matter how trivial, should automatically be treated as relevant to a defendant's credibility and, at the other end of the spectrum, that the admission of certain of an accused's previous convictions might prove too prejudicial, when the Crown applies for leave to cross-examine on bad character the courts may employ their discretion to limit the scope of such questioning. At the lower end of the scale, judges routinely refuse the prosecution leave to cross-examine on stale, trivial offences if the defendant has not re-offended for an appreciable length of time ...

At the upper end of the scale, on the other hand, two strands of reasoning emerge from the case law. First, when defendants have convictions for theft and related offences, the courts sometimes seize upon the notion that such 'offences of dishonesty' are especially relevant to the issue of a defendant's creditworthiness. Lord Lane CJ brought out this point in his judgment in *Watts* [(1983) 77 Cr App R 126, 129-30], although the Lord Chief Justice in *Powell* [[1985] 1 WLR 1364, 1370] and Neill LJ in *Owen* [(1986) 83 Cr App R 100, 105] subsequently moderated the emphasis on the relevance of offences of dishonesty. In other jurisdictions, too, courts have been lured into treating offences of dishonesty as possessing particular probative value. Linguistically, the elision between testimonial dishonesty and criminal dishonesty is easily made. But as Mischel has pointed out, 'the data on moral behaviour provide no support for the widespread psychodynamic belief in ... a unitary entity of conscience or honesty' [*Personality and Assessment* (New York, 1968), p 26]. Behaviour is widely believed to be in essence situational. The findings of Hartshorne and May's imposing Character Education Enquiry in the late 1920s included the conclusion that 'when situations involving the possibility of deception were almost identical the behaviour of individuals did not greatly vary from occasion to occasion. But when the situations permitting dishonesty were altered ... then there was found greater and greater diversity of behaviour, so that one could not predict from what a person did in one situation what he would do in a different situation.' [Hartshorne, May & Shuttleworth, *Three Studies in the Organization of Character* (New York, 1930), p 1]. The link drawn by the courts, then, is substantially intuitive – at best approximate guesswork, at worst a deceptive comforter which gives tribunals of fact added confidence to disbelieve the word of defendants who have chalked up convictions for offences of dishonesty. The calculus can conceivably be refined and a rough-hewn, commonsensical case made that convictions for offences like perjury, perverting the course of justice and other crimes which involve cocking a snook at the law are even more relevant in demonstrating an absence of respect variously for the oath, for judicial proceedings and for the lawful elucidation of the truth. Applied psychologists seem largely agreed that gauging subjects' credibility is extremely difficult. Some may entertain a belief that 'new findings on the measurement of facial expression, body movement, voice and verbal behavior ... show that the combination of facial and vocal measures allows highly accurate identification of deceptive behaviour' [Ekman, 'Why Lies Fail and What Behaviors Betray a Lie', in Yuille (Ed) *Credibility Assessment* (Dordrecht, 1988), p 71], but the conventional wisdom is still that some individuals lie better than others, that techniques for the detection of lying are far from fool-proof, that we do not really know what makes some individuals appear credible when lying and that the connection, if any, between behavioural and psychophysiological indications of deception remains a mystery. The self-confidence of many legal pronouncements on the relevance of character evidence to credibility contrasts sharply with the tentative judgments of the psychologists in the matter of credibility assessment.

A second guiding principle which has evolved in the case law is that convictions for offences similar to those for which the defendant is standing trial may be viewed as particularly relevant. This line of authority is unsettling as it both brings home the difficulty of crisply separating matters of issue from matters of credit and, whatever one pretends, must also serve to entice jurors into employing 'the forbidden reasoning' and into convicting defendants on the basis that their past characters show that they are the sort of people to commit the offences with which they are currently charged. If it emerges in cross-examination that a defendant charged with assault has previous convictions for assault and violence, two problems are posed. First, a tribunal of fact will find it nigh impossible to use such knowledge uniquely to gauge the defendant's credibility as a witness. As Lord Goddard CJ remarked in *Samuel* [(1956) 40 Cr App R 8, 12], 'it is very difficult to see how if it is permissible to cross-examine a prisoner with regard to convictions, for example, if he is a thief, and he is cross-examined on previous convictions for larceny, the jury is not in effect being asked to say: "The prisoner is just the sort of man who will commit these crimes and therefore it is highly probable he did." Evidence going to credit blurs into evidence to issue at this point. Secondly, even if in theory the division between issue and credit can be maintained in this situation, in jury cases it is dependent upon the efficacy of a judicial direction delivered to the jury during the summing-up. Practitioners have for long questioned the effectiveness of such evidentiary warnings, the Court of Appeal has 'acknowledge[d] unreservedly the difficulty of formulating an intelligible direction to a jury on a matter which is so opaque even to lawyers' [*Wright* (1989) 90 Cr App R 325, 335], and a growing body of psychological research cautions that such instructions are of little effect. Just like judicial instructions to disregard evidence, the concept of the warning is all very well; but as defending counsel inquired of the court at the trial of Jack Ruby, when the jury was told to disregard the fact of Ruby's previous arrest, 'You cannot unring a bell, can you?'

The Court of Appeal wrestled with this dilemma in a cluster of cases in the mid-1980s. In *Watts* [(1983) 77 Cr App R 126] the court at first took the view that to ask a jury in an indecent assault case to use the accused's record for indecent assaults on very young girls merely as information to assist them in deciding whether to accept him as a truthful witness and not as evidence to show that he had a propensity to commit indecent assaults was to demand of them impossible feats of 'mental gymnastics'. Within a matter of months, however, the Lord Chief Justice recanted, admitting in *Powell* that 'those views were wrong' [[1985] 1

WLR 1364, 1370]. Henceforth courts were not to inhibit cross-examination simply on account of the similarity of the previous offending. In reaching this conclusion Lord Lane CJ relied heavily on the House of Lords decision in *Selvey v DPP* [[1970] AC 304] and on two previous unreported decisions of the Court of Appeal ... One suspects that not merely has this ruling resulted in a greater willingness of trial judges to permit cross-examination to credit under section 1(f) on similar previous convictions and in a laxer attitude in the Court of Appeal in such cases, but more generally the decision has further blurred the line which supposedly divides evidence going to issue from evidence going to credit and, quite possibly, contributed to stimulating the latest developments in the field – a class of case which extends the scope of cross-examination beyond the traditional point of merely adverting to the fact of the previous conviction or to the sort of matters detailed in the defendant's certificate of conviction to an exploration of the details of those other offences, if the court adjudges them 'relevant'.

Before passing to this subject, however, the point should be made that the courts rarely make clear what exactly renders a defendant's previous bad character 'relevant' to his credibility. Indeed, sometimes their rulings are highly ambiguous. Take the case of *Shaw* [(1993) 97 Cr App R 218]. S and a co-accused were jointly charged with burglary. Successful appeal was taken against conviction on the ground that the trial judge had failed to give the jury any direction on the issue of S's good character. Owen J was of the view that this might have been attributed to the Court of Appeal's earlier ruling in *Gibson* [(1991) 93 Cr App R 9], which had counselled that in cases where one defendant is of good character and the other has previous convictions a trial judge will be wise to say very little, if anything, concerning the former's good character for fear that this might imply to the jury that the latter's character leaves something to be desired. In *Shaw* there was a basic similarity in that S's co-accused had what the court termed 'relevant convictions' [(1993) 97 Cr App R 218, 221]. The count in the indictment was one of burglary; the co-accused's previous record comprised 'convictions for dishonesty and indeed in one case for burglary'. The question that is left unresolved in *Shaw* is whether the particular 'relevance' of those convictions derives from their being offences of dishonesty – the line suggested, say, in Lord Lane CJ's judgment in *Watts*, whether it can be deduced from the circumstance that the previous offending is of a similar type, and indeed is identical in one case, to the offence charged in the indictment – as is now permissible, in the court's discretion, under *Powell*; or whether it is the combination of both these features.

Exploring the Details of the Record

Once evidence of propensity shades so thoroughly into evidence to credit and once cross-examination can focus on previous convictions similar to the offence charged, the temptation is strong to press matters harder and, where they shed light on the accused's story, to explore the details of his previous offending, particularly if these reveal generally similar patterns of behaviour. Although the courts have traditionally rejected applications by prosecuting counsel to explore these areas, occasionally they now relent, allowing the Crown to probe the details of the defendant's prior record. Such decisions further erode an already fragile dividing-line between issue and credit and, under cover of evidence of credibility, trespass deeper into a zone conventionally known as 'the forbidden reasoning' – proof of guilt by propensity. The issue has arisen under both sub-provisos (ii) and (iii) of section 1(f) ...

1 Sub-proviso (ii). The classical scope of cross-examination under section 1(f) is illustrated in *Khan* [[1991] Crim LR 51]. K's convictions for affray and common assault were quashed on the grounds that cross-examination concerning his previous convictions had been too wide-ranging. The offences, arising out of an altercation in the early hours of the morning outside a night-club, included an assault on a police officer whom the appellant had kicked whilst already under arrest in a panda car. Having cast imputations on the character of Crown witnesses, Khan was cross-questioned on a criminal record which included an assault upon the police. Defence counsel, knowing that the nature of the defence would inevitably lead to the defendant's record being revealed to the jury, had already informed the court of his client's conviction. Prosecuting counsel, however, proceeded 'to cross-examine the appellant as to the details of the manner in which it was alleged he had committed the previous offence'. No attempt was made to invoke the similar fact evidence principles – although the Court of Appeal did hint that, in its opinion, this avenue might conceivably have been open. Simply, with the possible active encouragement of the judge and with no objection being made by the defence, the Crown taxed Khan with 'the obvious similarity between what he was contending for now and what had been stated in a previous case' in 'an attempt obviously to demonstrate to the jury that the way in which he behaved on this occasion was almost precisely similar to the way he had behaved previously'. Watkins LJ placed reliance on the authority of *Vickers* [[1972] Crim LR 101], a case in which the Court of Appeal had quashed a malicious wounding conviction because the defendant's previous record had improperly been picked over in detail with a view to implying that he had a violent disposition. The court concluded in *Khan* that prosecuting counsel's cross-examination had been 'such as to show unmistakably that [Khan] was predisposed to using violence, bad language and other misbehaviour of the kind which was alleged against him in the indictment'. Since it was authoritatively established that cross-examination under section 1(f)(ii) 'is related, and must only relate, to the matter of credibility', Khan's convictions had to be quashed, Watkins LJ having by implication answered his own question to the effect that counsel exercising his right to put questions under sub-proviso (ii), 'is ... confined merely to asking the witness if he needs to (that is to say if it has not already been brought out by the defendant himself) if he has previously been convicted of the like offence to that with which he is charged in the indictment, and, if so, when and where'. A similar view had been taken by the Court of Appeal in *John and Brathwaite* [(1983) 24 Nov, unreported], where the trial judge had mistakenly allowed the Crown to highlight the similarities in *modus operandi* between the purse-snatching charges and the defendants' previous convictions for thefts from the person.

In the later case of *Whelan* [(1992) 18 June, unreported], however, there were signs that the Court of Appeal was becoming less resistant to such applications from Crown counsel. At his trial on two counts of assault occasioning actual bodily harm to two police officers, the defendant volunteered the information that although he had a record for violence, imprisonment had taught him a lesson. He had not therefore attacked the police on this occasion. Prosecuting counsel seized the opportunity to introduce all the defendant's previous convictions for violent crime and to extract from them the particular feature that the prior violence took a similar form to the offence charged, 'just fists and feet'. Although the defendant had introduced his prior record in evidence-in-chief, Waterhouse J noted that, given the nature of Whelan's defence, the trial judge would in any case have been bound to allow cross-examination under sub-proviso (ii). Therefore, this decision is equally applicable to such cases.

At first sight the Court of Appeal looks to have disapproved of Crown counsel's line of questioning. But the criticism is muted. Waterhouse J observed: 'It may well be that, as a matter of perfectionist criticism, counsel for the prosecution in the instant case did stray over the line by asking a question about the specific form of violence used in the offence of street robbery, but it is right that the matter was not pursued and that the previous record of the appellant occupied only a very short period of the cross-examination.'

Although 'it would have been better ... if the question about the particular form of violence ... had not been put', the *de minimis* principle could be applied, not least thanks to the trial judge having thrice warned the jury not to treat those convictions for similar acts of violence as evidence of propensity. The extent to which jurors comprehend judicial instructions is of course doubtful, as is their ability to put prejudicial matters from their minds. As John Parris put it, in a slightly different context: 'Jurors can be told to put out of their minds whatever they have previously read, but this is like asking them to remove their own skin. What they have read and the conclusions they have drawn become part of their own bodies' [*Scapegoat* (London, 1991), p 14].

Moreover, the Crown's strategy in *Whelan* appears to have been deliberately to focus on propensity, for it was decided not to 'develop a much wider ranging cross-examination in relation to a number of offences of dishonesty committed previously by the appellant'. In the context of *Whelan's* case it can only be self-delusion to imagine that the likely juror reaction would not have been: 'Whelan is charged with very violently assaulting a policeman in Soho Square with his fists and feet – the officer claimed, the most violent behaviour he had witnessed in thirteen years on the force. Whelan previously received a stiff, five-year sentence for street "robbery times seven", offences in which he had used "just fists and feet". He is therefore the type of hooligan who brawls with his fists and feet. He is likely to be guilty in this case.' The specifics of the previous offending may only have been briefly alluded to. Nevertheless, they significantly accentuated the propensity-value of Whelan's criminal record.

Whelan reveals other questionable features. First, the Court of Appeal intimates that Crown cross-examination might legitimately have extended to 'the defences that (Whelan) had put forward in relation to previous allegations of assault on the police, because it appeared that he had not pleaded guilty to those offences'. This idea has been floated before. As we have argued elsewhere, to treat previous unsuccessful pleas of not guilty as proven cases of perjury is a hazardous exercise, just as *Archbold's* argument (now abandoned) that defendants with records of similar offending know that they have more to lose and hence a greater incentive to lie is unconvincing as a proof that similar offending is particularly relevant to such a defendant's credibility. Nevertheless, the Court of Appeal has once again endorsed this approach to cross-examination under section 1(f)(ii) in *McLeod* [[1994] 3 All ER 25], a case where leave to appeal was granted with the avowed design of giving clearer guidance to prosecuting counsel on how far they are entitled to go in cross-examining defendants on previous convictions. Having reviewed the authorities, Stuart-Smith LJ reiterated that similarities of defence which have been rejected by juries on previous occasions – for example, false alibis, the defence that an incriminating substance had been planted, whether or not the accused pleaded guilty or was disbelieved having given evidence on oath – *could* be a legitimate matter for questions. This approach poses problems. As the court implicitly acknowledges in McLeod, certain defences do tend to be routinely advanced. In assaults on police officers, mistaken identity, self-defence or the gambit that 'the officer is lying' hardly display originality. Previous recourse to such defences will rarely prove illuminating, and this species of cross-examination will tend to generate more heat than light. Additionally, there may even be a problem in proving the details of defences run by defendants in previous cases. Apart from those trials in which the defence's line is relatively unclear or those cases in which the accused switches horses in mid-stream provoking a dispute over the exact nature of the defence, if the defendant denies prosecuting counsel's suggestions or affects not to recall the details of his defence, can the Crown prove them? It is submitted that the Crown may not.

Since questions on previous convictions under sub-proviso (ii) are only relevant to credit, a witness's answers would normally be treated as final. Rebuttal evidence is only admissible under limited exceptions to the collateral-finality rule. Section 6 of the Criminal Procedure Act 1865 (even as amended by PACE) only contemplates proof of the *fact* of a conviction, should any witness seek to deny that he has been convicted of an offence. Sections 73 to 75 of PACE, which now complement this provision by allowing proof of further details by production of informations, complaints, indictments and charge-sheets, do not authorise production of the transcript. At common law, it is now accepted that depositions or authenticated transcripts of testimony given at a previous criminal trial may become admissible in subsequent criminal proceedings. But this restricted exception to the hearsay rule seems only to apply in the case of witnesses who are ill or unavailable at the subsequent hearings of the same proceedings and is not intended to afford a means of contradicting an accused's account of evidence he has given in previous proceedings on different charges. Similarly, because matters of credit are collateral, the Crown cannot call witnesses to prove what was said on any previous occasion. Nor does it seem likely that the Crown can avail itself of sections 4 and 5 of the Criminal Procedure Act 1865, which allow proof of a witness's previous inconsistent statements during cross-examination, given that these sections only cover 'a former statement made by [the witness] relative to the subject matter of the indictment or proceeding'. Unless given an unusually wide interpretation, evidence given at trial on another indictment and in unconnected proceedings will necessarily fall outside these provisions. If this analysis is correct – and the point seems never to have been argued – the question arises whether the prosecution should be allowed to pursue matters of detail which will be of devastating effect but which it is in no position to prove?[24]

CROSS-EXAMINATON OF A CO-ACCUSED GENERALLY

Miller (1952) and *Bracewell* (1978) show that cross-examination under s 1(f)(iii), like any other cross-examination, must be relevant. The extent of such cross-examination, once ruled relevant, is illustrated by *Lui Mei-lin v R* (1989).

R v Miller (1952, Winchester Assizes)

Trial on indictment

At Winchester Assizes, before Devlin, J, and a jury, Alfred Miller, Nathan Mercado and Leonard Harris were charged on an indictment that between 1 January 1949 and 6 October 1951 they conspired together and with others fraudulently to evade duties of customs payable on the importation of nylon

---

24. Pages 305-309, 311-317.

stockings. At the trial evidence was tendered for the prosecution in respect of 21 importations, the first in February 1949 and the last in September 1951. The prosecution alleged that Miller started the illegal importations, conspiring with members of the crews of ships docking at Southampton, and that later he was joined in the conspiracy by Harris and Mercado. Between 28 November 1949 and 16 September 1950, Harris was serving a sentence of imprisonment for an offence unconnected with the present charges, and during that period there were no illegal importations. The defence of Mercado, as appeared from the cross-examination by his counsel of a witness for the prosecution, was that he was not concerned in the illegal importations, but that Harris, masquerading as Mercado, by whom he was employed, used Mercado's office for that purpose. In support of this defence and to show that Harris was primarily responsible for the importations, counsel asked the witness whether he was aware that Harris was in prison during a period when the importations were suspended. Counsel for Harris then applied for an order that the jury be discharged from giving a verdict in respect of Harris and that there should be a new trial with respect to him on the ground that his trial must be so prejudiced by the question asked by Mercado's counsel that that would be the proper course for a judge to take in the exercise of his discretion.

Devlin J: The fundamental principle, equally applicable to any question that is asked by the defence as to any question that is asked by the prosecution, is that it is not normally relevant to enquire into a man's previous character, and, particularly, to ask questions which tend to show that he has previously committed some criminal offence. It is not relevant because the fact that he has committed an offence on one occasion does not in any way show that he is likely to commit an offence on any subsequent occasion. Accordingly, such questions are, in general, inadmissible, not primarily for the reason that they are prejudicial, but because they are irrelevant. There is, however, this difference in the application of the principle. In the case of the prosecution, a question of this sort may be relevant and at the same time be prejudicial, and, if the court is of the opinion that the prejudicial effect outweighs its relevance, then it has the power, and, indeed, the duty, to exclude the question. Therefore, counsel for the prosecution rarely asks such a question. No such limitation applies to a question asked by counsel for the defence. His duty is to adduce any evidence which is relevant to his own case and assists his client, whether or not it prejudices anyone else.

Accordingly, the question which I have to ask myself in the first instance is whether it was relevant to inquire where Harris was at a certain period of time. The answer is, I think, that it was relevant, and indeed, no real objection has been taken on that ground. It was plainly relevant to the case which was being developed on behalf of the accused Mercado – that the time when the conspiracy was, as he says, quiescent was a time when Harris was unable to take part in it. So far no real evidence has been adduced, but the question indicates what I presume will be the case: that counsel for Mercado will seek to tender proof of where Harris was at the relevant period, and what I am doing, in effect, is determining whether evidence of that character is admissible or not. For the reasons that I have given I think it is relevant, and, therefore, admissible.

Although there was no irregularity in the form of the question under consideration, I have dealt with it in this way to make clear how far my ruling goes. First, it does not open the field to any question of this kind by counsel for an accused person against the character of another accused. It is admissible in the present case because it happens to be relevant. In the ordinary way the character of the accused is no more relevant at the hands of the defence than it is at the hands of the prosecution. Secondly, while counsel is not bound by the same considerations of restraint that would affect counsel for the prosecution in such a matter, care ought to be taken not to go any further than is strictly necessary for the proof of the relevant point on which the defence desires to rely. In such a matter the court is very much in the hands of counsel. I have indicated that at this stage proof of where Harris was at a given period during the conspiracy appears to me to have relevance, but I think that counsel for the defence ought to follow, so far as possible in the very different circumstances of appearing for the defence, the same restraint as counsel for the prosecution would, and ought not to introduce material of this sort further than is necessary or unless it is strictly required for the purpose of his case. Thirdly, I think that any question of this sort that is being asked by counsel for one accused that will affect the other accused ought to be communicated to counsel for the other accused in advance, so that he may consider whether he desires to take any objection to it.[25]

R v Bracewell (1978, Court of Appeal)

Appeal against conviction

On 22 February 1977 at Leeds Crown Court (Boreham J) the appellant was convicted of the murder of Isaac Blakey (count 1). On arraignment he pleaded guilty to burglary (count 3). He was sentenced to life imprisonment on count 1 and to one year's imprisonment concurrent on count 3. His co-accused, one Lockwood (who did not appeal) was convicted on the same indictment of the manslaughter of Blakey (count 1) and of burglary (count 3). He was sentenced to to six years' imprisonment on count 1 and to one year's imprisonment concurrent on count 3.

The following facts are taken from the judgment.

On 19 July 1974, the deceased, who lived alone in a house at Gipton Wood Crescent, Leeds, was found dead, lying across his bed with his legs hanging over the side of the bed. He had been severely battered about the face and head; he had a black eye and multiple bruises to the face and head and bruises on his hands and elsewhere; at post-mortem a fracture of the nasal bones was found and the inside of his mouth was split in several places. The most important post-mortem findings, however, were numerous discrete bruises in the tissues of the neck, indicating that his neck had been gripped, probably by two hands, in two or more positions, and the fact that, in spite of considerable bleeding of the nose and mouth, very little blood was found in the trachea and bronchi, and none in the smaller bronchi, suggesting that he had survived his injuries only for a very short time. The room in the house appeared to have been ransacked, but a sum of money, which was hidden in the bed, had been missed by the thief or thieves. Under his body there was found a length of what was described as mutton-cloth.

Some two years elapsed before the police arrested the two accused. At the time of the killing they had been living in the same house and were, in effect, brothers-in-law. Bracewell and his wife lived at Horsforth, near Leeds, and

---

25. [1952] 2 All ER 667.

Lockwood and Mrs Firth, who was Mr Bracewell's sister, had been sharing the house with them for some time. By July 1974 this arrangement was causing considerable domestic stress in the Bracewell family, and on the evening before the killing, Mrs Bracewell had walked out of the house and gone to her mother's. Bracewell was greatly upset by this, and he and Lockwood went out drinking that night at various places including a club and a 'shabeen'. Both men made long statements to the police after their arrests, admitting that, at Lockwood's suggestion, they had decided to burgle the house occupied by the deceased. At that time, the applicant, Bracewell, who was 29 years of age, was in regular employment and had no previous experience of crime; Lockwood, on the other hand, had no occupation and was an experienced thief and burglar, making his living by crime. He knew something about the deceased and believed that he kept money concealed in a sofa in the house. Both men made preparations for the offence, including taking several lengths of mutton-cloth with them, although Lockwood maintained throughout that he was not aware that Bracewell had this until after they had entered the deceased's house.

Having driven to the house they broke in through a window over the front porch. From this point in their story their respective statements diverge completely, each claiming to have had nothing to do with the attack on the deceased, and asserting that it had taken place while he was out of the bedroom. Both men gave evidence at the trial substantially to the same effect as their respective statements to the police. Lockwood's case was that having found the old man asleep in the bedroom he told Bracewell to stay outside the bedroom door and see that he did not come out while he, Lockwood, searched the house. He went downstairs and while searching the ground-floor rooms, heard noises upstairs and Bracewell calling him. He went up to the bedroom and found the old man dead and Bracewell in the room with him. Bracewell's version was that Lockwood entered the house first; he followed but had difficulty in climbing, owing to his overalls which restricted his movements, so that some time elapsed before he got in. When he entered the bedroom he found the old man lying as he was afterwards found, obviously seriously injured and semi-conscious. He cried, 'Help', once or twice and was moving his arms about. Lockwood was standing on the far side of the bed. They then tied the old man's wrists with the mutton-cloth but, as he was making a noise, Lockwood, using another piece of the mutton-cloth, put a gag in his mouth. Lockwood then searched the bedroom while he, Bracewell, stayed with the deceased trying to reassure him; patting his hands and talking to him. Lockwood then went downstairs to continue looking for the money. The old man made a gurgling noise. Bracewell then removed the gag and tried to revive him but realised that he was dead. Both men panicked and hurriedly left the house and eventually drove home.

Lockwood made immediate arrangements to get out of the neighbourhood, expecting that the police would be looking for him, and went to Newcastle. Bracewell remained at home; his wife returned, but found him in a severely depressed and anxious state, which developed into something like a nervous breakdown. He eventually gave his wife and Mrs Firth some account of what had happened. Lockwood later returned to Bracewell's house and resumed his association with Mrs Firth. Nothing further happened until the two men were arrested some two years later, in September 1976.

The grounds of appeal were: (1) the trial judge misdirected the jury on the medical evidence and the cause of death; (2) the trial judge was wrong in law in disallowing the appellant's counsel from cross-examining Mrs Firth with a view to showing that Lockwood and not the appellant had perpetrated the violence on the deceased which caused his death; and (3) the trial judge failed to warn the jury at all or adequately upon the danger of acting upon the uncorroborated evidence of Lockwood against the appellant.

Ormod LJ: ... It is apparent ... that the jury were faced with an exceedingly difficult task in deciding (if it was not a joint enterprise with violence as a common purpose) which of these two men actually killed the deceased. There was no evidence other than their own which threw any direct light on this point. Indirect evidence, of which there was some but not very much, assumed a crucial importance in the attempt to distinguish between the two accused men. It was of two kinds, the medical evidence and the evidence of the nature and disposition of each of them ...

[After rejecting the first ground of appeal, he continued.]

The second ground of appeal raises an entirely different and more difficult question. It challenges a ruling on evidence which was made by the learned judge in the course of the evidence of Mrs Firth, Lockwood's mistress, who was a witness for the prosecution. She was called to give evidence of conversations with both Bracewell and Lockwood after the crime.

Her witness statement, however, included the following passage: 'Brian Lockwood was a very violent man especially after drink. Whilst we were at Brenda's house he struck me with the back of his hand on my nose, after he had come home drunk one night. This assault on me caused a broken nose and I had to have an operation to re-set it. We have had numerous fights, Brian and I, but the trouble with Brian is that once he starts he doesn't stop. About 12 months ago, whilst we were at 31 King Edward Avenue, Horsforth, Brian assaulted me again. This was because he had made an insulting remark about me at Brenda's and I walked home and locked him out. He broke a window in the back living room and he also broke the door window trying to get in. He came into the house and came upstairs. I had locked the bedroom door but he broke that off its hinges. He dragged me downstairs, thumped me about the head and body and after I had fallen to the floor he then kicked me everywhere over my whole body with his boots on. It was on this occasion that he tried to strangle me with his hands round my neck. I had severe bruising to my head and body and I couldn't move for two days nor could I swallow or move my head. Once he started these assaults he did not appear to be able to stop himself.'

The prosecution, of course, did not refer to this part of her statement, but Mr Steer, on behalf of the applicant, wished to introduce it and proposed to cross-examine her upon it. Counsel for the prosecution and for Lockwood both objected that the evidence was inadmissible on the ground that it was simply evidence of propensity and, therefore, irrelevant. Boreham J accepted their submissions and disallowed Mr Steer's cross-examination upon it.

In this court, Mr Steer submitted that the learned judge was wrong. He relied upon *Miller* (1952) and *Lowery v R* (1973), contending that in the case of a co-accused the only test of admissibility was relevance to the defence of the co-accused; unlike the prosecution, he did not have to get over what he called 'the hurdle of prejudice', and so the judge had no discretion in the matter. He particularly relied upon the phrase, 'the trouble with Brian is that once he starts he doesn't stop', in relation to the severity of the attack on the deceased.

A clear statement of the principle is to be found in an extract from the judgment of the Supreme Court of Victoria in *Lowery's* case (*supra*) which was cited with approval by Lord Morris in giving the opinion of the Privy Council in that case: 'It is, however, established by the highest authority that in criminal cases the Crown is precluded from leading evidence that does no more than show that the accused has a disposition or propensity or is the sort of person likely to commit the crime charged ... It is, we think, one thing to say such evidence is excluded when tendered by the Crown in proof of guilt, but quite another to say it is excluded when tendered by the accused in disproof of his own guilt. We see no reason of policy or fairness which justifies or requires the exclusion of evidence relevant to prove the innocence of an accused person.' Lord Morris went on to say that evidence was relevant if it tended to show that the version of the facts put forward by the one co-accused was more probable than that put forward by the other.

The question, therefore, is not whether the evidence goes to disposition or propensity but whether it is relevant, in the sense that it has some probative value.

In practice it is usually unnecessary to inquire too closely whether evidence of this kind has any probative value. The problem generally arises in connection with evidence tendered by the Crown, so that marginal cases can be dealt with by the exercise of the discretion. 'When in doubt, exclude', is a good working rule in such cases. But where the evidence is tendered by a co-accused, the test of relevance must be applied, and applied strictly, for if irrelevant, and therefore inadmissible evidence is admitted, the other accused is likely to be seriously prejudiced, and grave injustice may result. The judge has, of course, an overriding duty to prevent injustice, so far as the rules of evidence permit. Moreover, in doubtful cases there is considerable scope for differences of judicial opinion as to whether the evidence does or does not make it more likely that one of the co-accused committed the act in question.

In the present case the proposition upon which the applicant relies, in its broadest terms, can be formulated in this way: 'A man who has a history of violence towards his wife or mistress is more likely to attack a man in the course of a burglary, than a man who has no history of domestic violence.' Most people would regard such a proposition as highly dubious, if not definitely unsound, and Mr Steer did not attempt to support it in that form. He argued, however, that in a narrower sense the proposition was sound. He put it in this form: 'A man who, when he uses violence to his mistress, does not know when to stop, is more likely to have been guilty of a violent assault on a man in the course of a burglary than a man who has not used violence to his wife or mistress.' Opinions upon the validity of this proposition may differ widely. Without the benefit of statistical correlations or experience, it can only be a matter of opinion, and in such a case as the present the onus of satisfying the judge as to its validity must be on the party tendering the evidence.

There is a further point of some importance in this case. In both Miller (*supra*) and *Lowery v R* (*supra*) the evidence tendered was incontrovertible. In *Miller*, (*supra*) it was the fact that between certain specified dates the co-accused was in prison; in *Lowery's* case (*supra*) it was the results of certain psychological tests which could not be disputed, although the proper inference to be drawn from them might be in issue. In the instant case, the evidence of Mrs Firth was likely to be strongly denied by Lockwood, so that before they could use her evidence the jury would have had to decide whether it was true. It could, of course, only be relevant, ie of probative value, at that stage, if it were true. There are obvious objections to putting a co-accused in a position of having to fight two quite different battles at the same time.

For these reasons we think that the learned judge was right to exclude this evidence at the stage when his ruling was made. We shall, however, have to come back to this matter later ...

[After rejecting the third ground of appeal, he continued.]

In the ordinary way, all the grounds of appeal having been rejected, the application for leave to appeal would be dismissed, but there are a number of matters which have caused us considerable anxiety and have led us to consider whether in the light of the evidence as a whole this verdict of murder can be regarded as safe and satisfactory.

Our principal concern is whether there was, in fact, sufficient evidence to justify the jury in discriminating between these two men and identifying either one of them as the killer ...

There is another factor which may have worked an injustice to Bracewell. As the trial proceeded it became clear that an important aspect of Lockwood's defence was that he was an experienced burglar of a strictly non-violent type with a cool head in emergencies, whereas Bracewell was inexperienced, nervous, excitable and possibly to some extent under the influence of drink. By developing this line of defence Lockwood clearly put in issue, and therefore made relevant, his disposition or 'propensity', because he was relying upon it himself. The evidence of his behaviour to his mistress, Mrs Firth, might well be thought to be inconsistent with the portrait of himself which he was painting. Consequently, this material became relevant at this stage. Mr Steer would have been fully entitled to cross-examine Lockwood upon it and, if he disputed it, to call Mrs Firth or have her recalled for cross-examination. This is not intended in any way as a criticism of Mr Steer's conduct of this case, because, as he explained to us, he thought that all he would get from Lockwood would be a strong denial which might prejudice Bracewell in the eyes of the jury. Nonetheless, this evidence, if known to the jury, might have led them to be, at least, sceptical about Lockwood's picture of himself as a self-controlled man who could keep his head in a crisis.

For these reasons, coupled with the absence of any strong warning of the dangers of relying on the evidence of either of the accused, we are left in real doubt about this verdict; we do not feel that it is safe and, accordingly, we think it our duty to quash the conviction for murder against Bracewell and to treat the two men alike by substituting a conviction for manslaughter, and imposing the same sentence in Bracewell's case as in the case of Lockwood.[26]

Lui Mei-lin v R (1989, Privy Council)

Lord Roskill: ... The appellant was one of three defendants jointly charged on two counts (the first and second counts in the indictment), one of having forged dies with intent to defraud, the other of having forged valuable securities. The first defendant was named Lui Kan-por. The appellant was the third defendant. Yick Hak-kan was the second defendant. Yick Wai-ming was the fourth defendant. The third and fourth counts in the indictment were against the second defendant

---

26. 68 Cr App R 44.

alone, while a fifth count was against the first defendant alone. The first defendant, the appellant and the fourth defendant were all convicted on counts one and two. The second defendant was acquitted on counts three and four. The first defendant was also convicted on the fifth count. Substantial prison sentences were imposed on all three defendants so convicted. Subsequent appeals to the Court of Appeal by the first and fourth defendants against their convictions on counts one and two succeeded on the ground of misdirection by the trial judge. Retrials were ordered. The appellant's appeal against her convictions was dismissed.

The issue involved in the appellant's appeal to the Court of Appeal and now to this Board is entirely different from the issues involved in the appeals by the other defendants. On 11 June 1986 the first defendant was interviewed by and made a statement to the police. That statement, which their Lordships have read, beyond doubt incriminated the appellant. The prosecution sought to adduce that statement in evidence against its maker, the first defendant. The admissibility of the statement was challenged. At the outset of the trial a *voir dire* was held to determine whether or not the statement had been made voluntarily. The trial judge held that the statement was made as a result of inducements by a police officer. He accordingly excluded the statement on the ground that it was not made voluntarily. The first defendant in due course gave evidence in his own defence. He admitted that he had taken part in the arrangements for printing stamps, but had done so innocently, having been misled by the appellant. He was cross-examined on behalf of the second and fourth defendants. There is no doubt that his oral evidence differed in a number of material respects (the details do not now matter), from what he had said in the excluded statement. The appellant's counsel naturally cross-examined the first defendant on the basis that the oral evidence was false. He sought the leave of the trial judge further to cross-examine the first defendant on the excluded statement as being an inconsistent statement previously made by the first defendant. Counsel for the Crown opposed the application, relying on a previous decision of the Court of Appeal in *Yu Tit-hoi v R* [1983] HKLR 7. The trial judge was of course bound by that decision and refused the application for leave to cross-examine the first defendant on his statement. A further application on behalf of the appellant for a separate trial was also refused.

When the appellant appealed to the Court of Appeal that court also held that the appeal must fail because it too was bound by the decision in *Yu Tit-hoi v R* and indeed by later decisions following that decision. Power JA in a separate judgment, while accepting that the court was so bound, expressed the view that it was 'unfortunate that [the court was] not free to consider the [appellant's] arguments ...'. On 18 December 1987 special leave to appeal to the Board was given.

Since the Hong Kong decisions to which their Lordships have just referred were given, the same issue arose for decision in England in *R v Rowson* (1985). In that case the trial judge had ruled that a statement made by one co-accused was inadmissible in that the relevant rule of the Judges' Rules (see *Practice Note* (1964)) had been broken. Counsel for other co-accused in due course sought to cross-examine the maker of that statement on its content when he gave evidence. The trial judge allowed the facts alleged in the statement to be put to the maker of the statement but declined to allow the jury to be told that the facts emanated from the statement which he had already excluded. All the accused were convicted but the two co-accused appealed on the ground that their counsel had an unfettered right to cross-examine on the statement and had been prevented from exercising that right. The Court of Appeal, Criminal Division, in a judgment delivered by Robert Goff LJ, held that the submission was well-founded though the court applied the proviso and dismissed the appeals. The attention of the court was not, it seems, drawn to the relevant Hong Kong decisions. It is therefore clear that there has been a divergence of view between the Court of Appeal in Hong Kong on the one hand and in England on the other which their Lordships must now resolve.

The decision in *Yu Tit-hoi v R* was founded on the decisions of the Court of Criminal Appeal in *R v Treacy* (1944) and *R v Rice* (1963). In the former case the Crown had not sought to put in evidence, as part of the prosecution case, a statement made by a defendant charged with murder (there was no co-accused in that case) but when the defendant gave evidence in his own defence he was allowed to be cross-examined on that statement. This, as the Court of Appeal held, was plainly wrong and the conviction for murder was quashed. Much reliance was placed by the Court of Appeal in *Yu Tit-hoi v R* on the statement in the judgment of the Court of Criminal Appeal delivered by Humphreys J that a statement made by a person under arrest was either admissible or not admissible. The judge went on: 'If it is admissible, the proper course for the prosecution is to prove it, give it in evidence, let the statement if it is in writing be made an exhibit, so that everybody knows what it is and everybody can inquire into it and do what they think right about it. If it is not admissible, nothing more ought to be heard of it, and it is quite a mistake to think that a document can be made admissible in evidence which is otherwise inadmissible simply because it is put to a person in cross-examination.'

In *R v Rice* the same principle was applied to the use by the prosecution of a statement made by one co-accused against another co-accused. But their Lordships emphasise that neither case was concerned, as the present case is concerned and as *Yu Tit-hoi v R* and *R v Rowson* were concerned, with the attempted use by a co-accused of an excluded statement made by another co-accused.

Counsel for the appellant placed great reliance on the decision of the House of Lords in *Murdoch v Taylor* (1965). The question there arose under s 1(f)(iii) of the Criminal Evidence Act 1898. The House decided that, once a co-accused had 'given evidence against' another co-accused, the latter was under the statute entitled without restriction to cross-examine the former as to character and to put his previous convictions to him ...

Counsel for the Crown invited their Lordships to distinguish *Murdoch v Taylor* on the ground that the rights there in question arose under a statute and that what was there allowed to be put in cross-examination were the previous convictions of the co-accused. Their Lordships agree that this is so but find no sufficient ground of distinction in that fact. Ever since s 5 of the Criminal Procedure Act 1865 ... was enacted (this section is exactly reproduced in s 14 of the Evidence Ordinance (Cap 8) of Hong Kong) it has been permissible in every criminal and indeed in every civil trial to cross-examine a witness as to any previous inconsistent statement made by him in writing or reduced into writing subject, where the inconsistent statement is said to be in writing, to his attention first being called to those parts of any writing which were to be used in order to contradict him. The only limit on the right of a co-accused to cross-examine another co-accused in these circumstances is, in their Lordships' opinion, relevancy. If one co-accused has given evidence incriminating another it must be relevant for the latter to show, if he can, that the former has on some other occasion given inconsistent evidence and thus is unworthy of belief.

Counsel for the Crown also argued before their Lordships that *R v Rowson* was wrongly decided and should not be followed. With respect their Lordships disagree. That decision is entirely in line with the principles which their Lordships have endeavoured to enunciate and is clearly consistent with the decisions in *R v Miller* and *Murdoch v Taylor*. Their Lordships respectfully agree with the distinction which the Court of Appeal, Criminal Division, drew in *R v Rowson* between *R v Treacy* and *R v Rice* on the one hand and the case then before that court where it was, as already stated, counsel for one co-accused who sought to cross-examine another co-accused on his excluded statement. When Humphreys J said in *R v Treacy* that 'nothing more ought to be heard of it' he clearly meant that nothing more ought to be heard of the excluded statement, as between the prosecution and the defendant. The judge plainly did not have in mind the possibility of a co-accused subsequently seeking to make use of the excluded statement, for in that case there was no co-accused. It follows that their Lordships have also reached the conclusion, with great respect to the Court of Appeal, that *Yu Tit-hoi v R* and the later Hong Kong cases following it were wrongly decided and should not be followed. As already pointed out, their Lordships have noted that in the present case Power JA clearly had reservations as to the correctness of those decisions.

Counsel for the Crown pressed on their Lordships the submission that to allow a co-accused complete freedom to cross-examine on an excluded statement could give rise to difficult questions how far, if at all, a trial judge should explain to a jury why it was that they were suddenly hearing of this statement and perhaps even seeing it for the first time at a comparatively late stage of the trial ... Their Lordships doubt if it is possible to state general principles which should be uniformly applied in every case where the question arises. But ... they are clearly of the view that the trial judge should warn the jury that they must not use the statement in any way as evidence in support of the prosecution's case and that its only relevance is to test the credibility of the evidence which the maker of the statement has given against his co-accused. Their Lordships consider that as a general rule the trial judge should briefly tell the jury why the statement had previously been excluded and cannot therefore be relied on by the prosecution to prove its case, as for example that it was or may well have been procured by inducement. It should be remembered that in cross-examination as to credit the cross-examiner is bound by the answers which he receives and that it is not legitimate to reopen all the circumstances in which the excluded statement was taken. In many cases, as in the present, the trial judge may well think it right to remind the jury that the maker of the statement may well have a motive for incriminating a co-accused and that his or her evidence should be approached with extreme caution.

It was also suggested on behalf of the Crown that, if cross-examination on the excluded statement were to be permitted, the trial judge might have to carry out what was described as a balancing exercise, balancing the interests of the maker of the statement against the interests of the co-accused on whose behalf it was sought to cross-examine, before deciding whether or not to permit the proposed cross-examination. Their Lordships disagree. In their view the right to cross-examine is, as Lord Donovan stated in *Murdoch v Taylor*, unfettered, the only limit being relevancy. If the statement contains irrelevant matter the trial judge would no doubt insist that that irrelevant matter should not be referred to and, if necessary, excised from any copies of the statement which the jury might be allowed to see ...[27]

---

27. [1989] 1 All ER 359.

CHAPTER 10

THE COURSE OF TESTIMONY

There are three golden rules which, if followed faithfully, will ensure that you understand this part of evidence law. The first rule is that you should leave your books and go into a court. The second is that, once you are there, you should watch and listen carefully. The third rule is that you should repeat this process frequently. When you have got use to doing this, the rather dry topics dealt with in chapters like this will make much more sense and will consequently be remembered more readily. Watching films of American trials, whether fictional or otherwise, is not a substitute for going into court yourself. American and English procedures and terminology differ and it is indiscreet to confuse the two. Do not copy the mistakes of journalists who use expressions such as 'take the stand' instead of 'go into the witness-box'. It doesn't matter to them, but it will matter to you one day if you follow their example and are made to look foolish in court when you are appearing for a client.

I have divided what follows into five sections, each dealing with a particular type of problem. The first is concerned with the extent to which a witness may refresh his memory from an earlier written account of the events about which evidence is to be given. The second section covers the situation where a witness wants to support the credibility of his testimony by showing that he was giving the same account of the events under investigation before trial – in other words, that his story has not changed in any significant way.

The third section deals with witnesses who are allegedly 'hostile'. A hostile witness is *one who is not desirous of telling the truth at the instance of the party calling him*. This definition, by JF Stephen, is better than any other because it makes it clear that a witness may be 'hostile' through fear, and that it is not *necessary* for there to be hostility in the ordinary sense of the word.

The fourth section, on cross-examination, highlights a case which has important things to say about the general approach to be adopted by counsel, and which is too often ignored in practice. Three particular difficulties are then considered: cross-examination on a previous inconsistent statement, cross-examination of police about their behaviour in other cases where this may be relevant to a current prosecution, and cross-examination under the restrictions imposed by the Sexual Offences (Amendment) Act 1976.

It is sometimes said that answers given to 'collateral questions' in cross-examination are 'final' or 'conclusive'. This is often misunderstood by students who think that if you are cross-examining about a collateral matter and you get an answer, you are stuck with it and cannot pursue the point any further. It does not mean this at all. What it does mean is that if you are cross-examining about a collateral matter you may not later call evidence to contradict an answer given by the witness. To this general rule there are some exceptions, and they are referred to in the fifth section.

REFRESHING MEMORY

Maugham v Hubbard (1828, Court of King's Bench)

ASSUMPSIT for money had and received. Plea, not guilty. At the trial before Lord *Tenterden* CJ, at the *Middlesex* sittings after last term it appeared that the action was brought to recover from the assignees of the bankrupt 20*l*. paid by the plaintiff to the bankrupt before his bankruptcy. The bankrupt being called as a witness on the part of the plaintiff stated, that he had dealt with the plaintiff several years; that in *November* 1822, 20*l*. was received from the plaintiff, which was not carried to the account. A rough cash-book kept by the plaintiff was then put into his hands; in which there was the following entry: '4th of *November* 1822. Dr–R Lancaster. Check 20*l*. RL.' The bankrupt then said, 'The entry of 20*l* in the plaintiff's book has my initials, written at the time; I have no recollection that I received the money; I know nothing but by the book; but seeing my initials, I have no doubt that I received the money.' It was contended that the paper on which this entry was made ought to have been stamped as a receipt; but Lord *Tenterden* CJ was of opinion, that though it was not itself admissible in evidence to prove the payment of the money the witness might use it to refresh his memory; and that his having said that he had no doubt that he received the money was sufficient evidence of the fact. A verdict was found for the plaintiff, but liberty was reserved to the defendant to move to enter a nonsuit, if the Court should be of opinion that this evidence ought not to have been received.

Robinson now moved accordingly, and contended, that as the entry in the plaintiff's own book could be used for no other purpose than that of proving the receipt of the money by the bankrupt, it ought to have been stamped. Here the witness stated that he had no recollection of the fact of the receipt of the money. The effect of allowing the witness to look at the entry to refresh his memory was to make it operate as a receipt, and it ought, therefore, to have been stamped ...

Lord Tenterden CJ: In order to make the paper itself evidence of the receipt of the money it ought to have been stamped. The consequence of its not having been stamped might be, that the party who paid the money, in the event of the death of the person who received it, would lose his evidence of such payment. Here the witness, on seeing the entry signed by himself, said that he had no doubt that he had received the money. The paper itself was not used as evidence of the receipt of the money, but only to enable the witness to refresh his memory; and when he said that he had no doubt he had received the money there was *sufficient* parol evidence to prove the payment.

Bayley J: Where a witness called to prove the execution of a deed sees his signature to the attestation, and he says that he is, therefore, sure that he saw the party execute the deed, that is a sufficient proof of the execution of the deed, though the witness add that he has no recollection of the fact of the execution of the deed.

Rule refused.[1]

Topham v M'Gregor (1844)

In the course of the trial, one of the witnesses stated that she knew that a certain circumstance, with reference to which she had been examined, occurred at the

---

1. 8 B & C 14, 108 ER 948.

time mentioned by her (namely, in the month of March 1830), because she remembered, that, some time during that month, the weather was for several days extremely warm for the season of the year; and because she knew that it was whilst the weather was in this state that the occurrence of which she was called upon to speak took place. In order to corroborate her testimony as to the peculiar state of the weather at the period mentioned, it was proposed to read an article from a newspaper, which had been published at the time, and which contained a statement confirmatory of the witness's evidence. This having been objected to, the gentleman who had edited and published the newspaper was called, and he stated that the article referred to had been furnished by a gentleman who had, in the year 1830 and for some time previous, been in the habit of writing such articles for the newspaper in question; he likewise stated that the manuscript of the said article had been diligently searched for, but that it could not be found. The writer of the article was then called, and he stated that he had no recollection of having communicated the particular article referred to; he stated, however, that, at the time mentioned by the editor, he had been in the habit of furnishing him with articles with reference to phenomena connected with the weather, and he swore that the statements contained in those articles were invariably true.

Kelly [for the defendants] then submitted that the article should be read.

Knowles [for the plaintiffs] objected that the article could not be read, because it amounted to mere evidence of a declaration by the witness, which could not be evidence in the cause.

Rolfe B, however, thought that the article might be used for the purpose of refreshing the witness's memory; and that he might be asked, whether, looking at the article in question, he had any doubt that the fact really was as therein stated.[2]

R v Richardson (1971, Court of Appeal)

The defendant was tried for offences of burglary and attempted burglary committed about 18 months earlier. The civilian witnesses called for the prosecution were told outside court before giving evidence that they might refresh their memories, if they wished, by reading the statements which they had made to the police a few weeks after the offences. Each of the witnesses did this. On appeal, the question arose whether this had been proper.

Sachs LJ: ... [I]t is necessary to consider what should be the general approach of the court to there being shown in this way to witnesses their statements – which were not 'contemporaneous' within the meaning of that word as normally applied to documents used to refresh memory.

First, it is to be observed that it is the practice of the courts not to allow a witness to refresh his memory in the witness-box by reference to written statements unless made contemporaneously. Secondly, it has been recognised in a circular issued in April 1969 with the approval of the Lord Chief Justice and the judges of the Queen's Bench Division (the repositories of the common law) that witnesses for the prosecution in criminal cases are normally (though not in all circumstances) entitled, if they so request, to copies of any statements taken from them by police officers. Thirdly, it is to be noted that witnesses for the defence

---

2. 1 Car & Kir 320, 174 ER 829.

are normally, as is known to be the practice, allowed to have copies of their statements and to refresh their memories from them at any time up to the moment when they go into the witness-box – indeed, Mr Sedgemore [for the defendant] was careful not to submit that there was anything wrong about that. Fourthly, no one has ever suggested that in civil proceedings witnesses may not see their statements up to the time when they go into the witness-box. One has only to think for a moment of witnesses going into the box to deal with accidents which took place five or six years previously to conclude that it would be highly unreasonable if they were not allowed to see them.

Is there, then, anything wrong in the witnesses in this case having been offered an opportunity to see that which they were entitled to ask for and to be shown on request? In a case such as the present, is justice more likely to be done if a witness may not see a statement made by him at a time very much closer to that of the incident?

Curiously enough, these questions are very bare of authority. Indeed, the only case which has a direct bearing on this issue is one which was decided not in this country but on appeal in the Supreme Court of Hong Kong in 1966: *Lau Pak Ngam v The Queen* (1966). In the view of each member of this court this case contains some sage observations, two of which are apt to be quoted. One of them is: 'Testimony in the witness-box becomes more a test of memory than of truthfulness if witnesses are deprived of the opportunity of checking their recollection beforehand by reference to statements or notes made at a time closer to the events in question.'

The other is: 'Refusal of access to statements would tend to create difficulties for honest witnesses but be likely to do little to hamper dishonest witnesses.'

With those views this court agrees. It is true that by the practice of the courts of this country a line is drawn at the moment when a witness enters the witness-box; when giving evidence there in chief he cannot refresh his memory except by a document which, to quote the words of *Phipson on Evidence*, 11th edn (1970), p 634, para 1528: 'must have been written either at the time of the transaction or so shortly afterwards that the facts were fresh in his memory.' (Incidentally, this definition does provide a measure of elasticity and should not be taken to confine witnesses to an over-short period.) This is, moreover, a practice which the courts can enforce: when a witness is in the box the court can see that he complies with it.

The courts, however, must take care not to deprive themselves by new, artificial rules of practice of the best chances of learning the truth. The courts are under no compulsion unnecessarily to follow on a matter of practice the lure of the rules of logic in order to produce unreasonable results which would hinder the course of justice. Obviously it would be wrong if several witnesses were handed statements in circumstances which enabled one to compare with another what each had said. But there can be no general rule (which, incidentally, would be unenforceable, unlike the rule as to what can be done in the witness-box) that witnesses may not before trial see the statements which they made at some period reasonably close to the time of the event which is the subject of the trial. Indeed, one can imagine many cases, particularly those of a complex nature, where such a rule would militate very greatly against the interests of justice ...[3]

---

3.   [1969] QB 299.

R v Westwell (1976, Court of Appeal)

Bridge LJ: ... There is no general rule that prospective witnesses may not, before giving evidence at a trial, see the statements which they made at or near the time of the events of which they are to testify. They may see them whether they make a request to do so or merely accept an offer to allow them to do so. On the other hand, there is no rule that witnesses must be allowed to see their statements before giving evidence. There may be cases where there is reason to suppose that the witness has some sinister or improper purpose in wanting to see his statement and it is in the interests of justice that he should be denied the opportunity. Examples are suggested in the Home Office circular and in the judgment of this court in *R v Richardson* (1971). However, in most cases and particularly where, as often happens, there is a long interval between the alleged offence and the trial, the interests of justice are likely to be best served and witnesses will be more fairly treated if, before giving evidence, they are allowed to refresh their recollection by reference to their own statement made near the time of the events in question. As was said by the Supreme Court of Hong Kong in 1966, in passages quoted with approval by this court in *R v Richardson*, if a witness is deprived of this opportunity his testimony in the witness-box becomes more a test of memory than truthfulness; and refusal of access to statements would tend to create difficulties for honest witnesses but would be likely to do little to hamper dishonest witnesses. We have all, from time to time, seen the plight of an apparently honest witness, subject to captious questioning about minor differences between his evidence in the witness-box and the statement he made long ago and has never seen since, although his tormentor has it in his hand and has studied it in detail. Although such cross-examination frequently generates in the jury obvious sympathy with the witness and obvious irritation with the cross-examiner, it must leave a witness who has come to court to do his honest best with a smarting sense of having been treated unfairly.

Neither in the approved statement in the Home Office circular, nor in the judgment of the court in *R v Richardson*, is it laid down that the Crown must inform the defence that a prosecution witness has been allowed to look at his written statement before giving evidence. In *R v Richardson* the defence first discovered the fact for themselves in the course of cross-examination of a prosecution witness. The court made no criticism of the Crown on that account, nor was it invited to do so. Moreover, the decision of the trial judge, refusing to allow previous witnesses to be recalled for cross-examination about their statements, was upheld because in the particular facts of that case no prejudice was thereby caused to the defence.

Since hearing the argument in this appeal, our attention has been called to the decision of the Divisional Court in *Worley v Bentley* (1976) in which the same point arose. The court held that it was desirable but not essential that the defence should be informed that the witnesses have seen their statements. We agree. In some cases the fact that a witness has read his statement before going into the witness-box may be relevant to the weight which can properly be attached to his evidence and injustice might be caused to the defendant if the jury were left in ignorance of that fact.

Accordingly, if the prosecution is aware that statements have been seen by witnesses it will be appropriate to inform the defence. But if, for any reason, this is not done, the omission cannot of itself be a ground for acquittal. If the prosecution tell the defence that the witness has been allowed to see his statement the defence can make such use of the information as it thinks prudent, but in any event the defence, where such fact may be material, can ask the witness directly when giving evidence whether the witness has recently seen his statement. Where such information is material it does not ultimately matter whether it is volunteered by the prosecution or elicited by the defence. If the mere fact that the prosecution had not volunteered the information were a bar to conviction, this would be an artificial and arbitrary rule more appropriate to a game or a sporting contest than to a judicial process. The question for the court is whether, in the event, the trial can be continued without prejudice or risk of injustice to the defendant ...[4]

R v Cheng (1976, Court of Appeal)

The defendant was charged with selling Chinese heroin in Soho. Over a considerable period of time police officers had kept observation and had made detailed notes of what they had seen. The defendant did not stand trial until some three years after the alleged offences. During this period one of the officers in the case transferred from the Metropolitan Police to another police force and handed in the relevant notebook with all his others to the Metropolitan Police. The notebook was then lost. There existed a statement which the officer had made with the assistance of his notes. It was not a full transcription of the notes because the statement omitted references to other persons who were under observation. The prosecution did not claim that the statement was a document made reasonably soon after the event to which it referred, but the trial judge allowed the officer to refresh his memory from it while giving evidence. Was he right to do so?

Lawton LJ: The sole question in this case has been whether the judge acted properly and in accordance with law in allowing Constable Moore to refresh his memory from the statement.

Mr Wright, on behalf of the Crown, has reminded the court that in *Richardson* (1971) Sachs LJ giving the judgment of the court said this: 'The courts, however, must take care not to deprive themselves by new, artificial rules of practice of the best chances of learning the truth. The courts are under no compulsion unnecessarily to follow the lure of the rules of logic in order to produce results on a matter of practice which are unreasonable and would hinder the course of justice.'

It is because of that approach by this court as recently as 1971 that we have felt it necessary to find out how the rules about refreshing memory developed. As far as the researches of counsel go (and their researches seem to be supported by text books), the first reported case in which the problem of what documents a witness could use to refresh his memory was discussed was *Doe d Church and Phillips v Perkins* (1790). It is clear from the facts of that case that up to that time there had been no certain rule about what witnesses could look at when giving evidence for the purpose of making a deposition. The witness whose evidence was under consideration in that case had been allowed to refer to a document which had been substantially prepared by her solicitor. Lord Kenyon CJ ruled that this was irregular.

In the 60 years which followed, the problem of what witnesses could look at to refresh their memories came before the courts in a number of cases. It is manifest that as the years went by the courts came to the conclusion that too strict a rule was not in the interest of justice. It is not necessary for us to deal with each of the

---

4.   [1976] 2 All ER 812.

cases which were considered in the 60 odd years after the decision in *Doe d Church and Phillips v Perkins (supra)*. It suffices to refer to two.

In *Burton v Plummer* (1834), the question before the court was whether a witness could look at a copy of an original note which he made. The court adjudged that he could; but he had to be able to say that the copy was an accurate copy of the original note.

It was almost inevitable after that case that some lawyer would raise the question as to what was an accurate copy. That very problem was considered by the House of Lords in *Horne v Mackenzie* (1839). The point arose in this way: I read from the headnote: 'A, a surveyor, made a survey or report, which he furnished to his employers: being afterwards called as a witness, he produced a printed copy of this report, on the margin of which he had, two days before, to assist him in giving his explanations as a witness, made a few jottings. The report had been made up from his original notes, of which it was in substance, though not in words, a transcript ... In other words, as appears clear when one looks at the details of the case what he was looking at in the witness-box was not strictly a copy at all of his original note. He was allowed to refresh his memory from it and the House of Lords seems to have taken the view, albeit *obiter*, that there was nothing wrong in his doing so.

The judgment of the House was delivered by Lord Cottenham: he said at p 645: 'If your Lordships think that there should be a new trial on this ground, it will be unnecessary to give any decision on the question of evidence. But I may say that in my opinion the witness was, under the circumstances of this case, entitled to refer to the paper to refresh his memory.'

In our judgment that opinion of the Lord Chancellor resolves this case. What the police constable was doing in this case was what the surveyor had done in that case. He had transcribed that part of his note which he thought was relevant. We can see nothing wrong in that. Indeed if we had felt bound to say that it was wrong for him to refresh his memory from his statement, we would have brought about an absurdity, because it is now established by *Richardson (supra)* to which I have already referred that a witness can see his original statement outside court. If he could read it right up to the court door and learn it off by heart, but was forbidden in the witness-box to look at it at all, this would be a triumph of legalism over common sense.

What seems to us to be the position is this. If the statement in this case, or any other transcription of notes in other cases, is substantially what is in the notes and there is evidence to that effect, then the judge should allow the witness to refresh his memory from the statement or transcription as the case may be. But if, after investigation, it turns out that the statement or transcription bears little relation to the original note, then a different situation arises. The judge in the exercise of his discretion would be entitled to refuse to allow a witness to refresh his memory from such an imperfect source of information ...[5]

R v Da Silva (1990, Court of Appeal)

The defendant was charged with robbery. One of the prosecution witnesses was allowed, after having begun his evidence, to retire and refresh his memory from a statement which he had given earlier to the police but had not been shown before going into the witness-box.

---

5.   63 Cr App R 20.

Stuart-Smith LJ: ... There are two main grounds of appeal. The first relates to the evidence of Collina. He was called by the Crown to give evidence of a conversation with the defendant which had taken place on 21 November 1986, in which the defendant had admitted his involvement in the crime. Collina had made a statement to this effect on 22 December 1986, in which he gave details of the conversation. He had not seen his witness statement before he came into the witness-box. When he came to give evidence, he said, to adopt the judge's summary since we do not have a transcript of Collina's evidence: 'I cannot remember now. It is a year ago. I did make a statement at the time.' Thereupon the judge intervened and invited the witness to withdraw and read his statement in the cells, he being a serving prisoner, under the supervision of a prison officer.

It appears that this incident occurred just before the midday break. This being done, counsel for the defendant submitted, in the absence of the jury, that this procedure was irregular. That submission has been renewed in this court. Mr Bradshaw [for the appellant] submits that there is a hard and fast division between contemporaneous statements, that is to say statements made at a time while the events that the witness is recording are fresh in his memory and those that are made at a later time. He submits that in the case of a contemporaneous statement, the witness can be permitted to refresh his memory from it provided he does so in the witness-box and the ground for the application for permission is properly laid. In the case of a statement that is not contemporaneous, a witness may refresh his memory by looking at the statement before he goes into the witness-box but not thereafter. In this case he submits that the statement, having been made a month after the events related, was not contemporaneous and was not treated as such by the judge. The judge did not make it clear whether he was treating the statement as a contemporaneous one or not.

Mr Kay, on behalf of the Crown, submits that in effect he did so, and that it was only as a matter of convenience, because the incident occurred just before the natural break in the proceedings, that the witness was invited to read the statement in the cells.

Mr Bradshaw has drawn our attention to *Reg v Graham* (1973), in which the court said that a judge should hesitate before deciding that a statement made 27 days after the event was contemporaneous. But the court was not saying that a statement made after that length of time could not be contemporaneous. It is a question of fact and degree in each case, and the matter should be investigated to see that the events were fresh in the witness's mind after the lapse of time. Much will depend on the nature of the evidence to be given. Where, for example, a witness purports to give a verbatim account of a conversation, the note will need to have been made much nearer the time than if he merely purports to give the general effect of a conversation.

We do not think that the judge treated the statement as a contemporaneous one. It does not appear that the proper foundation for so doing was laid, namely to ask the witness whether events were fresh in his mind when he made the statement. Moreover, if the statement had been treated as contemporaneous, the witness would have been allowed to refresh his memory in the witness-box and refer to it if need be.

In the alternative, Mr Kay submits that there is no rigid rule that even if the statement is not contemporaneous, a witness may in no circumstances look at it once he has started to give evidence. In *Archbold, Criminal Pleading Evidence & Practice*, 43rd edn (1988), p 470, the rule is stated in such terms. It is said, at para 4-294: 'A line is drawn at the moment when a witness enters the witness-box.' When giving evidence there in chief he cannot refresh his memory 'unless the document he wishes to use falls within the conditions prescribed by the memory refreshing rule'.

The quotations are from the judgment of the court given by Sachs LJ in *Reg v Richardson* (1971). The actual decision in that case was that where a long interval had elapsed between statements made fairly soon after events forming the subject matter of the prosecution, but not contemporaneously within the meaning given to that expression, witnesses might be shown their statements before going into the witness-box.

The passage cited in *Archbold* was therefore *obiter*, though it may be said to represent the generally accepted principle. But since in either case, that is to say both with contemporaneous statements and those that do not fall within that class, the witness is refreshing his memory, it may fairly be said that there is no logical reason why in the one case he must do it in the witness-box and in the other he must do it before he enters the witness-box and not once he has done so. Moreover, if a witness needs to refresh his memory, there is much to be said for it being apparent to the jury that he is doing so and for the jury knowing when the statement was made. What must be avoided is a witness simply reading his statement when he has no real recollection of events; but that can be avoided by removing the statement from him once he has read it to refresh his memory ...

In our judgment, therefore, it should be open to the judge, in the exercise of his discretion and in the interests of justice, to permit a witness who has begun to give evidence to refresh his memory from a statement made nearer to the time of events in question, even though it does not come within the definition of contemporaneous, provided he is satisfied: (1) that the witness indicates that he cannot now recall the details of events because of the lapse of time since they took place; (2) that he made a statement much nearer the time of the events and that the contents of the statement represented his recollection at the time he made it; (3) that he had not read the statement before coming into the witness-box; (4) that he wished to have an opportunity to read the statement before he continued to give evidence.

We do not think that it matters whether the witness withdraws from the witness-box and reads his statement, as he would do if he had had the opportunity before entering the witness-box, or whether he reads it in the witness-box. What is important is that if the former course is adopted, no communication must be had with the witness, other than to see that he can read the statement in peace. Moreover, if either course is adopted, the statement must be removed from him when he comes to give his evidence and he should not be permitted to refer to it again, unlike a contemporaneous statement which may be used to refresh memory while giving evidence.

In this case the initiative came from the judge, but it is clear that it is no ground of objection if the judge thinks it is in the interests of justice that he intervene: see *Reg v Fotheringham* (1975) and *Reg v Tyagi* (1986). In our judgment, it was open to the judge to permit the witness Collina to refresh his memory from the witness statement in the exercise of his discretion, because the conditions set out above were satisfied ...[6]

Senat v Senat (1965)

Sir Jocelyn Simon P: ... In my view the mere inspection of a document does not render it evidence which counsel inspecting it is bound to put in. I think that the

---

6.   [1990] 1 All ER 29.

true rules are as follows: Where a document is used to refresh a witness's memory, cross-examining counsel may inspect that document in order to check it, without making it evidence. Moreover he may cross-examine upon it without making it evidence provided that his cross-examination does not go further than the parts which are used for refreshing the memory of the witness: *Gregory v Tavernor* (1833). But if a party calls for and inspects a document held by the other party, he is bound to put it in evidence if he is required to do so: *Wharam v Routledge* (1805) ...[7]

Owen v Edwards (1983, Divisional Court)

At a trial before magistrates a police officer gave evidence against the accused without referring in the witness-box to any notes. He admitted in cross-examination that he had made notes and that he had referred to them outside court before giving evidence. Counsel for the defendant asked to see the notebook and was allowed to do so. But she was not allowed to cross-examine upon any of the entries relating to the case, on the basis that the book was not an exhibit and had not been referred to by the witness while giving evidence.

McNeill J: ... Curiously, the point whether or not an accused's representative may ask to see the notebook of a police officer, or indeed the statement of a witness, from which the witness has refreshed his memory not in the witness-box but outside the door of the court, has not been decided in England. There is a passage in *Archbold* (41st edn, 1982) para 4-324, which reads as follows: 'If the witness has not referred to any book in his evidence for the purpose of refreshing his memory, and has merely admitted in cross-examination that he did make a note, it has been held in Scotland that he cannot be compelled to produce the book: *Hinshelwood v Auld* (1926) SC (J) 4 (police officer's notebook).' The learned editors continue: 'It is unlikely that this decision would be applied in England or Wales. If, for example, the witness admitted that he had been refreshing his memory from the notebook outside the court door, it would be odd indeed if he could not be required to produce the document after entering the witness-box ...

The whole tenor of authority appears to indicate that the defence is entitled to see such documents, including notebooks and statements, from which memory has been refreshed subject, of course, only to the well-established rules that a witness can be cross-examined having refreshed his memory upon the material in his notebook from which he has refreshed his memory without the book being made evidence in the case, whereas if he is cross-examined beyond those limits into other matters, the cross-examiner takes the risk of the material being evidence and the document being exhibited and therefore available for use by the fact-finding tribunal.

As I say, the justices came to the conclusion that counsel was entitled to inspect the notebook but not entitled to cross-examine the witness on matters contained in it and which had not been referred to by the witness. It seems to me that on that aspect of the case I am in total agreement with the learned editors of *Archbold* in saying that the rules which apply to refreshing memory in the witness-box should be the same as those which apply if memory has been refreshed outside the door of the court or, in the words of the learned editor: 'It would be odd if it were otherwise.' It is not for this court on these facts to determine how much earlier than giving evidence the line is to be drawn. That

---

7.   [1965] P 172.

will be for the fact-finding tribunal or some other court to consider, if necessary. On the point of law as posed by the justices, my answer would be that they were wrong in law ...[8]

R v Virgo (1978, Court of Appeal)

The appellant was the head of the Obscene Publications Squad of the Metropolitan Police. He and a number of other officers were charged with conspiracy to accept bribes. Part of the evidence against Virgo came from a dealer in pornography called Humphreys who, when giving evidence, had refreshed his memory from contemporaneous diary entries which he had made.

Geoffrey Lane LJ: ... Mr Farquharson [for the appellant] submits that the judge was guilty of error in the way in which he dealt with those entries in the diaries ...

The diaries in question related to two years: 1971 and 1972 ... The prosecution, not unnaturally, sought to allow Humphreys to use various entries in those diaries to refresh his memory whilst giving evidence. The necessary permission was given and defending counsel, very properly, realising that it would be necessary to cross-examine the witness *in extenso* about the contents of the diaries, did not object; indeed may actually have encouraged the jury to have copies of the documents. At any rate copies were before the jury. The defence had no material upon which they could suggest to Humphreys that the entries were other than contemporaneous to the incidents which they purported to record, although they did not accept or concede that the entries were contemporaneously made.

The main attack was directed, as it had to be, towards showing that any references to 'Wally' in the diaries, of which there were many, were not references to Wally Virgo, the appellant, but were references to one of the other two Wallys with whom undoubtedly the witness Humphreys was acquainted or whom he knew. It that attack had succeeded, it would undoubtedly have destroyed Humphreys as a witness and would have resulted in Virgo's acquittal on the two specific counts 26 and 27. It is quite obvious that the attack did not succeed.

There is always a danger in circumstances such as these when attention has been focussed on a particular document for a long period of time, and when the document has been subjected to a minute and line by line analysis, as these diaries were, that the document will achieve an importance which it does not warrant. It was most important in this case that the status of these diaries should be clearly understood throughout the trial and particularly at the end of the trial when the learned judge came to sum up the matter to the jury.

Those diaries were never more, at best, than a means whereby Humphreys might be able to give accurate dates and accurate chapter and verse for the incidents in respect of which he was giving evidence. They were never more than documents prepared by Humphreys and Humphreys was a self-confessed dealer in pornography. He was an accomplice and he was, on any view, a highly unsavoury character in many other ways. His evidence, par excellence, required corroboration.

The learned judge made perfectly plain to the jury, in impeccable language at the outset of his direction, the general law relating to corroboration. No one complained about that for a moment, nor could they complain. So far as

---

8.   77 Cr App R 191.

Humphreys' diaries were concerned, not only did his evidence in general require corroboration, but by the same token, the answers which he gave about his diaries required corroboration. At the very highest, if the jury were convinced that the diaries were genuine, they showed a degree of consistency in Humphreys which otherwise might have been lacking, just as a complaint by the victim of a sexual assault, if made at the first reasonable opportunity thereafter, may show consistency in his or her evidence, though that analogy, one concedes, is not altogether apt. What the diaries could not under any circumstances do, was to support the oral evidence of Humphreys other than in a very limited way which we have already endeavoured to describe. In no way were they evidence of the truth of their contents ...[9]

PREVIOUS CONSISTENT STATEMENTS

R v Roberts (1942, Court of Criminal Appeal)

The defendant was convicted of the murder of his former girlfriend by shooting her with a rifle. The defence was that the death had been accidentally caused. At trial, the defence wished to call evidence from the defendant's father to the effect that his son, shortly after being arrested, had told him that there had been an accident. The trial judge held this evidence inadmissible.

Humphreys J: ... The second of the grounds of appeal is put in this way: 'That the learned judge was wrong in law in refusing to admit the evidence of the appellant's father as to the statement made to him by the appellant after his arrest.' That relates to a statement alleged to have been made by the accused to his father after his arrest and while he was in custody. The father, naturally, was allowed to see his son. In our view the judge was perfectly right in refusing to admit that evidence, because it was in law inadmissible. It might have been, and, perhaps, by some judges would have been, allowed to be given on the ground that it was the evidence which the defence desired to have given, was harmless, and there was no strenuous opposition on the part of the prosecution. Such evidence might have been allowed to be given, but the judge was perfectly entitled to take the view which he did, that in law that evidence was inadmissible. The law upon the matter is well-settled. The rule relating to this is sometimes put in this way, that a party is not permitted to make evidence for himself. That law applies to civil cases as well as to criminal cases. For instance, if A and B enter into an oral contract, and some time afterwards there is a difference of opinion as to what were the actual terms agreed upon and there is litigation about it, one of those persons would not be permitted to call his partner to say: 'My partner a day or two after told me what his view of the contract was and that he had agreed to do' so and so. So, in a criminal case, an accused person is not permitted to call evidence to show that, after he was charged with a criminal offence, he told a number of persons what his defence was going to be, and the reason for the rule appears to us to be that such testimony has no evidential value. It is because it does not assist in the elucidation of the matters in dispute that the evidence is said to be inadmissible on the ground that it is irrelevant. It would not help the jury in this case in the least to be told that the appellant said to a number of persons, whom he saw while he was awaiting his trial, or on bail if he was on bail; that his defence was this, that or the other. The

---

9.   67 Cr App R 323.

evidence asked to be admitted was that the father had been told by his son that it was an accident. We think the evidence was properly refused. Of course, if the statement had been made to the father just at the time of the shooting, that would have been a totally different matter, because it has always been regarded as admissible that a person should be allowed to give in evidence any statement accompanying an act so that it may explain the act. It was put by counsel for the appellant that the statement might be admissible on the ground that the accused had been asked in cross-examination, and it had been suggested to him in cross-examination that this story of accident was one which he had recently concocted. If any such question had been put, undeniably the evidence would have been admissible as showing it was not recently concocted, because the accused had said so on the very day the incident occurred. The answer is that no such question had been put, and no suggestion made, to the accused ...[10]

R v Storey & Anwar (1968, Court of Appeal)

Widgery LJ: ... We think it right to recognise that a statement made by the accused to the police, although it always forms evidence in the case against him, is not in itself evidence of the truth of the facts stated. A statement made voluntarily by an accused person to the police is evidence in the trial because of its vital relevance as showing the reaction of the accused when first taxed with the incriminating facts. If, of course, the accused admits the offence, then as a matter of shorthand one says that the admission is proof of guilt, and, indeed, in the end it is. But if the accused makes a statement which does not amount to an admission, the statement is not strictly evidence of the truth of what was said, but is evidence of the reaction of the accused which forms part of the general picture to be considered by the jury at the trial ...[11]

R v Pearce (1979, Court of Appeal)

The Lord Chief Justice: The judgment which I am about to read is the judgment of the court prepared by Lloyd J.

On July 5 1978 the appellant was convicted at Newport Crown Court of two counts of handling and fined £100 on each count. He now appeals against conviction by leave of the single judge.

The case raises an unusual question. It has been the practice to admit in evidence all unwritten and most written statements made by an accused person to the police whether they contain admissions or whether they contain denials of guilt. The only exception which readily comes to mind is the exclusion of any admission of a previous conviction. In this case however the judge has excluded two voluntary statements and part of an interview on the grounds that they are self-serving statements and as such are not admissible. If the judge is right it would mean that the practice of the courts over the last fifty years or more has been erroneous ...

In our view the present case can be disposed of within the principles stated in *Storey and Anwar* (1968) and *Donaldson* (1977). Those decisions will be found to contain all the guidance that is necessary in practice. We would ourselves summarise the principles as follows:

(1)   A statement which contains an admission is always admissible as a declaration against interest and is evidence of the facts admitted. With this

10.   [1942] 1 All ER 187.
11.   52 Cr App R 334.

exception a statement made by an accused person is never evidence of the facts in the statement.

(2) (a) A statement that is not an admission is admissible to show the attitude of the accused at the time when he made it. This however is not to be limited to a statement made on the first encounter with the police. The reference in *Storey* to the reaction of the accused 'when first taxed' should not be read as circumscribing the limits of admissibility. The longer the time that has elapsed after the first encounter the less the weight which will be attached to the denial. The judge is able to direct the jury about the value of such statements. (b) A statement that is not in itself an admission is admissible if it is made in the same context as an admission, whether in the course of an interview, or in the form of a voluntary statement. It would be unfair to admit only the statements against interest while excluding part of the same interview or series of interviews. It is the duty of the prosecution to present the case fairly to the jury; to exclude answers which are favourable to the accused while admitting those unfavourable would be misleading. (c) The prosecution may wish to draw attention to inconsistent denials. A denial does not become an admission because it is inconsistent with another denial. There must be many cases however where convictions have resulted from such inconsistencies between two denials.

(3) Although in practice most statements are given in evidence even when they are largely self-serving, there may be a rare occasion when an accused produces a carefully prepared written statement to the police, with a view to it being made part of the prosecution evidence. The trial judge would plainly exclude such a statement as inadmissible ...[12]

R v Sharp (1988, House of Lords)

Lord Havers: My Lords, the question certified for your Lordships' decision is in the following form: 'Where a statement made to a police officer out of court by a defendant contains both admissions and self-exculpatory parts do the exculpatory parts constitute evidence of the truth of the facts alleged therein?'

... In *Duncan* (1981) Lord Lane CJ said: 'Where a "mixed" statement is under consideration by the jury in a case where the defendant has not given evidence, it seems to us that the simplest, and, therefore, the method most likely to produce a just result, is for the jury to be told that the whole statement, both the incriminating parts and the excuses or explanations, must be considered by them in deciding where the truth lies. It is, to say the least, not helpful to try to explain to the jury that the exculpatory parts of the statement are something less than evidence of the facts they state. Equally, where appropriate, as it usually will be, the judge may, and should, point out that the incriminating parts are likely to be true (otherwise why say them?), whereas the excuses do not have the same weight. Nor is there any reason why, again where appropriate, the judge should not comment in relation to the exculpatory remarks upon the election of the accused not to give evidence.'

... My Lords, the weight of authority and common sense leads me to prefer the direction to the jury formulated in *Duncan* to an attempt to deal differently with the different parts of a mixed statement. How can a jury fairly evaluate the facts in the admission unless they can evaluate the facts in the excuse or explanation? It is only if the jury think that the facts set out by way of excuse or explanation

---

12. 69 Cr App R 365.

might be true that any doubt is cast on the admission, and it is surely only because the excuse or explanation might be true that it is thought fair that it should be considered by the jury. I agree with Lawton LJ that a jury will make little of a direction that attempts to draw a distinction between evidence which is evidence of facts and evidence in the same statement which whilst not being evidence of facts is nevertheless evidentiary material of which they may make use in evaluating evidence which is evidence of the facts. One only has to write out the foregoing sentence to see the confusion it engenders. I cannot improve upon the language of Lord Lane CJ in *Duncan* and will not attempt to do so. It is in my opinion rightly decided and should be followed.

I would therefore dismiss the appeal and answer the certified question in the affirmative but amend it by substituting for the words 'a police officer' the words 'a person', to make it clear that this exception is of general application and not limited to statements to the police.[13]

Fox v General Medical Council (1960, Privy Council)

Lord Radcliffe: This is an appeal against a decision of the General Medical Council, acting by its Disciplinary Committee, that the appellant, Dr Kenneth Merrall Fox, had been guilty of infamous conduct in a professional respect and that his name should be erased from the Register of Medical Practitioners. The decision of the council was arrived at on November 27 1959 after a three-day hearing. The charge preferred against the appellant was that for a period of some three years ending in April 1959 he had improperly associated with a patient of his, the late Mrs Kathleen Margery Thomas, and committed adultery with her on numerous occasions. The course of proceedings before the committee and on the appeal before this Board made it plain that the charges of improper association and of adultery were to be considered as interdependent, and that the decision to remove the appellant's name from the register must stand or fall according to the view taken of the relevance and cogency of the evidence on the adultery charge ...

The remaining objection taken relates to what was said to be the wrongful refusal to admit a piece of relevant evidence for the appellant. It was sufficiently apparent that the appellant's solicitor wished to call a Mr Frampton – an old friend of the appellant – to confirm that on April 15 the appellant had told him the same general story about his relations with Mrs Thomas, in particular that her outburst of the previous day was not induced by any improper conduct of his, that constituted his defence to the charge before the committee. The purpose of such evidence of a witness's previous statement is and can only be to support his credit, when his veracity has been impugned, by showing a consistency in his account which adds some probative value to his evidence in the box. Generally speaking, as is well known, such confirmatory evidence is not admissible, the reason presumably being that all trials, civil and criminal, must be conducted with an effort to concentrate evidence upon what is capable of being cogent and, as was remarked by Humphreys J in *Rex v Roberts* (1942), it does not help to support the evidence of a witness, who is the accused person, to know that he has frequently told other persons before the trial what his defence was. Evidence to that effect is therefore in a proper sense immaterial.

There are, however, certain special exceptions, or at any rate one head of exception, from this general rule. If in cross-examination a witness's account of some incident or set of facts is challenged as being a recent invention, thus

---

13. 86 Cr App R 274. The other Law Lords agreed. *Sharp* was followed by the House of Lords in *Aziz* [1995] 3 All ER 149.

presenting a clear issue as to whether at some previous time he said or thought what he has been saying at the trial, he may support himself by evidence of earlier statements by him to the same effect. Plainly the rule that sets up the exception cannot be formulated with any great precision, since its application will depend on the nature of the challenge offered by the course of cross-examination and the relative cogency of the evidence tendered to repel it. Its application must be, within limits, a matter of discretion, and its range can only be measured by the reported instances, not in themselves many, in which it has been successfully invoked ...

Perhaps the best example of the way in which the exception can be properly invoked and applied is offered by *Flanagan v Fahy* (1918). There a witness who had testified to the forging of a will was cross-examined to the effect that he had invented his story because of enmity between him and the accused, the beneficiaries under the propounded will. He was allowed to call confirmatory evidence to show that before the cause of this enmity had arisen he had told a third party the story he was now telling. In that situation the issue raised by the cross-examination was clearly defined: a recent invention due to a specified cause, and if the witness could show that his account had been the same before the cause existed he was certainly adding a relevant fact in support of his credibility.

Did Mr Frampton's evidence, as tendered, come within the exception? In their Lordships' opinion it did not. It is impossible to say that its exclusion was wrongful in the legal sense. The cross-examination of the appellant on behalf of the respondents had not in fact challenged his account of what had passed between him and Mrs Thomas on April 14. It did not need to, since nearly everything that, according to him, was said could have been said consistently with either view of the case. What was, no doubt, challenged was his whole story that there had been no adulterous relations between them, and that her outburst of April 14 had come as a complete surprise to him. According to him he was 'appalled' by the predicament in which this placed him; he had become 'more and more worried by the turn of events.' In that state he went to seek advice from an old friend. Could it have made any contribution to the committee's judgment on the veracity of his whole account for them to know that in such a situation he had told the old friend substantially the same story as to his innocence of the matters charged as he was now telling the hearing? Their Lordships do not think that it could. In their view, the challenge to the appellant's evidence that was raised by the cross-examination was not of the order that could be affected by proof of statements made by him of that kind at that date. No tribunal that was not otherwise prepared to accept the appellant's general story could have been led to do so by hearing what he had told Mr Frampton on April 15. So regarded, the evidence rejected is no more than the previous assertion of the defence story told at the trial, which Humphreys J pointed out in *Rex v Roberts* is clearly inadmissible ...[14]

R v Oyesiku (1971, Court of Appeal)

Karminski LJ: ... The real point in this case, in our view, is a comparatively short one. The appellant, having been arrested, was taken away in custody where he remained for the time being, and was later bailed. But about two days later – the date is not wholly certain – the wife went to his solicitors and made a statement on her own in writing. The effect of it can be summarised as being that the

---

14.   [1960] 1 WLR 1017.

aggressor in that sense was the sergeant; the appellant was trying to find out what it was all about and was trying to break away, and did not realise that Sergeant Evans was a police officer. That statement (we have an affidavit from the solicitors) was made about two days after the offence took place and the appellant was arrested. It is said, and I do not think it is contradicted, if that date is right, that it was made two days after the offence. The wife had not by that time seen her husband, who was in custody. She saw him not very long afterwards.

She was of course cross-examined by counsel for the prosecution, who put it to her that this statement given to the solicitors was something she had made up. The suggestion was that she had coloured her evidence. Counsel objected to the jury looking at the statement. There is no doubt that counsel for the prosecution made it quite clear that he was attacking the wife's evidence on the grounds that she had made her evidence up, to help her husband.

The learned judge refused to allow her written statement to go before the jury ...

Our attention has also been drawn to a recent decision in the High Court of Australia, *Nominal Defendant v Clements* (1961). I desire to read only one passage from the full judgment of Dixon CJ. He said this (at p 479): 'The rule of evidence under which it was let in is well recognised and of long standing. If the credit of a witness is impugned as to some material fact to which he deposes upon the ground that his account is a late invention or has been lately devised or reconstructed, even though not with conscious dishonesty, that makes admissible a statement to the same effect as the account he gave as a witness, if it was made by the witness contemporaneously with the event or at a time sufficiently early to be inconsistent with the suggestion that his account is a late invention or reconstruction. But, inasmuch as the rule forms a definite exception to the general principle excluding statements made out of court and admits a possibly self-serving statement made by the witness, great care is called for in applying it. The judge at the trial must determine for himself upon the conduct of the trial before him whether a case for applying the rule of evidence has arisen and, from the nature of the matter, if there be an appeal, great weight should be given to his opinion by the appellate court. It is evident however that the judge at the trial must exercise care in assuring himself not only that the account given by the witness in his testimony is attacked on the ground of recent invention or reconstruction or that a foundation for such an attack has been laid by the party, but also that the contents of the statement are in fact to the like effect as his account given in his evidence and that having regard to the time and circumstances in which it was made it rationally tends to answer the attack. It is obvious that it may not be easy sometimes to be sure that counsel is laying a foundation for impugning the witness's account of a material incident or fact as a recently invented, devised or reconstructed story. Counsel himself may proceed with a subtlety which is the outcome of caution in pursuing what may prove a dangerous course. That is one reason why the trial judge's opinion has a peculiar importance.'

Dealing with the last paragraph of that quotation from Dixon CJ, there is no doubt at all that in this case counsel was making an attack, because it was clear from what he said at the trial and indeed what he said to us today. That judgment of the Chief Justice of Australia, although technically not binding upon us, is a decision of the greatest persuasive power, and one which this court gratefully accepts as a correct statement of the law applicable to the present appeal.

That is the position in law, and in our view the learned trial judge was wrong to refuse to allow that evidence to be given ...[15]

HOSTILE WITNESSES

Criminal Procedure Act 1865

3   A party producing a witness shall not be allowed to impeach his credit by general evidence of bad character, but he may, in case the witness shall, in the opinion of the judge, prove adverse, contradict him by other evidence, or, by leave of the judge, prove that he has made at other times a statement inconsistent with his present testimony; but before such last mentioned proof can be given the circumstances of the supposed statement, sufficient to designate the particular occasion, must be mentioned to the witness, and he must be asked whether or not he has made such statement.

R v Thompson (1976, Court of Appeal)

The Lord Chief Justice: On January 16 1976 at the Central Criminal Court the appellant was convicted of two counts of incest with his daughter Anne, one of indecent assault with the same girl, one of attempted incest with his daughter Sylvia, and one of indecent assault on Sylvia. He was sentenced to a variety of terms of imprisonment in respect of those offences, the total sentence being one of five years' imprisonment.

He now appeals against his conviction by leave of the single judge.

The case raises points of some interest which have been very clearly and compactly argued by counsel whose assistance we have had this morning, and I can take the background facts quite quickly. The two girls mentioned in the indictment, together with the appellant, their father, and their mother, lived together as a family. Their daughter Anne, who was 16 at the time of the trial, was called as a witness. She had given a statement to the police earlier implicating her father in these offences, and at the trial she was called into the witness-box to be sworn, and was sworn, but then refused to give evidence.

We have a transcript and we have been able to check the detail of it. It is not necessary to go into the matter in great detail, but one sees her acknowledging her name and address and her age, and then when counsel for the prosecution begins to ask questions dealing with the merits of the case she said: 'I'm not saying nothing, I'm not going to give evidence.' The learned judge said: 'Oh yes you are.' She answered: 'I'm not.' The learned judge said: 'Unless you want to spend some time in prison yourself, do you?' to which she replied: 'No.' The judge continued 'You won't like it in Holloway I assure you. You answer these questions and behave yourself, otherwise you will be in very serious trouble. Do you understand that?' To which she replied: 'Yes.' Then, shortly after that, the learned judge gave counsel permission to treat the witness as hostile. She was asked leading questions accordingly, her statement was put to her, and in the end she agreed that her statement was true and that was of course the basis of the case against the appellant in respect of the daughter Anne.

When it came to the turn of the daughter Sylvia to give evidence she also refused as in the case of her sister, and the judge, who no doubt was getting a little tired of this sort of conduct in this case, gave an order that she should be detained

---

15.   56 Cr App R 240.

overnight in a remand home. The result of that was that on the following morning when she was brought back into the witness-box she agreed to give evidence and she was examined perfectly normally without leading questions and without being treated as hostile. She thereby sustained the case so far as it was directed to offences against her ...

Thus, one comes from there to Mr Mylne's main point today, his best point as he described it, which is that the girl Anne ought never to have been treated as hostile. He concedes that she was a hostile witness and that the provisions of section 3 of the Criminal Procedure Act 1865 applied to her, but he says, for a reason which I will endeavour to explain in a moment, that that section did not apply in this case ...

It is to be observed in the text of that section that the party producing a witness is permitted in certain circumstances to contradict, and that he may produce a statement inconsistent with present testimony. The argument of Mr Mylne is that in order to get the benefit of section 3 it is not enough to show, as in this case, that the girl was hostile and stood mute of malice. It is essential, so the argument goes, that there should be a contradiction of a previous statement and an inconsistent current statement, and since in this case there was no such contradiction, the previous statement standing alone and the girl refusing to produce a second statement either consistent or otherwise, it is contended that the section has no application.

We do not find it necessary to express any view upon the section as applied to cases where there is an inconsistent statement. We think this matter must be dealt with by the provisions of the common law in regard to recalcitrant witnesses. Quite apart from what is said in section 3, the common law did recognise that pressure could be brought to bear upon witnesses who refuse to co-operate and perform their duties. We have had the advantage of looking at one or two of the earlier cases prior to the Act to which I have already referred and their treatment of this matter.

The first is *Clarke v Saffery* (1824), and the issue before the Vice-Chancellor does not require to be considered in any detail. But it is to be observed that in the course of the trial the plaintiff's counsel called the defendant, who was also one of the assignees, as a witness, and objection was taken by the defendant's counsel to the mode of examining the defendant. There does not seem to be a second statement contradicting the earlier one there, yet Best CJ said, at p 126: 'there is no fixed rule which binds the counsel calling a witness to a particular mode of examining him. If a witness, by his conduct in the box, shows himself decidedly adverse, it is always in the discretion of the judge to allow a cross-examination ...'

I pause there because the rest of Best CJ's judgment is subject to comment in the later cases, but that part which I have read seems to me to stand uncontradicted. That is what we are dealing with here. We are dealing here with a witness who shows himself decidedly adverse, and whereupon, as Best CJ says, it is always in the discretion of the judge to allow cross-examination. After all, we are only talking about the asking of leading questions. If the hostile witness declines to say anything at all that was inconsistent with his or her duty as making a second and inconsistent statement about the facts, Best CJ is recognising as a feature of the common law the right in the discretion of the judge always to allow cross-examination in those circumstances.

Then in the case of *Bastin v Carew* (1824) Lord Abbott CJ said at p 127: 'I mean to decide this, and no further. But in each particular case there must be some discretion in the presiding judge as to the mode in which the examination should be conducted, in order best to answer the purposes of justice.'

That statement, which is consistently supported in later authorities, again seems to us to cover this case admirably. The short question after all is: was the judge right in allowing counsel to cross-examine in the sense of asking leading questions? On the authority of *Clarke v Saffery* (*supra*) and *Bastin v Carew* (*supra*), it seems to us that he was right and there is no reason to suppose that the subsequent statutory intervention into this subject has in any way destroyed or removed the basic common law right of the judge in his discretion to allow cross-examination when a witness proves to be hostile.

Accordingly, it seems to us that there is nothing in Mr Mylne's best point, as he characterised it, and this appeal must be dismissed.[16]

CROSS-EXAMINATION

R v Baldwin (1925, Court of Criminal Appeal)

The Lord Chief Justice [Lord Hewart]: The appellant was charged with having had unlawful carnal knowledge on three occasions of a young girl, named Maggie Prescoll, who was born on September 20th 1910. It is not necessary to enter into the history of the case. There came a time when the appellant at the trial gave evidence on his own behalf. He said that his acquaintance with the child was only slight before an interview on December 15th 1924 at which her mother told him that Maggie was pregnant and asked him what he was going to do about it. He said that he denied that he had had anything to with her. Mrs Baldwin's evidence was to the same effect. When the appellant was being cross-examined this passage in the evidence occurred. Counsel for the prosecution asked: 'The girl says until the beginning of the year she never knew you, but that then you used, quite naturally and properly, to say good-night to her. Is that wrong?' 'I have only spoken to that girl twice in my life.' Then comes this question: 'Then can you suggest any reason at all why this girl should invent this story against you? Has she got any particular "down" on you?' 'I do not know – not without it is regarding getting some money off me and my parents.' 'To put it plainly, you regard her story then as blackmail?' 'Certainly, sir.' 'I took down very carefully what my learned friend said to Maggie in putting questions. Do you agree that what she is doing is trying to shield some boy and not telling the truth with regard to you?' 'Yes.' 'In other words, she is an immoral girl, is that it?' Counsel continued: 'Are you a particularly moral man yourself?' 'Yes.' Counsel then said: 'I submit that I am entitled now to pursue a certain line of cross-examination.' Counsel on the other side said: 'Because my case is that this girl is untruthful?' The judge said: 'I think so.' Thereupon there followed cross-examination to show that the appellant was paying money under the terms of a bastardy order.

Some other questions have been mooted on this appeal; but this is without doubt the real question ... It seems quite clear in the present case that certain questions were asked at the beginning of the evidence-in-chief of the prisoner which it is difficult to suppose were likely to produce any other effect than to indicate at

---

16. 64 Cr App R 96. I have quoted a little more than was necessary for the purely legal point because of the interest which the case has a piece of social history. The trial judge was Melford Stevenson J, a man described by Lord Devlin as 'the last of the grand eccentrics'. He added that 'without knowing what bodies, political or other, Melford belonged to, it would be safe to say that he was on the right wing of all of them' (Patrick Devlin, *Easing the Passing: The Trial of Dr John Bodkin Adams* (London: Faber and Faber, 1986, p 38).

least to the jury that the defendant was a person of good character, a respectable family man, not in the least likely to commit the sort of offence with which he was then being charged. The questions were: 'Baldwin, what age are you?' 'Thirty-two, sir.' 'Are you a married man?' 'Yes.' 'What are you?' 'A joiner.' When questions of that kind are asked, no matter what degree of ingenuity they may be thought to display, the client on whose behalf they are asked is put in great peril; and it will not be in the least surprising if, when the case arises, some learned judge were to say: 'As the counsel for the defendant has thought it right to elicit the fact that this man is a married man with children, you, if you like, may elicit the fact, if you believe it to be the fact, that he is also a person who is the father of illegitimate children.' There cannot be licence to the defence if there is to be strictness for the prosecution. But [counsel for the Crown] has frankly admitted that it was on no such grounds as that that he cross-examined the appellant on character. He put the questions to which attention has been directed on the ground that, apart from what the appellant had said in answer to any questions, the nature and the conduct of the defence were such as to involve imputations on the character of the prosecutrix and the witnesses for the prosecution. He did not put them in order to provoke imputations and so prepare the way for cross-examination to character. It is not necessary to say that counsel's assurances upon this point are to be accepted. The fact remains that these questions were put, and that, whatever else might have been done or whatever other arguments might have been adduced, the judge admitted this cross-examination. The law on this matter is perfectly clear. One would have thought that it did not need a decision. It cannot be right for counsel for the Crown to ask questions for the purpose of eliciting answers which may be of such a kind as to involve the accused person inadvertently in the mischief provided for in this part of the statute. That was made quite plain, for example, in *Beecham* (1921). In that case it was said in the judgment of this court: 'With regard to the cross-examination, we are bound to say that we cannot approve of the manner in which the appellant was led by counsel for the prosecution into making the statement which it was contended amounted to putting his character in issue.'

There is a further matter involved here which goes far beyond the present case, and, it may be, beyond criminal cases. One so often hears questions put to witnesses by counsel which are really of the nature of an invitation to an argument. You have, for instance, such questions as this: 'I suggest to you that ...' or: 'Is your evidence to be taken as suggesting that ...?' If the witness were a prudent person he would say, with the highest degree of politeness: 'What you suggest is no business of mine. I am not here to make any suggestions at all. I am here only to answer relevant questions. What the conclusions to be drawn from my answers are is not for me, and as for suggestions, I venture to leave those to others.' An answer of that kind, no doubt, requires a good deal of sense and self-restraint and experience, and the mischief of it is, if made, it might very well prejudice the witness with the jury, because the jury, not being aware of the consequences to which such questions might lead, might easily come to the conclusion (and it might be true) that the witness had something to conceal. It is right to remember in all such cases that the witness in the box is an amateur and the counsel who is asking questions is, as a rule, a professional conductor of argument, and it is not right that the wits of the one should be pitted against the wits of the other in the field of suggestion and controversy. What is wanted from the witness is answers to questions of fact.

One even hears questions such as: 'Do you ask the jury then to believe ...?' The witness may very well reply: 'I am asking the jury nothing; my business is to tell whatever is relevant that I know and that I am asked to tell, and therefore my answer to your question and to all such questions is, "No, I do not".' But in practice, both in civil cases and in criminal cases, one finds this line of cross-examination employed. It is a mischievous line and it is never more mischievous than when it has the effect of inducing a witness, inadvertently or, it may be, even in a mood of irritation, to make the kind of attack that, under s 1 of the statute, lets in certain other evidence which, but for that attack, would not be let in. These matters are not to be ignored by counsel who appear for the prosecution. They are equally not to be ignored by counsel who appear for the defence, because so often questions are asked which are ingeniously calculated up to the very last point to be consistent with abstinence from putting the defendant's character in issue, while undoubtedly the probable, as it is the intended, effect of those questions is to exhibit the man to the jury as a person of good character. Counsel for the defence should refrain from such questions for prudential reasons. Counsel for the prosecution should refrain from them for reasons of fairness, because the Crown has no interest whatever in securing a conviction. Its sole interest is to convict the right man.

In these circumstances, we think that this evidence ought not to have been admitted. We are not satisfied that, if it had been excluded, the jury would inevitably have come to the like conclusion. It follows, therefore, that this appeal must be allowed and this conviction quashed.[17]

Criminal Procedure Act 1865

4   If a witness, upon cross-examination as to a former statement made by him relative to the subject matter of the indictment or proceeding, and inconsistent with his present testimony, does not distinctly admit that he has made such statement, proof may be given that he did in fact make it; but before such proof can be given the circumstances of the supposed statement, sufficient to designate the particular occasion, must be mentioned to the witness, and he must be asked whether or not he has made such statement.

5   A witness may be cross-examined as to previous statements made by him in writing or reduced into writing relative to the subject matter of the indictment or proceeding, without such writing being shown to him; but if it is intended to contradict such witness by the writing, his attention must, before such contradictory proof can be given, be called to those parts of the writing which are to be used for the purpose of so contradicting him; provided always, that it shall be competent for the judge, at any time during the trial, to require the production of the writing for his inspection, and he may thereupon make such use of it for the purpose of the trial as he may think fit.

R v Golder (1960, Court of Criminal Appeal)

The defendant was charged with receiving a gold watch, part of the proceeds of a burglary in relation to which he was also charged, together with two other defendants. At committal proceedings before magistrates a prosecution witness named Taylor deposed to the fact that Golder had given her a watch, but at the trial she changed her story.

Lord Parker CJ: ... At the trial [Taylor] went back on her story and counsel for the prosecution obtained leave to treat her as adverse and cross-examine her. He did

---

17.   18 Cr App R 175.

not, however, succeed in extracting from her an admission that her deposition was true, still less that it was the appellant Golder who handed her the gold watch.

In the course of summing up the deputy chairman dealt with the question of the watch and the conflicting testimony of Taylor in a way which plainly indicated to the jury that it was open to them to act upon the evidence contained in her deposition notwithstanding her repudiation of it. The whole of the deposition was in fact read to them when they returned for further direction. It is only necessary to refer to two passages in the summing-up: 'The only evidence which you have that he gave the gold watch to Mrs Taylor is the evidence of Mrs Taylor herself, and she, you may think, is a stranger to truth. You heard the evidence before the justices.' Later, he said: 'If you came to the conclusion that what she said before the magistrates was accurate then of course it all starts to tie up.'

In the judgment of this court the direction to the jury in regard to Mrs Taylor's deposition was wrong in law ... A long line of authority has laid down the principle that while previous statements may be put to an adverse witness to destroy his credit and thus to render his evidence given at trial negligible, they are not admissible evidence of the truth of the facts stated therein ...

In the judgment of this court, when a witness is shown to have made previous statements inconsistent with the evidence given by that witness at the trial, the jury should not merely be directed that the evidence given at the trial should be regarded as unreliable; they should also be directed that the previous statements, whether sworn or unsworn, do not constitute evidence upon which they can act ...[18]

R v Governor of Pentonville Prison, ex p Alves (1993, House of Lords)

Lord Goff of Chieveley: ... [I]n the course of his submissions, Mr Nicholls [for the CPS] referred the Appellate Committee to Reg v Golder (1960), in which Lord Parker CJ delivering the judgment of the Court of Criminal Appeal, stated: 'In the judgment of this court, when a witness is shown to have made previous statements inconsistent with the evidence given by that witness at the trial, the jury should not merely be directed that the evidence given at the trial should be regarded as unreliable; they should also be directed that the previous statements, whether sworn or unsworn, do not constitute evidence upon which they can act.'

This statement was subsequently applied in Reg v Oliva (1965) and was relied on by Mr Newman in the course of his submissions on behalf of the appellant as applicable by analogy in the present case. In my opinion, however, too much can be read into it. It would, I consider, be wrong to read it as requiring that in every case where a witness is shown to have made a previous statement inconsistent with his evidence at the trial, the jury should be directed that such evidence should be regarded as unreliable ... Thus in Reg v Pestano (1981) it was held by the Court of Appeal that the credibility of evidence given by a witness inconsistent with a statement previously made by him was a matter for the jury to consider, subject to a proper warning by the judge as to the weight to be attached to the evidence. In any event, as appears from the context in both Golder and Oliva, the burden of Lord Parker CJ's statement is to be found in the second part of it, under which the jury is to be directed that the witness's previous statement will not as such be evidence upon which the jury can act ...[19]

---

18.   [1960] 1 WLR 1169.
19.   [1993] AC 284. The other Law Lords agreed.

R v Edwards (1991, Court of Appeal)

In the course of this appeal the court had to consider the extent to which police officers in one trial could be cross-examined about other cases in which they or their colleagues had been involved. The defence at trial had been that alleged admissions by Edwards had been concocted by the police, who were members of the West Midlands Serious Crime Squad.

Lord Lane CJ: ... Mr Hacking's submissions [on behalf of the appellant] concerned the behaviour in other cases of police officers involved in the instant case and the extent to which the court is entitled or obliged to enquire into such behaviour as possibly throwing light on the reliability of those officers at the trial of the appellant.

His argument runs as follows. (1) It would have been permissible to cross-examine each of the police officers at trial, had the appellant's then advisers known then what is known now, to allege a course of conduct or system. Such cross-examination would go not merely to credit or the lack of it, but would be probative of the appellant's assertion at trial that he was 'fitted up' with false evidence.

(2) The evidence of the behaviour of these police officers in other cases, together with the behaviour of other police officers in the West Midlands Serious Crime Squad (the Squad) in such cases and in further cases, establishes a consistent course of conduct or system of a strikingly similar pattern in 1986, 1987 and 1988 following the introduction of the Police and Criminal Evidence Act 1984 in January 1986. This, it is suggested, involved police officers in the Squad tampering with and fabricating evidence to the detriment of persons arrested by the Squad. This evidence is credible and admissible on the issue of whether evidence was fabricated in the appellant's case.

(3) The appellant, if he had known of the said course of conduct, would have been entitled to call evidence in his defence to establish that there was such a course of conduct in the Squad towards persons arrested and this would have been credible and admissible on the issue of fabrication. Such evidence was relevant and goes to the heart of the defence put forward at trial and provides, adopting the words of Neil LJ in *Reg v Shore* (1988), 'an underlying unity of probative value in relation to' the defence at trial.

(4) Mr Hacking points out correctly that it is now known that the police officers involved in the appellant's case are the subject of a large number of allegations by members of the public which are being investigated by the Police Complaints Authority.

(5) It is known that one of the officers involved has been charged with the offence of perjury in respect of which proceedings are likely to start very soon.

(6) It is known that other trials involving members of the West Midlands Serious Crime Squad have resulted in acquittals or in some cases the quashing of convictions by this court.

We turn now to consider whether those submissions are well founded.

If the defence had had this information at the trial, to what extent could they have made use of it? The test is primarily one of relevance, and this is so whether one is considering evidence-in-chief or questions in cross-examination. To be admissible questions must be relevant to the issue before the court.

Issues are of varying degrees of relevance or importance. A distinction has to be drawn between, on the one hand, the issue in the case upon which the jury will be pronouncing their verdict and, on the other hand, collateral issues of which the credibility of the witnesses may be one. Generally speaking, questions may be put to a witness as to any improper conduct of which he may have been guilty, for the purpose of testing his credit ...

The distinction between the issue in the case and matters collateral to the issue is often difficult to draw, but it is of considerable importance. Where cross-examination is directed at collateral issues such as the credibility of the witness, as a rule the answers of the witness are final and evidence to contradict them will not be permitted: see Lawrence J in *Harris v Tippett* (1811). The rule is necessary to confine the ambit of a trial within proper limits and to prevent the true issue from becoming submerged in a welter of detail.

There are however exceptions to that rule, of which one of the most important is to show bias on the part of the witness: *Reg v Shaw* (1888). 'Facts showing that the witness is biased or partial in relation to the parties or the cause may be elicited on cross-examination: or, if denied, independently proved': *Phipson on Evidence*, 14th edn (1990) p 265, para 12-34.

It has been suggested – see *Reg v Funderburk* (1990) – that a further exception now exists, namely to show 'that the police are prepared to go to improper lengths to secure a conviction'. That proposition is drawn from the decision in *Reg v Busby* (1981). In that case the prosecution had adduced evidence from police officers about statements suggesting guilt made by the accused man. The officers were cross-examined to suggest that they had fabricated the accused man's remarks and were biased against him. This they denied. The defence then called a witness to give evidence on another aspect of the case. From this witness they also sought to obtain evidence that the same two police officers had made threats against him (the witness) to prevent him giving evidence on behalf of the accused man.

Objection was taken, and the judge excluded the evidence on the ground that it went solely to the credit of the officers. Eveleigh LJ delivering the judgment of the Court of Appeal held that the evidence should not have been excluded. It would have tended to support the defendant's case that the officers concerned were prepared to go to improper lengths to secure a conviction. It was therefore, it was said, relevant to an issue which had to be tried.

A close study of the decision in *Reg v Busby* seems to show however that its true basis may well have been the suggestion of bias against those particular defendants in that particular case. The fact that the police were allegedly prepared to prevent a potential witness from giving evidence on behalf of the defendant falls within the rule as stated in *Reg v Shaw*; namely, that facts showing that the witness is biased or partial in relation to the parties or the cause may be elicited in cross-examination: or, if denied, independently proved. If the decision in *Reg v Busby* cannot be explained on that basis, it seems to us to be inconsistent with the central and long standing principle, and indeed inconsistent with the decision in *Harris v Tippett* itself where the facts were not dissimilar to those in *Reg v Busby*.

It follows that, had the suggested evidence been available, the present case would have raised these problems: first, what questions could properly be asked of the police witnesses in cross-examination, and secondly, whether evidence to contradict those answers would have been admissible.

So far as the matters advanced by Mr Hacking are concerned, the police officers could certainly be cross-examined as to any relevant criminal offences or disciplinary charges found proved against them.

That leaves the following matters: should questions be permitted as to: (1) complaints by members of the public about the behaviour of the witness on other occasions not yet adjudicated upon by the Police Complaints Authority; (2) discreditable conduct by other officers in the same squad; (3) other cases in which the witness has given evidence which have resulted in acquittal of the defendant at the trial or the quashing of the conviction on appeal.

This is an area where it is impossible and would be unwise to lay down hard and fast rules as to how the court should exercise its discretion. The objective must be to present to the jury as far as possible a fair, balanced picture of the witnesses' reliability, bearing in mind on the one hand the importance of eliciting facts which may show, if it be the case, that the police officer is not the truthful person he represents himself to be, but bearing in mind on the other hand the fact that a multiplicity of complaints may indicate no more than what was described before us as the 'bandwagon' effect.

We do not consider that it would have been proper to suggest to the officer in the present case that he had committed perjury or any other criminal offence by putting to him that he had been charged but not yet tried. Nor do we think that complaints to the Police Complaints Authority which have not been adjudicated upon would properly be the subject of cross-examination. It would not be proper to direct questions to an officer about allegedly discreditable conduct of other officers, whether or not they happened to be serving in the same squad.

There remains the problem of other cases in which the witness has, so to speak, unsuccessfully given evidence. We have the advantage in this respect of earlier decisions of this court.

In *Reg v Thorne (John)* (1977) the judge at trial had refused an application by the defence to have a police officer recalled for further cross-examination about verdicts of acquittal which had been returned by other juries in other cases in which he had been involved. Lawton LJ in the course of giving judgment said, at p 15: 'The fact that [the police officer] may have given evidence against other accused in other cases which did not lead to convictions, did not begin to prove that he was biased against any of the appellants in this case in any sense known to the law of evidence. The fact that a jury returns a verdict of not guilty does not go to prove that an important witness for the prosecution, albeit the sole witness, is a liar.'

The matter was further considered in *Reg v Cooke (Gary)* (1986) in which the earlier authorities, including *Reg v Thorne (John)*, were considered. The facts in the case were these. A police officer had allegedly obtained admissions in interviews with a number of different accused persons about the same group of offences. The interviews were part of a connected series which took place over a short period of time. The various accused persons were not all tried together. Two of the other defendants were acquitted. The evidence against them had consisted almost entirely of admissions said to have been made by them to a police officer as to whose evidence the jury must plainly have had doubt. At the trial evidence was given by the same police officer of admissions allegedly made by Cooke. The trial judge refused leave to cross-examine the police officer about the circumstances of the acquittal of the other accused persons.

Upon appeal Parker LJ, giving the judgment of the court, said, at pp 291-292: 'It seems to us that where a police officer has allegedly obtained admissions on interviews about the same group of offences from different accused as part of a connected series of interviews over a short period, where those interviews are alleged to have been fabricated, and where the alleged admissions were the essential evidence against one or more of the accused who were nevertheless acquitted, justice demands that the jury should know this when they are considering a challenge by another accused to the truth of evidence of admissions said to have been made by him to the same officer at about the same time and about the same series of events.'

There it was the behaviour of the officer in what was to all intents and purposes the same case as that being tried which was the subject of the proposed cross-examination. That was therefore a limited extension of the principle expressed in *Reg v Thorne (John)*.

The result of those two decisions seems to be this. The acquittal of a defendant in case A, where the prosecution case depended largely or entirely upon the evidence of a police officer, does not normally render that officer liable to cross-examination as to credit in case B. But where a police officer, who has allegedly fabricated an admission in case B, has also given evidence of an admission in case A, where there was an acquittal by virtue of which his evidence is demonstrated to have been disbelieved, it is proper that the jury in case B should be made aware of that fact. However, where the acquittal in case A does not necessarily indicate that the jury disbelieved the officer, such cross-examination should not be allowed. In such a case the verdict of not guilty may mean no more than that the jury entertains some doubt about the prosecution case, not necessarily that they believed any witness was lying ...[20]

Sexual Offences (Amendment) Act 1976

2 (1) If at a trial any person is for the time being charged with a rape offence to which he pleads not guilty, then, except with the leave of the judge, no evidence and no question in cross-examination shall be adduced or asked at the trial, by or on behalf of any defendant at the trial, about any sexual experience of a complainant with a person other than that defendant.

(2) The judge shall not give leave in pursuance of the preceding subsection for any evidence or question except on an application made to him in the absence of the jury by or on behalf of the defendant; and on such an application the judge shall give leave if and only if he is satisfied that it would be unfair to that defendant to refuse to allow the evidence to be adduced or the question to be asked.

(3) In subsection (1) of this section 'complainant' means a woman or a man upon whom, in a charge for a rape offence to which the trial in question relates, it is alleged that rape was committed, attempted or proposed.

(4) Nothing in this section authorises evidence to be adduced or a question to be asked which cannot be adduced or asked apart from this section.

7 (2) In this Act –

'a rape offence' means any of the following, namely rape, attempted rape, aiding, abetting, counselling and procuring rape or attempted rape, incitement to rape, conspiracy to rape and burglary with intent to rape.

R v Viola (1982, Court of Appeal)

Lord Lane CJ gave the following judgment of the court: On February 24 1982 at the Crown Court at Warwick, this applicant, Michael Viola, was convicted of rape and sentenced to four years' imprisonment. He now applies for leave to appeal

---

20. [1991] 1 WLR 207. *Cf R v Edwards (Maxime)* (1996) Times, 13 January.

against that conviction. We give him leave and, with Mr Wakerley's consent on his behalf, we treat this as the hearing of the appeal.

The issue for the jury was one of consent and the facts, in so far as they are material, were as follows. The complainant was 22 years of age. She lived in a maisonette in Coventry with two young children of her own. There was no dispute that about half an hour before midnight on Tuesday, September 8 1981 the appellant came to her door. The reason why he had come there was this. He had, it seems, been in some trouble with the police over the driving of a motor car, and he had parked the vehicle and then thrown the keys into a doorway. He knocked on the door of the complainant's maisonette in order to try, so he said, to find the keys. She by fetching a piece of lighted paper assisted him in that search and, according to her, let him inside the maisonette in order that he could look out of the window to see whether the police were still waiting for him or looking for him. There was a slight acquaintanceship between the two of them. It seems that he and she on one occasion had danced together.

The complainant's version of events thereafter is this. Once inside, the appellant told her that he fancied her, sat next to her on the sofa, whereupon she asked him to go and got up. Then, according to her, he seized hold of her, butted her in the face with his head, he pulled her hair and, when she started to scream, he threatened to knock her out and to stab her. He, according to her, ripped her knickers and when she was on the sofa he raped her.

On the other hand the appellant's version of events was that, when he knocked on the door in order to get assistance, the complainant invited him in for a drink. They sat on the sofa for a while, kissing and so on, and then intercourse took place between them with her fully consenting to the act.

The first complaint proper made by the complainant herself seems to have been on Friday, that is, some considerable time after the alleged event. It was after that complaint and after she had been seen by the police on the Friday that she was examined by the police doctor and also by her own doctor, and it is plain that at that stage she was found to have swelling across the bridge of her nose and bruising round the eye.

The police interviewed the appellant on Friday evening. He first of all said that he never touched her, that he had not been involved in any trouble with the police and when the complaint was put to him he said that it was all a lie and referred to the complainant in highly uncomplimentary terms. Then at the police station he changed his story, admitted that he had had intercourse with the complainant, but said that she consented to it and, according to the police, he admitted that he had butted her with the head, but he said that that took place after the intercourse and not before it. The appellant in evidence denied having made any admissions to the police with regard to butting the complainant in he face.

There were three defence witnesses who gave evidence that shortly after the alleged rape and a matter of 48 hours or so before the complainant was examined by the doctors, they had seen her and that she had no injuries upon her face. Certainly so far as Mr and Mrs Burns are concerned, they said that she did not appear to have any injuries. The complainant's boyfriend or ex-boyfriend – there is some dispute as to the precise state of affairs between them – said that he saw her shortly afterwards and saw a slight scratch on her nose but no more.

The jury came to the conclusion by a majority verdict that the offence had been made out. The principal ground of appeal is that the judge was wrong in preventing the defendant from cross-examining the complainant about three separate matters. The first matter was a suggestion that during the afternoon and evening of the Tuesday – it will be remembered that the rape was alleged to have taken place at very shortly before midnight on that day – and immediately prior to the alleged act of rape, this complainant was making sexual advances to two men who visited her flat; the next matter was that during the afternoon of September 9 1981 the complainant had sexual intercourse with her boyfriend, or recently discarded boyfriend; and finally, on the morning of September 9, that would be about eight or nine hours after the alleged act of rape, there was a man in the complainant's flat on the sofa wearing nothing except a pair of slippers.

So far as this aspect of the appeal is concerned, it raises once again the problem of the application of section 2 of the Sexual Offences (Amendment) Act 1976. We have to determine whether the judge was right or wrong in refusing to allow the suggested questions to be put ...

It is, we think, apparent from [the words of the section] that the first question which the judge must ask himself is this: are the questions proposed to be put relevant according to the ordinary common law rules of evidence and relevant to the case as it is being put? If they are not so relevant, that is the end of the matter ...

The second matter which the judge must consider is this. If the questions are relevant, then whether they should be allowed or not will of course depend on the terms of section 2, which limits the admissibility of relevant evidence. That section has been the subject of judicial consideration first of all by May J in *Reg v Lawrence* (1977); a passage, which is taken verbatim from the transcript of the ruling, reads, at p 493: 'The important part of the statute which I think needs construction are the words: "if and only if [the judge] is satisfied that it would be unfair to that defendant to refuse to allow the evidence to be adduced or the question to be asked." And, in my judgment, before a judge is satisfied or may be said to be satisfied that to refuse to allow a particular question or a series of questions in cross-examination would be unfair to a defendant he must take the view that it is more likely than not that the particular question or line of cross-examination, if allowed, might reasonably lead the jury, properly directed in the summing-up, to take a different view of the complainant's evidence from that which they might take if the question or series of questions was or were not allowed.'

That statement was approved by this court in *Reg v Mills (Leroy)* (1978) ...

That approval by this court of the decision in *Reg v Lawrence* (1977) means that we are bound by the words of May J to which we have referred. In the end the judge will have to ask himself the question whether he is satisfied in the terms expounded by May J. It will be a problem for him to apply that dictum to the particular facts of the case. In those circumstances it seems to us it would be both improper and, perhaps more importantly, very unwise for us to try to say in advance what may or may not be unfair in any particular case ...

It has been agreed on all hands, not only by the appellant and by the Crown but also by Mr Green who has assisted us as amicus curiae, that it is wrong to speak of a judge's 'discretion' in this context. The judge has to make a judgment as to whether he is satisfied or not in the terms of section 2. But once having reached his judgment on the particular facts, he has no discretion. If he comes to the conclusion that he is satisfied it would be unfair to exclude the evidence, then the evidence has to be admitted and the questions have to be allowed.

Having said that, when one considers the purposes which lay behind the passing of this Act ... it is clear that it was aimed primarily at protecting complainants from cross-examination as to credit, from questions which went merely to credit and no more. The result is that generally speaking – I use these words advisedly, of course there will always be exceptions – if the proposed questions merely seek to establish that the complainant has had sexual experience with other men to whom she was not married, so as to suggest that for that reason she ought not to be believed under oath, the judge will exclude the evidence. In the present climate of opinion a jury is unlikely to be influenced by such considerations, nor should it be influenced. In other words questions of this sort going simply to credit will seldom be allowed ...

On the other hand if the questions are relevant to an issue in the trial in the light of the way the case is being run, for instance relevant to the issue of consent, as opposed merely to credit, they are likely to be admitted, because to exclude a relevant question on an issue in the trial as the trial is being run will usually mean that the jury are being prevented from hearing something which, if they did hear it, might cause them to change their minds about the evidence given by the complainant. But, I repeat, we are very far from laying down any hard and fast rule.

Inevitably in this situation, as in so many similar situations in the law, there is a grey area which exists between the two types of relevance; namely, relevance to credit and relevance to an issue in the case. On one hand evidence of sexual promiscuity may be so strong or so closely contemporaneous in time to the event in issue as to come near to, or indeed to reach the border between, mere credit and an issue in the case. Conversely, the relevance of the evidence to an issue in the case may be so slight as to lead the judge to the conclusion that he is far from satisfied that the exclusion of the evidence or the question from the consideration of the jury would be unfair to the defendant.

We have had drawn to our attention some of the difficulties which face a judge. It is perfectly true to say that normally he has to make this decision at an early stage of the trial. It will be, generally speaking, when the complainant's evidence-in-chief is concluded that counsel in the absence of the jury will make the necessary application under section 2. At this stage it may not be easy for the judge to reach a conclusion, but this a problem which is continually being faced by judges, sometimes in even more trying circumstances; for example, when he is asked to determine whether a count should be tried separately or whether defendants should be tried separately and so on, before the trial has got under way at all. He has to reach the best conclusion that he can.

The second matter is: is this court entitled to differ from the conclusions of the judge? As already pointed out, this is the exercise of judgment by the judge not an exercise of his discretion. This court is in many respects in as good a position as the judge to reach a conclusion. The judge has certainly heard the complainant give evidence, but only in chief. So far as the proposed questions are concerned, the statements upon which the questions were to be asked or the way in which the matter was going to be put to the jury are presented in exactly the same way to this court as they were to the judge at first instance. We have been told what it was that counsel sought in the course of his submission to the judge and indeed we have been given the statements which were to be the basis of the questions which he was going to ask. So what we have to decide is whether the judge was right or wrong in the conclusion which he reached, applying the test of May J in *Reg v Lawrence* (1977). Like so many decisions in the grey area, it is not an easy decision to make. Let me turn therefore to the precise matters about which it was proposed to ask questions.

First of all the presence of the two men in her maisonette very shortly before the alleged rape took place. The facts of that were apparently these. The two men, whose names are not material, called at the maisonette occupied by the complainant, in the hope of finding the complainant's boyfriend, whose name was Willy, present. They arrived some time during the afternoon. They were equipped with considerable amounts of drink, amongst other things a gallon of wine. They discovered that Willy was not there. Nevertheless they went in at the invitation of the complainant. It was not suggested that she knew them very well. Indeed she probably did not, although she was acquainted with them. According to their evidence not only was a good deal of alcohol consumed by them and the complainant, but during the course of the several hours that they were there with her, she made sexual advances to them: she suggested that one or the other might like to try out her new bed; she made physical contact with one of them by rubbing his back, and so on; in other words indicated that she would not be averse to sexual intercourse with them. The precise timing is not available, perhaps not surprisingly, but it seems likely that the length of time which elapsed between the departure of these two men and the advent of the appellant was something like an hour and a half. Consequently it is suggested to us, and was suggested to the judge, that in the context of this case this evidence was very much material to an issue in the case, namely, the question of consent, owing, *inter alia*, to the similarity between the entry of these two men to the maisonette and the entry of the appellant and to the close proximity in time of the two incidents.

The next matter was the fact that she had had sexual intercourse with her boyfriend during the afternoon of September 9, that was about 14 hours after the alleged act of rape. The relevance, it was suggested, in respect of this question was that it was said in the complainant's statement to the police that after the so-called rape her vagina was sore, the inference being that it was because the sexual intercourse had been without consent that she suffered that pain. We are told, although it is not in evidence, that there was some difficulty about the real cause for the girl's soreness; it was suggested perhaps it was the size of the appellant's male member that had caused the soreness rather than the lack of consent.

The final matter which it was sought to introduce was that on the morning of September 9, a very few hours after the alleged act of rape, a woman friend of the complainant had come to the maisonette to pick up the complainant's little boy to take him to school. There was no reason apparently to doubt the veracity of this lady and what she said was that in the maisonette there was lying on the sofa this man naked apart from a pair of slippers.

All those matters have to be read against the somewhat unusual features of this case, the unusual features being first of all the dispute about the injuries, some people saying that they observed them on the Friday, and others apparently saying that they did not earlier on; and the remarkable feature that no complaint was made to anyone apparently between the time of the event, at about midnight on Tuesday night, and Friday.

In those circumstances it seems to us that the presence of the two men in the maisonette prior to the incident in question and the presence of the naked man in the maisonette immediately after the event are matters which went to the question of consent and were matters which could not be regarded as so trivial or of so little relevance as for the judge to be able to say that he was satisfied that no injustice would be done to the appellant by their exclusion from the evidence. This case differs from those to which we have been referred, because those were cases when the questions sought to be put in were questions solely as to credit. These questions were not mere questions as to credit.

It need hardly be said that one differs from a judge on a point such as this with the greatest possible reluctance, and it is only after very serious consideration that we have come to the conclusion that in this particular case the judge was wrong in the conclusion which he reached: he was wrong in respect of the two men in the flat and wrong in respect of the naked man in the flat. We would not say the same of the second of the three allegations, about sexual intercourse with the boyfriend. If the appeal had rested upon that alone, we would not have interfered. We think he was right in the conclusion he reached in respect of that, but he was wrong in respect of the other two ...[21]

R v Barton (1987, Court of Appeal)

O'Connor LJ read the judgment of the court: On March 10 1986 in the Crown Court at Coventry the appellant was convicted of rape and sentenced to six years' imprisonment. He appeals against conviction by leave of the single judge.

At the trial the only issue was consent in both its forms: (1) that the complainant consented to intercourse; alternatively (2) if she did not consent the appellant genuinely but mistakenly believed that she was consenting to intercourse. The main ground of appeal is that the trial judge wrongly refused to permit the cross-examination of the complainant about her sexual past and the adduction of evidence on that topic ...

Mr Henry [for the appellant] has submitted that the topics on which he wished to cross-examine and lead evidence did not go solely to the credit of the complainant but were relevant to the issue of consent both as to the question of whether the complainant in fact consented and alternatively to the question whether the appellant genuinely but mistakenly believed that she was consenting. He submitted that a defendant charged with rape was entitled as of right to put before the jury any matter which he said had persuaded him to believe that the complainant was consenting including his knowledge of her previous promiscuity. In support of that submission he relied on section 1(2) of the Sexual Offences (Amendment) Act 1976 which provides: 'It is hereby declared that if at a trial for a rape offence the jury has to consider whether a man believed that a woman was consenting to sexual intercourse, the presence or absence of reasonable grounds for such a belief is a matter to which the jury is to have regard, in conjunction with any other relevant matters, in considering whether he so believed.'

This subsection is declaratory of the law as it was (see Smith and Hogan Criminal Law, 5th edn (1983), pp 404-405).

Mr Henry submitted that that subsection expressly provided for the jury to consider whether the grounds put forward by a defendant for his belief that the complainant consented were reasonable or unreasonable and that they could not do that unless they were told what the grounds were. He submitted that where the issue was genuine but mistaken belief in consent and a ground was the defendant's knowledge of the complainant's previous promiscuity, the prohibition in section 2(1) did not apply. Alternatively, that a refusal to permit the defendant to tell the jury what his grounds were must be necessarily unfair to him within the meaning of that word in section 2(2). He submitted that the interpretation put on section 2(2) by May J (as he then was) in Lawrence (1977),

---

21. [1982] 1 WLR 1138.

approved by this court in *Mills (Leroy)* (1979) and declared binding on us in *Viola* (1982), has no application in cases where genuine but mistaken belief in consent is an issue. In *Lawrence* May J said: 'The important part of the statute which I think needs construction are the words "if and only if he (the judge) is satisfied that it would be unfair to that defendant to refuse to allow the evidence to be adduced or the question to be asked", and, in my judgment, before a judge is satisfied or may be said to be satisfied that to refuse to allow a particular question or a series of questions in cross-examination would be unfair to a defendant he must take the view that it is more likely than not that the particular question or line of cross-examination, if allowed, might reasonably lead the jury, properly directed in the summing-up, to take a different view of the complainant's evidence from that which they might take if the question or series of questions was or were not allowed.'

The court was not concerned with genuine but mistaken belief in any of the three cases, *Lawrence*, *Mills (Leroy)* or *Viola*, and the wording of May J's *dictum* is not appropriate when the judge is considering whether it would be unfair to a defendant where the issue is genuine but mistaken belief. On that issue the complainant's credit is not being attacked but only arises where it is accepted that she did not consent.

If the construction which Mr Henry submits to be the correct construction of section 1(2) is correct, then it will be seen that for practical purposes the protection given to complainants by section 2 of the Act would disappear in consent cases. We cannot accept that the subsection has that effect. As was pointed out in *Viola* (1982) the protection given by section 2 of the Act is not required for questions in cross-examination and/or evidence which is not relevant. It follows that Parliament must have intended to exclude relevant matters by section 2 of the Act. We think that the answer to Mr Henry's submission is to be found in the wording of section 1(2). The presence or absence of reasonable grounds has to be considered by the jury 'in conjunction with any other relevant matter'. In the light of section 2 of the Act these words must mean 'relevant matters properly before the jury' and the wording of section 1(2) does not permit a defendant to circumvent the prohibition found in section 2, because that section controls what matters can be properly placed before the jury.

When an application is made in a case such as the present; that is, where both consent and a genuine but mistaken belief are in issue, the trial judge has a difficult task. On the one hand the application necessarily involves an attack upon the credit of the complainant who has asserted in her evidence that she did not consent to intercourse and this aspect has to be considered in the context of the dictum of May J in *Lawrence (supra)*. On the other hand when considering the effect of the complainant's past sexual promiscuity upon the defendant's belief that she was consenting to intercourse the judge must decide in the context of the facts of the case. It must be remembered that there is a difference between believing that a woman is consenting to intercourse and believing that a woman will consent if advances are made to her. In the end it is the application of common sense to the facts of the individual case ...[22]

---

22. 85 Cr App R 5. The appeal was dismissed.

EVIDENCE IN REBUTTAL

R v Funderburk (1990, Court of Appeal)

Henry J read the following judgment of the court: On 28 September 1988 in the Crown Court at Reading, before McNeill J, the appellant was convicted on three counts of sexual intercourse with a girl of 13 years – in law, a child – and was sentenced to consecutive terms of 18, 15, and 12 months' imprisonment. These three counts were specimen counts covering 10 or 11 alleged acts of intercourse.

The first count covered the month of November 1987, the second, December 1987, and the third, February 1988. He now appeals against conviction and sentence by the leave of the single judge.

The facts are that the appellant was a master sergeant in the United States Air Force who lived with Joanne Potts in Berkshire. Until about Christmas 1987 a friend of his had lived with a lady who was the mother of the child, the complainant, who was then aged 13. The mother herself was only 31.

At Christmas the child, who had been living with the grandparents, began to live with her mother and stepbrothers. They moved in with the appellant and Miss Potts as lodgers. They left at the beginning of March after arguments concerning money. It was after that parting that these events came to the notice of the authorities.

The complainant gave evidence that she began to have a crush on the appellant when in November 1987 he took her to a night-club as a reward for baby-sitting for him. She described in some detail in the witness-box the acts of intercourse which had occurred, as I say, on 10 or 11 occasions.

The transcript of her evidence shows that it came out in a way which strongly suggested that on the occasion of the first act of intercourse, which she said was a week or so after the night-club visit, she was a virgin. She had been asked in the introductory questions during her evidence-in-chief about her previous boyfriends and the innocence of her association with them. She said that the appellant had said to her: 'You've got to do it one day; why not now?' Then followed her description of the penetration, the pain caused by it and the bleeding which she later discovered.

It being made clear at the time that she was not then menstruating, it seems to us that it must have been perfectly clear to the jury that in giving that description of the first occasion she was describing the loss of her virginity.

The appellant's defence was that the child was lying from beginning to end. Her motive in this was to support her mother who – as the child agreed in the witness-box – had it in for the appellant as a result of the disputes which had arisen between them.

One difficulty which the defence had to meet was that if she was lying, how could so young a girl have given so detailed and varied accounts as the accounts that she in fact gave of the acts of intercourse? The answer which the defence suggested as to this was that despite her age she was both experienced and sexually interested, and that she had either transposed experiences which she had had with others to this appellant and/or fantasised about experience with the appellant on whom she freely admitted having had a crush. In support of that, defence counsel wished, and it is this matter which gives rise to the appeal against conviction, first to put to her that she had told Miss Potts, a potential defence witness, that before the first incident complained of she had had sexual intercourse with two named men and consequently she had wanted to undergo a pregnancy test.

As will be seen, counsel was not permitted to put those questions in cross-examination. For convenience we refer to them as 'the disputed questions'. Having laid the basis in cross-examination, counsel wished subsequently to call Miss Potts to give evidence of that conversation. As will be seen, he was not able to do that either, and we call this 'the disputed evidence'.

Counsel made application on the basis not only that it went to her credibility but also on the basis that it went to an issue in the case. Somewhat surprisingly when the application was originally made there was no mention of the Criminal Procedure Act 1865 ('Lord Denman's Act') until the judge brought it up himself after the overnight adjournment. This was one of the difficulties with which the judge had to cope.

The case was heard on circuit. Library facilities are often scant there, as they seem to have been in this case. None of the authorities which have been cited to us were cited to the trial judge. He had a difficult task.

The rule which is challenged in this appeal is the judge's ruling that whether or not the child was a virgin at the time of the first incident was not an issue material to the charge of unlawful sexual intercourse. He commented that the prosecution had rightly avoided any inquiry as to her virginity.

It is right to say that the prosecution had never asked her directly the question, 'Were you a virgin at the time?' although it was clearly implicit from her evidence that that was what she was saying she was. The judge went on to rule that if the child had, as the defence contended, implicitly averred her previous virginity, her previous inconsistent statement, namely, that she had had sexual intercourse with two other men before this date, could not be put to her as a challenge to her credibility, as her virginity was, in the judge's words, 'immaterial to establishing or refuting the charge that this defendant had sexual intercourse with the girl'.

For our part we are quite satisfied that both the prosecution and the child herself were putting her forward as a virgin before the first incident and that the jury cannot have doubted she was telling them of the loss of her virginity.

Before we come to answering the questions posed we think it necessary to go back to first principles. One starts with the obvious proposition that in a trial relevant evidence should be admitted and irrelevant evidence excluded. 'Relevant' means relevant according to the ordinary common law rules of evidence and relevant to the case as it is being put, as Lord Lane CJ put it in *Reg v Viola* (1982).

But as relevance is a matter of degree in each case, the question in reality is whether or not the evidence is or is not sufficiently relevant. For in order to keep criminal trials within bounds and to assist the jury in concentrating on what matters and not being distracted by doubts as to marginal events, it is necessary in the interests of justice to avoid multiplicity of issues where possible. In every case this is a matter for the trial judge on the evidence and on the way the case is put before him.

When one comes to cross-examination, questions in cross-examination equally have to be relevant to the issues before the court, and those issues of course include the credibility of the witness giving evidence as to those issues. But a practical distinction must be drawn between questions going to an issue before the court and questions merely going either to the credibility of the witness or to facts that are merely collateral. Where questions go solely to the credibility of the witness or to collateral facts the general rule is that answers given to such questions are final and cannot be contradicted by rebutting evidence. This is because of the requirement to avoid multiplicity of issues in the overall interests of justice.

The authorities show that the defence may call evidence contradicting that of the prosecution witnesses where their evidence: (a) goes to an issue in the case (that is obvious); (b) shows that the witness made a previous inconsistent statement relating to an issue in the case (Denman's Act, which we deal with below); (c) shows bias in the witness: *Rex v Phillips* (1936); (d) shows that the police are prepared to go to improper lengths to secure a conviction: *Reg v Busby* (1981); (e) in certain circumstances proves the witness's previous convictions; (f) shows that the witness has a general reputation for untruthfulness; (g) shows that medical causes would have affected the reliability of his testimony.

All those categories listed, other than category (a), might be considered exceptions to the general rule as to the finality requirement of questions put on issues of credibility and collateral matters. They demonstrate the obvious proposition that a general rule designed to serve the interests of justice should not be used where so far from serving those interests it might defeat them. On that basic summary of the law two questions arise in this case. First, should the disputed questions have been permitted as questions either going to an issue or going to the credibility of the child? Second, if so, were her answers to such questions final or could evidence be given of previous inconsistent statements relating to previous sexual activities?

We deal first with admission of the questions as going to credit. Originally counsel for the prosecution conceded that the disputed questions could be asked as going to credit, subject to the answers being final, but in the course of submissions he withdrew this concession. The question of roaming cross-examinations as to the credit of complainants in rape cases rightly exercised Parliament and such cross-examination was statutorily restricted by section 2 of the Sexual Offences (Amendment) Act 1976 ...

[T]hough the limits on cross-examination as to credit imposed by that Act do not apply to this case, the court will not wish to see the mischief sought to be prevented by that Act perpetrated in this context and therefore will be astute to see that such cross-examination is not abused or extended unnecessarily. McNeill J was rightly concerned as to the ordeal of this child.

So far as concerns the general test as to the limits of cross-examination as to credit, the *locus classicus* of that is to be found in the judgment of Lawton J in *Reg v Sweet-Escott* (1971). There the witness was cross-examined as to his credit in relation to convictions 20 years ago. As a general test Lawton J, having found that the question should not have been allowed, said: 'What, then, is the principle upon which the judge should draw the line? It seems to me that it is this. Since the purpose of cross-examination as to credit is to show that the witness ought not to be believed on oath, the matters about which he is questioned must relate to his likely standing after cross-examination with the tribunal which is trying him or listening to his evidence.'

... As is clear from our summary of the judge's refusal of the application in this case, that is not the test that the trial judge here applied. He applied the test set out in section 4 of Denman's Act as to the admissibility of proof of previous inconsistent statements. I should read that section to show the test he applied. Section 4 of that Act deals with oral statements and provides: 'If a witness, upon cross-examination as to a former statement made by him' – and these are the important words – 'relative to the subject matter of the indictment or proceeding, and inconsistent with his present testimony, does not distinctly admit that he has made such statement, proof may be given that he did in fact make it; but before such proof can be given the circumstances of the supposed statement, sufficient to designate the particular occasion, must be mentioned to the witness, and he must be asked whether or not he has made such a statement'.

It was on the basis of that section that the application as to Joanne Potts' evidence could, it seems to us, have most strongly been made. The trial judge, having found that the virginity or non-virginity of the child on the occasion of the first alleged act of intercourse was not a material issue, disallowed both the disputed questions and the calling of the witness to make good what would have been put in the disputed questions.

Was the trial judge right to apply the test set out in section 4 of that Act (dealing with the calling of evidence relating to the cross-examination) instead of the ordinary test set out in *Reg v Sweet-Escott* relating to allowing questions going to the credibility of a witness? We see nothing in section 4 which would prevent a witness's previous statement inconsistent with his testimony before the judge being put to him to challenge his credibility even where the section did not allow the evidence of the making of the inconsistent statement to be given. So this court assumed in *Reg v Hart* (1957). There the appellant was convicted of wounding with intent to do grievous bodily harm, the wound being a severe knife wound concerning one Humphreys. The defence case was that the wound was caused accidentally when Humphreys came at him with a bottle. The prosecution case was that Humphreys had no bottle. It was put to him in cross-examination that he, the prosecution witness, had told a defence witness the opposite. However, the judge did not allow the defence witness to give evidence on this matter on the erroneous basis that the Act only applied to sworn statements. The court held that the judge was wrong in excluding the evidence but in that case applied the proviso. In giving the judgment of the court Devlin J made the distinction between questions going to the issue and questions going merely to credit: 'The provision under which that evidence was sought to be made admissible' – and this is the inconsistent statement – 'is now contained in section 4 of the Criminal Procedure Act 1865, which re-enacted the Common Law Procedure Act 1854. Before that it had probably been the common law that, quite apart from any statute, questions were admissible – certainly in the ordinary common law courts – whereby if a witness gave evidence of a fact that was relevant to the issue (*and that is important, because if the question merely goes to credit, he cannot be contradicted)'*– I stress that parenthesis – 'it could be put to him that on some earlier occasion he had made a contrary statement to somebody else and, if he denied it, that somebody else could be called'.

There the distinction is clearly made between questions going to the issue and questions going to credit. Examination of the judgment suggests that the court proceeded on the basis that the question went to the issue 'accident or not', because the jury might have thought the point as to whether Humphreys had a bottle important.

Accordingly we can see no basis either on the authorities or as a matter of principle for applying the Denman's Act test, relating to the calling of contradictory evidence, to the question of allowing cross-examination as to credit. To that problem it seems to us that the test suggested by Lawton J in *Reg v Sweet-Escott* is appropriate: how might the matter put to him affect his standing with the jury after cross-examination?

Applying that test it seems to us that the jury, having heard a graphic account from the child's evidence-in-chief as to how she had lost her virginity, might reasonably have wished to re-appraise her evidence and her credibility if they had heard that on other occasions she had spoken of experiences which, if true, would indicate that she could not have been a virgin at the time of the incident she so vividly described. Her standing as a witness might have been reduced.

Therefore, in our judgment, prosecuting counsel was wrong to withdraw his original concession (as he frankly conceded in the course of submissions before us) and the trial judge was wrong not to allow the disputed questions to be put in cross-examination.

The trial judge did not therefore have to go on to consider whether Denman's Act would permit the disputed evidence to be called if the questions were put. In any event it would have been premature to do so before the reaction to such cross-examination was known and the application to call the disputed evidence was made. However, his reasoning makes it clear that had he had to take that decision prematurely at the time of his ruling, he would not have allowed that evidence to be called. But as the Crown seek to rely on the proviso to support the convictions, and as Mr Shears for the defence has realistically acknowledged that the defence would have been much stronger had the disputed evidence been called to support the disputed questions, it is necessary for us to consider whether, on the likely scenario that the child had denied making inconsistent statements, the disputed evidence could have been called ...

When it came to the detail which she gave it seems clear to us that the transcript shows that the account she gave in her evidence-in-chief of the first of those incidents was a clear and pathetically moving account of the loss of virginity. If that account is true the tears, which we see from the transcript, accompanying the giving of that evidence were wholly unsurprising. Though the loss of virginity was never spelled out by any direct question from the Crown it would, in our judgment, have been superfluous to do so, not only because of the detail the child had gone into, but because of the Crown's introductory questions, which were cited by the judge in his summing-up in relation to the innocence of her previous experiences with her boyfriends.

It seems to us very likely that this particular detailed account of that first incident would be the most vivid picture which the jury took with them into their retiring room. Even disregarding the tears and the pathos, it was an account of something which only happens once in a lifetime.

Accordingly we do not find it surprising that the defence submit that it was necessary for them to challenge that account in order properly to put their defence, namely, a denial that there had been any acts of intercourse between the parties. Unchallenged, the descriptive details could give the account the stamp of truth: detail often adds verisimilitude, and it seems to us that it certainly would have here. But if a detail of such significance is successfully challenged it can destroy both the account and the credit of the witness who gave it. Therefore, it is submitted that this is not a challenge which goes merely to credit but that the disputed questions go directly to the issue and not merely to a collateral fact or, alternatively at least, in the words of Denman's Act, that her accounts of having lost her virginity on a previous occasion were statements 'inconsistent with her present testimony' made by her 'relative to the subject matter of the indictment.'

We are disposed to agree with the editors of *Cross on Evidence*, 6th edn (1985), p 295 that where the disputed issue is a sexual one between two persons in private the difference between questions going to credit and questions going to the issue is reduced to vanishing point. I read from that work: 'It has also been remarked that sexual intercourse, whether or not consensual, most often takes place in private, and leaves few visible traces of having occurred. Evidence is often effectively limited to that of the parties, and much is likely to depend on the balance of credibility between them. This has important effects for the law of evidence since it is capable of reducing the difference between questions going to credit and questions going to the issue to vanishing point.'

Similar problems arise when considering what facts are collateral. Again, we cite from *Cross* at p 283: 'As relevance is a matter of degree, it is impossible to devise an exhaustive means of determining when a question is collateral for the purpose of the rule under consideration; Pollock CB said in the leading case of *Attorney-General v Hitchcock* (1847) 1 Exch 91, 99: "The test of whether the matter is collateral or not is this: if the answer of a witness is a matter which you would be allowed on your own part to prove in evidence – if it have such a connection with the issues, that you would be allowed to give it in evidence – then it is a matter on which you may contradict him."'

The difficulty we have in applying that celebrated test is that it seems to us to be circular. If a fact is not collateral then clearly you can call evidence to contradict it, but the so-called test is silent on how you decide whether that fact is collateral. The utility of the test may lie in the fact that the answer is an instinctive one based on the prosecutor's and the court's sense of fair play rather than any philosophic or analytic process. Applying the test in argument, Morland J put to Mr Hillman for the Crown the hypothetical question, 'If the defence had medical evidence that this child was not a virgin before the date on which she gave her account of losing her virginity, would the defence be allowed to call such evidence?' On reflection, Mr Hillman accepted that they would be allowed to call such evidence, and we think that answer to the question not only right but inevitable. Otherwise there would be the danger that the jury would make their decision as to credit on an account of the original incident in which the most emotive, memorable and potentially persuasive fact was, to the knowledge of all in the case save the jury, false.

If that is right, then *a fortiori* conflicting statements must be 'relative to the subject matter of the indictment' within the meaning of Lord Denman's Act. It seems to us that on the way the prosecution presented the evidence the challenge to the loss of virginity was a challenge that not only did the jury deserve to know about on the basis that it might have affected their view on the central question of credit, but was sufficiently closely related to the subject matter of the indictment for justice to require investigation for the basis of such a challenge.

That is how the matter appears to us, but Mr Shears in the discharge of his duties to the court has referred us to an authority adverse to the submissions he has made to us, namely, the decision of this court in *Rex v Cargill* (1913) ... We do not doubt that decision in any way but in our view that case is clearly distinguishable from the instant case where, as we have attempted to indicate, the disputed evidence went far beyond a mere question of credibility.

Before leaving that authority we feel we should comment on one comment made by Channell J, in giving the judgment of the court, which reads strangely to modern eyes. He said: 'It is said an injustice has been done. I think that the ordinary rules of evidence do sometimes do an injustice. The rules are made to meet the general run of cases, and it cannot be helped if in particular cases they work an injustice. It is better to apply the rules strictly than to allow it to be supposed that a judge has a discretion to relax them if he thinks they will work an injustice.'

He then went on to find that he was in no doubt that in that case no injustice had been done. However, in relation to the general statement we would say that the rules of evidence are to foster the interest of justice and are made for that purpose, as we have attempted to indicate. That is why they impose restrictions on multiplicity of issues. But as we have also indicated the courts have evolved various exceptions to that rule under the category that we have given. The reason that the court evolved those exceptions is that where it is found that rules designed to promote justice interfere in any given case with justice, then the court must look anxiously to see whether this is an exceptional category of case. It may be that the categories of exception we have already listed are not closed. It is impossible to tell the circumstances in which some problems may arise in the future.

Accordingly it seems to us that the defence should have been allowed to put the disputed questions and, if met with a denial, to call the disputed evidence ...[23]

Criminal Procedure Act 1865

6   A witness may be questioned as to whether he has been convicted of any felony or misdemeanour, and upon being so questioned, if he either denies or does not admit the fact, or refuses to answer, it shall be lawful for the cross-examining party to prove such conviction.

R v Richardson (1968, Court of Appeal)

Edmund Davies LJ, giving the judgment of the court, summarised the facts and continued: The principal ground relied upon by both accused involves a point of pure law and it, therefore, is one upon which they are entitled to appeal as of right, and in respect of this and other points of law to be mentioned we treat this as the hearing of the appeals based upon them. It arises from what transpired at the trial when counsel for Longman sought to discredit the vital evidence of Mrs Clemence by calling a witness to establish that her testimony could not be relied upon. The method resorted to for this purpose, although little known, has considerable antiquity in the law ... The legal position may be thus summarised:

1   A witness may be asked whether he has knowledge of the impugned witness's general reputation for veracity and whether (from such knowledge) he would believe the impugned witness's sworn testimony.

2   The witness called to impeach the credibility of a previous witness may also express his individual opinion (based upon his personal knowledge) as to whether the latter is to be believed upon his oath and is not confined to giving evidence merely of general reputation.

3   But whether his opinion as to the impugned witness's credibility be based simply upon the latter's general reputation for veracity or upon his personal knowledge, the witness cannot be permitted to indicate during his examination-in-chief the particular facts, circumstances or incidents which formed the basis of his opinion, although he may be cross-examined as to them ... [24]

---

23.   90 Cr App R 466.
24.   51 Cr App R 381.

Toohey v Metropolitan Police Commissioner (1965, House of Lords)

Lord Pearce: The appellant and two other men were convicted on indictment of together assaulting Madden, a youth of 16, with intent to rob him. The episode took place in the dark in an alleyway beside and behind a cinema. The main evidence for the prosecution was that of Madden. There was also evidence from two police officers who saw two men standing in the shadows outside the cinema, and, being suspicious, turned their car. A faint crying noise directed them to the alleyway where they found Madden with his back to the wall and the three accused standing round him. The appellant was holding his arm. Madden's face was tear-stained; he was in a very distressed and hysterical condition, and his clothes were dishevelled. The accused claimed that they had done nothing wrong to him and were going to take him home. The boy said that he was going to the police station. He attempted to run away from the police officers, but they caught him and took him to the police station where he was examined by the divisional police surgeon, Dr Patrick Warren. At the trial Madden gave evidence that he was dragged into the dark alleyway, that the appellant hit him in the stomach and on the head until he 'saw sparks'; and that one of the accused searched him but took nothing since he did not find the 10s note which was in an inside pocket.

The defence was that Madden appeared to have been drinking and was behaving strangely, laughing and joking, and apparently incapable of taking care of himself. The three accused men were going to take him home but one of them wanted to make water; so they went down the alleyway behind the cinema. While the appellant was relieving himself, Madden bumped into him from behind, banged himself against a wall, and became hysterical, saying that someone had hit him and that they were after his money. They held his arm and took him up the alleyway to calm him down and get him home. They claimed that his account was an hysterical invention.

The police surgeon gave evidence for the defence to the effect that no bruises or signs of injury were found on Madden; that there was a definite smell of alcohol on his breath; that throughout the examination he was weeping and in a state of acute hysteria; that he was unable to reply sensibly to any question; and that at the end of the examination he just 'flopped down' on the floor. The doctor was, however, prevented by a ruling of the commissioner from giving certain further evidence. That exclusion was the ground of the present appeal.

There had been a previous abortive trial at which the jury disagreed. At that trial the doctor had given evidence, *inter alia*, that Madden's fall to the ground was a typically hysterical fall, a careful fall to avoid hitting himself on the furniture. He also said that, 'normal people do not have hysterical attacks like that and [that] anyone who presented a hysteria like that would be prone to that sort of thing and would be unstable'. Neither at that trial nor at the second trial did the prosecution object to any of the doctor's evidence. The commissioner at the second trial however, having presumably seen the notes of the doctor's evidence at the first trial, raised with counsel for the defence the question of admissibility before the doctor gave evidence. Relying on the case of *Rex v Gunewardene* (1951) he ruled that the doctor could say nothing, 'by way of medical opinion as to the boy's condition other than what he actually saw', and that he could not give 'a medical opinion, but ... such facts as anybody could have ascertained by looking at that boy'.

The Court of Criminal Appeal fairly summarised under two heads the evidence of whose exclusion the appellant was complaining: 'The first was the doctor's opinion as to what part was played by alcohol in the hysterical condition of

Madden ... The second was the doctor's opinion from what he observed by his examination of Madden of what Madden's normal behaviour might be like; in other words, as counsel put it, was he more prone to hysteria than a normal person, according to the doctor's observation?' The Court of Criminal Appeal came to the conclusion that the evidence was properly excluded on the principle set out in *Gunewardene's* case.

On the same ground, they also rejected an application to tender additional evidence which was not available at the trials as to the medical condition of Madden, as shown by matters which occurred after the alleged crime. Within two months of it Madden had pleaded guilty to loitering with intent. He was then certified as being subnormal, and an order was made under the Mental Health Act 1959 for his detention in a hospital. The reports since his admission showed him to be an hysterical, fanciful and untrustworthy person.

The Court of Criminal Appeal certified that a point of law of general public importance was involved, namely: 'Whether, having regard to *Rex v Gunewardene* or otherwise, counsel for the defence ought to have been permitted to put to a medical witness called on behalf of the accused a question designed to obtain an expression of the witness's opinions on a matter relating to the general mental condition of the witness who had given evidence for the prosecution, namely whether he was normally of an unstable or hysterical disposition.'

... The second question, whether it was permissible to impeach the credibility of Madden, *qua* witness, by medical evidence of his hysterical and unstable nature, raises a wider and more important problem which applies to evidence in criminal and civil cases alike ...

Human evidence shares the frailties of those who give it. It is subject to many crosscurrents such as partiality, prejudice, self-interest and, above all, imagination and inaccuracy. Those are matters with which the jury, helped by cross-examination and common sense, must do their best. But when a witness through physical (in which I include mental) disease or abnormality is not capable of giving a true or reliable account to the jury, it must surely be allowable for medical science to reveal this vital hidden fact to them. If a witness purported to give evidence of something which he believed that he had seen at a distance of 50 yards, it must surely be possible to call the evidence of an oculist to the effect that the witness could not possibly see anything at a greater distance than 20 yards, or the evidence of a surgeon who had removed a cataract from which the witness was suffering at the material time and which would have prevented him from seeing what he thought he saw. So, too, must it be allowable to call medical evidence of mental illness which makes a witness incapable of giving reliable evidence, whether through the existence of delusions or otherwise.

It is obviously in the interest of justice that such evidence should be available ... Medical evidence is admissible to show that a witness suffers from some disease or defect or abnormality of mind that affects the reliability of his evidence. Such evidence is not confined to a general opinion of the unreliability of the witness but may give all the matters necessary to show, not only the foundation of and reasons for the diagnosis, but also the extent to which the credibility of the witness is affected.

I would therefore allow the appeal.[25]

---

25. [1965] AC 595. The other Law Lords agreed.

CHAPTER 11

OPINION EVIDENCE

The sources in this chapter cover three main problems. First, when is opinion evidence admissible? The second problem arises when it has been decided that opinion evidence is, in principle, admissible. At that stage it is necessary to examine the basis on which the opinion has been reached because this, too, may affect admissibility. The third problem is one which has been seen to arise with some frequency in criminal trials. To what extent is the evidence of psychiatrists or psychologists admissible?

WHEN IS OPINION EVIDENCE ADMISSIBLE?

The basic rule is that witnesses testify about *facts* but are not entitled to give testimony about conclusions which they have drawn from facts, ie about their opinions. This basic rule is only rough and ready; quite often a 'fact' is an opinion in disguise. For example, if I say that I saw my neighbour Mary in the supermarket, there lurks behind this apparent statement of fact an opinion based on my knowledge of Mary and conclusions which I have reached about her characteristics and those of the person whom I saw in the supermarket. Further, an expression of opinion may actually be a shorthand way of stating perceived facts. Thus, if at the scene of a motor accident a bystander who observed what happened says, 'That pedestrian never gave the driver a chance to stop', he probably means that the pedestrian walked into the road quickly and without paying any attention to the traffic. The basic rule is not pressed too far. But there is also an important exception to it: an expert's opinion is admissible to furnish the court with scientific information which is likely to be outside the experience or knowledge of a judge or jury.

Civil Evidence Act 1972

3 (1) Subject to any rules of court made in pursuance of this Act, where a person is called as a witness in any civil proceedings, his opinion on any relevant matter on which he is qualified to give expert evidence shall be admissible in evidence.

(2) It is hereby declared that where a person is called as a witness in any civil proceedings, a statement of opinion by him on any relevant matter on which he is not qualified to give expert evidence, if made as a way of conveying relevant facts personally perceived by him, is admissible as evidence of what he perceived.

(3) In this section 'relevant matter' includes an issue in the proceedings in question.

R v Silverlock (1894, Court for Crown Cases Reserved)

The defendant was convicted on an indictment containing two counts of obtaining a cheque by false pretences. After his conviction the chairman of quarter sessions stated a case for the opinion of the court. It included the question whether it was necessary, in the case of proving handwriting by comparison, for the person drawing attention to the points of resemblance to be a professional expert or a person whose ordinary business led him to have special experience in questions of handwriting, or whether the evidence of any person who had, or stated he had, for some years studied handwriting would be admissible for that purpose.

Lord Russell of Killowen CJ: ... We now come to the second objection, as to the proof of the handwriting, which affords a good illustration of that class of evidence called evidence of opinion. It is true that the witness who is called upon to give evidence founded on a comparison of handwritings must be *peritus*; he must be skilled in doing so; but we cannot say that he must have become *peritus* in the way of his business or in any definite way. The question is, is he *peritus*? Is he skilled? Has he an adequate knowledge? Looking at the matter practically, if a witness is not skilled the judge will tell the jury to disregard his evidence. There is no decision which requires that the evidence of a man who is skilled in comparing handwriting, and who has formed a reliable opinion from past experience, should be excluded because his experience has not been gained in the way of his business. It is, however, really unnecessary to consider this point; for it seems from the statement in the present case that the witness was not only *peritus*, but was *peritus* in the way of his business. When once it is determined that the evidence is admissible, the rest is merely a question of its value or weight, and this is entirely a question for the jury, who will attach more or less weight to it according as they believe the witness to be *peritus*. ...[1]

THE BASIS FOR THE OPINION

An expert gives his opinion on the basis of facts in a particular case, and those facts must themselves be proved by admissible evidence. But the rule against hearsay, if strictly applied, would often prevent the expert from giving his opinion because his reasoning and conclusions will be governed by matters which he has come to know in the course of his training and profession from what he has read, or from what he has heard from others who have the same specialisation.

English Exporters (London) Ltd v Eldonwall Ltd (1973, Chancery Division)

This was an application under Part II of the Landlord and Tenant Act 1954 by the plaintiff tenants for the grant by the defendant landlords of a new tenancy. Amongst other things, the judge had to determine what should be the rent under the new tenancy, and in order to do this he heard expert evidence.

Megarry J: ... As is usual in these cases, a number of comparables was adduced. Eight were put forward by the landlords: the tenants put in none of their own. As is also far from unknown, some of the comparables were less comparable than others, and some turned out to be supported only by hearsay evidence, or by evidence that was in other respects less than cogent. There was no formal process of a ruling being made to exclude those comparables which were supported only by hearsay evidence; but I was discouraging, and in the event [counsel for the landlords] though rueful, did not seriously argue the point, or press it. I nevertheless think that I ought to make more explicit the reasons for my having

---

1. [1894] 2 QB 766. The other judges concurred.

been discouraging, for in my experience the status of hearsay evidence of comparables in valuation cases is a matter that is often misunderstood, and not only by valuers ...

Let me put on one side the cases in which exceptions to the rule excluding hearsay evidence have grown up, whether by case law or by statute ... and in particular I exclude cases in which, subject to observing the statutory safeguards, hearsay evidence has been made admissible under the Civil Evidence Act 1968. Let me further ignore cases in which questions in cross-examination may have let in evidence that otherwise would be inadmissible, and confine myself to the admissibility of hearsay in chief and in re-examination in these valuation cases. In such circumstances, two of the heads under which the valuers' evidence may be ranged are opinion evidence and factual evidence. As an expert witness, the valuer is entitled to express his opinion about matters within his field of competence. In building up his opinions about values, he will no doubt have learned much from transactions in which he has himself been engaged, and of which he could give first-hand evidence. But he will also have learned much from many other sources, including much of which he could give no first-hand evidence. Textbooks, journals, reports of auctions and other dealings, and information obtained from his professional brethren and others, some related to particular transactions and some more general and indefinite, will all have contributed their share. Doubtless much, or most, of this will be accurate, though some will not; and even what is accurate so far as it goes may be incomplete, in that nothing may have been said of some special element which affects values. Nevertheless, the opinion that the expert witness expresses is none the worse because it is in part derived from the matters of which he could give no direct evidence. Even if some of the extraneous information which he acquires in this way is inaccurate or incomplete, the errors and omissions will often tend to cancel each other out; and the valuer, after all, is an expert in this field, so that the less reliable the knowledge that he has about the details of some reported transaction, the more his experience will tell him that he should be ready to make some discount from the weight that he gives it in contributing to his overall sense of values. Some aberrant transactions may stand so far out of line that he will give them little or no weight. No question of giving hearsay evidence arises in such cases; the witness states his opinion from his general experience.

On the other hand, quite apart from merely expressing his opinion, the expert often is able to give factual evidence as well. If he has first-hand knowledge of a transaction, he can speak of that. He may himself have measured the premises and conducted the negotiations which led to a letting of them at £x, which comes to £y per square foot; and he himself may have read the lease and seen that it contains no provisions, other than some particular clause, which would have any material effect on the valuation; and then he may express his opinion on the value. So far as the expert gives factual evidence, he is doing what any other witness of fact may do, namely, speaking of that which he has perceived for himself. No doubt in many valuation cases the requirement of first-hand evidence is not pressed to an extreme: if the witness has not himself measured the premises, but it has been done by his assistant under his supervision, the expert's figures are often accepted without requiring the assistant to be called to give evidence. Again, it may be that it would be possible for a valuer to fill a gap in his first-hand knowledge of a transaction by some method such as stating in his evidence that he has made diligent enquiries of some person who took part in the transaction in question, but despite receiving full answers to his enquiries, he discovered nothing which suggested to him that the transaction had any unusual features which would affect the value as a comparable. But basically, the expert's factual evidence on matters of fact is in the same position as the factual evidence of any other witness. Further, factual evidence that he cannot give himself is sometimes adduced in some other way, as by the testimony of some other witness who was himself concerned in the transaction in question, or by proving some document which carried the transaction through, or recorded it; and to the transaction thus established, like the transactions which the expert himself has proved, the expert may apply his experience and opinions, as tending to support or qualify his views.

That being so, it seems to me quite another matter when it is asserted that a valuer may give factual evidence of transactions of which he has no direct knowledge, whether *per se* or whether in the guise of giving reasons for his opinion as to value. It is one thing to say, 'From my general experience of recent transactions comparable with this one, I think the proper rent should be £x': it is another thing to say, 'Because I have been told by someone else that the premises next door have an area of x square feet and were recently let on such and such terms for £y a year, I say the rent of these premises should be £z a year'. What he has been told about the premises next door may be inaccurate or misleading as to the area, the rent, the terms and much else besides. It makes it no better when the witness expresses his confidence in the reliability of his source of information: a transparently honest and careful witness cannot make information reliable if, instead of speaking of what he has seen and heard for himself, he is merely retailing what others have told him. The other party to the litigation is entitled to have a witness whom he can cross-examine on oath as to the reliability of the facts deposed to, and not merely as to the witness's opinion as to the reliability of information which was given to him not on oath, and possibly in circumstances tending to inaccuracies and slips. Further, it is often difficult enough for the courts to ascertain the true facts from witnesses giving direct evidence, without the added complication of attempts to evaluate a witness's opinion of the reliability, care and thoroughness of some informant who has supplied the witness with the facts that he is seeking to recount.

It therefore seems to me that details of comparable transactions upon which a valuer intends to rely in his evidence must, if they are to be put before the court, be confined to those details which have been, or will be, proved by admissible evidence, given either by the valuer himself or in some other way. I know of no special rule giving expert valuation witnesses the right to give hearsay evidence of facts: and notwithstanding many pleasant days spent in the Lands Tribunal while I was at the Bar, I can see no compelling reasons of policy why they should be able to do this. Of course, the long-established technique in adducing expert evidence of asking hypothetical questions may also be employed for valuers. It would, I think, be perfectly proper to ask a valuer, 'If in May 1972 No 3, with an area of 2,000 sq ft, was let for £10,000 a year for seven years on a full repairing lease with no unusual terms, what rent would be appropriate for the premises in dispute?' But I cannot see that it would do much good unless the facts of the hypothesis are established by admissible evidence; and the valuer's statement that someone reputable had told him these facts, or that he had seen them in a reputable periodical, would not in my judgment constitute admissible evidence ...[2]

H v Schering Chemicals Ltd (1983, Queen's Bench Division)

The plaintiffs sued the defendants for damages for personal injuries allegedly caused by the defendants in the manufacture and marketing of a drug. There

---

2. [1973] Ch 415.

were two main issues: whether the defendants had been negligent, and whether the injuries complained of had in fact been caused by the drug. The court had to consider the admissibility of a variety of documents, some summarising the results of research, others taking the form of articles or letters published in medical journals. It was common ground between the parties that the contents of the journals could be referred to by expert medical witnesses as part of the body of medical knowledge within their expertise. In the judgment the following comment was made:

Bingham J: It is, as I have said, common ground that these articles can be referred to by experts as part of the general corpus of medical knowledge falling within the expertise of an expert in this field. That of course means that an expert who says ... 'I consider that there is a causal connection between the taking of the drug and the resulting deformity', can fortify his opinion by referring to learned articles, publications, letters as reinforcing the view to which he has come. In doing so, he can make reference to papers in which a contrary opinion may be expressed but in which figures are set out which he regards as supporting his contention. In such a situation one asks: Are the figures and statistics set out in such an article strictly proved? And I think the answer is, No. I think that they are none the less of probative value when referred to and relied on by an expert in the manner in which I have indicated. If an expert refers to the results of research published by a reputable authority in a reputable journal the court would, I think, ordinarily regard those results as supporting inferences fairly to be drawn from them, unless or until a different approach was shown to be proper.[3]

R v Abadom (1983, Court of Appeal)

The appellant was convicted of robbery. His appeal raised the question of what materials could be used by expert witnesses when giving evidence.

Kerr LJ: ... During the afternoon of Saturday 25 August 1979 four masked and gloved men broke into the office of a family business run by a Mr and Mrs Williams who were working there together with other members of the family. The men were all wearing Balaclava helmets with slits for the eyes, so that it was only possible for those present to form some general impression of their description, without being able to identify them thereafter. They were armed with cudgels and the leader broke an internal window in the office, no doubt in order to contribute to the fright which was naturally experienced by those present. They then demanded where the money was kept and, on this being indicated to them, made off with a sum of over £5,000 in cash from a drawer in the office.

The case for the prosecution was that the appellant was the leader who had broken the window. The main evidence against him was that a pair of his shoes removed by the police from his home after his arrest were found to have fragments of glass adhering and embedded in them, which, as the prosecution contended, had formed part of the broken window. There was evidence concerning the position of the fragments of glass which was consistent with the incident, in that some were found on the upper part and inside the shoes, while others were embedded in the sole, suggesting that some of the fragments had fallen from above and others had been trodden on by the appellant.

---

3.   [1983] 1 WLR 143.

In order to seek to establish the likelihood of the fragments of glass having come from the broken window, the prosecution called two expert witnesses who were principal scientific officers at the Home Office forensic laboratories with considerable experience in the analysis of fragments of glass, a Mr RA Cooke and a Mr KW Smalldon ...

Mr Cooke explained that all glass has a refractive index, capable of being determined to five decimal places, which constitutes a measure as to how the light is bent when it passes into a particular piece of glass. He described the method of determining this index which he had used in this case. Using this method, he had compared several of the fragments of glass found in and on the shoes with each other and with the control sample, the glass of the broken window, and found that they all had the identical refractive index. Before expressing any opinion as to the likelihood or otherwise of the fragments of glass having come from the window, he was then asked about the frequency with which this particular refractive index is found to occur. In this connection he explained that it had been the practice of the Home Office Central Research Establishment to collate statistics of the refractive index of broken glass which had been analysed in forensic laboratories over a period of years, and that, having consulted these statistics, he found that this particular refractive index only occurred in 4% of all the analyses which had been made. If the analyses were limited to window glass, the frequency of occurrence was marginally lower. He was then asked whether, on the basis of his expert knowledge and the further analysis made by Mr Smalldon which he had seen and to which I turn in a moment, he was able to express any opinion as to the likely relationship of the glass fragments with the control sample. He answered this by saying: 'Well, considering that only 4% of controlled glass samples actually have this refractive index I consider there is very strong evidence that the glass from the shoes is in fact the same as the glass from the window; in fact it originated from the window.'

Mr Smalldon then gave evidence that he had carried out a chemical analysis of the fragments of glass and of the control sample, and that he had found that 'the two samples were similar on analysis and the analysis was typical of modern flat production glass', ie window glass ...

The point taken on this appeal was that the evidence of Mr Cooke, that the identical refractive index of the fragments of glass with that of the control sample occurred in only 4% of all controlled glass samples analysed and statistically collated in the Home Office Central Research Establishment, was inadmissible because it constituted hearsay evidence. It was said to be hearsay because Mr Cooke had no personal knowledge of the analyses whose results were collated in these statistics, save possibly a few for which he may have been personally responsible. This submission was challenged on behalf of the Crown, but no point was taken, in our view clearly rightly, on the ground that the admissibility of this evidence had not been challenged on behalf of the defence at the trial. In our view, the evidence was not inadmissible as hearsay. It is convenient to deal with this issue first on the basis of general principle and then to consider the authorities.

Mr Cooke was admittedly an expert, and was giving evidence as an expert, on the likelihood or otherwise of the fragments of glass having come from the control sample, the broken window. As an expert in this field he was entitled to express an opinion on this question, subject to laying the foundation for his opinion and subject, of course, to his evidence being tested by cross-examination for evaluation by the jury. In the context of evidence given by experts it is no more than a statement of the obvious that, in reaching their conclusion, they must be entitled to draw on material produced by others in the field in which their expertise lies. Indeed, it is part of their duty to consider any material which may be available in their field, and not to draw conclusions merely on the basis of their own experience, which is inevitably likely to be more limited than the general body of information which may be available to them. Further, when an expert has to consider the likelihood or unlikelihood of some occurrence or factual association in reaching his conclusion, as must often be necessary, the statistical results of the work of others in the same field must inevitably form an important ingredient in the cogency or probative value of his own conclusion in the particular case. Relative probabilities or improbabilities must frequently be an important factor in the evaluation of any expert opinion and, when any reliable statistical material is available which bears on this question, it must be part of the function and duty of the expert to take this into account.

However, it is also inherent in the nature of any statistical information that it will result from the work of others in the same field, whether or not the expert in question will himself have contributed to the bank of information available on the particular topic on which he is called on to express his opinion. Indeed, to exclude reliance on such information on the ground that it is inadmissible under the hearsay rule might inevitably lead to the distortion or unreliability of the opinion which the expert presents for evaluation by a judge or jury. Thus, in the present case, the probative value or otherwise of the identity of the refractive index as between the fragments and the control sample could not be assessed without some further information about the frequency of its occurrence. If all glass of the type in question had the same refractive index, this evidence would have virtually no probative value whatever. The extent to which this refractive index is common or uncommon must therefore be something which an expert must be entitled to take into account, and indeed must take into account, before he can properly express an opinion about the likelihood or unlikelihood of the fragments of glass having come from the window in question. The cogency or otherwise of the expert's conclusion on this point, in the light of, *inter alia*, the available statistical material against which this conclusion falls to be tested, must then be a matter for the jury.

We therefore consider that Mr Cooke's reliance on the statistical information collated by the Home Office Central Research Establishment, before arriving at his conclusion about the likely relationship between the fragments of glass and the control sample, was not only permissible in principle, but that it was an essential part of his function as an expert witness to take account of this material ...

However, it was submitted that the present case was indistinguishable from the decision in *Myers v DPP* (1964) since Mr Cooke had not been personally responsible for the compilation of the Home Office statistics on which he relied, so that the inferences which he drew from them must be inadmissible because they were based on hearsay. In our view this conclusion does not follow, either as a matter of principle or on the basis of authority. We are here concerned with the cogency or otherwise of an opinion expressed by an expert in giving expert evidence. In that regard it seems to us that the process of taking account of information stemming from the work of others in the same field is an essential ingredient of the nature of expert evidence. So far as the question of principle is concerned, we have already explained our reasons for this conclusion. So far as the authorities are concerned, the position can be summarised as follows.

First, where an expert relies on the existence or non-existence of some fact which is basic to the question on which he is asked to express his opinion, that fact must be proved by admissible evidence: see *English Exporters (London) Ltd v Eldonwall Ltd* (1973) and *R v Turner* (1975). Thus, it would no doubt have been inadmissible if Mr Cooke had said in the present case that he had been told by somebody else that the refractive index of the fragments of glass and of the control sample was identical, and any opinion expressed by him on this basis would then have been based on hearsay. If he had not himself determined the refractive index, it would have been necessary to call the person who had done so before Mr Cooke could have expressed any opinion based on this determination. In this connection it is to be noted that Mr Smalldon was rightly called to prove the chemical analysis made by him which Mr Cooke was asked to take into account. Second, where the existence or non-existence of some fact is in issue, a report made by an expert who is not called as a witness is not admissible as evidence of that fact merely by the production of the report, even though it was made by an expert ...

These, however, are in our judgment the limits of the hearsay rule in relation to evidence of opinion given by experts, both in principle and on the authorities. In other respects their evidence is not subject to the rule against hearsay in the same way as that of witnesses of fact: see *English Exporters (London) Ltd v Eldonwall Ltd* (1973) and *Phipson on Evidence* (12th edn, 1976) para 1207. Once the primary facts on which their opinion is based have been proved by admissible evidence, they are entitled to draw on the work of others as part of the process of arriving at their conclusion. However, where they have done so, they should refer to this material in their evidence so that the cogency and probative value of their conclusion can be tested and evaluated by reference to it.

Thus, if in the present case the statistical tables of analyses made by the Home Office forensic laboratories had appeared in a textbook or other publication, it could not be doubted that Mr Cooke would have been entitled to rely on them for the purposes of his evidence. Indeed, this was not challenged. But it does not seem to us, in relation to the reliability of opinion evidence given by experts, that they must necessarily limit themselves to drawing on material which has been published in some form. Part of their experience and expertise may well lie in their knowledge of unpublished material and in their evaluation of it. The only rule in this regard, as it seems to us, is that they should refer to such material in their evidence for the reasons stated above.

We accordingly conclude that Mr Cooke's reliance on the Home Office statistics did not infringe the rule against hearsay and we dismiss the appeal against conviction ...[4]

EVIDENCE FROM PSYCHIATRISTS AND PSYCHOLOGISTS

Judges have an ambivalent attitude towards evidence from experts on mental conditions. To some extent they recognise that a psychiatrist or psychologist may be able to provide useful testimony about matters that are outside the experience of judge or jurors. At the same time, they think there is a danger that mental experts will usurp the role of the jury or other triers of fact unless a clear line is drawn between abnormal and normal mental states. The latter include

---

4. [1983] 1 All ER 364.

lust, anger and other undesirable emotions which, judges believe, are perfectly capable of being understood by ordinary people without expert assistance. The attempt to make such a distinction has led to some unhappy compromises, the most bizarre being the distinction that has been drawn between expert evidence that is relevant to the reliability of a confession and expert evidence relevant to *mens rea*.

DPP v A & BC Chewing Gum Ltd (1968, Divisional Court)

Lord Parker CJ: This is an appeal by way of case stated from a decision of justices for the North East London Commission Area, sitting at Romford, who dismissed an information preferred by the Director of Public Prosecutions against the defendant company for that they on a day in March 1966 had for publication for gain divers obscene articles, to wit, 43 'bubble gum' battle cards, contrary to section 2(1) of the Obscene Publications Act 1959 and section 1(1) of the Obscene Publications Act 1964.

What had been found in the present case was that a Mr O'Connell took over a tuck shop at 19, Storey Road, N6, opposite an elementary and infants' school. He had a stock of bubble gum which had been obtained by the previous owners from the defendant company, and he found that this sold like wildfire. The children came and bought the bubble gum and so did parents, and the real attraction appeared to be the cards – rather a glorified edition of the old form of cigarette cards – which came in a numbered series with the bubble gum. Children and grown-ups would come to buy the bubble gum not only for the gum but in order to obtain these cards and swop them amongst themselves. He was in fact asked to stop and did stop selling them at the request of the headmistress of the school.

The police were informed, and they approached the defendant company, who quite frankly let them have a complete set of 73 cards. Of those, 42 or 43 were selected as subjects for this prosecution. The only finding of the justices which is important here is that the defendant company had in contemplation that it was likely that (a) the cards and copies thereof would be sold in and with packets of chewing gum and be read and seen by children of all ages from five upwards, and (b) such children would swop cards amongst themselves in order to obtain a complete set of 73 cards, and would therefore see and read a complete set. The justices, however, came to the conclusion that none of the 43 cards, either by itself or in conjunction with the others, was such as to tend to deprave and corrupt a child of the age of five or upwards, and accordingly dismissed the information.

For myself, I see, though I might change my mind on argument, great difficulty in saying that that was a perverse decision in the sense of a decision which no reasonable bench of justices, properly directing themselves as to the law, could arrive at, but I find it unnecessary to go into that matter for this reason: the prosecution at the trial tendered expert witnesses, in the form of psychiatrists, experienced in child psychiatry, to give evidence as to the likely effect upon children of various ages of the 43 cards taken singly and together. The justices, however, refused to hear that expert evidence. If they were wrong in so doing, then clearly this case must go back for retrial.

Now what was submitted to the justices and has been submitted to this court is that, as a general rule, a long-standing rule of common law, evidence is inadmissible if it is on the very issue the court has to determine. For my part, and I am only dealing with this case, I cannot think that the evidence tendered was on that very issue. There were two matters really for consideration. What sort of effect would these cards singly or together have upon children, and no doubt children of different ages; what would it lead them to do? Secondly, was what they were led to do a sign of corruption or depravity? As it seems to me, it would be perfectly proper to call a psychiatrist and to ask him in the first instance what his experience, if any, with children was, and to say what the effect on the minds of children of different groups would be if certain types of photographs or pictures were put before them, and indeed, having got his general evidence, to put one or more of the cards in question to him and say what would their effect be upon the child. For myself, I think it would be wrong to ask the direct question as to whether any particular cards tended to corrupt or deprave, because that final stage was a matter which was entirely for the justices. No doubt, however, in such a case the defence might well put it to the witness that a particular card or cards could not corrupt, and no doubt, whatever the strict position may be, that question coming from the defence would be allowed, if only to give the defence an opportunity of getting an answer, 'No', from the expert.

On that ground alone, as it seems to me, the evidence in the present case was admissible.

I myself would go a little further in that I cannot help feeling that with the advance of science more and more inroads have been made into the old common law principles. Those who practise in the criminal courts see every day cases of experts being called on the question of diminished responsibility, and although technically the final question, 'Do you think he was suffering from diminished responsibility?', is strictly inadmissible, it is allowed time and time again without any objection. No doubt when dealing with the effect of certain things on the mind science may still be less exact than evidence as to what effect some particular thing will have on the body, but that, as it seems to me, is purely a question of weight.

I said that I was confining my observations to this particular case, because I can quite see that when considering the effect of something on an adult an adult jury may be able to judge just as well as an adult witness called on the point. Indeed, there is nothing more that a jury or justices need to know. But certainly when you are dealing here with children of different age groups and children from five upwards, any jury and any justices need all the help they can get, information which they may not have, as to the effect on different children. For those reasons, I think that certainly in so far as this objection is based on common law it fails ...[5]

R v Anderson (1972, Court of Appeal)

This was the appeal in the notorious case involving *Oz No 28 School Kids' Issue*, in which the defendants were charged, *inter alia*, with an offence under s 2 of the Obscene Publications Act 1959.

Lord Widgery CJ [delivering the judgment of the court]: ... The second matter which arose in the court below, and which requires some general comments by this court, relates to the expert evidence which was called. The defence called expert evidence for something more than twenty days. A great mass of expert evidence was called. Part of that evidence was directed to what is called the 'public good' defence contained in section 4 of the Act. I need not read the section in full but under section 4(1) a defence can be put forward in respect of an obscene article that its publication is desirable in the public good, and section 4(2) specifically

---

5. [1968] QB 159.

provides that the opinion of experts as to the literary, artistic, scientific or other merit of such an article may be admitted. What is contemplated there is that, if an article is found to be obscene, evidence of experts as to its merits under those heads may be called and it is then for the jury to balance the merit and demerit of the article and conclude whether they find it acceptable or not. So far as evidence was called under that section, no question arises on it now, but a majority of the expert evidence called by the defence in this case bore no relation to the defence of the public good under section 4, but was rather directed to showing that the article was not obscene. In other words, it was directed to showing that in the opinion of the witness it would not tend to deprave or corrupt. Now whether the article is obscene or not is a question exclusively in the hands of the jury, and it was decided in this court in *Reg v Calder & Boyars Ltd* (1969) that expert evidence should not be admitted on the issue of obscene or not. It is perfectly true that there was an earlier Divisional Court case in which a somewhat different view had been taken. It was the *Director of Public Prosecutions v A and BC Chewing Gum Ltd* (1968). That case in our judgment should be regarded as highly exceptional and confined to its own circumstances, namely, a case where the alleged obscene matter was directed at very young children, and was of itself of a somewhat unusual kind. In the ordinary run of the mill cases in the future the issue 'obscene or not' must be tried by the jury without the assistance of expert evidence on that issue, and we draw attention to the failure to observe that rule in this case in order that that failure may not occur again.

We are not oblivious of the fact that some people, perhaps many people, will think a jury, unassisted by experts, a very unsatisfactory tribunal to decide such a matter. Those who feel like that must campaign elsewhere for a change of the law. We can only deal with the law as it stands, and that is how it stands on this point ...[6]

Lowery v The Queen (1974, Privy Council)

Lowery and King were convicted of the sadistic and otherwise motiveless murder of a girl aged 15. At trial they ran 'cut throat' defences, each saying that the other was solely responsible for the crime. King called in his defence a psychologist, the effect of whose testimony was to support King's allegations against Lowery. In the event, both defendants were convicted. Lowery appealed, arguing that the psychologist's evidence should not have been admitted.

Lord Morris of Borth-y-Gest: [T]he evidence given by Lowery ... was that the killing was entirely the work of King and that he (Lowery) had made strong efforts to stop King. Beyond this, as the judge said in his report to the Court of Criminal Appeal: 'Lowery himself had not only called evidence as to his reputation with a view to showing that his disposition made him entirely unlikely to have committed such a crime as this, but in addition he had for the same purpose given evidence that he had never been charged with any serious offence, that he had been happy in his marriage, happy in the prospect of the birth of the child and happy in the prospect of moving into his new house, and that he had had good hopes for his financial future. He also called his wife to confirm his evidence on some of these matters.'

In his re-examination Lowery, in support of his evidence to the effect that after what had happened he was in fear of King and feared what King might do, said

6.   [1972] 1 QB 304.

that King was a member of an organisation called Hell's Angels whereas he (Lowery) was not. In answer to a question by his counsel Lowery proceeded to say that he had expectation about his father's business. When inquiry was made as to the relevance of this evidence the questions being put were justified as being put (a) to show that, 'his prospects were just opening before him and in those circumstances such an activity as is suggested to him would completely wreck them', and (b), 'in rebuttal of the suggestion that he was interested in this sort of behaviour or would wish to plan such a venture over a period of time or follow it through.' Finally in re-examination Lowery was asked whether he had any motive whatsoever to take a girl away and kill her: he answered that he had not.

When the time came for the evidence by and on behalf of King to be presented the position was that not only was there the Crown case that both accused had acted in concert but there was the testimony of Lowery that it was King who had been the killer and that he (Lowery) had been physically overborne when he tried to stop King and had afterwards been put in fear by King's threats of what he might do (including a threat of violence to Lowery's wife if he (Lowery) did not say certain things that King wished him to say) and further that he (Lowery) was not only of good character but was not 'interested in this sort of behaviour'. As the central theme of King's defence (if issues concerning insanity and automatism failed) was that it was Lowery who had been the killer it is manifest that it became necessary in King's interests that the suggestions made by and on behalf of Lowery should be displaced.

It was in this setting that the witness Professor Cox was called on behalf of King. Before referring to the substance of the evidence which the witness gave it will be convenient to indicate the nature of the objections which at the trial or on appeal were submitted against its admissibility. It was said that the evidence was not relevant to any issue and was of no probative value in considering the guilt of the accused: that evidence of the psychological condition of an accused person as tending to prove his guilt ought never to be introduced either by the prosecution or by the defence of a co-accused person: that the evidence whether adduced by prosecution or by defence ought to have been excluded as a matter of law because its introduction would merely show disposition: that the evidence did not fall within any of the exceptions denoted in *Makin v Attorney General for New South Wales* (1894) to the general rule there stated.

When considering evidence which is tendered to a court it is always helpful to distinguish between relevance and admissibility and weight ... Questions of weight are for a jury. In the present appeal attention is focused upon the evidence of one witness out of very many who were called in the course of a lengthy trial. How far the evidence assisted the jury must be a matter of speculation. Their Lordships are only concerned to consider whether the Court of Criminal Appeal were right in upholding the admissibility of the evidence. The questions arise whether the evidence was (a) relevant and (b) admissible: not all evidence that is relevant is admissible. In some circumstances evidence that may have some relevance is not admissible because its prejudicial effect heavily overbalances its probative value and as a matter of fairness or of public policy a court will not allow the prosecution to call such evidence ...

Professor Cox had interviews in turn with Lowery and with King. In each case he applied certain well-known tests. His evidence was as to the results of the tests in each case. These tests were 'the main stock in trade' of clinical psychologists. The tests were partly intelligence tests but primarily were tests as to the general personality of the person interviewed. The judge at the trial after objection and argument allowed evidence to be given as to the respective results of the tests of the two men in so far as they threw light on qualities of dominance or leadership or dependence or submission or on the general personality of the two men ...

The witness gave the results of the two tests in the case of King and combining the two test records the witness said that the picture was, 'of an immature – by that I mean immature for a young man of his age – an immature, emotionally shallow youth who seems likely to be led and dominated by more aggressive or dominant men and who conceivably could act out or could behave aggressively to comply with the wishes or the demands or orders of another person.'

The record of the tests was consistent with King's statement in evidence that he was frightened by Lowery while the events were taking place.

The same two tests for personality were used by the witness in regard to Lowery. The resultant findings of the witness were that Lowery showed little evidence of capacity to relate adequately to others, that he had a strong aggressive drive with weak controls over the expression of aggressive impulses, and a basic callousness and impulsiveness. The attribute of callousness had not been found in King. Another finding ... was only given in evidence after further arguments had been addressed to the court in the absence of the jury. The ruling of the judge was that the witness should confine himself to those personality traits which would be relevant to the question as to which account of the killing was the more probable and that the witness should not go into any which related to tendencies such as tendencies to lying or fraud or deceit or the like. The further finding was that one of the tests indicated in Lowery's case that some sadistic pleasure was obtained from observing the suffering of other people. In relation to King the results of the tests had given no such indication. Lowery's personality could be described as a psychopathic personality, it being made clear that in this context the word 'psychopathic' conveyed no suggestion of insanity or of mental disease but merely of personality disorder. To be shaken in this assessment the witness said that he would need evidence of non-psychopathic characteristics. King also showed some features of a psychopathic personality but they were less severe than in Lowery's case. Lowery showed little evidence of capacity to feel for others: King's capacity to feel for others was below the average. Both men showed aggressive tendencies with weak control over them but Lowery's aggressiveness was more intense. Both men showed impulsiveness: that in Lowery being a little more but not a great deal more marked ...

Having referred fully to the nature of the evidence given by Professor Cox the question as to its admissibility may now be considered. There was no doubt that Rosalyn Mary Nolte was killed in the bush area some 10 miles out of Hamilton when Lowery and King were present and when no one else was present. As was pointed out in the Court of Criminal Appeal the very nature of the killing showed that it was 'a sadistic and otherwise motiveless killing'. Any prospect of the acquittal of either of the two accused could only have been on the basis that one alone was the killer and that the other took no part whatsoever. That was what Lowery alleged when he said that King alone was the killer and that he (Lowery) was powerless to save the girl. In *Rex v Miller* (1952), Devlin J referred to the duty of counsel for the defence to adduce any admissible evidence which is strictly relevant to his own case and assists his client whether or not it prejudices anyone else. The case for King was that Lowery had alone been the killer and that King had been heavily under the influence of drugs and had been powerless to stop Lowery ... In all these circumstances it was necessary on behalf of King to call all relevant and admissible evidence which would exonerate King and throw responsibility entirely on Lowery. If in imaginary circumstances similar to those of this case it was apparent that one of the accused was a man of great physical strength whereas the other was a weakling it could hardly be doubted that in forming an opinion as to the probabilities it would be relevant to have the disparity between the two in mind. Physical characteristics may often be of considerable relevance: see *Reg v Toohey* (1965). The evidence of Professor Cox was not related to crime or criminal tendencies: it was scientific evidence as to the respective personalities of the two accused as, and to the extent, revealed by certain well-known tests. Whether it assisted the jury is not a matter that can be known. All that is known is that the jury convicted both the accused. But in so far as it might help in considering the probabilities as to what happened at the spot to which the girl was taken it was not only relevant to and indeed necessary for the case advanced by King but was made relevant and admissible in view of the case advanced by Lowery and in view of Lowery's assertions against King.

The case being put forward by counsel on behalf of King involved posing to the jury the question, 'Which of these two men is the more likely to have killed this girl?', and inviting the jury to come to the conclusion that it was Lowery. If the crime was one which was committed apparently without any kind of motive unless it was for the sensation experienced in the killing then unless both men acted in concert the deed was that of one of them. It would be unjust to prevent either of them from calling any evidence of probative value which could point to the probability that the perpetrator was one rather than the other.

Lowery put his character in issue. If an accused person puts his character in issue in the sense of asserting that he has never been convicted of any offence then provided that it is fair to do so it may be shown that he has had convictions. If an accused person puts his character in issue in the sense of adducing evidence that he is of good general reputation then it may be legitimate to call rebutting evidence of an equally general nature. When an accused person puts his character in issue he is in effect asking a jury to take the view that he is not one who would be disposed to have committed or would be likely to have committed the crime in question. An accused person of good character is permitted to advance such a consideration. But if an accused person is not of good character the law has been firm in the principle recognised by Lord Herschell LC in *Makin v Attorney General for New South Wales* (1894), when he said: 'It is undoubtedly not competent for the prosecution to adduce evidence tending to show that the accused has been guilty of criminal acts other than those covered in the indictment, for the purpose of leading to the conclusion that the accused is a person likely from his criminal conduct or character to have committed the offence for which he is being tried.'

Lord Herschell LC proceeded to refer to certain well-known exceptions from the general rule.

It may here be stated that it was not suggested by the Solicitor-General that the contested evidence either could or would have been adduced by the prosecution.

In reference to this matter the Court of Criminal Appeal said, and in their Lordships' view rightly said: 'It is, however, established by the highest authorities that in criminal cases the Crown is precluded from leading evidence that does no more than show that the accused has a disposition or propensity or is the sort of person likely to commit the crime charged ...' and further: 'It is, we think, one thing to say that such evidence is excluded when tendered by the Crown in proof of guilt, but quite another to say that it is excluded when tendered by the accused in disproof of his own guilt. We see no reason of policy or fairness which justifies or requires the exclusion of evidence relevant to prove the innocence of an accused person.'

The evidence of Professor Cox as will have been seen was not as such evidence in regard to the character of Lowery and King but rather was evidence as to their respective intelligences and personalities ... Lowery and King were each asserting that the other was the completely dominating person at the time Rosalyn Nolte was killed: each claimed to have been in fear of the other. In these circumstances it was most relevant for King to be able to show, if he could, that Lowery had a personality marked by aggressiveness whereas he, King, had a personality which suggested that he would be led and dominated by someone who was dominant and aggressive. In support of King's case the evidence of Professor Cox was relevant if it tended to show that the version of the facts put forward by King was more probable than that put forward by Lowery. Not only however was the evidence which King called relevant to this case: its admissibility was placed beyond doubt by the whole substance of Lowery's case. Not only did Lowery assert that the killing was done by King and not only did he say that he had been in fear of King but, as previously mentioned, he set himself up as one who had no motive whatsoever in killing the girl and as one who would have been likely to wreck his good prospects and furthermore as one who would not have been interested in the sort of behaviour manifested by the killer. While ascribing the sole responsibility to King he was also in effect saying that he himself was not the sort of man to have committed the offence. The only question now arising is whether in the special circumstances above referred to it was open to King in defending himself to call Professor Cox to give the evidence that he gave. The evidence was relevant to and necessary for his case which involved negativing what Lowery had said and put forward: in their Lordships' view in agreement with that of the Court of Criminal Appeal the evidence was admissible.

For these reasons their Lordships have humbly advised Her Majesty that the appeal should be dismissed.[7]

R v Turner (1975, Court of Appeal)

I have reproduced the whole of this judgment because, as well as dealing with the admissibility of psychiatric evidence, it provides an excellent example of the analytical approach which should be adopted towards any expert evidence. The first question must always be: *What*, precisely, is this expert saying? And then: *On what* is he basing his opinion?

Lawton LJ read the following judgment of the court: On February 14 1974 at Bristol Crown Court after a trial before Bridge J the defendant was convicted of murder and sentenced to life imprisonment. He has appealed against his conviction on the ground that the judge refused to admit evidence which a psychiatrist was prepared to give in support of his defence of provocation. He has asked this court to receive that evidence.

At about midnight on October 26/27 1973 at Swindon while sitting in a motor car with a girl named Wendy Butterfield the defendant killed her by battering her about the head and face with a hammer. Fifteen blows were struck. Very shortly after striking these blows he went to a nearby farmhouse and told the occupants there he had killed his girlfriend. The police were sent for. When they arrived he said: 'I've killed my girlfriend ... I bashed her head in with a hammer. I didn't mean to do it. I didn't mean to do it, honestly.' Later when told he would be arrested on suspicion of murder he said: 'I know, I know. I just kept hitting her.'

---

7. [1974] AC 85.

His defence was provocation. In the circumstances it could not have been any other. The basis for this defence was that he was deeply in love with the girl, whom he thought was pregnant by him. While he was in the motor car with her he said that she had told him with a grin that while he had been in prison she had been sleeping with two other men, that she could make money in this way and that the child she was carrying was not his. He claimed that he had been very upset by what she had said. His hand had come across the hammer which was down by the side of the seat and he had hit her with it. He said: 'It was never in my mind to do her any harm. I did not realise what I had in my hand. I knew it was heavy ... When I realised it was a hammer I stopped.'

If the jury rejected his evidence as to how the girl came to be killed (it was challenged by the prosecution) there was no foundation for the defence put forward. The defendant's credit as a witness was an important issue.

After the defendant had given evidence his counsel, Mr Mildon, told Bridge J he wanted to call a psychiatrist. He explained why. He said: 'First of all, it may help the jury to accept as credible the defendant's account of what happened and, second, it may tell them why this man was provoked.'

The judge queried whether the evidence of a psychiatrist was admissible on these matters. There was some discussion, at the end of which the judge said that he wanted to see the evidence which the psychiatrist proposed to give. Mr Mildon then handed to the judge a lengthy psychiatric report dated February 2 1974 which had been prepared by a Dr Smith. It was in a form with which judges have become familiar in recent years. At the beginning the doctor said that he had been asked to deal with various matters and in particular to assess the defendant's personality, his present mental state and to consider from the psychiatric point of view his emotional state and reaction at the time of the crime. Then followed a long account of the defendant's personality and medical history and his family background. Some of the information had come from medical records: most of it from the defendant himself but a little from his family and friends as is shown by the following passage: 'From all accounts his personality has always been that of a placid, rather quiet and passive person who is quite sensitive to the feelings of other people. He was always regarded by his family and friends as an even-tempered person who is not in any way aggressive ... In general until the night of the crime he seems to have always displayed remarkably good impulse control.'

This passage surprised Mr Calcutt, who appeared for the Crown, because he knew that in November 1971 the defendant had been convicted of being in unlawful possession of an offensive weapon and in May 1972 of assault with intent to rob. The defendant himself had not put his character in issue. If the psychiatrist had given evidence in accordance with his report, the defendant would have been put before the jury by the psychiatrist as having a character and disposition which the prosecution considered in the light of his record he had not got. The opinion expressed at the end of this report was as follows: 'At no time has this man appeared to show any evidence of mental illness as defined by the Mental Health Act 1959. His homicidal behaviour would appear to be understandable in terms of his relationship with Wendy Butterfield which, as I have endeavoured to outline above, was such as to make him particularly vulnerable to be overwhelmed by anger if she confirmed the accusation that had been made about her. If his statements are true that he was taken completely by surprise by her confession he would have appeared to have killed her in an explosive release of blind rage. His personality structure is consistent with someone who could behave in this way. There is no demonstrable clinical evidence to suggest that brain damage or organic disease of the brain diminished his sense of responsibility at the time he killed her, and since her death his behaviour would appear to have been consistent with someone suffering from profound grief. Although he would obviously benefit from psychotherapeutic counselling, in the absence of formal psychiatric illness there are no indications for recommending psychiatric treatment.'

Mr Calcutt pointed out to the judge the difficulty presented by the references in the report to the defendant's alleged disposition and character. Thereupon the judge commented that the report contained 'hearsay character evidence' which was inadmissible. He could have said that all the facts upon which the psychiatrist based his opinion were hearsay save for those which he observed for himself during his examination of the defendant such as his appearance of depression and his becoming emotional when discussing the deceased girl and his own family. It is not for this court to instruct psychiatrists how to draft their reports, but those who call psychiatrists as witnesses should remember that the facts upon which they base their opinions must be proved by admissible evidence. This elementary principle is frequently overlooked.

Mr Mildon appreciated that problems would arise about character if the psychiatrist gave evidence along the lines of his report. He submitted that he would be entitled to ask the following questions: Have you examined this man? Over what period of time did you examine him? Are you able to help the jury as to the intensity of his feelings for Wendy? Assuming what the defendant has said here in court as to the nature of the provocation is true, how would you have expected him to react? The judge did not rule specifically upon these suggested questions: he directed his attention to the report and ruled that it was irrelevant and inadmissible.

Before dealing with the submission made on behalf of the defendant in this court we would like briefly to refer to the questions which Mr Mildon suggested he could properly put to the psychiatrist. What he was proposing to do was to use a common forensic device to overcome objections of inadmissibility based on hearsay. The use of this device was criticised by Lord Devlin in *Glinski v McIver* (1962): he thought it was objectionable. It was certainly unhelpful. Before a court can assess the value of an opinion it must know the facts upon which it is based. If the expert has been misinformed about the facts or has taken irrelevant facts into consideration or has omitted to consider relevant ones, the opinion is likely to be valueless. In our judgment, counsel calling an expert should in examination-in-chief ask his witness to state the facts upon which his opinion is based. It is wrong to leave the other side to elicit the facts by cross-examination.

Before this court Mr Mildon submitted that the psychiatrist's opinion as to the defendant's personality and mental make-up as set out in his report was relevant and admissible for three reasons: first, because it helped to establish lack of intent; secondly, because it helped to establish that the defendant was likely to be easily provoked; and thirdly, because it helped to show that the defendant's account of what had happened was likely to be true. We do not find it necessary to deal specifically with the first of these reasons. Intent was not a live issue in this case. The evidence was tendered on the issues of provocation and credibility. The judge gave his ruling in relation to those issues. In any event the decision which we have come to on Mr Mildon's second and third submissions would also apply to his first.

The first question on both these issues is whether the psychiatrist's opinion was relevant. A man's personality and mental make-up do have a bearing upon his conduct. A quick-tempered man will react more aggressively to an unpleasing situation than a placid one. Anyone having a florid imagination or a tendency to exaggerate is less likely to be a reliable witness than one who is precise and careful. These are matters of ordinary human experience. Opinions from knowledgeable persons about a man's personality and mental make-up play a part in many human judgments. In our judgment the psychiatrist's opinion was relevant. Relevance, however, does not result in evidence being admissible: it is a condition precedent to admissibility. Our law excludes evidence of many matters which in life outside the courts sensible people take into consideration when making decisions. Two broad heads of exclusion are hearsay and opinion. As we have already pointed out, the psychiatrist's report contained a lot of hearsay which was inadmissible. A ruling on this ground, however, would merely have trimmed the psychiatrist's evidence: it would not have excluded it altogether. Was it inadmissible because of the rules relating to opinion evidence?

The foundation of these rules was laid by Lord Mansfield in *Folkes v Chadd* (1782) and was well laid: the opinion of scientific men upon proven facts may be given by men of science within their own science. An expert's opinion is admissible to furnish the court with scientific information which is likely to be outside the experience and knowledge of a judge or jury. If on the proven facts a judge or jury can form their own conclusions without help, then the opinion of an expert is unnecessary. In such a case if it is given dressed up in scientific jargon it may make judgment more difficult. The fact that an expert witness has impressive scientific qualifications does not by that fact alone make his opinion on matters of human nature and behaviour within the limits of normality any more helpful than that of the jurors themselves; but there is a danger that they may think it does.

What, in plain English, was the psychiatrist in this case intending to say? First, that the defendant was not showing and never had shown any evidence of mental illness, as defined by the Mental Health Act 1959, and did not require any psychiatric treatment; secondly, that he had had a deep emotional relationship with the girl which was likely to have caused an explosive release of blind rage when she confessed her wantonness to him; thirdly, that after he had killed her he behaved like someone suffering from profound grief. The first part of his opinion was within his expert province and outside the experience of the jury but was of no relevance in the circumstances of this case. The second and third points dealt with matters which are well within ordinary human experience. We all know that both men and women who are deeply in love can, and sometimes do, have outbursts of blind rage when discovering unexpected wantonness on the part of their loved ones; the wife taken in adultery is the classical example of the application of the defence of 'provocation'; and when death or serious injury results, profound grief usually follows. Jurors do not need psychiatrists to tell them how ordinary folk who are not suffering from any mental illness are likely to react to the stresses and strains of life. It follows that the proposed evidence was not admissible to establish that the defendant was likely to have been provoked. The same reasoning applies to its suggested admissibility on the issue of credibility. The jury had to decide what reliance they could put upon the defendant's evidence. He had to be judged as someone who was not mentally disordered. This is what juries are empanelled to do. The law assumes they can perform their duties properly. The jury in this case did not need, and should not have been offered, the evidence of a psychiatrist to help them decide whether the defendant's evidence was truthful.

Mr Mildon submitted that such help should not have been rejected by the judge because in *Lowery v The Queen* (1974) the Privy Council had approved of the admission of the evidence of a psychologist on the issue of credibility. We had to consider that case carefully before we could decide whether it had in any way put a new interpretation upon what have long been thought to be the rules relating to the calling of evidence on the issue of credibility, viz that in general evidence can be called to impugn the credibility of witnesses but not led in chief to bolster it up. In *Lowery v The Queen* evidence of a psychologist on behalf of one of two accused was admitted to establish that his version of the facts was more probable than than put forward by the other. In every case what is relevant and admissible depends on the issues raised in that case. In *Lowery v The Queen* the issues were unusual; and the accused to whose disadvantage the psychologist's evidence went had in effect said before it was called that he was not the sort of man to have committed the offence. In giving the judgment of the Board, Lord Morris of Borth-y-Gest said: 'The only question now arising is whether in the special circumstances above referred to it was open to King in defending himself to call Professor Cox to give the evidence that he gave. The evidence was relevant to and necessary for his case which involved negativing what Lowery had said and put forward; in their Lordships' view in agreement with that of the Court of Criminal Appeal the evidence was admissible.'

We adjudge *Lowery v The Queen* (1974) to have been decided on its special facts. We do not consider that it is an authority for the proposition that in all cases psychologists and psychiatrists can be called to prove the probability of the accused's veracity. If any such rule was applied to our courts, trial by psychiatrists would be likely to take the place of trial by jury and magistrates. We do not find that prospect attractive and the law does not at present provide for it.

In coming to the conclusion we have in this case we must not be taken to be discouraging the calling of psychiatric evidence in cases where such evidence can be helpful within the present rules of evidence. These rules may be too restrictive of the admissibility of opinion evidence. The Criminal Law Revision Committee in its eleventh report thought they were and made recommendations for relaxing them: see paragraphs 266-271. The recommendations have not yet been accepted by Parliament and until they are, or other changes in the law of evidence are made, this court must apply the existing rules: see *Myers v Director of Public Prosecutions* (1965). We have not overlooked what Lord Parker CJ said in *Director of Public Prosecutions v A and BC Chewing Gum Ltd* (1968) about the advance of science making more and more inroads into the old common law principle applicable to opinion evidence; but we are firmly of the opinion that psychiatry has not yet become a satisfactory substitute for the common sense of juries or magistrates on matters within their experience of life. The appeal is dismissed.[8]

R v Coles (1995, Court of Appeal)

In *Silcott* (1991) the Court of Appeal acknowledged that it was the regular practice of judges to admit psychiatric or psychosocial evidence when considering submissions under the Police and Criminal Evidence Act 1984 as to the admissibility of confessions. The reason for this was that the mental condition of the defendant at the time of interview was one of the circumstances to be considered by the trial judge on a submission under s 76(2)(b). In *Silcott* the Court of Appeal had to consider evidence about the mental state of a co-defendant named Raghip. The psychological evidence showed that Raghip's IQ of 74 placed him outside, but not far outside, the mental defective range. The

---

8.   [1975] QB 834.

court found it unattractive to allow an arbitrary division affecting admissibility to be made between cases where a defendant came within the range and cases where he did not. It held that the evidence would have supported a submission under s 76(2)(b) that Raghip's confession was inadmissible. However, Farquharson LJ made it clear that the court recognised a distinction between the admission of psychiatric or psychological evidence going to the reliability of a confession and the admission of such evidence going to a defendant's *mens rea*. The latter situation had to be considered in the next case, in which the defendant had been charged with arson, being reckless as to whether life was endangered.

Hobhouse LJ [reading the judgment of the court]: ... After the prosecution evidence had been given and the defendant Lee Coles had himself given evidence, Mr Maynard, counsel for Lee Coles, applied to adduce the expert evidence of a psychologist, Mr Kirby Turner ...

[The trial judge] refused to admit the evidence of the psychologist on two grounds: first, that it was not relevant to any issue which the jury had to consider; secondly, that since the psychological evidence was not evidence of any mental abnormality, merely that the defendant was of low average mental capacity, expert evidence was not admissible.

Following these rulings the defendant changed his plea on count two to one of guilty and the jury, on that plea, returned a verdict of guilty. They were not required to give a verdict on the alternative count of simple arson ...

The evidence of Mr Kirby Turner which was tendered on behalf of Lee Coles was based upon a report and interview with Lee and (it appears) a subsequent reading of the committal papers and certain psychometric assessments which had been made of Lee on two occasions in connection with his educational requirements. The report purports to express opinions about precisely those matters which were explored in evidence at the trial with Lee Coles himself. It inevitably was based upon assumptions about the veracity of what Lee had told Mr Kirby Turner. It is accepted that part of Mr Kirby Turner's opinion would not be admissible. However, it is suggested that the opinion he expressed based upon the psychometric assessment of Lee's 'verbal comprehension factor' and 'perceptual organisational factor', that 'Lee operates in the low average range of intellectual functioning' were admissible. At another point in his report he describes Lee as being in 'the low average range of ability' or in 'the range of thinking characteristic of pre-adolescent children'. Elsewhere his IQ results were given in terms which whilst below the average were well within the range of normality. He reports that Lee saw himself as the 'ideas man' in the group and that Lee needed to impress both others and himself; Lee 'was locked into the excitement-seeking in rather a thoughtless way'. It was suggested by counsel for Lee that this evidence provided a possible basis for a conclusion that he lacked a capacity for foresight ...

The other ground of appeal advanced on behalf of the appellant related to the exclusion of the evidence of Mr Kirby Turner. The judge rightly refused to admit this evidence. It was not evidence of any abnormality of the mind of the defendant. It related to characteristics of the defendant which could be completely evaluated by a jury by reference to the facts of the actual case without the assistance of expert evidence. Adolescents of varying stages of maturity and brightness are all within the common experience of jurors. The appellant relied upon the case of *Raghip, Silcott and Braithwaite, The Times*, December 9 1991 where the Court of Appeal held that expert evidence as to the mental characteristics of a defendant ought to have been admitted. But this was expressly in relation to the exercise of a judge's discretion whether or not he ought to admit a confession under section 76 of the Police and Criminal Evidence Act 1984. Such evidence had been admitted in the case of *Everett* (1988), and the court was of the opinion that such evidence ought to have been admitted in the case of *Raghip* in order to assist the judge in deciding whether or not the defendant was particularly susceptible to suggestion and whether or not it was fair to him to admit in evidence what he had said in response to questions by the police. The Court of Appeal expressly drew a distinction between such evidence and evidence which was said to go to the defendant's *mens rea*: 'We emphasise that nothing we say in this judgment is intended to reflect upon the admissibility of psychiatric or psychological evidence going to the issue of the defendant's *mens rea*.'

Unless some factor of the mental health or psychiatric state of the defendant is raised, such evidence is not admissible ...[9]

---

9. [1995] 1 Cr App R 157.

CHAPTER 12

PRIVILEGE AND PUBLIC POLICY

PRIVILEGE

In this section I have concentrated on those topics where the subject of privilege is most likely to arise: legal professional privilege and the privilege attaching to 'without prejudice' correspondence. The cases frequently cover several aspects of the law. Special attention in reading should be paid to the following:

- the scope of legal professional privilege
- its justification
- waiver, especially accidental, and its remedy
- scope and justification of 'without prejudice' privilege
- the purposes for which 'without prejudice' correspondence may be used.

Police and Criminal Evidence Act 1984

(The scope of the privilege, determined by the common law, was said by Lord Goff in *R v Central Criminal Court, ex parte Francis & Francis* (1988) to be accurately reflected in s 10 of PACE, which limits police powers to search for and seize evidence.)

10 (1) Subject to subsection (2) below, in this Act 'items subject to legal privilege' means –

(a) communications between a professional legal adviser and his client or any person representing his client made in connection with the giving of legal advice to the client;

(b) communications between a professional legal adviser and his client or any person representing his client or between such an adviser or his client or any such representative and any other person made in connection with or in contemplation of legal proceedings and for the purposes of such proceedings; and

(c) items enclosed with or referred to in such communications and made

(i) in connection with the giving of legal advice; or

(ii) in connection with or in contemplation of legal proceedings and for the purposes of such proceedings,

when they are in the possession of a person who is entitled to possession of them.

(2) Items held with the intention of furthering a criminal purpose are not items subject to legal privilege.

Wheeler v Le Marchant (1881, Court of Appeal)

In an action for specific performance the defendants tried to keep from production letters which had passed between their solicitors and their surveyors. Bacon VC held that the letters were privileged. The plaintiffs appealed.

Jessel MR: As regards the main question in dispute, this appears to be an attempt on the part of the present respondents to extend the rule as to the protection from discovery. It was fairly admitted by their counsel that no decided case carries the rule to the extent to which they wish it carried, but they urged that as a matter of principle it ought to be so extended. What they contended for was that documents communicated to the solicitors of the defendants by third parties, though not communicated by such third parties as agents of the clients seeking advice, should be protected, because those documents contained information required or asked for by the solicitors, for the purpose of enabling them the better to advise their clients. The cases, no doubt, establish that such documents are protected where they have come into existence after litigation commenced or in contemplation, and when they have been made with a view to such litigation, either for the purpose of obtaining advice as to such litigation, or of obtaining evidence to be used in such litigation, or of obtaining information which might lead to the obtaining of such evidence, but it has never hitherto been decided that documents are protected merely because they are produced by a third person in answer to an inquiry made by the solicitor. It does not appear to me to be necessary, either as a result of the principle which regulates this privilege or for the convenience of mankind, so to extend the rule. In the first place, the principle protecting confidential communications is of a very limited character. It does not protect all confidential communications which a man must necessarily make in order to obtain advice, even when needed for the protection of his life, or of his honour, or of his fortune. There are many communications which, though absolutely necessary because without them the ordinary business of life cannot be carried on, still are not privileged. The communications made to a medical man whose advice is sought by a patient with respect to the probable origin of the disease as to which he is consulted, and which must necessarily be made in order to enable the medical man to advise or to prescribe for the patient, are not protected. Communications made to a priest in the confessional, on matters perhaps considered by the penitent to be more important even than his life or his fortune, are not protected. Communications made to a friend with respect to matters of the most delicate nature, on which advice is sought with respect to a man's honour or reputation, are not protected. Therefore it must not be supposed that there is any principle which says that every confidential communication which it is necessary to make in order to carry on the ordinary business of life is protected. The protection is of very limited character, and in this country is restricted to the obtaining the assistance of lawyers, as regards the conduct of litigation or the rights to property. It has never gone beyond the obtaining legal advice and assistance, and all things reasonably necessary in the shape of communication to the legal advisers are protected from production or discovery in order that that legal advice may be obtained safely and sufficiently.

Now, keeping that in view, what has been done is this: The actual communication to the solicitor by the client is of course protected, and it is equally protected whether it is made by the client in person or is made by an agent on behalf of the client, and whether it is made to the solicitor in person or to a clerk or subordinate of the solicitor who acts in his place and under his direction. Again, the evidence obtained by the solicitor, or by his direction, or at his instance, even if obtained by the client, is protected if obtained after litigation has been commenced or threatened, or with a view to the defence or prosecution of such litigation. So, again, a communication with a solicitor for the purpose of obtaining legal advice is protected though it relates to a dealing which is not the subject of litigation, provided it be a communication made to the solicitor in that character and for that purpose. But what we are asked to protect here is this. The solicitor, being consulted in a matter as to which no dispute has arisen, thinks he would like to know some further facts before giving his advice, and applies to a surveyor to tell him what the state of a given property is, and it is said that the information given ought to be protected because it is desired or required by the solicitor in order to enable him the better to give legal advice. It appears to me that to give such protection would not only extend the rule beyond what has been previously laid down, but but beyond what necessity warrants. The idea that documents like these require protection has been stated, if I may say so, for the first time today, and I think the best proof that the necessities of mankind have not been supposed to require this protection is that it has never heretofore been asked. It seems to me we ought not to carry the rule any further than it has been carried. It is a rule established and maintained solely for the purpose of enabling a man to obtain legal advice with safety. That rule does not, in my opinion, require to be carried further ...[1]

[Brett and Cotton LJJ also delivered judgments allowing the appeal.]

Calcraft v Guest (1898, Court of Appeal)

Lindley MR: In the course of this appeal a question has arisen as to whether certain documents are privileged by reason of their being confidential communications, as I will call them, and, if they are, whether secondary evidence can be given of some of them of which the appellants have copies ...

[Having concluded that the documents were privileged, he continued:]

Then comes the next question. It appears that the appellant has obtained copies of some of these documents, and is in a position to give secondary evidence of them; and the question is whether he is entitled to do that. That appears to me to be covered by the authority of *Lloyd v Mostyn* (1842). I need not go closely into the facts of that case. That was an action on a bond which was said to be privileged from production on the ground of its having come into the hands of the solicitor in confidence, and the learned judge at the trial allowed the objection, and nobody seems to have quarrelled with it. The plaintiff then tendered in evidence a copy of the bond, and proposed to give secondary evidence of it. This was rejected on the ground that notice to produce was necessary. The plaintiff then proved a notice to produce, the sufficiency of which was disputed. The learned judge being of opinion that the notice was sufficient, held that the copy was admissible, and the jury found a verdict for the plaintiff for the full amount of the bond, leave being given to the defendant to move to enter a nonsuit if the court should be of opinion that the copy of the bond ought not to have been received in evidence. In support of the motion to enter a nonsuit Sir Fitzroy Kelly relied on a passage in *Phillipps on Evidence*, 8th edn p 182, and a case there cited of *Fisher v Heming*, decided by Bayley J *at nisi prius* in 1809. That passage runs as follows: 'If a deed deposited confidentially with an attorney has been obtained out of his hands for the purpose of being produced in evidence by another witness, it cannot be received. Thus, in a case tried before Bayley J, the plaintiff's counsel having proved a certain deed in the possession of the defendant, and the defendant refusing to produce it, though he admitted having received notice, the counsel of the plaintiff offered in evidence a copy of the deed, which had been obtained from one who many years ago acted as an attorney for the person under whom the defendant claimed, and who had been intrusted by him with the original deed in his professional character. The counsel on the part of the defendant objected that this evidence ought not to be received, as the original deed had been deposited confidentially with the attorney; and Bayley J refused to admit it. He said, the attorney could not give parol evidence

---

1. 17 Ch D 675.

of the contents of the deed which had been intrusted to him; so neither could he furnish a copy. He ought not to have communicated to others what was deposited with him in confidence whether it was a written or verbal communication. It is the privilege of his client, and continues from first to last.' That is the passage from *Phillipps on Evidence*. Upon that Parke B said: 'I have always doubted the correctness of that ruling. Where an attorney intrusted confidentially with a document communicates the contents of it, or suffers another to take a copy, surely the secondary evidence so obtained may be produced. Suppose the instrument were even stolen, and a correct copy taken, would it not be reasonable to admit it?' The matter dropped there; but the other members of the court (Lord Abinger, Gurney B, and Rolfe B) all concurred in that, which I take it is a distinct authority that secondary evidence in a case of this kind may be received ...[2]

Lord Ashburton v Pape (1913, Court of Appeal)

Appeal from a decision of Neville J

This was an action brought by Lord Ashburton against Edward James Pape, Charles William Langford, Thomas Howard Redfern, and William Nocton for an injunction 'restraining the defendants and each of them from publishing, circulating, disclosing, divulging, or parting with, otherwise than to the plaintiff or by deposit in Court, and from allowing to be published, circulated, disclosed, or divulged any correspondence, letters or other documents received by or communicated to the defendant Nocton as solicitor of the plaintiff, or the effect thereof, or copies thereof, or extracts therefrom, and from informing any person or persons of their or any of their contents.'

Mr Pape was a bankrupt and his discharge was opposed by, amongst others, Lord Ashburton, who was a creditor for over 139,000*l*. In the course of those proceedings it appeared that Mr Pape had in his possession a number of letters written by Lord Ashburton to his late solicitor, Mr W Nocton, which were admitted to be privileged. These letters had been obtained by Mr Pape by serving on one of Mr Nocton's clerks called Brooks a *subpoena duces tecum* requiring him to produce the letters in the Bankruptcy Court. Brooks did so, and whilst in attendance there complained of not feeling well, handed over the letters to Mr Pape, and left the court. Mr Pape's solicitors, Messrs Langford & Redfern, took copies of the letters and gave the originals back to Mr Pape. Lord Ashburton's present solicitor heard of this and wrote to Messrs Langford & Redfern for copies of the letters, and these, after an application in the Bankruptcy Court, were supplied to him. On a motion by Lord Ashburton in the action Neville J made an order that the defendant Edward James Pape do forthwith hand over to the defendant William Nocton all original letters from the plaintiff to the said William Nocton or his firm in his the defendant Edward James Pape's possession or control. 'And it is ordered that the defendants Edward James Pape, Charles William Langford and Thomas Howard Redfern their servants and agents be restrained until judgment or further order from publishing or making use of any of the copies of such letters or any information contained therein except for the purpose of the pending proceedings in the

---

2. [1898] 1 QB 759.

defendant Edward James Pape's bankruptcy and subject to the direction of the Bankruptcy Court.' And the defendant William Nocton undertaking in the terms of the prayer to refrain from publishing any correspondence received by him as solicitor of the plaintiff, the court made no order against him.

Lord Ashburton appealed and asked that the order might be varied by striking out the words 'except for the purpose of the pending proceedings in the defendant Edward James Pape's bankruptcy and subject to the direction of the Bankruptcy Court'.

Cozens-Hardy MR: ... The rule of evidence as explained in *Calcraft v Guest* merely amounts to this, that if a litigant wants to prove a particular document which by reason of privilege or some circumstance he cannot furnish by the production of the original, he may produce a copy as secondary evidence although that copy has been obtained by improper means, and even, it may be, by criminal means. The court in such an action is not really trying the circumstances under which the document was produced. That is not an issue in the case and the court simply says, 'Here is a copy of a document which cannot be produced; it may have been stolen, it may have been picked up in the street, it may have improperly got into the possession of the person who proposes to produce it, but that is not a matter which the court in the trial of the action can go into'. But that does not seem to me to have any bearing upon a case where the whole subject matter of the action is the right to retain the originals or copies of certain documents which are privileged. It seems to me that, although Pape has had the good luck to obtain a copy of these documents which he can produce without a breach of this injunction, there is no ground whatever in principle why we should decline to give the plaintiff the protection which in my view is his right as between him and Pape, and that there is no reason whatever why we should not say to Pape in pending or future proceedings, 'You shall not produce these documents which you have acquired from the plaintiff surreptitiously, or from his solicitor, who plainly stood to him in a confidential relation'. For these reasons I think the appeal ought to be allowed so far as it asks, and only so far as it asks, to strike out the exception.

Kennedy LJ: ... I agree that the better view seems to me to be that although it is true that the principle which is laid down in *Calcraft v Guest* must be followed, yet, at the same time, if, before the occasion of the trial when a copy may be used, although a copy improperly obtained, the owner of the original can successfully promote proceedings against the person who has improperly obtained the copy to stop his using it, the owner is none the less entitled to protection, because, if the question had arisen in the course of a trial before such proceedings, the holder of the copy would not have been prevented from using it on account of the illegitimacy of its origins ...

Swinfen Eady LJ: ... The principle upon which the Court of Chancery has acted for many years has been to restrain the publication of confidential information improperly or surreptitiously obtained or of information imparted in confidence which ought not to be divulged. Injunctions have been granted to give effectual relief, that is not only to restrain the disclosure of confidential information, but to prevent copies being made of any record of that information, and, if copies have already been made, to restrain them from being further copied, and to restrain persons into whose possession that confidential information has come from themselves in turn divulging or propagating it ... If [Pape] is allowed to retain possession of these copies or to divulge the contents, he is availing himself of the breach of contract by Brooks the clerk, by means of which these letters have come into his hands ... There are many ... cases ... where the use of information improperly obtained has been restrained and the parties into whose possession it has come have been restrained from using or divulging it. Down to that point there can be no dispute as to the law. Then objection was raised in the present case by reason of the fact that it is said that Pape, who now has copies of the letters, might wish to give them in evidence in certain bankruptcy proceedings, and although the original letters are privileged from production he has possession of the copies and could give them as secondary evidence of the contents of the letters, and, therefore, ought not to be ordered either to give them up or to be restrained from divulging their contents. There is here a confusion between the right to restrain a person from divulging confidential information and the right to give secondary evidence of documents where the originals are privileged from production, if the party has such secondary evidence in his possession. The cases are entirely separate and distinct. If a person were to steal a deed, nevertheless in any dispute to which it was relevant the original deed might be given in evidence by him at the trial. It would be no objection to the admissibility of the deed in evidence to say you ought not to have possession of it. His unlawful possession would not affect the admissibility of the deed in evidence if otherwise admissible. So again with regard to any copy he had. If he was unable to obtain or compel production of the original because it was privileged, if he had a copy in his possession it would be admissible as secondary evidence. The fact, however, that a document, whether original or copy, is admissible in evidence is no answer to the demand of the lawful owner for the delivery up of the document, and no answer to an application by the lawful owner of confidential information to restrain it from being published or copied ...[3]

Butler v Board of Trade (1971, Chancery Division)

Goff J: In this action the plaintiff, who is being prosecuted by the Board of Trade for alleged offences under section 332(3) of the Companies Act 1948 in connection with two companies now in compulsory liquidation, claims a declaration as follows: 'that the defendants', the Board of Trade, 'are not entitled by themselves, their servants or agents to publish, disclose, divulge or otherwise make use of the contents of a letter dated July 31 1964 written to the plaintiff by Phyllis Edith Newman, a solicitor, or any information contained therein'.

The object is to prevent the defendants from adducing in evidence against the plaintiff at the criminal trial a copy of a letter written to him by Mrs Newman, a solicitor then in charge of the practice of another solicitor, one Miss Berman.

The facts which have to be assumed are set out in the special case and it is unnecessary to recite them, save paragraphs 7, 8 and 12 which read as follows:

7. Shortly after the dates of the respective winding up orders a representative of the Official Receiver being the provisional liquidator of Curzon and Capricorn called upon Miss Berman and collected the papers of the company concerned. A copy of the letter was found amongst these papers. 8. The department of the Official Receiver in Companies Liquidation is a department of the defendant ... 12. For the purpose of the special case it is to be assumed (i) that the letter was unsolicited by the plaintiff and (ii) that it was written by Mrs Newman as the plaintiff's own solicitor and not, or not only, as solicitor to Curzon and Capricorn.

---

3. [1913] 2 Ch D 469.

The last-mentioned paragraph postulates alternatives, but I can only deal with the matter on this special case on one footing which must be that most favourable to the plaintiff, that is to say, ignoring the words 'or not only'.

The question for the opinion of the court, set out in paragraph 14, is 'whether there is any equity to prevent the defendants from tendering a copy of the letter in evidence in any of the said criminal proceedings'.

The plaintiff claims that the original of the letter is protected by legal professional privilege, and that therefore the copy is a confidential document, and I agree that if the premise be right the conclusion follows. Further, in my judgment it is right *prima facie* because, although the special case tells me nothing about the solicitor's instructions, I must, as it seems to me, assume that the advice contained in the letter was given by her as legal adviser and within the ambit of her retainer, and indeed that is really implicit in paragraph 12 of the special case.

It is submitted on behalf of the defendants, however, that as the plaintiff is charged with criminal offences, and the letter is relevant thereto, which it undoubtedly is, the privilege does not apply. Now, it is clear that a sufficient charge of crime or fraud will in certain circumstances destroy the privilege, but there is a dispute between the parties as to what it is necessary to show for that purpose.

The defendants say that relevance is alone sufficient ... The plaintiff submits, however, that it is necessary to go further and to show that the professional advice was in furtherance of the crime or fraud ... or in preparation for it ... or parts of it ...

As questions of this nature have to be determined on a *prima facie* basis, often without seeing the documents or knowing what was orally communicated, the two tests will, I think, in many and probably most cases be found in practice to produce the same result because in most cases of relevance the proper *prima facie* inference will be that the communication was made in preparation for or in furtherance or as part of the criminal or fraudulent purpose. However, the two tests are not the same and in the present case cannot, I think, possibly produce the same result. On the information before me the letter was nothing but a warning volunteered – no doubt wisely, but still volunteered – by the solicitor that if her client did not take care he might incur serious consequences, which she described. I cannot regard that on any showing as being in preparation for or in furtherance or as part of any criminal designs on the part of the plaintiff.

I must, therefore, decide which test is correct, and I prefer the narrower view ...

If relevance alone is the test, it follows that privilege could never be claimed in cases of crime or fraud, except as to communications in connection with the defence ...

In my judgment, therefore, on the limited facts before me the original letter is privileged and the copy confidential ...

It was then argued that the copy letter having left the care of the solicitor and come into the hands of the defendants, so that one is no longer in the realm of privilege but of confidence, there can be no equity which the plaintiff can set up because of the principle succinctly summed up by Wood VC in *Gartside v Outram* (1856), in the phrase, 'there is no confidence as to the disclosure of iniquity' ...

In my judgment, however, that does not apply to the present case. At the trial the defendants may or may not prove the criminal offences with which the plaintiff is charged, and the letter, if received in evidence, may or may not help them to do so, but although, if more were known of the facts, one might find some communication falling within this exception, I cannot see in this bare warning any element of vice which the umbrella of confidence may not in general cover.

There remains, however, the final question whether the law or equity as to breach of confidence operates, in the terms of paragraph 14 of the special case, to give the plaintiff 'any equity to prevent the defendants from tendering a copy of the letter in evidence in any of the said criminal proceedings', where if tendered it would, as I see it, clearly be admissible: see *Calcraft v Guest* (1898), subject of course to the overriding discretion of the trial court to reject it if it thought its use unfair.

The plaintiff relies on the decision of the Court of Appeal in *Ashburton v Pape* (1913), where a party to certain bankruptcy proceedings, having by a trick obtained a copy of a privileged letter, Neville J granted an injunction restraining him and his solicitors from publishing or making use of it, save for the purposes of those proceedings, and the Court of Appeal varied the order by striking out the exception, so that the injunction was unqualified ...

In the present case there was no impropriety on the part of the defendants in the way in which they received the copy, but that, in my judgment, is irrelevant because an innocent recipient of information conveyed in breach of confidence is liable to be restrained. I wish to make it clear that there is no suggestion of any kind of moral obliquity on the part of the solicitors, but the disclosure was in law a breach of confidence. Nevertheless, *Ashburton v Pape* does differ from the present case in an important particular, namely, that the defendants are a department of the Crown and intend to use the copy letter in a public prosecution brought by them.

As far as I am aware, there is no case directly in point on the question whether that is merely an immaterial difference of fact or a valid distinction, but in my judgment it is the latter because in such a case there are two conflicting principles, the private right of the individual and the interest of the state to apprehend and prosecute criminals ...

In my judgment it would not be a right or permissible exercise of the equitable jurisdiction in confidence to make a declaration at the suit of the accused in a public prosecution in effect restraining the Crown from adducing admissible evidence relevant to the crime with which he is charged. It is not necessary for me to decide whether the same result would obtain in the case of a private prosecution, and I expressly leave that point open.

My reasons for the conclusion I have reached are as follows: First, it is clear that if the copy letter were in the hands of a third party I would in restraining him have to except the power of the trial court to subpoena him to produce the letter and his obligation to comply with that order: see *per* Bankes LJ in *Weld-Blundell v Stephens* (1919). It would be strange if the defendants could subpoena a witness to produce this document yet, having it themselves, not be allowed to tender it in evidence. Secondly, and even more compelling, is the effect of the conflict between the two principles to which I have already referred. In *Elias v Pasmore* (1934) it was held accordingly by Horridge J that the police were justified in retaining and using at the trial of Hannington documents belonging to Elias which they had seized irregularly when entering the premises to arrest Hannington. True it is that in *Ghani v Jones* (1970), Lord Denning MR criticised the dictum of Horridge J as being too wide in that he gave the police the right to use the documents in the trial of any person, but with that qualification Lord Denning accepted what Horridge J had said. Thus *Elias v Pasmore* is authority for the proposition that the right and the duty of the police to prosecute offenders prevails over the accused's right of ownership. He cannot demand his own goods back. By analogy it seems to me that the interest and duty of the defendants as a department of the state to prosecute offenders under the Companies Act must prevail over the offender's limited proprietary right in equity to restrain a breach of confidence, and here, of course, the doubt suggested by Lord Denning does not arise because the accused and the person entitled to the benefit of the confidence are one and the same ...

For these reasons, in my judgment, the answer to the question propounded in paragraph 14 of the special case is in the negative and the action must be dismissed ...[4]

Barclays Bank plc v Eustice (1995, Court of Appeal)

Schiemann LJ: ... On 21 June we dismissed an appeal against an order for discovery made by Judge Raymond Jack QC. These are my reasons for approving that course. The action in which that order was made was one in which the plaintiff bank sought, amongst other relief, a number of declarations pursuant to the provisions of section 423 of the Insolvency Act 1986 to the effect that various transactions entered into by the defendants were void because they defrauded the creditor bank. In the interlocutory proceedings with which this appeal is concerned the bank sought an order that the defendants should disclose all documents containing or evidencing communications between the defendants and their legal advisers relating to the transactions. The defendants claimed that these documents were privileged from disclosure on the basis of legal professional privilege. The judge ruled in favour of the bank and the defendants appeal against that order by leave of this court.

The appeal raises two questions the first of which is of interest only to the parties but the second of which is of some general significance. The first question is whether the judge was entitled to find that the evidence disclosed a strong *prima facie* case in favour of making the section 421 order sought by the bank. The second question arises only if the answer to the first question is in the affirmative. It is this: does legal professional privilege attach to documents containing or evidencing communications between the transferor and his legal advisers relating to transactions entered into by the transferor at an undervalue for the purpose of prejudicing the interest of persons making a claim against him? This is, so far as the researches of counsel go, the first time that this question has fallen for decision ...

I turn therefore to the question of general interest in relation to the law governing discovery. We start for this purpose from the position that there is a strong *prima facie* case that Mr. Eustice ('the transferor') entered into transactions at an undervalue and that his purpose in so doing was to prejudice the interests of the bank ('the claimant'). It is also common ground that these documents are relevant to the issues between the parties and therefore disclosable. The question which falls to be resolved is whether legal professional privilege attaches to documents containing or evidencing communications between the transferor and his legal advisers relating to transactions entered into by the transferor at an undervalue for the purpose of prejudicing the interest of persons making a claim against him. If it does then the documents need not be produced for inspection.

---

4. [1971] Ch 680.

In the resolution of this question there are two conflicting desiderata in the background. (1) Discovery of every relevant document is desirable to help the court decide what happened and why. The right answer is more likely to be arrived at by the court if it is in possession of all relevant material. (2) It is desirable that persons should be able to go to their legal advisers knowing that they can talk frankly and receive professional advice knowing that what each party has said to the other will not be revealed to third parties. This second desideratum has recently been expressed thus by Bingham LJ in *Ventouris v Mountain* [1991] 1 WLR 607, 611 and I gratefully adopt his words: 'The doctrine of legal professional privilege is rooted in the public interest. which requires that hopeless and exaggerated claims and unsound and spurious defences be so far as possible discouraged, and civil disputes so far as possible settled without resort to judicial decision. To this end it is necessary that actual and potential litigants, be they claimants or respondents, should be free to unburden themselves without reserve to their legal advisers, and their legal advisers be free to give honest and candid advice on a sound factual basis, without fear that these communications may be relied on by an opposing party if the dispute comes before the court for decision. It is the protection of confidential communications between client and legal adviser which lies at the heart of legal professional privilege ... Without the consent of the client, and in the absence of iniquity or dispute between client and solicitor, no inquiry may be made into or disclosure made of any instructions which the client gave the solicitor or any advice the solicitor gave the client, whether in writing or orally.'

It will be noted that in the last sentence cited Bingham LJ referred to the 'absence of iniquity.' In so doing he was recognising the effect of a line of cases which have established that advice sought or given for the purpose of effecting iniquity is not privileged. The present appeal is concerned essentially with the question whether the effecting of transactions at an undervalue for the purpose of prejudicing the interests of a creditor can be regarded as 'iniquity' in this context. 'Iniquity' is, I believe, without having done any research on the point, Bingham LJ's word. The case law refers to 'crime or fraud' (*Reg v Cox and Railton* (1884) 14 QBD 153, 165), 'criminal or unlawful' (*Bullivant v Attorney-General for Victoria* [1901] AC 196, 201), and 'all forms of fraud and dishonesty such as fraudulent breach of trust, fraudulent conspiracy, trickery and sham contrivances' (*Crescent Farm (Sidcup) Sports Ltd v Sterling Offices Ltd* [1972] Ch 553, 565). The case law indicates that 'fraud' is in this context used in a relatively wide sense ...

On the other hand the courts have shown themselves reluctant to extend the concept indefinitely and have warned against an indiscriminate setting aside of legal privilege ...

In *Crescent Farm (Sidcup) Sports Ltd v Sterling Offices Ltd* (1972), the court was not willing to extend the concept to the tort of inducing a breach of contract.

One of the factors which the court will often find relevant and which may be decisive in a particular case is the purpose for which the advice is sought. Is it sought to explain the legal effect of what has already been done and is now the subject of existing or imminent litigation? Or is it sought in order to structure a transaction which has yet to be carried out. In the former class of case the court will be more hesitant to lift the cloak of privilege than in the latter ... Thus the court would be reluctant – it is not presently necessary to decide the point – to force a legal adviser to give evidence or produce documents as to what a client had said when seeking advice as to how to respond to a criminal charge which had been preferred against him. That, normally at any rate, would be unjustifiably to invade the defendant's rights to silence and would be against the public interest to which Bingham LJ referred in the passage I have cited.

I regard the present case however as being essentially one about advice sought on how to structure a transaction. I accept that it must have been obvious to the defendants that the bank might, once it learnt of the challenged transactions, start proceedings. It was faintly submitted on behalf of the defendants that therefore advice as to structuring the transaction was to be regarded as advice coming into existence for the dominant purpose of being used in contemplated proceedings. That submission I reject. The dominant purpose was to stop the bank from interfering with the defendants' use of what they regarded as family assets.

The first main submission made by Mr Morgan was based on the decision of Scott J in *A L I Finance Ltd v Havelet Leasing Ltd* (1992) In that case Scott J was prepared to accept that an intention to put a debtor's assets out of the reach of a creditor was not necessarily a dishonest motive but held that even so it could suffice for the purposes of section 423. Mr Morgan relied on this and went on to submit that the case law had in effect confined the possibility of lifting the privilege to cases where there was dishonesty.

I reject this submission. Scott J was not concerned with whether legal professional privilege should be lifted. His use of the word 'dishonest' was not in that context. In any event he was merely indicating that he was prepared to accept something which he did not need to decide and which had been submitted by the losing party. Moreover, as I have indicated, various words other than 'dishonest' have been used in the course of the cases in which privilege has been in issue. However, to me the most important consideration is that we are here engaged not in some semantic exercise to see what adjective most appropriately covers the debtor's course of conduct but in deciding whether public policy requires that the documents in question are left uninspected. I do not think it does. Adopting the approach of Vinelott J in *Derby & Co Ltd v Weldon (No 7)* (1990) discovery followed by inspection would not here result in an unjustified interference with the defendants' property or right to privacy ...

Mr Morgan submitted that the cloak of privilege should only be lifted if either the solicitor was a party to the 'crime' or the client uses the solicitor's advice or assistance for a criminal or fraudulent purpose not contemplated by the solicitor so that the solicitor is an unwitting accomplice to the client's fraud or crime. He submitted that no one had alleged that the solicitors in question were engaged in crime and that the defendants and the solicitors had jointly and openly engaged in a purpose which was both overt and lawful, namely seeking and giving advice as to how to remove Mr Eustice's assets out of the temporary reach of the bank without rendering the transactions liable to be set aside under section 423.

These submissions were attractively presented but I reject them. For reasons given earlier in this judgment we start here from a position in which, on a *prima facie* view, the client was seeking to enter into transactions at an undervalue the purpose of which was to prejudice the bank. I regard this purpose as being sufficiently iniquitous for public policy to require that communications between him and his solicitor in relation to the setting up of these transactions be discoverable.

If that view be correct, then it matters not whether either the client or the solicitor shared that view. They may well have thought that the transactions would not fall to be set aside under section 423 either because they thought that the transactions were not an undervalue or because they thought that the court would not find that the purpose of the transactions was to prejudice the bank. But if this is what they thought then there is a strong *prima facie* case that they were wrong. Public policy does not require the communications of those who misapprehend the law to be privileged in circumstances where no privilege attaches to those who correctly understand the situation.

These cases can indeed throw up difficult problems of policy and one sees frequent references in the case law to the desirability of deciding each case on its facts. The evidence in the present case reveals a strong *prima facie* case of what the sidenote to section 423 refers to as 'Transactions defrauding creditors.' The evidence which is sought to be inspected may help the plaintiffs overcome a detriment to which they ought not to have been exposed and to which they were exposed by the action of the defendants. Mr Morgan, when asked to identify the prejudice which inspection might cause to his client, could do no more than indicate that material might emerge which would indicate to the plaintiffs various weaknesses in the defendant's position. In those circumstances I do not consider that the public interest requires these communications to be kept secret. If the strong *prima facie* case turns out to be correct then the defendants have deliberately indulged in something which I would categorise as sharp practice. I do not consider that the result of upholding the judge's order in the present case will be to discourage straightforward citizens from consulting their lawyers. Those lawyers should tell them that what is proposed is liable to be set aside and the straightforward citizen will then not do it and so the advice will never see the light of day. In so far as those wishing to engage in sharp practice are concerned, the effect of the present decision may well be to discourage them from going to their lawyers. This has the arguable public disadvantage that the lawyers might have dissuaded them from the sharp practice. However, it has the undoubted public advantage that the absence of lawyers will make it more difficult for them to carry out their sharp practice. In my judgment the balance of advantage is in permitting inspection of the material as ordered by the judge. I would dismiss the appeal ...[5]

Waugh v British Railways Board (1980, House of Lords)

This is a famous instance – no doubt there are others – of an order of a Queen's Bench Master which was rejected by the judge and the Court of Appeal but ultimately upheld in the House of Lords. 'In my judgment,' Lord Edmund-Davies said, 'a grievous wrong might have been done had Master Bickford Smith's original order in favour of disclosure not been finally upheld.'

Lord Wilberforce: My Lords, the appellant's husband was an employee of the British Railways Board. A locomotive which he was driving collided with another so that he was crushed against a tank wagon. He received injuries from which he died. The present action is brought under the Fatal Accidents Acts 1846-1959 and this appeal arises out of an interlocutory application for discovery by the board of a report called the 'joint inquiry report', made by two officers of the board two days after the accident. This was resisted by the board on the ground of legal professional privilege. The Court of Appeal, Eveleigh LJ and Sir David Cairns, Lord Denning MR dissenting, refused the application.

When an accident occurs on the board's railways, there are three reports which are made. 1. On the day of the accident a brief report of the accident is made to the Railway Inspectorate. 2. Soon afterwards a joint internal report is prepared incorporating statements of witnesses. This too is sent to the Railway Inspectorate. Preparation of this report, it appears, is a matter of practice: it is not

---

5. [1995] 1 WLR 1238. Aldous and Butler-Sloss LJJ agreed.

required by statute or statutory regulation. 3. In due course a report is made by the Railway Inspectorate for the Department of the Environment.

The document now in question is that numbered 2. ... [It] was prepared for a dual purpose: for what may be called railway operation and safety purposes and for the purpose of obtaining legal advice in anticipation of litigation, the first being more immediate than the second, but both being described as of equal rank or weight. So the question arises whether this is enough to support a claim of privilege, or whether, in order to do so, the second purpose must be the sole purpose, or the dominant or main purpose. If either of the latter is correct, the claim of privilege in this case must fail.

My Lords, before I consider the authorities, I think it desirable to attempt to discern the reason why what is (inaccurately) called legal professional privilege exists. It is sometimes ascribed to the exigencies of the adversary system of litigation under which a litigant is entitled within limits to refuse to disclose the nature of his case until the trial. Thus one side may not ask to see the proofs of the other side's witnesses or the opponent's brief or even know what witnesses will be called: he must wait until the card is played and cannot try to see it in the hand. This argument cannot be denied some validity even where the defendant is a public corporation whose duty it is, so it might be thought, while taking all proper steps to protect its revenues, to place all the facts before the public and to pay proper compensation to those it has injured. A more powerful argument to my mind is that everything should be done in order to encourage anyone who knows the facts to state them fully and candidly – as Sir George Jessel MR said, to bare his breast to his lawyer: *Anderson v Bank of British Columbia* (1876). This he may not do unless he knows that his communication is privileged.

But the preparation of a case for litigation is not the only interest which calls for candour. In accident cases, ' ... the safety of the public may well depend on the candour and completeness of reports made by subordinates whose duty it is to draw attention to defects': *Conway v Rimmer* (1968) *per* Lord Reid. This however does not by itself justify a claim to privilege since, as Lord Reid continues: '... no one has ever suggested that public safety has been endangered by the candour or completeness of such reports having been inhibited by the fact that they may have to be produced if the interests of the due administration of justice should ever require production at any time.'

So one may deduce from this the principle that while privilege may be required in order to induce candour in statements made for the purposes of litigation it is not required in relation to statements whose purpose is different – for example to enable a railway to operate safely.

It is clear that the due administration of justice strongly requires disclosure and production of this report: it was contemporary; it contained statements by witnesses on the spot; it would be not merely relevant evidence, but almost certainly the best evidence as to the cause of the accident. If one accepts that this important public interest can be overridden in order that the defendant may properly prepare his case, how close must the connection be between the preparation of the document and the anticipation of litigation? On principle I would think that the purpose of preparing for litigation ought to be either the sole purpose or at least the dominant purpose of it: to carry the protection further into cases where that purpose was secondary or equal with another purpose would seem to be excessive, and unnecessary in the interest of encouraging truthful revelation. At the lowest such desirability of protection as might exist in such cases is not strong enough to outweigh the need for all relevant documents to be made available ...

[The other Law Lords delivered speeches restoring the order of Master Bickford Smith and upholding the 'dominant purpose' test.][6]

Alfred Crompton Amusement Machines Ltd v Customs and Excise Commissioners (No 2) (1972, Court of Appeal)

Amongst other things, the Court of Appeal in this case clarified the application of legal professional privilege to salaried legal advisers. Forbes J had held that the privilege did not apply to communications between lawyers in this category and their employers. The decision of the Court of Appeal on this point was not challenged in the subsequent appeal to the House of Lords.

Lord Denning MR: ... The law relating to discovery was developed by the Chancery courts in the first half of the 19th century. At that time nearly all legal advisers were in independent practice on their own account. Nowadays it is very different. Many barristers and solicitors are employed as legal advisers, whole time, by a single employer. Sometimes the employer is a great commercial concern. At other times it is a Government department or a local authority. It may even be the Government itself, like the Treasury Solicitor and his staff. In every case these legal advisers do legal work for their employer and for no one else. They are paid, not by fees for each piece of work, but by a fixed annual salary. They are, no doubt, servants or agents of the employer. For that reason Forbes J thought they were in a different position from other legal advisers who are in private practice. I do not think this is correct. They are regarded by the law as in every respect in the same position as those who practise on their own account. The only difference is that they act for one client only, and not for several clients. They must uphold the same standards of honour and of etiquette. They are subject to the same duties to their client and to the court. They must respect the same confidences. They and their clients have the same privileges. I have myself in my early days settled scores of affidavits of documents for the employers of such legal advisers. I have always proceeded on the footing that the communications between the legal advisers and their employer (who is their client) are the subject of legal professional privilege: and I have never known it questioned. There are many cases in the books of actions against railway companies where privilege has been claimed in this way. The validity of it has never been doubted.

I speak, of course, of their communications in the capacity of legal advisers. It does sometimes happen that such a legal adviser does work for his employer in another capacity, perhaps of an executive nature. Their communications in that capacity would not be the subject of legal professional privilege. So the legal adviser must be scrupulous to make the distinction. Being a servant or agent too, he may be under more pressure from his client. So he must be careful to resist it. He must be as independent in the doing of right as any other legal adviser. It is true, as the Law Reform Committee said in their report in 1967 on *Privilege in Civil Procedure* (Cmd 3472), that the 'system is susceptible to abuse', but I have never known it abused. So much so that I do not think the law should be changed in the way that Forbes J would have it. There is a safeguard against abuse. It is ready to hand. If there is any doubt as to the propriety or validity of a claim for privilege, the master or the judge should without hesitation inspect the documents himself so as to see if the claim is well-founded, or not ... The affidavit should not be treated as conclusive, nor anything like it. A party cannot

---

6.   [1980] AC 521.

use the affidavit as a taboo or spell to prevent anyone looking at the documents. When the master or judge sees the documents, he will see if the privilege is rightly claimed – or not – and make an order accordingly ...

[Karminski and Orr LJJ also delivered judgments in which they agreed with the reasoning and conclusions of Lord Denning.][7]

Rush & Tompkins Ltd v GLC (1988, House of Lords)

Lord Griffiths: ... The 'without prejudice rule' is a rule governing the admissibility of evidence and is founded on the public policy of encouraging litigants to settle their differences rather than litigate them to a finish ...

The rule applies to exclude all negotiations genuinely aimed at settlement whether oral or in writing from being given in evidence. A competent solicitor will always head any negotiating correspondence 'without prejudice' to make clear beyond doubt that in the event of the negotiations being unsuccessful they are not to be referred to at the subsequent trial. However, the application of the rule is not dependent on the use of the phrase 'without prejudice' and if it is clear from the surrounding circumstances that the parties were seeking to compromise the action, evidence of the content of those negotiations will, as a general rule, not be admissible at the trial and cannot be used to establish an admission or partial admission ...

Nearly all the cases in which the scope of the without prejudice rule has been considered concern the admissibility of evidence at trial after negotiations have failed. In such circumstances no question of discovery arises because the parties are well aware of what passed between them in the negotiations. These cases show that the rule is not absolute and resort may be had to the without prejudice material for a variety of reasons when the justice of the case requires it. It is unnecessary to make any deep examination of these authorities to resolve the present appeal but they all illustrate the underlying purpose of the rule which is to protect a litigant from being embarrassed by any admission made purely in an attempt to achieve a settlement. Thus the without prejudice material will be admissible if the issue is whether or not the negotiations resulted in an agreed settlement, which is the point that Lindley LJ was making in *Walker v Wilsher* (1889) and which was applied in *Tomlin v Standard Telephones and Cables Ltd* (1969). The court will not permit the phrase to be used to exclude an act of bankruptcy (see *Re Daintrey, ex p Holt* (1893)), or to suppress a threat if an offer is not accepted (see *Kitcat v Sharp* (1882)). In certain circumstances the without prejudice correspondence may be looked at to determine a question of costs after judgment has been given: see *Cutts v Head* (1984). There is also authority for the proposition that the admission of an 'independent fact' in no way connected with the merits of the case is admissible even if made in the course of negotiations for a settlement. Thus an admission that a document was in the handwriting of one of the parties was received in evidence in *Waldridge v Kennison* (1794). I regard this as an exceptional case and it should not be allowed to whittle down the protection given to the parties to speak freely about all issues in the litigation both factual and legal when seeking compromise and, for the purpose of establishing a basis of compromise, admitting certain facts. If the compromise fails the admission of the facts made for the purpose of the compromise should not be held against the maker of the admission and should therefore not be received in evidence.

7. [1974] AC 405.

I cannot accept the view of the Court of Appeal that *Walker v Wilsher* is authority for the proposition that if the negotiations succeed and a settlement is concluded the privilege goes, having served its purpose. In *Walker v Wilsher* the Court of Appeal held that it was not permissible to receive the contents of a without prejudice offer on the question of costs and no question arose as to the admissibility of admissions made in the negotiations in any possible subsequent proceedings. There are many situations when parties engaged on some great enterprise such as a large building construction project must anticipate the risk of being involved in disputes with others engaged on the same project. Suppose the main contractor in an attempt to settle a dispute with one subcontractor made certain admissions, it is clear law that those admissions cannot be used against him if there is no settlement. The reason they are not to be used is because it would discourage settlement if he believed that the admissions might be held against him. But it would surely be equally discouraging if the main contractor knew that if he achieved a settlement those admissions could then be used against him by any other subcontractor with whom he might also be in dispute. The main contractor might well be prepared to make certain concessions to settle some modest claim which he would never make in the face of another far larger claim. It seems to me that if those admissions made to achieve settlement of a piece of minor litigation could be held against him in a subsequent major litigation it would actively discourage settlement of the minor litigation and run counter to the whole underlying purpose of the without prejudice rule. I would therefore hold that as a general rule the without prejudice rule renders inadmissible in any subsequent litigation connected with the same subject matter proof of any admissions made in a genuine attempt to reach a settlement. It of course goes without saying that admissions made to reach settlement with a different party within the same litigation are also inadmissible whether or not settlement was reached with that party ...

[The other Law Lords agreed with the speech of Lord Griffiths.][8]

R v Derby Magistrates' Court, ex p B (1995, House of Lords)

In this case, the House of Lords, overruling earlier decisions, held that legal professional privilege would be upheld even where the witness no longer had any recognisable interest in preserving confidentiality.

Lord Taylor of Gosforth CJ: ...

Mr Richards, as amicus curiae, acknowledged the importance of maintaining legal professional privilege as the general rule. But he submitted that the rule should not be absolute. There might be occasions, if only by way of rare exception, in which the rule should yield to some other consideration of even greater importance. He referred by analogy to the balancing exercise which is called for where documents are withheld on the ground of public interest immunity, and cited the speech of Lord Simon of Glaisdale in *D v National Society for the Prevention of Cruelty to Children* [1978] AC 171, 233, and in *Waugh v British Railways Board* [1980] AC 521, 535. But the drawback to that approach is that once any exception to the general rule is allowed, the client's confidence is necessarily lost. The solicitor, instead of being able to tell his client that anything which the client might say would never in any circumstances be revealed without his consent, would have to qualify his assurance. He would have to tell the client that his confidence might be broken if in some future case the court were to hold

---

8. [1988] 3 All ER 737.

that he no longer had 'any recognisable interest' in asserting his privilege. One can see at once that the purpose of the privilege would thereby be undermined.

As for the analogy with public interest immunity, I accept that the various classes of case in which relevant evidence is excluded may, as Lord Simon of Glaisdale suggested, be regarded as forming part of a continuous spectrum. But it by no means follows that because a balancing exercise is called for in one class of case, it may also be allowed in another. Legal professional privilege and public interest immunity are as different in their origin as they are in their scope. Putting it another way, if a balancing exercise was ever required in the case of legal professional privilege, it was performed once and for all in the 16th century, and since then has applied across the board in every case, irrespective of the client's individual merits ...

[I]t is not for the sake of the applicant alone that the privilege must be upheld. It is in the wider interests of all those hereafter who might otherwise be deterred from telling the whole truth to their solicitors. For this reason I am of the opinion that no exception should be allowed to the absolute nature of legal professional privilege, once established. It follows that *Reg v Barton* (1973) and *Reg v Ataou* (1988) were wrongly decided, and ought to be overruled ...[9]

PUBLIC POLICY

As with privilege, the cases on public policy frequently cover several aspects of the topic. The main points to concentrate on are:

- the rule in *Marks v Beyfus* – see also the subject of prosecution disclosure in Chapter 9;
- the distinction drawn between the *class* and the *contents* of a particular communication;
- the judge's power to inspect;
- judicial comment on circumstances when it would be proper to rely on public policy to avoid disclosure;
- justification for exclusion on public policy grounds;
- the presence, or absence, of an underlying rationale for the operation of the rule;
- the operation of s 10 of the Contempt of Court Act 1981.

Marks v Beyfus (1890, Court of Appeal)

Appeal from a decision of the Queen's Bench Division (Lord Coleridge CJ and Mathew J), refusing a new trial

The action was brought against several defendants for maliciously and without reasonable and probable cause conspiring to institute and instituting a prosecution for fraud against the plaintiff, upon the trial of which he was acquitted; alternatively the defendants were charged with conspiring to cause the Director of Public Prosecutions to institute the prosecution ... At the trial before Huddleston B and a special jury, the plaintiff, who conducted his case in

---

9.   [1995] 3 WLR 681.

person, put in the sworn information of the defendant, Alfred Beyfus, which had been used upon the application for a summons against the plaintiff, and also put in the depositions taken before the magistrate upon which the plaintiff had been committed for trial. The plaintiff then called the Director of Public Prosecutions, who, in answer to questions put to him by the plaintiff, said that the prosecution had been instituted by himself and not by the defendants, and that he had a statement in writing which had been supplied to him, but declined, on grounds of public policy, to give the names of his informants or to produce the written statement; he offered, however, to answer the questions if the learned judge was of opinion that they were such questions as ought to be answered; but Huddleston B refused to order him to answer the questions or to produce the statement, and, no other evidence being produced on behalf of the plaintiff, he was nonsuited.

The Divisional Court refused a new trial, and the plaintiff appealed.

Lord Esher MR: ... The ground taken on behalf of the Director of Public Prosecutions is that this was a public prosecution, ordered by the Government (or by an official equivalent to the Government) for what was considered to be a public object, and that therefore the information ought not on grounds of public policy to be disclosed. The question whether this was a public prosecution in this sense depends upon the true construction of the statutes by which the office of Director of Public Prosecutions was created, and we have to say whether, when that officer acts under the rules ordinarily regulating his duties or under the direction of the Attorney General, the case is put in the category of public prosecutions instituted by the Government for the public protection ...

[Having concluded that a prosecution instituted or conducted by the DPP was a public, not a private, prosecution, he continued:]

What, then, is the rule as to the disclosure of the names of informants, and the information given by them in the case of a public prosecution? In the case of *Attorney General v Briant* (1846), Pollock CB discussing the case of *Rex v Hardy* (1794), says that on all hands it was agreed in that case that the informer, in the case of a public prosecution should not be disclosed; and later on in his judgment, Pollock CB says: 'The rule clearly established and acted on is this, that in a public prosecution a witness cannot be asked such questions as will disclose the informer, if he be a third person ... and we think the principle of the rule applies to the case where a witness is asked if he himself is the informer.' Now, this rule as to public prosecutions was founded on grounds of public policy, and if this prosecution was a public prosecution the rule attaches; I think it was a public prosecution, and that the rule applies. I do not say it is a rule which can never be departed from; if upon the trial of a prisoner the judge should be of opinion that the disclosure of the name of the informant is necessary or right in order to shew the prisoner's innocence, then one public policy is in conflict with another public policy, and that which says that an innocent man is not to be condemned when his innocence can be proved is the policy that must prevail. But except in that case, this rule of public policy is not a matter of discretion; it is a rule of law, and as such should be applied by the judge at the trial, who should not treat it as a matter of discretion whether he should tell the witness to answer or not. The learned judge was, therefore, perfectly right in the present case in applying the law, and in declining to let the witness answer the questions ...

Lindley LJ: I agree. It is obvious that the plaintiff could not hope to succeed in his action without the evidence of the Director of Public Prosecutions, and I am satisfied, for the reasons given by the Master of the Rolls, that the learned judge at the trial was perfectly right in the course he took.

Bowen LJ: I am of the same opinion ... The only question which remains for our decision is, whether the Director of Public Prosecutions was right in objecting to answer the questions put to him, and whether the judge was right in saying that on grounds of public policy he ought not to be asked to disclose the name of his informant. That depends upon whether this was a public prosecution; if so, then neither upon the criminal trial nor upon any subsequent civil proceedings arising out of it, ought the Director of Public Prosecutions, upon grounds of general policy, to be asked to disclose the name of his informant. The only exception to such a rule would be upon a criminal trial, when the judge if he saw that the strict enforcement of the rule would be likely to cause a miscarriage of justice, might relax it in *favorem innocentiae*; if he did not do so, there would be a risk of innocent people being convicted ... [10]

Duncan v Cammel Laird & Co (1942, House of Lords)

On 1 June 1939 the submarine *Thetis*, which had been built by the respondents under contract with the Admiralty, was undergoing submergence tests in Liverpool Bay. While engaged in a trial dive she sank to the bottom owing to the flooding of her two foremost compartments and failed to return to the surface. Ninety-nine men died. Many actions for negligence were begun by representatives of the deceased against the respondents. All these actions save two were stayed until after the trial of two test actions, which were consolidated. The plaintiffs in those actions were the appellants in this appeal. The respondents in their affidavit of documents had objected to having to produce a number of documents on the basis that, the attention of the First Lord of the Admiralty having been drawn to their nature and contents, the Treasury Solicitor had directed the respondents to object to production, except under order of the court, on the ground of Crown privilege. The First Lord of the Admiralty had sworn an affidavit stating that all the documents had been considered by him with the assistance of technical advisers and that he had formed the opinion that disclosure would be injurious to the public interest.

Viscount Simon LC: ... It will be observed that the objection is sometimes based upon the view that the public interest requires a particular class of communications with, or within, a public department to be protected from production on the ground that the candour and completeness of such communications might be prejudiced if they were ever liable to be disclosed in subsequent litigation rather than on the contents of the particular document itself ...

Two further matters remain to be considered. First, what is the proper form in which objection should be taken that the production of a document would be contrary to the public interest? And, secondly, when this objection is taken in proper form, should it be treated by the court as conclusive, or are there circumstances in which the judge should himself look at the documents before ruling as to their production?

On the first question, it is to be observed that the matter may arise at either of two stages in the course of a civil suit. It may arise (as in the present instance) before the trial begins out of an application for inspection of documents referred to in the affidavit of one of the parties, but it may also arise at the trial itself when

---

10. 25 QBD 494.

a subpoena or corresponding process has been served calling for the production of the documents and there is a refusal to comply on the ground that production would be contrary to the public interest. ... The essential matter is that the decision to object should be taken by the minister who is the political head of the department, and that he should have seen and considered the contents of the documents and himself have formed the view that on grounds of public interest they ought not to be produced, either because of their actual contents or because of the class of documents, eg departmental minutes, to which they belong. Instances may arise where it is not convenient or practicable for the political minister to act (eg he may be out of reach, or ill, or the department may be one where the effective head is a permanent official) and in such cases it would be reasonable for the objection to be taken, as it has often been taken in the past, by the permanent head. If the question arises before trial, the objection would ordinarily be taken by affidavit ... If the question arises on subpoena at the hearing it is not uncommon in modern practice for the minister's objection to be conveyed to the court, at any rate in the first instance, by an official of the department who produces a certificate which the minister has signed, stating what is necessary. I see no harm in that procedure, provided it is understood that this is only for convenience and that if the court is not satisfied by this method, it can request the minister's personal attendance.

The remaining question is whether, when objection has been duly taken, the judge should treat it as conclusive. There are cases in the books where the view has been expressed that the judge might properly probe the objection by himself examining the documents ... On the other hand, it has been several times laid down that the court ought to regard the objection, when validly and formally taken, as conclusive ...

The practice in Scotland, as in England, may have varied, but the approved practice in both countries is to treat a ministerial objection taken in proper form as conclusive ... As Lord Parker said in another connection: 'Those who are responsible for the national security must be the sole judges of what the national security requires': *The Zamora* (1916) ... The withholding of documents, on the ground that their publication would be contrary to the public interest, is not properly to be regarded as a branch of the law of privilege connected with discovery. 'Crown privilege' is for this reason not a happy expression. Privilege, in relation to discovery, is for the protection of the litigant and could be waived by him, but the rule that the interest of the state must not be put in jeopardy by producing documents which would injure it is a principle to be observed in administering justice, quite unconnected with the interests or claims of the particular parties in litigation, and, indeed, is a rule on which the judge should, if necessary, insist, even though no objection is taken at all ...

Although an objection validly taken to production, on the ground that this would be injurious to the public interest, is conclusive, it is important to remember that the decision ruling out such documents is the decision of the judge ... It is the judge who is in control of the trial, not the executive, but the proper ruling for the judge to give is as above expressed. In this connection, I do not think it is out of place to indicate the sort of grounds which would not afford to the minister adequate justification for objecting to production. It is not a sufficient ground that the documents are 'State documents' or 'official' or are marked 'confidential'. It would not be a good ground that, if they were produced, the consequences might involve the department or the Government in parliamentary discussion or in public criticism, or might necessitate the attendance as witnesses or otherwise of officials who have pressing duties elsewhere. Neither would it be good ground that production might tend to expose a want of efficiency in the administration or tend to lay the department open to claims for compensation. In a word, it is not enough that the minister of the department does not want to have the documents produced. The minister, in deciding whether it is his duty to object, should bear these considerations in mind, for he ought not to take the responsibility of withholding production except in cases where the public interest would otherwise be damnified; for example, where disclosure would be injurious to national defence, or to good diplomatic relations, or where the practice of keeping a class of documents secret is necessary for the proper functioning of the public service. When these conditions are satisfied and the minister feels it is his duty to deny access to material which would otherwise be available, there is no question but that the public interest must be preferred to any private consideration. The present opinion is concerned only with the production of documents, but it seems to me that the same principle must also apply to the exclusion of oral evidence which, if given, would jeopardize the interests of the community ... After all, the public interest is also the interest of every subject of the realm, and while, in these exceptional cases, the private citizen may seem to be denied what is to his immediate advantage, he, like the rest of us, would suffer if the needs of protecting the interests of the country as a whole were not ranked as a prior obligation ...

[The other Law Lords concurred.][11]

Conway v Rimmer (1968, House of Lords)

The facts, stated by Lord Reid were as follows: In April 1963, the appellant became a probationer police constable in the Cheshire Constabulary for a period of two years. The respondent was a superintendent in that force. In December 1964 another probationer constable lost an electric torch worth 15s 3d. He found a torch in the appellant's locker which he said was his torch and reported this to his superiors. The matter was investigated by the respondent. The appellant asserted that this torch was his torch. In the course of the investigation the respondent stated to the appellant that his probationary reports were adverse and he urged him to resign. The appellant refused. The respondent then prepared a report which he submitted to the chief constable apparently with a view to its being sent to the Director of Public Prosecutions for advice whether the appellant should be charged with theft of the torch. It did not appear what advice was received from the Director of Public Prosecutions but after a short time the respondent was instrumental in bringing a charge of larceny against the appellant. He was tried at quarter sessions in Chester and the respondent gave evidence. At the close of the prosecution case the jury stopped the case and returned a verdict of not guilty. Shortly thereafter another probationary report was prepared – by whom it did not appear – and then the appellant was dismissed. He had no right of appeal.

The appellant then sued the respondent for damages for malicious prosecution. He said that as a result of those events he had found it impossible to obtain suitable employment. On discovery of documents being sought, the existence of five documents was disclosed. Both the appellant and the respondent stated to the Appellate Committee through their counsel that they

---

11. [1942] AC 642.

wished these documents to be produced but production had been withheld on the ground of Crown privilege. These documents were (1) and (3) 'probationary reports' on the appellant dated 1 January and 21 July 1964; (2) a report on the appellant by a district police training centre; (4) a report by the respondent to his chief constable of 13 January 1965, which admittedly was the report prepared for submission to the Director of Public Prosecutions; and (5) a probationary report on the appellant dated 9 April 1965. None of the contents of these documents had ever been disclosed to the appellant.

Production of these documents had been refused by reason of an affidavit sworn by the Home Secretary on 15 July 1966, which was as follows:

I, the Right Honourable Roy Harris Jenkins, one of Her Majesty's Principal Secretaries of State, make oath and say as follows:

1   On or about June 3 1966 my attention was drawn to a copy of a list of documents delivered in these proceedings on behalf of the defendant and to the documents referred to in the second part of the first schedule to the said list of documents being numbered therein 38; 39; 40; 47 and 48.

2   I personally examined and carefully considered all the said documents and I formed the view that those numbered 38; 39; 40 and 48 fell within a class of documents comprising confidential reports by police officers to chief officers of police relating to the conduct, efficiency and fitness for employment of individual police officers under their command and that the said document numbered 47 fell within a class of documents comprising reports by police officers to their superiors concerning investigations into the commission of crime. In my opinion the production of documents of each such class would be injurious to the public interest.

3   Accordingly I gave instructions that Crown privilege was to be claimed for the said documents and by letter dated June 7 1966, from the Treasury Solicitor, the defendant's solicitors were so informed.

4   I have been informed of an order made by this Honourable court in these proceedings on June 9 1966, that the said above-mentioned documents should be produced as therein mentioned unless an affidavit sworn by me should be filed in these proceedings on or before July 21 1966.

5   I object to the production of each of the said documents on the grounds set forth in paragraph 2 of this affidavit.

Lord Reid continued: ... The question whether such a statement by a Minister of the Crown should be accepted as conclusively preventing any court from ordering production of any of the documents to which it applies is one of very great importance in the administration of justice. If the commonly accepted interpretation of the decision of this House in *Duncan v Cammell Laird & Co Ltd* (1942) is to remain authoritative the question admits of only one answer – the minister's statement is final and conclusive. Normally I would be very slow to question the authority of a unanimous decision of this House only 25 years old which was carefully considered and obviously intended to lay down a general rule. But this decision has several abnormal features.

Lord Simon thought that on this matter the law in Scotland was the same as the law in England and he clearly intended to lay down a rule applicable to the whole of the United Kingdom. But in *Glasgow Corporation v Central Land Board* (1956) this House held that that was not so, with the result that today on this question the law is different in the two countries. There are many chapters of the law where for historical and other reasons it is quite proper that the law should be different in the two countries. But here we are dealing purely with public policy – with the proper relation between the powers of the executive and the powers of the courts – and I can see no rational justification for the law on this matter being different in the two countries.

Secondly, events have proved that the rule supposed to have been laid down in *Duncan's* case is far from satisfactory. In the large number of cases in England and elsewhere which have been cited in argument much dissatisfaction has been expressed and I have not observed even one expression of whole-hearted approval. Moreover a statement made by the Lord Chancellor in 1956 on behalf of the Government, to which I shall return later, makes it clear that that Government did not regard it as consonant with public policy to maintain the rule to the full extent which existing authorities had held to be justifiable.

I have no doubt that the case of *Duncan v Cammell Laird & Co Ltd* was rightly decided. The plaintiff sought discovery of documents relating to the submarine *Thetis* including a contract for the hull and machinery and plans and specifications. The First Lord of the Admiralty had stated that, 'it would be injurious to the public interest that any of the said documents should be disclosed to any person'. Any of these documents might well have given valuable information, or at least clues, to the skilled eye of an agent of a foreign power. But Lord Simon LC took the opportunity to deal with the whole question of the right of the Crown to prevent production of documents in a litigation. Yet a study of his speech leaves me with the strong impression that throughout he had primarily in mind cases where discovery or disclosure would involve a danger of real prejudice to the national interest. I find it difficult to believe that his speech would have been the same if the case had related, as the present case does, to discovery of routine reports on a probationer constable ...

It is universally recognised that here there are two kinds of public interest which may clash. There is the public interest that harm shall not be done to the nation or the public service by disclosure of certain documents, and there is the public interest that the administration of justice shall not be frustrated by the withholding of documents which must be produced if justice is to be done. There are many cases where the nature of the injury which would or might be done to the nation or the public service is of so grave a character that no other interest, public or private, can be allowed to prevail over it. With regard to such cases it would be proper to say, as Lord Simon did, that to order production of the document in question would put the interest of the state in jeopardy. But there are other cases where the possible injury to the public service is much less and there one would think that it would be proper to balance the public interests involved. I do not believe that Lord Simon really meant that the smallest probability of injury to the public service must always outweigh the gravest frustration of the administration of justice ...

There are now many large public bodies, such as British Railways and the National Coal Board, the proper and efficient functioning of which is very necessary for many reasons including the safety of the public. The Attorney General made it clear that Crown privilege is not and cannot be invoked to prevent disclosure of similar documents made by them or their servants even if it were said that this is required for the proper and efficient functioning of the public service. I find it difficult to see why it should be *necessary* to withhold whole classes of routine 'communications with or within a public department' but quite unnecessary to withhold similar communications with or within a public corporation. There the safety of the public may well depend on the candour and completeness of reports made by subordinates whose duty it is to draw attention to defects. But, so far as I know, no one has ever suggested that public safety has been endangered by the candour or completeness of such reports having been inhibited by the fact that they may have to be produced if the interests of the due administration of justice should ever require production at any time.

I must turn now to a statement made by the Lord Chancellor, Lord Kilmuir, in this House on June 6 1956. When counsel proposed to read this statement your Lordships had doubts, which I shared, as to its admissibility. But we did permit it to be read, and, as the argument proceeded, its importance emerged. With a minor amendment made on March 8 1962, it appears still to operate as a direction to, or at least a guide for, ministers who swear affidavits. So we may assume that in the present case the Home Secretary acted in accordance with the views expressed in Lord Kilmuir's statement.

The statement sets out the grounds on which Crown privilege is to be claimed. Having set out the first ground that disclosure of the contents of the particular document would injure the public interest, it proceeds: 'The second ground is that the document falls within a class which the public interest requires to be withheld from production, and Lord Simon particularised this head of public interest as "the proper functioning of the public service".'

There is no reference to Lord Simon's exhortation [in *Duncan v Cammell Laird*] that a minister ought not to take the responsibility of withholding production of a class of documents except where the practice of keeping a class of documents secret is necessary for the proper functioning of the public service. Then the statement proceeds: 'The reason why the law sanctions the claiming of Crown privilege on the "class" ground is the need to secure freedom and candour of communication with and within the public service, so that Government decisions can be taken on the best advice and with the fullest information. In order to secure this it is necessary that the class of documents to which privilege applies should be clearly settled, so that the person giving advice or information should know that he is doing so in confidence. Any system whereby a document falling within the class might, as a result of a later decision, be required to be produced in evidence, would destroy that confidence and undermine the whole basis of class privilege, because there would be no certainty at the time of writing that the document would not be disclosed.'

But later in the statement the position taken is very different. A number of cases are set out in which Crown privilege should not be claimed. The most important for present purposes is: 'We also propose that if medical documents, or indeed other documents, are relevant to the defence in criminal proceedings, Crown privilege should not be claimed.'

The only exception specifically mentioned is statements by informers. That is a very wide ranging exception, for the Attorney General stated that it applied at least to all manner of routine communications and even to prosecutions for minor offences. Thus it can no longer be said that the writer of such communications has any 'certainty at the time of writing that the document would not be disclosed'. So we have the curious result that 'freedom and candour of communication' is supposed not to be inhibited by knowledge of the writer that his report may be disclosed in a criminal case, but would still be supposed to be inhibited if he thought that his report might be disclosed in a civil case.

The Attorney General did not deny that, even where the full contents of a report have already been made public in a criminal case, Crown privilege is still claimed for that report in a later civil case. And he was quite candid about the reason for that. Crown privilege is claimed in the civil case not to protect the document – its contents are already public property – but to protect the writer from civil liability should he be sued for libel or other tort. No doubt the Government have weighed the danger that knowledge of such protection might encourage malicious writers against the advantage that honest reporters shall not be subjected to vexatious actions, and have come to the conclusion that it is an advantage to the public service to afford this protection. But that seems very far removed from the original purpose of Crown privilege.

And the statement, as it has been explained to us, makes clear another point. The minister who withholds production of a 'class' document has no duty to consider the degree of public interest involved in a particular case by frustrating in that way the due administration of justice. If it is in the public interest in his view to withhold documents of that class, then it matters not whether the result of withholding of a document is merely to deprive a litigant of some evidence on a minor issue in a case of little importance or, on the other hand, is to make it impossible to do justice at all in a case of the greatest importance. I cannot think that it is satisfactory that there should be no means at all of weighing, in any civil case, the public interest involved in withholding the document against the public interest that it should be produced.

So it appears to me that the present position is so unsatisfactory that this House must re-examine the whole question in light of all the authorities.

Two questions will arise: first, whether the court is to have any right to question the finality of a minister's certificate and, secondly, if it has such a right, how and in what circumstances that right is to be exercised and made effective.

A minister's certificate may be given on one or other of two grounds: either because it would be against the public interest to disclose the contents of the particular document or documents in question, or because the document belongs to a class of documents which ought to be withheld, whether or not there is anything in the particular document in question disclosure of which would be against the public interest. It does not appear that any serious difficulties have arisen or are likely to arise with regard to the first class. However wide the power of the court may be held to be, cases would be very rare in which it could be proper to question the view of the responsible minister that it would be contrary to the public interest to make public the contents of a particular document. A question might arise whether it would be possible to separate those parts of a document of which disclosure would be innocuous from those parts which ought not to be made public, but I need not pursue that question now. In the present case your Lordships are directly concerned with the second class of document ...

Lord Simon did not say that courts in England have no power to overrule the executive. He said (*Duncan's* case): '... the decision ruling out such documents is the decision of the judge ... It is the judge who is in control of the trial, not the executive, but the proper ruling for the judge to give is as above expressed.'

That is, to accept the minister's view in every case. In my judgment, considering what it is 'proper' for a court to do we must have regard to the need, shown by 25 years' experience since *Duncan's* case, that the courts should balance the public interest in the proper administration of justice against the public interest in withholding any evidence which a minister considers ought to be withheld.

I would therefore propose that the House ought now to decide that courts have and are entitled to exercise a power and duty to hold a balance between the public interest, as expressed by a minister, to withhold certain documents or other evidence, and the public interest in ensuring the proper administration of justice. That does not mean that a court would reject a minister's view: full weight must be given to it in every case, and if the minister's reasons are of a character which judicial experience is not competent to weigh, then the minister's view must prevail. But experience has shown that reasons given for withholding whole classes of documents are often not of that character. For example a court is perfectly well able to assess the likelihood that, if the writer of a certain class of document knew that there was a chance that his report might be produced in legal proceedings, he would make a less full and candid report than he would otherwise have done.

I do not doubt that there are certain classes of documents which ought not to be disclosed whatever their contents may be. Virtually everyone agrees that Cabinet minutes and the like ought not to be disclosed until such time as they are only of historical interest. But I do not think that many people would give as the reason that premature disclosure would prevent candour in the Cabinet. To my mind the most important reason is that such disclosure would create or fan ill-informed or captious public or political criticism. The business of Government is difficult enough as it is, and no Government could contemplate with equanimity the inner workings of the Government machine being exposed to the gaze of those ready to criticise without adequate knowledge of the background and perhaps with some axe to grind. And that must, in my view, also apply to all documents concerned with policy making within departments including, it may be, minutes and the like by quite junior officials and correspondence with outside bodies. Further it may be that deliberations about a particular case require protection as much as deliberations about policy. I do not think that it is possible to limit such documents by any definition. But there seems to me to be a wide difference between such documents and routine reports. There may be special reasons for withholding some kinds of routine documents, but I think that the proper test to be applied is to ask, in the language of Lord Simon in *Duncan's* case, whether the withholding of a document because it belongs to a particular class is really 'necessary for the proper functioning of the public service'.

It appears to me that, if the minister's reasons are such that a judge can properly weigh them, he must, on the other hand, consider what is the probable importance in the case before him of the documents or other evidence sought to be withheld. If he decides that on balance the documents probably ought to be produced, I think that it would generally be best that he should see them before ordering production and if he thinks that the minister's reasons are not clearly expressed he will have to see the documents before ordering production. I can see nothing wrong in the judge seeing documents without their being shown to the parties. Lord Simon said (in *Duncan's* case) that 'where the Crown is a party ... this would amount to communicating with one party to the exclusion of the other'. I do not agree. The parties see the minister's reasons. Where a document has not been prepared for the information of the judge, it seems to me a misuse of language to say that the judge 'communicates with' the holder of the document by reading it. If on reading the document he still thinks that it ought to be produced he will order its production.

But it is important that the minister should have a right to appeal before the document is produced. This matter was not fully investigated in the argument before your Lordships. But it does appear that in one way or another there can be an appeal if the document is in the custody of a servant of the Crown or of a person who is willing to co-operate with the minister. There may be difficulty if it is in the hands of a person who wishes to produce it. But that difficulty could occur today if a witness wishes to give some evidence which the minister unsuccessfully urges the court to prevent from being given. It may be that this is a matter which deserves further investigation by the Crown authorities ...

It appears to me to be almost improbable that any harm would be done by disclosure of the probationary reports on the appellant or of the report from the police training centre. With regard to the report which the respondent made to his chief constable with a view to the prosecution of the appellant there could be more doubt, although no suggestion was made in argument that disclosure of its contents would be harmful now that the appellant has been acquitted. And, as I have said, these documents may prove to be of vital importance in the litigation.

In my judgment, this appeal should be allowed and these documents ought now to be required to be produced for inspection. If it is then found that disclosure would not, in your Lordships' view be prejudicial to the public interest, or that any possibility of such prejudice is, in the case of each of the documents, insufficient to justify its being withheld, then disclosure should be ordered.

[The other Law Lords also delivered speeches allowing the appeal.][12]

Rogers v Home Secretary (1973, **House of Lords**)

Lord Reid: My Lords, by 1968 it had become notorious that the control of many gaming establishments was passing into the hands of very undesirable people. The Gaming Act 1968 provides for licensing of premises used for gaming and by section 10 it established the Gaming Board for Great Britain with a special duty to keep under review the extent and character of gaming. One of its duties is to deal with applications for its consent to apply for a gaming licence. No licences can be granted to any applicant unless he has obtained such consent from the board. The functions and duties of the board in this regard are set out in Schedule 2 to the Act, paragraph 4. The board are required to make unusually extensive enquiries not only into the capacity and diligence of all applicants but also into their character, reputation and financial standing and any other circumstances appearing to the board to be relevant.

Applications were made by a company of which the appellant was a director and by the appellant himself. All were refused after the appellant had been interviewed by the board.

It is the custom of the board to obtain confidential information about applicants from the police. The appellant says that there came into his possession from an anonymous source a copy of a letter written about him to the board by Mr Ross, assistant chief constable of Sussex. Obviously this letter had been abstracted by improper means from files of the board or from the police. The appellant says that this letter contains highly damaging libellous statements about him and that he wishes to take proceedings to clear his reputation. The means he chose for doing that was to seek to prosecute Mr Ross for criminal libel. To succeed he must prove that the letter was sent, so he applied for witness summonses against representatives of the board and the chief constable requiring them to produce, *inter alia*, this letter. The Attorney General then sought an order of *certiorari* to quash the summonses on the ground that the documents called for were the subject of Crown privilege and he succeeded ...

The ground put forward has been said to be Crown privilege. I think that that expression is wrong and may be misleading. There is no question of any privilege in the ordinary sense of the word. The real question is whether the

---

12. [1968] AC 910.

public interest requires that the letter shall not be produced and whether that public interest is so strong as to override the ordinary right and interest of a litigant that he shall be able to lay before a court of justice all relevant evidence. A Minister of the Crown is always an appropriate and often the most appropriate person to assert this public interest, and the evidence or advice which he gives to the court is always valuable and may sometimes be indispensable. But, in my view, it must always be open to any person interested to raise the question and there may be cases where the trial judge should himself raise the question if no one else has done so. In the present case the question of public interest was raised by both the Attorney General and the Gaming Board. In my judgment both were entitled to raise the matter. Indeed I think that in the circumstances it was the duty of the board to do as they have done.

The claim in the present case is not based on the nature of the contents of this particular letter. It is based on the fact that the board cannot adequately perform their statutory duty unless they can preserve the confidentiality of all communications to them regarding the character, reputation or antecedents of the applicants for their consent.

Claims for 'class privilege' were fully considered by this House in *Conway v Rimmer* (1968). It was made clear that there is a heavy burden of proof on any authority which makes such a claim. But the possibility of establishing such a claim was not ruled out. I venture to quote what I said in that case: 'There may be special reasons for withholding some kinds of routine documents, but I think that the proper test to be applied is to ask, in the language of Lord Simon in *Duncan v Cammell Laird & Co Ltd* (1942), whether the withholding of a document because it belongs to a particular class is really "necessary for the proper functioning of the public service".'

I do not think that 'the public service' should be construed narrowly. Here the question is whether the withholding of this class of documents is really necessary to enable the board adequately to perform its statutory duties. If it is, then we are enabling the will of Parliament to be carried out.

There are very unusual features about this case. The board require the fullest information they can get in order to identify and exclude persons of dubious character and reputation from the privilege of obtaining a licence to conduct a gaming establishment. There is no obligation on anyone to give any information to the board. No doubt many law-abiding citizens would tell what they know even if there was some risk of their identity becoming known, although many perfectly honourable people do not want to be thought to be mixed up in such affairs. But it is obvious that the best source of information about dubious characters must often be persons of dubious character themselves. It has long been recognised that the identity of police informers must in the public interest be kept secret and the same considerations must apply to those who volunteer information to the board. Indeed, it is in evidence that many refuse to speak unless assured of absolute secrecy.

The letter called for in this case came from the police. I feel sure that they would not be deterred from giving full information by any fear of consequences to themselves if there were any disclosure. But much of the information which they can give must come from sources which must be protected and they would rightly take this into account. Even if information were given without naming the source, the very nature of the information might, if it were communicated to the person concerned, at least give him a very shrewd idea from whom it had come.

It is possible that some documents coming to the board could be disclosed without fear of such consequences. But I would think it quite impracticable for the board or the court to be sure of this. So it appears to me that, if there is not to be very serious danger of the board being deprived of information essential for the proper performance of their difficult task, there must be a general rule that they are bound not to produce any document which gives information to them about an applicant.

We must then balance that fact against the public interest that the course of justice should not be impeded by the withholding of evidence. We must, I think, take into account that these documents only came into existence because the applicant is asking for a privilege and is submitting his character and reputation to scrutiny. The documents are not used to deprive him of any legal right. The board have a wide discretion. Not only can they refuse his application on the ground of bad reputation although he may say that he has not deserved that reputation; it is not denied that the board can also take into account any unfavourable impression which he has made during an interview with the board.

Natural justice requires that the board should act in good faith and that they should so far as possible tell him the gist of any grounds on which they propose to refuse his application so that he may show such grounds to be unfounded in fact. But the board must be trusted to do that; we have been referred to their practice in this matter and I see nothing wrong in it.

In the present case the board told the appellant nothing about the contents of the letter because they say that they had sufficient grounds for refusing his application without any need to rely on anything in the letter. Their good faith in this matter is not subject to any substantial challenge. If the appellant had not by someone's wrongful act obtained a copy of the letter there was no reason why he should ever have known anything about it.

In my judgment on balance the public interest clearly requires that documents of this kind should not be disclosed, and that public interest is not affected by the fact that by some wrongful means a copy of such a document has been obtained and published by some person. I would therefore dismiss the appellant's appeal ...

[The other Law Lords delivered speeches dismissing the appeal by Mr Rogers.][13]

D v NSPCC (1978, House of Lords)

Lord Diplock: My Lords, in form this is an interlocutory appeal upon a summons relating to the discovery of documents by the National Society for the Prevention of Cruelty to Children (NSPCC) in a pending action brought against them by the respondent (Mrs D). In substance, the question for your Lordships is whether the NSPCC can be compelled in legal proceedings to disclose the identity of persons who give them information that a child is being ill-treated or neglected.

The NSPCC is a voluntary society founded in 1889 and incorporated by royal charter in 1895. Its purposes are: 1. To prevent the public and private wrongs of children, and the corruption of their morals. 2. To take action for the enforcement of laws for their protection. 3. To provide and maintain an organisation for the above objects. 4. To do all other such lawful things as are incidental or conducive to the attainment of the above objects ...

Although empowered to bring care proceedings, neither constables nor the NSPCC are under any statutory duty to do so. In this respect their position differs from that of a local authority ...

13. [1973] AC 388.

Before this House the claim of the NSPCC to refuse discovery of documents which could reveal the identity of their informant was based squarely upon the public interest in maintaining the confidentiality of information given to the society so that it may take steps to promote the welfare of a child, whether, as happens in the great majority of cases, by giving support, advice and guidance to the family of which the child is a member or, if this be necessary in the interest of the child, by instituting care proceedings in respect of him or prosecuting those who have committed offences against him.

To assist them to carry out the purposes of their charter and their functions as a person authorised to take care proceedings under section 1 of the Children and Young Persons Act 1969, the NSPCC invite the help of the general public in telling the society's officers of any child of whom they know who may be suffering because of misfortune, ignorance, neglect or ill-treatment. The leaflets, which the society distributes widely to enlist the public's aid, contain the promise: 'Your name, and the information you give for the purpose of helping children, will be treated as confidential.' The uncontradicted evidence of the director of the NSPCC is that the work of the society is dependent upon its receiving prompt information of suspected child abuse and that, as might be expected, the principal sources of such information are neighbours of the child's family or doctors, schoolteachers, health visitors and the like who will continue to be neighbours or to maintain the same relationship with the suspected person after the matter has been investigated and dealt with by the NSPCC. The evidence of the director is that without an effective promise of confidentiality neighbours and others would be very hesitant to pass on to the society information about suspected child abuse. There is an understandable reluctance to 'get involved' in something that is likely to arouse the resentment of the person whose suspected neglect or ill-treatment of a child has been reported by the informant, however true the information may be. Unless the NSPCC can guarantee the anonymity of its informants, its ability to learn of cases where children are at risk would be drastically reduced.

The fact that information has been communicated by one person to another in confidence, however, is not of itself a sufficient ground for protecting from disclosure in a court of law the nature of the information or the identity of the informant if either of these matters would assist the court to ascertain facts which are relevant to an issue upon which it is adjudicating: *Alfred Crompton Amusement Machines Ltd v Customs and Excise Commissioners (No 2)* (1974). The private promise of confidentiality must yield to the general public interest that in the administration of justice truth will out, unless by reason of the character of the information or the relationship of the recipient of the information to the informant a more important public interest is served by protecting the information or the identity of the informant from disclosure in a court of law.

The public interest which the NSPCC relies upon as obliging it to withhold from the plaintiff and from the court itself material that could disclose the identity of the society's informant is analogous to the public interest that is protected by the well-established rule of law that the identity of police informers may not be disclosed in a civil action, whether by the process of discovery or by oral evidence at the trial: *Marks v Beyfus* (1890).

The rationale of the rule as it applies to police informers is plain. If their identity were liable to be disclosed in a court of law, these sources of information would dry up and the police would be hindered in their duty of preventing and detecting crime. So the public interest in preserving the anonymity of police informers had to be weighed against the public interest that information which might assist a judicial tribunal to ascertain facts relevant to an issue upon which it is required to adjudicate should be withheld from that tribunal. By the uniform practice of the judges which by the time of *Marks v Beyfus* had already hardened into a rule of law, the balance has fallen upon the side of non-disclosure except where upon trial of a defendant for a criminal offence disclosure of the identity of the informer could help to show that the defendant was innocent of the offence. In that case, and in that case only, the balance falls upon the side of disclosure ...

For my part I would uphold the decision of Croom-Johnson J and reverse that of the Court of Appeal. I would do so upon what in argument has been referred to as the 'narrow' submission made on behalf of the NSPCC. I would extend to those who give information about neglect or ill-treatment of children to a local authority or the NSPCC a similar immunity from disclosure of their identity in legal proceedings to that which the law accords to police informers. The public interests served by preserving the anonymity of both classes of informants are analogous; they are of no less weight in the case of the former than in that of the latter class, and in my judgment are of greater weight than in the case of informers of the Gaming Board to whom immunity from disclosure of their identity has recently been extended by this House.

In the Court of Appeal, as in this House, counsel for the NSPCC advanced, as well as what I have referred to as the narrow submission, a broad submission that whenever a party to legal proceedings claims that there is a public interest to be served by withholding documents or information from disclosure in those proceedings it is the duty of the court to weigh that interest against the countervailing public interest in the administration of justice in the particular case and to refuse disclosure if the balance tilts that way. This broad submission, or something rather like it confined to information imparted in confidence, was adopted in his dissenting judgment by Lord Denning MR, but as I have already indicated there is the authority of this House that confidentiality of itself does not provide a ground of non-disclosure; nor am I able to accept the proposition that the basis of all privilege from disclosure of documents or information in legal proceedings is to prevent the breaking of a confidence. For my part, I think this House would be unwise to base its decision in the instant case upon a proposition so much broader than is necessary to resolve the issue between the parties ...

I see no reason and I know of no authority for confining public interest as a ground for non-disclosure of documents or information to the effective functioning of departments or organs of Central Government. In *Conway v Rimmer* (1968) the public interest to be protected was the effective functioning of a county police force; in *Re D (Infants)* (1970) the interest to be protected was the effective functioning of a local authority in relation to the welfare of boarded-out children. In the instant case the public interest to be protected is the effective functioning of an organisation authorised under an Act of Parliament to bring legal proceedings for the welfare of children. I agree with Croom-Johnson J that this is a public interest which the court is entitled to take into consideration in deciding whether the identity of the NSPCC's informants ought to be disclosed. I also agree that the balance of public interest falls on the side of non-disclosure.

I would allow this appeal.

[The other Law Lords also delivered speeches allowing the appeal.][14]

14. [1978] AC 171.

Science Research Council v Nassé (1980, House of Lords)

Lord Wilberforce: My Lords, Mrs Nassé and Mr Vyas, who are the two appellants in these conjoined appeals, have complained to industrial tribunals of discrimination against them by their employers.

Mrs Nassé was employed as a clerical officer by the Science Research Council ('SRC'), a body incorporated by royal charter. She sought, unsuccessfully, promotion to the grade of executive officer and complained, originally, that she had been discriminated against on the ground of her activities in her trade union. Later she added a complaint of discrimination under the Sex Discrimination Act 1975.

Mr Vyas was employed as a methods analyst by Leyland Cars (BL Cars Ltd) – 'Leyland.' He sought, unsuccessfully, a level transfer to another division in the company, and complained of discrimination on racial grounds: he is of Asian origin.

Each appeal raises the question whether and to what extent a complainant under the Employment Protection Act 1975, or the Sex Discrimination Act 1975, or the Race Relations Act 1976, may obtain discovery and inspection of documents, and in particular, whether she or he is entitled to see confidential assessments, references, reports or other documents relating to the complainant and to other persons, particularly those persons who have been preferred to the complainant. In each case the employer has been willing to produce for inspection a certain amount of material. But in each case it objects to the disclosure of matters revealed in confidence on the ground, broadly, that this would involve a breach of the confidence under which the material came into existence, and would undermine the whole system and structure of promotion and employer management ...

In cases under the Sex Discrimination Act and the Race Relations Act the necessary information and material to support or refute a claim will rarely be in the possession of the employee, but, on the contrary, is likely to be in the possession of the employer. Discrimination, at least in promotion cases, involves an allegation that, although the unselected complainant is as well-qualified as the person selected, or indeed better qualified, he was not chosen, an allegation which almost necessarily involves a careful comparison of qualifications, and an inquiry into the selection process. The employer is likely to have information on these matters. So, in order to ensure its production, each of the Acts contains a powerful inquisitorial procedure enabling the statutory commission set up under each Act to obtain information. They may conduct a 'formal investigation' and in the course of it require any person to give oral information and produce documents; there is however the limitation that a person cannot be required to give information, or produce documents, which he could not be compelled to give in evidence or produce in civil proceedings before the High Court. If an individual considers that he may have been discriminated against, the relevant commission may assist him (by advice or 'legal aid') and may help him to question the employer by means of a questionnaire. If the employer refuses to answer, or if his answer appears evasive or equivocal, inferences adverse to him may be drawn. Furthermore, industrial tribunals have powers – of their own motion – to ask for particulars of the grounds on which a person relies and of any facts or contentions relevant thereto ... The relevant point to be made is that, by reason of these powers, employees and the tribunals have the means, before any question of discovery arises, to obtain a great deal of information which may assist the employees' case, and indeed by conferring them Parliament has shown that its policy is that they should have every chance to lay before the tribunal or the court all material that may be relevant to a discrimination claim.

That brings me to the question of discovery (in which I include inspection) as to which the situation, as I see it, is formally simple. By a number of cross-references between regulations, the Industrial Tribunals (Labour Relations) Regulations 1974, the County Court Rules and the Rules of the Supreme Court the position is reached that the tribunal, or the county court, has a general discretion to order discovery, coupled with the qualification that 'discovery shall not be ordered if and so far as the court is of the opinion that it is not necessary either for disposing fairly of the proceedings or for saving costs' (County Court Rules, Ord 14, r 2(2)). These provisions, applied as they have been since their introduction, are sufficient to provide a solution for the issues in these appeals. These are, broadly, two: First, is there in relation to confidential documents, or any relevant class of confidential documents, any immunity from disclosure? Second, if not, how should the tribunal exercise its discretion as to discovery in relation to confidential documents in this field? (Here and elsewhere I use the word 'tribunal' so as to include, where appropriate, a county court.)

On these points my conclusions are as follows:

1   There is no principle of public interest immunity, as that expression was developed from *Conway v Rimmer* (1968), protecting such confidential documents as those with which these appeals are concerned. That such an immunity exists, or ought to be declared by this House to exist, was the main contention of Leyland. It was not argued for by the SRC; indeed that body argued against it.

2   There is no principle in English law by which documents are protected from discovery by reason of confidentiality alone. But there is no reason why, in the exercise of its discretion to order discovery, the tribunal should not have regard to the fact that documents are confidential, and that to order disclosure would involve a breach of confidence. In the employment field, the tribunal may have regard to the sensitivity of particular types of confidential information, to the extent to which the interests of third parties (including their employees on whom confidential reports have been made, as well as persons reporting) may be affected by disclosure, to the interest which both employees and employers may have in preserving the confidentiality of personal reports, and to any wider interest which may be seen to exist in preserving the confidentiality of systems of personal assessments.

3   As a corollary to the above, it should be added that relevance alone, though a necessary ingredient, does not provide an automatic sufficient test for ordering discovery. The tribunal always has a discretion. That relevance alone is enough was, in my belief, the position ultimately taken by counsel for Mrs Nassé thus entitling the complainant to discovery subject only to protective measures (sealing up, etc). This I am unable to accept.

4   The ultimate test in discrimination (as in other) proceedings is whether discovery is necessary for disposing fairly of the proceedings. If it is, then discovery must be ordered notwithstanding confidentiality. But where the court is impressed with the need to preserve confidentiality in a particular case, it will consider carefully whether the necessary information has been or can be obtained by other means, not involving a breach of confidence.

5   In order to reach a conclusion whether discovery is necessary notwithstanding confidentiality the tribunal should inspect the documents. It

will naturally consider whether justice can be done by special measures such as 'covering up', substituting anonymous references for specific names, or, in rare cases, hearing *in camera* ...

To these considerations I will now add some supporting arguments. I make these briefly since a large part of the ground is familiar, and to deal fully with all the contentions we have heard would require treatment disproportionate to the case. In the end the issue between the parties, apart from the claim to public interest immunity, is a narrow one.

1   I reject the contention of public interest immunity basically on three grounds. First there is no acceptable analogy, still less any precedent, on which such a claim could be admitted. The area in which the immunity is claimed is essentially one of private right even though interests beyond those of the particular employer concerned may be involved. Secondly, to admit such a claim in this field would conflict with the clear public interest accepted and emphasised by Parliament in the Sex Discrimination Act 1975 and the Race Relations Act 1976 that the fullest information should be before the tribunals. Thirdly, to admit such a claim would produce most undesirable results in excluding classes of documents altogether from use in the proceedings, since documents covered by immunity on grounds of public interest not only may but must be withheld.

2   No authority is needed for the negative proposition that confidentiality alone is no ground for protection. ... English law as to discovery is extremely far reaching: parties can be compelled to produce their private diaries; confidences, except between lawyer and client, may have to be broken however intimate they may be. But there are many examples of cases where the courts have recognised that confidences, particularly those of third persons, ought, if possible, in the interests of justice, to be respected ... This principle was accepted by this House in *D v National Society for the Prevention of Cruelty to Children* (1978). Employment cases, and indeed all cases involving selection, involve a wide dimension of confidentiality, affecting other candidates or applicants, who may be numerous, and a number of reporting officers and selection bodies. No court attempting to administer these Acts can fail to give weight to this, though it is not, as above stated, the only element. It is sometimes said that in taking this element into account, the court has to perform a balancing process. The metaphor is one well worn in the law, but I doubt if it is more than a rough metaphor. Balancing can only take place between commensurables. But here the process is to consider fairly the strength and value of the interest in preserving confidentiality and the damage which may be caused by breaking it; then to consider whether the objective – to dispose fairly of the case – can be achieved without doing so, and only in a last resort to order discovery, subject if need be to protective measures. This is a more complex process than merely using the scales: it is an exercise in judicial judgment ...

Lord Salmon: ... I do not consider that an order to produce for the employees' inspection such documents as those to which I have referred could be contrary to public interest; nor do any such documents bear any resemblance to the kind of documents which are normally accepted as immune from production in the public interest. I therefore consider that the main argument relied on by British Leyland (but rejected by the Science Research Council in the second appeal) must fail. The next question that arises is whether and to what extent the fact that the documents concerned are considered to be confidential affects the complainant's right to discovery and inspection. In most cases, whether before the High Court, the county court or an industrial tribunal, there has been discovery of documents with no claim to privilege or immunity from production; and the documents are normally produced for inspection as a matter of course. This however does not always apply to cases in which the documents which one of the parties wishes to inspect have come into the hands of the other party in confidence. It has long been established, however, that no documents which have been acquired in confidence can for that reason be privileged from production or inspection. This point was not challenged by counsel for the Science Research Council or British Leyland; and no doubt this also explains why counsel for British Leyland relied almost entirely upon public interest immunity.

Since confidential documents are not privileged from inspection and public interest immunity fails, the tribunal which for this purpose is in the same position as the High Court and the county court, may order discovery (which includes inspection) of any such documents as it thinks fit – with this proviso: 'Discovery shall not be ordered if and so far as the court [tribunal] is of the opinion that it is not necessary either for disposing fairly of the proceedings or for saving costs.'

If the tribunal is satisfied that it is necessary to order certain documents to be disclosed and inspected in order fairly to dispose of the proceedings, then, in my opinion, the law requires that such an order should be made; and the fact that the documents are confidential is irrelevant.

The law has always recognised that it is of the greatest importance from the point of view of public policy that proceedings in the courts or before tribunals shall be fairly disposed of. This, no doubt, is why the law has never accorded privilege against discovery and inspection to confidential documents which are necessary for fairly disposing of the proceedings. What does 'necessary' in this context mean? It, of course, includes the case where the party applying for an order for discovery and inspection of certain documents could not possibly succeed in the proceedings unless he obtained the order; but it is not confined to such cases. Suppose, for example, a man had a very slim chance of success without inspection of documents but a very strong chance of success with inspection, surely the proceedings could not be regarded as being fairly disposed of, were he to be denied inspection.

I, of course, recognise that the tribunal, like the courts, has a discretion in the exercise of its power to order discovery. It would, however, in my view, be a wholly wrongful exercise of discretion, were an order for discovery and inspection to be refused because of the court's or the tribunal's natural aversion to the disclosure of confidential documents notwithstanding that the proceedings might not be fairly disposed of without them ...

Lord Scarman: ... For myself, I regret the passing of the currently rejected term 'Crown privilege'. It at least emphasised the very restricted area of public interest immunity. As was pointed out by Mr Lester QC who presented most helpful submissions on behalf of the two statutory bodies as well as specifically for the appellant, Mr Vyas, the immunity exists to protect from disclosure only information the secrecy of which is essential to the proper working of the Government of the State. Defence, foreign relations, the inner workings of Government at the highest levels where ministers and their advisers are formulating national policy, and the prosecution process in its pre-trial stage are the sensitive areas where the Crown must have the immunity if the Government of the nation is to be effectively carried on. We are in the realm of public law, not private right. The very special case of *D v National Society for the Prevention of Cruelty to Children* (1978) is not to be seen as a departure from this well-established principle. Immunity from disclosure existed in that case because the House recognised the special position of the NSPCC in the enforcement process of the provisions of the Children Act 1969: a position which the House saw as comparable with that of a prosecuting authority in criminal proceedings. But I would not, with respect, go as far as my noble and learned friend, Lord Hailsham of St Marylebone, when he said in that case: 'The categories of public interest are not closed'; nor can I agree with the dictum of my noble and learned friend, Lord Edmund-Davies, that, where a confidential relationship exists and disclosure would be in breach of some ethical or social value involving the public interest, the court may uphold a refusal to disclose relevant evidence, if, on balance, the public interest would be better served by excluding it.

I do not find anything in *Conway v Rimmer* (1968) or the cases therein cited which would extend public interest immunity in this way. On the contrary, the theme of Lord Reid's speech is that the immunity arises only if 'disclosure would involve a danger of real prejudice to the national interest'. The public interest protected by the immunity is that 'harm shall not be done to the nation or the public service by disclosure': Lord Reid. Whatever may be true generally of the categories of public interest, the 'public interest immunity', which prevents documents from being produced or evidence from being given is restricted, and is not, in my judgment, to be extended either by demanding ministers or the courts. And, though I agree with my noble and learned friend, Lord Edmund-Davies, in believing that a court may refuse to order production of a confidential document if it takes the view that justice does not require its production, I do not see the process of decision as a balancing act. If the document is necessary for fairly disposing of the case, it must be produced, notwithstanding its confidentiality. Only if the document should be protected by public interest immunity, will there be a balancing act. And then the balance will not be between 'ethical or social' values of a confidential relationship involving the public interest and the document's relevance in the litigation, but between the public interest represented by the state and its public service, ie the executive Government, and the public interest in the administration of justice: see Lord Reid. Thus my emphasis would be different from that of my noble and learned friends. 'Public interest immunity' is, in my judgment, restricted to what must be kept secret for the protection of Government at the highest levels and in the truly sensitive areas of executive responsibility ...[15]

Air Canada v Secretary of State for Trade (1983, House of Lords)

Note the division of opinion in this case on the test to be applied by a judge who has to make a decision whether or not to inspect documents for which public immunity has been claimed.

Lord Wilberforce: We are concerned with a claim for discovery of documents in which the parties' respective positions are familiar and one could say ritualised. The relevant pleas in the action (and they are only some of many) challenge the validity of certain actions said to have been taken by the Secretary of State for Trade in relation to the fixing by the BAA [British Airports Authority] of charges for the use by the appellant airlines of Heathrow Airport. The Secretary of State, it is said, has acted beyond his powers, and/or has exercised his powers and discretion for purposes other than those for which they were conferred, viz (briefly) for the purpose of reducing the Government's public sector borrowing

---

15.   [1980] AC 1028.

requirement. In support of these allegations, discovery is sought of a number of documents which, it is claimed, might throw light on the manner in which, and the purpose for which, the Secretary of State exercised his power or his discretion: such documents appear to satisfy the threshold test of relevancy. The Secretary of State's answer is to claim public interest immunity: certificates are put in and signed by top-ranking civil servants (this is because the actions of successive Governments are involved and a powerful convention prevents ministers having access to papers of their predecessors) ... The documents now in issue ... relate directly to the making of decisions as to Government policy in a sensitive area, *viz* the economic and financial policy of the Government, particularly in relation to nationalized industries, by ministers and civil servants prior to consideration in Cabinet, and familiar contentions are put forward as to the need to protect them against disclosure in the interest of the confidentiality of the inner working of Government and of the free and candid expression of views. It is relevant to add that it is shown that there are in existence Cabinet papers bearing on these same matters. These are not asked for, but their existence underlines the high level status and confidentiality of those whose production is sought. It is not, at this stage, disputed that the documents in question fall within the class for which protection is claimed, nor that the claim for protection is put on what is accepted to be the highest grade.

The appellants' claims for discovery and production rests, as it must, upon their assertion that they are necessary for the disposal fairly of the case: see RSC, Ord 24, r 13. There is a public interest, they say, in justice being done to their case and this public interest has to be weighed against the contrary public interest for immunity which the Secretary of State puts forward. As it is not known what the documents may contain, it is not possible for this weighing process to be carried out unless they are inspected. Consequently, and their counsel prudently confined himself to this contention, they ask that the court should privately inspect the documents, as, under the rule (Ord 24, r 13(2)) it has power to do. The judge accepted this submission, but the Court of Appeal reversed his decision.

What then are the criteria upon which a decision should be made to inspect, or not to do so? This matter was discussed at length in the opinions of the House of Lords in the *Burmah Oil* case (1980). The main difference of opinion between the majority and the minority opinions related to the likelihood, on the facts of that case, that the documents, inspection of which was claimed, would be supportive of the plaintiffs' case, the minority regarding this likelihood as purely speculative, the majority as amounting to a degree (differently expressed) of probability. Leaving this difference aside as not relevant here, there are three questions which have now to be answered: (1) What is it that the documents must be likely (in whatever degree) to support? (2) What is the degree of likelihood that must be shown? (3) Is that degree of likelihood attained?

(1) On this point there was a difference in opinion between Bingham J and the Court of Appeal. The learned judge held that documents would be necessary for fairly disposing of a case or (his gloss) for the due administration of justice, if they give substantial assistance to the court in determining the facts upon which the decision in the case would depend. He considered that they were very likely to affect the outcome 'one way or the other'. The Court of Appeal, on the other hand, held that there must be a likelihood that the documents would support the case of the party seeking discovery.

On this point I agree with the Court of Appeal. In a contest purely between one litigant and another, such as the present, the task of the court is to do, and be seen to be doing, justice between the parties – a duty reflected by the word 'fairly' in the rule. There is no higher or additional duty to ascertain some independent truth. It often happens, from the imperfection of evidence, or the withholding of it, sometimes by the party in whose favour it would tell if presented, that an adjudication has to be made which is not, and is known not to be, the whole truth of the matter: yet if the decision has been in accordance with the available evidence and with the law, justice will have been fairly done. It is in aid of justice in this sense that discovery may be ordered, and it is so ordered upon the application of one of the parties who must make out his case for it. If he is not able to do so, that is an end of the matter. There is no independent power in the court to say that, nevertheless, it would like to inspect the documents, with a view to possible production, for its own assistance ...

(2)   The degree of likelihood (of providing support for the plaintiff's case) may be variously expressed: 'Likely' was the word used by Lord Edmund-Davies in *Burmah Oil*: a 'reasonable probability' by Lord Keith of Kinkel. Both expressions must mean something beyond speculation, some concrete ground for belief which takes the case beyond a mere 'fishing' expedition. One cannot attain greater precision in stating what must be a matter of estimation. I would accept either formula ...

Lord Scarman: ... The issue is specific and within a small compass. The Crown having made its objection to production in proper form, in what circumstances should the court inspect privately the documents before determining whether they, or any of them, should be produced?

The court, of course, has a discretion: but the discretion must be exercised in accordance with principle. The principle governing the production of disclosed documents is embodied in RSC, Ord 24, r 13. No order for the production of any documents for inspection or to the court shall be made unless the court is of the opinion that the order is necessary either for disposing fairly of the cause or matter or for saving costs: r 13(1). And the court may inspect the document for the purpose of deciding whether the objection to production is valid: r 13(2). The rule provides a measure of protection for a party's documents irrespective of the class or contents and independently of any privilege or immunity. While the existence of all documents in a party's possession or control relating to matters in question in the action must be 'discovered', that is to say disclosed, to the other party (or parties), he is not obliged to produce them unless the court is of the opinion that production is necessary.

It may well be that, where there is no claim of confidentiality or public interest immunity or any objection on the ground of privilege, the courts follow a relaxed practice, allowing production on the basis of relevance ... But very different considerations arise if a reasoned objection to production is put forward. In *Science Research Council v Nassé* (1980) your Lordships' House ruled that, even where there is no question of public interest immunity but the documents are confidential in character, the court should not order production unless it thought it necessary. An objection based on public interest immunity, if properly formulated, must carry at least as much weight as an objection on the ground of confidentiality.

Faced with a properly formulated certificate claiming public interest immunity, the court must first examine the grounds put forward. If it is a 'class' objection and the documents ... are routine in character, the court may inspect so as to ascertain the strength of the public interest in immunity and the needs of justice before deciding whether to order production. If it is a 'contents' claim, eg a specific national security matter, the court will ordinarily accept the judgment of the minister. But if it is a class claim in which the objection on the face of the certificate is a strong one – as in this case where the documents are minutes and memoranda passing at high level between ministers and their advisers and concerned with the formulation of policy – the court will pay great regard to the minister's view (or that of the senior officer who has signed the certificate). It will not inspect unless there is a likelihood that the documents will be necessary for disposing fairly of the case or saving costs. Certainly, if, like Bingham J in this case, the court should think that the documents might be 'determinative' of the issues in the action to which they relate, the court should inspect: for in such a case there may be grave doubt as to which way the balance of public interest falls: *Burmah Oil Co Ltd v Governor and Company of the Bank of England* (1980). But, unless the court is satisfied on the material presented to it that the documents are likely to be necessary for fairly disposing of the case, it will not inspect for the simple reason that unless the likelihood exists there is nothing to set against the public interest in immunity from production.

The learned judge, Bingham J, correctly appreciated the principle of the matter. He decided to inspect because he believed that the documents in question were very likely to be 'necessary for the just determination of the second and third issues in the plaintiffs' ... case'. Here I consider he fell into error. For the reasons given in the speech of my noble and learned friend, Lord Templeman, I do not think that the appellants have been able to show that the documents whose production they are seeking are likely to be necessary for fairly disposing of the issues in their 'constitutional' case. Indeed, my noble and learned friend has demonstrated that they are unnecessary. Accordingly, for this reason, but for no other, I would hold that the judge was wrong to decide to inspect the documents.

On all other questions I find myself in agreement with the judge. In particular, I am persuaded by his reasoning that the public interest in the administration of justice, which the court has to put into the balance against the public interest immunity, is as he put it: 'In my judgment, documents are necessary for fairly disposing of a cause or for the due administration of justice if they give substantial assistance to the court in determining the facts upon which the decision in the cause will depend.'

The learned judge rejected, in my view rightly, the view which has commended itself to the Court of Appeal and to some of your Lordships that the criterion for determining whether to inspect or not is whether the party seeking production can establish the likelihood that the documents will assist his case or damage that of his opponent. No doubt that is what he is seeking; no doubt also, it is a very relevant consideration for the court. But it would be dangerous to elevate it into a principle of the law of discovery. Discovery is one of the few exceptions to the adversarial character of our legal process. It assists parties and the court to discover the truth. By so doing, it not only helps towards a just determination: it also saves costs. A party who discovers timeously a document fatal to his case is assisted as effectively, although less to his liking, as one who discovers the winning card; for he can save himself and others the heavy costs of litigation. There is another important aspect of the matter. The Crown, when it puts forward a public interest immunity objection, is not claiming a privilege but discharging a duty. The duty arises whether the document assists or damages the Crown's case or if, as in a case to which the Crown is not a party, it neither helps nor injures the Crown. It is not for the Crown but for the court to determine whether the document should be produced. Usually, but not always, the critical factor will be whether the party seeking production has shown the document will help him. But it may be necessary for a fair determination or for saving costs, even if it does not. Therefore, although it is likely to make little difference in practice, I would think it better in principle to retain the formulation of the interests to be balanced which Lord Reid gave us in *Conway v Rimmer* (1968): 'It is universally recognised that here there are two kinds of public interest which may clash. There is the public interest that harm shall not be done to the nation or the public service by disclosure of certain documents, and there is the public interest that the administration of justice shall not be frustrated by the withholding of documents which must be produced if justice is to be done.'

And I do so for the reasons given by Lord Pearce in the same case. Describing the two conflicting interests, he said of the administration of justice that the judge, 'can consider whether the documents in question are of much or little weight in the litigation, whether their absence will result in a complete or partial denial of justice to one or other of the parties or perhaps to both, and what is the importance of the particular litigation to the parties and the public.'

Basically, the reason for selecting the criterion of justice, irrespective of whether it assists the party seeking production, is that the Crown may not have regard to party advantage in deciding whether or not to object to production on the ground of public interest immunity. It is its duty to bring the objection, if it believes it to be sound, to the attention of the court. It is for the court, not the Crown, to balance the two public interests, that of the functioning and security of the public service, which is the sphere within which the executive has the duty to make an assessment, and that of justice, upon which the executive is not competent to pass judgment.

For these reasons I would dismiss the appeal.

[All the Law Lords agreed that the appeal should be dismissed. The test for inspection proposed by Lord Wilberforce was supported by Lord Fraser of Tullybelton and Lord Edmund-Davies. The test proposed by Lord Scarman was supported by Lord Templeman.][16]

Contempt of Court Act 1981

10　No court may require a person to disclose, nor is any person guilty of contempt of court for refusing to disclose, the source of information contained in a publication for which he is responsible, unless it be established to the satisfaction of the court that disclosure is necessary in the interests of justice or national security or for the prevention of disorder or crime.

X Ltd v Morgan-Grampian (Publishers) Ltd (1990, House of Lords)

Lord Bridge of Harwich: ... But the question whether disclosure is necessary in the interests of justice gives rise to a more difficult problem of weighing one public interest against another. A question arising under this part of s 10 has not previously come before your Lordships' House for decision. In discussing the section generally Lord Diplock said in *Secretary of State for Defence v Guardian Newspapers Ltd* (1984): 'The exceptions include no reference to "the public interest" generally and I would add that in my view the expression "justice", the interests of which are entitled to protection, is not used in a general sense as the antonym of "injustice" but in the technical sense of the administration of justice in the course of legal proceedings in a court of law, or, by reason of the extended definition of "court" in s 19 of the 1981 Act, before a tribunal or body exercising the judicial power of the state.'

16.　[1983] 2 AC 394.

I agree entirely with the first half of this dictum. To construe 'justice' as the antonym of 'injustice' in s 10 would be far too wide. But to confine it to 'the technical sense of the administration of justice in the course of legal proceedings in a court of law' seems to me, with all respect due to any dictum of Lord Diplock, to be too narrow. It is, in my opinion, 'in the interests of justice', in the sense in which this phrase is used in s 10, that persons should be enabled to exercise important legal rights and to protect themselves from serious legal wrongs whether or not resort to legal proceedings in a court of law will be necessary to attain these objectives. Thus, to take a very obvious example, if an employer of a large staff is suffering grave damage from the activities of an unidentified disloyal servant, it is undoubtedly in the interests of justice that he should be able to identify him in order to terminate his contract of employment, notwithstanding that no legal proceedings may be necessary to achieve that end.

Construing the phrase 'in the interests of justice' in this sense immediately emphasises the importance of the balancing exercise. It will not be sufficient, *per se*, for a party seeking disclosure of a source protected by s 10 to show merely that he will be unable without disclosure to exercise the legal right or avert the threatened legal wrong on which he bases his claim in order to establish the necessity of disclosure. The judge's task will always be to weigh in the scales the importance of enabling the ends of justice to be attained in the circumstances of the particular case on the one hand against the importance of protecting the source on the other hand. In this balancing exercise it is only if the judge is satisfied that disclosure in the interests of justice is of such preponderating importance as to override the statutory privilege against disclosure that the threshold of necessity will be reached.

Whether the necessity of disclosure in this sense is established is certainly a question of fact rather than an issue calling for the exercise of the judge's discretion, but, like many other questions of fact, such as the question whether somebody has acted reasonably in given circumstances, it will call for the exercise of a discriminating and sometimes difficult value judgment. In estimating the weight to be attached to the importance of disclosure in the interests of justice on the one hand and that of protection from disclosure in pursuance of the policy which underlies s 10 on the other hand, many factors will be relevant on both sides of the scale.

It would be foolish to attempt to give comprehensive guidance as to how the balancing exercise should be carried out. But it may not be out of place to indicate the kind of factors which will require consideration. In estimating the importance to be given to the case in favour of disclosure there will be a wide spectrum within which the particular case must be located. If the party seeking disclosure shows, for example, that his very livelihood depends on it, this will put the case near one end of the spectrum. If he shows no more than that what he seeks to protect is a minor interest in property, this will put the case at or near the other end. On the other side the importance of protecting a source from disclosure in pursuance of the policy underlying the statute will also vary within a wide spectrum. One important factor will be the nature of the information obtained from the source. The greater the legitimate public interest in the information which the source has given to the publisher or intended publisher, the greater will be the importance of protecting the source. But another and perhaps more significant factor which will very much affect the importance of protecting the source will be the manner in which the information was itself obtained by the source. If it appears to the court that the information was obtained legitimately this will enhance the importance of protecting the source. Conversely, if it appears that the information was obtained illegally, this will diminish the importance of protecting the source unless, of course, this factor is counterbalanced by a clear public interest in publication of the information, as in the classic case where the source has acted for the purpose of exposing iniquity. I draw attention to these considerations by way of illustration only and I emphasise once again that they are in no way intended to be read as a code ...

[The other Law Lords delivered speeches agreeing with Lord Bridge.][17]

17. [1990] 2 All ER 1.

INDEX